Lecture Notes in Computer Sci

T0230542

Commenced Publication in 1973
Founding and Former Series Editors:
Gerhard Goos, Juris Hartmanis, and Jan van Leeuwen

Peter Herrmann   Valérie Issarny
Simon Shiu (Eds.)

Trust
Management

Third International Conference, iTrust 2005
Paris, France, May 23-26, 2005
Proceedings

Volume Editors

Peter Herrmann
University of Dortmund, Department of Computer Science
44221 Dortmund, Germany
E-mail: peter.herrmann@udo.edu

Valérie Issarny
INRIA Rocquencourt, Domaine de Voluceau
78153 Le Chesnay Cedex, France
E-mail: valerie.issarny@inria.fr

Simon Shiu
Hewlett-Packard Labs
Bristol BS34 8QZ, UK
E-mail: simon.shiu@hp.com

Library of Congress Control Number: 2005925757

CR Subject Classification (1998): H.4, H.3, H.5.3, C.2.4, I.2.11, K.4.3-2, K.5

ISSN   0302-9743
ISBN-10   3-540-26042-0 Springer Berlin Heidelberg New York
ISBN-13   978-3-540-26042-4 Springer Berlin Heidelberg New York

Springer is a part of Springer Science+Business Media

springeronline.com

© Springer-Verlag Berlin Heidelberg 2005
Printed in Germany

Typesetting: Camera-ready by author, data conversion by Scientific Publishing Services, Chennai, India
Printed on acid-free paper   SPIN: 11429760   06/3142   5 4 3 2 1 0

Preface

This volume constitutes the proceedings of the 3rd International Conference on Trust Management, held in Paris, France, during 23–26 May 2005. The conference follows successful International Conferences in Crete in 2003 and Oxford in 2004. All conferences were organized by iTrust, which is a working group funded as a thematic network by the Future and Emerging Technologies (FET) unit of the Information Society Technologies (IST) program of the European Union.

The purpose of the iTrust working group is to provide a forum for cross-disciplinary investigation of the applications of trust as a means of increasing security, building confidence and facilitating collaboration in dynamic open systems. The notion of trust has been studied independently by different academic disciplines, which has helped us to identify and understand different aspects of trust.

The aim of this conference was to provide a common forum, bringing together researchers from different academic branches, such as the technology-oriented disciplines, law, social sciences and philosophy, in order to develop a deeper and more fundamental understanding of the issues and challenges in the area of trust management in dynamic open systems.

The response to this conference was excellent; from the 71 papers submitted to the conference, we selected 21 full papers and 4 short papers for presentation. The program also included two keynote addresses, given by Steve Marsh from National Research Centre Canada, Institute for Information Technology, and Steve Kimbrough from the University of Pennsylvania; an industrial panel; 7 technology demonstrations; and a full day of tutorials.

The running of an international conference requires an immense effort from all involved parties. We would like to thank the people who served on the Program Committee and the Organizing Committee for their hard work. In particular, we would like to thank the people at INRIA Rocquencourt for handling the logistics for the conference.

May 2005

Peter Herrmann
Valerie Issarny
Simon Shiu

Organization

The 3rd International Conference on Trust Management was organized by iTrust, a Working Group on Trust Management in Dynamic Open Systems, and INRIA Rocquencourt. The conference was partially funded by the Future and Emerging Technologies (FET) unit of the European IST program.

Executive Committee

Conference Chair	Valerie Issarny, INRIA, France
Program Chairs	Peter Herrmann, University of Dortmund, Germany
	Simon Shiu, Hewlett-Packard, UK
Tutorials	Yuecel Karabulut, SAP AG, Germany
Demonstrations	Nikolaos Georgantas, INRIA, France
Panels	Paul Kearney, BT Exact, UK
Local Arrangements	Dominique Potherat, INRIA, France

Local Organizing Committee

Emmanuelle Grousset	INRIA
Jinshan Liu	INRIA
Marie-Francoise Loubressac	INRIA

Program Committee

Adrian Baldwin	HP Labs, UK
Yolanta Beres	HP Labs, UK
Elisa Bertino	University of Milan, Italy
Jon Bing	NRCCL, University of Oslo, Norway
Jeremy Bryans	University of Newcastle, UK
Cristiano Castelfranchi	CNR, Italy
David Chadwick	University of Salford, UK
Andrew Charlesworth	University of Bristol, UK
Mark Roger Dibben	University of St Andrews, UK
Theo Dimitrakos	CLRC, UK
Rino Falcone	CNR, Italy
Peter Herrmann	University of Dortmund, Germany
Valerie Issarny	INRIA, France
Keith Jeffery	CLRC, UK

Table of Contents

Third International Conference on Trust Management

III   Short Papers

IV   Demonstration Overviews

Foraging for Trust: Exploring Rationality and the Stag Hunt Game

Steven O. Kimbrough

University of Pennsylvania, Philadelphia, PA 19104, USA
kimbrough@wharton.upenn.edu
http://opim-sun.wharton.upenn.edu/~sok/

Abstract. Trust presents a number of problems and paradoxes, because existing theory is not fully adequate for understanding why there is so much of it, why it occurs, and so forth. These problems and paradoxes of trust are vitally important, for trust is thought to be the essential glue that holds societies together. This paper explores the generation of trust with two simple, but very different models, focusing on repeated play of the Stag Hunt game. A gridscape model examines creation of trust among cognitively basic simple agents. A Markov model examimes play between two somewhat more sophisticated agents. In both models, trust emerges robustly. Lessons are extracted from these findings which point to a new way of conceiving rationality, a way that is broadly applicable and can inform future investigations of trust.

1 Introduction

Can trust arise spontaneously—by an invisible hand as it were—among strategically interacting individuals? If so, under what conditions will it arise? When will it be stable and when will it not be stable? What interventions might be effective in promoting or undermining stability? If trust is established, under what conditions will it be destroyed? What are the rôles of social structure, game structure, and cognition in establishing or disestablishing trust? These questions belong to a much longer list of important and challenging issues that the problem of trust presents. Answering them fully and adequately constitutes a research program to challenge a community over a period of many years.

I aim in this paper to contribute in two ways to that program. In the end, although progress will be made, more work will have been added. First, I shall present findings, focusing on the Stag Hunt game, that bear more or less directly on at least some of these questions. I shall focus on the Stag Hunt game for several reasons. The game does capture well and succinctly certain aspects of the problem, the dilemma, of trust. It has the happy virtue of not being the (over-worked but still worthwhile) game of Prisoner's Dilemma. Also, it has fruitfully received new attention of late (e.g., [Sky04]), so that what I will add here will, I hope, enrich a topic that is very much in play.

The second way in which I aim to contribute to the trust research program is more indirect. Trust is a problem or a puzzle, even paradox, in part because there

P. Herrmann et al. (Eds.): iTrust 2005, LNCS 3477, pp. 1–16, 2005.

seems to be more of it naturally occurring than can be explained by received theory (classical game theory). I shall say little by way of documenting this claim because space is limited and I take it that the claim is widely accepted. (Chapter 3, "Mutual Aid," of [Sky96] is a discussion of how and why nature is *not* "red in tooth and claw." Also behavioral game theory, reviewed in [Cam03] amply documents the imperfect fit between theory and observation in this domain. Those with a taste for blunt talk might consult [Gin00].) Instead, I hope to say something about how the puzzle of trust might be investigated. I will submit that the puzzle of trust arises, at least in part, because of a presupposed account of agent rationality. This account goes by different names, among them *expected utility theory* and *rational choice theory*. I want to propose, in outline form, a very different approach to conceiving of rationality. By way of articulating this general approach, which I shall call a *theory of exploring rationality*, I shall present a model of agent behavior which, in the context of a Stag Hunt game (as well as other games), explains and predicts the presence of trust.

2   Stag Hunt and a Framing of the Program

The Stag Hunt game (also known as the Assurance game [Gam05a]) gets its name from a passage in Jean Jacques Rousseau's *A Discourse on the Origin of Inequality,* originally published in 1755.

> Was a deer to be taken? Every one saw that to succeed he must faithfully stand to his post; but suppose a hare to have slipped by within reach of any one of them, it is not to be doubted but he pursued it without scruple, and when he had seized his prey never reproached himself with having made his companions miss theirs. [Rou04–Second Part]

Here is a representative summary of the Stag Hunt game.

> The French philosopher, Jean Jacques Rousseau, presented the following situation. Two hunters can either jointly hunt a stag (an adult deer and rather large meal) or individually hunt a rabbit (tasty, but substantially less filling). Hunting stags is quite challenging and requires mutual co-operation. If either hunts a stag alone, the chance of success is minimal. Hunting stags is most beneficial for society but requires a lot of trust among its members. [Gam05b]

This account may be abstracted to a game in strategic form. Figure 1 on the left presents the Stag Hunt game with payoffs that are representative in the literature.[1] Let us call this our *reference game*. On the right of figure 1 we find the Stag Hunt game presented in a generic form. Authors differ in minor ways. Often, but not always, the game is assumed to be symmetric, in which

---

[1] For example, although it is not called the Stag Hunt, the game with these payoffs is discussed at length in [RGG76], where it is simply referred to as game #61.

	Hunt stag (S)	Chase hare (H)
Hunt stag (S)	4	3
	4	1
Chase hare (H)	1	2
	3	2

	Hunt stag (S)	Chase hare (H)
Hunt stag (S)	R'	T'
	R	S
Chase hare (H)	S'	P'
	T	P

Fig. 1. Stag Hunt (aka: Assurance game)

case R=R', T=T', P=P', and S=S'. I will assume symmetry. It is essential that R>T>P≥S.[2]

Thus formalized, the Stag Hunt game offers its players a difficult dilemma, in spite of the fact that their interests coincide. Each does best if both hunt stag (S,S). Assuming, however, that the game is played once and that the players lack any means of coming to or enforcing a bargain,[3] each player will find it tempting to "play it safe" and hunt hare. If both do so, (H,H), the players get 2 each in our reference game, instead of 4 each by playing (S,S). Both of these outcomes— (S,S) and (H,H)—are Nash equilibria. Only (S,S), however, is Pareto optimal. There is a third Nash equilibrium for Stag Hunt: each player hunts stag with probability $\frac{P-S}{((R+P)-(T+S))}$ For our reference game, this amounts to a probability of $\frac{1}{2}$ for hunting stag (and $\frac{1}{2}$ for hunting hare). At the mixed equilibrium each player can expect a return of $2\frac{1}{2}$. Notice that if, for example, the row player hunts hare with probability 1, and the column player plays the mixed strategy, then the row player's expected return is $2\frac{1}{2}$, but the column player's expected return is $1\frac{1}{2}$. Uniquely, the safe thing to do is to hunt hare, since it guarantees at least 2. Hunting hare is thus said to be *risk dominant* and according to many game theorists (H,H) would be the predicted equilibrium outcome.[4]

We can use the Stag Hunt game as a model for investigation of trust. A player hunting stag trusts the counter-player to do likewise. Conversely, a player hunting hare lacks trust in the counter-player. Deciding not to risk the worst outcome (S) is to decide not to trust the other player. Conversely, if trust exists then risk can be taken. There is, of course, very much more to the subject of trust than can be captured in the Stag Hunt game. Still, something is captured. Let us see what we can learn about it.

Before going further it is worth asking whether Rousseau has anything else to say on the matter to hand. Typically in the game theory literature nothing else in this *Discourse* or even in other of Rousseau's writings is quoted.   As is well known, Rousseau wrote in praise of the state of nature, holding that people

---

[2] Usually, and here, P>S. Some authors allow T≥P with P>S. None of this matters a great deal for the matters to hand.

[3] In the jargon of game theory, this is a *noncooperative* game.

[4] I'm using the term risk dominant in a general way, since adverting to its precise meaning would divert us. See [HS88] for the precise meaning.

were free of war and other ills of society, and on the whole were happier. That needn't concern us here. What is worth noting is that Rousseau proceeds by conjecturing (his word, above) a series of steps through which man moved from a state of nature to the present state of society. Rousseau is vague on what drives the process. The view he seems to hold is that once the equilibrium state of nature was broken, one thing led to another until the present. Problems arose and were solved, one after the other, carrying humanity to its modern condition. He laments the outcome, but sees the process as more or less inevitable. With this context in mind, the passage immediately before the oft-quoted origin of the Stag Hunt game puts a new light on Rousseau's meaning. He is describing a stage in the passage from the state of nature to civil society.

> Such was the manner in which men might have insensibly acquired some gross idea of their mutual engagements and the advantage of fulfilling them, but this only as far as their present and sensible interest required; for as to foresight they were utter strangers to it, and far from troubling their heads about a distant futurity, they scarce thought of the day following. Was a deer to be taken? ... [Rou04–Second Part]

Rousseau is describing behavior of people not far removed from the state of nature. Language, for example, comes much later in his account. These people end up hunting hare because "as to foresight they were utter strangers to it, and far from troubling their heads about a distant futurity, they scarce thought of the day following." If we *define* the game to be one-shot, then there is no future to worry about. Rousseau is right: if there is no future or if the players cannot recognize a future, then stag will roam unmolested. Rousseau is also right in presuming that in the later development of civil society the future matters, agents can recognize this, and much coordination and hunting of stag occurs. Rousseau is *not* agreeing with contemporary game theorists in positing hunting of hare as the most rational thing to do in the Stag Hunt game.

More generally, trust happens. Our question is to understand how and why. We assume that there is a future and we model this (initially) by repeating play of a basic game, called the *stage game*, here the Stag Hunt. Given repeated play of a stage game, there are two kinds of conditions of play that call out for investigation. The first is condition is the *social aspect* of play. We investigate a simple model of this in §3. The second condition might be called the *cognitive aspect* of play. How do learning and memory affect game results? We discuss this second aspect in §4.

3   The Gridscape: A Simple Society

We shall work with a very simple model of social aspects of strategic interaction, called the *gridscape*. The gridscape is a regular lattice—think of a checkerboard—which we will assume is two-dimensional and wraps around on itself (is technically speaking a torus). Agents or players occupy cells on the gridscape and each has 8 neighbors. Figure 2(a) illustrates. Cell (3,2) has neighbors (2,1), (2,2),

	1	2	3	4	5	6
1						
2						
3						
4						
5						
6						

(a) Labeled 6×6 gridscape

Generation	Ss	Hs	Total Points
0	7167	7233	344960.0
1	8715	5685	451224.0
2	12288	2112	599424.0
3	13891	509	668312.0
4	14306	94	686720.0
5	14392	8	690712.0
6	14400	0	691200.0

(b) Representative run on a 120×120 gridscape. R=3, T=2, P=1, S=0.

	1	2	3	4	5	6
1	S	S	H	S	S	S
2	S	S	H	S	S	S
3	S	S	H	S	S	S
4	S	S	H	S	S	S
5	S	S	H	S	S	S
6	S	S	H	S	S	S

(c) Stable 6×6 gridscape, for R=3, T=2.5, P=1, S=0

Fig. 2. Labeled 6×6 gridscape

(2,3), (3,1), (3,3), (4,1), (4,2), (4,3).[5] Every cell has eight neighbors. Thus, the neighbors of (1,1) are (6,6), (6,1), (6,2) (1,6), (1,2) (2,6), (2,1), and (2,2). With the gridscape as a basis it is now possible to undertake a variety of experiments. We'll confine ourselves to a simple one.

Protocol 1 (Basic Gridscape Stag Hunt Protocol). *Each cell in the gridscape is initialized by placing on it either a hare hunter, H, or a stag hunter, S. H and S are the consideration set of policies of play for the experiment. Players using the H policy always hunt hare; and players using the S policy always hunt stag. Initialization is random in the sense that every cell has the same probability of being initialized with an H (or an S). After initialization, play proceeds by discrete generations. Initialization concludes generation 0. At the start of each subsequent generation each player (at a cell) plays each of its 8 neighbors using its policy in use from the consideration set. The player records the total return it gets from playing the 8 neighbors. After all players have played their neighbors, each player updates its policy in use. A player changes its policy in use if and only if one of its neighbors is using the counter-policy and has achieved a strictly higher total return in the current generation than has the player or any of its neighbors with the same policy in use achieved. (This is called the* IMITATE THE BEST NEIGHBOR *policy.) Policy updating completes the generation. Play continues until a maximum number of generations is completed.*

The table in figure 2(b) shows representative data when the gridscape is seeded randomly (50:50) with stag hunters (Ss) and hare hunters (Hs) and protocol 1 is executed. Here, after 5 generations the Hs go extinct. The stag hunters conquer the board. This is the usual case, but it is not inevitable. To see why, consider

[5] This is called the *Moore neighborhood*. The *von Neumann neighborhood*, consisting of the four neighbors directly above, below, to the left, and to the right, is also widely studied. The results we report here are not sensitive to which of the two neighborhood definitions is in force.

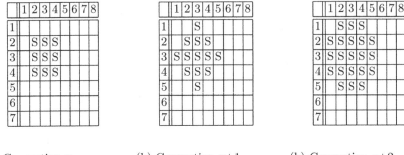

(a) Generation x   (b) Generation x+1   (b) Generation x+2

Fig. 3. Growth of a block of stag hunters when R=4, T=3, P=2, and S=1

the examples in figure 3, which shows a 3×3 block of stag hungers (Ss). The remaining cells are blank and for the purposes of the discussion may be filled in as needed.

The first thing to notice is that in figure 3(a) at (3,3) we have an S that is completely surrounded by Ss. This cell obtains a total reward of $8 \times R = 8 \times 4 = 32$ in our reference example. It is impossible to do equally well or better, given the setup. In consequence, given the protocol, once a 3×3 block of Ss is created none of its members will ever change to H. This is true for all versions of the Stag Hunt game (under protocol 1). We say that a 3×3 block of Ss cannot be invaded. More generally, it is easy to see that no rectangular block of Ss larger than 3×3 can be invaded either. (Note further that blocks of hare hunters are not so advantaged. An internal hare hunter gets $8T < 8R$ in all Stag Hunt games.)

Can a block of stag hunters grow? Assume that in figure 3(a) the blank cells are all hare hunters. In general, the stag hunter at (2,3) will get a return of $5R + 3S$ which is $5 \times 4 + 3 \times 1 = 23$ in our reference game. The hare hunter at (1,3) will get $5P + 3T$ in general and $5 \times 2 + 3 \times 3 = 19$ in the reference game. And in general, so long as $5R + 3S > 5P + 3T$ a hare hunter in this position will convert to stag hunting. Note that not all Stag Hunt games will support this conversion. For example, R=101, T=100, P=99, and S=0 will not. Figures 3(b) and (c) show the next two generations and the pattern is clear: the stag hunters will drive the hare hunters to extinction.

Is conquest by stag hunters inevitable if a 3×3 block is created and the game rewards are sufficient for it to grow in a field consisting entirely of hare hunters? Equivalently, if $5(R - P) > 3(T - S)$ and a 3×3 block (or larger) of stag hunters forms, is it inevitable that hare hunters are driven to extinction? No it is not. For example, the configuration in figure 2(c) is stable for the given payoff values.

There are many nice questions to ask and many interesting variations on the basic gridscape model for the Stag Hunt game. For present purposes, however, the following points are most on topic.

1. The gridscape Stag Hunt results described above are robust. What happens— whether Hs come to dominate or not, whether a stable mixture results and

so on—depends on the game payoffs (What is it worth if both players hunt stag? etc.) and the initial configuration. For a broad range of cases, however, hunting stag will eventually dominate the society. Trust—in the form of hunting stag predominately—can arise spontaneously among strategically interacting individuals. In fact, this is far from an implausible outcome.

2. Trust in Stag Hunt on the gridscape is also robust in a second sense: once it is established in large part, it is not easily dislodged. Mutations occurring at a small rate in a field of stag hunters will create mostly isolated hare hunters who will convert to S in the next generation. If stag hunters do well without noise they will do reasonably well with it.

3. The gridscape model under protocol 1 evidences a clear social effect. What we may call the *shadow of society* appears and affects the outcome. The policies played by one's neighbors may be, and usually are, influenced by policies played by players who are not one's neighbors. Recalling figure 3(a), what happens to a hare hunter at (1,3) depends very much on the fact that the neighboring stag hunters are themselves adjacent to other stag hunters. Thus, while the hare hunter at (1,3) beats the stag hunter at (2,3), in the sense that it gets more points in the one-on-one play, the stag hunter at (2,3) in aggregate does better and it is the hare hunter who is converted.

4. The Prisoner's Dilemma game arguably presents a trust dilemma in more extreme form than does the Stag Hunt. Can cooperators largely take over the gridscape? Yes, under certain, more restricted conditions. In Prisoner's Dilemma, we require $T > R > P > S$ and $2R > T + S$. Further, we relabel the policies. Hunt Stag becomes Cooperate and Hunt Hare becomes Defect. On the gridscape, the 3×3 (and larger) block is key in the analysis. If, for example, we set $T = R + 1$, $P = 1$ and $S = 0$ in Prisoner's Dilemma, then so long as $R > 4$, a 3×3 (and larger) block of cooperators will be able to expand in a field of defectors. Defectors may not be eliminated, but they may become very much minority constituents of the gridscape. Note further that if Prisoner's Dilemma games are repeated (either infinitely with discounting or finitely), and the TIT FOR TAT policy replaces ALWAYS COOPERATE, then the payoff structure will, under broad conditions, become a Stag Hunt (cf. [Cam03–chapter 7], [Sky04–chapter 1]).

5. The agents on the gridscape have an update policy, IMITATE THE BEST NEIGHBOR, which they use to choose policies for play from their consideration sets. Under this update policy, from protocol 1, agents change their policies of play if, after a round of play, one of their neighbors has used the alternative policy and gotten more points than either the player or one its neighbors playing with the player's policy of play. This is a reasonable update policy, but there are reasonable alternatives. Is there a sense in which it is optimal? Is some other update policy optimal? Is there a sense in which it is an ESS (evolutionarily stable strategy) [May82]?

These are all interesting questions, well worth investigation. Space is limited, however, and doing so would divert us from the main theme. A larger issue raised is this. Any reasonable update policy, including ours, may be interpreted as taking a stand on the uncertainty faced by the agent.[6] Agents in games may be interpreted as seeking maximum return. That indeed is a presumption underlying the strategic framework. It is not a presumption that the agents are conscious or have intentions.

Regarding the stand on uncertainty, agents following our update policy are engaging in risky behavior whenever they opt for hunting stag. Yet when all agents so behave collective stag hunting robustly follows. Note the "Total Points" column in figure 2(b). In the first generation the agents collectively garnered 344960 points from the gridscape. If the agents had not updated their policies of play this is where it would stay. As we see, with the update policy used (IMITATE THE BEST NEIGHBOR) the agents collectively more than doubled their take from the gridscape. IMITATE THE BEST NEIGHBOR has this to commend itself: it does well when playing against itself. In Prisoner's Dilemma the same can be said for TIT FOR TAT. Notice as well that NEVER UPDATE, ALWAYS HUNT STAG does well against itself in Stag Hunt and ALWAYS COOPERATE does well against itself in Prisoner's Dilemma. Further, IMITATE THE BEST NEIGHBOR does well against NEVER UPDATE, ALWAYS HUNT STAG, as TIT FOR TAT does well against ALWAYS COOPERATE. Before pursuing these comments further, indeed as a means of doing so, let us turn to a more sophisticated model of learning by agents in games.

4   A Model for Exploring Rationality

We turn now to a more sophisticated model for learning by two agents engaged in repeated play of a stage game.[7] The model—MLPS: Markov Learning in Policy Space—is highly stylized and has quite unrealistic assumptions. It is, however, valid as an approximation of realistic conditions; I ask for the reader's indulgence.

The key idea is that agents have a *consideration set of policies for play, S*. The *supergame* consists of an indefinitely long sequence of *games*, each of which is a finite sequence of *rounds of play* of a stage game (e.g., Stag Hunt). Agents draw elements from their Ss and use them as *focal policies* for a period of time, or number of rounds of play, called a *game*. Each game is divided into n_e epochs of length l_e. Thus, the number of rounds of play in a game is $n_e l_e$. During an epoch an agent plays its current focal policy with probability $(1 - \varepsilon)$, and other policies from its consideration set the rest of the time, with probability ε.

At the end of each game, g_{t-1}, a player, p, picks a focal policy, f_p^t, from its consideration set, S, for play in game g_t. The players use the *fitness-proportional* choice rule. Let $\widehat{V}(p, i, j, k)$ be the average value per round of play returned to player p for policy i, when p has focal policy j and $-p$ (the counter-player) has

---

[6] I am using *uncertaintly* here in its technical sense, which contrasts with risk [LR57]. In a decision under risk we have an objectively supported probability distribution (or density) on the outcomes. Not so in a decision under uncertainty.

[7] More extensive treatment of this model may be found in [Kim04b].

Table 1. State 1: Payoffs to Row in Stag Hunt example when the system is in state 1 and $l_e = 10$

	$1-\varepsilon$: TFT	ε: ALLD	Total
$1-\varepsilon$: TFT	$(1-\varepsilon)(l_e R)$ $(1-\varepsilon)40$	$\varepsilon((l_e-1)P+S)$ 9ε	$40-31\varepsilon$
ε: ALLD	$(1-\varepsilon)(T+(l_e-1)P)$ $12(1-\varepsilon)$	$\varepsilon(l_e P)$ 10ε	$12-2\varepsilon$

Table 2. State 2: Payoffs to Row in Stag Hunt example when the system is in state 2 and $l_e = 10$

	ε: TFT	$1-\varepsilon$: ALLD	Total
$1-\varepsilon$: TFT	$\varepsilon(l_e R)$ $\varepsilon40$	$(1-\varepsilon)((l_e-1)P+S)$ $9(1-\varepsilon)$	$9+31\varepsilon$
ε: ALLD	$\varepsilon(T+(l_e-1)P)$ 12ε	$(1-\varepsilon)(l_e P)$ $10(1-\varepsilon)$	$10+2\varepsilon$

Table 3. State 3: Payoffs to Row in Stag Hunt example when the system is in state 3 and $l_e = 10$

	$1-\varepsilon$: TFT	ε: ALLD	Total
ε: TFT	$(1-\varepsilon)(l_e R)$ $(1-\varepsilon)40$	$\varepsilon((l_e-1)P+S)$ 9ε	$40-31\varepsilon$
$1-\varepsilon$: ALLD	$(1-\varepsilon)(T+(l_e-1)P)$ $12(1-\varepsilon)$	$\varepsilon(l_e P)$ 10ε	$12-2\varepsilon$

Table 4. State 4: Payoffs to Row in Stag Hunt example when the system is in state 4 and $l_e = 10$

	ε: TFT	$1-\varepsilon$: ALLD	Total
ε: TFT	$\varepsilon(l_e R)$ $\varepsilon40$	$(1-\varepsilon)((l_e-1)P+S)$ $9(1-\varepsilon)$	$9+31\varepsilon$
$1-\varepsilon$: ALLD	$\varepsilon(T+(l_e-1)P)$ 12ε	$(1-\varepsilon)(l_e P)$ $10(1-\varepsilon)$	$10+2\varepsilon$

focal policy k. (Similarly, $V(p,i,j,k)$ is the value realized in a particular round of play.) Then

$$\Pr(f_p^{t+1} = i | f_p^t = j, f_{-p}^t = k) = \widehat{V}(p,i,j,k) / \sum_i \widehat{V}(p,i,j,k) \qquad (1)$$

That is, the probability that a player chooses a policy for focus in the next game is the proportion of value it returned per round of play, compared to all the player's policies, during the previous game.

There is nothing egregiously unrealistic about these assumptions. The MLPS model strengthens them for the sake of mathematical tractability. Specifically,

Table 5. Stag Hunt transition matrix data assuming fitness proportional policy selection by both players, based on previous Tables 1–4. Numeric example for $\varepsilon = 0.1 = \varepsilon_1 = \varepsilon_2$

	s(1)=(1,1)	s(2)=(1,2)	s(3)=(2,1)	s(4)=(2,2)
s(1)	$0.7577 \cdot 0.7577$	$0.7577 \cdot 0.2423$	$0.2423 \cdot 0.7577$	$0.2423 \cdot 0.2423$
	= 0.5741	= 0.1836	= 0.1836	= 0.0587
s(2)	$0.5426 \cdot 0.7577$	$0.5426 \cdot 0.2423$	$0.4574 \cdot 0.7577$	$0.4574 \cdot 0.2423$
	= 0.4111	= 0.1315	= 0.3466	= 0.1108
s(3)	$0.7577 \cdot 0.5426$	$0.7577 \cdot 0.4574$	$0.2423 \cdot 0.5426$	$0.2423 \cdot 0.4574$
	= 0.4111	= 0.3466	= 0.1315	= 0.1108
s(4)	$0.5426 \cdot 0.5426$	$0.5426 \cdot 0.4574$	$0.4574 \cdot 0.5426$	$0.4574 \cdot 0.4574$
	= 0.2944	= 0.2482	= 0.2482	= 0.2092

it is assumed that a mechanism is in place so that the two players are exactly coordinated. Each has its games begin and end at the same time (round of play in the sequence). Further, each game is neatly divided into epochs and the random choices are arranged so that each player's $\widehat{V}$ values exactly realize their expected values. The upshot of this is that the $\widehat{V}$ values seen by the players are constant, as are the underlying expected values. The resulting system is a stationary Markov process with states $S_p \times S_{-p}$ and the equilibrium distribution of states can be analytically determined.

To illustrate, assume the stage game is Stag Hunt with $R = 4, T = 3, P = 1$, and $S = 0$. Assume that each player has a consideration set of two policies of play: (1) TIT FOR TAT (TFT) in which the player begins (in the epoch) by hunting stag and subsequently mimics the behavior of the counter-player on the previous round of play, and (2) ALWAYS DEFECT (ALLD) in which the player always hunts hare. This system has four possible states: (1) both players in the game have TFT as their focal policy, (TFT, TFT), (2) player 1 (Row) has TFT as its focal policy and player 2 (Column) has ALLD as its focal policy, (TFT, ALLD), (3) (ALLD, TFT), and (4) (ALLD, ALLD). With $l_e = 10$ we get the payoffs for the various states as shown in tables 1–4.

Letting $\varepsilon = 0.1$, routine calculation leads to the transition matrix indicated in table 5.

At convergence of the Markov process:

Pr(s(1))	Pr(s(2))	Pr(s(3))	Pr(s(4))
0.4779	0.2134	0.2134	0.0953

So 90%+ of the time at least one agent is playing TFT. Note the expected take for Row per epoch by state:

1. $(1 - \varepsilon)(40 - 31\varepsilon) + \varepsilon(12 - 2\varepsilon) = 34.39$
2. $(1 - \varepsilon)(9 + 31\varepsilon) + \varepsilon(10 + 2\varepsilon) = 11.91$
3. $\varepsilon(40 - 31\varepsilon) + (1 - \varepsilon)(12 - 2\varepsilon) = 14.31$
4. $\varepsilon(9 + 31\varepsilon) + (1 - \varepsilon)(10 + 2\varepsilon) = 10.39$

Further, in expectation, Row (and Column) gets $(0.4779\ 0.2134\ 0.2134\ 0.0953) \cdot$ $(34.39\ 11.91\ 14.31\ 10.39)' = 23.02$ (per epoch of length $l_e = 10$, or 2.302 per round of play), much better than the 10.39 both would get if they played ALLD with ε-greedy exploration. Note that even the latter is larger than the return, 10 per epoch or 1 per round, of settling on the risk-dominant outcome of mutually hunting hare. There is a third, mixed, equilibrium of the one-shot Stag Hunt game. For this example it occurs at $((\frac{1}{2}S, \frac{1}{2}H), (\frac{1}{2}S, \frac{1}{2}H))$. At this equilibrium each player can expect a return of 2 from a round of play. Players playing under the MLPS regime learn that trust pays. A few points briefly before we turn to the larger lessons to be extracted from these examples.

1. Markov models converge rapidly and are quite robust. The results on display here hold up well across different parameter values (e.g., for ε). Further, relaxation of the mechanism of play so that agents get imperfect, but broadly accurate, estimates of the expected values of the V quantities will not produce grossly different results. We get a nonstationary Markov process, but in expectation it behaves as seen here.
2. The MLPS model also has attractive behavior for different kinds of games. Players in Prisoner's Dilemma games will learn a degree of cooperation and do much better than constant mutual defection. In games of pure conflict (constant sum games) the outcomes are close to those predicted by classical game theory. And in coordination games players go far by way of learning to coordinate. See [Kim04b] for details.
3. If we retain the core ideas of the MLPS model, but entirely relax the synchronization conditions imposed by the game mechanism, simulation studies produce results that qualitatively track the analytic results: the players learn to trust and more generally the players learn to approach Pareto optimal outcomes of the stage game [KLK04].

5 Discussion

Neither the gridscape model nor the MLPS model with protocol 1 nor the two together are in any way definitive on the emergence of trust in repeated play of Stag Hunt games. They tell us something: that trust can arise spontaneously among strategically interacting agents, that this can happen under a broad range of conditions, that it can be stable, and so on. The models and their discussion here leave many questions to be investigated and they raise for consideration many new questions. Much remains to be done, which I think is a positive result of presenting these models. I want now to make some remarks in outline by way of abstracting the results so far, with the aim of usefully framing the subject for further investigation.

LPS models: learning in policy space. Both the gridscape model and the MLPS model with protocol 1 are instances of a more general type of model, which I call an LPS (learning in policy space) model. In an LPS model an agent has a consideration set of policies or actions it can take, $\mathcal{S}$, and a learning or update,

L/U, policy it employs in selecting which policies to play, or actions to take, at a given time. In the gridscape model, $\mathcal{S} = \{H, S\}$ for every player. In the MLPS model with protocol 1, $\mathcal{S} = \{\text{TFT}, \text{ALLD}\}$ for both players. In the gridscape model the L/U policy employed by all players was IMITATE THE BEST NEIGHBOR. In the MLPS model, the players used the fitness-proportional update rule, in the context of the mechanism described in the previous section.

LPS models categorize strategies. In classical game theory the players are conceived as having *strategies,* complete instructions for play, which they can be thought of as choosing before the (super)game starts. The possible strategy choices constitute what we call the consideration set, $\mathcal{S}$. Because strategies are picked *ex ante* there is no learning, although the strategies can be conditioned on play and can mimic any learning process. The agents employ what we might call the *null learning/update rule, $L/U_\emptyset$.* In an LPS model with a non-null L/U policy, the consideration set of policies of play does not include all possible strategies in the game. Policies in $\mathcal{S}$ are tried sequentially and played for a limited amount of time, then evaluated and put into competition with other members of $\mathcal{S}$. The L/U policy constitutes the rules for comparison, competition and choice. The total number of possible strategies is not affected by imposition of the LPS framework, but the strategies are implicitly categorized and the agents choose among them during the course of play (instead of *ex ante*). The consideration set of *strategies* used by an agent is implicit in its consideration set of policies, its L/U policy, the structure of the game, and the play by the counterplayers. Thus, LPS models subsume standard game-theoretic models. A *proper* LPS model, however, has a non-null L/U policy. Normally, when I speak of an LPS model I shall be referring to a proper LPS model.

Folk Theorem undercuts. According to the Folk Theorem,[8] nearly any set of outcomes in an indefinitely repeated game can be supported by some Nash equilibrium. In consequence, the Nash equilibrium becomes essentially worthless as a predictive or even explanatory tool, in these contexts. The problems of trust arise against this backdrop and against the following point.

Refinements unsatisfying. Refinements to the classical theory, aimed at selecting a subset of the Nash equilibria in predicting outcomes, have been less than fully satisfying. This is a large subject and it takes us well beyond the scope of the present paper. However, the favored refinement for Stag Hunt would be universal hunting of hare, because it is the risk dominant equilibrium. (For a general discussion see [VBB91, VBB90].) Agents playing this way might well be viewed as "rational fools" [Sen77] by LPS agents.

LPS agents may be rational. At least naïvely, the L/U regimes employed by our gridscape and MLPS agents are sensible, and may be judged rational, or at least not irrational. Exploring the environment, as our LPS agents do, probing it with play of different policies, informed by recent experience, is on the face it entirely reasonable. Why not try learning by experience if it is not obvious what

---

[8] A genuine theorem, described in standard texts, e.g., [Bin92].

to do in the absence of experience? I shall now try to articulate a sense in which LPS agents may be judged rational, even though they violate the rationality assumptions of classical game theory and rational choice theory.

Contexts of maximum taking (MT). Given a set of outcomes whose values are known, perhaps under risk (i.e., up to a probability distribution), given a consistent, well-formed preference structure valuing the outcomes, and given a set of actions leading (either with certainty or with risk) to the outcomes, rational choice theory (or utility theory) instructs us to choose an action that results in our taking the maximum expected value on the outcomes. Presented with valued choices under certainty or risk, we are counseled to take the maximum value in expectation. Although the theory is foundational for classical game theory and economics, it has also been widely challenged both from a normative perspective and for its empirical adequacy.[9]

Contexts of maximum seeking (MS). In an MS context an agent can discriminate among outcomes based on their values to the agent, but the connection between the agent's possible actions and the resulting outcomes is uncertain in the technical sense: the agent does not have an objectively well grounded probability distribution for associating outcomes with actions. In seeking the maximum return for its actions, the agent has little alternative but to explore, to try different actions and to attempt to learn how best to take them.[10]

Exploring rationality is appropriate for MS contexts. The claim I wish to put on the table is that in MS as distinct from MT contexts, rationality is best thought of as an appropriate learning process. An agent is rational in an MS context to the extent that it engages effectively in learning to obtain a good return. In doing so, it will be inevitable that that agent engages in some form of trial and error process of exploring its environment. Rationality of this kind may be called an *exploring rationality* to distinguish it from what is often called *ideal rationality,* the kind described by rational choice theory and which is, I submit, typically not appropriate in MS contexts. See [Kim04a] for further discussion of the concept of an exploring rationality.

Evaluate exploring rationalities analytically by performance. LPS models with their articulated L/U regimes afford an excellent framework for evaluating forms of exploring rationality. Such evaluation will turn largely on performance under a given L/U regime. For starters and for now informally, an L/U regime may be assessed with regard to whether it is generally a strong performer. Rational admissibility is a useful concept in this regard.

---

[9] Good, wide-ranging discussion can be found in [Fri96, GS94]. A classic paper [KMRW82] develops a model in which for the finitely repeated Prisoner's Dilemma game it is sometimes rational for a player to cooperate, *provided the player believes the counter-player is irrational.* Since both players would benefit by mutual cooperation it seems a stretch to call all attempts to find it irrational.

[10] Classical game theory seeks to finesse this situation by assuming classical rationality and common knowledge. The present essay may be seen as an exploration of principled alternatives to making these very strong assumptions.

General Definition 1 (Rational Admissibility). *A learning (update) regime for policies of play in an indefinitely repeated game is* <u>*rationally admissible*</u> *if*

1. *It performs well if played against itself (more generally: it performs well if universally adopted).*
2. *It performs well if played against other learning regimes that perform well when played against themselves (more generally: the other learning regimes perform well if universally adopted).*
3. *It is not vulnerable to catastrophic exploitation.*

To illustrate, in the gridscape model IMITATE THE BEST NEIGHBOR performs well against itself in that when everyone uses it, as we have seen, trust breaks out and stag hunting prevails robustly. The null L/U policy of ALWAYS HUNT STAG also does well against itself, and both IMITATE THE BEST NEIGHBOR and ALWAYS HUNT STAG will do well against each other. ALWAYS HUNT STAG, however, is catastrophically vulnerable to ALWAYS HUNT HARE. IMITATE THE BEST NEIGHBOR on the other hand will do better, although how much better depends on the payoff structure of the stage game. Some stag hunters may open themselves up to exploitation because they have one neighbor who hunts stag and is surrounded by stag hunters. In sum, with reference to the set of these three L/U policies, IMITATE THE BEST NEIGHBOR is uniquely rationally admissible (robustly, across a wide range of stag game payoff structures). A similar point holds for the MLPS model discussed above.

Two additional comments. First, "not vulnerable to catastrophic exploitation" is admittedly vague. It is not to my purpose to provide a formal specification here. I believe that more than one may be possible and in any event the topic is a large one. The motivating intuition is that a learning regime is vulnerable to exploitation if it learns to forego improving moves for which the counter-players have no effective means of denial. Thus, an agent that has learned to hunt stag in the face of the counter-player hunting hare is being exploited because it is foregoing the option of hunting hare, the benefits of which cannot be denied by the counter-player. Similarly, agents cooperating in Prisoner's Dilemma are not being exploited. Even though each is foregoing the temptation to defect, the benefits of defecting can easily be denied by the counter-player following suit and also defecting. Second, the similarity between the definition, albeit informal, of rational admissibility and the concept of an ESS (evolutionarily stable strategy, [May82]) is intended. In a nutshell, a main message of this paper is that for repeated games it is learning regimes and consideration sets of policies, rather than strategies alone, that are key to explanation. (And dare one suggest that rational play in one-shot games may sometimes draw on experience in repeated games?)

Evaluate exploring rationalities empirically, for descriptive adequacy. As no-ted, it is well established that rational choice theory (ideal rationality) is not descriptively accurate at the individual level. In light of the results and observations given here, one has to ask to what degree subjects at variance from the received theory are perceiving and responding to contexts of maximum seeking (MS), rather than the postulated MT contexts. In any event, it is worth noting that foraging by animals—for food, for mates, for shelter or other resources—is a ubiquitous natural form of behavior in an MS context [GC00, SK86], for which models under the LPS framework would seem a good fit. Experimental investigation is only beginning. I think it shows much promise.

In conclusion, the problems and paradoxes of trust are vitally important on their own. Trust is the "cement of society".[11] Understanding it is crucial to maintenance and design of any social order, including and especially the new social orders engendered by modern communications technologies, globalization, global warming, and all that comes with them. I have tried to contribute in a small way to understanding how and when trust can emerge or be destroyed. The gridscape and MLPS models are helpful, but they can be only a small part of the story and even so their depths have barely been plumbed. But it's a start; it's something. The more significant point, I think, is that the problems of trust lead us, via these very different models, to a common pattern that abstracts them: LPS, learning in policy space, and contexts of maximum seeking (MS), as distinguished from contexts in which maximum taking (MT) is appropriate. The fact, demonstrated here and elsewhere, that agents adopting this stance generate more trust and improve their take from the environment, is encouraging. So is the observation that such behavior is analogous to, if not related to or even a kind of, foraging behavior.

Acknowledgements. Many thanks to Alex Chavez and James D. Laing for comments on an earlier version of this paper.

References

[Bin92]   Ken Binmore, *Fun and games: A text on game theory*, D.H. Heath and Company, Lexington, MA, 1992.

[Cam03]   Colin F. Camerer, *Behavioral game theory: Experiments in strategic interaction*, Russell Sage Foundation and Princeton University Press, New York, NY and Princeton, NJ, 2003.

[Els89]   Jon Elster, *The cement of society: A study of social order*, Studies in rationality and social change, Cambridge University Press, Cambridge, UK, 1989.

[Fri96]   Jeffrey Friedman (ed.), *The rational choice controversy*, Yale University Press, New Haven, CY, 1996, Originally published as *Critical Review*, vol. 9, nos. 1–2, 1995.

[Gam05a]   GameTheory.net, *Assurance game*, http://www.gametheory.net/Dictionary/Games/AssuranceGame.html, Accessed 8 February 2005.

[Gam05b]   _____, *Stag hunt*, http://www.gametheory.net/Dictionary/Games/StagHunt.html, Accessed 8 February 2005.

---

[11] Elster's term [Els89], after Hume who called causation the cement of the universe.

[GC00]   Luc-Alain Giraldeau and Thomas Caraco, *Social foraging theory*, Princeton University Press, Princeton, NJ, 2000.

[Gin00]   Herbert Gintis, *Game theory evolving: A problem-centered introduction to modeling strategic interaction*, Princeton University Press, Princeton, NJ, 2000.

[GS94]   Donald P. Green and Ian Shapiro, *Pathologies of rational choice theory: A critique of applications in political science*, Yale University Press, New Haven, CT, 1994.

[HS88]   John C. Harsanyi and Reinhard Selten, *A general theory of equilibrium selection in games*, MIT Press, Cambridge, MA, 1988.

[Kim04a]   Steven O. Kimbrough, *A note on exploring rationality in games*, Working paper, University of Pennsylvania, Philadelphia, PA, March 2004, Presented at SEP (Society for Exact Philosophy), spring 2004. http://opim-sun.wharton.upenn.edu/~sok/comprats/2005/exploring-rational\%ity-note-sep2004.pdf.

[Kim04b]   _____, *Notes on MLPS: A model for learning in policy space for agents in repeated games*, working paper, University of Pennsylvania, Department of Operations and Information Management, December 2004, http://opim-sun.wharton.upenn.edu/~sok/sokpapers/2005/markov-policy.pdf\%.

[KLK04]   Steven O. Kimbrough, Ming Lu, and Ann Kuo, *A note on strategic learning in policy space*, Formal Modelling in Electronic Commerce: Representation, Inference, and Strategic Interaction (Steven O. Kimbrough and D. J. Wu, eds.), Springer, Berlin, Germany, 2004, pp. 463–475.

[KMRW82]   David M. Kreps, Paul Milgrom, John Roberts, and Robert Wilson, *Rational cooperation in the finitely repeated prisoners' dilemma*, Journal of Economic Theory **27** (1982), 245–252.

[LR57]   R. Duncan Luce and Howard Raiffa, *Games and decisions*, John Wiley, New York, NY, 1957, Reprinted by Dover Books, 1989.

[May82]   John Maynard Smith, *Evolution and the theory of games*, Cambridge Univesity Press, New York, NY, 1982.

[RGG76]   Anatol Rapoport, Melvin J. Guyer, and David G. Gordon, *The 2×2 game*, The University of Michigan Press, Ann Arbor, MI, 1976.

[Rou04]   Jean Jacques Rousseau, *A discourse upon the origin and the foundation of the inequality among mankind*, http://www.gutenberg.org/etext/11136, 17 February 2004, Originally published, in French, in 1755.

[Sen77]   Amartya K. Sen, *Rational fools: A critique of the behavioural foundations of economic theory*, Philosophy and Public Affairs **6** (1977), 317–344.

[SK86]   David W. Stephens and Jorn R. Krebs, *Foraging theory*, Princeton University Press, Princeton, NJ, 1986.

[Sky96]   Brian Skyrms, *Evolution of the social contract*, Cambridge University Press, Cambridge, UK, 1996.

[Sky04]   _____, *The stag hunt and the evolution of social structure*, Cambridge University Press, Cambridge, UK, 2004.

[VBB90]   John B. Van Huyck, Raymond C. Battalio, and Richard O. Beil, *Tacit coordination games, strategic uncertainty, and coordination failure*, The American Economic Review **80** (1990), no. 1, 234–248.

[VBB91]   _____, *Strategic uncertainty, equilibrium selection, and coordination failure in average opinion games*, The Quarterly Journal of Economics **106** (1991), no. 3, 885–910.

Trust, Untrust, Distrust and Mistrust – An Exploration of the Dark(er) Side

Stephen Marsh[1] and Mark R. Dibben[2]

[1] National Research Council Canada, Institute for Information Technology
steve.marsh@nrc.gc.ca
[2] Lincoln University, New Zealand
dibbenm@lincoln.ac.nz

Abstract. There has been a lot of research and development in the field of computational trust in the past decade. Much of it has acknowledged or claimed that trust is a good thing. We think it's time to look at the other side of the coin and ask the questions why is it good, what alternatives are there, where do they fit, and is our assumption always correct?

We examine the need for an addressing of the concepts of Trust, Mistrust, *and* Distrust, how they interlink and how they affect what goes on around us and within the systems we create. Finally, we introduce the phenomenon of 'Untrust,' which resides in the space between trusting and distrusting. We argue that the time is right, given the maturity and breadth of the field of research in trust, to consider how untrust, distrust and mistrust work, why they can be useful in and of themselves, and where they can shine.

1 Introduction

Computers, and the world they touch, are interesting. For example, issues of IT security mean that, to coin a phrase, everyone is distrusted equally, but some are distrusted more equally than others[1], while 'trusted computing' would have us believe that we are capable of trusting our computers and our networks, as it were, with just a little more effort in the design and implementation process. ECommerce vendors compete for the trust of consumers, tweaking websites, designing online experiences and generally falling over themselves in their eagerness to put right what has been pointed out as wrong (a major research area in its own right, that of trust in online experiences, see for example [1, 2, 3, 4, 5, 6]), which is odd considering that distrust is an important motive force in such transactions as result [7]. A great deal of excellent research has gone into computational trust, trust management, online trust, and so on in the past decade or so, and now, we find ourselves at a crossroads.

---

[1] As an aside, we believe that the use of the term 'trust' in IT security requires much more careful thought, but that's a story, and a recurrent argument, for another time.

P. Herrmann et al. (Eds.): iTrust 2005, LNCS 3477, pp. 17–33, 2005.

There is, in the literature and the world, an overwhelming consideration that trust is a fundamentally positive force that, when applied in many different areas, from society to computation, will bear positive fruit. As trust researchers, we tend to agree, but there's a caveat – Trust has a 'darker' side, Distrust, and this is almost uniformly ignored, or glossed over as something to be addressed at another time. Invariably, distrust causes problems with computational formulae – what exactly is it, how does it get represented and, when it is represented, what does it really *mean*? Just as invariably, we promise we'll think about it another time and head off with a greater understanding of trust and none of distrust. The time is right to examine the darker side of trust. Distrust is not a simple reversal of the concept, although it *is* tightly coupled [8]. It's also not *Mis*trust or *Un*trust, although again it's related. To our knowledge, the question of how it's related, where, and to what extent it comes into play, and how one can become another, has not been adequately addressed in the computational sciences literature ([7, 9, 10] notwithstanding). For the sake of a complete understanding, it's time this was done. Finally, it's also time to discuss what the space between trusting and distrusting is, and how it works.

This paper serves as a next step in that process, as a call to arms to the Trust researchers and developers to turn their thoughts to Untrust, Distrust and Mistrust, to consider them as unique entities in their own right, and to develop systems and architectures that utilise their strengths in a concrete manner that acknowledges where one ends and another begins. The organisation of this paper is as follows. Firstly, we believe that it is necessary to understand our terms of reference before we proceed. Accordingly, section 2 presents and discusses definitions of trust, untrust, distrust, and mistrust, and by doing so creates a concrete foundation from which to move into our explorations. To discuss the concepts further, in section 3 we expand the formalisation in [11] to include explicit consideration of distrust and mistrust, and to make it more applicable to computational trust as it now stands. Section 4 discusses why the phenomena of untrust, distrust and mistrust are important, where they can be used and why, and how they contribute to trust research and the ultimate conception of trust as a positive thing.Finally, we apply the new formalisation and end with a call to arms for understanding and further work in this area in section 5.

2   Definitional Issues and Discussions

A short review of trust literature in the social sciences reveals an increasing interest in distrust. What was once regularly considered as a side-effect of trust violation [12, 13], rather than necessarily a construct of its own, has now assumed more significance. Most understandings of distrust appear to take their cue from Luhmann's [14] suggestion that those who choose not to trust "must adopt another negative strategy to reduce complexity" [15–page 24] and that Golembiewski and McConkie's 'self-heightening cycle of trust' [16] applies in the opposite way to its supposed corollary [17–page 38]. The significance of distrust as a separate concept is brought into stark relief when coupled with ideas from risk management and social, or public, trust – and this is an area we will develop later. Suffice to say that from the perspective of risk communication, public distrust is a 'cultural tendency' [18–page 60], ameliorated by better information [19] which recognises that "lay-people's conceptions of risk reflect a richer and broader rationality" [20–page 130]. That is to say, distrust is a human response to a lack of information. Thus, distrust is often considered as the "negative mirror-image of trust" [21–page 26], a "confident negative expectation regarding anothers conduct" [22–page 439] in a situation entailing risk to the trusting party. Mistrust, for its part, can be considered as "either a former trust destroyed, or former trust healed" [21–page 27].

While we've mentioned (and criticised) before [23] that it seems that every paper in computational trust at least seems to have its own need for a definition of trust, that's certainly true here. Not only that, but we also need definitions for distrust untrust, and mistrust. Importantly, we argue that in fact they are *not* the same.

In many ways, this paper represents an evolution from [11], where we discussed distrust and ignorance. There, we stated that distrust was negative of trust. Here, we're evolving that definition because of the work that has been done in the area, and a greater understanding of the concept because of this work. That given, it's still surprisingly difficult to find definitions of distrust that don't use mistrust as synonymous (even the otherwise excellent [9] confuses the two). In fact, we believe this is a mistake because it removes a tool for trust researchers to be able to focus on what they are researching. We use a corollary with information as a pointer to the direction we will take. From the Oxford English Dictionary, we find that the term 'misinformation' can be taken to mean information that is incorrect. This can be a mistake on the part of the informer, and generally speaking, it can be spotted after the fact. The term 'disinformation' removes all doubt – it's information that is deliberately false and intended to deceive. That is, disinformation is misinformation that is deliberately and knowingly planted. From this, we can move to a better understanding of distrust and mistrust, and what untrust is.

A simple comparison between the concepts is probably necessary. For the sake of argument, following [24, 25, 26, 27, 14, 11], let's say that trust, in general, is taken as the belief (or a measure of it) that a person (the trustee) will act in the best interests of another (the truster) in a given situation, even when controls are unavailable and it may not be in the trustee's best interests to do so. Given this, we can now examine untrust, distrust and mistrust in the following ways.

Given that Misinformation is passive in some form (that is, it may or may not be intentional, and is a judgment usually attained after the fact), we conjecture that **Mistrust** is misplaced trust. That is, in a situation where there was a positive estimation of the trustee and trust was betrayed, we can say that trust has been misplaced (not always 'betrayed,' since the trustee may not have had bad intentions). Thus, the truster mistrusted the trustee. Thus, as we see in [28] mistrust is defined so "When a trustee betrays the trust of the truster, or, in other words, defaults on trust, we will say that a situation of mistrust has occured, or that the truster has mistrusted the trustee in that situation." (p.47).

Somewhere between distrust and trust there is a potentially large gap. In this gap exists 'Untrust'. **Untrust** is a measure of how *little* the trustee is actually trusted. That is to say that if we say a trustee is untrusted, then the truster has little confidence (belief, faith) in the trustee acting in their best interests in that particular situation. This is not quite the same as being the opposite of trust. In [11] the concept of untrust, while not explicitly acknowledged as such at the time, is covered in the situation of Situational Trust being less than Cooperation Threshold – I trust you, but not enough to believe you'll be of any help in this situation if push comes to shove. Thus, untrust is positive trust, but not enough to cooperate. In this instance, as has been noted elsewhere [9], it is possible to put into place measures that can help increase trust, or at least remove the need to rely on the trustee. These can include legal necessities such as contracts, or verification techniques, for example observation until the truster is satisfied, and so on: "Trust, but verify," as Reagan said.

Distrust, by comparison is a measure of how much the truster (we obviously use the term loosely here!) believes that the trustee will actively work against them in a given situation. Thus, if I distrust you, I expect you'll work to make sure the worst (or at least not the best) will happen in a given situation. Interestingly, while trust (and mistrust and untrust) are situational, it's hard to imagine many examples where a distrusted person can be trusted by the same truster in a different situation, but there may well be some. Again, [28] defines distrust as "to take an action as if the other agent is not trusted, with respect to a certain situation or context. To distrust is different from now having any opinion on whether to trust or not to trust ... Although distrust is a negative form of trust, it is *not the negation* of trust" (p.47, my emphasis). As will be seen in section 3, it is possible to represent distrust as negative trust, which is not the same as the negation *of* trust.

For further clarification, consider the statements 'I mistrusted the information John just gave me,' 'I don't trust the information Bill just handed me' and 'I distrust what Paula just told me' – in the first, the information was trusted but revealed to be incorrect, in the second, it may or may not be correct, but what we're saying is that we'd need more assurance before trusting it. In the third case, we are actively sure that the information is incorrect; moreover, that Paula intended it to be incorrect. Mis- versus dis-information relates here to mis- versus dis-trust.

Luhmann [14] states that distrust is functionally equivalent to trust. That is, it is possible to imagine distrust working in a complex situation *to the detriment* of the (dis)truster. Distrust results in the *need* for evidence, verification, and so on, and thus increases the complexity of a situation (where, as Luhmann claims, trust reduces that complexity). While Untrust is passive in the sense that it allows the truster to know that a trustee *may* be trustworthy in a situation, but isn't for this truster, Distrust is active, and allows the (dis)truster to know that

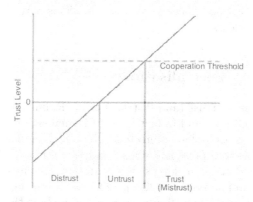

Fig. 1. The Continuum: From Distrust to Trust

a trustee is *not* to be trusted in this situation. Untrust is a measure of how much a person is trusted (and is a positive measure), Distrust is a negative measure.

Figure 1 illustrates how untrust, mistrust and trust conceptually relate. With some thought, it can be seen that there are still avenues in need of work (what *is* a trust value of zero anyway?). However, the diagram serves to illustrate where our definitions of Untrust, Distrust and Trust lie. Mistrust doesn't fit on this diagram because it's a misplaced value that was positive and misplaced. As such, it would usually be in the trust section of the graph before cooperation.

Distrust, and untrust, are important not because of what they potentially stop, but because of what they can allow to continue. Thus, while I may mistrust or distrust you, this gives me a measure of what it is necessary for me to do or for you to undertake before I can be comfortable relying on you. This can include recourse to legal niceties, but can also include guarantees or other personal activities. Mistrust is important because of what it tells a truster after everything goes horribly wrong.

There is evidence to suggest that distrust, untrust[2] and mistrust are at least as important as trust, for example in E-Commerce [7], in government and organizations [29, 30], and in life [14, 8]. In fact, we conjecture, given the recent drops in trust in government, for example in the US [29], that distrust has become a more prevalent way to manage relationships that are at arms length than trust. That is to say, trust is the grease in the wheels of personal, private relationships, while distrust is the means by which every other relationship is measured and controlled. While this may seem to be something of a dark conjecture, it holds a certain amount of promise. Distrust (and its cousins) really can be important in high risk situations [7], limiting exposure, being more risk averse, and exposing more gradually in risky situations than trust would result in. Since the spiral of trust can hopefully lead to more exposure and more trust as trustworthy behaviour is exhibited [11, 16], it is reasonable to assume that untrust, placed

---

[2] Although no-one calls it that, in fact, no-one calls it *anything*.

correctly, can lead to trust. There exist more problems with distrust, of course, that we will address below.

3 Introductory Formalisations

Several formalisations of trust (and distrust) exist. Rahman's thesis documents them particularly well [28], and in fact his own formalisation is one of the more flexible ones. However, we're less interested in how such models work with trust, but how it is possible to represent *dis*trust, and/or *un*trust.

Bearing in mind that distinct trust levels are ambiguous at best (at least in terms of semantics and subjectivity [28–p.124]), we'll use them anyway. We believe benefits far outweigh their disadvantages, and include the ability to narrow down and discuss subconcepts (as is shown below), (computational) tractability and the ability to discuss and compare to some extent, and given a limited amount of space here, we'll argue the point at length elsewhere. From [11] we use the notation shown in table 1. For more information discussions on the use of values and their ultimate frailties, see [11, 31, 32], amongst others.

The formalisations in [11] attempted to answer questions about trust in cooperative situations. That is, given the choice between cooperation and non-cooperation, whether to cooperate with a specific trustee or not. Two formulae are used, the first being to estimate Situational Trust. To estimate situational trust, x uses:

$$T_x(y, \alpha) \;=\; U_x(\alpha) \times I_x(\alpha) \times \widehat{T_x(y)} \tag{1}$$

The second formulae considers a Cooperation Threshold:

$$\text{Cooperation\_Threshold}_x(\alpha) = \frac{\text{Perceived\_Risk}_x(\alpha)}{\text{Perceived\_Competence}_x(y, \alpha) + \widehat{T_x(y)}} \times I_x(\alpha) \tag{2}$$

Table 1. Summary of notation ('Actors' are truster, trustee and others)

Description	Representation	Value Range
Situations	$\alpha, \beta, \ldots$	
Actors	$a, b, c, \ldots$	
Set of Actors	$\mathcal{A}$	
Societies of Actors	$\mathcal{S}_1, \mathcal{S}_2 \ldots$ $\mathcal{S}_n \in \mathcal{A}$	
Knowledge (e.g., x knows y)	$K_x(y)$	True/False
Importance (e.g., of α to x)	$I_x(\alpha)$	$[0, +1]$
Utility (e.g., of α to x)	$U_x(\alpha)$	$[-1, +1]$
Basic Trust (e.g., of x)	T_x	$[-1, +1)$
General Trust (e.g., of x in y)	$T_x(y)$	$[-1, +1)$
Situational Trust (e.g., of x in y for α)	$T_x(y, \alpha)$	$[-1, +1)$

Finally we state that,

$$T_x(y, \alpha) \geq \text{Cooperation\_Threshold}_x(\alpha) \Rightarrow \text{Will\_Cooperate}(x, y, \alpha)$$

The specifics of the formulae are not overly relevant here. What we are considering is a situation where, given some information, knowledge, and experience, x has to decide whether to cooperate or not with y. While a simplification, we have always seen this as a decision founded on trust.

The next question that naturally arises is 'what if the thresholds are too high?' That is, what if x doesn't trust y enough in a situation, or what if the resultant values are negative. These are, respectively, situations of untrust and distrust.

3.1   Modeling Untrust

For a situation of mistrust, the following must be true:

$$T_x(y, \alpha) > 0 \ \& \ T_x(y, \alpha) < \text{Cooperation\_Threshold}_x(\alpha) \Rightarrow \text{Untrust}(x, y, \alpha) \quad (3)$$

That is, if $T_x(y, \alpha)$ is less than the Cooperation Threshold but larger than 0, x is in a state of *untrust* in y. That is, x 'doesn't trust' y. Generally speaking, that means x will not enter into cooperation with y in this situation. In fact, this is somewhat simplistic because of course there may be little choice but for x to rely on y in α (note that it is possible to rely on someone without trusting them [28]). As has been noted above, this puts x into an interesting situation. She knows that y is not trusted enough to cooperate with (but note that y is trusted to some extent) but there's not much of a choice about who else to work with. As will be seen, there are answers to this dilemma.

3.2   Modeling Distrust

Distrust, as discussed above, is an active judgment in the negative intentions of the other. That is to say:

$$T_x(y, \alpha) \ < 0 \Rightarrow \text{Distrust}(x, y, \alpha) \quad (4)$$

Because of the way the formulae work, this can occur in situations where there is a negative importance or utility for α. This is a potential shortcoming of the formalisation that has already been pointed out (see [11] for indepth discussions), but is easily checked in computational trust. However, while outside the scope of this article, it is worth thinking about what negative importance or negative utility might actually mean.

Whatever the case, a negative situational trust value can be taken to mean that the truster expects the trustee to behave contrary to their best interests in the situation. Clearly, the truster should not then enter into the situation. Again, questions arise as to what happens if there is no choice. Of course, we argue that distrust in this circumstance gives one a choice – it may be better not to enter in and face the consequences than to jump into the situation with the trustee, and distrust can give a measure of whether or not the consequences of *not* entering into the situation are worse than those of entering into it and a (subjectively estimated) subsequent betrayal. Ultimately, this can be a question of risk, consequences, utility and so on.

Consider an example. A security program controls access to data warehouse that is queried by an autonomous agent searching for information. To attain access to the information, the agent must be given some security clearance. Calculations suggest a distrust (negative trust) in the agent, but if the program does not grant access, there may be legal costs involved, or the reputation of the data warehouse could be adversely affected, so what to do? The program could grant access, knowing that the other will steal or perhaps alter valuable information, or it could deny access, with the resultant negative effects. Importantly, knowing that there may be a violation of trust means the security program can create defences (backing up data more frequently, for example). The resultant damage to the reputation of the repository could well be more damaging than the cost of making ready for violations of trust. As another example, consider my need to fly to Europe to give a talk. In an examination of sub-goals, I can calculate that I do not trust (in fact, this could be distrust or untrust, depending somewhat on my notions of a global baggage handler conspiracy!) the baggage handlers to get my luggage to me correctly (perhaps something can be damaged or stolen, or simply routed wrongly). The costs are potentially minimal, but could include the loss of all my clothes for the week I am in Europe. The cost of not going is loss of reputation when I cancel last minute, subsequent shame, and so on. Despite the fact I mistrust baggage handlers, I consider that the cost of losing reputation is higher than that of a t-shirt and a pair of socks. I board the plane with a change of underwear in my carry on bag...

3.3   Dealing with Lack of Trust: Making x Comfortable

One of the most important aspects of trust is that it enables a decision maker to act in situations of doubt, distrust, or untrust [33]. In equation 3, x is in a state of mistrust in y for situation α. As we've noted, there is still the possibility of x having no choice but to rely on y, or perhaps of yy, despite a low trust value, being the most trusted of several alternatives[3]. This, or other similar situations where x is constrained, being the case, it falls to x and y to negotiate a way in which x can become comfortable enough to enter into α with y.

Because of the way in which the formulae above work, we can examine some options[4]:

- Reduce the Perceived Risk inherent in α
- Reduce the Importance of α
- Increase the Perceived Competence of y
- Reduce the potential Utility of α for x

---

[3] Note here that the main strength of using values, whether subjective or not, is this inherent ability to perform such rankings internally to the actor.

[4] Given other formalisations, this list would alter. What is important to us is that a list is available for the actors to work through.

Examining these, we can come up with solutions for the dilemma x finds herself in. We consider some (a non-exhaustive list) now. To reduce risk, x xan get some assurances from y that y will behave carefully, or be bound in some way. To increase the perceived competence, y could present credentials or examples of previous experience.

Reducing the importance of a situation, and the utility of a situation, are more interesting. In both cases, it would seem that such actions require that α in fact become a completely different situation (let's call it β). It could also, for example, involve splitting α into two or more other situations, each of which lead toward the goal of α but each of which has less importance than α. This is of course a goal-directed approach. What if α is not workable in this way? Then, other considerations must be made.

Conceptually, it's easy to understand this dilemma. In practice, it's often difficult for an actor to work through solutions. The use of the formalisation allows an actor to at least see the considerations. From there, they can make alternative plans.

3.4   When It All Goes Horribly Wrong: Mistrust

As discussed above, Mistrust is misplaced trust, that is trust that was placed and was subsequently betrayed in some way. In [11, 34], we briefly examined how betrayal of trust affects the general trust of the trustee by the truster, and determined that the disposition of the truster had an effect on both general trust and subsequent adjustments of how much the trustee is trusted from them on.

Put simply, there is an adjustment to make to trust in the trustee following the conclusion of a situation. For time t:

$$T_x(y)^{t+1} = T_x(y)^t + \Delta(T_x(y)) \tag{5}$$

What the Δ is here is what is of interest. Much work remains to be done in this area, but briefly consider two circumstances and how this can affect trust subsequently. In the first instance, the trustee betrayed the trust of the truster but did not intend to (this can be as a result of lack of competence, circumstances outside the control of the trustee, and so forth). In other words, they should have been *un*trusted. In this circumstance, the Δ can be a small percentage of original $T_x(y)^t$. However, if it turns out that the trustee was disposed to betray the truster *before* the situation took place, in other words should have been *dis*trusted, then the Δ would be a great deal larger. This is in keeping with the behaviour of trust that has been observed across various disciplines (see e.g. [24, 35, 14, 36]).

4   Related Work, Discussions and Pointers

Thus far we have raised the issue of distrust (i.e. a 'confident negative expectation...' as opposed to trust's 'confident positive expectation...') and untrust (i.e. insufficient trust of the other party in the particular situation under consideration) as concepts certainly not as well recognised in computer science as in social science. Recognising the need to develop information systems modelling that more accurately reflects the behaviour of human agents, we have then put together a formalisation of the impact of distrust and untrust on the co-operative behaviour of autonomous agents. This, however, is only a first step.

Our purpose in the remainder of the paper is to move the discussion forward by considering what implications recent advances in the understanding of trust, confidence and distrust in specific branches of the social sciences (most notably public policy, health care and management studies) may have for 'information systems trust management' (iTrust). We do this by briefly (1) critically comparing the formalism with Lewicki et als formal distinctions between trust and distrust [22]; and (2) exploring the almost taken-for-granted association between confidence and trust arising out of the adoption of Luhmanns [8] connection between the two concepts (that Lewicki et al also adopt), in the light of what has been termed the problem of 'public sector accountability' through clinical governance and performance indicators (e.g. [37, 38]). Such discussions lend themselves to areas for further research.

4.1   Questioning the Bi-polar Construct Principle

The formalism we have developed thus far is characterised by an understanding that trust relationships are both situation specific (i.e. they are mutlifaceted) and that they are processual (i.e. ever-changing; [39]). This is in contrast to more normative views arising largely out of traditional sociologies of exchange (e.g. [40, 41]) that see trust relationships as rather more homeostatic and consistent states [42, 43]. However, the formalism does entertain an assumption that trust and distrust can be described as one bi-polar construct. This assumption has its basis in early psychological research that viewed them as being at opposite ends of a single continuum [44]). This has a natural implication for co-operation in terms of no co-operation arising from distrust and co-operation arising from trust (e.g. [45, 46, 47]). While we have already said here and elsewhere [11, 48, 49] that such a stark distinction is perhaps misleading and that no co-operation might be more indicative of insufficient trust ('untrust') rather than any active distrust, the inherent bi-polar construct principle has been brought into question by [22].

Basing their thinking on Luhmanns [14] argument that both trust and distrust simplify the social world by allowing actors to (differently) manage social uncertainty (the principle of functional equivalency), Lewicki et al suggest that in fact trust and distrust are entirely separate dimensions. This is because "low distrust is not the same as high trust, and high distrust is not the same as low trust" [22–page 445]. They argue that it is perfectly possible to have conditions of a) simultaneous low trust and low distrust, b) simultaneous high trust and low distrust, c) simultaneous low trust and high distrust and d) simultaneous high trust and high distrust. This rendering can be seen as a description of the history of the relationship between two actors, as perceived from one actors perspective.

For example, low trust, low distrust is characteristic of a relationship where there are no grounds for either high trust or high distrust in a situation, most common in newly established relationships. We wonder whether this may be an extension of the notion of blind trust, or even Meyerson et al's swift trust [50]. High trust, low distrust is characteristic of a relationship in which the actor has a situational trust that has been rewarded with positive experiences and few, if any, instances of trust violation. Low trust, high distrust is perhaps the most difficult relationship to manage, according to Lewicki et al, since "they must find some way to manage their distrust" [22–page 447]. Most often, this is achievable by the establishment of clearly identified and defined parameters within which the relationship proceeds, and through which "constrained trust relations that permit functional interaction within the constraints" (ibid.) can emerge and be fruitful. High trust, high distrust relations are characterised by actors having some conflicting and some shared objectives. This leads to many positive experiences and many negative experiences, reinforcing both trust and distrust. In these circumstances, the relationship can be managed by limiting the actors dependence to those situations that reinforce the trust and strongly constrain those situations that engender distrust, to the extent that the outcome can be contained, if not entirely predicted.

The importance of such a rendering of trust and distrust as co-existing to our understanding of artificial intelligence agents and their operation in (for example) search engines, may lie in the practical importance of building and maintaining trust relationships with sources of information while at the same time treating with suspicion much of the information received from those sources. Lewicki et al argue that dysfunction in relationships arises not from distrust, but rather from trust without distrust and from distrust without trust. They argue that it is the "dynamic tension" between trust and distrust that allows relationships between actors to be productive, in the best interests of both confiding parties and as a source of long-lasting stability for relationships [22–page 450]. This dynamic tension is certainly evident in studies of doctor patient relations (e.g. [39], where the blind faith in a doctors ability to cure illness is replaced – often after considerable trust violation – with what has been termed a relationship of 'guarded alliance' [51, 52]. This is one in which the patient recognises the limitations of the doctor and works within them to manage their illness while seeking (or not) a cure. We wonder:

- Whether and how it would be possible to model such trust and distrust relations in more formal (computational) terms;
- What impact this may have on the behaviour of such agents; and
- Whether such behaviour would be productive from a user perspective – even if it were more 'realistic,' i.e. closer to the experience of human relations.

4.2   The Confidence Problem – And Carole Smith's Solution

The complexity and risk-laden nature of health care scenarios has also led to a re-evaluation of the nature and role of confidence in human interaction. While at the heart of much trust research, the understanding (often associated with Luhmann; [43]) of confidence in terms of an association with willingness to confide in another, or have a positive belief about another party, has recently been implicitly called into question through a quite different interpretation of the concept. In sum, this interpretation, having a risk and operations management basis derived from the need to achieve clinical governance and public sector accountability, suggests that the search for confidence is indicative of – at best – insufficient trust in the other party [53]. More likely, it is indicative of the need to explicitly and critically compare the performance of others rather than take their word for it [37] – something which in our eyes seems more akin to distrust. We shall now proceed to examine this definitional problem more closely.

It is interesting to note that Luhmann drew a very clear distinction between trust and confidence that calls into question research suggesting trust is a 'confident expectation...' Luhmann suggested that confidence is indicated by a lack of consideration for the risks involved [whereas] trust is indicated by a consideration of the risks involved [8–pages 97–103]; see also [48–page 274] for further discussion). We may ask how confidence can then be a part of trust at all? To complicate matters further, there is also the issue of self-trust, the trust of the trusting agent in itself to act in the best interests of itself. To avoid an explicitly psychological emphasis that would lead one away from an account of the situation and the other party, we have previously handled this in terms of perceptions of self-competence [48]; i.e. as a co-operation criterion). In other words, a more complete account of the behaviour of the trusting agent requires an estimation of that agents confidence in itself to act in its best interests according to its recognised abilities in the situation, and as compared with its perceived competence of the other agent. In sum, therefore, we can surmise four different interpretations of competence. First, confidence as concerning a trust of another party sufficient to be willing to confide in that party (e.g. [10]). Second, confidence as being confident in ones own decision to place trust (or distrust) in another (e.g. [24]. Third, confidence as self-assuredness to the extent of acting without consideration for risk [8]. Fourth, confidence in oneself as an agent based on ones assessment of ones own competence, as a conceptual proxy for self-trust [48]. Is there any new means by which to better clarify the distinction between trust and confidence?

One contentious, but potentially helpful way of understanding the difference has been proposed by Carole Smith as a result of studying social work and the public sector accountability of such activity. Research in public policy and management has revealed the need to better comprehend how trust sustains well-functioning organisations, 'especially those agencies in the public sector that lack market discipline [54, 38, 55, 56]. The impact of public trust comes to the fore in such circumstances, as it has an impact on the nature and extent of the accountability systems put in place by public sector managers (e.g., [57, 58, 51]). Such accountability systems are intended to provide appropriate reassurance to the public and enable effective corrective action to be taken to ensure public safety. These accountability systems, however, rely largely on explicit measurement of individual performance and organisational outcomes to establish confidence intervals that can be proven to be an accurate account of the organisation and the work of its employees. Such intense focus on performance measurement, coupled with a range of potential indictments for any failure to meet organisational objectives has,[53] argues, eroded the trust between employees and managers necessary for effective professional relationships, such as those found in hospitals. In this sense, therefore the drive for public accountability through the establishment of explicit quantitative measures of performance standards, i.e. the drive for the establishment of public confidence, is in direct conflict with interpersonal trust [59].

To unpack this problematic, Smith [53] draws a stark distinction between trust and confidence, suggesting the two concepts are indeed very different, but not in the way Luhmann proposed. For Smith, trust concerns uncertainty about outcomes, an ambiguity of objective information and the exercise of discretion about action. It is also an internal attribution, a moral exercise of free will that assumes most significance in situations where there is a lack of regulation or means of coercion. Confidence, on the other hand, concerns the establishment of explicitly predictable outcomes, information is objective, standardised and scientific and there is little opportunity or even need to exercise discretion about action. In this sense, therefore, systemic confidence is seen an external attribution lacking morality that assumes most significance in situations where there are extensive regulatory mechanisms and / or opportunities for coercion of individual agents.

In sum, according to Carole Smith, the institutional or managerial search for confidence is indicative of a lack of trust, perhaps even genuine distrust. Further, such a search for confidence may in fact have a tendency to instil distrust among professional colleagues, as a result of the increased sense of scrutiny and critical peer comparison. This is clearly a very different interpretation of what is mean by confidence. We wonder:

- Whether and how it would be possible to model such trust vs. confidence distinctions and inter alia impact in more formal (computational) terms;
- What impact this may have on the behaviour of such agents; and again
- Whether such behaviour would be productive from a user perspective – even if it were more realistic, i.e. closer to the experience of human relations.

5   Conclusions and a Call to Arms

We have noticed in recent literature that, some notable exceptions aside, there is an overarching acceptance that trust is a positive phenomenon that should be encouraged, for example to get people to buy more stuff, or get jobs done, or share information. While lack of trust is paid attention to, it is seen more as a byproduct of the trust phenomenon everyone has to adhere to.

We argue that Distrust and Untrust, respectively negative and 'not enough Trust,' allied under the wider umbrella of trust, are valuable and positive means to achieving concrete foundations to action in environments of uncertainty and doubt. We argue that there are ways to estimate and work with values for these phenomena that allow autonomous agents or other actors to behave sensibly in such situations. This behaviour can include, but is not limited to, recourse to other authorities, adjustment of resources or expectations, manipulation of situations to achieve comfort, and so on. Finally, we argue that Mistrust, the misplacing of trust, can tell an agent a great deal more about who to trust next time, or what went wrong, when allied with Untrust and Distrust information or conjecture.

To an extent, this paper represents something of a 'call to arms' to trust researchers to examine the phenomena and strengths and weaknesses of trust, untrust, distrust and mistrust to achieve their goals in a more rounded way. This includes the need for better models of the darker side of trust. We have made a first effort at this discussion and look forward to much more detailed explorations in the research to come.

For our part, we are examining how the phenomena work in multi-agent systems and information sharing architectures to allow partial access, modified access, or simply curtailed access to information, for example in CSCW, P2P architectures or community-based information sharing agents (cf [60]). Taking the concept further, we are examining how the related phenomenon of *forgiveness* can work in conjunction with trust and its darker components to create a gentler side to the security 'arms race' we find ourselves embroiled in.

References

1. Nielsen, J.: Trust or bust: Communicating trustworthiness in web design. Alertbox (http://www.useit.com/alertbox/990307.html) (1999)
2. Cheskin/Studio Archetype: Ecommerce trust (available online at: http://www.cheskin.com/p/ar.asp?mlid=7&arid=40&art=0). Technical report (1999)
3. Cheskin/Studio Archetype: Trust in the wired americas (available online at: http://www.cheskin.com/p/ar.asp?mlid=7&arid=12&art=0). Technical report (2000)
4. Head, M., Hassan, K.: Building online trust through socially rich web interfaces. In Marsh, S., ed.: Proceedings of PST 2004, International Conference on Privacy, Security and Trust (http://dev.hil.unb.ca/Texts/PST/). (2004)
5. Egger, F.: From Interactions to Transactions: Designing the Trust Experience for Business-to-Consumer Electronic Commerce. PhD thesis, Eindhoven University of Technology (2003)
6. Sillence, E., Briggs, P., Fishwick, L., Harris, P.: Trust and mistrust of online health sites. In: Proceedings of the 2004 conference on Human factors in computing systems. (2004) 663–670
7. McKnight, D.H., Kacmar, C., Choudhury, V.: Whoops... Did I use the Wrong concept to Predict E-Commerce Trust? Modeling the Risk-Related Effects of Trust versus Distrust Concepts. In: 36th Hawaii International Conference on Systems Sciences. (2003)
8. Luhmann, N.: Familiarity, confidence, trust: Problems and alternatives. In Gambetta, D., ed.: Trust. Blackwell (1990) 94–107
9. McKnight, D.H., Chervany, N.L.: Trust and distrust definitions: One bite at a time. In Falcone, R., Singh, M., Tan, Y.H., eds.: Trust in Cyber-Societies. Volume 2246 of Lecture Notes in Artificial Intelligence. Springer-Verlag, Berlin, Heidelberg (2001)

10. Lewicki, R.J., McAllister, D.J.B., Bies, R.J.: Trust and distrust: New relationships and realities. Academy of Management Review **23** (1998) 438–458
11. Marsh, S.: Formalising Trust as a Computational Concept. PhD thesis, Department of Computing Science, University of Stirling (1994) Available online via http://www.stephenmarsh.ca/Files/pubs/Trust-thesis.pdf.
12. Kramer, R.M.., Tyler, T.R.: Trust in Organisations: Frontiers of Theory and Research. Thousand Oaks: Sage (1996)
13. Hollis, M.: Trust Within Reason. Cambridge University Press (1998)
14. Luhmann, N.: Trust and Power. Wiley, Chichester (1979)
15. Lane, C., Bachmann, R., eds.: Trust Within and Between Organisations: Conceptual Issues and Empirical Applications. Oxford University Press (1998)
16. Golembiewski, R.T., McConkie, M.: The centrality of interpersonal trust in group processes. In Cooper, C.L., ed.: Theories of Group Processes. Wiley (1975) 131–185
17. Sydow, J.: Understanding the constitution of interorganisational trust. In Lane, C., Bachmann, R., eds.: Trust Within and Between Organisations. Oxford University Press (1998)
18. Cvetkovich, G.: The attribution of social trust. In Cvetkovich, G., Lofstedt, R., eds.: Social Trust and the Management of Risk. London: Earthscan (1999) 53–61
19. Earle, T.C., Cvetkovich, G.: Social trust and culture in risk management. In Cvetkovich, G., Lofstedt, R.E., eds.: Social Trust and the Management of Risk. London: Earthscan (1999) 9–21
20. Gowda, M.V.R.: Social trust, risk management and culture: Insights from native america. In Cvetkovich, G., Lofstedt, R.J., eds.: Social Trust and the Management of Risk. London: Earthscan (1999) 128–139
21. Sztompka, P.: Trust: a Sociological Theory. Cambridge University Press (1999)
22. Lewicki, R.J., McAllister, D.J., Bies, R.J.: Trust and distrust: New relationships and realities. The Academy of Management Review **23** (1998) 438–458
23. Marsh, S., Briggs, P., Wagealla, W.: Enhancing collaborative environments on the basis of trust. Available online at http://www.stephenmarsh.ca/Files/pubs/CollaborativeTrust.pdf (2004)
24. Boon, S.D., Holmes, J.G.: The dynamics of interpersonal trust: resolving uncertainty in the face of risk. In Hinde, R.A., Groebel, J., eds.: Cooperation and Prosocial Behaviour. Cambridge University Press (1991) 190–211
25. Low, M., Srivatsan, V.: What does it mean to trust an entrepreneur? In Birley, S., MacMillan, I.C., eds.: International Entrepreneurship. Routledge, London (1995) 59–78
26. Noteboom, B., Berger, H., Noordehaven, N.: Effects of trust and governance on relational risk. Academy of Management Journal **40** (1997) 308–338
27. Deutsch, M.: Cooperation and trust: Some theoretical notes. In Jones, M.R., ed.: Nebraska Symposium on Motivation, Nebraska University Press (1962)
28. Abdul-Rahman, A.: A Framework for Decentralised Trust Reasoning. PhD thesis, Department of Computer Science, University College London (2004 (Submitted))
29. Nye, Jr., J.S., Zelinkow, P.D., King, D.C., eds.: Why People Don't Trust Government. Harvard University Press (1997)
30. Kramer, R.M.: Trust and distrust in organizations: Emerging perspectives, enduring questions. Annual Review of Psychology **50** (1999) 569–598
31. Mui, L.: Computational Models of Trust and Reputation: Agents, Evolutionary Games, and Social Networks. PhD thesis, Massachusetts Institute of Technology, Department of Electrical Engineering and Computer Science (2002)

32. Seigneur, J., Jensen, C.D.: The role of identity in pervasive computational trust. In Robinson, P., Vogt, H., Wagealla, W., eds.: Privacy, Security and Trust within the Context of Pervasive Computing. Volume 780 of Kluwer International Series in Engineering and Computer Science. Kluwer (2005)

33. Kramer, R.M.: Trust rules for trust dilemmas: How decision makers think and act in the shadow of doubt. In Falcone, R., Singh, M., Tan, Y.H., eds.: Trust in Cyber Societies. Springer Verlag, Lecture Notes in Artificial Intelligence, LNAI 2246 (2001) 9–26

34. Marsh, S.: Optimism and pessimism in trust. In Ramirez, J., ed.: Proceedings Iberoamerican Conference on Artificial Intelligence/National Conference on Artificial Intelligence (IBERAMIA94/CNAISE94), McGraw-Hill (1994)

35. Lagenspetz, O.: Legitimacy and trust. Philosophical Investigations 15 (1992) 1–21

36. Daughtrey, T.: Costs of trust for e-business. Quality Progress (2001)

37. Davies, H., Mannion, R.: Clinical governance: Striking a balance between checking and trusting. In Smith, P.C., ed.: Reforming Markets in Health Care: An Economic Perspective. London: Open University Press (1999)

38. Davies, H.T.O.: Falling public trust in health services: Implications for accountability. Journal of Health Service Research and Policy 4 (1999) 193–194

39. Dibben, M.R.: Exploring the processual nature of trust and co-operation in orgnisations: A whiteheadian analysis. Philosophy of Management 4 (2004) 25–40

40. Blau, P.: Exchange and Power in Social Life. New York: John Wiley and Sons (1964)

41. Berger, P.: Sociology Reinterpreted. London: Penguin (1982)

42. Lewicki, R.J., Bunker, B.B.: Trust in relationships: A model of trust, development and decline. In Bunker, B.B., Rubin, J.Z., eds.: Conflict, Cooperation and Justice. San Francisco: Josey Bass (1985) 133–173

43. Lewicki, R.J., Bunker, B.B.: Developing and maintaining trust in working relationships. In Kramer, R.M., Tyler, T.R., eds.: Trust in Organizations: Frontiers of Theory and Research. Thousand Oaks: Sage (1996) 114–139

44. Rotter, J.B.: Generalized expectancies for interpersonal trust. American Psychologist 25 (1971) 443–452

45. Arrow, K.J.: The Limits of Organization. New York: Norton (1974)

46. Axelrod, R.: The Evolution of Cooperation. Basic Books, New York (1984)

47. Coleman, J.S.: The Foundations of Social Theory. The Belknap Press of the University of Harvard (1990)

48. Dibben, M.R.: Exploring Interpersonal Trust in the Entrepreneurial Venture. London: MacMillan (2000)

49. Marsh, S., Dibben, M.R.: The role of trust in information science and technology. In Cronin, B., ed.: Annual Review of Information Science and Technology. Volume 37. Information Today Inc. (2003) 465–498

50. Meyerson, D., Weick, K., Kramer, R.M.: Swift trust and temporary groups. In Kramer, R., Tyler, T., eds.: Trust in Organisations: Frontiers of Theory and Research. Thousand Oaks: Sage (1996) 166–195

51. Mechanic, D.: Changing medical organization and the erosion of trust. Millbank Quarterly 74 (1996) 171–189

52. Mechanic, D., Meyer, S.: Concepts of trust among patients with serious illness. Journal of Social Science and Medicine 51 (2000) 657–668

53. Smith, C.: Trust and confidence: Possibilities for social work in 'high modernity'. British Journal of Social Work 31 (2001) 287–305

54. Cvetkovich, G., Lofstedt, R.E., eds.: Social Trust and the Management of Risk. London: Earthscan (1999)

55. Waren, M.E.: Democracy and Trust. Cambridge University Press (1999)
56. Waterhouse, L., Beloff, H., eds.: Hume Papers on Public Policy: Trust in Public Life. Volume 7 of Hume Papers on Public Policy. Edinburgh: Edinburgh University Press (1999)
57. Davies, H., Lampell, J.: Trust in performance indicators? Quality in Health Care **7** (1998) 159–162
58. Harrison, S., P. J, L.: Towards a High-Trust NHS: Proposals for Minimally Invasive Reform. London: Her Majesty's Stationery Office (1996)
59. Dibben, M.R., Davis, H.T.O.: Trustworthy doctors in confidence-building systems. Quality & Safety in Health Care **13** (2004) 88–89
60. Marsh, S., Ghorbani, A.A., Bhavsar, V.C.: The ACORN Multi-Agent System. Web Intelligence and Agent Systems **1** (2003) 65–86

Security and Trust in the Italian Legal Digital Signature Framework

Stefano Zanero

Dip. di Elettronica e Informazione,
Politecnico di Milano,
via Ponzio 34/5, 20133 Milano, Italy
zanero@elet.polimi.it

Abstract. The early adoption of a national, legal digital signature framework in Italy has brought forth a series of problems and vulnerabilities. In this paper we describe each of them, showing how in each case the issue does not lie in the algorithms and technologies adopted, but either in faulty implementations, bad design choices, or legal and methodological issues. We also show which countermeasures would be appropriate to reduce the risks. We show the reflex of these vulnerabilities on the trust-based framework which gives legal value to digital signatures. We think that this study can help to avoid similar mistakes, now that under EU directives a similar architecture is planned or under development in most EU countries.

1 Introduction

In 1997, the concept of "law-strong" digital signature (we will call it ILDS, Italian Legal Digital Signature, in the rest of this paper, for the sake of clarity and to distinguish it from the more general concept of "digital signatures") was introduced in Italy [1]. The decree was revolutionary for its time, giving to electronically signed documents (prepared with prescribed methods) the same value of signed paper documents, "trusting" them to show the will of the signatory.

Just as it happened with the early introduction of a law on privacy protection (see, for a commentary, [2]), the early adoption of a legal digital signature scheme has brought forth a series of issues and vulnerabilities, which we helped to identify in at least one well-known case.

A popular misconception, during the ensuing debate, was that such vulnerabilities were defects of the digital signature technology itself. In this paper, we describe these issues, and we show that in each case the problem does not lie in the choice of algorithms and technologies, but either in faulty software implementations, in bad design choices, or in legal and methodological issues. We also show that there exist countermeasures which can be adopted, in order to make the process more secure.

The remainder of the paper is organized as follows: in Section 2 we describe the original Italian law on digital signature, and its recent modifications. In

P. Herrmann et al. (Eds.): iTrust 2005, LNCS 3477, pp. 34–44, 2005.

Section 3 we describe four cases of failures and bugs, in particular the bug we discovered, and show how appropriate countermeasures could avoid such problems, or at least diminished their potential impact. Finally, in Section 4 we draw some conclusions about what can be learned from the vulnerabilities of ILDS.

2   The Italian Law on Digital Signatures

In [1] the underlying concept is that if the procedure (*protocol*) used to generate the ILDS signature is secure, the electronic document can be trusted to show the actual will of the signer, giving to the electronic signature the same meaning and force as the traditional handwritten one. Really, the law recognized that a chain of trusted processes could build a trusted proof, such as the handwritten signature traditionally is.

Truly, in the original legal framework the digital signature was valued more than a traditional one: the law declared that it could not be "unrecognized". In the Italian civil framework, a written but unsigned document has proof value only if the author recognizes it, a signed document has value unless the author unrecognizes the signature, while an authenticated signature, which has been stamped by a public notary, cannot be unrecognized. This is because the notary authenticates the signatory securely. The law thus made the digital signatures similar in strength to an authenticated signature, even if the Certification Authority itself is not a public notary and does not follow notary procedures. This is a strange juridical status, see for a discussion [3]. Since the algorithms used to generate the signature are backed up by strong mathematical principles, *a digital signature cannot be claimed to be forged*, unless proof is given that, for instance, the private key was lost before the signature was placed (for a more detailed discussion, see [4]).

Technical regulations were subsequently released to describe a PKI architecture which could enforce such level of trust. The ILDS system, described in [5] is based on standard X.509 certificates, and on the usage of tamper-proof hardware devices "that can be programmed only at the origin" for generating the keys (i.e. requiring the use of smart cards). Thus, the only way for user to claim the loss of his private key is to declare that his smart card has been lost or stolen, in which case the certificate must be immediately revoked.

The original version of the law required ILDS certificates to be created and signed by trusted certification authorities, and the regulatory agency AIPA[1] was entrusted as the keeper of the CA registry. Requirements for these trusted CAs were:

- to be "S.p.A.", which is a particular societary form, and to have a minimum capital of about 6.500.000 EUR

---

[1] Agenzia per l'Informatica nella Pubblica Amministrazione: Regulatory Agency for IT in the Government, now called CNIPA, Consiglio Nazionale per l'Informatica nella Pubblica Amministrazione, National Council for IT in the Government.

- particular requirements of "honorability" for their administrators (e.g. they must never have been filed for bankruptcy, have been forbidden from taking public offices as a result of a penal process, and so on)
- their technicians must show due diligence and competence to meet with technical regulations
- their IT processes must respect international standards for quality assurance.

A new regulation [6], introduced to incorporate the recent EU directive on digital signatures [7], has introduced different "levels of trust" for different types of electronic signatures. It is beyond the scope of this article to fully discuss the official EU terminology and its differences with the Italian one, but the definitions can be summed up as follows:

Electronic Signature: a set of data in electronic format, which is attached to or logically linked with some other electronic data and which is used for the signatory's authentication.

Advanced Electronic Signature: an electronic signature which is unambiguously linked with the signatory, can identify the signatory, is created with a method or device which can be controlled solely by the signatory, and is attached to the signed data so that any changes in the data can be noticed.

Qualified Electronic Signature: an advanced signature based on a qualified certificate and made with a secure signature creation device; this is the type of signature which has similar value to traditional handwritten signatures.

Qualified Certificate: a certificate with particular requirements of security.

Digital Signature: a qualified electronic signature created with asymmetric cryptography algorithms; this definition has been added in order to make the new law backward-compatible with the old ILDS definition.

Entering the public registry of CAs which are certified to create qualified certificates is now called "accreditation". In this paper we will be mainly talking about the requirements for "digital signatures", because part of it was developed under the old ILDS framework. We refer the reader to [8, 9] for a more complete discussion on the legislative evolution of the italian law on digital and electronic signatures, and to [10] for a commentary on international trends in law.

An important point which follows from the history of the development of the ILDS scheme is that each authorized CA implemented its own application for the creation and the verification of digital signatures. This has created a number of problems for interoperability, in addition to the vulnerabilities we address in this article.

There is a wide debate on the validity of the different types of signature. For our discussion, it suffices to say that a "digital signature" can be used to sign contracts or documents destined to government agencies and branches, with full effect. It still cannot be used, for instance, in order to buy a house (since the Italian law requires the presence of buyer and seller in front of a public notary) or to sign a petition for a referendum consultation (for this will require you to be recognized by a public officer). In either case, you could use the ILDS certificate, providing that the notary or the officer have adequate means to let you sign the documents with it.

There are also some fields where a scheme of legal digital signature is probably not worth the effort: for example, small business to consumer e-commerce transactions have been done and will be done without using strong digital signatures [11].

3   The Failures of the Digital Signature

3.1   Word Macros and Fields

The first serious vulnerability we found in a ILDS application deals with the use of Word macro scripting and dynamic fields.

The vulnerability consists of a flaw in the application design, which we originally discovered in the digital signature software DiKe, developed by InfoCamere (as we said earlier, each CA implemented and released its own toolkit for generating signatures). A quick survey showed afterwards that most of the applications from other CAs were similarly affected.

The principle of the vulnerability is simple. If a Microsoft Office document containing a dynamic field (e.g. a self-updating time and date field) is signed by the means of DiKe, and then verified at a later time, the application shows it in an integrated viewer along with the updated field, without either detecting the variation or alerting the user that a dynamic field is present. This class of vulnerabilities was described also in [12].

This can end up in rather anomalous results, as can be seen in Figure 1. We can see multiple repetition of the documents' date and time. The first is a dynamic field, which is displayed differently each time the document is opened by DiKe, without warning the user in any way. If opened in Word, the changing field would at least show up.

The vendors, alerted by us with a short vulnerability advisory [13], tried to minimize, pointing out that:

– the defect had little impact because another regulation [14] required government agencies and offices to use document formats which cannot contain macros or executable code
– DiKe, like any other ILDS software, digitally signs (and verifies) not the textual content of a document, but an hash of the file containing the document. The execution of the macro does not alter the file contents, but just its representation, thus DiKe correctly reports that the document integrity has not been broken
– Office macros cannot be deactivated from the document viewer APIs used by third party developers. Microsoft, after our advisory and the discussion which ensued, acknowledged this design flaw (which affects all the versions of Office) and released on the Italian market an add-in to deal with it [15].

Fig. 1. The behavior of dynamic fields in DiKe. DiKe displays the field on the fourth line, which is a changing date, without alerting the user in any way

In our opinion, this does not reduce the impact of the problem. There is no doubt that DiKe implements correctly the cryptographic algorithms: the sequence of bits of the file containing the document does not change, and thus the algorithm cannot detect any change. But still, the result is not what the end user - or the law - would expect.

One possible solution to this particular issue is to disqualify files that contain macros. This is the simplest solution, and following our advisory (and, according to [16], because of it), it was adopted as part of the new regulations on digital documents and signatures [17], at article 3. Giving a handle to turn off the updating of fields, as Microsoft did, is helpful in this particular case, but does not solve a more general problem.

In Italian (and particularly in law terminology), the word "document" does not have the same meaning as "file". A legal document is "the representation of acts and facts of judiciary relevance" [18], so an electronic document is not the "file", but rather the representation of the contents, i.e. what the reader can see, or even better, what the author actually wanted to show. A digital signature software, in order to be compliant with the spirit and the letter of the Italian law, should then verify that the *representation* is still authentic, not the file itself. In addition, in [5], article 10 states further that the signature applications must represent to the signer "in an unambiguous manner" what he is going to sign. In other words, the signature framework should preserve the proper representation of the will of the signer, building a chain of trusted transformations that grants a correct, non-repudiable and non forgeable end-to-end transmission of this act of will.

A document containing dynamic fields is just one of the examples of a large class of possible problems. For example, another issue could rise from the large amount of metadata that is attached to some file formats, notably Office platform files [19]. Usually, the user is unaware of the metadata contents, and a number of curious cases (such as involuntary disclosure of deleted and corrected parts of documents on press releases) happened because of this. Are these data part of the signed document? If so, how is the signer supposed to know what is embedded into these hidden tags?

A solution could be that the signature application could automatically generate an image or PDF copy of the document, and let the signer sign this copy. This could create a problem of royalties and patents for the application developers, but could be a viable short-term solution. But going in depth, any decoding system used to represent the document to the signer, i.e. any viewer for any file format, should be validated and incorporated into a secure ILDS application. This is evidently impractical.

Choosing a standard format for data, such as XML, combined with "XML Signature" proposed standards [20], could be the ideal solution for this type of problems. Possible problems have also already been identified [21]. We think that this is an interesting topic for further research.

3.2   The PostECom Failure

Firma&Cifra is the application released by PostECom, another accredited CA. This application contains a vulnerability [22], reported by an anonymous researcher, which makes it totally insecure. Exactly as in the case of the previous bug, the problem does not reside in the cryptographic algorithms.

The bug leverages the fact that in ILDS signatures, as in most standards, the digital certificate used to generate the signature is appended to the signature itself, using a PKCS#7 envelope [23]. The certificate should be verified first (using the trusted certificates of the authorized CNIPA CAs already stored), and then added to a cache list of verified certificates. If a root certificate is inserted in the PKCS#7 envelope, it should be discarded, because the storage of Firma&Cifra is pre-loaded with the approved root certificates of the accredited CAs, or at least the user should be warned before trusting it. Firma&Cifra instead does not discard it, but imports it automatically to the certificate storage area, and then uses it to verify other certificates.

This incredible error leads to astonishing results, such as those described in Figure 2: here we see that the software has gladly accepted as authentic the certificate in name of "Arsène Lupin", which is obviously fake.

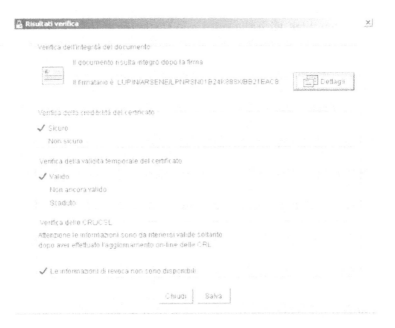

Fig. 2. The certificate of Arsène Lupin in Firma&Cifra. Please note that there is no hint that it has not been signed by a recognized root CA

We must note that also in this case the response from the software vendor has been less than prompt and vaguely worrying, describing this as a feature, and not a bug. This shows a worrying trend in the attention of accredited CAs about the security of their own products. Fortunately, after a while, an update correcting this bug was released.

3.3   Procedural Issues with Token Distribution

A number of procedural issues have also come up. As it may be guessed, one of the most important and delicate points in the certificate roll-out procedure is the proper identification of the subject on whose name a digital certificate is going to be created, and how the smart card with the private key is handed over to this person. This is the fundamental building block of the trust preservation chain which the ILDS framework strives to build.

In many documented cases which were reported to us, a CA (whose name will be omitted) created a number of certificates for the clients of various professional accountants, which were given (along with their PIN) to the accountants themselves, instead of the clients. The accountants were in most cases blissfully unaware of the full possibilities of these smart cards, which they used only to sign and deposit balances and filings on behalf of the customers. In most cases they also kept all the smartcards, with their PIN sticked on the top, in a nice binder on an office shelf.

This kind of problems is not unheard-of in commercial, private CAs. However, when the digital signature becomes, by force of law, totally equivalent to an handwritten signature, the procedure must be considerably strengthened. The PIN and the smart card should be given only to the person on whose name the certificate has been created, verifying that he or she actually knows the full extent of the law concerning its use.

Since the Italian authorities now require some filings to be done only in electronic form, with the use of ILDS, and since in Italy almost always filings are done by accountants on behalf of their customers, we also feel that proper education on the real value of the smart card and the PIN would be necessary, in order to avoid that, after receiving their devices, less-than-knowledgeable people will give them to a potentially untrusted third party.

A possible solution, requiring technical and legal modifications, would be to create *limited trust* digital signature certificates, with predefined usage limits (e.g. "This certificate can be used to sign only financial filings"), which can then be delegated to third parties according to their responsibilities.

While the law does not explicitly allow this (since the electronic document, signed with a qualified digital signature, is substantially equivalent to a written and undersigned paper document), a regulation (in [18], article 27-bis, third paragraph) says that "The qualified certificate may contain, on request of the owner... [eventual] delegations of powers; b) usage restrictions for certificate, as defined by article 28-bis, paragraph 3; c) limitations on the values of acts and contracts for which the certificate can be used [...]". Article 28-bis, paragraph 3, introduced in D.Lgs. 10/02, explicitly states that "The C.A. can indicate in a qualified certificate usage limitations for said certificate, or a limitation on the value of the contracts the certificate can be used for", provided that third parties can check these limitations. But note that neither of the texts explicitly states that, if said limits are exceeded, the signed document is invalid. Article 43 of the cited [17] states more strongly that the C.A. "must, on request, insert into the certificate any usage limitations".

3.4 Insecurity of the Host System

In [24] a further attack on digital signature systems is presented. It basically uses a vulnerability in the Java class loader to trojanize the digital signature application on the host PC, in order to sign documents without the user's acknowledgment. The work underlines how to exploit a shortcoming of the JVM to make an user unwittingly sign a document, but from a security point of view the issue is far more general, and quite well known: an insecure system (one on which a trojan can be present, as it is assumed in this work) cannot generally be used for generating trusted, secure digital signatures, and this was already demonstrated a number of times (e.g. in [25]). The vulnerability in the class loading and certification scheme is one of the many possible attack paths that are opened if the basic assumption that the host system is secure fails. This discovery once again received great attention from the italian press as the "first practical realization worldwide of an attack against the digital signature devices", which is evidently not the case.

These demonstrations, however, mark a point: how can a digital signature be trusted to the full extent required by ILDS if it has been generated on a computer whose security is not granted? And if digital signatures are to be used by average computer users, how can we ensure or assume the security of their host systems?

If this assumption does not hold any more, we need to completely rethink the transmission paths between applications and signature devices, and we need to insert somehow "trusted checkpoints" on which the user can check what he is really going to sign. For instance, a new card reader device could display on a small embedded screen the fingerprint of the document that is being signed, and ask for further confirmation by the user (for instance by pressing a button on the device). In the same line of thought, devices that require the user to enter the PIN directly on a number keyboard attached to the smart card reader could reduce the risk of exposure to trojanized applications and similars. A more radical approach is the proposal of a dedicated, trusted device, similar to a small PDA, for signature purposes [26].

All these ideas, however, are not very practical, since standard readers already show interoperability problems, and such extensions could magnify them unbearably. In addition, creating nonstandard devices would significantly heighten the costs. However, no solutions based simply on software can prevent a trojan from capturing and replaying the PIN or altering the data flow.

A viable solution is proposed in [27]. The authors rely on the presence of a Trusted Platform Module, as proposed in the TCPA alliance Trusted Computing Platform specifications, and on the Intelligent Adjunct solution proposed in [28].

4   Conclusions

In this paper we have briefly presented two technological issues with two different ILDS applications, and we have shown that in each case the issue does not lie in the cryptographic algorithms: in one case, the abnormal behavior is a matter of a bad design choice, while in the other case the culprit is a faulty implementation of the certificate checking process. We have also shown that certifying the representation of a document, as opposed to the file containing the document, is not a trivial problem, and more research is required in order to properly solve it.

In addition, we have reported an example of methodological issue dealing with certificate distribution and user education. We have also generalized an attack recently reported on a particular architecture as being one facet of the many, well-known problems in the generation of trusted signatures on an un-trusted machine. In these two cases, the cryptographic algorithms are not even challenged: they are completely bypassed by other issues. Solutions exist, but they have not been applied in the commercially developed signing devices for the ILDS.

In conclusion, this case study shows once more that the sound security of the cryptographic algorithms is just one of the issues to be solved in order to properly implement a Public Key Infrastructure, or indeed any secure system. As an old maxim of cryptographers has it, "If you think cryptography can solve your problem, then you don't understand your problem and you don't understand cryptography"[29].

The Italian law on digital signature focused on the robustness of the algorithms as a sufficient proof of trust and security of the ILDS. However, as we have shown, mathematical proofs of correctness and security do not always translate seamlessly to the real world, where the design, the implementation, and above all people behavior constitute the true, weak component of any security architecture.

Acknowledgments

This work was partially supported by the Italian FIRB-Perf project. We also thank dr. Pierluigi Perri of the University of Milano and prof. Andrea Monti of the University of Chieti for their helpful comments on legal issues. The images are a courtesy of the InterLex archive [30, 31].

References

1. D.P.R. 10-11-1997, n. 513, "Regolamento contenente i criteri e le modalitá per la formazione, l'archiviazione e la trasmissione di documenti con strumenti informatici e telematici a norma dell'articolo 15, comma 2, della legge 15 marzo 1997, n. 59". Gazzetta Ufficiale n. 60 (13 mar.), in Italian (1998)
2. Perri, P., Zanero, S.: Lessons learned from the italian law on privacy. Computer Law and Security Report 20 (2004)
3. Monti, A.: Il documento informatico nei rapporti di diritto privato. InterLex website, in Italian (1997)
4. Borruso, R., Buonomo, G., Corasaniti, G., D'Aietti, G.: Profili penali dell'informatica. Giuffré (1994)
5. D.P.C.M. 08-02-1999, "Regole tecniche per la formazione, la trasmissione, la conservazione, la duplicazione, la riproduzione e la validazione, anche temporale, dei documenti informatici". Gazzetta Ufficiale n. 87 (15 apr.), in Italian (1999)
6. D.P.R. 07/04/2003, n. 137, "Regolamento recante disposizioni di coordinamento in materia di firme elettroniche a norma dell'articolo 13 del decreto legislativo 23 gennaio 2002, n. 10". in Italian (2003)
7. Directive 1999/93/EC of the European Parliament and of the Council of 13 december 1999, "On a Community framework for electronic signatures". Official Journal L013 (19 jan.) (2000)
8. Cammarata, M., Maccarone, E.: La firma digitale sicura. Il documento informatico nell'ordinamento italiano. Giuffré, Milan (2003)
9. Dumortier, J.: Legal status of qualified electronic signatures in europe. In Paulus, S., Pohlmann, N., Reimer, H., eds.: ISSE 2004-Securing Electronic Business Processes, Vieweg (2004) 281–289
10. Brazell, L.: Electronic signatures: law and regulation. Sweet & Maxwell, London (2004)

11. Winn, J.K.: The emperor's new clothes: The shocking truth about digital signatures and internet commerce. Idaho Law Review Symposium on Uniform Electronic Transaction Act (2001)
12. Kain, K., Smith, S., Asokan, R.: Digital signatures and electronic documents: A cautionary tale. In: Advanced Communications and Multimedia Security, IFIP TC6/TC11 6th Joint Working Conference on Communications and Multimedia Security. Volume 228 of IFIP Conference Proceedings., Kluwer Academic (2002) 293–308
13. Zanero, S.: Sconfinati campi di cavoli amari. Vulnerability Advisory, in Italian (2002)
14. Autoritá per l'informatica nella pubblica amministrazione: Deliberazione n. 51/2000, "regole tecniche in materia di formazione e conservazione di documenti informatici delle pubbliche amministrazioni ai sensi dellart. 18, comma 3, del decreto del presidente della repubblica 10 novembre 1997, n. 513". In Italian (2000)
15. Firma digitale sicura in Microsoft Word. Press Release, in Italian (2003)
16. Cammarata, M.: Regole tecniche per bachi legali. InterLex website, in Italian (2003)
17. D.P.C.M. 13 gennaio 2004, "Regole tecniche per la formazione, la trasmissione, la conservazione, la duplicazione, la riproduzione e la validazione, anche temporale, dei documenti informatici". Gazzetta Ufficiale n. 98 (27 apr.), in Italian (2004)
18. D.P.R. 28-12-2000, n. 445, "Testo unico delle disposizioni legislative e regolamentari in materia di documentazione amministrativa". Gazzetta Ufficiale n. 42 (20 feb), in Italian (2001)
19. How to minimize metadata in Word 2003. Microsoft Knowledge Base (2004)
20. XML signature requirements. Request For Comments 2807 (2000)
21. Jsang, A., Povey, D., Ho, A.: What you see is not always what you sign. In: The proceedings of the Australian UNIX User Group. (2002)
22. Anonymous: Security Advisory, in Italian (2003)
23. Pkcs #7: RSA cryptographic message syntax standard. RSA Laboratories (1993) version 1.5.
24. Bruschi, D., Fabris, D., Glave, V., Rosti, E.: How to unwittingly sign non-repudiable documents with Java applications. In: 9th Annual Computer Security Applications Conference. (2003)
25. Spalka, A., Cremers, A.B., Langweg, H.: The fairy tale of what you see is what you sign: Trojan horse attacks on software for digital signature. In: Proceedings of the IFIPWG9.6/11.7 Working Conference, Security and Control of IT in Society-II (SCITS-II). (2001)
26. Weber, A.: See what you sign: Secure implementations of digital signatures. In: Proceedings of the 5th International Conference on Intelligence and Services in Networks, LNCS 1430, Springer-Verlag (1998) 509–520
27. Spalka, A., Cremers, A.B., Langweg, H.: Protecting the creation of digital signatures with trusted computing platform technology against attacks by trojan horse programs. In: Proceedings of the 16th International Conference on Information Security: Trusted Information. (2001) 403–419
28. Balacheff, B., Chan, D., Chen, L., Pearson, S., Proudler, G.: Securing intelligent adjuncts using trusted computing platform technology. In: Proceedings of the 4th Working Conference on Smart Card Research and Advanced Applications, Kluwer Academic Publishers (2001) 177–195
29. Schneier, B.: A hacker looks at cryptography. In: Black Hat Conference. (1999)
30. Gelpi, A.: La firma è sicura, il documento no. InterLex website, in Italian (2002)
31. Cammarata, M.: Il certificato di Arsène Lupin. InterLex website, in Italian (2003)

Specifying Legal Risk Scenarios Using the CORAS Threat Modelling Language

Experiences and the Way Forward

Fredrik Vraalsen[1], Mass Soldal Lund[1], Tobias Mahler[2],
Xavier Parent[3], and Ketil Stølen[1]

[1] SINTEF, Norway
{fvr, msl, kst}@sintef.no
[2] Norwegian Research Center for Computers and Law,
University of Oslo, Norway
tobias.mahler@jus.uio.no
[3] King's College London, UK
xavier@dcs.kcl.ac.uk

Abstract. The paper makes two main contributions: (1) It presents experiences from using the CORAS language for security threat modelling to specify legal risk scenarios. These experiences are summarised in the form of requirements to a more expressive language providing specific support for the legal domain. (2) Its second main contribution is to present ideas towards the fulfilment of these requirements. More specifically, it extends the CORAS conceptual model for security risk analysis with legal concepts and associations. Moreover, based on this extended conceptual model, it introduces a number of promising language constructs addressing some of the identified deficiencies.

1 Introduction

The notion of trust is tightly interwoven with notions like security and usability [1, 2]. Furthermore, it is difficult to separate trust from the expectation of a legal framework that offers protection in the cases where the trust relationship fails [3]. An analysis of trust should therefore encompass a number of issues including technological, legal, sociological and psychological aspects.

Since the trustor may be unable to monitor or control the trustee, it is essential that there are protective measures in place to solve situations that arise from lack of trustworthiness of the trustee. For example, Jones et al. [3] argue that "although businesses and consumers may consider underlying systems to be completely secure, they may not trust these systems with their business or personal interests unless there is a suitable legal framework they can fall back on, should problems arise." In this case, the legal framework is seen as a treatment to potential risks, e.g. economic loss. Hence, the proper foundation of trust is dependent on legal means of protection, as well as the security mechanisms that are employed to protect the system and its data [1]. Security measures, e.g.

P. Herrmann et al. (Eds.): iTrust 2005, LNCS 3477, pp. 45–60, 2005.

logging, may, however, conflict with rules and regulations for data protection and privacy. Hence, the risk of breaking existing legal rules may limit the use of trust-enhancing technologies.

Understanding how to exploit legal risk analysis [4] to achieve well-founded trust and security is seen as an important issue for research. For example, legal risk analysis can be used to do a preliminary identification and prioritisation of legal risks, based on the assets determined by the stakeholders. Risk analysis may in this way help guide the application of conventional legal analysis to the areas which are of highest business importance, thus increasing effectiveness. Some, like Richard Susskind, predict a shift from legal problem solving to legal risk management [5]. Legal risk analysis is based on traditional risk analysis methods. It focuses upon an asset and analyses possible risks to this asset.

The result of a general risk analysis may indicate where a flow of information should be controlled, e.g. by erecting legal or technological barriers. In many cases legal and technological measures can not be strictly separated. Technological measures will often reflect their own set of rules, and can be seen as a *lex informatica*, as indicated by Reidenberg [6]. Hence, risk analysis can be used to identify the necessity for rules, be it binding legal rules or non-binding but effective policies. In particular, a legal risk analysis can be conducted from the perspective of a party who is interested or involved in the flow of information, as an owner, sender, recipient or intermediate. In this case, the involved party can analyze legal risks and bring about a strategy to manage these risks, e.g. through a contract that addresses liability issues. As a final step, risk analysis can be used to analyze and test the contract, in order to control whether previously identified risks are reduced or eliminated and in order to identify additional risks that arise as consequences of the chosen treatment.

Risk analysis requires a clear understanding of the system to be analysed. Normally, this understanding can be obtained only through the involvement of different stakeholders, e.g. legal experts, security experts, system developers and users. In fact, most methods for risk identification make use of structured brainstorming sessions of one kind or another, involving 5-7 stakeholders with different backgrounds. This poses a challenge with regards to communication and understanding between stakeholders. The effectiveness of such sessions depends on the extent to which the stakeholders and analysts involved understand and are understood by each other.

The CORAS language for threat modelling [7, 8, 9] has been designed to mitigate this problem within the security domain. This paper evaluates the suitability of this language to specify legal risk scenarios. It also presents ongoing research focusing on how to increase the expressiveness to provide specific support for the legal domain. The remainder of this paper is structured as follows. In Sect. 2 we give an overview of the existing CORAS language. Models resulting from applying CORAS for the analysis of legal issues are presented in Sect. 3. Section 4 is devoted to ongoing work on extending the language to specifically support legal risk analysis. Finally, Sect. 5 draws the main conclusions and outlines future work.

2   The CORAS Threat Modelling Language

The CORAS language for threat modelling is a graphical language allowing documentation of undesirable behaviour in the form of threat scenarios. The CORAS language covers notions like asset, threat, risk and treatment, and supports communication among particpants with different backgrounds through the definition of easy-to-understand icons (symbols) associated with the modelling elements of the language. The CORAS language is an extension of the UML 2.0 [10] specification language, the de facto standard modelling language for information systems. It is defined as a UML profile [11], and has recently become part of an OMG standard [12].

The underlying assumption when modelling threats with the CORAS language is that the threats are part of the behaviour of a computerized system, whereas vulnerabilities are features of the system, even though these are negative or unwanted features. This basically means that the same modelling techniques may be used for modelling threats as for modelling the desired features and functionality of a system. The CORAS language provides a number of specialized UML diagrams supporting threat modeling, such as asset diagrams, threat & unwanted incident diagrams, and treatment diagrams.

Assets. Figure 1 shows a subset of the CORAS risk analysis conceptual model [11]. This sub-model defines part of the context of a risk analysis. The context consists of the *stakeholders* and *assets* of the system under analysis. A risk analysis is asset-driven, which means that the analysis is carried out relative to the identified assets. A stakeholder is a person or organisation that has interests in the target of evaluation (ToE). In the general case, an asset may be anything that stakeholders of the target find to have value. An *entity* is a physical or abstract part or feature of the target that becomes an asset when assigned value by a stakeholder.

Threats and unwanted incidents. A threat is described in the CORAS language using a *threat agent*, e.g. a disloyal employee or a computer virus. The threat agent initiates a *threat scenario*, which is a sequence of events or activities leading to an *unwanted incident*, i.e. an event resulting in a reduction in the value of the target asset.

Each threat agent is related to one or more threat scenarios, represented by ovals with ignited bombs. The threat scenarios are again related to the assets

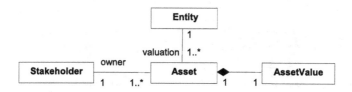

Fig. 1. Risk analysis context sub-model

they threat, represented as stacks of coins. Even though a threat exists, this does not mean that something bad will necessarily happen. The actual incident may also be the result of interplay between a number of threats. We model this by the use of unwanted incidents, represented as ovals with warning signs. The «include» arrow is used for expressing that an unwanted incident includes a threat scenario. The threat scenario pointed at describes a subscenario of the scenario associated with the unwanted incident. Further, an unwanted incident may lead to another unwanted incident, forming a chain of events. This is modelled by the «Initiate» arrow.

Figure 2 shows an example threat & unwanted incident diagram. In this example we have modelled threats to a telemedicine system. The system uses a dedicated network for transmitting medical data, allowing a general practitioner and a cardiology expert to examine a patient together even though they are physically located at different sites. This involves retrieving the patient's health record from a database and transmitting the relevant data to be provided to the application clients (presentation layer) running at both medical doctors' computers.

Taking the patient's view, the target of the threats is his/her medical data, more specifically the health record. There are two threats to this health record (1) input of wrong data, resulting in a health record containing misleading medical information; (2) illegal access to the data when transmitted over the network, with the result that the data get known by unwanted people which again may result in the data being used against the patient's interests.

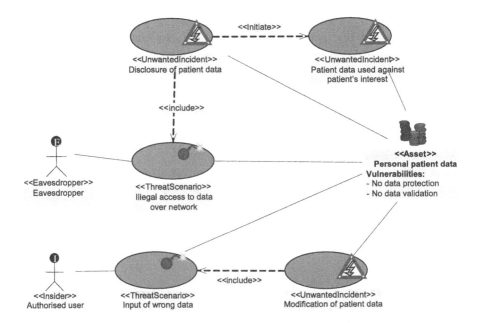

Fig. 2. Threat & unwanted incident diagram

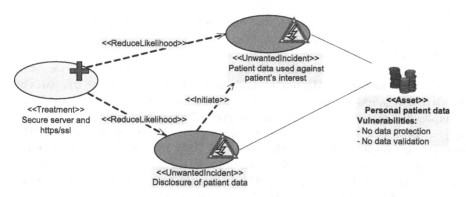

Fig. 3. Treatment diagram

In the example, the unwanted incident "Disclosure of patient data" includes the threat that an eavesdropper gets illegal access to the network, and may lead to the unwanted incident that the patient data is used against the patient's interests. As wee see, both unwanted incidents are related to the asset, meaning that the occurrence of these events have consequences for the asset.

Treatments. Once the threats have been identified and analysed, we go on to identifying treatments in order to reduce the risks. As with threats and unwanted incidents, treatments are modelled by specialized use cases. Treatment options are shown as ovals with a red cross in the corner, and are connected to the threats and unwanted incidents they treat with dashed arrows. One obvious treatment to the threats in the example above is introduce protection mechanisms like encryption of the data being transmitted over the network. This is shown in the example treatment diagram in Fig. 3.

3   Using CORAS Within the Legal Domain

We have evaluated the applicability of the CORAS language for legal risk analysis using two legal risk scenarios defined in the TrustCoM project [13]. The scenarios deal with issues related to data protection law and intellectual property rights (IPR), respectively. Some of the modelling results from the latter scenario are presented in Sect. 3.1. Based on these trials, we have come up with requirements to an extended language, which are discussed in Sect. 3.2.

3.1   Analysis Results

The scenario forming the basis for the following results deals with a group of engineering companies who are forming a Virtual Organisation (VO) in order to collaborate on a project to design an aircraft. To accomplish this, they of course need to share information, such as design drawings for the various aircraft components. A number of challenges related to intellectual property rights arise from this scenario, such as who has the right to access and distribute the data, as well as possible remedies when non-disclosure agreements are broken. These issues are of course also tightly connected to technical issues, such as security infrastructure and policies.

Before we are able to start identifying threats, we need to define the target of evaluation through e.g. UML models and natural text documenting the parts of the virtual organisation and its processes we are interested in. Consider a small example of company A and company B collaborating in the above mentioned project. Both companies hold intellectual property, "A's information" and "B's information" respectively, that they want to keep confidential (trade secrets) but which they agree to share with each other in the project in order to reach a common goal. Furthermore, they need to discuss the project idea with a potential customer C. Figure 4 shows a UML diagram documenting some of the activities that A may perform in relation to B's intellectual property.

Assume that company B is the client of a risk analysis. That is, B is regarded as stakeholder, and threats are identified from the viewpoint of B. In order to protect their interests, the involved parties set up an agreement that deals with the use of confidential information and its non-disclosure to third parties. Through the risk analysis, the probabilities and consequences, e.g. monetary loss, of the various risks are determined. These results may form the basis for determining which aspects should be included in e.g. non-disclosure agreements, such as who may receive the information and the required level of security, as well as appropriate legal sanctions if the agreement is broken.

Hazard and Operability (HazOp) analysis [14] was employed to identify threats. HazOp is a form of structured brainstorming session where the knowledge and expertise of all the participants is exploited in order to find as many relevant threats as possible. There are two broad classes of risks in this example as seen from B's perspective: (1) The disclosure of B's confidential information to a competitor, caused by either A or a third party. (2) A possible liability for B himself disclosing A's confidential information in breach of the non-disclosure agreement. Figure 5 shows a threat & unwanted incident diagram documenting some of the threats and unwanted incidents which were identified in relation to the disclosure of confidential information.

An example of a legal threat is the possibility of a lawsuit against B if B is responsible for A's information being leaked to a third party (competitor),

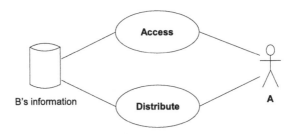

Fig. 4. Target of Evaluation (ToE)

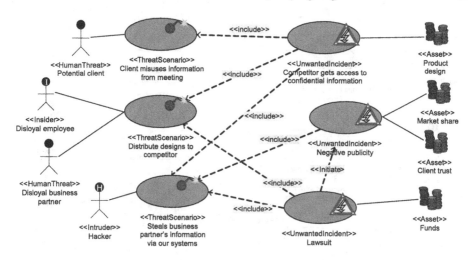

Fig. 5. Threat & unwanted incident diagram

either on purpose, e.g. a disloyal employee, or through negligence, e.g. insufficient security measures. One benefit of legal risk analysis is that legal risks may be incorporated into a larger risk management picture. Non-legal consequences of legal risks, e.g. negative media exposure as a result of a lawsuit, may turn out to be equally important from a business perspective but are typically not considered in conventional legal analysis.

Once the risks have been identified and evaluated, one can identity and assign treatments to reduce the risks. Treatments may for example be to establish a non-disclosure agreement with the potential client C to regulate what they may do with the information provided to them in the meeting. Alternatively, the companies may agree to not disclose any confidential information to each other in the meeting. Legal treatments may be used both against legal threats, e.g. contract clauses limiting liability to reduce the consequence of a potential lawsuit, or against non-legal threats, e.g. hackers may be prosecuted by law. Similarly, treatments to legal threats may also be of a non-legal nature, e.g. improvements to the security infrastructure to reduce the likelihood of a lawsuit. These treatments are shown in the treatment diagram in Fig. 6.

3.2   Requirements to an Extended Language

As the examples above have shown, we are able to use the CORAS language to document and analyse some aspects of legal risks and the current language seems to be a good starting point for legal risk analysis. However, we wish to be able to model and analyze more legal aspects, for example whether the act of disclosing certain information, as shown in Fig. 4, infringes upon a non-disclosure agreement. To enable this, we need facilities for:

– specifying ownership, which is highly relevant when determining e.g. the rights and obligations of an actor,

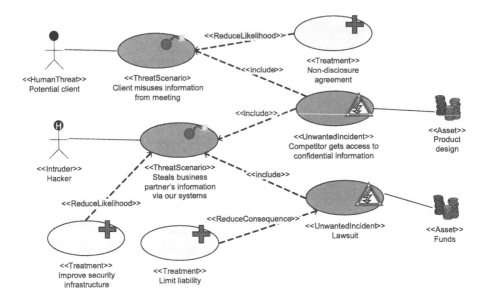

Fig. 6. Treatment diagram

- specifying legal effects on different roles and activities, and
- correlating these effects with the relevant legal sources, e.g. which contract clause is the source of the legal effect in question.

We thus see the need to incorporate more information relevant to legal aspects into the graphical language. Furthermore, to facilitate the use of the graphical modelling language for documentation and communication of legal risk analysis results, the users of the language need a clear understanding of what the graphical models express. A graphical language for legal risk analysis should on the one hand be easily understandable for practitioners and on the other hand be sufficiently precise to allow in-depth analysis. We must be able to explain the meaning of the diagrams as well as how they can be combined and refined. Furthermore, to support automated analysis of the graphical models, tools must be able to extract and process relevant information. To enable this, the semantics of the graphical language need to be defined, with particular emphasis on the notions of trust, security, privacy, data protection and intellectual property rights.

4   Towards a More Expressive Language

To meet the requirements stated above, we are extending the CORAS language with concepts and relationships relevant to legal analysis. A central conjecture is that modal logic [15] may be an important source of inspiration with respect to what kind of language constructs are required. In particular, we are looking at deontic logic, a form of modal logic which deals with the notion of obligation.

This will enable us to specify e.g. which activities are permitted, obligated and forbidden.

Formal conceptual modelling is employed in Sect. 4.1 to provide a semantic basis for the graphical language. Some examples of how the extended conceptual model may be used to improve the expressiveness of the graphical language are presented in Sect. 4.2.

4.1   Conceptual Model for Legal Risk Analysis

In this section we propose a conceptual model for legal risk analysis, described using UML 2.0 [10]. The following introduces the various parts of our conceptual model.

Central to legal risk analysis are *legal norms*, which describe legal requirements and consequences. Legal norms have the general structure of an *antecedent* and a *consequent*: if A then B.

The antecedent describes the *criteria* for the norm to apply, i.e. which factual *circumstances* have to be present. The *consequent* indicates the *legal effects* of the norm being applied. Often, an effect is only a link to further norms, which chained together will represent the norms governing the case at hand. When law is applied to a case or situation, the legal criteria are compared with the circumstances of the case. Figure 7 shows a UML diagram depicting the concepts outlined above and the relationships between them.

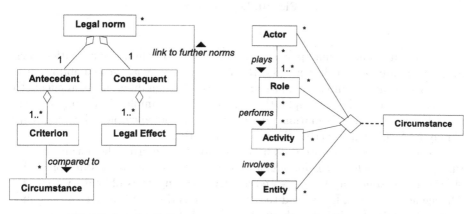

Fig. 7. Legal norm   **Fig. 8.** Circumstance

The legal effect a particular norm has on an actor depends on the activity being performed as well as the roles that actor plays, e.g. student, employer, (system) owner, etc. A circumstance thus consists of an *actor*, an *activity* being performed by that actor, and the *role* which the actor is in while performing the activity. Another *entity* may also be involved in the activity. For example, a circumstance may be that a person (*actor*) who is an employee of company A (*role*) accesses (*activity*) some information (*entity*) which belongs to company B. Figure 8 shows the concepts and relationships related to circumstance.

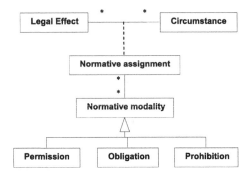

Fig. 9. Normative modalities and effects of legal norms

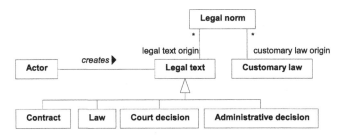

Fig. 10. Legal sources

In general, an actor may play several roles and perform many activities, each involving a number of other entities. However, by looking at each combination of these as separate circumstances, this allows us to assign different legal effects to each circumstance. For example, the person in the example above may be permitted to access the information, whereas another person employed by company C may be forbidden to access the same information.

Normative modalities are used in deontic logic to describe the normative status (*permitted, obligatory, forbidden,* and so on) assigned to a state of affairs A [15]. *Obligation* may be expressed as OA, meaning "it is obligatory that A." The agency operator, E_i, is used to express propositions such as OE_iA, meaning "agent i is obliged to bring it about that A" [16]. *Permission* is the dual of obligation, i.e. $PE_iA = \neg O\neg E_iA$ ("agent i is permitted to bring it about that A"), and *prohibition* (forbidden) is simply the negation of permission, e.g. $\neg PE_iA$ ("agent i is forbidden/not permitted to bring it about that A"). We assign normative modalities to the relationship between legal effect and circumstance to specify which circumstances are permitted, obligatory and forbidden by the legal norm in question, as depicted in Fig. 9. The legal criteria are derived from legal reasoning based on the relevant source material, which may include statutes, regulations, court or administrative decisions, etc. The identification of such sources itself is an essential part of a legal decision making process. Figure 10 shows an example of some legal sources. Figure 11 shows how the various concepts from

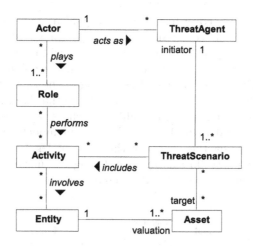

Fig. 11. Integrating threat scenario

the CORAS risk analysis conceptual model are integrated with the concepts described above. On the left hand side are the concepts related to circumstance, and on the right hand side are the concepts from the CORAS model. An actor may act as a threat agent, i.e. initiating the threat scenario. The threat scenario may include a number of activities. Entity and asset are related in the CORAS conceptual model, as shown in Fig. 1.

The client of the risk analysis may not be interested in trust as such, but rather in assets such as market share and income. *Trust* and *reputation*, however, are clearly important factors that affect customers' behaviour, and may therefore be viewed as assets of their own [17]. As mentioned in Sect. 2, an *entity* is a physical or abstract part or feature of the target that becomes an asset when assigned value by a stakeholder. We therefore also view trust and reputation as subtypes of entities. Of particular interest in the context of legal risk analysis of data protection issues and intellectual property rights (IPR) are *information* assets, as well as the notion of *ownership*.

Studies of trust distinguish between the trustor, that is, the agent that trusts another agent, and the trustee; the agent being trusted. Trust can be modelled as a binary relationship from the trustor to the trustee, denoted as *source* and *target* of the trust, respectively. Ownership is modelled as a relationship between an actor, the *owner*, and an entity. These concepts and relationships are shown in Fig. 12. The actor also plays the role of stakeholder with regards to an asset. This is the same as the stakeholder shown in Fig. 1. Actor is another specialisation of entity. An actor may be a natural person or a juristic person, e.g. an organization, as well as other types of behavioral entities, e.g. a software agent.

4.2   Exploiting the Improved Expressiveness

In legal risk analysis, parts of the target of evaluation will originate from legal issues formulated in legal texts such as laws and contracts. This motivates that

ToE descriptions not only cover technical and organizational aspects but also the legal issues. Legal texts have a tendency to be complex and also hard to read by laymen. Since participants of legal risk analyses will include people that are not legal experts, we claim that standard modelling techniques can be applied to give these participants a better understanding of the legal issues.

As discussed in Sect. 4.1, legal norms have effects that bind the roles involved in certain activities by normative modalities, such as "it is permitted for A to do X" and "it is forbidden for B to do Y". When modelling legal issues, we concentrate on modelling the *effects* of the relevant legal texts (not the legal texts themselves), and we do this by introducing the normative modalities as modelling elements in the form of UML stereotypes.

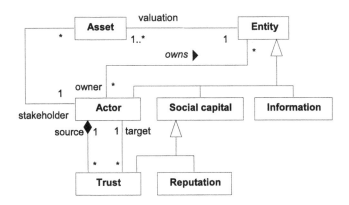

Fig. 12. Incorporating trust

Consider the example from Sect. 3, where company A and company B decide to cooperate on a shared project to reach some goal. An extract of the legal effects of the contract between A and B are modelled in the diagram of Fig. 13, which is a specialisation of Fig. 4. In this example, one of the effects of the contract is that A has permission to access B's information, modelled using the stereotype «permitted» on the association between A and the use case "access". Similarly, the effect that A is forbidden to distribute B's information is modelled using the stereotype «forbidden». The diagram also shows where these effects originate from (e.g. contract clause 3) by attaching a constraint to the association. Ownership is modelled using the «owns» stereotype on the association between B and B's information.

The CORAS language has proved useful in threat modelling [18]. In order to model threats related to legal issues, we integrate the approach above with the threat modelling features of the CORAS language. Figure 14 shows a threat and how this is related to one of the legal effects in the previous figure. Company B acts as stakeholder and company A acts a threat agent in this example, modelled using the «acts as» stereotype. Furthermore, B's information is viewed as one of B's assets, and the threat scenario includes an activity that is forbidden for A,

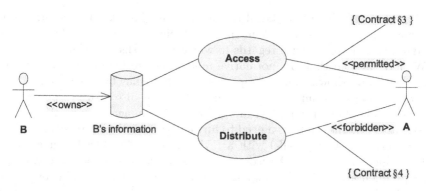

Fig. 13. Modelling legal effects

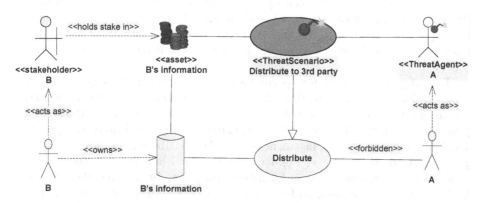

Fig. 14. Modelling legal threats

modelled using the standard UML «includes» stereotype. The structure of this diagram is similar to the one of Fig. 11, which shows the relationship between the CORAS conceptual model for risk analysis and the new concepts presented in this paper. Here, A is the actor, performing the "Distribute" activity involving the entity "B's information".

5 Conclusion

Our preliminary results from using the CORAS language for security risk analysis in legal risk scenarios show that this language may also be utilised successfully for the specification of legal risk scenarios. Furthermore, conventional legal analysis focuses primarily on the purely legal consequence of legal risks, i.e. legal sanctions such as fines. However, these legal sanctions may lead to a number of other consequences which may turn out to be equally important from a business perspective, e.g. negative media exposure and loss of market share. Technical aspects, such as protection of electronic information, will often also have legal implications, and vice versa. Legal risk analysis enables us to integrate the legal aspects into the overall risk management picture, thus providing a better foundation for decisions with regards to which legal risks to tackle.

We have argued that the normative modalities are highly relevant to legal risk analysis and shown some examples of how these may be integrated into the language. However, a number of other notions might also prove to be relevant, e.g., the notion of exception plays an important role in agreements. We are thus investigating whether there is a need to further increase the expressiveness. This work is carried out in parallel with a revision of the CORAS language where both the meta model and the icons are revised based on experience from use and experimentation with the language. We are also currently working on various approaches for assigning semantics to our graphical language, e.g., by mapping it to a logical language which would provide an unambiguous reference point. Our approach is to formalize the conceptual model in a first order logic framework [19] and to formalize the use case based language in the STAIRS semantics [20] for sequence diagrams. A mapping between these two formalizations and an interpretation in the model theoretic foundations of deontic logic will also be provided.

The language facilities for specifying obligations and permissions may also prove useful for e.g. specification of policies. The normative modalities in Sect. 4.1 are used as the basis for policy specifications described in the ODP enterprise viewpoint [21]. Ponder [22] is a declarative, object-oriented language for specifying security and management policies for distributed systems. Unlike the graphical CORAS language, Ponder uses a textual language for specification of policies. An interesting topic for future study may be whether the extended CORAS language can be used for graphical modelling of (a subset of) the Ponder language. A number of other text-based policy languages and frameworks exist, such as XACML [23] for specification of access control policies, REFEREE [24] for specification and evaluation of trust policies, the KeyNote [25] trust and public key based authorisation system, as well as various other PKI- and credential-based approaches [26, 27].

Tropos [28] is a methodology and graphical modelling language for development of agent-oriented systems. Like our extended language for legal risk analysis, actors and roles are central concepts in the Tropos language. However, unlike the CORAS language, which is asset-oriented and targeted at threat modelling, the Tropos language is goal-oriented and is targeted at modelling agents and their goals, plans, capabilities, beliefs, etc. In our future work we will investigate the need for incorporating concepts from languages such as TROPOS as well as other conceptual models such as the one presented in [29].

Acknowledgements

The research on which this paper reports has partly been carried out within the context of the EU-projects TrustCoM (IST-2003-01945) and iTrust (IST-2001-34910).

References

1. Jøsang, A., Ismail, R., Boyd, C.: A Survey of Trust and Reputation Systems for Online Service Provision. Decision Support Systems (to appear) http://security.dstc.edu.au/papers/JIB2005-DSS.pdf.
2. Egger, F.N.: Towards a model of trust for e-commerce system design. In: CHI 2000: Workshop Designing Interactive Systems for 1-to-1 E-commerce. (2000) http://www.zurich.ibm.com/~mrs/chi2000/contributions/egger.html.
3. Jones, S., Wilikens, M., Morris, P., Masera, M.: Trust requirements in e-business. Communications of the ACM **43** (2000) 81–87
4. Wahlgren, P.: Juridisk riskanalys - Mot en säkrare juridisk metod. Jure, Stockholm (2003) (In Swedish).
5. Susskind, R.: The Future of Law. Clarendon Press, Oxford (1996)
6. Reidenberg, J.: Lex Informatica: The Formulation of Information Policy Rules Through Technology. In: Texas Law Review. Volume 76. (1998) 553–593
7. CORAS: The CORAS project (2005) http://coras.sourceforge.net/ (visited February 2005).
8. Dimitrakos, T., Ritchie, B., Raptis, D., Aagedal, J.Ø., den Braber, F., Stølen, K., Houmb, S.H.: Integrating model-based security risk managament into eBusiness systems development: The CORAS approach. In: I3E2002, Kluwer (2002) 159–175
9. Raptis, D., Dimitrakos, T., Gran, B.A., Stølen, K.: The CORAS approach for model-based risk management applied to e-commerce domain. In: CMS-2002, Kluwer (2002) 169–181
10. OMG: UML 2.0 Superstructure Specification. (2004) OMG Document: ptc/2004-10-02.
11. Lund, M.S., Hogganvik, I., Seehusen, F., Stølen, K.: UML profile for security assessment. Technical Report STF40 A03066, SINTEF Telecom and informatics (2003)
12. OMG: UML Profile for Modeling Quality of Service and Fault Tolerance Characteristics and Mechanisms, Draft Adopted Specification (2004) OMG Document: ptc/2004-06-01.
13. TrustCoM: Trust and Contract Management in Virtual Organisations (2005) http://www.eu-trustcom.com/ (visited February 2005).
14. Redmill, F., Chudleigh, M., Catmur, J.: HazOp and software HazOp. Wiley (1999)
15. Chellas, B.F.: Modal Logic - An Introduction. Cambridge University Press, Cambridge, UK (1980)
16. Elgesem, D.: The Modal Logic of Agency. Nordic Journal of Philosophical Logic **2** (1997)
17. Brændeland, G., Stølen, K.: Using risk analysis to assess user trust - a net-bank scenario. In: Proceedings of 2nd International Conference on Trust Management (iTrust 2004). Volume 2995., LNCS, Springer (2004) 146–160
18. den Braber, F., Lund, M.S., Stølen, K.: Using the CORAS Threat Modelling Language to Document Threat Scenarios for several Microsoft relevant Technologies. Technical Report STF90 A04057, SINTEF ICT (2004)
19. Berardi, D., Calì, A., Calvanese, D., De Giacomo, G.: Reasoning on UML Class Diagrams. Technical Report 11-03, Dipartimento di Informatica e Sistemistica, Università di Roma "La Sapienza" (2003)
20. Haugen, Ø., Husa, K.E., Runde, R.K., Stølen, K.: Why timed sequence diagrams require three-event semantics. To appear in LNCS (2005)
21. ISO/IEC: FCD 15414: Information Technology - Open Distributed Processing - Reference Model - Enterprise Viewpoint. JTC1/SC7 N2359, ISO/IEC (2000)

22. Damianou, N., Dulay, N., Lupu, E., Sloman, M.: The Ponder Specification Language. In: Workshop on Policies for Distributed Systems and Networks, Bristol, UK (2001)

23. OASIS: eXtensible Access Control Markup Language (XACML) Version 1.0. Technical report, OASIS (2003)

24. Chu, Y.H., Feigenbaum, J., LaMacchia, B., Resnick, P., Strauss, M.: Referee: Trust management for web applications. In: Sixth International World Wide Web Conference, Santa Clara, CA, USA (1997)

25. Blaze, M., Feigenbaum, J., Ioannidis, J., Keromytis, A.D.: The KeyNote Trust Management System, Version 2. Request For Comments (RFC) 2704, AT&T Labs and University of Pennsylvania (1999)

26. Biskup, J., Karabulut, Y.: A Hybrid PKI Model with an Application for Secure Mediation. In: 16th Annual IFIP WG 11.3 Working Conference on Data and Application Security, Cambridge, England, Kluwer Academic Press (2002) 271–282

27. PERMIS: Privilege and Role Management Infrastructure Standards Validation (2004) http://sec.isi.salford.ac.uk/permis/ (visited December 2004).

28. Bresciani, P., Giorgini, P., Giunchiglia, F., Mylopoulos, J., Perini, A.: TROPOS: An Agent-Oriented Software Development Methodology. In: Journal of Autonomous Agents and Multi-Agent Systems. Volume 8., Kluwer Academic Publishers (2004) 203–236

29. Sagri, M.T., Tiscornia, D., Gangemi, A.: An ontology-based model for Representing "Bundle-of-rights". In: The second International Workshop on Regulatory Ontologies (WORM 2004). LNCS, Larnaca, Cyprus, Springer (2004)

On Deciding to Trust

Michael Michalakopoulos and Maria Fasli

University of Essex, Department of Computer Science,
Wivenhoe Park, Colchester CO4 3SQ, UK
{mmichag, mfasli}@essex.ac.uk

Abstract. Participating in electronic markets and conducting business online inadvertedly involves the decision to trust other participants. In this paper we consider trust as a concept that self-interested agents populating an electronic marketplace can use to take decisions on who they are going to transact with. We are interested in looking at the effects that trust and its attributes as well as trust dispositions have on individual agents and the electronic market as a whole. A market scenario is presented which was used to build a simulation program and then run a series of experiments.

1 Introduction

With the advent of Internet related technologies and the increased availability of broadband access, the number of individuals and businesses that participate in e-commerce transactions has increased rapidly. This has resulted in a mounting interest in deploying agent-based and multi-agent systems to fully automate commercial transactions. Semi-autonomous software agents are continuously running entities that can negotiate for goods and services on behalf of their users reflecting their preferences and perhaps negotiation strategies. As transactions on the Internet do not require the physical presence of the participants involved, this creates situations that can be exploited by some that seek to make an extra profit even at the expense of others. As a number of studies indicate [19, 20, 21], various forms of fraud on the Internet have been on the increase in the last few years. Although a range of technologies exist to make the transactions more secure (secure payment methods, secure communication protocols, trusted third parties), the ultimate decision whom to trust falls on the shoulders of the individuals.

As human agents, when trading in financial markets we need to have trust on the other parties that they are going to comply with the rules of the marketplace and carry out their part of the agreement. The same attitude of trust that we require needs to be reflected on the software agents too. Hence, the notion of trust needs to be built into software agents and taken into account by their decision making process. In this paper we discuss the issue of trust in the e-marketplace and present the results from experiments run on a market simulation. The paper is organized as follows: Next we discuss trust in general and some related work. The presentation of the market simulation follows. Section 5 presents the experiments run and discusses the results. Finally, the paper closes with the conclusions and further work.

P. Herrmann et al. (Eds.): iTrust 2005, LNCS 3477, pp. 61–76, 2005.

2   Trust Concepts

Trust: Trust has received a lot of attention from social as well as natural sciences. Though it is difficult to give a single definition, most of the researchers working on this area seem to agree that trust is a belief or cognitive stance that can be measured [5, 12, 10, 8]. Briefly, this belief is about the expectation that an agent will be competent enough to effectively perform a task that was delegated to it by another agent or if we are talking about trust in a market, trust can be perceived as the expectation that the other party will comply with the protocol used and honour the deal or carry out their part of the agreement reached.

The formation of such an expectation is not trivial; it is based on many parameters and quite often an agent may have to take a decision on whether to trust or not, in the absence of solid evidence that such an action will be beneficial to its interests. If fact, it is this uncertainty that necessitates the existence of a trust mechanism; if an agent is certain about the outcome of an action it does not need to bother with the costs of the mechanisms involved for estimating trust. These costs may involve third parties that act as guarantors, time to gather information about one's credibility or even loss of resources after a bad decision to trust the wrong agent. The agent which delegates the task is known to be the truster and the agent which the task is delegated to is the trustee.

Risk: Inevitably, the decision to trust involves risk [17]. Risk may derive from the fact that the trustee's trustworthiness is low or not known for a given context, or it may be due to external factors beyond the agent's control that will cause the trustee to fail in accomplishing the task. In deciding whether to trust or not, an agent needs to consider the possible gain or loss of delegating the task to someone else. In electronic markets the outcome of a transaction is usually expressed in monetary terms and delegating a task refers to honouring a previously reached agreement (e.g. a seller needs to deliver the goods as agreed, a buyer needs to make a payment). In certain cases, it may be enough to estimate a trust threshold [16] that serves as a safety net: if the trust for a trustee falls below the threshold it is unlikely that a trusting decision will take place.

Reputation: Whereas subjective trust is completely dependant on one's opinion and is usually formed by individual past experiences and perceived stimuli, reputation derives from the aggregate of individual opinions of the members of a group about an agent's trustworthiness. Reputation systems are often used to enhance the effectiveness of transactions in auction web sites (eBay, yahoo), or rate opinions and products (amazon, epinions, dabs). They are particularly useful in cases where the trustee is completely unknown to the truster but well-known to another group. However, reputation systems are not immune to manipulation [13]. Trustee agents can change their identity and discard previous negative reputation and additionally there is always the question of the reliability of the agents that actually participate in the process of reputation forming.

As agents may have different trust dispositions [16], personalities [4], risk behaviours and may have perceived different experiences in the past [15], their trusting decisions will differ even when they perceive the same facts in a society and are presented with the same choices.

3   Related Work

In [10] the authors provide a concise overview of the conceptual and measurable constructs that are related to trust and build a typology of trust across the various disciplines. An analogous study, but specifically towards e-commerce and oriented at providing a trust model for first trade situations is given in [6].

Modelling trust has been the focus of many works: [16] discusses the various components of trust and provides methods to derive the value of trust and the cooperation threshold taking into account trust dispositions, the importance of the goal, the competence of the trustee and the memory of the agent. However, as the author points out there are certain shortcomings in the suggested formalism. In [15], trust is explicitly based on rating experiences and integrating the rating into the existing trust. The validity of the presented model is confirmed by a series of experiments in which humans participated [1]. In [4, 12], the authors indicate that "trust is more than a subjective probability" and present a model of trust based on Fuzzy Logic that takes into account many different beliefs and personality factors. The models presented in the literature quite often exhibit different aspects of trust and behaviours. For example, the authors in [3] perform experiments of reputation in the marketplace with a trust model that tends to be forgiving for the unreliable agents. On the other hand, in [9] a model of trust is presented in which negative outcomes of transactions, cause a steep decline in the trusting relationships. Such an attitude represents the fact that trust is difficult to build, but can be destroyed easily. While most of the works focus mainly on trust, another important aspect closely related to it, is that of risk. In [2] a mechanism based on expected utility theory that integrates the two concepts together by considering the possible gain and loss of a transaction in relation with a trust value is studied.

In the area of e-Commerce [14] have suggested a mechanism for contracting with uncertain levels of trust by using advanced payments on the buyers' behalf, however, this may not always be feasible. Moreover, they do not discuss how the involved parties derive their trust estimates. [11] present a market scenario and experimental results related to trade partnerships in which trust is important, but use pre-fixed values for the impact of positive and negative ratings after a transaction has finished. On the other hand, [5] describe a more dynamic model of trust, which takes into account various attributes of a contract. They argue that their trust model can reduce the negotiation phase of a transaction, but do not discuss how these findings may affect the market as a whole.

On the topic of reputation, [8] present a model in which agents can revise their beliefs based on information gathered from other agents and use Bayesian belief networks to filter out information they regard as false. Problems with reputation have to do with disproportionately positive feedback (making an agent appear more reliable than it really is), and defamation (making an agent appear unreliable although it is not). To address these issues [7] suggest a reputation mechanism for an information sharing multi-agent society, which is based on different roles. However, as the authors point out the roles of these agents will differ from the roles of the agents in an e-commerce society.

4   Market Simulation

Next, we describe the main properties of our simulation, the roles and utilities, the market protocol and the attributes for modelling the trust concepts.

4.1   Market Roles and Utilities

In our simulation the market is populated by a number of agents that are divided into buyers and sellers. All the agents are self-interested, and their goal is to maximise their profit by participating in market transactions. As described previously, a number of reliability issues can come up when agents transact in the electronic marketplace. We have chosen to apply a simple case of fraud, in which a seller will not ship all the items that a buyer requested, or a buyer will not pay the whole amount that was agreed.

Sellers are registered with a Directory Facilitator (DF), so they can advertise their ability to sell a specific good or service for a certain price.

Buyers wish to obtain certain quantities of goods from agents that claim they can make the deliveries. Each Buyer has a personal valuation for the good it would like to obtain and this is higher than the offered market prices. As in the real world, this latter statement needs to be true in order for the Buyer agents to enter into a transaction with any seller. The monetary gain that a buyer agent gets when transacting with a seller is given by:

$$G_{Buyer} = (DI \cdot PV) - M \tag{1}$$

where DI is the number of items the supplier delivered, PV is the buyer's personal valuation for the good, and M is the money the buyer paid to the seller.

The sellers ship the requested items to buyers and their monetary gain is analogous to that of buyers:

$$G_{Seller} = M - (IS \cdot UC) \tag{2}$$

where M is the money the seller received from a buyer, IS is the number of items the supplier sent to the buyer and UC is the unit cost for each item.

4.2   Market Protocol

The market protocol consists of three phases:

- Phase 1, initial registration: Sellers register with the DF and buyers decide on the quantity and personal valuation for the items they wish to obtain.
- Phase 2, selecting partners: Buyer agents query the DF so as to see which agents can offer their desired good. Then, they query the sellers for the asked price. Each buyer evaluates the utility it will get from each seller it found via the DF and makes a request to one of them for buying the items. The seller evaluates its trust towards the buyer and either rejects the request or accepts it. At this point a mutual agreement is understood by both members: sellers agree to deliver the items, and buyers agree to make the payments.

– Phase 3, completing the transaction: The seller delivers the requested items and the buyer pays the seller. These steps of making the deliveries and the payments take place simultaneously, therefore no member can see in advance whether the other participant fulfilled its own part of agreement. At the end of this phase, the agents actually perceive the quality of the service they have received (items delivered or payment made), calculate their monetary gains, and update their trust values for the participant they transacted with.

During phase 3, unreliable agents may deviate from the market protocol. There may be a lot of types of fraud in the marketplace; however our approach to this issue is that unreliable agents will behave in such a way that the utility of the other member with which they transacted will not be the expected one. For example, sellers may deliver items of poor quality, or deliver them late and buyers may not pay the whole amount as agreed or may be late in their payments. In our simulation, deviation from the market's protocol for the sellers is materialized by not delivering the requested quantities to the buyers and for the buyers by not making a full payment to the sellers. Whereas, trusted third parties (e.g. banks, law enforcement bodies) can often intervene and provide credentials for the identity of the involved parties or punish cheaters, we wish to see the effects of the agents' behaviour in a market where these are absent.

4.3   Trust Attributes

Each agent has a certain set of features, which are directly related to the way in which trust is measured. We describe these in the next paragraphs.

Trust Formula: In order to calculate trust we adopt the notion of a trust update function [15], which is based on experience rating and further enrich it using trust dispositions [16]. In our formalism, trust is perceived as a value that represents the positive expectation that the selected partner will behave as expected, that is, it will comply with the market's protocol and honour its part in the agreement reached. Therefore, the resulting trust is in the range [0..1] where 0 represents a complete distrust, and 1 represents complete trust. The formula that agent A uses to calculate trust towards agent B is given by:

$$T_{A \to B} = T'_{A \to B} \cdot w + E_{A \to B} \cdot (1 - w) \qquad (3)$$

where $T'_{A \to B}$ is the previously calculated trust value or initial trust, w is a factor in the range [0..1] and biases the result towards existing trust or new experiences and $E_{A \to B}$ is the agent's A rating of the experience this agent had with agent B, also in the range [0..1].

Initial Trust Value: The value $T'_{A \to B}$ is used as the value of trust in the cases where the agent that needs to calculate the trust towards another agent does not have a record of previous experiences with it. Agents can enter the market using any trust value in the range [0..1]. A value towards 0 means that the agent enters the market with a pessimistic disposition, whereas a value towards 1 shows that the agent has a more optimistic stance. However, an agent can enter the market with a low initial trust value and at the same time be a realist or an optimist.

Trust Disposition and Memory: Agents remember a number of experiences E they had with another agent, depending on their memory capacity n:

$$SE_{A \to B} = \{E_1, E_2, .., E_{n-1}, E_n\} \tag{4}$$

In our simulation agents have a trust disposition, which allows them to take a different approach when calculating trust. As in [16], three cases are considered: optimists, realists and pessimists. The trust disposition is important when the agents choose the value of the experience E to use in the formula: Optimists expecting or hoping a very positive outcome will come next, will use the $Max(SE)$ experience value they can remember. Pessimists on the other hand, anticipating a rather bad outcome, use $Min(SE)$ from all their remembered values, and realists come between the extremes and use the $Avg(SE)$. The amount of experiences the agents can remember depends on their memory capacity. Trust dispositions and memory, contribute to the dynamics of trust: for example there may be a steep decline in trust (such as in [8]), should the agent decide to switch from optimism to pessimism.

Rating an experience: Agents rate their experiences, based on the amount of the trustworthiness they have perceived from the other member of the market and their own commitment they have put on the specific transaction. In our case, each agent's commitment is synonymous to the degree the agent complied with the market's protocol and is expressed with a percentage on the delivered items (for the sellers), or the payment made (for the buyers) after each session. The following rules are applied when rating an experience:

1. If $C_{in} > C_{out}$ set $E = C_{in}$
2. If $C_{in} < C_{out}$ set $E = C_{in} - \epsilon$
3. If $C_{in} = C_{out}$ set $E = C_{in}$

C_{in} is the commitment value agent A perceived from agent B after completing a transaction with it, and C_{out} is agent's A commitment towards B. The second rule shows that agents punish the other participant, when the latter one does not comply with the protocol at least as much as they do. In such a case, one of the agents spends more resources only to see that after the transaction, the outcome is not the expected one. The parameter ϵ represents this punishment quantity and is set to a small random value, which depends on the difference $d = C_{out} - C_{in}$, so that $\epsilon = RND[0..d]$; the higher the difference is, the higher the probability that the experience will receive a rating lower than C_{in}.

Risk Behaviour and Seller Selection: In our simulation, the only risk the agents face derives from the unreliability of the other market participants. Different behaviours towards risk for the buyer agents are modelled using the expected utility method, a concept well-founded in decision theory and economics [18]. During the second phase of the protocol, buyers evaluate the trust and the potential gain they can get from buying the items from each seller and decide to buy the items from the agent for which they can get the maximum utility:

$$EU = T \cdot U(G) \tag{5}$$

where T is the trust value as in (3), G is the expected gain from the transaction (1), and $U(G)$ is the utility the agent assigns to the monetary gain G. An agent with a risky behaviour can choose an exponential function for the utility, a risk neutral can choose a linear one and a risk averse agent a logarithmic. The combination of the memory, trust dispositions and risk functions allows us to map a different range of behaviours in our formalism. For example, an optimist with a risky behaviour has a completely different trusting behaviour from a pessimist, risk-neutral agent.

Threshold: Buyer agents that use (5) as a criterion to select the seller from whom to buy goods, will not always be better off, especially if the market is populated by unreliable agents. In this case all the expected utilities will be quite low, and simply selecting the highest one does not guarantee the agent a profit. The seller agents also need to have a mechanism to reject unreliable buyers if they wish to. Each agent in the marketplace has a trust threshold: if trust towards another agent is below this threshold, the truster will not go into a transaction with the trustee. Buyers and sellers have this value updated after every transaction: a positive utility contributes towards reducing the threshold and a negative utility towards increasing it. Agents update the threshold by considering the average trust value they have towards sellers or buyers:

$$H = H \pm (avgTrust \cdot H) \qquad (6)$$

Contrary to trust, where each agent has a trust value for every member it queries in the marketplace, the threshold is a single quantity which applies to all the agents, a buyer or seller meets in the market[1].

5   Experimental Work

Table 1 describes the parameters and their values used in our experiments. In the following sections the words trustworthy and reliable are used interchangeably, i.e. we have made the assumption that agents being reliable are trustworthy.

5.1   The Ideal Marketplace

In our first experiments we simulated a marketplace where all the participants are trustworthy and complied with the market's protocol. In such a marketplace, we expected that all the agents would manage to gain their expected profits. The results from these experiments are obtained under ideal conditions and can therefore serve as a reference point for our second series of experiments.

Experiment I1: First we experimented with the trust disposition and the initial trust attributes. The market was populated by 27 risk neutral buyers (3 agents×3 trust dispositions×3 settings for initial trust) and 10 sellers. Under conditions of

---

[1] The threshold formula may result in values beyond the range [0..1]; in such a case, the agents stop transacting.

Table 1. Parameters used in experiments

Parameter	Value			
Trust Disposition (td)	Pessimist, Realist, Optimist			
Risk Behavioutr (rb)	Risk averse, Risk neutral, Risky			
Memory (m)	Unbounded, Bounded to 5 experiences			
Initial Trust (it)	Low(0.1), Average(0.5), High(1)			
Trustworthiness (tw)	*Trustworthy*		*Not Trustworthy*	
	Probability	*Commit. Value*	*Probability*	*Commit. Value*
	1	100	0.45	[10..50]
			0.45	[51..79]
			0.05	[80..90]
			0.05	[91..100]
Weights	$w = 0.5$			

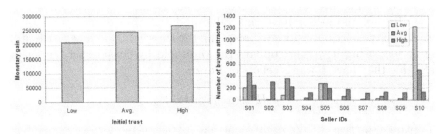

Fig. 1. a) Accumulative profits for buyers with different initial trust values, b) Number of buyers with different initial trust values attracted by sellers

complete trustworthiness in the marketplace, all the agents managed to receive their anticipated profits. However, buyers with a higher initial trust managed to gather higher monetary gains, than buyers with lower initial trust (fig.1a). These agents developed trust bonds with all the reliable sellers in the marketplace and chose to buy their goods from the sellers that offered them at lower prices. On the contrary, buyers that started with a low trust did not often change sellers; they developed a strong bond with the agents they chose in the first few rounds and stayed with them for long periods. As a result, they missed out some opportunities to improve their profits by buying their goods from unknown (trustworthy), sellers.

This behaviour also affected the welfare of the sellers: In the case of buyers with a low trust, only few sellers managed to attract these buyers, whereas in the case of a high initial trust, all the sellers attracted almost an equal number of buyers in every session (fig.1b). In this experiment the trust dispositions and the memory, of the agents did not make any significant difference to their profits, since buyers always rated their experiences using the highest value.

Experiment I2: We introduced the three different risk behaviours among 27 buyers that shared an average initial trust and a bounded memory (3 agents×3

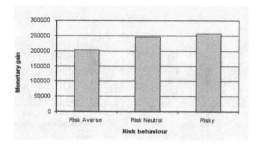

Fig. 2. Monetary gain for buyers with different risk behaviours in a reliable marketplace

trust dispositions×3 risk behaviours). Under conditions of complete trustworthiness, the highest monetary gains were achieved by the agents that demonstrated a risky behaviour (fig2). These agents were willing to try out different sellers after every session. On the other hand, risk averse agents preferred to stay longer with the agent they cooperated first making less profits, and risk neutral agents came between the two extremes. Again, the trust disposition did not turn out to be important as all the agents always rated their experience as 1.

The outcomes of these experiments showed that in a healthy marketplace, everyone manages to gather their expected profits. However, a cautious approach (low initial trust, risk averse behaviour) in a marketplace where all the participants are honest is not always beneficial for the agents. When the buyers develop a strong bond with a reliable seller, they miss out other opportunities in the marketplace. Naturally, the attachment to few sellers also affects the rest of the marketplace, since a lot of sellers are never asked to go into a transaction. In these initial experiments, the trust dispositions and the memory did not affect the results, unlike the risk behaviours that made a difference on the profits of the buyers. The next series of experiments seeks to find out whether and how unreliable agents may affect these findings.

5.2   A More Realistic Marketplace

In an unreliable marketplace, it seems intuitive that cautious agents will be better off than agents that seem to exercise trust in a non-chary way, for example optimists or risky agents.

Experiment R1. We gradually introduced a number of unreliable sellers in a marketplace populated by buyers as in experiment I1. The results showed that under the new conditions, both trust dispositions and memory capacity, (when the majority of the sellers is unreliable) are important for the agents (fig.3a,fig3b).

When unreliable agents populate the 20 and 40 percent of the marketplace, optimists manage to make slightly higher profits than the realists and the pessimists. Moreover, the different memory setting does not significantly affect the agents' utilities, since most of the time, they choose reliable sellers. Figure 4a shows the average trust value that agents of different trust dispositions have

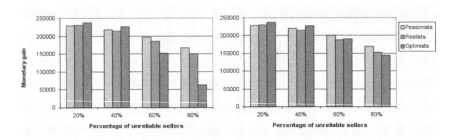

Fig. 3. Monetary gain for buyers with different trust dispositions and memory capacity in unreliable marketplaces. a)unbounded memory, b)bounded memory

in relation to the market honesty when 20% of the sellers are unreliable. The market honesty represents sellers' trustworthiness and is defined as the ratio between the delivered and the requested quantities towards buyers. As it can be seen, optimists build a trust value which is higher than that of realists and pessimists. Initially, all the agents show a decline in their trust towards sellers since the market honesty is also low. As the buyers continue transacting, they discover the reliable agents and soon the trust towards them increases. Since the buyers have now found the reliable sellers the market honesty also starts to increase and both average trust and market honesty converge. Under these conditions, exercising a high trust gives the optimists a slight advantage, since when making a selection in this case, the agents take into account the aspect of profit as well.

However, when the market is mostly populated by unreliable sellers (60 and 80 percent), the situation is reversed for the benefit of the pessimists. In such an environment, being an optimist is not helpful, as these buyers tend to have high trust values even for the unreliable agents. Pessimists, on the other hand manage to do better since their trust towards unreliable sellers is quite low and a few selections of reliable agents stand out from the rest of the alternatives. Figure 4b demonstrates this effect: optimists have a high trust estimate towards sellers from the first few sessions, as opposed to pessimists that exhibit a more cautious behaviour. In a marketplace where the majority of the sellers is not reliable building a high trust value is not beneficial. Again, as the agents continue to transact, the market honesty and the trust values of the buyers towards sellers converge, but in the case of the optimists the trust belief is higher than the actual honesty, an indication that these agents made excessive use of their trust.

In the case where the memory is unbounded, optimists make significantly less profits than other buyers, since they tend to stay with unreliable sellers for long periods. Although, optimists were sometimes trapped in their optimism by choosing unreliable sellers, they did not stop transacting; their threshold value never exceeded their trust towards sellers. Additionally, as the results showed, realists were most of the time between the two extremes.

Regarding the initial trust, the experiments showed that entering the market with a low initial trust was beneficial only in the case where the market was

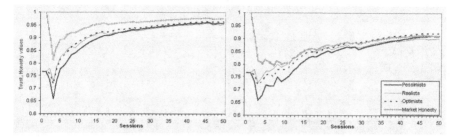

Fig. 4. Average trust value of the buyers towards sellers in a) a market populated by 20% unreliable sellers, b) a market populated by 80 unreliable sellers

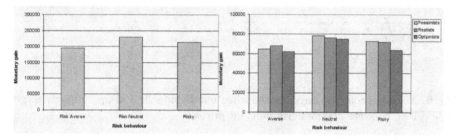

Fig. 5. Monetary profits for a)buyers with different risk behaviours, b) buyers with different trust dispositions and risk behaviours

mostly populated by unreliable sellers. Again, this is in accordance with our previous finding: with a low initial trust and a marketplace mostly populated with reliable sellers, buyers are slow in building trust and prefer few sellers, missing out other opportunities. On the contrary, when the marketplace is populated by unreliable agents, having a more cautious approach becomes beneficial.

Experiment R2. In addition to trust dispositions, we introduced risk behaviours in a setup analogous to experiment I2. The number of unreliable sellers was set to 50 percent and all the sellers initially advertised their goods with prices drawn from the same range. As the results show, the agents that were better off were the risk neutral ones (fig.5a) and among these the pessimists (fig.5b). Among the buyers, the risk averse agents were able to find the reliable sellers for the 95% of their transactions, risk neutral ones for the 85% and risky agents bought their goods from reliable agents in 70% of their transactions. Although the risk averse agents managed to find the reliable sellers in the majority of their transactions in comparison with the other buyers, they still did not gain a higher monetary value than them. This phenomenon is related to experiment I2, where risk averse agents prefer to stay with the agent they initially trust. In this case, risk averse agents found a reliable seller and stayed with it for a very long period, almost ignoring the other trustworthy sellers. Risk neutral agents also managed to find the trustworthy agents and achieved a nice distribution regarding their

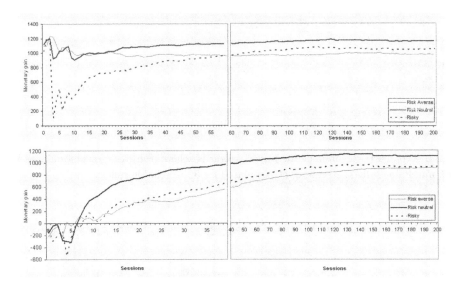

Fig. 6. Average profit the buyers make when unreliable sellers a)-upper diagram: give same prices, b)-lower diagram:give different prices

selections taking into account the aspect of profit. Finally, risky agents made the most unsafe selections and were sometimes lured by the unreliable sellers even when they had an average trust for them.

Figure 6a) shows the average profit of buyers during the experiment, in relation to their different risk behaviours. As illustrated, during the first few sessions risk averse agents are better off than the risk neutral and the risky ones, but this later changes in favour of the risk neutral agents. Additionally, risky agents manage to gain a higher profit than the risk averse agents, once they manage to get a good picture of the sellers' trustworthiness. However, our experiments showed that having suffered great losses in the beginning, risky agents cannot catch up with the profits of the risk neutral agents. A second run of this experiment in which unreliable agents were biased to make cheaper offers than the reliable ones, did not significantly alter the results (fig. 6b): risk neutral agents still made the highest profits, but this time the difference between the risky and risk averse agents became smaller. Running the experiment for another 200 sessions did not change the fact that risky agents made a higher profit than the risk averse ones. The cheaper prices the unreliable sellers initially offered, attracted risk neutral and to a greater extent risky agents, but since trust for these sellers became very low quite soon, the agents started making other selections.

6   Conclusions

This work presented the results from a simulation in a marketplace in which sellers, may not be reliable and sometimes choose to deviate from the reached agreements with the buyers. We focused on unreliable sellers, although our software can simulate marketplaces in which both, buyers and sellers can deviate from the market's protocol (see next section).

There has been an increasing number of computational models for different aspects of trust as described in the related work section. These existing works can be largely divided in two categories: a) the ones that present a trust model and explain how it can help agents learn cooperation, increase their utilities by selecting reliable partners or isolate cheaters in a multi-agent environment, and b) works that present a trust model and look into various aspects of it and their effects in a specific domain. Our work falls in the second category.

The approach presented here is different and adds to current work in the literature in a number of ways. Firstly, although we use a mechanism of experiences as in [15], we also provide a simple mechanism for agents to rate their experiences based not only on the amount of trustworthiness they perceive, but also on their own resources they spent when agreeing to transact. Secondly, since our abstraction of trust represents a belief, we chose to measure trust in the scale [0..1] in contrast to [15, 16] where the [-1..1] range is used. The trust model was inspired by the trust dispositions as described in [16] and this resulted different behaviours in our agents. A number of works on the topic often make the assumption that agents simply select the partner for whom they have the highest trust [5, 11]. However, when trust is very low towards others, agents may choose to trust noone [3, 9]. We therefore used a threshold mechanism which allows the agents to decide not to enter a transaction, if their trust has been abused. Another direction in which our work contributes to the topic of trust is related to the integration of risk behaviours in the trusting decision. Our approach is slightly different from [2], in that we do not follow a gain-loss approach and we choose a simpler concept from utility theory for modelling risk behaviours. Last, to our knowledge, our work is the first experimental work that combines the concepts of trust and risk attitudes for agents in the electronic marketplace.

Although we are using trust as a subjective probability during the selection phase, we still believe that trust is a complex mental process. In our experiments we seek to find out how certain characteristics related to trust (initial trust, trust dispositions, memory, risk behaviour) can lead to different decisions and consequently in different payoffs in an electronic marketplace. Our findings from the experiments can be summarized as follows:

1. The trust dispositions and the number of experiences the agents can remember are not important in a marketplace in which everyone is reliable. However, in marketplaces that are populated by both reliable and unreliable sellers, these attributes are important. Optimism is beneficial for the cases where the majority of the agents are reliable, whereas pessimism is preferable for the cases that the market is mostly populated by unreliable agents. A short term memory is helpful for the optimists when there are a lot of unreliable agents in the marketplace.
2. In a marketplace that all the agents behave reliably, the ones that enter the market with a high initial trust make a higher profit than the ones with a

low initial trust, an indication that being cautious and unwilling to trust in a healthy marketplace is not beneficial. When the conditions change and unreliable sellers appear in the marketplace, a high initial trust is good when the percentage of unreliable sellers is small.

3. In terms of risk, agents operating in a healthy environment are better off when they are willing to take risks, followed by risk neutral and risk averse agents. In marketplaces populated by unreliable sellers, risk neutral buyers manage to gather the highest profits. Risky agents manage to gather higher profits than the risk averse ones, even in the case where unreliable sellers operate in the marketplace. This does not come as a surprise, the agents choose their partners taking into account both the trust value towards sellers and their risk attitude. Once the risky buyers manage to find the reliable sellers, their profits start increasing.

Our results related to memory confirm some previous works on this topic. For example, [16], where it is mentioned that under certain conditions, the trust dispositions are not important, and in [2], where remembering past experiences for ever is not beneficial for the agents. Our experiments have led us to results that in most cases seem intuitive - for example, optimism is good when the market consists mainly of reliable sellers, pessimism is good when the majority of the agents are unreliable. Other results that at first seem less intuitive, for example, the case of risk neutral agents, making higher profits than the risk averse ones in an uncertain marketplace, can also be explained by taking into account the fact that the agents do not make "blind" decisions about where to buy their goods from, but they take into account both their trust towards sellers and their risk behaviour.

7   Further Work

There are many aspects of the presented work that we are currently working on. We are experimenting with introducing unreliable buyers in addition to unreliable sellers in the marketplace. Our findings so far, indicate that trustworthy agents manage to find each other rejecting unreliable participants. At the moment, reliable agents in our simulation are committed to a complete trustworthiness. In the real world however, even reliable agents can sometimes deviate from an agreement. We are running a series of experiments analogous to the ones presented here, where the reliable agents do not always have the highest commitment level. The first results indicate that under these conditions, pessimists agents are worse off in most cases and they choose to leave the marketplace after a certain number of sessions.

We also wish to see in more detail, how the trust dispositions relate to risk behaviours under different conditions in the marketplace. Our experiments included all the combinations of these, and although pessimists, risk neutral agents did marginally better than realists and optimists (exp. R2), it may be the case that in other markets, the results are different. Although, it initially seems out of the norms to consider the extreme cases (for example, pessimists who take risks, optimists who are risk averse), these can still be found in our world.

Another aspect of trust not addressed in the experiments presented here, is reputation. Apart from helping agents to isolate unreliable participants, reputation can probably address other issues as well: for example cases of exploitation where the sellers are reliable but they charge their loyal customers more than their occasional ones[2], or cases where the agents initially behave reliably, but later on decide to switch to a non-reliable behaviour. These assumptions remain to be tested in future experiments.

We are not interested in developing different strategies that relate to the degree the agents comply with the market's protocol in a prisoner's dilemma fashion. We have a made a simple assumption regarding the trustworthiness of the agents, given them certain characteristics and seen how these affect their individual welfare, as well as the marketplace. Our ultimate goal is to understand how the mechanisms presented in this work affect individual agents under different conditions. Doing so will help us enhance the decision making process of agents that participate in marketplaces. For example, agents under certain conditions could benefit by deciding to switch to a different trust disposition, or alter their risk behaviour.

Acknowledgments

This research has been supported by the Greek State Scholarship Foundation (IKY) grant number 2000/421.

References

1. Catholijn M. Jonker, Joost J. P. Schalken, Jan Theeuwes and Jan Treur. Human Experiments in Trust Dynamics In *Proceedings of the second International Conference on Trust Management (iTrust 2004)*, pages.195-210, 2004.
2. Jøsang, A. and Lo Presti, S. Analysing the Relationship Between Risk and Trust. In *Proceedings of Second International Conference on Trust Management (iTrust 2004)*, pages 135-145, Springer 2004.
3. Jøsang A., Shane Hird, and Eric Faccer. Simulating the effects of Reputation Systems on E-markets. In *Proceedings of the first International Conference on Trust Management (iTrust 2003)*, pages.179-194, 2003.
4. Castelfranchi C., Falcone R. and Pezzulo G. Integrating Trustfulness and Decision Using Fuzzy Cognitive Maps. In *Proceedings of the first International Conference on Trust Management (iTrust 2003)*, pages.195-210, 2003.
5. Ramchurn S. D., Sierra C., Godo L. and Jennings, N. R. A Computational Trust Model for Multi-agent Interactions based on Confidence and Reputation. In *Proceedings of 6th International Workshop of Deception, Fraud and Trust in Agent Societies*, pages 69-75, 2003.

---

[2] Amazon case, visit Google and search for keywords: amazon loyal customers dynamic pricing.

6. Yao-Hua Tan. A Trust Matrix Model for Electronic Commerce. In *Proceedings of the first International Conference on Trust Management (iTrust 2003)*, pages.33-45, 2003.

7. Jonathan Carter, Elijah Bitting, and Ali A. Ghorbani: Reputation Formalization for an Information-Sharing Multi-Agent System. In *Computational Intelligence*, Vol 18, No. 4, pages. 45-64, 2002.

8. Barber, S. and Kim, J. Belief Revision Process based on Trust: Agents Evaluating Reputation of Information Access. In *Trust In Cyber-societies*, Volume 2246 of Lecture Notes in Computer Science, pages. 111-132, Springer, 2001.

9. Nooteboom B, Klos T. and Jorna R, Adaptive Trust and Cooperation: An Agent-based Simulation Approach. In *Trust In Cyber-societies*, Volume 2246 of Lecture Notes in Computer Science, pages. 83-108, Springer, 2001.

10. McKnight, D. H. and Chervany, N. L. Trust and Distrust Definitions: One Bite at a Time. In *Trust In Cyber-societies*, Volume 2246 of Lecture Notes in Computer Science, pages 27-54, Springer, 2001.

11. M. Witowski, A. Artikis and J. Pitt. Experiments in Building Experiential Trust in a Society of Objective Trust Based Agents. In *Trust In Cyber-societies*, Volume 2246 of Lecture Notes in Computer Science, pages 111-132, Springer, 2001.

12. Castelfranchi C. and Falcone R. Trust is Much More Than Subjective Probability: Mental Components and Sources of Trust. In *Proceedings of the 33rd Hawaii International Conference on System Sciences, Vol. 6*, pages 10-12, 2000.

13. Dellarocas C. Immunizing online reputation reporting systems against unfair ratings and discriminatory behavior. In *Proceedings of the 2nd ACM Conference on Electronic Commerce*, Minneapolis, pages 150-157, 2000.

14. Brainov S. and Sandholm T. Contracting with Uncertain Level of Trust. In *Proceedings of the First ACM Conference on Electronic Commerce*, pages 15-21, 1999.

15. C. Jonker and J. Treur. Formal Analysis of Models for the Dynamics of Trust based on Experiences. In *Proceedings of the 9th European Workshop on Modelling Autonomous Agents in a Multi-Agent World: MultiAgent System Engineering*, pages: 221-231, 1999.

16. Marsh S. Formalising Trust as a Computational Concept, PhD Thesis, University of Stirling, 1994.

17. Luhmann, N. Familiarity, Confidence, Trust: Problems and Alternatives. In *Gambetta, D. (ed.) Trust: Making and Breaking Cooperative Relations*. Electronic edition, Department of Sociology, University of Oxford. 6, pages 94-107, 1988.

18. French, S. Decision Theory: An Introduction to the Mathematics of Rationality. Chichester: Ellis Horwood, 1988

19. www.fraud.org, Internet Fraud Watch.

20. www.econsumer.gov, site for cross-border e-commerce complaints.

21. www.ifccfbi.gov, Internet Fraud Complaint Center

Trust Management Survey

Sini Ruohomaa and Lea Kutvonen

University of Helsinki, Finland
{Sini.Ruohomaa, Lea.Kutvonen}@cs.helsinki.fi
http://www.cs.helsinki.fi/group/tube/

Abstract. Trust is an important tool in human life, as it enables people to cope with the uncertainty caused by the free will of others. Uncertainty and uncontrollability are also issues in computer-assisted collaboration and electronic commerce in particular. A computational model of trust and its implementation can alleviate this problem.

This survey is directed to an audience wishing to familiarize themselves with the field, for example to locate a research target or implement a trust management system. It concentrates on providing a general overview of the state of the art, combined with examples of things to take into consideration both when modelling trust in general and building a solution for a certain phase in trust management, be it trust relationship initialization, updating trust based on experience or determining what trust should have an effect on.

1 Introduction

Trust plays an important role in virtual organisations, countering uncertainty caused by the business requirement for openness. The requirement seeks to make marketable services openly available to all potential, highly autonomous clients, which increases a service provider's vulnerability to an attack. As there is no central authority to provide support for traditional authentication for a rapidly changing actor base, making sensible authorisation decisions concerning new, previously unknown partners is difficult. Manual updates to policy or access control settings quickly become laborious, which drives organisations into making only very broad decisions concerning large parts of the user base to avoid the overly heavy process of personalizing the security settings. Trust management can provide a basis for more detailed and better-informed authorisation decisions, while allowing for a high level of automation.

This paper aims to provide an overview of trust management research in the field of computer science, without going too deeply into any implementation specifics. It was written as a part of a state-of-the-art analysis for the TuBE (Trust Based on Evidence) project [1]. The paper is organized in two parts. The first part discusses trust as a concept, how it has been modelled and how the concept could be introduced to computer security. Noteworthy ideas are drawn from all sources alike.

P. Herrmann et al. (Eds.): iTrust 2005, LNCS 3477, pp. 77–92, 2005.
© Springer-Verlag Berlin Heidelberg 2005

The second part describes the different tasks of the trust management system: determining initial trust, observing the trustee's actual behaviour and updating trust accordingly. Technologies and ideas to support a particular task are brought up together with the general discussion of the challenges related to that task. This forms a loose application taxonomy through which trust management research is presented. The task set, or trust life cycle, is taken to begin from choosing a partner and determining a suitable initial trust in them. Reputation systems are discussed as an aid in this task, although their usability does not end there. After the partner is allowed to use the provided services, the system moves to observation and gathering evidence of the partners' behaviour. Intrusion detection and prevention systems (IDS/IPS) play a central role here. From the data gathered from various pieces of evidence and possible updates from a reputation system, different actions can be taken, the most central being the adjustment of the trust estimate.

The rest of this paper is organized as follows: Chapter 2 discusses concepts for trust management and how to model it, covering the aforementioned first part of the paper. Chapter 3 covers the second part, discussing the initialization of trust relationships, identifying methods for observing the trustee and considering the various decisions to base on trust and the observations. Finally, chapter 4 offers some conclusions.

2   On the Nature of Trust

Trust and reputation, a closely related term, are firmly rooted in sociology, and those roots should not be forgotten [2]. However, trust is quite a complicated phenomenon, the concept itself carrying many meanings. As our interest in purely sociological or psychological studies on trust has been limited, this section will only give a brief overview of the trust phenomenon before moving on to how systems should trust. It is not certain that we want to even try imitating human trust fully in computer systems, as humans do not seem to always make fully rational trust decisions [3, 4].

2.1   Concepts for Trust Management

In the following chapters of this work, we consider trust as it is directed at independent actors. The **trustor** is a service provider practicing electronic commerce on the Internet, and the **trustee** is either a business partner or an individual requiring access to the trustor's services, as represented by an identifiable agent in the network. The trustees are independent in the sense that their actions cannot directly be controlled by outsiders such as the service provider, i.e. the trustor. The business partners and individuals behind the trustee agents can have control over several different identities through agents which cannot be reliably traced back to them or to each other.

Trust seems to essentially be a means for people to deal with uncertainty about the future and their interaction partners. Stephen Marsh considers the protection of law, a lack of options for possible outcomes and other kinds of limitations, reducing the aforementioned independence of actors, as examples of factors reducing the need to trust [5]. In a more technical environment, "trusted" hardware for monitoring [6] or cryptographically secure communications [7] also work towards reducing uncertainty.

Trust is defined as *the extent to which one party is willing to participate in a given action with a given partner, considering the risks and incentives involved* (adjusted from [8, 9]). **A trust decision** is binary and based on the balance between trust and risk, and it has some sort of effect on the trustee. Usually it is made with a class of applicable situations in mind, such as concerning a particular trustee in performing a certain action only. **Actions** involve using services provided by the trustor. The effect of the trust decision on the trustee varies: depending on the situation, trust may directly affect whether the action is *authorised* at all. Even if access is granted, there may be a need to *limit resources* available during the action or tighten the *observation* of the trustee.

The effect of trust comes with a **risk**: an authorisation decision means that we expose something in our control to attack or abuse, while reduced observation means that misbehaviour may proceed undetected and more resources allocated means that more of them may go to waste or be misused. The connection of risk and trust is emphasised by many researchers, such as [5, 8, 10]. Risks are tied to assets [11]. If money or system security are assets, the related risks involve losing money or experiencing a breach in security. The risks considered here are limited to those known to the trustor; balancing against something unknown may prove difficult. The **action importance**, or its business value, affects trust similarly to good reputation, increasing the willingness to make a positive trust decision.

Reputation is defined as a *perception a party creates through past actions about its intentions and norms* [2]. Reputation exists only in a community which is observing its members in one way or another, and is as such meaningless outside its native environment. It can be transmitted from one community context to another, however, by means of recommendations. As the definition implies, it is affected by experience; directly if the experience is shared by the entire community, or through negotiations if only a sub-community has borne witness.

A **recommendation** is simply *an attempt at communicating a party's reputation from one community context to another*. A poor recommendation may be detrimental to one's reputation, and there is no separate term for "negative recommendation". The word *attempt* should remind us that the source and target communities are seldom compatible enough to be able to use a recommendation directly. Instead, the recommendation may be tuned down in various means, including tagging it as "uncertain information" or giving it a lowered weight in appropriate calculations. In order for reputation to exist in larger than the trivial one-member communities, the members must come to an agreement about their shared perception for each given party in that community. Various reputation systems suggest different ways of coming to this agreement. There is no objective truth to be found—or lost—in reputation itself, but some perceptions come closer to the target party's real intentions and norms than others.

Despite the earlier dismissal of human trust as somewhat irrational and overly complex, it is an important research topic for computer scientists as well. After all, there is a human actor somewhere behind the user agents and client programs, making trust-involving decisions e.g. on whether to use our trust management system or not. If the human users disagree with their trust management system more often than not, they will probably change the system accordingly. Research on how to appear trustworthy to users shows that trustworthiness estimates are determined by much more than just past success or failure to comply to expectations [11, 12, 13, 14]. It has been suggested that contracts, as they make implicit expectations explicit, can encourage more trust [13, 14]. An agreement on social norms does help in building human trust, but binding contracts can also be used to reduce uncertainty in electronic commerce. In case of a breach of contract, a means for dealing with the violation may be given by the contract itself, with the backing of law, if necessary and available. Contracts are in this sense another measure of control, like insurances, and they may well reduce risk even more than encourage more trust to balance with the remaining risk. The effect of contracts in trust management has been discussed in relation to transaction modelling as well [15, 16].

2.2   The Trust Management Model

Trust management research has its roots in authentication and authorisation. In the context of authentication, trust is established by means such as digital certificates. These certificates are proof of either identity directly or membership in a group of good reputation. Authentication-related trust is discussed for example in [17, 7]. Policy languages, such as [18, 19, 20], then make it possible to automatically determine whether certain credentials are sufficient for performing a certain action, to authorise the trustee. The Sultan trust management framework [21] includes a language for describing trust and recommendation relationships in the system. Constraints can be attached to these relationships, and through them the relationships can be connected to the Ponder policy language [22].

Credentials are sufficient when the system is either convinced of the trustee's identity or knows her to be a member of some sufficiently trusted group—or one of the credentials may be an authorisation certificate, signed by someone with the right to delegate such authority. At the authentication level, trust is monotonic across time and attached to a certain identity or membership. Updating the level of trust based on evidence of actual behaviour is not yet considered; the focus is on credentials matching policy.

Sufficiently flexible policy systems provide the backbone for a trust management system. Tonti et al. compare three languages for policy representation and reasoning [23]. KAoS [24, 25], Rei [26] and the aforementioned Ponder are used as a basis for sketching some general properties desirable in future work on policy semantics. Delegent has strong roots in authorisation administration research [27], and it has also been developed into software [28].

To make trust more dynamic, the behaviour of the trustee should be considered as well. In 2000, monitoring users could be achieved by intrusion detection systems, but the information gleaned was not being used to evolve trust or reputation. None of the existing systems then yet covered monitoring and re-evaluation of trust [29]. Since then, behaviour history collection has been included in one form or another in numerous trust models. Behaviour information can be gathered locally [30, 9], or it can be received as third-party observations through a reputation system [31]. Involving third parties, however, requires some sort of trust in their statements, as well as comparability between the trustor's and the third party's views on reputation. Reputation systems are discussed in more detail in chapter 3.1.

Much work has also gone to identifying factors which either are considered to affect trust directly or which are used together with trust decisions. It was mentioned earlier that uncertainty is involved in increasing the need for trust. Uncertainty is not always problematic to the trustor, however, but mostly when it is related to risk. While the exact relationship between risk and trust is not entirely clear [8, 10], it is agreed that increased risk and increased need to trust go hand in hand [32, 33]. Risk is relative to the trustor taking the risk; for example, the risk of losing a specific monetary sum is less important if the sum is only a small fraction of the usable funds. It has also been noted that increased potential profits in making a decision to trust encourages coping with relatively higher risk [9]. Potential profits can be considered a part of the action importance mentioned in chapter 2.1. The protection of law and other factors limiting the need to trust according to Marsh may also be considered means to reduce risk [5].

Applications where a more dynamic trust management is beneficial may have a rapidly-changing user base. Newcomers create a problem for a trust management system based on behaviour history alone. The system must determine how much these unknown individuals should be trusted, sometimes without knowing anything about them. While certification may provide a means to introduce an initial trust out of band, it may not be plausible for some applications. Similarly, reputation systems are only helpful if the user has interacted with other systems gathering reputation before. For fully unknown users, a default level of trust must be determined. If it is set too low, the user may not be allowed access to the system at all, which makes proving trustworthiness through one's actions rather difficult [34]. If it is set very high, there may be a need to limit the possibility for users to "start over" by re-registration after misbehaving. Otherwise the punishment from having behaved badly becomes void, as a user with a trustworthiness estimate below that given to a newcomer will re-register herself to the system to become one herself.

2.3   The Trust Information Model

The problem of somehow representing human thought and feeling in a computer system is quite evident in trust management, albeit still in a somewhat limited sense compared to some other fields. Sociologists and psychologists, as well as economists in the field of game theory, have attempted to model trust and concepts closely related to it, such as reputation and reciprocity. Reciprocity is the *mutual exchange of deeds (such as favor or revenge)* [2]. That is, if one participant in a highly reciprocal society tends to be very cooperative, others should be cooperative towards him as well. The term has not been included in many trust models this far.

Current trust models have been criticised for not making the relationship between trust and reputation clear and for treating them as independent of context or time [2]. Grandison and Sloman [21] find that while the current (in 2002) logic-based frameworks suffer from problems related to applicability and limit themselves to a subsection of the trust management problem, the existing solutions such as PolicyMaker [19], KeyNote [20], REFEREE [18] and Trust-Builder, a negotiation architecture for sensitive credential exchange [17], merely concentrate on certificates and access control, with no trust re-evaluation based on available information.

Early forms of trust management, as represented by the aforementioned four systems, began by automating authentication and authorisation decisions with the help of varying sets of credentials. In this kind of setting, a trust level is fixed in relationship to passed credentials, and trust is not re-evaluated based on experience information. It is outsourced, in a sense, to certificate authorities and the like, and the system using this kind of trust management is merely deciding how much it "trusts" a given credential or its issuer in the context of determining a reputation of sorts.

Research on trust can be divided into three groups based on its context. On the lowest, most fundamental level, trust is a part of the *infrastructure*. Early trust research has been concentrating on this level. As electronic commerce has gained a foothold and open systems become more common, trust forms an important part on the *service* level as well, where much of this paper is positioned. There are still many problems to be solved on this level before research on the highest level, the *community*, can proceed freely.

Marsh was one of the first to introduce a computational model for trust in his doctorate thesis [5]. His model is relatively simple, based on a scalar value of trust, and does not discuss reputation. Abdul-Rahman and Hailes criticize the model for overvariabilisation [35]. Mayer looked for a differentiation between factors contributing to trust, trust itself and its outcomes [8]. Two years later Essin wrote a socio-technologically focused model for trust and policy, with a goal to make them work better in computer systems [36].

Various different aspects of trust are highlighted in the different ways it is defined. Gambetta sees trust as a subjective *probability* in the trustee performing a particular action ([37], used by e.g. Abdul-Rahman and Hailes [35]). Not far apart, Mui et al. consider it as a subjective *expectation* about the trustee's future behaviour [2]. On the other hand, Mayer, Jøsang and Lo Presti define trust as an extent of *willingness* to depend on somebody [8,9]. Demolombe places his definitions of trust in a framework of modal logic, and considers it to be a strong *belief about a given property* of the trustee, for example sincerity, cooperativity or credibility [38].

Jøsang draws our attention to being clear about the target of trust [39]. He points out that a machine or a program (a rational entity) does not trust; it only implements the trust policy given by a human (a passionate entity). On the other hand, while trusting another passionate entity concerns speculation on things such as their motives and intentions, trusting a rational entity, who only acts according to lists of commands and rules, is based on trusting its ability to withstand manipulation by a passionate entity [39]. This also implies that when placing trust in an agent, which is a rational representation of a passionate entity, i.e. a human user, we are not only placing trust in the user behind the agent, but also indirectly in the person who coded the agent and anyone who would be capable of assuming control of the agent. While all this can be summarised as trusting the user to only use a "secure" agent, being explicit about the implications of that trust will aid not only fellow scientists but, possibly even more importantly, the users of the trust models, frameworks and implemented solutions produced from trust management research.

Egger [40, 12] has developed a model for trust-relevant factors from a customer's perspective. Some factors are relevant for the perspective of a service provider as well, such as reputation, propensity to trust and transference. As mentioned before, risk is an important factor in trust management. Mayer points out, in light of his definition of trust as a willingness to depend on someone, that risk is not directly tied to the willingness itself, but on the behavioural manifestation of a willingness to be vulnerable [8].

While Marsh's trust model represented trust in the form of a scalar [5], SECURE represents it as a range to include a measure of uncertainty in the value [41]. Jøsang and Lo Presti include a three-dimensional decision surface for balancing trust and risk in their model [9]. Trust could also be represented as an n-dimensional vector, with parameters such as the trustee's reputation, the action to perform and the risk and business importance related to it. As described before, a trust decision related to a particular action in a given situation remains binary, with the system possibly providing also a third option for "yes, if the following constraints are met".

3   The Tasks of a Trust Management System

In the previous section, we built some theoretical basis for trust management, categorized the effects of trust to the trustee into those related to authorisation, observation and resource allocation, and identified different factors weighed in a trust decision. In this section, we take a look at different challenges set for a trust management system. The section begins with the initialization of trust relationships, and goes on to identify different means to observe the trustee's behaviour during the actions. Finally, actions to take based on the new experience are discussed.

3.1   Initializing a Trust Relationship

Sometimes partners can be found with traditional out-of-band means like word of mouth, but in a highly dynamic and possibly automated environment a discovery service of some sort is necessary [42]. The lack of background information constitutes a problem both for determining an initial trust in a partner as well as choosing the suitable partner for one's current needs. A search using a discovery service may result in a plethora of potential partners, some of which may be incompetent or even malicious. Once a number of potential partners has been found, a reputation system may aid in locating the most trustworthy one, based on their past behaviour with other principals in the network.

A reputation system aggregates information about the past behaviour of a group of entities in the form of the community's shared perception of them. This information may include information from book reviewers' perceived fairness to on-line companies' perceived competence and reliability. Reputation systems have been found to benefit of computer-aided human-to-human interaction, by reducing the level of uncertainty about new acquaintances to an endurable level [31, 33].

Experience or reputation information gathering and storage can be organized centrally or be distributed across peers. EBay (http://www.ebay.com), an on-line marketplace, gathers performance ratings from its users distributedly, but the results are kept on a central server [33]. Organizations like The International Chamber of Commerce, who act as advisors and certifiers in first-trade situations and provide information about other organizations' reputation, represent a fully centralized approach [43]. Everyone wishing to use a reputation system must be able to trust the information provider to not insert false ratings or omit information at will. While this may be a small challenge in a centralized approach, it is considerably more difficult to achieve with a fully distributed approach. The problem escalates when reputation is more valuable; competitors may be given bad ratings to disrupt their business, or good ratings may be sold for money, unrelated to actual performance. Gathering negative feedback may also be a problem: human reviewers in eBay tend to avoid giving negative feedback to others and prefer to resolve conflicts out-of-band *before* making a rating [31].

Obreiter suggests the use of evidence in the form of trade receipts, which can be used as a sort of certificate of having behaved well at some point [44]. Pinocchio rewards honest participation in a recommendation system, which might rate users as well as e.g. books, with a sort of virtual currency which is then needed to use the system. It approximates an honest user (measured as a scalar) as one who does not disagree with other users more than other users on the average disagree with each other. On the other hand, it also punishes poor "reputation" as a recommender by stopping the rewards for a probationary period [45].

Dishonesty in the expression of perceptions should be somewhat difficult to detect, let alone prove, but in the context of reputation systems we can understand dishonesty as relatively similar to Pinocchio's view—either too agreeing or too disagreeing to be likely to be useful for others. Kalcklösch and Herrmann apply statistical methods in ad hoc networks where trust information communication is automatic [46]. While these methods may not be the approach of choice for an established web service provider looking for partners, they serve well in their context. One must note that solutions on different levels, from infrastructure to service to community level, have very different needs.

Even if the recommending party is known to be honest and knowledgeable, their statements may be useless if the principals are not known by the same name by the recommender and the receiver, or if the principles behind the recommendations are not comparable to those of the receiver. A good reputation as a trader in an on-line auctioning system does not necessarily mean that the user should be given e.g. wider access privileges in a distributed software development project. This makes representing trust or reputation as a single numeric value somewhat problematic: If a reputation statement says that a user is trustworthy by "3 on a scale from 1 to 5", what does it mean in the receiver's context? Has the default been 1 or 3 and how easily is it increased or decreased? If this is a trader's reputation, should I trust them to sell a car to me if they got their reputation by selling pocket lighters [31]? This causes difficulties for porting ratings from one system to another as well. Recommendations remain an *attempt* at communicating reputation information between communities.

Resnick et al. describe three requirements for a successful reputation system: first, the entities must be long-lived and have use for reputation; second, feedback must be captured, distributed and made available in the future; third, the feedback must be used to guide trust decisions [31]. The first property implies some problems that newcomers have with reputation systems. Besides having the problem of finding a trustworthy information provider, they must gain a reputation themselves [34].

The usability of reputation information from outside sources is not limited to choosing a partner. It can also be included as a factor in the trust estimate of a partner, along with their locally gathered reputation based on first-hand experience. Initially, as there is no local information about the partner's behaviour, external reputation information may hold considerable weight in a trust decision.

Besides reputation systems, various kinds of authentication and credential systems may help determine an initial level of trust through e.g. membership in a group with a good reputation. The Web Services standard WS-Trust approaches authorisation and authentication via security tokens requested from on-line servers [47]. Karabulut proposes a hybrid public key infrastructure model to ease the delegation of trust, in the sense of allowing third parties to produce credentials usable for authorisation trust management in the target system [48].

A trust management system also tends to have some sort of a default value to assign to complete strangers. This value represents the system's general tendency to trust, or its *trust propensity*. This default may be raised or lowered based on a general view of the world the system operates in. If the average partner seems to be a somewhat unreliable opportunist, the trust propensity may be reduced. On the other hand, if the system operates in an environment of honest cooperation, the trust propensity may be increased.

As the initial trust value is even at best based on the experiences of others with the partner, it may prove to be a poor estimate. Observing the partner's actions and updating their local reputation based on the observation strengthens the system against misplaced expectations. Evolving reputation and trust is discussed in more detail in chapter 3.3.

3.2   Observation

Observation can be done in two different roles: either as an active participant of a collaboration, or as an outsider, a silent third party. In the first case, the actions of the observed are seen through a personal context, which gives more depth to the analysis. Intrusion detection software can benefit greatly from "insider" information from the observed application, if it is available. As an example, Zamboni [49] suggests using internal sensors inside the observed applications themselves, but such modifications are not always possible.

The principles and research in the field of intrusion detection can be put to use in observing users or partners in a trust management system. The traditional approach to intrusion detection looks at system calls or network traffic, while application-level intrusion detection adds "insider" understanding to the analysis by being aware of the particular applications observed instead of trying to understand network traffic or system calls for the entire system.

We can divide intrusion detection into two main approaches. Anomaly detection attempts to model normal behaviour, often by learning from experience gained during an observation period [50, 51], and considers abnormalities potential signs of an attack. The second approach, misuse detection, constructs models to match the attacks instead [52]. While such specifications are less likely to yield false positives than detecting previously unseen behaviour in general, keeping them up to date is problematic—only known attacks can be detected. The approaches are not mutually exclusive, as is shown by IDES [53].

Specification-based anomaly detection attempts to combine the best of both worlds [54]. A specification for normal behaviour can be built with the help of e.g. source code. In the context of Web Services, contracts of acceptable behaviour may have already been made, possibly with the help of e.g. the Web Service Description Language (WSDL) [55]. If a suitable set of interface specifications for a particular Web Service can be found, it could be used as a basis for the specification of acceptable behaviour as well.

Thorough observation ties up resources, which may make it simply impossible to keep close track of what every user is doing at all times. Herrmann and Krumm, who study monitoring and trust or lack thereof directed towards a set of system components, suggest adjusting the intensity of monitoring and behaviour checks according to the level of trust in the observed component, its hosting environment and its vendor [56].

Suspicious activity can in the most straightforward case be actual misbehaviour in the form of breaking system policy or not following other forms of orchestration. It can, however, also be an action which either should only be taken by actors in a different role or is simply highly unusual behaviour for the observed. A change in an actor's behaviour may give reason to suspect that communications with the actor have been compromised, either on the way or in the source by subverting the actor or its representee somehow. The exact reason behind the unusual behaviour is not necessarily of consequence; the actor is not behaving as it should, and the observing system wants to protect itself against these possibly malicious influences.

When an observation system has detected suspicious activity, a decision must be made on what to do with the information. In the literature, the most visibly noted actions are updating the trust value or reputation (see the following chapter) and, if the analysis is done in real time, stopping the suspicious activity altogether. An Intrusion Prevention System (IPS) extends the concept of intrusion detection by also considering preemptive measures.

Automated reaction to detected attacks requires very accurate, real-time intrusion detection. The anomaly intrusion detection approach, with is tendency towards false positives, would therefore be sub-optimal if used alone in intrusion prevention. On the other hand, misuse intrusion detection would also miss some attacks due to not knowing them beforehand. Specification-based anomaly detection shows some promise, but building specifications of normal behaviour may not be feasible for all applications. It has been applied to network protocols [54], and could maybe find a place in the field of Web Services. Specifications of acceptable behaviour could potentially be composed based on the architecture's various specification languages, mainly the Web Service Description Language (WSDL) combined with probably necessary additional semantic information. Taking the step from merely being a language validator to observing trust-relevant activity may be challenging, however.

The idea of preventing policy-breaking or otherwise suspicious activity is not new. Access control lists have for long prevented users without specific identity-tied privileges from accessing certain files or services, and policy languages can be used to further limit access according to other constraints. They can also be used to lower the resources allocated for a slightly risky task which is not considered to be in direct conflict with policy, and as mentioned earlier, the task can be allowed to proceed normally, but under tighter observation as with trust decisions discussed earlier. Similar adjustments could be based on trust instead of more static, pre-set constraints.

Besides detecting suspicious activity, an observation system could be used as a witness of "normal" behaviour. Good experiences lead to better or at least more "certain" reputation in many reputation systems where the users themselves act as witnesses. On the other hand, if a reputation estimate includes a measure of confidence, i.e. how certain the estimate is, a lengthy period of observation showing behaviour in agreement with the current reputation may be taken as increased confidence in the reputation estimate.

3.3   Evolving Reputation and Trust

The evolution of reputation stands at the heart of a trust management system. It also seems to be a subject which is seldom discussed in detail in a practical context. One reason for this may be the need for configurability; research should not impose any particular policy on trust updates upon its applications. Some detailed examples in the right context can prove invaluable, however.

Mathematical models give tools and formulae for dealing with experience as it is represented as a binary for "cooperated vs. defected" [2] or by scalars [57]. The SECURE project provides a formal model of incorporating new evidence to trust information [30, 41]. The Sultan project has also included an experience collection module in its architecture description [21, 58]. Translating experience into updates in reputation seems to largely be work in progress.

As the user's reputation is updated based on their actions, information about the changes can be sent as recommendations to reputation systems spanning larger communities, such as those used by the local reputation system to estimate the initial reputation of newcomers. The information can then be used to adjust the user's reputation in the target community as well. This requires that the recommendation includes a representation of the user's identity that is recognized in both communities. It is noteworthy that the reputation changes communicated across systems are not an objective truth by our definition, and the updates involve agreements on how the information is dealt with. This topic is central in the development of reputation systems.

4   Conclusions

Trust management is a young area of research. Trust as a concept has many very different applications, which causes divergence in trust management terminology. Also, conceptually separating trust from reputation is not always done, or nothing is said about how one affects the other [2]. Yet if either is forgotten, the remaining term's definition is left to bear both the aspect of perceptions and predictions as well as the willingness to depend and the related analysis of risks and benefits. Similarly, associating trust specifically to known actions instead of principals in general can make trust models more adaptable and understandable.

There has been some progress in the field of updating trust and reputation based on evidence of the actors' behaviour in the system. Yet while some projects include experience-collection modules in their systems [58, 10], practical studies on how to translate various suspicious or encouraging events into updates of reputation or trust are scarce. Theoretical models considering the topic assume that experiences have already been coded into either binary or scalar [2, 57]. Observation alone is a difficult task to automatize well; intrusion detection systems seek an automated way to answer to "is this an attack or just something resembling one?", and face similar problems. High configurability is a requirement for the observation system, or at least for its interpretation engine. As collaborative systems allow autonomic and dynamic policy changes at individual enterprises, conflicts in policy or expectations need to be detected run-time; static verification is no longer sufficient.

As a phenomenon, trust is such a multi-faceted research target that finding a satisfactory representation of it for computer systems must either be done based on a relatively limited context or not at all. The three-level view of trust research, from infrastructure to communities, was presented to keep these limitations of context in mind when evaluating earlier work. Still, there is work to do on all levels. An increased automation in trust management is needed for collaborative systems, especially for routine tasks. There should be room for human intervention, however, for exceptions of the rule or new kinds of situations where the routine rules may not be applicable.

On one hand, it is reassuring to remember that trust is only a tool and as such can be simplified and toned down to suit our purposes. On the other hand, a tool which gives poor counsel due to not considering factors the user would want to give weight to is a tool easily abandoned. A tool might also be considered faulty to the degree of being unusable even if it knows better, according to a suitable definition of better, but constantly disagrees with its users in ways they do not comprehend.

References

1. Kutvonen, L., Viljanen, L., Ruohomaa, S.: The TuBE approach to trust management in collaborative enterprise systems. (2005) Manuscript.
2. Mui, L., Mohtashemi, M., Halberstadt, A.: A computational model of trust and reputation. In: 35th Annual Hawaii International Conference on System Sciences (HICSS'02). Volume 7., IEEE Computer Society (2002)
3. Fogg, B., Soohoo, C., Danielson, D., Marable, L., Stanford, J., Tauber, E.R.: How do people evaluate a web site's credibility? Technical report, Stanford Persuasive Technology Lab (2002)
4. Jonker, C.M., Schalken, J.J.P., Theeuwes, J., Treur, J.: Human experiments in trust dynamics. In: Trust Management: Second International Conference, iTrust 2004, Oxford, UK, March 29–April 1, 2004. Proceedings. Volume LNCS 2995/2004., Springer-Verlag (2004) 206–220
5. Marsh, S.: Formalising Trust as a Computational Concept. PhD thesis, University of Stirling, Department of Computer Science and Mathematics (1994)
6. Baldwin, A., Shiu, S.: Hardware security appliances for trust. In: Trust Management: First International Conference, iTrust 2003, Heraklion, Crete, Greece, May 28–30, 2003. Proceedings. Volume LNCS 2692/2003. (2003) 46–58
7. Djordjevic, I., Dimitrakos, T.: Towards dynamic security perimeters for virtual collaborative networks. In: Trust Management: Second International Conference, iTrust 2004, Oxford, UK, March 29–April 1, 2004. Proceedings. Volume LNCS 2995/2004. (2004) 191–205
8. Mayer, R.C., Davis, J.H.: An integrative model of organizational trust. The Academy of Management Review **20** (1995) 709–734
9. Jøsang, A., Presti, S.L.: Analysing the relationship between risk and trust. In: Trust Management: Second International Conference, iTrust 2004, Oxford, UK, March 29–April 1, 2004. Proceedings. Volume LNCS 2995/2004. (2004) 135–145
10. English, C., Terzis, S., Wagealla, W.: Engineering trust based collaborations in a global computing environment. In: Trust Management: Second International Conference, iTrust 2004, Oxford, UK, March 29–April 1, 2004. Proceedings. Volume LNCS 2995/2004. (2004) 120–134
11. Brændeland, G., Stølen, K.: Using risk analysis to assess user trust - a net-bank scenario -. In: Trust Management: Second International Conference, iTrust 2004, Oxford, UK, March 29–April 1, 2004. Proceedings. Volume LCNS 2995/2004. (2004) 146–160
12. Egger, F.N.: From Interactions to Transactions: Designing the Trust Experience for Business-to-Consumer Electronic Commerce. PhD thesis, Eindhoven University of Technology (2003)

13. Grimsley, M., Meehan, A., Tan, A.: Managing Internet-mediated community trust relations. In: Trust Management: Second International Conference, iTrust 2004, Oxford, UK, March 29–April 1, 2004. Proceedings. Volume LNCS 2995/2004. (2004) 277–290

14. Ishaya, T., Mundy, D.P.: Trust development and management in virtual communities. In: Trust Management: Second International Conference, iTrust 2004, Oxford, UK, March 29–April 1, 2004. Proceedings. Volume LNCS 2995/2004. (2004) 266–276

15. Gordijn, J., Akkermans, H.: Designing and evaluating e-Business models. IEEE Intelligent Systems 16 (2001) 11–17

16. Tan, Y.H., Thoen, W., Gordijn, J.: Modeling controls for dynamic value exchanges in virtual organizations. In: Trust Management: Second International Conference, iTrust 2004, Oxford, UK, March 29–April 1, 2004. Proceedings. Volume LNCS 2995/2004. (2004) 236–250

17. Winsborough, W.H., Seamons, K.E., Jones, V.E.: Automated trust negotiation. In: DARPA Information Survivability Conference and Exposition, 2000. DISCEX '00. Proceedings. Volume 1., IEEE (2000) 88–102

18. Chu, Y.H., Feigenbaum, J., LaMacchia, B., Resnick, P., Strauss, M.: REFEREE: Trust management for Web applications. Computer Networks and ISDN Systems 29 (1997) 953–964

19. Blaze, M., Feigenbaum, J., Lacy, J.: Decentralized trust management. In: Proceedings of the IEEE Symposium on Security and Privacy, IEEE (1996)

20. Blaze, M., Feigenbaum, J., Keromytis, A.D.: KeyNote: Trust management for public-key infrastructures (position paper). In: Security Protocols: 6th International Workshop, Cambridge, UK, April 1998. Proceedings. Volume LNCS 1550/1998., Springer-Verlag (1998) 59–63

21. Grandison, T., Sloman, M.: Specifying and analysing trust for Internet applications. In: Proceedings of 2nd IFIP Conference on e-Commerce, e-Business, e-Government I3e2002, Lisbon, Portugal. (2002)

22. Damianou, N., Dulay, N., Lupu, E., Sloman, M.: The Ponder policy specification language. In: Workshop on Policies for Distributed Systems and Networks (Policy2001), HP Labs Bristol, 29-31 Jan 2001. Volume 1995. (2001) 18–

23. Tonti, G., Bradshaw, J.M., Jeffers, R., Montanari, R., Suri, N., Uszok, A.: Semantic Web languages for policy representation and reasoning: A comparison of KAoS, Rei, and Ponder. In: The SemanticWeb - ISWC 2003. Volume LCNS 2870/2003. (2003) 419–437

24. Uszok, A., Bradshaw, J.M., Jeffers, R.: KAoS: A policy and domain services framework for grid computing and Semantic Web services. In: Trust Management: Second International Conference, iTrust 2004, Oxford, UK, March 29–April 1, 2004. Proceedings. Volume LNCS 2995/2004. (2004) 16–26

25. Bradshaw, J.M.: KAoS: An open agent architecture supporting reuse, interoperability, and extensibility. In: Proceedings of Tenth Knowledge Acquisition for Knowledge-Based Systems Workshop. (1995)

26. Kagal, L., Finin, T., Joshi, A.: A policy language for a pervasive computing environment. In: Proceedings of IEEE 4th International Workshop on Policies for Distributed Systems and Networks (POLICY 2003), IEEE (2003) 63–74

27. Firozabadi, B.S., Sergot, M.: Revocation in the privilege calculus. In: Workshop on Formal Aspects of Security and Trust (FAST2003) at FM2003. Volume IIT TR-10/2003., IIT-CNR, Italy (2003) 39–51 URL http://www.iit.cnr.it/FAST2003/fast-proc-final.pdf (TR-10/2003).

28. Rissanen, E.: Server based application level authorisation for Rotor. IEE Proceedings Software **150** (2003) 291–295
29. Grandison, T., Sloman, M.: A survey of trust in Internet applications. IEEE Communications Surveys and Tutorials **3** (2000) 2–16
30. Wagealla, W., Carbone, M., English, C., Terzis, S., Nixon, P.: A formal model on trust lifecycle management. In: Workshop on Formal Aspects of Security and Trust (FAST2003) at FM2003. Volume IIT TR-10/2003. IIT-CNR, Italy (2003) 184–195 URL http://www.iit.cnr.it/FAST2003/fast-proc-final.pdf (TR-10/2003).
31. Resnick, P., Zeckhauser, R., Friedman, E., Kuwabara, K.: Reputation systems. Communications of the ACM **43** (2000) 45–48
32. Gray, E., Seigneur, J.M., Chen, Y., Jensen, C.: Trust propagation in small worlds. In: Trust Management: First International Conference, iTrust 2003, Heraklion, Crete, Greece, May 28–30, 2003. Proceedings. Volume LNCS 2692/2003. (2003) 239–254
33. Jøsang, A., Hird, S., Faccer, E.: Simulating the effect of reputation systems on e-markets. In: Trust Management: First International Conference, iTrust 2003, Heraklion, Crete, Greece, May 28–30, 2003. Proceedings. Volume LNCS 2692/2003. (2003) 179–194
34. Barber, K.S., Fullam, K., Kim, J. In: Challenges for Trust, Fraud and Deception Research in Multi-agent Systems. Volume 2631/2003 of Lecture Notes in Artificial Intelligence. Springer-Verlag (2003) 8–14
35. Abdul-Rahman, A., Hailes, S.: Supporting trust in virtual communities. In: Hawaii International Conference on System Sciences 33,HICSS. (2000)
36. Essin, D.J.: Patterns of trust and policy. In: Proceedings of 1997 New Security Paradigms Workshop, ACM Press (1997)
37. Gambetta, D.: Can we trust trust? Trust: Making and Breaking Cooperative Relations (2000) 213–237 Electronic edition.
38. Demolombe, R.: Reasoning about trust: A formal logical framework. In: Trust Management: Second International Conference, iTrust 2004, Oxford, UK, March 29–April 1, 2004. Proceedings. Volume LNCS 2995/2004. (2004) 291–303
39. Jøsang, A.: The right type of trust for computer networks. In: Proceedings of the ACM New Security Paradigms Workshop, ACM (1996)
40. Egger, F.N.: "Trust me, I'm an online vendor": Towards a model of trust for e-Commerce system design. In: Conference on Human Factors in Computing Systems, CHI'00 extended abstracts on Human factors in computing systems, ACM Press (2000)
41. Cahill, V., et al.: Using trust for secure collaboration in uncertain environments. Pervasive Computing **2** (2003) 52–61
42. Kutvonen, L.: Automated management of inter-organisational applications. In: Proceedings of the Sixth International Enterprise Distributed Object Computing Conference (EDOC '02). (2002) 27–38
43. Tan, Y.H.: A trust matrix model for electronic commerce. In: Trust Management: First International Conference, iTrust 2003, Heraklion, Crete, Greece, May 28–30, 2003. Proceedings. Volume LNCS 2692/2003. (2003) 33–45
44. Obreiter, P.: A case for evidence-aware distributed reputation systems overcoming the limitations of plausibility considerations. In: Trust Management: Second International Conference, iTrust 2004, Oxford, UK, March 29–April 1, 2004. Proceedings. Volume LNCS 2995/2004. (2004) 33–47

45. Fernandes, A., Kotsovinos, E., string, S., Dragovic, B.: Pinocchio: Incentives for honest participation in distributed trust management. In: Trust Management: Second International Conference, iTrust 2004, Oxford, UK, March 29–April 1, 2004. Proceedings. Volume LNCS 2995/2004. (2004) 64–77

46. Kalcklösch, R., Herrmann, K.: Statistical trustability (conceptual work). In: Trust Management: First International Conference, iTrust 2003, Heraklion, Crete, Greece, May 28–30, 2003. Proceedings. Volume LNCS 2692/2003. (2003) 271–274

47. Kaler, C., Nadalin, A., et al.: Web Services Trust Language (WS-Trust). (2004) Version 1.1.

48. Karabulut, Y.: Implementation of an agent-oriented trust management infrastructure based on a hybrid PKI model. In: Trust Management: First International Conference, iTrust 2003, Heraklion, Crete, Greece, May 28–30, 2003. Proceedings. Volume LNCS 2692/2003. (2003) 318–331

49. Zamboni, D.: Using Internal Sensors for Computer Intrusion Detection. PhD thesis, Purdue University (2001)

50. Teng, H.S., Chen, K., Lu, S.C.Y.: Adaptive real-time anomaly detection using inductively generated sequential patterns. In: 1990 IEEE Symposium on Research in Security and Privacy, May 7–9, 1990, IEEE Computer Society (1990) 278–284

51. Forrest, S., Hofmeyr, S., Somayaji, A., Longstaff, T.: A sense of self for Unix processes. In: 1996 IEEE Symposium on Security and Privacy, May 6–8, 1996, Oakland, California. (1996)

52. Kumar, S., Spafford, E.H.: A Pattern Matching Model for Misuse Intrusion Detection. In: Proceedings of the 17th National Computer Security Conference, Baltimore, Maryland, October 1994. (1994) 11–21

53. Denning, D.: An intrusion-detection model. IEEE Transactions on Software Engineering **13** (1987) 222–232

54. Sekar, R., Gupta, A., Frullo, J., Shanbhag, T., Tiwari, A., Yang, H., Zhou, S.: Specification-based anomaly detection: a new approach for detecting network intrusions. In: Proceedings of the 9th ACM Conference on Computer and Communications Security, Washington, DC, USA. (2002) 265–274

55. Chinnici, R., Gudgin, M., Moreau, J.J., Schlimmer, J., Weerawarana, S.: Web Services Description Language (WSDL) version 2.0 part 1: Core language, W3C working draft 10 November 2003. Technical report, World Wide Web Consortium (2003)

56. Herrmann, P., Krumm, H.: Trust-adapted enforcement of security policies in distributed component-structured applications. In: Proceedings of the 6th IEEE Symposium on Computers and Communications. Hammamet, Tunisia, IEEE Computer Society Press (2001) 2–8

57. Liu, J., Issarny, V.: Enhanced reputation mechanism for mobile ad hoc networks. In: Trust Management: Second International Conference, iTrust 2004, Oxford, UK, March 29–April 1, 2004. Proceedings. Volume LNCS 2995/2004. (2004) 48–62

58. Grandison, T.W.A., Sloman, M.: Sultan - a language for trust specification and analysis. In: Eighth Workshop of the HP OpenView University Association, Berlin, June 24-27, 2001, HP OpenView University Association (2001) URL `http://www.hpovua.org/PUBLICATIONS/PROCEEDINGS/8_HPOVUAWS/Papers/Paper01.2-Grandison-Sultan.pdf`.

Can We Manage Trust?

Audun Jøsang[1], Claudia Keser[2], and Theo Dimitrakos[3]

[1] DSTC*,
UQ Qld 4072, Australia
ajosang@dstc.edu.au
[2] IBM T.J. Watson Research Center,
P.O. Box 218, Yorktown Heights, NY 10598, USA
ckeser@us.ibm.com
[3] British Telecom, 2A Rigel House, Adastral Park, Martlesham Heath,
Ipswich, Suffolk, IP5 3RE, UK
Theo.Dimitrakos@bt.com

Abstract. The term trust management suggests that trust can be managed, for example by creating trust, by assessing trustworthiness, or by determining optimal decisions based on specific levels of trust. The problem to date is that trust management in online environments is a diverse and ill defined discipline. In fact, the term trust management is being used with very different meanings in different contexts. This paper examines various approaches related to online activities where trust is relevant and where there is potential for trust management. In some cases, trust management has been defined with specific meanings. In other cases, there are well established disciplines with different names that could also be called trust management. Despite the confusion in terminology, trust management, as a general approach, represents a promising development for making online transactions more dependable, and in the long term for increasing the social capital of online communities.

1 Introduction

How can we manage trust? This question is increasingly catching the attention of stakeholders in the Internet and online services industry as concerns regarding privacy, online payment security or reliability of service providers and vendors seems to negatively affect the growth of the Internet.

Lack of trust is like sand in the social machinery, and represents a real obstacle for the uptake of online services, for example for entertainment, for building personal relationships, for conducting business and for interacting with governments. Lack of trust also makes us waste time and resources on protecting ourselves against possible harm, and thereby creates significant overhead in economic transactions.

Positive trust on the other hand is a like catalyst for human cooperation. It enables people to interact spontaneously and helps the economy to operate smoothly. A high

---

* The work reported in this paper has been funded in part by the Co-operative Research Centre for Enterprise Distributed Systems Technology (DSTC) through the Australian Federal Government's CRC Programme (Department of Education, Science, and Training).

P. Herrmann et al. (Eds.): iTrust 2005, LNCS 3477, pp. 93–107, 2005.

level of well placed general trust is therefore very desirable for the prosperity of a community.

However, the ability to distrust, when warranted, enables us to avoid harm when confronted with unreliable systems or dishonest people and organisations. Similarly, trust, when unwarranted, results in exposure to risk and hazards. Trust is like a compass for guiding us safely through a world of uncertainty, risk and moral hazards.

The important role that trust plays for online interaction has resulted in the emergence of trust management as a new research discipline in the intersection between sociology, commerce, law and computer science. It focuses on understanding and facilitating people's trust in each other, in the network infrastructure and in the environment within which online interactions are embedded. An important goal of trust management, is to stimulate people's and organisations' acceptance of online environments as safe places for interacting and doing business.

This paper takes a closer look at current approaches to trust management, with the goal of assessing their potential for stimulating online activities and increasing the quality of online communities. In many cases, trust management simply represents a specific approach to activities that are often already well established under different names. The unique aspect of trust management is that it specifically focuses on assessing and increasing the dependability of systems and players in the online environment, and thereby on stimulating the growth and prosperity of online communities.

2   Understanding Trust Management

Trust is a directional relationship between two parties that can be called *trustor* and *trustee*. One must assume the trustor to be a "thinking entity" in some form, whereas the trustee can be anything from a person or physical entity, to abstract notions such as software or a cryptographic key [20].

A trust relationship has a *scope*, meaning that it applies to a specific purpose or domain of action, such as "being authentic" in the case of a an agent's trust in a cryptographic key. Mutual trust is when both parties trust each other for the same purpose, but this is obviously only possible when both parties are thinking entities. Trust influences the trustor's attitudes and actions, but can also have effects on the trustee and other elements in the environment, for example, by stimulating reciprocal trust [12].

The literature uses the term trust with a variety of meanings [30]. A distinction between *context independent trust*, (which we nickname *"reliability trust"*), and *context dependent trust* (which we nickname *"decision trust"*), can often be recognised in the literature, although usually not explicitly expressed in those terms.

As the name suggest, reliability trust can be interpreted as the reliability of something or somebody independently of the context, and the definition by Gambetta (1988) [15] provides an example of how this can be formulated:

Definition 1 (Reliability Trust). *Trust is the subjective probability by which an individual, A, expects that another individual, B, performs a given action on which its welfare depends.*

In Def.1, trust is primarily defined as the trustor's estimate of the trustee's reliability (in the sense of probability), and includes the concept of *dependence* on the trustee. It can be noted that this definition does not take the context into account.

However, trust can be more complex than Gambetta's definition indicates. For example, Falcone & Castelfranchi (2001) [13] recognise that having high (reliability) trust in a person in general is not necessarily enough to decide to enter into a situation of dependence on that person. In [13] they write: *"For example it is possible that the value of the damage per se (in case of failure) is too high to choose a given decision branch, and this independently either from the probability of the failure (even if it is very low) or from the possible payoff (even if it is very high). In other words, that danger might seem to the agent an intolerable risk."*

For example, consider a person who distrusts an old rope for climbing from the third floor of a house during a fire exercise. Imagine now that the same person is trapped in a real fire in the same house, and that the only escape is to climb from the third floor window with the same old rope. In a real fire, most people would trust the rope. Although the *reliability trust* in the rope is the same in both situations, the *decision trust* changes as a function of the utility values associated with the possible courses of action.

The following definition captures the concept of trust seen within a context.

Definition 2 (Decision Trust). *Trust is the extent to which a given party is willing to depend on something or somebody in a given situation with a feeling of relative security, even though negative consequences are possible.*

In Def.2, trust is primarily defined as the willingness to rely on a given object, and specifically includes the notions of *dependence* on the trustee, and its *reliability*. In addition, Def.2 implicitly also covers contextual elements such as *utility* (of possible outcomes), *environmental factors* (law enforcement, contracts, security mechanisms etc.) and *risk attitude* (risk taking, risk averse, etc.).

Both reliability trust and decision trust are based on positive belief about the object that the trustor depends on for his welfare. People hold this type of beliefs about almost everything around them, and would in fact be unable to live without it, as commented by Luhmann (1979):

> *"But a complete absence of trust would prevent him even from getting up in the morning. He would be prey to a vague sense of dread, to paralysing fears. He would not even be capable of formulating distrust and making that a basis for precautionary measures, since this would presuppose trust in other directions. Anything and everything would be possible. Such abrupt confrontation with the complexity of the world at its most extreme is beyond human endurance."* [29].

Trying to define trust management around this broad view of trust would create an extremely general, and effectively useless notion, because it would have to deal with our beliefs about almost everything around us. Simplifying assumptions about the stability of the world and our existential situation are therefore necessary.

Fortunately, we are concerned only with the online environment, such as the Internet, and this allows us to reduce the scope of trust management to a level where it can be useful [16, 23]. Because trust is an asymmetric relationship between a trustor and a trustee, trust management can be seen from two sides. The ability to gain the trust of others is an important criterion for the success and survival of an entity, because it makes others willing to collaborate. Humans and animals therefore have a set of genetically determined and culturally acquired strategies for appearing trustworthy. The safest and most used strategy is probably to simply act in a responsible and trustworthy manner. However, it is not uncommon that people attempt to give a false impression of trustworthiness for various reasons, such as for personal gain. The ability to correctly assess the trustworthiness of a target is therefore an equally important criterion for the performance, success or survival of an entity. Humans and animals have a strong ability to assess trustworthiness of other entities, based on a multitude of cognitive and affective factors. Based on this duality of trust, we define trust management for online environments as follows:

Definition 3 (Trust Management). *The activity of creating systems and methods that allow relying parties to make assessments and decisions regarding the dependability of potential transactions involving risk, and that also allow players and system owners to increase and correctly represent the reliability of themselves and their systems.*

Computer networks are removing us from a familiar direct style of interacting. We may now collaborate online with people or organisations we have never met, perhaps never heard of before, and that we might never meet again. Many of the traditional strategies for representing and assessing trustworthiness in the physical world can no longer be used in online environments. It can therefore be difficult to assess whether the services and information provided by a remote party are reliable and correctly represented. Organisations that engage in online service provision also face the challenge of building online systems and online customer relationships which engender trust.

There is thus a need for methodologies that enable relying parties to determine the trustworthiness of remote parties through computer mediated communication and collaboration. At the same time, trustworthy entities need methodologies that enable them to be recognised as such. In a nutshell, developing and applying these methodologies can be called trust management.

3   Sociological and Economic Interpretations of Trust

Online activities are directly and indirectly influenced by the social and economic environment in which they are embedded. It is therefore useful to understand the role trust plays in socio-economic activities in general. The following two subsections will look at trust from sociological and economic perspectives respectively, in order to assess the meaning and value trust management in those domains.

3.1   Trust and Sociology

From a sociological viewpoint, Fukuyama (1995) [14] and Putnam (1995) [36] argue that trust creates *social capital*. Social capital has been defined by Coleman (1988) [10] as *"the ability of people to work together for common purposes in groups and organizations"*.

The social capital embedded in trusting relationships is present in communities of all sizes, ranging from families to corporations and nations. Fukuyama argues that social capital fuels a society's economic performance. Based on a historical analysis he demonstrates that low trust countries tend to show a lower overall economic performance than high trust countries.

According to Fukuyama, the ability of a society to develop strong civic institutions and efficient organisations depends to a large degree on its social capital:

> *"One of the most immediate consequences of a culture with a high propensity for spontaneous sociability is the ability to form large modern corporations. The emergence of large, professionally managed corporations was driven, of course, by a host of technological and market-size factors as producers and distributors sought optimum scale efficiencies. But the development of large organisations able to exploit such efficiencies was greatly facilitated by the prior existence of a culture inclined to spontaneous social organization. It would appear to be no accident that three high-trust societies, Japan, Germany and the United States, pioneered the development of large-scale, professionally managed enterprises. Low trust societies like France, Italy and noncommunist Chinese states including Taiwan and Hong Kong, by contrast, were relatively late in moving beyond large family businesses to modern corporations."* [14], p.338.

Knack and Keefer (1997) [27] provide empirical support to Fukuyama's thesis based on general measures of trust derived from the *World Values Survey* of the National Opinion Research Center. Knack and Keefer took the percentage of respondents from each country with a high trust attitude as a measure of how trusting that country's populace was. They found a strong correlation between a trusting attitude and economic growth.

While the sociological interpretation of trust as social capital described above was aimed at explaining patterns in traditional cultures and societies, it seems quite obvious that social capital also is important in online communities, by stimulating their creation and prosperity [19, 35]. Huang *et al.* (2003) [17] show that trust has a statistically significant influence on levels of Internet penetration across countries, thereby reflecting this effect.

3.2   Trust and Economic Exchange

Neoclassical economic theory is based on the paradigm of self-interested rational behaviour. This postulated egoism of the economic agents leaves no room for trustworthy behaviour or trust. As a result, game theoretic economic models often predict breakdown in collaboration and inefficient economic exchange [3].

In real life however, people behave less selfishly than postulated by economic theory. In an experimental economics laboratory setting, Keser (2000) observed that people do trust, although the level of trust may depend on many factors [24]. For example, as already pointed out, the level of trust varies across countries. It may also play a role whether and how well the interacting parties know each other and whether the interaction is going to be repeated or not. Obviously, people are less inclined to trust a stranger with whom they interact for the first and probably only time than they are inclined to trust someone whom they have known from many previous interactions.

Repeated interaction with the same partner allows for reciprocal behaviour: cooperative behaviour by the others may be rewarded by cooperation while failure to cooperate may be punished by avoidance of cooperation. Mutual cooperation can be easily established and maintained if all of the players start out by playing cooperatively, hereby signalling their willingness to cooperate, and then adhere to the reciprocity principle. Axelrod (1984)[2], Selten *et al.* (1997) [41] and Keser (2000) [24] demonstrate that this kind of strategy tends to be very successful over many encounters with other players.

The reciprocity principle can play a role in a single encounters with others. This is due to *indirect reciprocity*(i.e. *"I'm doing a good deed today, hoping that it will come back to me at an other occasion"*) . However, as shown for example by Keser and van Winden (2000) [26], the efficiency level observed in single encounters is significantly lower than in repeated encounters. This implies for the Internet, as it increases the likelihood of single anonymous encounters, that we can expect reciprocity to play a lesser role, than in more traditional types of interactions. Fortunately, technological mitigation strategies, e.g. by using trust and reputation systems, can be used to change this trend.

Williamson (1993) [44] discusses the role of trust in the economic organisation. The economic approach to economic organisation is principally calculative. The awkwardness of including the notion of trust in calculative models leads him to reject trust as a computational concept. Williamson argues that the notion of trust should be avoided when modelling economic interactions because it adds nothing new, and that well known notions such as reliability, utility and risk are adequate and sufficient for that purpose. Because these terms already have a clear meaning, they give us better model control than the term trust provides.

A question arises whether trust related to the environment can be dissected in the similar way that direct calculative trust in agents can. By trust in the environment, we mean trust in elements of the environment within which economic transactions are embedded. This influences economic exchange in an indirect way. According to Williamson (1993) [44], that is because the need for transaction specific safeguards varies systematically with the institutional environments within which transactions are embedded. Changes in the conditions of the environment are therefore factored in, by adjusting transaction specific controls in cost-effective ways. In effect, institutional environments that provide general purpose safeguards relieve the need for added transaction specific controls. Accordingly, transactions that are viable in contexts that provide strong safeguards may not be viable in contexts that are weak, because it is not cost effective for the parties to craft transaction specific governance in the latter circumstances.

4   Principles for Building Trust

Trust requires two parties, and can therefore be seen from two sides. The relying party is interested in assessing the trustworthiness of the trustee as correctly as possible. The trustee, on the other hand, is interested in painting the best possible picture of himself, which is often done through marketing. This section briefly explains the model for establishing trust in e-commerce, and situations where it can be ethical to deceive by deliberately creating false trust.

4.1   Building Trust in e-Commerce

The following Trust Transition Model is adapted from Cheskin (1999) [8] and extended to give a more complete description of realistic transition stages for trust. The various technologies for building trust used by e-commerce players [33] fit into this model.

A distinction can be made between *extrinsic trust factors* which roughly speaking are information elements that are communicated between parties, and *intrinsic trust factors* which roughly speaking are information elements emerging from personal experience. These take precedence at different stages in the trust transition model of Fig.1.

Cheskin found that an unaware (potential) person first has to be attracted to, or made aware of a service provider, in order for that person to be able to develop trust in that service provider. Let us assume that the principal is aware of several service providers with similar offerings regarding specified price and quality. Then in the initial phase, the extrinsic trust factors will determine the principal's choice of service provider. These extrinsic factors can be, for instance, that the service provider has a well-known brand with a good reputation, that the web site offers ease of navigation, that the service provider presents satisfactory privacy and complaint policies, and that the communication channel is encrypted.

The customer then gets first hand experience with the chosen service provider. A good experience will improve trust, whereas a bad experience normally will cause the trust level to drop below the purchase threshold, as indicated by the dotted arrow in Fig.1. There are techniques for regaining lost trust. The provider must be able to determine when something has gone wrong and give the dissatisfied customer adequate apology and compensation. Studies show that a dissatisfied customer who receives compensation can end up having stronger trust that a satisfied customer. The obvious explanation is that receiving apology and compensation is evidence of good fulfilment, which in the end becomes a very strong positive intrinsic trust factor.

Over time, assuming that the extrinsic aspects of the service provider have not dramatically changed, the customer's mental model of the service provider, and its perceived trustworthiness, tends to become implicit, becoming an internalised product of

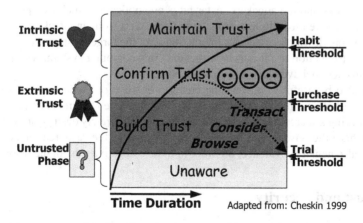

Fig. 1. e-Commerce trust transition model

interacting with that service provider. The personal direct experience represents intrinsic trust factors that overtime will outweigh the extrinsic factors.

Since deep and stable trust is based on experience over time, establishing initial trust can be a major challenge to newcomers in e-commerce, particularly those who do not have well established off-line brands. Without initial trust, merchants can not build a good transaction history - and without a good transaction history, consumers may not build trust in these merchants. Pichler [34] describes how, to some extent, merchants can 'buy' trust though advertising: this evidence of financial investment implies to consumers that a firm will not engage in quick gain deception.

Economic theory indicates that there is a balance between the cost of establishing a brand with a good reputation, and the financial benefit of having a it, leading to an equilibrium [28, 40]. Variations in the quality of services or goods can be a result of deliberate management decisions or uncontrolled factors, and whatever the cause, the changes in quality will necessarily lead to variations in the perceived trustworthiness. Although a theoretic equilibrium exists, there will always be fluctuations, and it is possible to characterise the conditions under which oscillations can be avoided [42] or converge towards the equilibrium [18].

4.2   Deception by Creating False Trust

Attempts to create false trust is normally seen as unethical. However, there are situations where most people would agree that it is morally acceptable to create false trust, and self defence is one such case.

In case a system is being attacked, counter attack against the perpetrators' system is generally illegal. Since attackers normally trust systems to provide genuine resources and services, an effective and legal defence strategy may be to let the attacked systems deceive [39]. This would waste the attacker's time and resources, and give the system owners the opportunity to organise an appropriate defence, and to collect, if needed, forensic information.

Honeypots, *tar pits* and *poisoning* are examples of computer deception. A honeypot is a system with no purpose, except to encourage attacks, so that data can be collected about the attacks and the attackers. A tar pit is an application, such as a protocol layer entity, that will intentionally respond slowly to requests from an attacker, with the purpose of slowing down the attacker's interaction with the target system. Poisoning is the deliberate introduction of false or incorrect data in a computer system, with purpose of making attackers believe that it is correct data.

It can also be useful to prevent the creation of trust, or even to create distrust, in order to divert attention away from an attractive but scarce resource. Agents who want to avoid sharing a scarce resource with others could deliberately destroy or hide positive evidence that otherwise would increase peoples trust in the resource, or deliberately fabricate false negative evidence, on order to induce negative trust in the resource.

5   Trust and Security

In a general sense, the purpose of security mechanisms is to provide protection against malicious parties. Traditional security mechanisms will typically protect resources from malicious users by restricting access to only authorised users. However, in many situations we have to protect ourselves from those who offer resources, so that the problem in fact is reversed. In this sense there is a whole range of security challenges that are not met by traditional approaches. Information providers can for example act deceitfully by providing false or misleading information, and traditional security mechanisms are unable to protect against this type of threat. Trust and reputation systems on the other hand can provide protection against such threats. The difference between these two approaches to security was first described by Rasmussen & Jansson (1996) [37], who used the term *hard security* for traditional mechanisms like authentication and access control, and *soft security* for what they called social control mechanisms in general, of which trust and reputation systems are examples. This section discusses trust related traditional security activities, whereas soft security and reputation systems will be described in more detail in Sec.6

5.1   Trust and Computer Systems Security

Security mechanisms protect systems and data from being adversely affected by malicious and non-authorised parties. The effect of this is that those systems and data can be considered more reliable, and thus more trustworthy. The concepts of Trusted Systems and Trusted Computing Base have been used in the IT security jargon (see e.g. Abrams 1995 [1]), but the concept of security assurance level is more standardised as a measure of security[1]. The assurance level can be interpreted as a system's strength to resist malicious attacks, and some organisations require systems with high assurance levels for high risk or highly sensitive applications. In an informal sense, the assurance level expresses a level of public (reliability) trust in a given system. However, it is evident that additional information, such as warnings about newly discovered security flaws, can carry more weight than the assurance level, when people actually form their own subjective trust in the system.

In case of multiple parties with conflicting interests, what is trusted by one party can be distrusted by another. For example, in the discussion around trusted computing (TC), there are two views on increasing security assurance regarding Digital Rights Management (DRM) by increasing monitoring of user activities. The service provider's perspective can be expressed as follows:

> *"A mildly charitable view of TC was put forward by the late Roger Needham who directed Microsoft's research in Europe: there are some applications in which you want to constrain the user's actions. For example, you want to stop people fiddling with the odometer on a car before they sell it. Similarly, if you want to do DRM on a PC then you need to treat the user as the enemy."*[2]

Although this would increase the digital content providers' trust, it would negatively affect the users' trust in those systems because it would threaten their privacy. This is an

---

[1] See e.g. the UK CESG at http://www.cesg.gov.uk/ or the Common Criteria Project at http://www.commoncriteriaportal.org/

[2] Quoted from Ross Anderson's "Trusted Computing FAQ" where he cites Roger Needham [31]. http://www.cl.cam.ac.uk/ rja14/tcpa-faq.html.

example of how measures to increase security assurance could possibly back-fire, thus making trust management controversial.

5.2   Trust in User Authentication and Access Control

Owners of systems and resources usually want to control who can access them. This is traditionally based on having a process for initial authorisation of identified parties, combined with operational mechanisms for authentication, and for controlling what resources those authenticated parties can access. There is thus a separation between authorisation, authentication and access control.

The first common use of the term trust management was closely linked to the combination of authorisation, authentication and access control in distributed systems, as expressed by by Blaze *et al.* (1996) [5]. The main idea behind their approach was that a system does not need to know the identities of those who are accessing its resources, only that they are trusted to do so. This type of trust management is thus about verifying access credentials without necessarily authenticating entities. Blaze *et al.* defined trust management as:

> "*a unified approach to specifying and interpreting security policies, credentials, relationships which allow direct authorisation of security-critical actions.*" [5]

The traditional purpose of X.509 and PGP public-key certificates is to link identities to public keys, not to specify access privileges. This contrasts with the approach by Blaze *et al.* which consists of assigning access privileges directly to a public key in the form of an access privilege certificate. Anyone possessing the corresponding private key then automatically has the access privileges assigned to the public key.

This model was implemented by AT&T Research Laboratories in PolicyMaker [6], and later enhanced in KeyNote [4]. REFEREE [9] is a system based on PolicyMaker aimed at controlling access to Web resources.

5.3   The Role of Trust in Security Protocols

From a trust perspective, security protocols can be described as mechanisms for propagating trust from where it initially exists to where it is needed [43]. Any security protocol relies on a set of initial assumptions about the protocol building blocks, participants and execution environment. More specifically, these assumptions can be divided into external and internal assumptions. The *external assumptions* are not specifically included when specifying and analysing a protocol, but are nevertheless needed in order for the implementation and instantiation of the protocol to be secure. The *Internal assumptions* are explicitly expressed in the formalism of the security protocol, and form the basis for deriving the conclusion of the protocol. This separation between internal and external assumptions can clearly be discerned in the description of BAN logic (1990) [7] for security protocol verification.

> "*Since we operate at an abstract level, we do not consider errors introduced by concrete implementations of a protocol, such as deadlock, or even inappropriate use of cryptosystems. Furthermore, while we allow for the possibility of hostile intruders, there is no attempt to deal with the authentication of*

an untrustworthy principal, nor detect weaknesses of encryption schemes or unauthorised release of secrets. Rather, our study concentrates on the beliefs of trustworthy parties involved in the protocols and in the evolution of these beliefs as a consequence of communication." [7]

Formalisms for security protocol verification can prove that the intended conclusion of the protocol can be derived from the initial internal assumptions and a correct instantiation of the protocol. However, because the internal assumptions only represent a subset of all the necessary assumption, these formalisms have limited scope for verifying the overall security of protocols. Nevertheless, security protocols are used in a broad range of security applications, and represent an efficient way of communicating and deriving security critical beliefs through otherwise insecure networks.

6   Systems for Deriving Trust and Reputation

There are two fundamental differences between traditional and online environments regarding how trust and reputation are, and can be used. Firstly, the traditional cues of trust and reputation that we are used to observe and depend on in the physical world are missing in online environments, so that electronic substitutes are needed. Secondly, communicating and sharing information related to trust and reputation is relatively difficult and normally constrained to local communities in the physical world, whereas IT systems combined with the Internet can be leveraged to design extremely efficient systems for exchanging and collecting such information on a global scale. In order to build good trust and reputation systems we therefore need to:

- Find adequate online substitutes for the traditional cues to trust and reputation that we are used to in the physical world, and identify new information elements (specific to a particular online application) which are suitable for deriving measures of trust and reputation.
- Take advantage of IT and the Internet to create efficient systems for collecting that information, and to derive measures of trust and reputation in order to support decision making and to improve the quality of online markets.

Reputation systems[38, 21] create word-of-mouth networks in online communities. Parties can rate each other, for example after the completion of a transaction. A reputation score can be derived from aggregated ratings about a given party, to assist other parties in deciding whether to transact with that party in the future. A natural side effect is the incentive this provides for good behaviour among participants. Examples of Web sites that use reputation systems are eBay, Epinions, Amazon, BizRate and Google.

For environments where trust is needed for any economic transaction to take place, it has been shown [25] that reputation systems can considerably increase the levels of both trust and good behaviour. This indicates that the introduction of reputation systems facilitates growth of online markets such as eBay. Reputation influences interactions between agents in two important ways. Firstly, it positively affects the trustor's reliability trust in the trustee. Secondly, it disciplines the trustee, because he knows that bad behaviour will be seen, and thereby sanctioned by the community. Trust and reputation are closely linked. Take e.g. the Concise Oxford dictionary's definition of reputation:

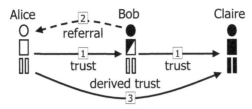

Fig. 2. Trust transitivity principle

Definition 4 (Reputation). *Reputation is what is generally said or believed about a person's or thing's character or standing.*

The difference between trust and reputation can be illustrated by the following perfectly normal and plausible statements:

1. *"I trust you because of your good reputation."*
2. *"I trust you despite your bad reputation."*

Assuming that the two statements relate to the same transaction, statement 1 reflects that the relying party bases his trust on the trustee's reputation. Statement 2 reflects that the relying party has some private knowledge about the trustee, e.g. through direct experience or intimate relationship, and that these factors overrule any positive or negative reputation that a person might have. Whenever trust is based on multiple factors, some will carry more weight than others. Personal experience (intrinsic factors) typically carries more weight than second hand trust referrals or reputation (extrinsic factors), but in the absence of personal experience, trust often has to be based on referrals from others.

While the basic principles of reputation systems are relatively easy to describe, what constitutes a *trust system* is less precise. Trust systems can include methods for analysing private information in addition to public ratings, and usually have a method for analysing transitive trust [21]. The idea behind trust transitivity is that when, for example, Alice trusts Bob, and Bob trusts Claire, then Alice can derive a measure of trust in Claire, as illustrated in Fig.2 below.

The type of trust considered in transitivity models is obviously reliability trust, not decision trust. In addition there are semantic constraints for the transitive trust derivation to be valid, e.g. that all involved trust relationships have the same purpose [22]. PKIs[3], PGP[4] [45], and even Google's PageRank algorithm [32], are all based on trust transitivity, and can be called trust systems.

7   Discussion and Conclusion

All is not as it should be in the online world. People have well based concerns about the reliability of players, systems and infrastructure, and this often represents a barrier for leveraging computer systems and the Internet to make communication and organisation

---

[3] Public-Key Infrastructure.

[4] Pretty Good Privacy.

more efficient. The emergence of trust management as a specific activity is aimed at mitigating this problem.

Trust is a relationship between two parties, and the goal of trust management can therefore be seen from two sides: Firstly, it aims at enabling players to efficiently assess the reliability of systems and remote parties. Secondly, it aims at allowing parties and system owners to increase the security and reliability of their systems, and correctly represent and communicate this to other players.

There can are of course be many different approaches to this. Some approaches are already well established under separate names, whereas other approaches have taken shape together with the emergence of trust management as a discipline in its own right. In order to avoid misunderstanding it is always good to be as specific as possible when using the term trust management, by providing additional information about its meaning in a given context. For example, if someone in the access control research community uses the term trust management without any further explanation when talking to a web marketing specialist, it is very likely to be misunderstood. This sort of confusion can easily be avoided by being more specific.

A current research project that combines multiple approaches to trust management is the European TrustCoM[5] initiative [11] that focuses on developing technologies that will enable multiple companies to integrate services, processes and resources, for example to provide integrated services through ad hoc virtual organisations, while at the same time allowing them to protect their respective assets. This builds on a framework for establishing trust between parties based on electronic contracts, policies and reputation systems, as well as a federated security architecture for authentication and access control. This can be seen as a very pragmatic approach to trust management.

A high level of general trust in a community is an important factor for the prosperity and economic fitness of that community. This applies to both traditional geographically bound communities as well as to online and virtual communities. Unfortunately, stakeholders in the development of online services and systems find it hard to ensure that systems are secure and that participants always behave in good faith. Finding ways to make the online environment more secure and dependable, and to increase the transparency regarding the participants' honesty and reliability, is crucial for attracting people and organisations to create and use online applications.

By leveraging the tremendous efficiency with which information can be disseminated and automatically analysed through computer systems and networks, trust management certainly has the potential of making the online environment an even safer place to interact and transact than the traditional environment currently is. Increased social capital in online communities will be the result of a successful outcome of this endeavour.

References

1. M.D. Abrams. Trusted System Concepts. *Computers and Security*, 14(1):45–56, 1995.
2. Robert Axelrod. *The Evolution of Cooperation*. Basic Books, New York, 1984.

---

[5] http://www.eu-trustcom.com/

3. J. Berg, J. Dickhaut, and K. McCabe. Trust, Reciprocity, and Social History. *Games and Economic Behavior*, 10:122–142, 1996.
4. Matt Blaze, Joan Feigenbaum, and Angelos D. Keromytis. KeyNote: Trust Management for Public-Key Iinfrastructures. In *Proceedings of the 1998 Secure Protocols International Workshop*, Cambridge, England, 1998.
5. Matt Blaze, Joan Feigenbaum, and Jack Lacy. Decentralized trust management. In *Proceedings of the 1996 IEEE Conference on Security and Privacy*, Oakland, CA, 1996.
6. Matt Blaze, Joan Feigenbaum, and Martin Strauss. Compliance Checking in the PolicyMaker Trust Management System. In *Proceedings of Financial Crypto*, 1998.
7. Michael Burrows, Marín Abadi, and Roger Needham. A logic of authentication. *ACM Transactions on Computer Systems*, 8(1):18–36, 1990.
8. Cheskin Research & Studio Archetype/Sapient. *eCommerce Trust Study*. Sapient, http://www.sapient.com/cheskin/, January 1999.
9. Y.-H. Chu, J. Feigenbaum, B. LaMacchia, P. Resnick, and M. Strauss. REFEREE: Trust Management for Web Applications. *World Wide Web Journal*, 2:127–139, 1997.
10. J. S. Coleman. Social Capital in the Creation of Human Capital. *American Journal of Sociology*, 94:95–120, 1988.
11. T. Dimitrakos. Towards a Trust and Contract Management Framework for Dynamic Virtual Organisations. In *Proceedings of eAdoptions and the Knowledge Economy: eChallenges 2004*. IOS Press, November 2004.
12. R. Falcone and C. Castelfranchi. How trust enhances and spread trust. In *Proceedings of the 4th Int. Workshop on Deception Fraud and Trust in Agent Societies, in the 5th International Conference on Autonomous Agents (AGENTS'01)*, May 2001.
13. R. Falcone and C. Castelfranchi. *Social Trust: A Cognitive Approach*, pages 55–99. Kluwer, 2001.
14. Francis Fukuyama. *Trust: The Social Virtues and the Creation of Prosperity*. The Free Press, New York, 1995.
15. D. Gambetta. Can We Trust Trust? In D. Gambetta, editor, *Trust: Making and Breaking Cooperative Relations*, pages 213–238. Basil Blackwell. Oxford, 1990.
16. T. Grandison and M. Sloman. Specifying and Analysing Trust for Internet Applications. In *Proceedings of the 2nd IFIP Conference on e-Commerce, e-Business and e-Government (I3E2002)*, Lisbon, 2002.
17. H. Huang, C. Keser, J. Leland, and J. Shachat. Trust, the Internet, and the Digital Divide. *IBM Systems Journal*, 42(3):507–518, 2003.
18. B.A. Huberman and F. Wu. The Dynamics of Reputations. *Computing in Economics and Finance*, 18, 2003.
19. Sirkka L. Järvenpää and D. E. Leidner. Communication and trust in global virtual teams. *Organization Science*, 10(6):791–815, 1999.
20. A. Jøsang. The right type of trust for distributed systems. In C. Meadows, editor, *Proc. of the 1996 New Security Paradigms Workshop*. ACM, 1996.
21. A. Jøsang, R. Ismail, and C. Boyd. A Survey of Trust and Reputation Systems for Online Service Provision (to appear). *Decision Support Systems*, 2005.
22. A. Jøsang and S. Pope. Semantic Constraints for Trust Tansitivity. In *Proceedings of the Asia-Pacific Conference of Conceptual Modelling (APCCM)*, Newcastle, Australia, February 2005.
23. A. Jøsang and N. Tran. Trust Management for e-Commerce. In *VirtualBanking2000*. Virtual Conference hosted at http://virtualbanking2000.com, 2000.
24. C. Keser. Strategically Planned Behavior in Public Goods Experiments. Technical report, CIRANO Scientific Series 2000s-35, Montreal, Canada, 2000.
25. C. Keser. Experimental Games for the Design of Reputation Management Systems. *IBM Systems Journal*, 42(3):498–506, 2003.

26. C. Keser and F. van Winden. Conditional Cooperation and Voluntary Contributions to Public Goods. *Scandinavian Journal of Economics*, 102:23–39, 2000.

27. S. Knack and P. Keefer. Does Social Capital Have an Economic Payoff? A Cross-Country Investigation. *Quarterly Journal of Economics*, 112(4):1251–1288, 1997.

28. D. Kreps and R. Wilson. Reputation and Imperfect Information. *Journal of Economic Theory*, 27(2):253–279, 1982.

29. N. Luhmann. *Trust and Power*. Wiley, Chichester, 1979.

30. D.H. McKnight and N.L. Chervany. The Meanings of Trust. Technical Report MISRC Working Paper Series 96-04, University of Minnesota, Management Information Systems Reseach Center, URL: http://misrc.umn.edu/wpaper/, 1996.

31. R.M Needham. *Security and open source*. Presentation at the Open Source Software Workshop, 2002. http://nats-www.informatik.uni-hamburg.de/view/OSS2004/PaperCollection.

32. L. Page, S. Brin, R. Motwani, and T. Winograd. The PageRank Citation Ranking: Bringing Order to the Web. Technical report, Stanford Digital Library Technologies Project, 1998.

33. M.A. Patton and A. Jøsang. Technologies for Trust in Electronic Commerce. *Electronic Commerce Research*, 4(1-2):9–21, 2004.

34. R Pichler. *Trust and Reliance - Enforcement and Compliance: Enhancing Consumer Confidence in the Electronic Marketplace*. Stanford Law School, www.oecd.org/dsti/sti/it/secur/act/online_trust/Consumer_Confidence.pdf, May 2000.

35. A. Powell, G. Piccoli, and B. Ives. Virtual teams: a review of current literature and directions for future research. *SIGMIS Database*, 35(1):6–36, 2004.

36. R.D. Putnam. Tuning in, tuning out: The strange disappearance of social capital in America. *Political Science and Politics*, 28(4):664–683, 1995.

37. L. Rasmusson and S. Janssen. Simulated Social Control for Secure Internet Commerce. In Catherine Meadows, editor, *Proceedings of the 1996 New Security Paradigms Workshop*. ACM, 1996.

38. P. Resnick, R. Zeckhauser, R. Friedman, and K. Kuwabara. Reputation Systems. *Communications of the ACM*, 43(12):45–48, December 2000.

39. N.C. Rowe. Designing Good Deceptions in Defense of Information Systems. In *Proceedings of the Annual Computer Security Applications Conferencen (ACSAC)*, Tucson, December 2004.

40. A. Schiff and J. Kennes. The Value of Reputation Systems. In *Proceedings of the First Summer Workshop in Industrial Organization (SWIO)*, Auckland NZ, March 2003.

41. R. Selten, M. Mitzkewitz, and G. Uhlich. Duopoly Strategies Programmed by Experienced Player. *Econometrica*, 65:517–555, 1997.

42. C. Shapiro. Consumer Information, Product Quality, and Seller Reputation. *The Bell Journal of Economics*, 13(1):20–35, 1982.

43. G.J. Simmons and C. Meadows. The role of trust in information integrity protocols. *Journal of Computer Security*, 3(1):71–84, 1995.

44. O.E. Williamson. Calculativeness, Trust and Economic Organization. *Journal of Law and Economics*, 36:453–486, April 1993.

45. P.R. Zimmermann. *The Official PGP User's Guide*. MIT Press, 1995.

Operational Models for Reputation Servers

D.W. Chadwick

Computing Laboratory, University of Kent, Canterbury, UK, CT2 7NF
d.w.chadwick@kent.ac.uk

Abstract. This paper devises a classification system for reputation systems based on two axes, namely: who performs the evaluation of a subject's reputation, and how the information is collected by the reputation system. This leads to 4 possible operational models for reputation systems, termed the Voting Model, the Opinion Poll Model, the MP Model and the Research Model, each of which is then analyzed. Finally, the paper postulates the inherent trustworthiness of each operational model, and concludes with a hypothesis of how these systems might evolve in the future.

1 Introduction

There is considerable interest in online reputation systems [1]. Many commercial web sites are employing different sorts of online reputation systems today. E-Bay [2] is probably the most well known example. QXL.com has a similar system. Slashdot.org also has its own rating system for ranking postings, based on the reputation (actually called *karma* by Slashdot) of the submitter. Prior to the evolution of online reputation systems the financial and banking world has had its own off-line reputation systems for very many years, in the shape of credit rating bureaus. For example, Dun and Bradstreet, now a global company, originally started in New York on 20th July 1841.

Users use reputation systems to determine the trustworthiness of the people, organizations or services they want to do business with. They determine their trustworthiness in part from the information obtained from these reputation systems, and in part from their own knowledge, feelings, intuitions etc. For unknown entities, reputation systems will contribute most, whilst for well known entities they will contribute much less. But this begs the question "how trustworthy is the reputation system itself?" In order to determine the trustworthiness of a potential transaction partner one first needs to be able to trust the reputation system that provides you with information about the potential partner. One clearly can have little trust in the reputations dispensed by a fraudulent, biased or badly managed reputation system. But if one were able to gain similar reputation scores for a potential partner from two or more unrelated reputation systems, then one could have more confidence or trust in the reputation of that potential partner and in each of the dispensing reputation systems. Further, if one knew the methods, or operational models, by which each of the reputation systems operated, then this might help a user to determine how reliable or trustworthy are the reputations dispensed by it.

The aim of this paper therefore is to classify the different types of reputation system that could exist, based on their operational models, and to postulate the

P. Herrmann et al. (Eds.): iTrust 2005, LNCS 3477, pp. 108 – 115, 2005.

inherent trustworthiness of these different types of reputation system, based solely on their operational models. The hypothesis is that some operational models are inherently more trustworthy than others, and therefore users can reasonably expect that the reputation information provided by them will be more reliable and trustworthy than that provided by other types of reputation system.

The rest of this paper is structured as follows. Section 2 proposes a classification scheme for the types of reputation system based on their operational models, and determines that there are 4 different types of reputation system. Sections 3 to 6 then analyze the properties of each of these models in more detail and postulates how they might be implemented. Section 7 discusses the inherent trustworthiness of each of these operational models and provides a ranking of them. Section 8 concludes and hypothesizes how these systems might evolve in the future.

2 Operational Models

This paper proposes two main axes for categorizing reputation servers. The primary axis distinguishes between who performs the evaluation of a subject's reputation based on the available information. The choice is between the actors who participate in transactions with the subject, or the reputation system itself. In the former case, each actor uses its own algorithm for computing the reputation of a subject. The reputation system then simply collates these values. In the latter case the reputation system takes raw data from the actors and uses its own algorithms to compute the reputation of the subjects.

The second axis distinguishes how the information is collected by the reputation service prior to collation and publishing the reputations. The reputation service can either gather and collate the data itself (the data pull mode) or the actors can spontaneously send data to the reputation service (the data push mode).

When these two axes are combined together we get the 2x2 matrix shown in Figure 1 below. Each of the four combinations has been given a name for ease of reference and this name is a metaphor to depict the primary characteristics of the operational model.

	Data Push	Data Pull
Actor evaluation	Voting model	Opinion Poll model
Reputation Server evaluation	MP[1] model	Research model

Fig. 1. The four operational models

Each of the four operational models is now discussed in more detail below.

---

[1] MP stands for Member of Parliament, an elected representative to the UK legislative body called the House of Commons.

3 The Opinion Poll Model

In this operational model, the reputation server actively collects reputation data from the actors. Each actor performs its own evaluation about the reputation of a subject, using its own algorithm, and based on its experiences of performing transactions with the subject. In real life humans do this sort of evaluation all the time about the shops they frequent, the people they meet, the political parties they vote for etc. The role of the reputation system is to find an appropriate sample of the actors and to gather and summarize the data, preferably using a simple publicly available algorithm. In the physical world opinion poll companies regularly collect this sort of information and publish the results. The most difficult operational aspect of this model for electronic reputation systems to implement is to discover who and where the actors are and how to contact them. In the physical world, when the actors are members of the public, opinion poll companies use electoral roles or telephone directories to determine who the actors are and where they live, or they simply stop a random sample of people in the street as they are passing by. If an opinion poll company is contracted by an organization to evaluate its reputation from the perspective of its customers, then the organization might provide the reputation service with its customer lists from which to obtain a sample of actors.

Engineering the latter in the virtual world is not difficult, because a directory of actors is available, but engineering the former is much more difficult since it involves finding out the opinions of the public. The difficulty lies in the fact that the equivalent of electoral rolls or public directory services do not exist on the Internet. The nearest thing we currently have to the electoral role is the Domain Name System (DNS) [3]. This lists all the publicly accessible services on the Internet, along with their IP addresses. The DNS is core to the functioning of the Internet. However, the DNS does not as yet hold reputation information or addresses of where it might be found by opinion poll servers. Two possibilities exist for this. One would be to define a new type of DNS resource record (RR), say the reputation (RP) record, that holds the name and reputation of the Internet service being reputed. The metric of the reputation e.g. a Likert scale, would need to be standardized. Actors would then write this DNS record into their DNS entry for each service they were assigning a reputation to. Opinion poll servers could then scan the DNS to sample these records and derive collective reputations for entities. The second method would be to define a new protocol for the gathering of reputation information from actors, say the Reputation Gathering Protocol (RGP), and then to register this protocol with the Internet Assigned Numbers Authority[2] (IANA) and get a well known port allocated to it. Once this is achieved, actors can simply register their RGP servers in the DNS, using the existing WKS RR [3], and this will allow opinion poll servers to contact them.

However both schemes suffer from a number of disadvantages. Firstly the granularity is wrong, since the DNS can only publish (reputation) information about Internet services, and not about individuals or organizations (unless they have their own Internet sites). Secondly the DNS is already heavily over-utilized and performs rather poorly. The IETF tries to keep tight control over it, and therefore is highly

---

[2] See www.iana.org

unlikely to sanction the definition of this new RR type or protocol, especially if it would cause significant performance penalties on existing DNS users. Finally, and most significantly, the DNS does not provide a scanning or search capability. DNS clients have to already know the DNS name of the entity they want to look up, before contacting the DNS to get its IP address. In the general case opinion poll servers won't know the DNS names of the actors they want to poll. Thus we need a search and discovery service that will allow opinion poll servers to search for all actors, or a subset of actors that meet pre-defined search criteria such as: size of business, no of transactions undertaken, currency of the data etc. before contacting the DNS. This implies that we need to either define schema for existing directories such as UDDI [10] or LDAP [11] (or both), or uses Web search engines such as Google, to enable this searching to take place. Web search engines already trawl the Internet for information, and so build their own internal directories of web pages available on the Internet. How complete these directories are depends upon the trawling methods used. The DNS on the other hand is guaranteed to be complete, since it holds the names of all publicly available services.

As can be seen from the above discussion, there are still a significant number of problems to be solved before opinion poll reputations systems become widely available.

4 The Voting Model

In this model, the actors evaluate the reputation of subjects, using their own algorithms and information, and then forward their decisions to a central Voting server. The role of the voting server is simply to collect messages that arrive, collate and summarize them (again using a simple publicly available algorithm), and then publish the results when asked. E-bay is one example of this type of reputation server in use today. Various shopping mall web sites also allow customers to register their votes about how well the stores in the mall are performing their various aspects of service provision, for example, timeliness of goods delivery, and quality of after sales service etc. This operational model is much easier to implement than the opinion poll model, since implicit in the voting model is a voter registration list, meaning that the system already has a full list of all actors that are allowed to vote. Thus a voting server does not need to have access to an external actor discovery or directory service, unlike the opinion poll model. Voting servers either keep their own lists of authorized actors, as in e-Bay, or have some way of authenticating a voter or a vote, as in e-voting systems [9]. They allow only these actors to lodge their votes with them. Very often these lists will be commercially sensitive, as in customer lists, and, if they contain personal data, will be protected by data protection legislation. Thus electronic voting type reputation systems are highly unlikely to make their lists public, or available to opinion poll servers. Therefore if a reputation subject is known to two or more voting type reputation systems, their reputation in each is likely to be calculated by different sets of actors.

5 The Research Model

In this model, the reputation server actively searches for information about subjects, and then evaluates it and publishes the results. The operations of the reputation server are complex and difficult to engineer. Not only does the reputation server have the problem of finding the actors, as in the Opinion Poll model, but also it has to determine what raw information to solicit from them and how to process and evaluate this in order to compute the reputations of the subjects. Such processes and algorithms are likely to be proprietary and commercially valuable.

Several examples of this model exist in the physical world, for example both Standard and Poor[3] and Dun and Bradstreet[4] provide credit ratings, and they are now global companies. Clearly this operational model can lead to a successful business model – if the reputation results are valuable they can be sold at a profit. If a client is considering whether to enter into a business venture with a subject or not, then knowing the subject's reputation can be worth a large amount of money to a client. But precisely because the server's operations are complex, the algorithms used to process the raw information are proprietary, and the results commercially valuable, then it is highly likely that the algorithms and processes used to calculate the reputations will be commercially sensitive and not open to public scrutiny. The implications of this on the trustworthiness of these types of reputation system are discussed below.

6 The MP Model

In this context, MP stands for Member of Parliament, a person elected to the UK House of Commons to represent a constituency. MPs should represent their constituency, but often they do not. When it comes to voting on issues in the House of Commons, they either usually follow the party line, or if a free vote is allowed, on such issues as capital punishment or hunting with dogs, they follow their own conscience. So even if constituents have sent them lots of letters imploring them to vote one way, they may quite freely decide to vote the opposite way.

A reputation server following the MP model, will be sent (pushed) raw data about subjects by the actors. Some of this may be data about transactions an actor has undertaken with a subject, others might be subject reputations evaluated by the actors themselves. The MP server will typically not have an actor list, and therefore not be able to tell which actors are genuine and which are not. Regardless of this, the MP server determines which data to use, which data to discard, and which other private information to use as well. Then using its own, usually unpublished, proprietary algorithms, it computes the reputation of subjects and publishes the results. The reputation results will primarily be based on the subjectivity of the MP server while the point of view of the actors submitting information may be ignored. Clearly this operational model is the most suspect in terms of reliability and trustworthiness.

---

[3] See http://www.standardandpoors.com/
[4] See http://www.dnb.com/us/

7   Trustworthiness of Reputation Servers

If one is relying on the reputations provided by a reputation server, one needs to ask how reliable or trustworthy are the reputations that the reputation server is providing. We now appraise the inherent trustworthiness or reliability of each of the four operational models.

The Opinion Poll model is inherently the most trustworthy and reliable, since the individual reputation scores have been calculated by very many actors. The opinion poll server merely needs to collate and sum the scores into an overall reputation for each subject, using a simple publicly available algorithm. Therefore it is very difficult for the reputation server to skew the results, unless it is configured to discard particular inputs, or bias the way actor selection is performed. Furthermore, it is difficult for an individual actor to try to skew the reputation of a subject, since they have no control over whether they are polled by the reputation server or not, and even if they are, they should be in a minority of one (a correctly operated opinion poll server should never poll the same actor twice, and each actor should only be registered once with the system). This indicates that the actor lists should have strong integrity protection against unauthorized modifications, and should have strong registration methods to prevent an actor registering multiple times. Of course, if many actors conspire together to inflate or deflate a subject's reputation, this is very difficult to protect against. Each actor's reputation scores are, in principle, available to be collected by any opinion poll server via the publicly available actor lists, therefore the resulting computed reputations are more easily validated and the results more easily repeatable by any opinion poll server (or any actor or subject for that matter). Therefore the published reputation results of any single opinion poll reputation server are not contingent on the reputations of the reputation server since their outputs can be independently validated. Any reputation server that was noted for publishing different results from other reputation servers would soon be ostracized and its results ignored.

The Voting model should provide the next most trustworthy set of results. The individual reputation scores have similarly been determined by many actors as in the Opinion Poll model, and therefore it should be difficult to skew the results, though it is not impossible. Because the list of actors is not public, it is not possible to independently validate the composite reputation results, nor is it possible for another reputation service to repeat the results. A dishonest reputation server could skew the results by discarding votes it did not like or by changing them. It was widely reported in the US that an electronic voting machine in Fairfax, Virginia "lost" one vote per hundred for a particular candidate [7]. Another recent paper showed how the results of the 2000 US presidential election could have been tipped either way by simply changing one vote per electronic voting machine from democrat to republican or vice versa [4]. Ballot stuffing, by either the reputation server itself, or by a group of colluding actors, could insert false votes to increase or decrease a subject's reputation. We are all familiar with this type of activity in real life, for example, the 2004 Ukrainian presidential election was accused of huge fraud [5] and had to be rerun. Dishonest actors can register false reputations. The consequences can be severe. Research has found that the appearance of a less than 100% positive reputation on e-Bay can seriously effect the price a seller is able to fetch for an item [8]. Actors that know how the summation algorithm of a reputation system works are able to fix the system. For example it is possible to get a high reputation on e-Bay by buying lots of worthless items that cost only a few cents. Once an actor has obtained a falsely high reputation it is possible to commit fraud on unsuspecting customers. For example, a Welsh schoolboy obtained £45,000 by selling non-existent electrical items through e-Bay [6]. So whilst electronic reputation systems that use the voting model, such as the one in e-Bay, should be able to provide trustworthy reputations of its subject, in reality, due to ballot stuffing or other nefarious actions by both the actors and the reputation system itself, this is not always the case, and the operational model has some inherent weaknesses in it.

The Research model provides the next lower level of trustworthy results. Because the reputation results are difficult to arrive at, both from a data collection and computational viewpoint, it is very difficult for actors to reproduce the results without an impossibly large investment of capital and time. Therefore an actor is left with no choice but to either trust or distrust the reputation service that is providing the results. Consequently it will take an appreciable amount of time for the reputation of a research model reputation service to be established, since trust in it will need to evolve over time and as its client base increases. Research model reputation systems might be expected to devote a considerable amount of their resources to ensuring the trustworthiness of the underlying data that they use, since ultimately their reputation will depend upon this. However, once their reputations have been established, they will become a great, if not the greatest, of the assets that the reputation systems possess. For example, it has taken Dun and Bradstreet over 160 years to build their reputation to the level it is now. We might therefore expect it will be many years before these type of electronic reputation servers will become a common feature of the Internet, unless companies with existing high reputations, such as D&B, move into this electronic world.

Finally, the MP model is inherently the least trustworthy and reliable of them all. This is because MP model reputations systems, like research model systems, will decide which data to keep, which data to discard, and how to evaluate it. But unlike research model systems, that actively solicit data from actors, so as to ensure that enough raw data is collected to compute meaningful results, MP model systems simply passively collect whatever information is provided to them, and might even be pre-programmed with particular biases that will skew whatever reputations they compute. The more trustworthy MP type reputation servers will be open to public scrutiny and will publish their algorithms and summaries of the raw data that they have used in their calculations (within the limits of the data protection act). But in general there is no requirement to do this, and therefore the trustworthiness of MP model reputation servers will at best be variable. It is for these reasons that we do not believe that this model is a viable one for reputation systems.

8 Conclusion

We have presented four different operational models for reputation servers, and evaluated the inherent trustworthiness of each model. We have shown that opinion poll model reputation servers, that use publicly accessible reputation information, and that summarize the results in an open and transparent way using publicly available algorithms are inherently the most trustworthy, whilst those reputation systems that do not disclose either the source of their data or the algorithms they use to compute reputations are inherently the least trustworthy.

Practical experience today with electronic reputation systems is limited to just the voting model type, since there are good business and operational reasons why this type of system has evolved. They are co-located with the e-business (usually of type B2C) that is hosting them, and they serve to enhance trust in the e-business itself. The actor lists (the consumers of the e-business) are readily available to the reputation system, making information collection easy, whilst the published reputations of the actors serve to increase the business of the hosting site itself. However, in a B2B world, where virtual organizations are continually being formed and dissolved from different sets of actors, and where there is no mandatory central hosting site such as e-Bay, then we believe that the opinion poll model for reputation systems will be the most effective and trustworthy to deploy. But before this can become a reality, there needs to be a publicly available actor list/directory service from which opinion poll servers can extract the sample of actors to poll for their opinions. In the longer term, research model reputation systems may become established, and this could be hastened by organizations that already enjoy a high reputation in the physical world moving into the electronic one.

References

[1] Paul Resnick , Ko Kuwabara , Richard Zeckhauser , Eric Friedman. "Reputation systems", Communications of the ACM, v.43 n.12, p.45-48, Dec. 2000

[2] Resnick, P., and Zeckhauser, R. (2002) "Trust Among Strangers in Internet Transactions: Empirical Analysis of eBay's Reputation System". In The Economics of the Internet and E-Commerce. Michael R. Baye, editor. Volume 11 of Advances in Applied Microeconomics, JAI Press.

[3] P.V. Mockapetris. "Domain names - implementation and specification" RFC 1035. Nov 1987

[4] Anthony Di Franco et al. "Small Vote Manipulations Can Swing Elections". Communications of the ACM, vol 47, no 10, pp 43-45. Oct 2004

[5] The Times Online. "Opposition overcomes 'total fraud' to claim victory in Ukraine elections". http://www.timesonline.co.uk/article/0,,3-1369632,00.html (viewed 24 Nov 04)

[6] Guardian Unlimited "Sharks target bargain-hungry surfers" http://www.guardian.co.uk/uk_news/story/0,,1328767,00.html (viewed 24 Nov 04)

[7] Washington Post "Fairfax Judge Orders Logs Of Voting Machines Inspected" http://www.washingtonpost.com/ac2/wp-dyn?pagename=article&contentId=A6291-2003Nov5 (viewed 25 Nov 04)

[8] D. Houser, J. Wooders, "Reputation in Auctions: Theory, and Evidence from eBay", University of Arizona. Paper under review.

[9] Q He, Z Su. "A new practical secure e-voting scheme". IFIP SEC'98, Austrian Computer Society, 1998, pp. 196–205. Also available from http://www.cs.huji.ac.il/~ns/Papers/He-Su.ps.gz

[10] OASIS. "UDDI Version 3.0.2". Oct 2004. Available from http://uddi.org/pubs/uddi_v3. htm

[11] Wahl, M., Howes, T., Kille, S. "Lightweight Directory Access Protocol (v3)", RFC 2251, Dec. 1997

A Representation Model of Trust Relationships with Delegation Extensions

Isaac Agudo, Javier Lopez, and Jose A. Montenegro

Computer Science Department, E.T.S. Ingenieria Informatica,
University of Malaga, Spain
{isaac, jlm, monte}@lcc.uma.es

Abstract. Logic languages establish a formal framework to solve authorization and delegation conflicts. However, we consider that a visual representation is necessary since graphs are more expressive and understandable than logic languages. In this paper, and after overviewing previous works using logic languages, we present a proposal for graph representation of authorization and delegation statements. Our proposal is based on Varadharajan et al. solution, though improve several elements of that work. We also discuss about the possible implementation of our proposal using attribute certificates.

Keywords: Attribute Certificate, Authorization, Delegation, Graph representation, Privilege Management Infrastructure (PMI).

1 Introduction

Traditional authorization schemes are typically based on the fact that the stakeholder has privileges to access the computer resource. That type of systems require that all users of a shared resource are locally registered. However, that requirement conforms a scenario where the authorization service does not scale well.

There are recent schemes where the authorization relies on elements that are external to the functional elements of the computer system. In these schemes, it is necessary to establish a trusted relation among the functional elements and the elements responsible for the authorization. On the other hand, they facilitate the situation in which several computer systems can share the same authorization method. Hence, the global information system results more scalable. We refer to this as *distributed authorization*: the authorization system publishes the authorization elements and the functional system use them to evaluate users' operations.

In many circumstances, delegation is a basic and necessary component to implement distributed authorization. The problem is that actual systems do not represent delegation concepts in a correct way. Several approaches have been proposed in order to manage delegation in distributed environments. The classic solution for knowledge reasoning is the use of logic, although there are other proposals that use a graphical representation.

P. Herrmann et al. (Eds.): iTrust 2005, LNCS 3477, pp. 116–130, 2005.

In this paper we introduce *Weighted Trust Graphs* (WTG) a graphical representation for authorization and delegation. As it can be deduced from its name, it is based on graphs, and provides a more flexible solution, in several ways, than other proposals, like those by Varadharajan and Ruan [1, 2]. One advantage of our solution is that WTG is a generalization of the other proposals. Additionally, WTG allows to define more complex policies. Even if in other solutions a delegation statement is usually issued together with an authorization statement, our solution can use both of them separately, allowing us to introduce the notion of negative delegation. We define negative and positive delegation statements as trust on negative and positive authorization, respectively. Moreover, we implement delegation as transitive trust.

The rest of the paper is structured as follows. Section 2 presents two variants to represent authorization and delegation statements: logic languages and visual representation using graphs. Section 3 describes our proposal based on graph representation, including the formalization of the system. In section 4, we discuss about the possible implementation of our proposal using attribute certificates. Finally, section 5 concludes the paper.

2 Representing Authorization and Delegation Statements

2.1 Logic-Based Schemes

This subsection introduces two formal proposals for delegation. These works are based on the use of logic languages to represent the authorization and delegation concepts. The Two significant proposals are, *Delegatable Authorization Program* and *RT Framework*.

Delegatable Authorization Program - DAP. Ruan et al proposed in [3] a logic approach to model delegation. Their language, $\mathcal{L}$, is a first order language, with four disjoint *sorts* $(S, <_S)$, $(O, <_O)$, $(A, <_A)$, and $T = \{-, +, *\}$, for *subject*, *object*, *access right* and *authorization* types, respectively.

In the constant set of authorization types, $T = \{-, +, *\}$, $-$ means negative, $+$ means positive, and $*$ means delegatable. A negative authorization specifies the access that must be forbidden, while a positive authorization specifies the access that must be granted. A delegatable authorization specifies the access that must be delegated as well as granted. The partial orders $<_S, <_O, <_A$ represent inheritance hierarchies of subjects, objects and access rights, respectively.

In DAP, *predicates* consist of a set of ordinary predicates defined by users, and one built-in predicate symbol, *grant*, for delegatable authorization. The later is a 5-term predicate symbol with type $S \times O \times T \times A \times S$, where the first argument is the grantee, the second one is the object, the third is the authorization type, the fourth is the access right and, finally, the fifth argument is the grantor of this authorization. Intuitively, $grant(s, o, t, a, g)$ means s is granted by g the access right a on object o with authorization type t. *grant* is called *authorization predicate*. There are two special predicates named *cangrant* and *delegate*, of type

$S \times O \times A$ and $S \times S \times O \times A$, respectively, that are used to model delegation. $cangrant(s, o, a)$ means subject s has the right to grant access a on object o to other subjects, while $delegate(g, s, o, a)$ means subject g has granted to subject s access a on object o with access type $*$.

A DAP consists of a finite set of rules of the form:

$$b_0 \leftarrow b_1, \ldots, b_k, not\ b_{k+1}, \ldots, not\ b_{k+m},\ m \geq 0$$

In [6], Ruan et al. extend their model with temporal capabilities, adding a new temporal parameter to predicates.

Example. Sorting of the language is defined as, $S = \{\#, s_1, s_2 : s_1 <_S s_2\}$, $O = \{o_1, o_2; o_1 <_O o_2\}$, $A = \{write, read; write <_A read\}$, and the rules of the DAP as:

```
r1 : dba(s₁) ←
r2 : ¬dba(s₂) ←
r3 : ¬secret(o₁) ←
r4 : secret(o₂) ←
r5 : grant(s₁,o₂,*,write,#)←
r6 : grant(s₂,o₂,-,write,s₁) ←
r7 : grant(_s,_o,-,write,#) ← secret(_o),not dba(_s)
```

RT Framework. Li et al. proposed in [5] logic programming as a way to model authorization and delegation relations. They use *Roles* for this purpose and they define a full general framework, RT for *Role Based Trust Management*. It comprise five different solutions, each of them with different characteristics. Roles can be interpreted as privileges or attributes, and are similar to what Ruan et al. call *access rights*. As in the previous logic-based proposal, the RT Framework defines a partial order in roles, establishing how rights can be inherited. Partial orders are used to represent other concepts too. Let u, p, r denote users, rights and roles, respectively; then:

- $r_1 \geq r_2$, is read as r_1 *dominates* r_2, and means that r_1 has all the rights r_2 has. It can also be read as r_2 contains r_1.
- $u \geq r$ assigns role r to user u.
- $r \geq p$ assigns right p to role r.

RT defines several types of credentials, an analogous concept to DAP. The basic credentials are:

1. $A.R \leftarrow D$: This credential means that A defines D to be a member of A's role R. In the attribute-based view, this credential can be read as D *has the attribute A.R*, or equivalently, A *says that D has the attribute R*.
2. $A.R \leftarrow B.R_1$: This credential means that A defines its role R to include all members of B's role $R1$. In the attribute-based view, this credential can be read as *if B says that an entity has the attribute R_1, then A says that it has the attribute R*.

3. $A.R \leftarrow A.R_1.R_2$: The expression on the right is called a *linked role*. It means that $A.R$ contains $B.R_2$ for all B in $A.R_1$. The attribute-based reading of this credential is: *if A says that an entity B has the attribute R_1, and B says that an entity D has the attribute R_2, then A says that D has the attribute R.*

4. $A.R \leftarrow B_1.R_1 \cap B_2.R_2 \cap \ldots \cap B_n.R_n$: This credential means that if an entity is a member of $B_1.R_1$, $B_2.R_2$, ... and $B_k.R_k$, then it is also a member of $A.R$. The attribute-based reading of this credential is *A believes that anyone who has all the attributes $B_1.R_1$, ..., $B_k.R_k$ also has the attribute R.*

```
EPub.disct ← EPub.preferred∩EPub.student
EPub.preferred ← EOrg.preferred
EOrg.prederred ← IEEE.member
EPub.student ← EPub.university.stuID
EPub.university ← ABU.accredited
ABU.accredited ← StateU
StateU.stuID ← Alice
IEEE.member ← Alice
```

2.2 Graphs-Based Schemes

Logic programming offers a powerful mechanism to represent authorization and access control decisions. Authorizations are represented as predicates and decisions are based on formulae verification. There are many logical solutions for formulae verification and it is easy to implement such a system in a standard way. A disadvantage of logical programming is that it is not well understandable and has an obscure transcription. The previous solutions are clear examples.

On the other hand, there are graphical solutions that are thought to be less powerful but more expressive and more understandable. A graphical solution may be based on the use of directed graphs to model authorization and delegation process. Basically, this maps each predicate to a directed arc in a graph. Arcs goes from the issuer of the authorization or delegation statement to the subject who is authorized or granted privileges. There are as many different arcs as different authorization/delegation statements to consider. As we model authorization and delegation, the graph we get is a tree and the root of the tree is (usually) the owner of the resource which we are reasoning about. With such a tree it is possible to study the relations between entities in the system in a graphical way.

Varadharajan and Ruan have proposed two solutions to represent authorization and delegation using directed graphs. In [1] they present a first approach to the problem. This approach considers three types of authorizations: negative authorization, positive authorization and delegatable authorization. As shown in figure 1, a cross line represents a negative authorization, a dashed line represents a positive authorization, and a simple line represents a delegatable one.

In [2] the same authors proposed a new approach, *weighted graphs*. In that proposal, each authorization is associated with a weight given by the grantor, representing the degrees of certainties about the authorization grants. The weight

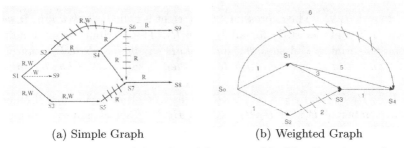

(a) Simple Graph   (b) Weighted Graph

Fig. 1. The two graph-based models proposed by Varadharajan et al

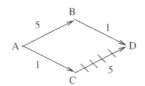

Fig. 2. Incomparable conflict

is a non-negative number, and a smaller number represents a higher certainty. When considering both negative and positive authorizations, we get conflicts if the same subject is issued a negative and a positive authorization. In this case, we need to define a conflict resolution method that allows us to decide which of them has to be considered.

These authors follow the idea of predecessor-take-precedence. However, there are still some conflicts that they do not solve. For instance, Figure 2 shows an incomparable conflict in the weighted graphs approach. We believe that ACD should override ABD because in the first link of the path A prefers C instead of B. This follows the predecessor-take-precedence philosophy as previous decisions take precedence over later ones. As shown later, our solution resolves this conflict.

3   Weighted Trust Graph

Weighted Trust Graphs (WTG) aims to generalize the proposal presented in [2]. However, our definition is more flexible. In fact, we support this proposal as a particular case of our framework.

As we consider negative and positive authorizations, conflicts between them may arise. We assign to each authorization a weight that, together with the security level policy, allow us to avoid many conflicts. In case the weights are the same, we follow a predecessor-take-precedence principle with some refinements; that is, a new conflict resolution method, that we call *strict-predecessor-take-precedence*.

This principle can also be used as a stand alone policy, where the owner of the resource establishes a hierarchy of subjects by assigning appropriated weights to their delegations, and any of the further delegations made for these subjects has to preserve this hierarchy. For instance, if A gets from S the higher priority in the hierarchy, all A's delegation or authorization statements take preference over the others ones.

In this paper we propose a security policy to avoid conflicts. We call it *Mean Policy*, where we use the *strict-predecessor-take-precedence* principle to solve conflicts.

Credentials are represented using arcs in a graph. Thus, both terms are used equally. We consider a credential as a 4-tuple:

$$(Issuer, Subject, Type, Right)$$

where (i) *Issuer* is the issuer of the authorization or delegation statement; (ii) *Subject* is whom this statement refers to; (iii) *Type*, as we will see later, is the type of the statement in a general way; and, (iv) *Right* is the right together with the resource we are reasoning about. We can represent *Right* as a 2-tuple consisting on the resource and the type of access, $Right = (Resource, Access)$. As with the *Right* of a credential, we can also express the *Type* as a 3-tuple[1] composed of the following parameters:

- *Weight*, which represents the level of trust in this authorization.
- *Delegatable*, which represents if the statement is delegatable or not.
- *Sign*, which represents the sign of the statement (negative or positive).

Then, we can define a credential as follows.

Definition 1. *A **credential** is a 4-tuple of the form (Issuer, Subject, Type, Right) where Issuer $\in \mathcal{S}$, Subject $\in \mathcal{S}$, Type $= (w, d, s) \in \mathcal{D} \times \{0, 1\} \times \{0, 1\}$ and Right $= (o, a) \in \mathcal{O} \times \mathcal{A}$.*

- $\mathcal{S}$ *is the set of subjects in the system;*
- $\mathcal{D}$ *is the domain where we evaluate the credential. In general, it could be any real number, but for our framework we restrict it[2] to $\mathcal{D} = [0, 1]$. We consider it as the level of trust that the issuer has on this credential: '1' stands for fully trustable credential, while '0' stands for non trustable credentials.*
- $\mathcal{O}$ *is the set of objects;*
- $\mathcal{A}$ *is the set of access types.*

We denote the set of all credentials by $\mathcal{G}$. Given a credential, we can refer to its *Type* components by the functions described next.

Definition 2. *Let m be a credential, then:*

- **Weight**, $|m|$ *defines the weight of the arc; according to Definition 1, $|m| \in [0, 1]$. When $m = 0$ we consider this credential as non existing.*

---

[1] If we consider validity intervals, it should be part of the credential *Type* and we should use a 4-tuple.

[2] Varadharajan et al. proposal could be derived from our framework, using non-negative numbers instead of $[0, 1]$.

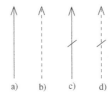

Fig. 3. Different types of arcs

- **Delegatable**, $d(m)$ is '0' for authorizations, and '1' for delegation statements.
- **Sign**, $s(m)$ is the sign of the credential ('1' if positive, '0' if negative).

Based on the proposal by Varadharajan et al., we define a graphical representation for the four types of credentials that we can obtain for the parameters d and s. Parameter w (the weight) is placed over the arcs in the graph. The different arc types that we support are represented in figure 3:

- Arc a) represents a positive delegation statement; i.e. $d(m) = 1$ and $s(m) = 1$. It means that the issuer trusts the subject about his/her positive authorizations or delegations. For simplicity, we suppose that this credential can be interpreted as a b or c credential.
- Arc b) represents a positive authorization statement; i.e. $d(m) = 0$ and $s(m) = 1$. It means that the issuer authorizes the subject to access the resource.
- Arc c) represents a negative delegation statement; i.e. $d(m) = 1$ and $s(m) = 0$. It means that the issuer trusts the subject about his/her negative authorizations or delegations.
- Arc d) represents a negative authorization statement; i.e. $d(m) = 0$ and $s(m) = 0$. It means that the issuer denies access to the subject over the resource.

We allow negative delegation statements which stands for trust about negations. In the example of figure 4, a bank could issue a negative delegation statement over granting credits to a company that maintains a customer blacklist, and at the same time could issue a (positive) delegation statement to one of its local offices. Even if the local office agrees on granting a credit to a specific citizen, they have to take into account the negative authorization issued by the black list company.

When taking decisions about granting access to a certain resource, we have to analyze the chains or paths of credentials from the owner of the resource to the subject. Next, we define paths of credentials.

Definition 3. A **path** C is a sequence of consecutive credentials, $m_1 m_2 \ldots m_n$. Every m_i is a credential and by 'consecutive' we mean that the issuer of m_{i+1} must be the subject of m_i for all $i \in \{1, \ldots, n-1\}$. The **length** of the path is defined as the number of credentials.

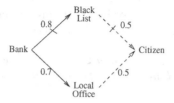

Fig. 4. Negative delegation

If there is only one path between the nodes, we can also note a path by its nodes instead of its arcs. Once we define a path, there could be conflictive paths between the same subjects, so we have to be able to compare them and decide which of them is valid and which not.

The key for conflict resolution is to define a metric over paths of credentials, which allow us to measure the priority of each authorization or, at least, to compare them. Such a metric should follow the predecessor-takes-precedence method. Therefore, a path should become less important as it grows (or, what is to say, as new arcs are added). We will use the term *metric*, even if it is not a metric in the mathematical sense.

Definition 4. *A metric is a non-negative function* $|\mathcal{C}| = f(|m_1||m_2| \ldots |m_n|)$ *where* $n = length(C)$. *In case there are different metrics, we denote it as* $| \cdot |_i$, *where the subindex refers to the particular metrics.*

The main property a metric has to fulfill in order to be considered as a metric for paths is *monotony*. This means that the weight or level of trust of the path decreases when going down in the path. As we want that larger paths are less important, we are interested in decreasing metrics, i.e., if we add one more credential to an existing path, the weight of the newer path can not be greater than the weight of the older path:

$$|m_1 m_2 \ldots m_i| \geq |m_1 m_2 \ldots m_i m_{i+1}| \tag{1}$$

Some examples of monotone metrics are,

- $|\mathcal{C}|. = |m_1||m_2| \cdots |m_n|$
- $|\mathcal{C}|_{min} = min(|m_1|, |m_2|, \ldots, |m_n|)$
- $|\mathcal{C}|_+ = |m_1| + |m_2| + \ldots + |m_n|$
- $|\mathcal{C}|_{max} = max(|m_1|, |m_2|, \ldots, |m_n|)$

The first two are decreasing metrics[3], and the last two are increasing metrics. With the help of these metrics we can define an order in the paths as follows:

$$\mathcal{C} > \mathcal{C}' \text{ if } |\mathcal{C}| > |\mathcal{C}'| \tag{2}$$

---

[3] $| \cdot |.$ is decreasing as we define $0 \leq |m|. \leq 1$ for all credentials in the system (see Definition 2).

Although there is a variety of orders that can be defined in this way, others can not. One example is the lexicographic or dictionary order.

Definition 5. *Given two paths C and C', let n be the minimum length of the two, $n := min\{lenght(C), lenght(C')\}$, we say that $C >_L C'$ if*

$$C >_L C' \; if \begin{cases} (|m_1| > |m'_1|) \\ or \\ (|m_1| = |m'_1|) \wedge |m_2| > |m'_2| \\ or \\ \ldots \\ or \\ (|m_1| = |m'_1|) \wedge \ldots \wedge (|m_{n-1}| = |m'_{n-1}|) \wedge |m_n| > |m'_n| \\ or \\ |m_i| = |m'_i| \, \forall i \in \{1, \ldots, n\} \wedge n = lenght(C) \end{cases}$$

When inspecting paths from one node to another, not all the possible paths need to be considered. It is necessary to define which are valid paths and which are not. If A trusts $B's$ negative authorizations, then paths containing $B's$ positive authorizations over $A's$ resources have to be discarded. If A authorizes B and B authorizes C, C is not authorized, as A does not trust B on positive authorizations. He just authorizes him, thus this path is also discarded. Next we define *valid paths*.

Definition 6. *Given a path, $C = m_1 m_2 \ldots m_n$, we say that C is valid or consistent if any of the following conditions holds:*

- *$length(C) = 1$*
- *$d(m_i) = 1$ for all $i \in \{1, .., n-1\}$ and $s(m_i) = -1$ for all $i \in \{1, .., n\}$*
- *$(d(m_i) = 1) \wedge (s(m_i) = 1) \forall i \in \{1, .., n-1\}$*

We define the function v to determine whether a path is valid or not,

$$v(C) := \begin{cases} 1 \; if \, C \; is \; consistent \\ 0 \; in \; other \; case \end{cases}$$

We have to keep in mind that, when taking access decisions, the last link in the path the user presents consists of an authorization and, therefore, provides the sign (positive or negative) for the path. We will consider that a path is positive/negative if the last link is positive/negative, respectively. We define, based in a given metric, a *pseudo-metric*, that takes into account all the details we have defined before. We denote it with double lines.

Definition 7. *Given a metric $|\cdot|$, a sign function $s(\cdot)$, a validity function $v(\cdot)$ and a path $C = m_1 m_2 \ldots m_n$, we define the associated **pseudo-metric** as*

$$\|C\| = |C| s(m_n) v(C)$$

As $|\mathcal{C}| \in [0,1]$, $\|\mathcal{C}\| \in [-1,1]$ then, given a number $x \in [-1,1]$, we define $\|x\|^{-1}$ as the set of all paths with pseudo-weight equal to x.

$$\|\mathcal{C}\|^{-1} := \{\mathcal{C} \in \mathcal{G} : \|\mathcal{C}\| = x\} \tag{3}$$

We choose for our proposal the metric, $|\mathcal{C}| = |\mathcal{C}|.$ and we omit the dot in the following.

Definition 8. *Given a set of paths $\mathcal{S}$, and the pseudo-metric $\|\mathcal{C}\|$, we define the **highest** and the **lowest** weight of the set $\mathcal{S}$ as,*

$$\mathcal{H}(\mathcal{S}) := max\{\|\mathcal{C}\| : \mathcal{C} \in \mathcal{S}\}$$

and

$$\mathcal{L}(\mathcal{S}) := min\{\|\mathcal{C}\| : \mathcal{C} \in \mathcal{S}\}$$

respectively. If $S = \emptyset$ then they are defined to be equal to '0'.

In particular, we can define the *higher/lower* weight between two nodes, as shown next.

Definition 9. *Let S_{AB} be the set of all valid paths $(v(\mathcal{C}) \neq 0)$ from A to B, then $\mathcal{H}_{AB} := \mathcal{H}(S_{AB})$ and $\mathcal{L}_{AB} := \mathcal{L}(S_{AB})$*

We can also define the average weight, compensating negative and positive authorization.

Definition 10. *Let S_B be the set of all credentials issued over B, and let X_m be the issuer of the credential m. Then, the average weight between principals A and B is defined as,*
$\mathcal{M}_{AB} := average\{|m|s(m)\mathcal{M}_{AX_m} : m \in S_B \wedge \mathcal{M}_{AX_m} > 0\}$
The initial case is $\mathcal{M}_{AA} := 1$.

Definition 10, is a recursive definition that can be seen as a graph exploration using a *branch and bound* algorithm where the strict lower bound for $\mathcal{M}_{AX}$ is set to zero. If we calculate $\mathcal{M}_{AB}$ from A to B, in the first step we inspect the principals conected from A with a single arc. Then we mark the negatives as "non useful", as they can not further delegate, so can not be part of any delegation path. With the rest we repeat the argument until we reach B. At the end, we have marked all the non useful nodes. When reasoning about two principals A and B, the non useful nodes are omitted and we get an effective graph containing only the useful nodes.The resulting graph is easier to inspect both visually and aritmetically.

In the following, we will explain how to calculate the previously defined functions with an example. We are going to calculate $\mathcal{M}_{AX}$, for all relevant nodes X in the full graph of Figure 5,

$$\mathcal{M}_{AB} = 1 \times 1 \times \mathcal{M}_{AA} = 1 \tag{4}$$

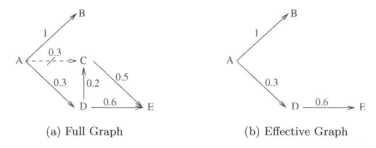

(a) Full Graph   (b) Effective Graph

Fig. 5. An example of a Delegation Graph and the Effective Graph

$$\mathcal{M}_{AD} = 0.3 \times 1 \times \mathcal{M}_{AA} = 0.3 \tag{5}$$

$$
\begin{aligned}
\mathcal{M}_{AC} &= \frac{0.3 \times (-1) \times \mathcal{M}_{AA} + 0.2 \times 1 \times \mathcal{M}_{AD}}{2} \\
&= \frac{-0.3 + 0.2 \times 0.3}{2} \\
&= -0.12
\end{aligned}
\tag{6}
$$

$$\mathcal{M}_{AE} = 0.6 \times (1) \times \mathcal{M}_{AD} = 0.6 \times 0.3 = 0.18 \tag{7}$$

What we actually do is the arithmetic average of all valid paths with all its nodes, X_i, having a positive $\mathcal{M}_{AX_i}$. Note that we have not considered the path ACE in the calculus of $\mathcal{M}_{AE}$ as $\mathcal{M}_{AC} < 0$ (see Definition 10 for more details). With the same example it is easy to calculate $\mathcal{L}_{AX}$ and $\mathcal{H}_{AX}$.

With these three elements we can define several types of policies for authorization. At this moment, we are working on a classification of the policies. One of the simplest policies is the **Mean Policy**. Easy speaking, A grant access to the resource to agent X if $\mathcal{M}_{AX} > 0$. Although this is an easy formula, there are cases in which $\mathcal{M}_{AX} = 0$, thus this formula does not grant authorization but, according to predecessor-takes-precedence method, we should grant it or implicitly deny it.

When $\mathcal{M}_{AX} = 0$, it could happen that there is no path from A to X or that they are both positive and negative. As the average is zero, we can not decide whether to grant authorization or not. Other proposals keep this situation as unsolvable. However, it is important to note that we try to solve it using the lexicographic order to decide about granting authorization.

Given a set of paths, we can also define another subset, including all the maximal elements according to the lexicographic order. We note it as $max_L(AB)$.

Definition 11. *Given a set of path, S, we define the **maximal lexicographic subset** of S as $max_L(S) := \{\mathcal{C} \in S : \text{ there are no } \mathcal{C}' \in S \text{ with } \mathcal{C}' >_L \mathcal{C}\}$.*
If the set S is the set of all paths from A to B, then we denote it as $max_L(AB)$

Using this set we can solve several cases in which $\mathcal{M}_{AX} = 0$. We allow access if any of the paths with the highest weight is greater (using the dictionary order) than all the paths with the lowest weight. In other case, we say the conflict in undecidable.

Now we can formally define this policy.

Definition 12. *According to the **Mean Policy**, A grants access to their resources to agent X if $\mathcal{M}_{AX} > 0$ or $\mathcal{M}_{AX} = 0$ and*

$$\exists\, \mathcal{C} \in \|\mathcal{H}_{AB}\|^{-1} : \mathcal{C} >_L \mathcal{C}' \,\forall\, \mathcal{C}' \in \|\mathcal{L}_{AB}\|^{-1}$$

Using this policy we can solve the problems mentioned when explaining Figure 2.

As mentioned in the introduction we also define a stronger principle than *predecessor-take-precedence*. We call it *strict-predecessor-take-precedence* and we implement it using the dictionary order. We order all path from A to X and choose the maximal ones; these are the preferred paths. If all of them are positive, then we grant authorization, but if there are positive and negative we can not say anything[4]. If there are only negative authorizations we deny access.

Definition 13. *According to **strict-predecessor-take-precedence**, A grants access to their resources to agent X if $max_L(AX)$ contains only positive authorizations.*

4   Implementation of Our Proposal Using Attribute Certificates

The last X.509 ITU-T Recommendation [7] introduces the concept of *Privilege Management Infrastructure* (PMI) as the framework for the extended use of *attribute certificates*. The Recommendation establishes four PMI models: (i) *General*, (ii) *Control*, (iii) *Roles* and (iv) *Delegation*. The first one can be considered as an abstract model, while the other ones can be considered as the models for implementation.

The implementation of the Control and Roles models are feasible tasks, though not free of complexity. However, the case of the Delegation model is substantially different because of the intrinsic difficult problems of the delegation concept. In this section, we discuss about the implementation of the Delegation model using our WTG solution in combination with attribute certificates.

The PMI area inherits many notions from the *Public Key Infrastructure* (PKI) area. In this sense, an *Attribute Authority* (AA) is the authority that assigns privileges (through attribute certificates) to users, and the *Source of Authorization* (SOA) is the root authority in the delegation chain. A typical PMI will contain a SOA, a number of AAs and a multiplicity of final users. As regarding our scheme, we will represent the previous elements as the nodes of the graph. The SOA will be the first node that outflows initial arcs. AAs will be the

---

[4] In fact, we can solve it combining the two policies presented in the paper or using other policies we are working on.

intermediary nodes while the final users will be the leaf nodes (that is, the nodes that do not outflow arcs but inflow authorization arcs only).

The ASN.1 [4] description of the structure of an attribute certificate is the following:

```
AttributeCertificate ::= SIGNED {AttributeCertificateInfo}
AttributeCertificateInfo ::= SEQUENCE
  {
      version                  AttCertVersion, --version is v2
      holder                   Holder,
      issuer                   AttCertIssuer,
      signature                AlgorithmIdentifier,
      serialNumber             CertificateSerialNumber,
      attrCertValidityPeriod   AttCertValidityPeriod,
      attributes               SEQUENCE OF Attribute,
      issuerUniqueID           UniqueIdentifier OPTIONAL,
      extensions               Extensions  OPTIONAL
  }


Extensions ::= SEQUENCE OF Extension
Extension ::= SEQUENCE {
    extnId      EXTENSION.&id ({ExtensionSet}),
    critical    BOOLEAN DEFAULT FALSE,
    extnValue   OCTET STRING
}


ExtensionSet EXTENSION      ::= { ... }
EXTENSION ::= CLASS {
    &id      OBJECT IDENTIFIER UNIQUE,
    &ExtnType }
    WITH SYNTAX {
    SYNTAX          &ExtnType
    IDENTIFIED BY      &id
    }
```

One of the fields is the *extensions* field. This is precisely the field than becomes essential for the practical implementation of our proposal. This field allows us to include additional information into the attribute certificate. The X.509 standard provides the following predefined extension categories:

Basic privilege management: Certificate extensions to convey information relevant to the assertion of a privilege.

Privilege revocation: Certificate extensions to convey information regarding location of revocation status information.

Source of Authority: These certificate extensions relate to the trusted source of privilege assignment by a verifier for a given resource.

Roles: Certificate extensions convey information regarding location of related role specification certificates.

Delegation: These certificate extensions allow constraints to be set on subsequent delegation of assigned privileges.

We focus on the Delegation extension category, that defines different extension fields. Among them, the Recommendation includes:

Authority attribute identifier: In privilege delegation, an AA that delegates privileges, shall itself have at least the same privilege and the authority to delegate that privilege. An AA that is delegating privilege to another AA or to an end-entity may place this extension in the AA or end-entity certificate that it issues. The extension is a back pointer to the certificate in which the issuer of the certificate containing the extension was assigned its corresponding privilege. The extension can be used by a privilege verifier to ensure that the issuing AA had sufficient privilege to be able to delegate to the holder of the certificate containing this extension.

That extension is close to our goals. However, it does not define the weight associated to the arc between the issuer and the holder of the certificate. Therefore, we define our own extension, in ASN.1, based on the *Authority attribute identifier* one.

This new extension determines a sequence between the SOA and the holder. Each sequence includes other sequence, *ArcsId*, where to include the information of the arcs in the graph, weight of the arc, origin node, and boolean information about statements, delegation and sign. The destination node must coincide with the serial number of the attribute certificate.

```
WeightPathIdentifier EXTENSION  ::=
{
     SYNTAX                WeightPathIdentifierSyntax
     IDENTIFIED BY    { id-ce-WeightPathIdentifier }
}
WeightPathIdentifierSyntax  ::= SEQUENCE SIZE (1..MAX) OF ArcsId

ArcsId ::= SEQUENCE {
             Origin      IssuerSerial,
             Destination HolderSerial,
             Weight      REAL (0..1),
             Delegable   BIT,
             Sign        BIT
}
```

5   Conclusions and Ongoing Work

Delegation is increasingly becoming a basic issue in distributed authorization. Actual systems do not represent delegation concepts in a correct way, and some approaches have been proposed for the management of delegation. The traditional solution for knowledge reasoning is the use of logic, although there are other proposals that use a graphical representation.

We have presented in this work the Weighted Trust Graphs (WTG) solution, a graphical representation for authorization and delegation. There are other solutions based on graphs. However, WTG provides a more flexible solution because it is a generalization of the other proposals. Additionally, WTG allows to define complex policies. Moreover, our solution can make use of authorization and delegation separately, allowing to manage negative delegations, which stands for trust on negative authorizations.

More complex policies than the one presented in the paper (at the end of section 3) are part of our actual research. The key to define policies is the use of general inequations on variables $\mathcal{H}_{AX}$, $\mathcal{M}_{AX}$ and $\mathcal{L}_{AX}$. These equations can be combined to produce more complex policies, using sequences of equations or systems of equations. Another importan ingredient for constructing policies is the use of the set $max_L(AX)$, or more generally, the use of the dictionay order.

The *Mean Policy* we have presented is the simplest inequation one can consider. Another simple policy, could be

$$\mathcal{L}_{AX} > 0$$

This equation holds only when there are no negative authorizations from A to X and there is at least one positive authorization. We are working on a classification of these policies, and are studying the efficiency of each solution.

In addition to the theoretic definition of the WTG scheme, this work has shown how to perform a practical implementation based on attribute certificates and the PMI framework defined by ITU-T.

Acknowledgements

This paper is an outcome of the work performed in three Research Projects where the different co-authors have been involved. We very much thank the support of: (i) the European Commission through the UBISEC Project (IST-506926), (ii) the Japanese National Institute of Information and Communication Technology (NICT) through the International Collaborative Research Project "Secure Privacy Infrastructure" and, (iii) the Spanish Ministry of Science and Technology through the project PRIVILEGE (TIC-2003-8184-C02-01). We also thank the Andalusian Regional Government, that supports Isaac Agudo's PhD work.

References

1. V. Varadharajan, C. Ruan. Resolving conflicts in authorization delegations. In *ACISP*, volume 2384 of *Lecture Notes in Computer Science*. Springer, 2002.
2. V. Varadharajan, C. Ruan. A weighted graph approach to authorization delegation and conflict resolution. In *ACISP*, volume 3108 of *Lecture Notes in Computer Science*. Springer, 2004.
3. Y. Zhang, C. Ruan, V. Varadharajan. Logic-based reasoning on delegatable authorizations. In *Foundations of Intelligent Systems : 13th International Symposium, ISMIS*, 2002.
4. B. Kaliski. *A Layman's Guide to a Subset of ASN.1, BER, and DER*, 1993.
5. N. Li, J. C. Mitchell, W. Winsborough. Design of a role-based trust management framework. In *Proceedings of the 2002 IEEE Symposium on Security and Privacy*, pages 114–130. IEEE Computer Society Press, May 2002.
6. C. Ruan, V. Varadharajan, Y. Zhang. A logic model for temporal authorization delegation with negation. In *6th International Information Security Conference, ISC*, 2003.
7. ITU-T Recommendation X.509. *Information Technology - Open systems interconnection - The Directory: Public-key and attribute certificate frameworks*, 2000.

Affect and Trust

Lewis Hassell

College of Information Science and Technology,
Drexel University, 3141 Chestnut St., Philadelphia, PA, USA
Telephone: 215-895-2492
Fax: 215-895-2494
lew.hassell@drexel.edu

Abstract. A number of models of trust, particularly vis à vis ecommerce, have been proposed in the literature. While some of these models present intriguing insights, they all assume that trust is based on logical choice. Furthermore, while these models recognize the importance of the subject's *perception* of reality in its evaluation, none of the proposed models have critically analyzed the nature of affective nature of perception, particularly in light of recent work in neurology and social psychology. This paper examines this concept of affect and then proposes a new, affect-based model in light of modern science. How this new model addresses previous shortcomings is demonstrated. Directions for future research are then proposed.

1 Introduction

Considerable research has been done that shows that affective computing – or emotional computing – is essential in advanced HCI design. Picard (2003) discusses the challenges and promises of affective computing in integrating human intelligence with machine intelligence. What has not been addressed, this author believes, is the part affect plays in intentional action. Thus we come to the matter of trust. Trust has become a very important concept for two domains within computer and information science: security and ecommerce. Almost all models presuppose what might be referred to as a "rational actor model". In fact, however, what they are presupposing is a "logical actor model". This model may be useful for artificial agents, certificate authorities, etc. However, this paper argues that the "logical actor model" is not a good model of how natural actors behave. There certainly must be machine-readable rules that govern interactions between computers and their software, but to deny the fact that to understand rational actors *qua* human beings one must take affect (emotion) into consideration flies in the face of modern neurobiology. This, in turn, is important because if computer and information scientists lose sight of the fact that human actors at times – perhaps often – behave in ways that is not in line with logic (first order, second order, fuzzy, what have you), computer systems will be doomed to be underused, misused, and, at worst, not used at all.

P. Herrmann et al. (Eds.): iTrust 2005, LNCS 3477 pp. 131 – 145, 2005.

2 Fundamental Distinctions

Distinction between reason and affect is central to this paper. By reason I mean the rather restrictive sense of our logical faculty. "Rationality" is then distinguished from reason. I will contend below that "rationality" and "rational" behavior are not solely based on reason, that is, logic. People whose actions are not properly guided by their affective faculties (emotion and socialization) do not appear to be "normal" (Brothers 1997). A couple of terms in the previous sentence require attention. The term "properly" is, of course, crucial. While acting like a robot, guided by the formal logic of your choice, is a recipe for disaster, so, too, is being driven strictly by your emotions. Modern psychology has shown this important relationship. The other phrase to be explicated is "affective faculties". There are various distinctions made between emotions and feelings. Closely related to emotions are values and socialization. I will use the phrase "affective faculties" for all of this.

Lastly, closely related to this distinction between reason and affect is a distinction between belief and trust. These distinctions will be discussed in the two subsections below. I will then give arguments based on both the natural and the social sciences to support my contention that trust arises from the affective centers of the brain.

2.1 Reason and Affect

It seems to be a common belief that self-reporting on trust ("I trust you", or "I will trust you") is the same as trust (i.e., actually *trusting* someone). Despite what seems to be the common contention, trust is an act, not a judgment. I do not trust you *when I say* that I trust you. I trust you *when I perform* an act of trust. Doing and reasoning are not the same thing, though they can be related – just as the perception of causality is different (and occurs in a different part of the brain) from reasoning about causality (Fonlupt 2003). The only true evidence of trust is the act of trust. The classic example of a person falling backwards into the arms of another illustrates this point. The person waiting to catch you is big, strong, honest, and relatively close. He asks if you trust him to catch you. You say, "yes". You may even mean yes. But you still don't fall. You are asked if you trust the big man to catch you. You reply that you do. When asked why you don't fall, you would probably respond that you are afraid. Fear is an emotion. It may be mitigated (or, perhaps justified) by calculation, but it is not controlled by it. The decision to trust or not to trust thus seems to be more governed by the emotional centers of the brain than the logical centers. It is well known in neurology that the emotions and socialization are intimately related. We shall have more to say about this below.

Thus, there is a distinction made between reason (the application of rules of logic to concepts) and emotion. Indeed, this contention should not be surprising. Pearce (1974), nearly thirty years ago, pointed out that the cognitive states antecedent to the particular choices in the Prisoner's Dilemma, a standard game used to test trust, are not unequivocally indicated by the subject's choices (i.e., either to trust or not to trust).

Reason (or logic) should not be equated completely with rationality, because what we, as human beings, would consider "rational behavior" is intricately bound up with the centers of the brain that control the emotions. If I am deprived of my emotions through brain disease or trauma, I am incapable of "acting rationally" (we will demonstrate this when discussing evidence from the brain sciences).

2.2 Belief and Trust

In the literature on trust, to date, what really seems to be being talked about is belief (e.g., Gefen et al 2003 or Ba, Whinston, & Zhang 2003), or perhaps trustworthiness. Gefen et al (2003) summarized 43 conceptualizations of trust in the literature. All 43 were based on belief, confidence, or faith that a person *would* perform as expected (i.e. was trustworthy) and did not recognize the emotional foundations of trust. This is significant because one might argue that belief is cognitive. Belief can be true or false, or at least correct or incorrect. This is not the case with trust. Trust is not true or false. It can only be considered correct or incorrect in a derivative sense. To wit, trust may be considered correct if it was, in fact, warranted and not betrayed. Furthermore, a person may be *adjudged* as being trustworthy or not. This, however, might only an *ex post facto* judgment and not the same as actually *acting* on that judgment – i.e. *trusting*. That to which most authors refer as trust, then, seems to be really a judgment of whether a person or institution is *trustworthy*. We may make these judgments logically based on appropriate input. This is not the same as the act of trusting that person or institution.

An example of e-commerce research that conflates trust and belief is Ba, Whinston, & Zhang (2003). What Ba and his colleagues describe as a trusted third party mechanism for building trust is really just a mechanism for lie (deception) detection, which only keeps participants honest for fear of being caught. Because there is a third party to whom we can go to check facts, we do not need to trust the second party. We can check up on them. The trust we show for the "trusted" third party is also of dubious character. Unless they are part of a social group or network that is known and trusted by us, we trust them only insofar as they can give us evidence that we can believe what they tell us and legal recourse in the event of fraud. Thus, again, we do not trust them. We are engaged in fact checking with the courts as a last resort. It is doubtful if this is what we ordinarily mean by 'trust'.

In a discussion of lie detection, Park et al (2002) have pointed out that when detecting a lie, people often rely on third parties. This, as Park admits, can be a long, drawn out process taking days, weeks or even months. Furthermore, one can assume, though it is not stated by Park, that the third party whose advice is sought is a member of the same community or social group – i.e., a *trusted member of the community* – as the person potentially being deceived. This will have significance for us later in this paper. This is also what would be expected based on Diffusion Theory (Rogers 1996). As for e-commerce and trust, it should be noted, "... studies of diffusion and mass communication have shown that people rarely *act* [authors italics] on mass-media information unless it is also transmitted through *personal* (italics mine) ties" (Granovetter 1973, p.1374).

Given not only the multitude of meanings of the word trust in e-commerce and other literature, and the additional confusion between trust, trustworthiness, and belief, one might argue, as does McEvily et al (2003), that we should learn to accept a multifaceted definition of trust. However, if we rush to such acceptance, we risk overlooking what may be a common, uniting thread in all the classifications of trust.

2.3   Trust and Affect

Trust, then, by our contention is not deductive. We may calculate and deduce all we wish, but when it comes time to trust or not to trust, there are other forces at work. Neither is trust coercive. We can be forced to *do* something, but we cannot be forced to choose to *trust* someone. Interestingly, there is considerable evidence for this both from the natural and the social sciences.

Evidence from the Brain Sciences

The scientific study of human emotions has a rich history, dating back at least as far as Darwin (1872). The latter half of the twentieth century saw a remarkable increase in the study of emotions. Recent studies in neurology and neuropsychology have shown that damage to the centers of the brain associated with the emotions causes a number of problems. Damasio (1995/2000, 1999, 2003) has shown that such damage prevents people from acting "rationally". Patients with damage to the amygdala, prefrontal cortex, and other affective centers of the brain (and who still have the logical centers of their brains, the cerebral cortex, perfectly in tact) are unable to enter into business agreements, know whom to trust, know when and how to minimize loss, and suffer a host of other ills. This is true despite the fact that these unfortunate souls can still make comparisons, perform deductions, and solve mathematical equations. For instance, damage particularly to the prefrontal region of the brain results in "a disturbance of the ability to decide advantageously in situations involving risk and conflict and a selective reduction of the ability to resonate emotionally in precisely those same situations ..." (Damasio 1995/2000, p. 41). Indeed, such patients become either socially paralyzed, or social miscreants (Hare and Quinn 1971, Bechara, Damasio, Damasio, & Anderson 1994). Prior to the brain damage, they were often leading very productive lives and were well respected by their peers.

Even more recently, research done by Zak (2003) seems to indicate that the chemical, oxytocin, is produced upon the act of trust, and oxytocin works on the amygdala, one of the emotional centers of the brain. This creates a bonding between the person trusting and the person trusted bio-chemically similar to the emotional bond created between a mother and child during breastfeeding.

Thus, modern research in neurology demonstrates that calculative processes (reason) do not govern trust (and much other social activity). Trust is not the result of a simple – or even strict – calculation of the truth-value of a speaker's utterances. We may calculate, but we weigh the affect of the propositions, and the referents of the terms of those propositions. If we do not like the result of our calculation, we find some reason for recalculating, or waiting to revisit the calculation until we "know more" (or can "justify" what "feels right"). (One might argue that this is what is going on in Kuhn's (1970) observation of scientists' allegiance to their paradigms.)

Evidence from the Social Sciences

Recent research in the "social sciences"—including psychology, CSCW, and linguistics—has been no kinder to the cognitive view of trust[1]. In the field of CSCW, research (Bos et al 2002) has shown that we tend to trust people most if we can meet them face-to-face. No real surprise here. Video conferencing (VTC) comes in a close second, with text chat being the worst. Audio-only (phone) conferencing came in somewhere between VTC and text chat for trust building.

In related research, Zheng et al (2002) determined that electronically mediated interaction is *almost* as good as face-to-face in generating trust, but it is more brittle and there is more of a time delay to the onset of trust. In effect, it would seem that we have to think more about whom and when to trust more in mediated than in face-to-face situations. Again, there should be no real surprises. Indeed, Zheng even showed that seeing a picture of the person with whom his subjects were interacting was better than nothing at all. What *may* be surprising is that the same research showed that his subjects tend to trust another more if they simply saw a picture than if they had a personal data sheet. Research by Platek et al (2002) has shown that we tend to prefer, and report we would be more likely to trust, children who are morphed to look like us. Greenspan et al (2000) showed that adding a voice channel to a Web page in e-commerce activities engendered higher trust.

If trust were merely deductive and logic-based, why does a fact sheet fare so poorly when contrasted with socially richer media, like face-to-face, voice, or even a still picture? One would think that logical deductions would be easier from a personal data sheet than a picture. What does voice add to a corporate Web page? Why would we trust someone whose photograph has been morphed to look more like us? Thus, one must wonder what exactly it is that we are getting from our interactions. I suggest that the standard information-seeking model is not adequate. Information is something that is identifiable, quantifiable, something that is capable of being pointed to. What we are getting in the above encounters is the gut feeling that we find difficult to further describe.

Another possible explanation is that it is difficult, if not impossible, to develop an authentic sense of community with another when we have not had first hand experience with them. Even a picture is sensory in this respect where a fact sheet is not. We can feel good or bad about someone we meet in person, or even a person we construct from some mediated means (such as a tele- or videoconference), or even a person we imagine from a picture. It is difficult, however, to "feel good" about data.[2]

---

[1] I should point out here that what I call the "cognitive view of trust" is not related to a common distinction between what is called "affective trust" and "cognitive trust". Cognitive Trust is defined as the extent to which the individual believes that the other party is competent to carry out a particular task. Affective Trust is defined as concerned about my welfare as I am about his or hers.

[2] We realize that there are other writers who address trust from a politico-economic perspective. Such a writer is Fukuyama (1995). While his arguments may have some currency among those more philosophically oriented, the reasons why we cannot subscribe to his neo-Hegelian, post-industrial, end-of-history approach to trust should be clear from our discussion above.

3   A New Model of Trust

With this background in the affective side of human nature and the distinction between reason and emotion, we may now propose a new model of trust that unpacks and explicates all the terms like "perceived", "cultural", "disposition", and "behavior" used in the models described above. Even our model must remain provisional. A detailed analysis of human nature, feeling, and thinking are far beyond the scope of this paper and are properly the domain of a work on epistemology.

Our model is depicted in Figure 1. The reader will notice that it looks as if we are depicting a sharp distinction between reason and emotion. We do not believe that one actually exists. There is no more a sharp distinction between affect and reason than there is a sharp distinction between the various regions of the brain. There are, however, general regions and that is what is being represented here. Many researchers up to now have created a distinction between affective trust and cognitive trust. This is a distinction that we completely reject. Trust is not a *judgment* – it is an *act*. We *trust* or we do *not*. We *maintain* trust or we *withdraw* it. We may *justify* it in one way or another. It is to be noted that while this model may be used as a model of online trust, it also shows how online trust is a subset of trust in general.

We must also note that while we accept the notion that we may trust a person, we may also trust a thing (a technology or other inanimate object). If we trust an object, however, we do so in a derivative manner. Physical objects *propter se* are actually governed by various physical laws. A physical object is predictable by the laws of physics, chemistry, and the other natural sciences and can be determined with mathematical exactitude (at least, above the quantum level). It would sound odd to say that we trust a photon. When we say that we trust that a photon travels at the speed of light what we are really saying is that photons traveling in a vacuum have been measured in the past and they all have traveled at 299,792,458 meters per second. Actually, it has been determined by physicists that the speed of light has actually changed over time (Montgomery and Dolphin 2004). Physicists, however, do not feel betrayed or hurt (the response to someone not honoring one's trust), but perplexed (the response to a scientific problem). Objects at the level of physics are not integrated into social organizations as a Web site or a machine like an automobile can be. Still, we do not really trust or feel betrayed by those things but by the humans behind them. We trust them because they are human-produced artifacts. If something goes wrong, we ask something like, "Why did they [human agent] design it that way?" We do not ask how, for example, the automobile could do that (to us). For the sake of simplicity, however, we will talk as if X can be an artifact.

We should also point out that this model includes two factors – Perceived Ease of Use and Attitude toward Using – that do not occur in all forms of trust, only those involving some form of technology. For this reason, we the edges (9, 12, and 13) connecting these nodes to the other nodes are represented by a dotted line.

In the next three subsections we will explain our model. We will analyze the two sides of our model – affect first, then logic. After that, we will discuss the interactions of the elements represented by the (numbered) edges of the model.

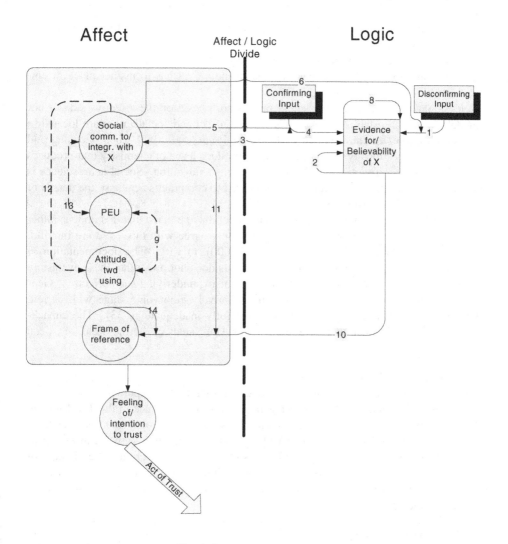

Fig. 1. Proposed model of trust

3.1 Affect

Again, as pointed out above, affect includes emotions, feelings, and socialization.

Social Commitment to and Integration with X

Social commitment to and integration with X is very complex in and of itself. It has to do with social history, the values embraced by the society, and social practices. By society, we do not necessarily mean just larger social organizations, such as nation states or ethnic groups, but also smaller organizational, regional groups, or even something as dispersed as a scientific community.

This node is affected by the individual's (it is, after all, the individual who ultimately trusts) commitment to and integration with the social group. This can be as strange as the lack of commitment to a society by a sociopath or as mundane as the relative commitment, or lack thereof, that an individual has to his/her place of employment.

It should not be strange that social factors are placed on the affective side of our model. It is well established in neurology that affect and socialization are located in the same regions of the brain (e.g., Damasio 1995/2000, 1999, 2003, Cushing and Carter 1999). Various types of socialization produce a sea of chemistry that produces various emotions. Emotions, in their turn, affect socialization. Social neuroscience is a relatively young science, even when compared to computer science, so the details of all this are still being worked out.

A justifiable criticism of this part of our model may be made that this node is rather large, and needs to be unpacked. We completely agree with this. We are mindful, however, of a comment by Cacioppo et al (2000), to wit: "The documentation of associations between social and biological events does not prove that these events are causally linked, nor does it speak to the mechanisms underlying such effects ... Generally speaking, however, the field is in a relatively embryonic stage with current knowledge about underlying mechanisms woefully inadequate" (833). The unpacking of this node must therefore be left for later analysis in the field of social neuroscience.

Perceived Ease of Use
Perceived ease of use (PEU) is closely bound up with prior experience. It plays an important role in many models, perhaps because of it importance in the TAM model. Prior experience, in turn, is bound up with the social context in which the user finds him/herself (Wiedenbeck and Davis 1996). Tighter integration with social organization will result in more use. One must also take into consideration the element of repetition that plays a part in ease of use. Repetition, however, rarely comes without a technology or practice being integrated into common social practices, so there is some interplay here.

Attitude Toward Using
The attitude toward trusting a particular thing or person is governed obviously by personal factors toward its use. This includes the individual's predilection for trust based on biology and personal history. It is also affected by emotional factors that are unique to the individual. Social pressures, being an integral element in the socialization/affect continuum, also play a role.

Frame of Reference
A particular person's frame of reference in influenced by a number of things. It is not simply an additive product of the number of things he/she has encountered, or the number of times something has been encountered. It is filtered and influenced by what counts or is accepted by ones' social organization. It is also filtered by one's own frame of reference. It should also be noted that not all parts of our frame of reference are necessarily conscious.

3.2 Logic

Here we do not wish to commit ourselves to any particular logic. By the term we simple mean something like the sort of standard rule-based deductions that we are all familiar with.

Input

Any particular belief can have both positive (confirming) and negative (disconfirming) input. We do not call this proof or disproof for a reason. While we are not adhering to a naïve form of idealism here, we wish to emphasize that what counts as a fact, or even as sensory input, does not follow the rules that a naïve realist would like. Truth is perspectival – often, wildly perspectival.

Evidence for Believability of X

This node is the accumulation of all the times one has seen, heard, or otherwise experienced X. In a purely logical world, this would be the sum, so to speak, of the times one has experienced confirmation of X minus the times one had a disconfirming experience for X. However, the world, at least as humans experience it, is not logical. The more we might experience X, the less likely we are to attend to disconfirming evidence (and, of course, vice versa). Thus, "total" evidence for the believability of X is not a simple matter of subtraction. This also addresses the concept of risk. In a purely logical world, like the one of actuaries, risk can be mathematically calculated based on confirming and disconfirming evidence. But risk for our purposes, as in other concepts to do with trust, is really our *perception* of risk and it is *filtered* by our emotions and our social world – that is, the affective centers of our brain.

3.3 Analysis of Node Interactions

The reader should note that there is no particular order to the numbering of the edges. This was done intentionally. While there *might* be some ordering of this sequence during the formative stages of infants and children, by the time we reach adulthood, the interaction is anything *but* orderly.

(1) Positive input provides evidence for X, but it does not immediately cause one to believe X.

(2) Continued input provides reinforcement or strengthening of the belief that X is true or that X is false. This is basically the predictability of the object. We must question the strength of this, however. The ability to take continued evidence for X into consideration is mitigated by the affective side of human nature.

(3) Continued evidence provides beginning integration into social structures, but only slowly and as governed by the "laws" of Diffusion Theory. It is also filtered by social structures and social and personal values. This is also the arena of relative profit and loss for the individual and the society. There is no absolute character of this profit or loss. Its nature could be physical (e.g., money) or psychosocial (e.g., pride or reputation). The exact strength of the perceived profit or loss has to do with the values of the involved social organization and the individual. Kuhn (1970)

showed that this sort of social influence as to what counts as evidence for X occurs even in the hardest of sciences. Medicine, too, has recognized the interrelationship between belief, social structures, and physical health (Cacioppo et al 2000).

(4) Contrary evidence is mitigated by prior evidence. But, again, it is filtered by what one is psychologically/socially prepared to believe.

(5) and (6). Existing social structures, values, etc. can "interfere" with positive or negative input. It is also important to note, after Lewicki (1992), that the impact that these edges have on their respective edges are not necessarily conscious to the individual. Indeed, their effect may be not only "below the radar screen" of the individual but might not be recognized if spelled out. This is also true for 11 below.

(7) However, social integration and/or commitment influence PEU and attitude toward using.

(8) Deception detection is actively engaged in based on level of conflicting inputs (pro or con) and economic or personal value at stake.

(9) One's attitude toward using X and PEU are mutually interacting.

(10) Believability of X impacts frame of reference *but only as mediated/permitted by* social commitment to or integration of X.

(11) While what we know or believe to be true feeds into our frame of reference, social and personal values filter this knowledge.

(12) and (13) In so many of the models where the word "perceived" comes into play, this is what they mean. It is the perception of the reality of X as filtered through the affective/social continuum that we see represented.

(14) In this edge we recognize that one prior frame of reference, once built, and permitted to be built by one's feelings, perceptions, and one's social structures, affect what one is willing to include into one's further frame of reference.

Thus, feelings of and/or inclination to trust come from the affective side of our brain, not from the logical side. The best the logical side can do is to retroactively defend the decision made by the affective side. This, at the appropriate time, results in an act of trust.

4 Discussion

Our model produces a number of questions for future research and amplifies those put forward by other authors. Our model adds clarity to many of Corritore's questions, such as: (1) How does the perception of expertise or predictability affect on-line trust? (2) How does the perception of risk affect on-line trust? This resolves to issues of how we perceptually filter input, both based on previous experience and on our affective world. (3) How does on-line trust transfer from one website to another?

If the contentions of this paper are proven out, however, numerous other questions arise.

1. Does the work of Zheng et al (2002) apply for all cultures and all age groups? Do they hold for all age and ethnic groups?

2. What is the impact of the size of a society or community or organization in the applications and usefulness of trust? A starting point for this might be along the lines of Roes and Raymond (2003) in their discussion of morality in different sized societies.

3. Are there mechanisms that facilitate *trust* (community-based) from that which facilitates *confidence* (which is individual-based)? Here, Zak (2003) has made some initial suggestions about how it would be useful to figure out how to "activate social attachment mechanisms" (p.23) in order to facilitate trust.

4. What is the role and importance of collaborative filtering and recommender systems in developing a sense of community and trust in online groups?

5. An additional overarching issue from the point of view of organizational computing in general and e-commerce in particular is the *cost* of trust versus the cost of a (complex) legal system to support interactions (McEvily et al 2003, p.100). Costs, however, must be viewed not just in monetary terms but also in cognitive and societal terms.

Lastly, all this may be considered a prelude to developing a complete pragmatics, so to speak, of trust. It is pragmatics that analyzes the *use* of language. Therefore, instead of talking of a "grammar" of trust, as do McKnight and Chervany (2001), we would be better served talking about a pragmatics of trust, because trust is a behavior.

Much work clearly needs to be done in the field of trust. While it is my contention that old presumptions as to what trust is, and how well it is "commonly" understood, should be challenged, we should not rush to judgment. The first thing to be determined is through functional MRI imagery to determine *scientifically* which portions of the brain are active during the act of trust and it this differs from determination of trustworthiness and belief. This may well sounds like the crassest of reductionisms. In the end, however, it would seem that only by identifying the underlying mechanisms at work at the moment that the act of trust takes place can we resolve any fundamental disputes (Churchland 1988).

5 Conclusion

One might think that, given the emotional nature of trust, it would be better to eliminate it from considerations concerning action. One look at the social impairment of those who have lost their "emotional intelligence" inclines us otherwise. Emotional intelligence (Gardner 1993) has its roots in Thorndike's (1920) concept of social intelligence, which "is a type of social intelligence that involves the ability to monitor one's own and others' emotions, to discriminate among them, and to use the information to guide one's thinking and actions." This is in keeping with the results of neuroscience discovered in the past two decades.

We should not be put off by assigning trust to the inner reaches of human "information processing". Lewicki (Lewicki 1986, Lewicki, Hill, & Czyzewska 1992), for instance, has pointed out that we are capable of dealing with enormous complexity at the nonconscious level. However, unlike Lewicki, there is real reason to believe that we are not "processing algorithms" at a level below that of consciousness (Holtgraves and Ashley 2001), but that other mechanisms are at play.

The concept of trust as choice (that is to say, activity), and not as the end product of reason, may not seem so strange if we remember Austin's (1962) groundbreaking work in speech act theory. Up to that time, most linguists and philosophers considered language as being made up of propositions that were either true or false. Austin showed that there was a (large) part of speech that could better be viewed as activity, which activity was either felicitous or infelicitous.

The reader should not feel that we are somehow asking our brave, new world to surrender to our darker past. Rules of logical reasoning are certainly important to rationality, but they are hard pressed to adequately and completely represent the way we represent and interact with the world (see, e.g., Waskan 2003). Rational behavior is impossible without *either* reason *or* emotion. Both are required for rationality. Both are required to pass any *real* Turing Test.

But if trust is not purely logical, but emanates from the affective centers of the brain, trust in a virtual world becomes more problematic – though not necessarily ineffable. The implications of this revised view of trust for the building trust in "virtual" societies must be addressed. If such issues are not resolved, trust may suffer the same, disappointing fate as artificial intelligence (Winograd 2000). If we proceed with an incomplete notion of trust, the prospect for the integration of agent technology with humans in cyberspace is poor. For these reasons, a deeper discussion of trust and its nature in a virtual world is needed. At the very least, we must understand that trust, and its betrayal, are not built and repaired like the algorithms of a computer program.

This being the case, talk of trust and a society of artificial agents is especially premature. Trust, as we know it, implies proximity (Weirich and Sasse 2002). What sort of proximity does an artificial agent have?

Until we *really* understand the essence of trust, we must put human agents together as the center of trusting agreement. Once we do really understand trust, we will realize we need to put human agents at the center of design. Simply supplying more data is not the answer. Culture is the foundation of the "trusted interface", not programming. Instead of stressing trustworthiness, or belief, or credibility, it would seem that the emphasis should be placed on demonstrating shared *values* between those wanting to be trusted and those expected to give trust.

It has been suggested that what we need is to build computers that recognize and then reason about human emotions. This, too, is problematic. Is the concept of "reasoning about emotions", practically speaking, an oxymoron (Hollnagel 2003, for a discussion of and rejoinders to this opinion, see Hudlicka 2003, McNeese 2003, Picard 2003)? Please understand that Hollnagel does not contend (nor do I) that we cannot understand emotion. But if all that reason is is making logical deductions based on input, is it sensible to "reason about emotions?" And if, on the other hand, reason entails emotion, is the concept of reasoning about emotion far more curious – yet at the same time more possible? Are we the creatures of pure reason? Or are we, at best (and most remarkably), creatures with the ability to reflect? Perhaps, at most (for the time being), computers should be built that recognize a breakdown in communication (Winograd and Flores 1986) and immediately check with a human being.

In the end, however, without trust, we can only rely on laws and the courts. While laws and the courts certainly have their place in modern society, we should ask if trust is a more efficient – or effective – mechanism for managing social interactions. And if so, are there size or other limitations on it?

Acknowledgement

The author would like to thank two anonymous reviewers for their comments, and for their attempts to call me back to my senses. I know that addressing their concerns has only improved this paper. Whatever weaknesses remain are purely my own.

References

Austin, J.L.: How to Do Things with Words. Harvard University Press, Cambridge, MA (1962)

Ba, S., Whinston, A.B., Zhang, H.: Building Trust in Online Markets through an Economic Incentive Mechanism. Decision Support Systems. 35 (2003) 273-286

Baier, A.: Trust and Antitrust. Ethics. 96(2) (1986) 231-260

Bechara, A., Damásio, A. R., Damásio, H., Anderson, S.: Insensitivity to future Consequences Following Damage to Human Prefrontal Cortex. Cognition. 50 (1994) 7-12

Bhattacharya, R., & Devinney, T.: A Formal Model of Trust Based on Outcomes. Academy of Management Review. 23(3) (1998) 459-472

Bos, N, Olson, J., Gergle, D., Olson, G., Wright, Z.: Effects of Four Computer-Mediated Communications Channels on Trust Development. HICSS. 2002 135-140

Brothers, L.: Friday's Footprints. Oxford University Press, Oxford (1997)

Cacioppo, J.T., Berntson, G.G., Sheridan, J.G., McClintock, M.K.: Multilevel Integrative Analysis of Human Behavior: Social Neuroscience and the Complementing Nature of Social and Biological Approaches. Psychological Bulletin. 126(6) (2000) 829-843

Churchland, P.M.: Matter and Consciousness. MIT Press, Cambridge, MA (1988)

Cushing, B.S., Carter, C.S.: Prior Exposure to Oxytocin Mimics the Effects of Social Contact and Facilitates Sexual Behavior in Females. Journal of Neuroendocrinology 11 (1999) 765-769

Damasio, A. R.: The Feeling of What Happens: Body and Emotion in the Making of Consciousness. Harcourt, New York (1999)

Damasio, A. R.: Descartes' Error: Emotion, Reason and the Human Brain. Quill, New York (2000)

Damasio, A. R.: Looking for Spinoza: Joy, Sorrow, and the Feeling Brain. Harcourt, New York (2003)

Darwin, C.: The Expression of the Emotions in Man and Animals. Philosophical Library, New York (1872)

Evans, D.: Emotion: The Science of Sentiment. Oxford University Press, Oxford (2002)

Fonlupt, P.: Perception and Judgment of Physical Causality Involve Different Brain Structures. Cognitive Brain Research. (2003) 17 248-254.

Fukuyama, F.: Trust : The Social Virtues and the Creation of Prosperity. The Free Press, New York (1995)

Gardner, H.: Multiple Intelligences. Basic Books, New York (1993)

Gefen, D., Karahanna, E., Straub, D.W.: Trust and TAM in Online Shopping: An Integrated Model. MIS Quarterly. 27(1) (2003) 51-90

Giddens, A.: The Consequences of Modernity. Stanford University Press, Stanford, CA (1990)

Granovetter, M.S.: The Strength of Weak Ties. The American Journal of Sociology, 78 (1973) 1360-1380

Greenspan, S., Goldberg, D. Weimar, D., Basso, A.: Interpersonal Trust and Common Ground in Electronically Mediated Communication. Proceedings of the Conference on Computer Supported Cooperative Work 2000 (2000) ACM Press 251-260

Hare, R. D., Quinn, M. J. (1971): Psychopathy and Autonomic Conditioning. Journal of Abnornal Psychology, 77, 223-235

Hollnagel, E. (2003): Is Affective Computing an Oxymoron?. International Journal of Human-Computer Studies, 59 (1-2), 65-70

Holtgraves, T., Ashley, A. (2001): Comprehending Illocutionary Force. Memory and Cognition, 29 (1), 83-90

Hudlicka, E. (2003): To Feel or Not to Feel: The Role of Affect in Human–Computer Interaction. International Journal of Human-Computer Studies, 59 (1-2), 1-32

Kuhn, T.: Structure of Scientific Revolution (2nd ed.). University of Chicago Press, Chicago (1970)

Lewicki, P.: Nonconscious Social Information Processing. Elsevier, Den Haag (1986)

Lewicki, P., Hill, T. Czyzewska, M.: Nonconscious Acquisition of Information. American Psychologist. 47 (1992) 796-801

McEvily, B., Perrone, V., Zaheer, A.: Trust as an Organizing Principle. Organization Science. 14(1) (2003) 91-103

McKnight, D. H. Chervany, N. L.: Trust and Distrust Definitions: One Bite at a Time. In: Falcone, R. Singh, M., Tan, Y. H. (Eds.) Trust in Cyber-Societies: Integrating the Human and Artificial Perspectives. Springer, Berlin (2001) 27-54

McNeese, M.D.: New Visions of Human–Computer Interaction: Making Affect Compute. International Journal of Human-Computer Studies. 59(1-2) (2003) 33-53

Montgomery, A., Dolphin, L.: Is the Velocity of Light Constant in Time? Downloaded from http://www.ldolphin.org/constc.shtml on June 30 (2004)

Park, H. S., Levine, T.R., McCornack, S. A., Morrison, K., Ferrara, M.: How People Really Detect Lies. Communication Monographs. 69 (2002) 144-157

Pearce, W.B.: Trust in Personal Communication. Speech Monographs. 41 (1974) 236-244

Picard, R.: Affective Computing: Challenges. International Journal of Human-Computer Studies. 59(1-2) (2003) 55-64

Platek, S.M., Burch, R.L., Panyavin, I.S., Wasserman, B.H., Gallup, G.G., Jr.: Reactions to Children's Faces: Resemblance Matters More for Males than Females. Evolution and Human Behavior. 23(3) (2002) 159-166

Roes, F.L., Raymond, M.: Belief in Moralizing Gods. Evolution and Human Behaviour. 24 (2003) 126-135

Rogers, E.: The diffusion of Innovation (4th ed.). New York: The Free Press (1996)

Thorndike, E.L.: Intelligence and its Uses. Harper's Magazine. 140 (1920) 227-235

Waskan, J.A.: Intrinsic Cognitive Models. Cognitive Science, 27 (2003) 259-283

Wiedenbeck, S., Davis, S.: The Influence of Interaction Style and Experience on User Perceptions of Software Packages. International Journal of Human–Computer Studies, 46 (1997) 563–587

Weirich, D., Sasse, M. A.: Pretty Good Persuasion: A First Step Towards Effective Password Security in the Real World. NSPW'01, ACM Press (2002) 137-143

Winograd, T., Flores, F.: Understanding Computers and Cognition. Addison Wesley, New York (1986)

Winograd, T.: Forward. In: Heidegger, Coping and Cognitive Science. Volume 1. Wrathall,M., Malpas, J. (eds.). MIT University Press, Cambridge, MA (2000) vii-ix

Woods, W.J. and Binson, D.: Gay bathhouses and public health policy. Hawthorne Press, Binghamton, NY (2003)

Zak, P. J.: Trust. Retrieved from http://faculty.egu.edu/~zakp/publications/CAPCOTrust.pdf on June 9 (2003)

Zheng, J., E. Neinott, N. Bos, J. S. Olson, & G. M. Olson: Trust Without Touch: Jumpstarting Long-Distance Trust with Initial Social Activities. HICSS (2002) 141-146

Reinventing Forgiveness: A Formal Investigation of Moral Facilitation

Asimina Vasalou and Jeremy Pitt

Intelligent Systems and Networks Group,
Electrical and Electronic Engineering Department,
Imperial College London,
Exhibition Road,
London SW7 2BT
{a.vasalou, j.pitt}@imperial.ac.uk

Abstract. Reputation mechanisms have responded to the ever-increasing demand for online policing by "collecting, distributing and aggregating feedback about participants' past behavior". But unlike in human societies where forbidden actions are coupled with legal repercussions, reputation systems fulfill a socially-oriented duty by alerting the community's members on one's good standing. The decision to engage in collaborative efforts with another member is chiefly placed in the hands of each individual. This form of people empowerment sans litigation brings forth a moral concern: in human-human interactions, a violation of norms and standards is unavoidable but not unforgivable. Driven by the prosocial benefits of forgiveness, this paper proposes ways of facilitating forgiveness between offender and victim through the use of personal 'moral' agents. We suggest that a richer mechanism for regulating online behaviour can be developed, one that integrates trust, reputation *and* forgiveness.

1 Introduction

Recently, there has been a push towards facilitating forgiveness in a number of fields such as law, psychology, theology and organizational management [5]. This is motivated by the homeostatic potential that forgiveness offers both to victim and offender as members of an autonomic society. In spite of the ongoing arguments on its suitability in certain situations, forgiveness, encompassing the *prosocial decision to adapt a positive attitude towards another,* warrants further investigation for its use in regulating online behavior. In this article we consider its role in online communities where, similar to physical worlds, certain forms of conduct that are expected of a member are frequently violated.

At present, the 'management' of human behavior online has been placed in the hands of technology. A number of trust and reputation mechanisms have emerged that operate *quantitatively* by "collecting, distributing and aggregating feedback about participants' past behaviors" [21]. But despite their success, dishonest members have persisted and found new ways to trick the system [6, 13]. In developing complementary 'behavior-controlling' solutions, there is a need to continue

P. Herrmann et al. (Eds.): iTrust 2005, LNCS 3477, pp. 146–160, 2005.

uncovering the roots of this phenomenon. Until now, research has focused on addressing the implications of anonymity [10, 7]. The lack of social context cues is also considered another cause for investigation [3, 23]. We argue that in addition to the above contributors, the "quantification" of human behavior (i.e. performance ratings) removes important human coping mechanisms which in physical worlds add value to human relationships and provide closure during their disruption (i.e. the ability to apologize). For example, the act of issuing forgiveness alone is known to stimulate the offender into positive actions of repair [2, 11]. In the absence of forgiveness or reversal mechanisms, the offender is deprived of those reparative outlets. Moreover, punishing the offender for a low intent action (i.e. tarred reputation for accidentally delivering the wrong product) will often result in anger and low-compliancy behaviors [11], in our context possibly leading to withdrawal from the unjust community. Consequently, alongside the continuous quantitative enhancements of trust and reputation mechanisms, we aim at a more *qualitative* proposal. Informed by its prosocial effects, we are interested in a technology-mediated facilitation of forgiveness as a way to motivate prosocial behaviors online and inhibit harmful ones.

Our future focus on the subject of forgiveness is threefold: first, we aim to develop a formal computational model inspired by human forgiveness; second, to design a tool that supports rule violation reports and links victim to offender to facilitate forgiveness; third, for evaluation purposes, to conduct observations of human behavior over time. We begin addressing the first point by presenting the theory of forgiveness as the basis for a formal computational model.

In section 2 of this article we describe the context of our work 'DigitalBlush', in which our model of forgiveness will be embedded. Section 3 presents the subject of forgiveness from the perspective of philosophy and psychology. We go on in section 4 to discuss the positive motivations that work to overturn one's initial censure and to facilitate forgiveness. In section 5 and 6, we propose a theoretical design and application domain for a forgiveness model, envisioned to integrate with current trust and reputation mechanisms. Finally in section 7, we conclude with a discussion on future directions.

2   DigitalBlush: Setting the Context

DigitalBlush is grounded on the belief that shame and embarrassment, if experienced during online interactions, can control otherwise uninhibited human behaviors. The controller function of shame and embarrassment within human societies is the guiding force behind this conviction [22]. Given time, DigitalBlush aspires to evolve into a transparent emotional and socio-cognitive layer subsumed within greater human-human networked interactions. The two layers will materialize the experience of shame and embarrassment by (1) strengthening one's sense of self and others awareness, (2) bridging cultural differences, (3) accounting for gender variances, (4) attaching value to one's identity and reputation as such, and (5) displaying social implications in response to one's actions [for a full discussion see 24].

The aforementioned tactics are directed towards inducing emotion and implicitly controlling unwanted behaviors. The process of reaching such an objective is complex and involves many facets, including the consequences of a shameful action. Assuming that one violates a standard and as a result experiences shame or embarrassment, what is the next natural progression within the cycle of emotion-reaction? According to the appeasement theory [12], the next progression, the relationship restoration between victim/observer and offender qualifies the very existence of embarrassment in the human species. Shame and embarrassment are followed by identifiable external signals (i.e. the blush) which in turn serve to appease and pacify observers or victims of social transgressions. Hence, the emotion display plays an important role in exposing the offender's violation acknowledgement. This acknowledgement may prompt sympathy or *forgiveness* from others during more serious transgressions and amusement during milder ones. Consequently, in the DigitalBlush setting, the interplay between one's acknowledgment and another's forgiveness is of paramount importance as it follows the natural cycle of emotion-reaction and extends even further than that to influence a fellow member's judgment. While DigitalBlush as a whole is not the focus of this article, our work on forgiveness will at times blend with shame and embarrassment as discussed in psychology.

Our work here considers a DigitalBlush community brought together in a distance learning setting. In this community, participants (i.e. students, professors and administrators) will connect with other members via their personal agents (see section 6 for more details). Each DigitalBlush member will participate in team activities such as project assignments and will carry certain responsibilities towards their fellow members. In the sections to follow, we will exemplify our forgiveness proposals through a number of hypothetical distance learning scenarios involving two members, Nick and Lidia.

We will be using several terms interchangeably. A 'violation of norms or standards', an 'immoral act', an 'offence' or a 'transgression' constitute of a rule being broken. The rules governing each community naturally vary and should be treated as independent factors (i.e. delivering a bad product in a transactional community vs. delivering a late assignment in a distance learning community). 'Observer' or 'victim' respectively refers to the witness or to the one harmed as a result of another's violation. The 'transgressor' or 'offender' is a member who violated a rule, may have harmed others in the process and who awaits their 'predicament' be that punishment, forgiveness or redemption from the observer or witness.

3 Forgiveness

3.1 A Formal Definition

Forgiveness is proposed to result from a *number of prosocial motivational changes which reverse one's initial desire to adopt negative strategies towards the transgressor* (i.e. revenge, avoidance). In this sense, forgiveness replaces malevolent motivations towards the transgressor with constructive and positive behaviors which work to reverse the initial censure [16]. The forgiveness process as described in psychology, is further illustrated in Fig. 1 where the offender, member x violates a rule with action A. Following victim y's, negative predisposition towards offending action A, six positive motivations collectively add up to possibly formulate forgiveness. The positive motivations we consider are empathy, actions of repair, historical relationship of victim-offender, frequency and severity of past actions, severity of current action and intent (see section 4 for a full discussion). The definition proposed, employs a degree of freedom in long-term relationships as one may forgive a single transgression without explicitly reversing their attitude as a whole [16]. Likewise, while a certain violation may be forgiven, other past behaviors may still impede one's trust towards another. Despite popular definitions of forgiveness, forgetting, condoning, trusting or removing accountability are not necessarily considered to be a part of forgiveness [5].

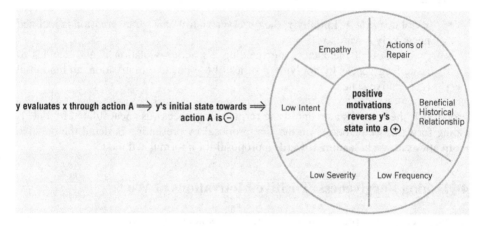

Fig. 1. A motivation-driven conceptualization of forgiveness where positive motivations add up to increase forgiveness

In the following discussion we adhere to an overarching moral tenet; in any social community, be that an agent environment or a human society, the transgressor and victim have equal value as people. The victim and the overall community value this tenet and as a result assess the transgressor's act rather than his/her worth as a person [9].

3.2 The Gray Areas

There are areas still unknown or controversial in nature on the subject of forgiveness. First, there are opposing arguments in granting forgiveness. On one hand, it has been empirically established that forgiveness may lead to constructive behaviors such as volunteering [11], attributed to the transgressor's reciprocal debt towards his 'benefactor'. This positive consequence may occur only when the transgressor takes responsibility and cares about his/her action. On the other end of the spectrum, it is argued that in the absence of punishment, the one in violation is spared of responsibility and is therefore encouraged to maintain a harmful position [9]. As a consequence, issuing forgiveness is risky and should be granted responsibly, with consideration for *relevant circumstances* surrounding the violation (e.g. the action's severity). Second, there is little known on what types of transgressions lead to forgiveness [5]. For example, there is no consensus on forgiveness in the event of a confidant revealing a friend's secret to another. In the proposed model to follow, we find answers in the motivation-driven definition of forgiveness as described above (see section 3.1). We consider the 'relevant circumstances' (e.g. severity, intent, actions of repair, etc.) to accumulatively stimulate a number of positive motivations, as a result, replacing ones' initial negative inclination and summing up to form forgiveness. By this choice, we circumvent subjective judgments on the transgression's type by adapting a more quantitative and multivariate approach. In sum, we propose the following:

Proposal 1

- x violates *rule A*. Initially y, the observer/victim of x's transgression is inclined negatively towards x
- y assesses all the factors surrounding x's action-violation A and decides to issue forgiveness by applying a series of (+) positive motivations to his initial (-) negative state

Proposal 1, the formal statement of the forgiveness process, is encapsulated by Fig. 1. Going forward, we elaborate on the first proposal by presenting in detail the positive motivations at work, leading towards a proposal for a formulated model.

4   Issuing Forgiveness: Positive Motivations at Work

In this section, we present three central components of a forgiveness model. We exclusively consider the positive motivations at work. Justifying our choice, is the victim's initial disposition which automatically factors negative coping mechanisms such as vengefulness into the agent's/actor's state (y's initial judgment towards action A is negative).

4.1   Violation Appraisal

Observers/victims of one's transgression make certain attributions by accounting for a number of factors surrounding the offence. First, the severity of the current act is assessed. More severe violations lead to harsher judgments [1, 2]. Furthermore, a historical trail of one's past behaviors is compared against the current violation. Together, frequency and severity of past acts impact one's inclination to forgive [2]. Additionally, apparent intent leads towards more negative attributions with low intent actions supporting more positive attributions [1, 14]. The interaction between intent and forgiveness has even stronger consequences on the transgressor's side. Low intent actions followed by retribution against the transgressor may result in low-compliancy, anger and even retaliation. On the other hand, low intent actions followed by forgiveness often motivate the transgressor into reciprocal actions of repair [11].

Proposal 2

- y assesses x's action by (severity) AND (frequency/severity of x's historical actions) AND (intent)

- x cares about action A. Upon receiving forgiveness, x repays y by offering reparative action B
- x cares about action A. Upon receiving retribution from y, x engages in a lower number of future interactions with y

Hypothetical example: Nick delivers a team assignment two days after its' due date. His tardiness will likely impact the overall team's grade. Although his action is considered very serious by his peers (high severity action), Nick has been timely during his past assignments. In addition to that, the previous week he had a number of school exams contributing to his tardiness (low intent). Upon receiving forgiveness from his teammates, Nick offers to do more work during the next assignment (reparative action).

4.2 Reversal and Restitution

Apology and restitution together constitute a strong partnership facilitating and even predicting forgiveness [25]. Furthermore, it is also possible to reverse one's immoral act by performing a good deed [2]. Inferred from the appeasement theory (see section 2), a truthful apology or a good deed, parallel to a disconcerted façade can in fact pacify the observer or victim and therefore lead to forgiveness. However, reversing one's violation with a reparative action brings up an important issue. Inevitably the weight of a good deed against a severe and frequently performed violation will have to be formulated.

Proposal 3

- y issues forgiveness if x offers (an apology) AND/OR (reparative action B $>=$ action A)

Hypothetical example: Nick contributes poor quality work for his final team project. Upon being confronted by his teammates, Nick apologizes (apology) and spends the next few days rewriting his team contribution (reparative action). Later in the week, he receives an email from his teammates thanking him for his work (forgiveness).

4.3 Pre-existing Factors: Historical Interactions and Personal Dispositions

There are several pre-existing factors positively predisposing the observer/victim towards the transgressor. First, prior familiarity and a relationship of commitment with the transgressor increase the likelihood of forgiveness [17]. Good friends or successful business partners rely on a richer and mutually-rewarding history fostering a propensity towards forgiveness. Second, empathy, one's emotional response towards another's affect [8] is regarded as a mediator, appeasing the victim and facilitating forgiveness. Empathy is evoked by transgressors' apologies among others, is a predictor of forgiveness and its intensity has been found to positively correlate to the extent of forgiveness the victim issues for the transgressor [18]. But even more pertinent to DigitalBlush, empathy manifests in embarrassment to form 'empathic embarrassment', a milder form of embarrassment 'incurred' by imagining oneself in another's place. Empathic embarrassment has several determinants:

- The salience of the transgressor's embarrassment controls the degree of felt empathic embarrassment. Visibly embarrassed transgressors elicit more empathic embarrassment from others.
- The emotion intensifies when the victim is somewhat familiar to the transgressor. The nature of past interactions (i.e. cooperative vs. competitive) appears to have little influence on the emotion experience although males tend to be more empathic towards competitive partners perhaps supporting known gender role differences, see e.g. [4].
- We foster stronger feelings of empathy towards those who are most similar to us in terms of personality or characteristics (i.e. a colleague or a cultural compatriot).
- The observer's propensity to embarrassment determines to a great degree the empathic embarrassment s/he may experience. A highly 'embarrassable' observer will experience increased empathic embarrassment [19]. At the same time, when the salience of the transgressor's embarrassment is visibly intense, propensity towards embarrassment is overpowered and plays a more secondary role [15].

If we consider the intricacies of judgment and violation appraisal (see section 4.1), an extensive history of severe violations and apparent intent should extinguish feelings of empathy or empathic embarrassment altogether. At the opposite end, observers who share a similar history of harmful behaviors with the transgressor may be more empathic and consequently more forgiving.

In sum, empathy and empathic embarrassment both share the same function mediated by different factors, a truthful apology versus a genuine façade respectively. Similar to the workings of empathy, a transgressors' visible embarrassment embodies an apology by acknowledgement of his/her act. Consequently, the transgressor's expression-genuineness will induce empathic embarrassment the same as a truthful apology will evoke empathy. On the basis of the previous discussion we propose the following:

Proposal 6

- y will issue forgiveness if y and x have had (a number of prior interactions) AND (x's past actions have been beneficial to y)

Hypothetical example: Nick contributes medium quality work (medium severity action) for his final team project. His teammates know that in the past, he has always paid attention to detail (past beneficial interaction) and as a result decide he should be forgiven.

Proposal 7

- The extent of y's forgiveness will vary by the (degrees of empathy/empathic embarrassment y feels for x)

- *y* will experience empathic embarrassment if (*x's* embarrassment is visibly intense) AND/OR (if *y* has met *x* before) AND/OR (if *x* shares similar characteristics to *y*) AND/OR (if *y's* propensity to embarrassment is high)
- *y* will feel more empathy for *x* if (*y's* past actions are similar in nature to *x's* current violation)

Hypothetical example: Nick contributes moderate quality of work for his final team project (medium severity action). Upon confrontation, his embarrassment becomes visibly intense (visible acknowledgment). Lidia who has experienced a similar situation in the past (similar past history) feels empathy towards Nick and as a result is more inclined to forgive.

In the section to follow, we discuss the complexity of the motivations' interactions through an example in psychology. In overcoming this challenge, we propose a solution that permits multiple interactions between motivations (e.g. empathy) and their constituent parts (e.g. visible acknowledgment) but also accommodates their variable weights.

5 Motivation Interactions Towards a Formal Model Proposal

5.1 Illustrating the Complexities

The theoretical work we have considered so far, with the exception of Boon and Sulsky's study [1], has measured each motivation's workings separately. A need prevails for a more elaborate model that describes the weights and interactions of each motivation. We briefly revisit Boon and Sulsky's work to better illustrate the challenge we are faced with. In an experiment examining forgiveness and blame attributions, the three judgment cues of *offense severity*, *avoidance* and *intent* were measured. Results of this study indicated different weights for each of these judgment cues, depending on blame or forgiveness attributions. More specific to our current interest, in forgiveness judgments, there was less inter-rating subject agreement in cue weights and interactions [1]. Most notably, through this example we are able to glimpse at the complexity of those interactions and identify an important issue: *how does one weigh one motivation against another and which one exerts the most influence?*

5.2 Model Proposal

In addressing the previous question, we accommodate the motivations, their underlying components and relevant weights in a model that functions as a shared-decision, illustrated in Fig. 2.

In the theoretical model shown in Fig. 2, the *judgment of offence* carries the most weight. Following its assessment, a forgiveness percentage is calculated. Next, the remaining three motivations (historical relationship, empathy and actions of repair) are calculated similarly and then compared against the judgment of offence percentage (see appendix A, tables 1-4). We justify this choice with the following example: If a truthful apology follows a low offence judgment, forgiveness may be possible, while the same apology following a high offence judgment may not suffice.

Crucially, the valence of the various motivations and their composite parts, will work in two opposite ways, increasing or decreasing the probability to forgive.

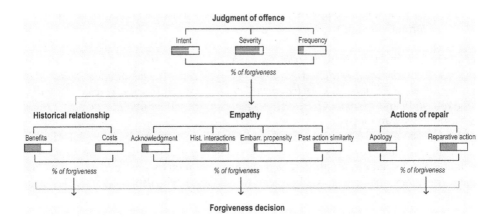

Fig. 2. A theoretical model of forgiveness: Each motivation contributes in degrees towards or against forgiveness

5.3 Context-Dependent Violations

Taking a brief look at ongoing online communities, it is apparent that what constitutes a violation in one, may not be considered a severe offence in another. A community driven by economic motives such as e-Bay may not find someone's contrived personality as serious as an emotional-support community. Each forum may experience a number of context-dependent violations making a rule-based model such as the one of forgiveness, reliant on context.

We employ a user-centered approach to address this issue. We plan to distribute two surveys to end users of our distance learning community. One will elicit possible violations through a series of open ended questions while the other will request users to attribute quantitative forgiveness ratings on the dimensions of intent, severity and frequency. These results, representing the community as a whole, will inform us in two ways. First, the list of given violations will encompass the community's rules. Second, the consensual judgment ratings (intent, severity, frequency) will be integrated into the 'judgment of offence' table (see appendix A, table 1). As a result, the final computational model will in part rely on violations users of the community have identified and judgment ratings as perceived by the community.

6 Application Domain and Platform Design

We employ the term *Socio-Cognitive grids* for our platform design and tool facilitation. This definition allows us to consider both resources of networked computing and human participants as constituent parts of a single, unified grid [20]. Consequently, the DigitalBlush community will be brought together in a distance learning setting. Participants of this community (i.e. students, professors and administrators) will connect with other members via their personal agents termed 'moral agents' (see Fig. 3). Each DigitalBlush member will perform team activities such as project assignments and will carry certain responsibilities towards their fellow members. Among other possibilities, in the context of this community a dishonest exchange of information (i.e. not delivering a promised assignment) will constitute a violation.

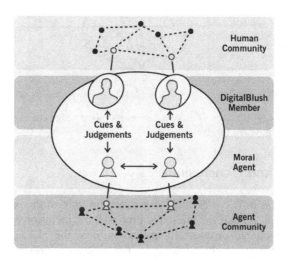

Fig. 3. Networked-Interaction between two actors where their moral agents promote cues which are lost during computer-mediated communication and support prosocial judgments

Our platform will support a number of exchanges. (1) Communication will be maintained across time, synchronously and asynchronously. (2) Each member will be represented in the community by their personal moral agent. (3) Moral agents will work as intelligent communicators. As illustrated in Fig. 3, they will carry social cues from one member to another and in reverse. Social cues will transmit emotional expressions from the sender and as a result they will support emotion interpretation by the receiver. But more to our current interest, moral agents will employ intelligence acquired over time to advise their human counterpart when forgiveness is appropriate (see Fig. 4). For example, in a low severity offence, a moral agent will assess the interaction partner's historical information and communicate a moral judgment to its human end. Ultimately, forgiveness will be issued by the human participant, making the role of the agent primarily one of intelligent and prosocial facilitation.

Hypothetical example: Nick's agent delivers low quality work to Lidia's agent. Upon receiving the work deliverable, Lidia notifies her agent about the violation. Her agent presents her with the benefits she has had from her collaboration with Nick (historical relationship), reminds her of a similar offence she had committed a few months ago (similarity of past actions) and that this incident is Nick's first offence (frequency). Lidia reconsiders her position and decides to give Nick another opportunity (reparative action).

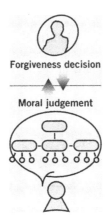

Fig. 4. Forgiveness facilitation: The agent carries its moral judgment to the actor who conveys back to his agent a possible forgiveness decision

7 Summary and Conclusions

To summarize, this article presented forgiveness in light of the prosocial and healing benefits it brings to human societies. We proposed the inclusion of forgiveness online as a way to encourage prosocial behaviors both in the victim and offender. The motivation behind our work is the reparative nature of forgiveness in some cases, while the destructive consequences of its absence in others. We went on to discuss the formation of forgiveness by the collective 'accumulation' of positive motivations. Resulting from this definition, we laid the foundation for a computational model, additively shaped by the motivations' interactions. Finally, we presented the preliminary design for a facilitation tool of forgiveness where agents' judgments are informed by historical, pertinent to the offence information and then effectively communicated to their human ends.

The objective of this article was to discuss the constituent parts of forgiveness and to bring forward this neglected but yet significant topic. Although psychology offers positive prospects for forgiveness applications, we cannot neglect the possible challenges we may face when implementing and integrating such a model in a computer-mediated environment. First, forgiveness may encourage harmful behaviors by withdrawing well-deserved punishment. As in many applications, users may 'hijack' the system and find ways to manipulate it to their advantage. Therefore, a coherent computational model of forgiveness is vital as well as responsible and careful facilitation. Second, colloquial beliefs of forgiveness demonstrate the confusion between forgiveness and other consequential ramifications. Forgiveness does not necessarily absolve one from their past harmful actions. It may be coupled with punishment or other mitigating reactions. We intend to address this second point with the design of clear and communicative language during agent-to-human facilitation. Third, the 'collection' and presentation of judgment factors may enhance prosocial decisions during offences that warrant forgiveness but they may have the opposite effect during severe offences that are well-deserving of punishment. Online users are overall more uninhibited and hostile [3, 23] compared to their offline conduct. One could clearly argue that due to this online disposition, higher severity offences emphasized by moral agents' assessments may support unjustifiably severe punishments. Although this argument is hypothetical, it can be adequately inferred by the current literature and its consequences should be accounted for. Concluding, we end this article by acknowledging the challenges we face and at the same time by emphasizing the promise of our proposal, where socio-cognitive and affective mechanisms may promote prosocial gestures amongst online members, ultimately contributing to a genuine social cohesion.

Acknowledgements

This research was funded by the HUMAINE IST Framework VI Network of Excellence. We would like to thank two anonymous reviewers for their comments.

References

1. Boon, S., & Sulsky, L.: Attributions of Blame and Forgiveness in Romantic Relationships: A Policy-capturing Study. Journal of Social Behavior and Personality, Vol. 12, (1997) 19-26
2. Buss, A. H.: Self-consciousness and social anxiety. San Francisco, CA: W. H. Freeman (1980)
3. Collins, M.: Flaming: The relationship Between Social Context Cues and Uninhibited Verbal Behaviour in Computer-mediated Communication. [On-line]. Available: http://www.emoderators.com/papers/flames.html (1992)
4. Efthim, P.W., Kenny, M.E., Mahalik, J.R.: Gender Role Stress in Relation to Shame, Guilt, and Externalization. Journal of Counseling & Development, Vol. 79, (2001) 430-438
5. Exline, J. J.,Worthington, E. L., Jr., Hill, P., & McCullough, M. E: Forgiveness and justice: A research agenda for social and personality psychology. Personality and Social Psychology Review, Vol. 7, (2003) 337-348
6. Grady, D.: Faking pain and suffering on the Internet. The New York Times, (1998)
7. Friedman, E. & Resnick, P. The Social Cost of Cheap Pseudonyms. Journal of Economics and Management Strategy, Vol. 10(2), (1999) 173-199
8. Gruen, R. J. & Mendelsohn, G.: Emotional responses to affective displays in others: The distinction between empathy and sympathy. Journal of Personality & Social Psychology, Vol. 51, (1986) 609-614
9. Holmgren, M.R.: Forgiveness and the intrinsic value of persons. American Philosophical Quarterly, Vol. 30(4), (1993) 341-451
10. Johnson, D.: Ethics Online: Shaping social behavior online takes more than new laws and modified edicts. Communications of the ACM, Vol. 40(1), (1997) 60-65
11. Kelln, B.R.C., & Ellard, J.H.: An equity theory analysis of the impact of forgiveness and retribution on transgressor compliance. Personality and Social Psychology Bulletin, Vol. 25, (1999) 864-872
12. Keltner, D., & Buswell, B. N.: Embarrassment: Its distinct form and appeasement functions. Psychological Bulletin, Vol. 122, (1997) 250-270
13. Kong, D. Internet auction fraud increases. USA Today, (2000)

14. Manstead, A.S.R., & Semin, G.R.: Social transgression, social perspectives, and social emotionality. Motivation and Emotion, Vol. 5, (1981) 249-261
15. Marcus, D. K., Wilson, J. R., & Miller, R. S.: Are perceptions of emotion in the eye of the beholder? A social relations analysis of judgments of embarrassment. Personality and Social Psychology Bulletin, Vol. 22, (1996) 1220-1228
16. McCullough, M.: Forgiveness who does it and how do they do it. (2001) Retrieved on 10.10.2005, http://www.psychologicalscience.org/members/journal_issues/cd/cdir1061.pdf
17. McCullough, M. E., Rachal, K.C., Sandage, S. J., Worthington, E. L., Brown, S. W., and Hight, T. L.: Interpersonal Forgiving in Close Relationships: II. Theoretical Elaboration and Measurement. Journal of Personality and Social Psychology, Vol. 75, (1998) 1586-1603
18. McCullough, M.E., Worthington, Jr., E.L., & Rachal, K.C.: Interpersonal forgiving in close relationships. Journal of Personality and Social Psychology, Vol. 73(2), (1997) 321-336
19. Miller, R. S.: Empathic embarrassment: Situational and personal determinants of reactions to the embarrassment of another. Journal of Personality and Social Psychology, Vol. 53, (1987) 1061-1069
20. Pitt J, Artikis A. Socio-cognitive grids: a partial ALFEBIITE perspective. In proceedings of the First international workshop on socio-cognitive grids. Santorini, Greece, (2003)
21. Resnick, P., Zeckhauser, R., Friedman, E., & Kuwabara, K.: Reputation Systems. Communications of the ACM, (2000)
22. Scheff, E.J.: The shame-rage spiral: A case study of an interminable quarrel. In H.B. Lewis (ed.): The role of shame in symptom formation. Hillsdale, NJ: Erlbaum (1987)
23. Sproull, L. & Kiesler, S.: Reducing social context cues: Electronic mail in organizational communication. Management Science, Vol. 32, (1986) 1492-1512
24. Vasalou, A. & Pitt, J.: DigitalBlush: Towards a self-conscious community. In proceedings of AISB, Conversational Informatics Symposium, (2005)
25. Witvliet, C.V.O., Worthington, E.L., Jr., Wade, N.G., & Berry, J. W.: Justice and forgiveness: Three experimental studies. Christian Association of Psychological Studies, Arlington Heights, (2002)

Appendix: A

Table 1. Judgment of Offence

#	1	2	3	4	5	6	7	8
Intent	++	++	++	++	--	--	--	--
Frequency	--	++	++	--	--	++	++	--
Severity	--	++	--	++	--	++	--	++
Forgiveness	%	%	%	%	%	%	%	%

Table 2. Repairative actions

#	1	2	3	4	5	6	7	8
Apology	++	++	++	++	--	--	--	--
Reparative Action	++	--	++	--	++	++	--	--
Judgment of Offence	++	++	--	--	++	--	++	--
Forgiveness	%	%	%	%	%	%	%	%

Table 3. Relationship

#	1	2	3	4	5	6	7	8
Benefits (social, economical)	++	--	++	--	++	--	++	--
Costs	++	++	++	++	--	--	--	--
Judgment of Offence	--	++	++	--	--	++	++	--
Forgiveness	%	%	%	%	%	%	%	%

Table 4.1. Empathy

#	1	2	3	4	5	6	7	8	9	10	11	12	13	14	15	16
Visible Acknow.	++	++	++	++	++	++	++	++	--	--	--	--	--	--	--	--
Past hist. interact.	--	--	--	--	++	++	++	++	++	++	++	++	--	--	--	--
Embar. propen.	--	--	++	++	--	--	++	++	--	--	++	++	--	--	++	++
Sim. past actions	--	++	++	--	--	++	++	--	--	++	++	--	--	++	++	--
Offence Judgm.	++	++	++	++	++	++	++	++	++	++	++	++	++	++	++	++
Forgiv.	%	%	%	%	%	%	%	%	%	%	%	%	%	%	%	%

Table 4.2. Empathy

#	1	2	3	4	5	6	7	8	9	10	11	12	13	14	15	16
Visible Acknow.	++	++	++	++	++	++	++	++	--	--	--	--	--	--	--	--
Past hist. interact.	--	--	--	--	++	++	++	++	++	++	++	++	--	--	--	--
Embar. propen.	--	--	++	++	--	--	++	++	--	--	++	++	--	--	++	++
Sim. past actions	--	++	++	--	--	++	++	--	--	++	++	--	--	++	++	--
Offence Judgm.	--	--	--	--	--	--	--	--	--	--	--	--	--	--	--	--
Forgiv.	%	%	%	%	%	%	%	%	%	%	%	%	%	%	%	%

Modeling Social and Individual Trust in Requirements Engineering Methodologies*

Paolo Giorgini[1], Fabio Massacci[1], John Mylopoulos[1,2], and Nicola Zannone[1]

[1] Department of Information and Communication Technology,
University of Trento - Italy
{massacci, giorgini, zannone}@dit.unitn.it
[2] Department of Computer Science,
University of Toronto - Canada
jm@cs.toronto.edu

Abstract. When we model and analyze trust in organizations or information systems we have to take into account two different levels of analysis: social and individual. Social levels define the structure of organizations, whereas individual levels focus on individual agents. This is particularly important when capturing security requirements where a "normally" trusted organizational role can be played by an untrusted individual.

Our goal is to model and analyze the two levels finding the link between them and supporting the automatic detection of conflicts that can come up when agents play roles in the organization. We also propose a formal framework that allows for the automatic verification of security requirements between the two levels by using Datalog and has been implemented in CASE tool.

Keywords: Information Technologies; Social; Security & Trust; Requirements and methodologies; Trust specification, analysis and reasoning; Realization of prototypes; Agent-Oriented Technologies.

1 Introduction

The last years have seen a major interest for methodologies for software engineering that could capture trust and security requirements from the very early stage of design [10, 12, 14, 18, 19]. Still all proposals (including our own) discuss the system or the organization looking at roles and positions rather than individual agents. From a certain viewpoint this is to be expected natural as a software engineer doesn't want to design and implement John Doe but rather the generic Cashier agent. However, in a recent study, the majority of Information Security Administrators said that their biggest worry is employee negligence and abuse

---

* This work has been partially funded by the IST programme of the EU Commission, FET under the IST-2001-37004 WASP project, by the FIRB programme of MIUR under the RBNE0195K5 ASTRO Project and by PAT MOSTRO project.

P. Herrmann et al. (Eds.): iTrust 2005, LNCS 3477, pp. 161–176, 2005.

[15]. Internal attacks can be more harmful than external attacks since they are being performed by trusted users that can bypass access control mechanisms. So, we need models that compare the structure of the organization (roles and relations among them) with the concrete instance of the organization (agents playing some roles in the organization and relations among them).

Among the requirements engineering methodologies, the Tropos agent-oriented requirements methodology [1] involves two different levels of analysis: *social* and *individual*. In the organization level we analyze roles and positions of the organization, whereas in individual level the focus is on single agents. Of course there is no explicit separation between the two levels, and so Tropos is not able to maintain the consistency between the social level (roles and positions) and the individual level (agent).

In the trust management setting, as far we know, there are only few proposals that analyze both social and individual levels and compare them. Huynh et al. [8] introduce role-based trust to model the trust resulting from the role-based relationships between two agents, but no requirements methodology is proposed. Sichman et al. [17] propose an approach where agents mental attitude is characterized by their personal mental attitude and the one which they have by playing a role. However, there is not a complete separation between the two levels. Therefore, this approach is not able to identify possible conflicts that can be arise by analyzing each level separately, and so system designers cannot verify the correctness and consistency of the structure of organizations.

In this paper we focus on the problem of identifying and solving conflicts emerging between the social and the individual level in the Secure Tropos model that we have proposed. Our goal is to:

- design models at both social level and individual level, independently;
- verify correctness and consistency of social level;
- map relations at social level into models at individual level;
- solve conflicts if needed;
- verify correctness and consistency of models at individual level.

The remainder of the paper is structured as follows. Next (§2) we provide an brief description of Tropos concepts and describe the basic ones that we use for modeling security. Then, we show how Tropos concepts are mapped into the Secure Tropos framework and vice versa (§3). Next (§4) we analyze how social relationships are propagate between social and individual levels, and show how this can generate conflicts. We present a formal framework for automatically identifying and solving conflicts (§5). Finally, we discuss related works and conclude the paper (§6).

2   Tropos and Secure Tropos

Tropos [1] is a development methodology, tailored to describe both the organizational environment of a system and the system itself. Tropos uses the concepts of actor, goal, soft goal, task, resource and social dependency for defining the obligations of actors (dependees) to other actors (dependers). An actor is an active entity that performs actions to achieve goals. Actors could have dependencies on other actors as well as dependencies from other actors. Actors can be decomposed into sub-units for modeling the internal structure of an actor preserving the intentional actor abstraction provided by modeling processes in terms of external relationships. Complex social actors can be modeled using three types of sub-units: agents, roles, and positions. An agent is an actor with concrete, physical manifestations, such as a human individual. The term agent is used instead of person since it can be used to refer to human as well as artificial agents. Agents are those that have characteristics not easily transferable to other individuals. A role is an abstract characterization of the behavior of a social actor within a certain domain. Its characteristics are easily transferable to other social actors. A position represents a set of roles played by an agent. A goal represents the strategic interests of an actor. A task specifies a particular course of action that produces a desired effect, and can be executed in order to satisfy a goal. A resource represents a physical or an informational entity. Finally, a dependency between two actors indicates that one actor depends on another to accomplish a goal, execute a task, or deliver a resource. In Tropos diagrams, actors are represented as circles; services - goals, tasks and resources - are respectively represented as ovals, hexagons and rectangles.

Secure Tropos [5] introduces four new concepts and relationships behind Tropos dependency: *trust*, *delegation*, *provisioning*, and *ownership*. The basic idea of ownership is that the owner of an service has full authority concerning access and disposition of his service. The distinction between owning (owns) and provisioning (provides) a service makes it clear how to model situations in which, for example, a client is the legitimate owner of his/her personal data and a Web Service provider that stores customers' personal data, provides the access to her/his data. We use the relation for delegation when in the domain of analysis there is a formal passage of authority (e.g. a signed piece of paper, a digital credential is sent, etc.). The trust relations have their intuitive meaning among agents. As for trust relations among roles or positions, the semantic is subtler as it refers to trust among organizations as we shall see in the next section.

3   Refining the Concept of Dependency

The new Secure Tropos concepts allow for a refinement of the dependency concept. In particular, we can now show how the dependency (depends) between two actors can be expressed in terms of trust and delegation. In order to do that, we introduce the distinction between delegation of permission and execution. In the *delegation of permission* (del_perm) the delegatee thinks "Now, I have the permission to fulfill the service", whereas in the *delegation of execution* (del_exec), the delegatee thinks "Now, I have to get the service fulfilled". Further, we want separate the concept of trust from the concept of delegation, as we might need to model systems in which some actors must delegate permission

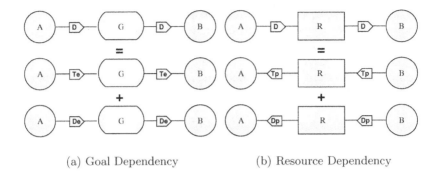

(a) Goal Dependency   (b) Resource Dependency

Fig. 1. Tropos dependency in terms of Secure Tropos

or execution to other actors they don't trust. Also in this case it is convenient to have a suitable distinction for trust in managing permission and trust in managing execution. The meaning of *trust of permission* (trust_perm) is that an actor (truster) trusts that another actor (trustee) uses correctly the service. The meaning of *trust of execution* (trust_exec) is that an actor (truster) trusts that another actor (trustee) is able to fulfill the service.

The distinction between *execution* and *permission* allows us to define a dependency in terms of trust and delegation. In particular, when the dependum is a goal or a task we have delegation and trust of execution, whereas when the dependum is a resource we have delegation and trust of permission. In symbols:

$$\mathsf{depends}(A, B, S) \Longleftrightarrow \mathsf{del\_exec}(A, B, S) \wedge \mathsf{trust\_exec}(A, B, S) \qquad (1)$$

where S is a goal or a task, and

$$\mathsf{depends}(A, B, S) \Longleftrightarrow \mathsf{del\_perm}(ID, B, A, S) \wedge \mathsf{trust\_perm}(B, A, S) \qquad (2)$$

where S is a resource.

A graphical representation of these formulas is given, respectively, in Fig. 1(a) and in Fig. 1(b). These diagrams use the label **D** for Tropos dependency and labels **De** and **Te** (**Dp** and **Tp**), respectively for delegation of execution and trust of execution (delegation of permission and trust of permission). Notice, also from Fig. 1 that the same dependency is mapped into differently oriented relations at the lower level.

Another refinement is the introduction of negative authorizations which are needed for some scenarios. Tropos already accommodates the notion of positive or negative contribution of goals to the fulfillment of other goals. We use negative authorizations to help the designer in shaping the perimeter of positive trust to avoid incautious delegation certificates that may give more powers than desired.

Suppose that an actor should not be given access to a service. In situations where authorization administration is decentralized, an actor possessing the right to use the service, can delegate the authorization on that service to the wrong actor. Since many actors may have the right to use a service, it is not always possible to enforce with certainty the constraint that a actor cannot access a particular service. We propose an explicit distrust relationship as an approach for handling this type of constraint. This is also sound from a cognitive point of view if we follow the definition of trust given by [2]: trust is a mental state based on a set of beliefs. We can say that if, on your own knowledge, you feel to trust me, then you trust me. Similarly, if you feel like distrusting me, then you distrust me. Obviously, there are various reasons of distrusting in agents such as unskillfulness, unreliability and abuse, but these situations are not treated here.

As we have done for trust, we also distinguish between distrust of execution (distrust_exec) and distrust of permission (distrust_perm). The graphical diagrams presented in this paper use the labels **Se** and **Sp**, respectively, for distrust of execution and distrust of permission. In the case there is no explicit trust relationship between agents, the label "?" is used.

4   Social Versus Individual Trust

In Tropos, stakeholders are presented as actors who depend on each other for goals to be achieved, tasks to be performed, and resources to be furnished. Since the concept of actor includes those of agent, role and position, the Tropos models involve two different levels of analysis: *social* and *individual*. In the social level we analyze roles and positions of the organization, whereas in individual level the focus is on single agents. In particular, at social level the structure of organizations are defined associating to every role (or position) objectives and responsibilities relating to the activities that such roles have to perform within the organizations. On the other hand, at individual level, agents not only are defined with their objectives and responsibilities, but also they are associated to role (or position) they can play.

This role-based approach takes advantage from specifying agents into two steps: assignment of objectives and responsibilities to role, and assignment of agents to roles. This allows to simplify the management of requirements. For instance, when new responsibilities are considered by the information system, the administrator needs only to decide to which roles such responsibilities have to be assigned. Then, all agents that play those roles inherit them. This means that relations spread from social level to individual level. Notice that when more agents play the same role, all instances inherit the properties associated to that role where the term property includes any relations presented above. Another advantage is that we can capture vested interested or conflict of interest explicitly during requirements phase.

Tropos supports also role hierarchy by using the relation ISA (is_a). Notice that this hierarchy is different from "standard" RBAC role hierarchy [9] where higher roles in the hierarchy are more powerful and the notion of domination is used. Instead our approach is based on the "standard" notion of hierarchy proposed in UML-base and Database-base approaches. Referring to the study case presented in [13] we have, for example, that Faculty Deans, Heads of De-

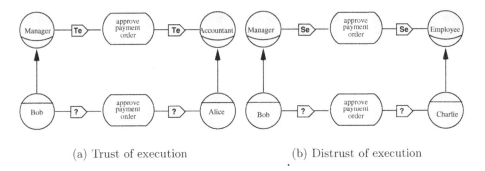

(a) Trust of execution   (b) Distrust of execution

Fig. 2. Missing (dis)trust relations at individual level

partment and Central Directorate Managers are Data Processors according the Italian Privacy legislations.

Definition 1. *Let r_1 and r_2 be roles. We say that r_1 is a* specialized sub-roles *of r_2 (or, equivalently, r_2 is* generalized super-role *of r_1) if* is_a(r_1, r_2). *Then, all specialized sub-roles inherit all properties of the generalized super-role.*

In above scenario, Faculty Deans, Heads of Department and Central Directorate Managers have all properties assigned to Data Processors.

Yet, in Tropos there is no explicit separation between the two levels, and it is very difficult to analyze and maintain the consistency between the social level (dependencies between roles and positions) and the individual level (dependencies between agents). For simplicity, in the remainder of the paper we don't distinguish role and position.

4.1   Missing Requirements

When we model and analyze functional trust and security relationships, it is possible that such requirements are given only at individual level or at social level. We would like to have a CASE tool that automatically completes models given at individual level from the social one when any relations are missing. Let us see why this is needed with examples from bank policies.

Example 1. In a bank context, branch managers have the objective to guarantee the availability and correct execution of payment orders. A bank policy states that a payment order should be issued only when it has been submitted and approved. Banks have also a policy stating that a branch bank manager should trust the chief accountants who work in his branch to approve payment orders (Fig. 2(a)). Suppose that Bob is the branch manager and Alice a new chief accountant and they have never met before. Then, Bob should trust Alice for approving payment orders to guarantee the availability of the service.

Example 2. Another bank policy states that a branch bank manager should distrust normal employees to approve payment orders (Fig. 2(b)). Suppose that

Bob is the branch manager and Charlie a newly employed cashier and they don't know each other. Then, Bob should distrust Charlie for approving payment orders.

We don't consider the case in which the relations are missing at social level because this level represents the structure of the organization which should be described explicitly in the requirements. The presence of a large number of trust relations at individual level that is not matched by a social level may be an indicator of a missing link at social level (or of a problem in the organization for distrust relations). On the contrary, Hannoun et al. [7] propose to detect the inadequacy of an organization regarding the relations existing among the agents involved in the system.

4.2   Conflicts on Trust Relations

In [5] we have only considered when trust is explicit, and we have not distinguished the case where there is explicit distrust and the case where no trust relation is given. Contrarily, in this paper we take in consideration all these three possibilities. The presence of positive and negative authorization at the same time could generate some conflicts on trust relationships. We define a *trust conflict* the situation where there are both a positive and a negative trust relation between two actors for the same service. Next, formal definitions are given.

Definition 2. *A conflict on trust of execution occurs when*

$$\exists x, y \in \mathsf{Agent} \; \exists s \in \mathsf{Service} \mid \mathsf{trust\_exec}(x, y, s) \wedge \mathsf{distrust\_exec}(x, y, s)$$

Definition 3. *A conflict on trust of permission occurs when*

$$\exists x, y \in \mathsf{Agent} \; \exists s \in \mathsf{Service} \mid \mathsf{trust\_perm}(x, y, s) \wedge \mathsf{distrust\_perm}(x, y, s)$$

A trust conflict may exist, for example, since system designers wrongly put both a (implicit) trust relation and the corresponding distrust relation.

Example 3. A manager depends on a short-term employee for a certain sensitive task, but short-term employees are distrusted for sensitive tasks (Figure 3(a)).

When we model and analyze security requirements, it is also possible that such requirements are specified at both individual and social levels, they could be in contrast with each other.

Example 4. Consider again Example 1 where bank managers trust accountants for approving payment orders, and Bob is the manager and Alice an accountant in a bank branch. What happen if Bob has had some problems with Alice in the past and he doesn't trust her? This scenario is presented in Fig.3(b).

Example 5. Consider again Example 2 where bank managers distrust employees for approving payment orders, and Bob is the manager and Charlie a employee in a bank branch. What happen if Bob trusts Charlie for approving payment orders? This scenario is presented in Fig. 3(c).

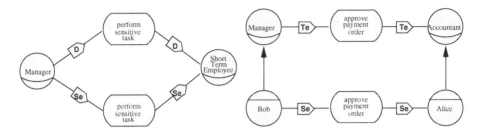

(a) Conflict due to implicit trust   (b) Social Trust vs Individual Distrust

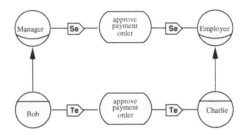

(c) Social Distrust vs Individual Trust

Fig. 3. Conflicts on (dis)trust relations

4.3   Solving Trust Conflicts

Our goal is to identify a solution in order to detect and, possibly, resolve conflicts on trust relations. To this end, we propose to use monitoring (monitoring) for solving conflicts since there is some evidence that it is good solution to prevent undesirable behaviors in information systems [6, 11]. Monitors rely on events and aim at observing, analyzing and controlling the execution of the information system in order to define its current behavior model and correct the undesirable behaviors, as well as unauthorized accesses.

Example 6. Referring to Example 4, we believe that Bob should monitor (or delegate this task to another actor) whether Alice does what she has to do since the organization imposes him to trust, but it is not his own choice.

4.4   Conflict of Interest

An agent can play (play) several roles. We assume that an agent is explicitly assigned to a given roles and this assignment gives him the rights and responsibilities assigned to that role. Conflicts of interest refer to scenarios where an individual occupies dual roles which should not be performed simultaneously. Because of the risk for abuse, performing both roles at the same time is considered to be inappropriate. In other words, the conflict of interest concerns the potential advantage an agent could take of his position.

Definition 4. *Let r_1 and r_2 be two roles that an agent cannot play at the same time. A conflict of interest occurs when*

$$\exists x \in \text{Agent} \mid \text{play}(x, r_1) \wedge \text{play}(x, r_2)$$

Example 7. In a bank context, payment orders should be issued only when they have been submitted and approved. A payment order should be submitted by an employee and approved by a different accountant. This means that an agent cannot play at the same time the role *accountant* and *employee*.

$$:- \text{play}(X, accountant) \wedge \text{play}(X, employee) \wedge \text{agent}(X)$$

Therefore, if we assume that the set of employees is disjoint from the set of managers this kind of conflicts doesn't exist.

The above notion of conflict of interest could be refined since it doesn't show why conflicts exist. Moreover, the definition we have done above could be too strong since some time a conflict could be only for some specific instances.

Example 8. The scenario presented in Example 7 is far from real life: accountant can usually execute employee tasks, but they cannot approve their own orders.

This example also reveals that, before verifying the consistency of the individual level, we should be sure on the consistency of the organization structure: it is also possible that a conflict arises by considering just the social level.

Further, some laws issued, for example, by Antitrust Division[1] or some enterprises' policies can impose that the same person must not own (be entitled) or provide some certain services at the same time. An agent could own or provide some service himself and could own or provide other services since he plays roles that owns or is able to provide such services. Now, we refine the Definition 4 as follows:

Definition 5. *Let s_1 and s_2 be two services that an actor cannot own at the same time. An ownership conflict occurs when*

$$\exists x \in \text{Actor} \mid \text{owns}(x, s_1) \wedge \text{owns}(x, s_2)$$

Definition 6. *Let s_1 and s_2 be two services that an actor cannot provide at the same time. A provisioning conflict occurs when*

$$\exists x \in \text{Actor} \mid \text{provides}(x, s_1) \wedge \text{provides}(x, s_2)$$

In this paper we define conflicts only on primitive properties, but similar definitions can be given also for the derived ones presented in [5].

Example 9. An instance of the bank policy presented in Example 8 can be formalized with the following integrity constraints.

$$:- \text{provides}(A, submit\_order\_25) \wedge \text{provides}(A, approve\_order\_25)$$

---

[1] http://www.usdoj.gov/atr/

5   Formalization

We distinguish between two main types of predicates: primitive and derived. These correspond to respectively extensional and intensional predicates in Datalog. Extensional predicates are predicates set directly with the help of ground facts and are the ones corresponding the edge and circles drawn by the requirements engineer on the CASE tool. Intensional predicates are implicitly determined with the help of rules. We start by presenting the set of extensional predicates (Table 1) and refer to [5] for all rules related to previously introduced concepts. Here we only present rules for the new concepts.

The left part of the table contains the primitives used for modeling Tropos framework. The unary predicates goal, task and resource are used respectively for identifying goals, tasks and resource. Note that type Goal, Task and Resource are sub-types of Service. We shall use letters S, G, T and R possibly with indices as metavariables ranging over the terms, respectively, of type Service, Goal, Task and Resource. The intuition is that agent(a) holds if instance a is an agent, position(a) holds if instance a is a position, and role(a) holds if instance a is a role. Note that type Agent, Position and Role are sub-types of Actor. We shall use letters X, Y and Z as metavariables ranging over the terms of type Actor, A, B and C as metavariables ranging over the terms of type Agent, and T, Q and V as metavariables ranging over the terms of type Role. Metalevel variables are used as a syntactic sugar to avoid to write the predicates that type variables. For example, when the metavariable G occurs in a rule, the predicate goal(G) should be put in the body of the rule. The predicate play(a, b) holds if agent a is an instance of role b. The intuition is that is_a(a, b) holds if role a is a specialization of role b. The predicate depends(a, b, s) holds if actor a depends from actor b for service s.

In the right part we have the additional predicates introduced by the Secure Tropos framework. When an actor has the capabilities to fulfill a service, he provides it. The intuition is that provides(a, s) holds if actor a provides service s.

Table 1. Predicates

Tropos Primitives	Secure Tropos Primitives
goal(Goal:g)	provides(Actor:a, Service:s)
task(Task:t)	wants(Actor:a, Service:s)
resource(Resource:r)	owns(Actor:a, Service:s)
agent(Agent:a)	del_exec(Actor:a, Actor:b, Service:s)
position(Position:a)	del_perm(id:idC, Actor:a, Actor:b, Service:s)
role(Role:a)	trust_exec(Actor:a, Actor:b, Service:s)
play(Agent:a, Role:b)	trust_perm(Actor:a, Actor:b, Service:s)
is_a(Role:a, Role:b)	distrust_exec(Actor:a, Actor:b, Service:s)
depends(Actor:a, Actor:b, Service:s)	distrust_perm(Actor:a, Actor:b, Service:s)
	monitoring(Actor:a, Actor:b, Service:s)
	trust_mon(Actor:a, Actor:b, Service:s)

Table 2. Axioms for mapping Tropos into Secure Tropos and vive versa

From Tropos to Secure Tropos
ST1: $\quad$ trust_exec(X, Y, G) :- depends(X, Y, G)
ST2: $\quad$ del_exec(X, Y, G) :- depends(X, Y, G)
ST3: $\quad$ trust_perm(Y, X, R) :- depends(X, Y, R)
ST4: del_perm(ID, Y, X, R) :- depends(X, Y, R)
From Secure Tropos to Tropos
ST5: $\quad$ depends(X, Y, G) :- trust_exec(X, Y, G) $\quad \wedge \quad$ del_exec(X, Y, G) $\quad \wedge$ $\quad$ **not** distrust_exec(X, Y, G)
ST6: $\quad$ depends(X, Y, R) :- trust_perm(Y, X, R) $\quad \wedge \quad$ del_perm(ID, Y, X, R) $\quad \wedge$ $\quad$ **not** distrust_perm(Y, X, R)

The predicate wants(a, s) holds if actor a has the objective of fulfilling service s. The predicate owns(a, s) holds if actor a owns service s. The owner of a service has full authority concerning access and usage of his services, and he can also delegate this authority to other actors. The predicate trust_exec(a, b, s) (resp. trust_perm(a, b, s)) holds is actor a trusts that actor b is able to fulfill (resp. uses correctly) service s where a is called truster and b trustee. The predicate distrust_exec(a, b, s) (resp. distrust_perm(a, b, s)) holds is actor a distrusts actor b for service s. The intuition is that monitoring(a, b, s) holds if actor a monitors actor b on service s. The intuition is that trust_mon(a, b, s) holds if actor a trust actor b for monitoring service s. The predicate del_perm(idC, a, b, s) holds if actor a delegates to actor b the permission on service s. The actor a is called the *delegater*; the actor b is called the *delegatee*; idC is the certificate identifier. The predicate del_exec(a, b, s) holds if actor a delegates to actor b the execution of service s.

Once the requirements engineer has drawn up the model (i.e. the extensional predicates) we are ready for the formal analysis. To derive the right conclusions from an intuitive model, we need to complete the model using *axioms* for the intensional predicates. Axioms are rules of the form L :- $L_1 \wedge ... \wedge L_n$ where L, called head, is a positive literal and $L_1, ..., L_n$ are literals and they are called body. Intuitively, if $L_1, ..., L_n$ are true in the model then L must be true in the model. We use the notation $\{L\}$:- $L_1, ..., L_n$ to indicate that if $L_1, ..., L_n$ are true then L *may* be true. Essentially, L will be added to the model only if some constraints demand its inclusion. This construction can be captured with a simple encoding in logic programs. Notice also that when a relation uses variables of type `Actor` the relation can apply to both social and individual levels, but separately.

In Table 2 there are the axioms to map Tropos dependency into Secure Tropos framework and vice versa. Notice that ST1-2 and ST5 have also to be repeated for the case where the dependum is a task.

Table 3 defines the intensional versions, entrust_exec and disentrust_exec (entrust_perm and disentrust_perm) of the extensional predicates trust_exec and distrust_exec (trust_perm and distrust_perm) that are used to build (dis)trust chains by propagating (dis)trust of execution (permission) relations. The in-

Table 3. Axioms on Trust and Distrust

Trust of execution
T1: disentrust_exec(X, Y, S) :- distrust_exec(X, Y, S)
T2: disentrust_exec(X, Z, S) :- entrust_exec(X, Y, S) $\wedge$ distrust_exec(Y, Z, S) $\wedge$ not disentrust_exec(X, Y, S)
T3: entrust_exec(X, Y, S) :- trust_exec(X, Y, S) $\wedge$ not disentrust_exec(X, Y, S)
T4: entrust_exec(X, Z, S) :- entrust_exec(X, Y, S) $\wedge$ entrust_exec(Y, Z, S) $\wedge$ not disentrust_exec(X, Z, S)
Trust of permission
T5: disentrust_perm(X, Y, S) :- distrust_perm(X, Y, S)
T6: disentrust_perm(X, Z, S) :- entrust_perm(X, Y, S) $\wedge$ distrust_perm(Y, Z, S) $\wedge$ not disentrust_perm(X, Y, S)
T7: entrust_perm(X, Y, S) :- trust_perm(X, Y, S) $\wedge$ not disentrust_perm(A, B, S)
T8: entrust_perm(X, Z, S) :- entrust_perm(X, Y, S) $\wedge$ entrust_perm(Y, Z, S) $\wedge$ not disentrust_perm(X, Z, S)
Confident of monitoring
T9: confident_mon(X, Y, S) :- trust_mon(X, Z, S) $\wedge$ monitoring(Z, Y, S)

tuitive meaning of rules T1-2 (and T5-6 for permission) is presented in the following examples.

Example 10. A branch manager depends on accountants for performing sensitive tasks. This implies that the manager trusts accountants for it. On the other hand, accountants distrust short-term employees for this goal. Therefore, the manager distrusts short-term employees. This explains also the conflict shown in Example 3.

Example 11. A bank policy states that the bank general manager should trust branch managers for correctly managing branch cash desks. Another branch policy states that the branch manager have not to permit (distrust of permission) short-term employees for managing branch cash desks. Therefore, the general manager distrusts short-term employees.

T3-4 (respectively T7-8) rules are used to build trust chains by propagating trust of execution (permission) relations. T9 introduces the intensional predicate confident_mon(a, b, s): actor a is confident that there exists someone that monitors actor b for service s. Also this set of axions applies to both social level and individual level, independently, and so A, B and C have to be typed as roles for the social level and as agents for the individual level.

Table 4 presents the axioms for role hierarchy and for mapping relations from social level to individual level. The predicate specialize is the intensional version of is_a, whereas instance is intensional version of play. Axioms Ax1-12 have to be repeated replacing the predicate instance with specialize and predicate agent with role for completing social level with respect to role hierarchy.

Properties are different from axioms: they are desirable design features, but may not be true (or too costly to implement) of the particular design at hand.

Table 4. Axioms for role hierarchy and for mapping social level into individual level

Role Hierarchy	
RH1:	$\text{specialize}(T, Q) :- \text{is\_a}(T, Q)$
RH2:	$\text{specialize}(T, Q) :- \text{specialize}(T, V) \wedge \text{is\_a}(V, Q)$
RH3:	$\text{instance}(A, T) :- \text{play}(A, T)$
RH4:	$\text{instance}(A, T) :- \text{instance}(A, Q) \wedge \text{specialize}(Q, T)$
From social level to individual level	
Ax1:	$\text{provides}(A, S) :- \text{provides}(T, S) \wedge \text{instance}(A, T)$
Ax2:	$\text{wants}(A, S) :- \text{wants}(T, S) \wedge \text{instance}(A, T)$
Ax3:	$\text{owns}(A, S) :- \text{owns}(T, S) \wedge \text{instance}(A, T)$
Ax4:	$\text{trust\_exec}(A, B, S) :- \text{trust\_exec}(T, Q, S) \wedge \text{instance}(A, T) \wedge \text{instance}(B, Q)$
Ax5:	$\text{trust\_perm}(A, B, S) :- \text{trust\_perm}(T, Q, S) \wedge \text{instance}(A, T) \wedge \text{instance}(B, Q)$
Ax6:	$\text{distrust\_exec}(A, B, S) :- \text{distrust\_exec}(T, Q, S) \wedge \text{instance}(A, T) \wedge \text{instance}(B, Q)$
Ax7:	$\text{distrust\_perm}(A, B, S) :- \text{distrust\_perm}(T, Q, S) \wedge \text{instance}(A, T) \wedge \text{instance}(B, Q)$
Ax8:	$\text{del\_exec}(A, B, S) :- \text{del\_exec}(T, Q, S) \wedge \text{instance}(A, T) \wedge \text{instance}(B, Q)$
Ax9:	$\text{del\_perm}(ID, A, B, S) :- \text{del\_perm}(ID, T, Q, S) \wedge \text{instance}(A, T) \wedge \text{instance}(B, Q)$
Ax10:	$\text{monitoring}(A, B, S) :- \text{monitoring}(T, Q, S) \wedge \text{instance}(A, T) \wedge \text{instance}(B, Q)$
Ax11:	$\text{trust\_mon}(A, B, S) :- \text{trust\_mon}(T, Q, S) \wedge \text{instance}(A, T) \wedge \text{instance}(B, Q)$
Ax12:	$\text{depends}(A, B, S) :- \text{depends}(T, Q, S) \wedge \text{instance}(A, T) \wedge \text{instance}(B, Q)$

Table 5. Properties for identifying conflicts

Pro1: :- $\text{entrust\_exec}(X, Y, S) \wedge \text{disentrust\_exec}(X, Y, S)$
Pro2: :- $\text{entrust\_perm}(X, Y, S) \wedge \text{disentrust\_perm}(X, Y, S)$
Pro3: :- $\text{entrust\_exec}(A, B, S) \wedge \text{disentrust\_exec}(T, Q, S) \wedge \text{instance}(A, T) \wedge \text{instance}(B, Q)$
Pro4: :- $\text{entrust\_perm}(A, B, S) \wedge \text{disentrust\_perm}(T, Q, S) \wedge \text{instance}(A, T) \wedge \text{instance}(B, Q)$
Pro5: :- $\text{disentrust\_exec}(A, B, S) \wedge \text{entrust\_exec}(T, Q, S) \wedge \text{instance}(A, T) \wedge \text{instance}(B, Q)$
Pro6: :- $\text{disentrust\_perm}(A, B, S) \wedge \text{entrust\_perm}(T, Q, S) \wedge \text{instance}(A, T) \wedge \text{instance}(B, Q)$

Table 5 presents the properties used to identifying conflicts that occur when both a trust and a distrust relations exist among two actors for the same service. Pro1-2 are used to identify generic conflicts and correspond to Definition 2 and 3. These properties apply to both social level and individual level, independently and so A and B have to be typed as role for the social level and as agents for the individual level. Pro1-2 can be refined in order to identify conflicts of the form of Fig. 3(c) (Pro3-4) and Fig. 3(b) (Pro5-6).

Table 6 formalizes the proposal for solving conflicts when there is a trust relation at social level and a distrust relation at individual level.

To accommodate C1-2 in our framework we have to modify axioms Ax6-7 in Table 4. The new version of these axioms is given in Table 7.

Table 6. Axioms for solving conflicts

C1: {monitoring(M, B, S)}:- disentrust_exec(A, B, S) $\wedge$ entrust_exec(T, Q, S) $\wedge$
instance(A, T) $\wedge$ instance(B, Q) $\wedge$ trust_mon(A, M, S)
C2: {monitoring(M, B, S)}:- disentrust_perm(A, B, S) $\wedge$ entrust_perm(T, Q, S) $\wedge$
instance(A, T) $\wedge$ instance(B, Q) $\wedge$ trust_mon(A, M, S)

Table 7. Axioms in order to support monitoring

Ax6': distrust_exec(A, B, S) :- distrust_exec$(T, Q, S) \wedge$instance$(A, T) \wedge$instance$(B, Q) \wedge$
not confident_mon(A, B, S)
Ax7': distrust_perm(A, B, S) :- distrust_perm$(T, Q, S) \wedge$instance$(A, T) \wedge$instance$(B, Q) \wedge$
not confident_mon(A, B, S)

6   Related Work and Conclusions

Computer Security is one of today's hot topic and the need for conceptual models
of security features have brought up a number of proposals especially in UML
community [4, 10, 12, 14, 18, 16].

Lodderstedt et al. [12] present a modeling language, based on UML, called SecureUML. Their approach is focused on modeling access control policies and how

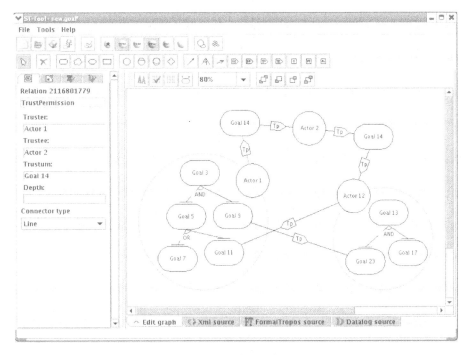

Fig. 4. STTool

these (policies) can be integrated into a model-driven software development process. To address security concerns during software design, Doan et al. [4] incorporate Mandatory Access Control (MAC) into UML. Ray et al. [16] propose to model RBAC as a pattern by using UML diagram template. Further, they represent constraints on RBAC model through the Object Constraint Language. Similarly, Jürjens [10] proposes an extension of UML to accommodate security requirements by using Abstract State Machine model and adding several stereotypes to accommodate its proposal towards security verification. McDermott and Fox adapt use cases [14] to capture and analyze security requirements, and they call the adaption an abuse case model. Sindre and Opdahl define the concept of a misuse case [18], the inverse of a use case, which describes a function that the system should not allow. CORAS [3] is a model-based risk assessment method for security-critical systems. It is essentially a risk management process based on UML and aims to adapt, refine, extend and combine existing methods for risk analysis.

We have presented here an enhanced trust and security requirements engineering methodology that is able to capture trust conflicts at social and individual level. Our framework is supported by a CASE tool called STTool.[2] A screenshot is shown in Fig. 4. This tool is implemented in JAVA and provides a user friendly interface within the DLV system to the requirements engineer for the verification of the correctness and consistency of trust and security requirements in the organization.

References

1. P. Bresciani, P. Giorgini, F. Giunchiglia, J. Mylopoulos, and A. Perini. TROPOS: An Agent-Oriented Software Development Methodology. *JAAMAS*, 8(3):203–236, 2004.
2. C. Castelfranchi and R. Falcone. Principles of trust for MAS: Cognitive anatomy, social importance and quantification. In *Proc. of ICMAS'98*, pages 72–79. IEEE Press, 1998.
3. F. den Braber, T. Dimitrakos, B. A. Gran, M. S. Lund, K. Stølen, and J. Ø. Aagedal. The CORAS methodology: model-based risk assessment using UML and UP. In *UML and the unified process*, pages 332–357. Idea Group Publishing, 2003.
4. T. Doan, S. Demurjian, T. C. Ting, and A. Ketterl. MAC and UML for secure software design. In *Proc. of FMSE'04*, pages 75–85. ACM Press, 2004.
5. P. Giorgini, F. Massacci, J. Mylopoulous, and N. Zannone. Requirements Engineering meets Trust Management: Model, Methodology, and Reasoning. In *Proc. of iTrust'04*, *LNCS* 2995, pages 176–190. Springer-Verlag, 2004.
6. Z. Guessoum, M. Ziane, and N. Faci. Monitoring and Organizational-Level Adaptation of Multi-Agent Systems. In *Proc. of AAMAS'04*, pages 514–521. ACM Press, 2004.
7. M. Hannoun, J. S. Sichman, O. Boissier, and C. Sayettat. Dependence Relations between Roles in a Multi-Agent System: Towards the Detection of Inconsistencies in Organization. In *Proc. of 1st. Int. Workshop on Multi-Agent Based Simulation*, *LNCS* 1534, pages 169–182. Springer-Verlag, 1998.

---

[2] http://sesa.dit.unitn.it/sttool/

8. D. Huynh, N. R. Jennings, and N. R. Shadbolt. Developing an Integrated Trust and Reputation Model for Open Multi-Agent Systems. In *Proc. of 7th Int. Workshop on Trust in Agent Societies*, pages 65–74, 2004.

9. S. Jajodia, P. Samarati, M. L. Sapino, and V. S. Subrahmanian. Flexible support for multiple access control policies. *TODS*, 26(2):214–260, 2001.

10. J. Jürjens. *Secure Systems Development with UML*. Springer-Verlag, 2004.

11. G. A. Kaminka, D. V. Pynadath, and M. Tambe. Monitoring Teams by Overhearing: A Multi-Agent Plan-Recognition Approach. *JAIR*, 17:83–135, 2002.

12. T. Lodderstedt, D. Basin, and J. Doser. SecureUML: A UML-Based Modeling Language for Model-Driven Security. In *Proc. of UML'02*, *LNCS* 2460, pages 426–441. Springer-Verlag, 2002.

13. F. Massacci, M. Prest, and N. Zannone. Using a Security Requirements Engineering Methodology in Practice: The compliance with the Italian Data Protection Legislation. *Comp. Standards & Interfaces*, 2005. To Appear. An extended version is available as Technical report DIT-04-103 at `eprints.biblio.unitn.it`.

14. J. McDermott and C. Fox. Using Abuse Case Models for Security Requirements Analysis. In *Proc. of ACSAC'99*, pages 55–66. IEEE Press, 1999.

15. L. Ponemon. What Keeps Security Professionals Up At Night?, April 2003. URL: http://www.darwinmag.com/read/040103/threats.html.

16. I. Ray, N. Li, R. France, and D.-K. Kim. Using UML to visualize role-based access control constraints. In *Proc. of SACMAT'04*, pages 115–124. ACM Press, 2004.

17. J. S. Sichman and R. Conte. On personal and role mental attitudes: A preliminary dependence-based analysis. In *Proc. of SBIA'98*, *LNCS* 1515, pages 1–10. Springer-Verlag, 1998.

18. G. Sindre and A. L. Opdahl. Eliciting Security Requirements by Misuse Cases. In *Proc. of TOOLS Pacific 2000*, pages 120 –131. IEEE Press, 2000.

19. A. van Lamsweerde, S. Brohez, R. De Landtsheer, and D. Janssens. From System Goals to Intruder Anti-Goals: Attack Generation and Resolution for Security Requirements Engineering. In *Proc. of RHAS'03*, pages 49–56, 2003.

Towards a Generic Trust Model – Comparison of Various Trust Update Algorithms

Michael Kinateder, Ernesto Baschny, and Kurt Rothermel

Institute of Parallel and Distributed Systems (IPVS),
Universität Stuttgart, Universitätsstr. 38,
70569 Stuttgart, Germany
{kinateder, rothermel}@informatik.uni-stuttgart.de
ernst@baschny.de

Abstract. Research in the area of trust and reputation systems has put a lot of effort in developing various trust models and associated trust update algorithms that support users or their agents with different behavioral profiles. While each work on its own is particularly well suited for a certain user group, it is crucial for users employing different trust representations to have a common understanding about the meaning of a given trust statement.

The contributions of this paper are three-fold: Firstly we present the UniTEC generic trust model that provides a common trust representation for the class of trust update algorithms based on experiences. Secondly, we show how several well-known representative trust-update algorithms can easily be plugged into the UniTEC system, how the mappings between the generic trust model and the algorithm-specific trust models are performed, and most importantly, how our abstraction from algorithm-specific details in the generic trust model enables users using different algorithms to interact with each other and to exchange trust statements. Thirdly we present the results of our comparative evaluation of various trust update algorithms under a selection of test scenarios.

1   Introduction

The phenomenal growth of the Internet that we experienced during the last couple of decades, together with the fact that computers can be found not only in business environments but also in many households almost to the point of being a commodity nowadays, led to a widespread public acceptance of this medium. There are plenty of reasons why people connect to the Internet. Among the most common usage scenarios are getting *access to information, communicating with people* and *buying or selling* goods.

There is no doubt that the Internet offers masses of information in all kinds of different areas, ranging from purely leisure-relevant possibly dispensable information, like who is currently number one in the US-single-charts, to more critical areas, like product reviews or even stock exchange data. Especially in these critical areas, the user needs *correct* information. Therefore the user needs to decide whether the information provider is trustworthy or not. In real life,

P. Herrmann et al. (Eds.): iTrust 2005, LNCS 3477, pp. 177–192, 2005.

we use social network structures of friends, colleagues etc. to find trustworthy persons whom to get advice or general information from. In the virtual environment of the Internet, *reputation systems* model these structures up to a certain degree supporting users in their decision whom to trust and whom to avoid. The goal of these systems is to minimize the risk of interactions with strangers.

One aspect, that research in trust and reputation systems strives to determine, is a suitable digital representation of trust, commonly referred to as a *trust model*. Tightly interwoven with trust models are the algorithms used to determine, how this trust is updated according to different usually discrete events. Such events might be a new experience with the person in question, or new information from other trusted sources regarding the reputation of this person etc. Numerous different models and trust update algorithms have been proposed in the literature and each approach is particularly well suited for a certain user group or application area. However, these trust models are not interoperable since there is a lack of a generic representation of trust. A generic trust model would allow users intending to use different models to translate their local representation to the generic one in order to understand each other's trust statements.

Our contribution is built on the observation that, although the algorithms used to compute a certain trust value are quite different from each other, the data that the algorithms are working upon and the outcome of the algorithms are not that different and can thus be mapped on a generic model. We suggest one approach for such a generic representation which we implemented in the context of the UniTEC distributed reputation system. This generic trust model allows us to easily integrate various existing trust update algorithms. Another contribution lies in a comparative analysis of these algorithms, which presents how the algorithms react on various test scenarios. This has – according to our knowledge – not been done in this depth before.

We structure our paper as follows: In the next section we give a brief overview of the UniTEC reputation system, in whose context this research is being conducted. After discussing several general aspects of trust and trust relationships in Sect. 3 we present in detail the components of the generic trust model in Sect. 4. We introduce in Sect. 5 a subset of trust update algorithms implemented in UniTEC and the necessary adaptations. In Sect. 6 we describe several test scenarios that the algorithms are subjected to which is followed in Sect. 7 by a presentation of the results of this evaluation. We conclude our paper in Sect. 8.

2   Application Area for a Generic Trust Model

In this section, we briefly point out the functionality of the UniTEC system as one sample application area for the introduced generic trust model. UniTEC is a completely decentralized reputation system and consists of a peer-to-peer network of agents residing on nodes with communication capabilities.

For privacy reasons, each user employs multiple virtual identities or pseudonyms instead of his real identity when interacting with the UniTEC system. Each pseudonym has an associated public and private key pair and is responsible for one or more context areas (see Sect. 3). The *identity management component* allows to create or remove pseudonyms and to assign context area responsibilities. The *anonymous peer-to-peer (P2P) communication component* provides communication mechanisms between pseudonyms while protecting the link between real user identities and their pseudonyms (see also [1]).

UniTEC can store and request trusted data items (TDI) about arbitrary products or services. TDIs are recommendations digitally signed with the key of the appropriate pseudonym and stored in the XML database of the *data management component* of the pseudonym owner's UniTEC agent. In order to retrieve a TDI, a requesting user poses a query to its own agent, which determines from the query context a neighborhood of already known pseudonyms deemed as capable of answering the query. The query is disseminated through the means offered by the anonymous P2P communication component to each neighborhood member and from there recursively further. During the query dissemination, a construct called the *trust chain* is built as part of the query, which consists of a set of trust statements, each specifying the trust of a node in its successor starting with the original requester. A node which has stored a TDI that satisfies the query sends a TDI response to the requester that contains this TDI and the then completed trust chain.

The *trust management component (TMC)* evaluates the trust chains contained in the TDI responses and presents to the requester the TDIs together with the calculated transitive trust in the TDI-issuer. Furthermore, the TMC keeps track of the user's trust in each pseudonym that she or he has been in contact with. More concretely, it stores trust in its database according to the specified trust model and updates the trust in these pseudonyms upon receipt of user feedback regarding the quality of the received TDIs according to the trust update algorithm specified in the user's preferences. This trust update influences the neighborhood selection the next time that a query is received for the trust context in question.

A generic representation of trust is essential especially for the trust statements inside the trust chains to enable the requester's TMC to compute the transitive trust in each TDI-issuer independently from the local trust models used at each intermediary. We are well aware of the fact, that this brief introduction leaves many questions unanswered. For more in-depth information regarding UniTEC, we would like to point the interested reader to [2] and our project website[1].

After having presented background information regarding the UniTEC reputation system as a whole, we focus in the following on the capabilities of its trust management component TMC. We start by introducing our view on the various aspects of a trust relationship.

3   The Phenomenon of Trust Relationships

In order to understand the phenomenon of trust relationships, we first need to understand the meaning of *trust*. In the related work, various different definitions

---

[1] `unitec.informatik.uni-stuttgart.de`

of the term trust have been proposed. One definition popular in the agent field is from Diego Gambetta [3] "trust (or, symmetrically, distrust) is a particular level of the subjective probability with which an agent assesses that another agent or group of agents will perform a particular action...". We identify two relevant points in this definition: firstly, trust is used in order to *predict* an entity's *future behavior*, secondly, trust is *subjective*. The subjectivity leads consequently to asymmetric trust relationships between *trustor*, the entity who is trusting, and *trustee*, the entity who is trusted. In the following, we identify various *dimensions of trust relationships* in addition to trustor and trustee:

Trust measure. refers to the quality of the trust relationship, which ranges from complete distrust over a neutral trust measure to full trust. The more a trustee is trusted, the higher the trust measure is supposed to be.

Trust certainty. specifies the confidence of the trustor in his or her estimation of the trustee. If this estimation is gained via only few personal experiences or just via word of mouth, the certainty is supposed to be low.

Trust context. People trust in a fine-grained manner depending on the area and goal in question, for instance person A might trust person B to babysit her child whereas she might not trust person B to repair a computer. A context can be represented by different categories as we described in [2].

Trust directness. Direct and indirect trust [4, 5] represent two distinct trust relationships. Direct trust means that the trustee can directly cooperate with the trustor. With indirect trust, the trustee is not supposed to cooperate directly himself, but should forward the cooperation request to a good expert. Consider for instance person A knowing that person B has many friends working in the computer business, although B is not schooled in this context herself. A will not trust B directly with a repair task but might very well trust recommendations received indirectly via B from one of B's expert friends.

Trust dynamics. A trust relationship is not static, but changes dynamically on various different incidents, e.g. on *own direct experiences*. If for instance the babysitting of A's child by B went well, the trust of A in B will increase. In addition to own experiences, *trust estimations received from others* influence the own trust assessment as well. If A's good friends C, D, and E warn A about the unreliable nature of B, A might refrain from relying on B's babysitting capabilities. Lastly, quite interestingly, *trust relationships may also change over time* when no experiences have been made, a fact, that is up to our knowledge not covered in the related work yet.

4   Towards a Generic Trust Model

Having presented the general concepts of trust relationships in the previous section, we describe in the following, how these concepts are mapped on the components of our generic trust model. The key components of our model result from an analysis of the characteristics of various existing trust models.

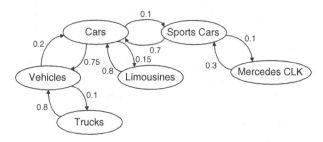

Fig. 1. Example snippet of a weighted directed trust context graph. The weights represent sample semantic distance of the context areas

4.1 Trust Measure and Certainty

Various different representations of trust values exist in the related work. Trust values can be depicted as real numbers in certain intervals like for instance $[-1, +1]$, as done by Jonker and Treur [6] and Sabater [7] or probabilities in $[0, 1]$, as proposed among others by Jøsang and Ismail [8], Yu and Singh [9], and Kinateder and Rothermel [2]. Others propose discrete values, like the binary representation by Blaze and Feigenbaum [10] or four discrete values introduced by Abdul-Rahman and Hailes [5].

The metric used for the *trust measure* in our proposed generic trust model is a real number in the interval of $[0, 1]$. Complete distrust is represented by 0 whereas 1 corresponds to full trust. This representation allows an easy transformation of any previously described measures in the generic measure as we will see in more detail in Sect. 5.

Not all investigated algorithms support the computation of a certainty value, which states the quality of the trust assessment represented in the trust measure. If uncertainty is mentioned [9, 8, 7] it is specified in the interval [0, 1].

The *trust certainty* in the generic trust model is represented similarly to the trust measure as a number in the interval of $[0, 1]$, whereas 0 describes complete uncertainty and 1 the total certainty.

4.2 Trust Context

As pointed out in the previous section, applications can define various context areas in which entities can be trusted. It is important to note, that these areas are not necessarily independent from each other. Different kinds of dependencies can exist among the context areas: *instance-of* relationships are one-level relationships for *classification*, *is-a* relationships provide *generalization*, *part-of* relationships enable *aggregation* and surely many other – potentially application-specific – forms of dependencies between context areas can be imagined.

For the sake of the trust model, however, we do not need to model all these relationships in detail. Instead, we model the *asymmetric semantic distance* between the context areas and therefore abstract from the kind of dependency. The metrics chosen for the semantic distance is a real number in the interval of $[0, 1[$. A distance close to 1 represents a high dependency, a distance of 0 refers to no dependency. Therefore, we organize the trust context areas as a weighted directed graph as can be seen in 1. This allows us to spread the impact of a trust update in one area to related areas. The context areas and the semantic distances between the areas are specified by the applications to be supported with trust management. However, due to the subjectivity of trust, each user is enabled to locally modify the distances to suit his or her personal views.

4.3   Trust Directness

Another dimension of a trust relationship is its directness. In our model, direct and indirect trust are two distinct instances, each with a specific trust measure, certainty etc. They are stored and updated separately by the trust algorithms.

4.4   Trust Dynamics

As already mentioned in the introduction, a change in trust occurs upon receipt of feedback regarding an experience of a trustor with a trustee. Various aspects are discussed in the following that influence the trust dynamics.

Quality Feedback. The trustor provides feedback about the subjective quality of a received information item. The metrics used to rate the quality is a real number in the interval of $[0, 1]$. A perfect information item is rated with 1, 0 describes a completely unsatisfactory one. The generic trust model does not dictate how this feedback is gained; e.g. for recommendations of a static attribute-value structure this feedback can be gained automatically in a collaborative filtering style.

Trustor Confidence. Trustors may specify a confidence in their own offered information items. This confidence is represented by a real number in the interval of $[0, 1]$. Similar to the trust certainty, 0 stands for no confidence whereas 1 stands for the highest possible confidence in the offered information. This confidence influences the trust update such that a weak statement with a low confidence leads to only a slight trust update, whether positive or negative.

Transaction Utility. Each information request, and the corresponding responses and feedback statements refers to a certain transaction the requester or trustor is about to take. Depending on the transaction's significance, the trustor specifies the utility as a real number in the interval of $[0, 1]$. We assume, that a "maximum utility" can be specified in such as utilities higher as this maximum utility will lead to the same trust update impact as with the specified maximum utility. 1 refers to the normalized maximum utility which leads to a trust update with a higher impact.

Experience Aging (Optional). The quality of trustees is not necessarily constant but may change over time, for instance due to gathered experience in a certain field. In order to determine trust as a prediction of the future behavior, it is possible to specify, that the latest experiences ought to weigh more than older experiences. We propose two options for experience aging: a *feedback window* and an *experience aging factor*. The feedback window limits the amount of considered experiences, either depending on a certain number of experiences or a certain maximum age. The aging factor in the interval of $[0, 1]$ determines the ratio of a new experience to previous experiences in the update computation. We describe in the following section how this aging factor is used in the algorithms.

Related Trust Context Areas (Optional). As mentioned before, an update in a single trust context area A may lead to an update of a lesser extent in related areas B_i according to the relationships in the context area graph. The semantic distance between two context areas that are linked via one or more intermediary areas can be computed by calculating the product of the semantic distances along the path. The proportion of the update of B_i to A is determined by the strongest semantic distance from A to B_i, in other words by calculating the maximum product of all paths from A to B_i. Context area that cannot be reached from A or where the distance is not known are not updated.

Trust Fading (Optional). When no experience with a trustee is made in a long time, the old trust relationship might no longer be valid. This usually means that the trust confidence level decreases over time. But there might be situations or time frames when also the trust level decreases without new experiences. We represent the magnitude of this fading effect with a *fading factor* as a real number $\lambda \geq 0$. A factor of 0 means no fading effect. The higher the fading factor, the faster trust relationship drops back to a state specified by the trust algorithm. This state might be a state of no trust and no confidence.

5   Supported Algorithms and Necessary Adaptations

The generic trust model presented in the previous section was conceived in such a way that existing trust models could be easily integrated into UniTEC. In the following, we present the mapping of the local trust models to the introduced generic model and suggest some algorithmic adaptations. The subset of investigated algorithms discussed here are Abdul-Rahman–Hailes, Beta Reputation, ReGreT and the original UniTEC algorithm. Due to space constraints, our results on the work of Yu and Singh [9], their previous suggestions [11] and Lik Mui's algorithm [12] are not covered here.

5.1   Abdul-Rahman – Hailes

The work on a trust model in [5] is based on sociological studies similar to the work of Marsh [13]. Here, interpersonal trust is context-dependent, subjective and based on prior experiences. A reputation information exchange amongst members of the community assists on trust decisions. All these aspects fit well in our generic trust model.

Trust is measured in a discrete metric with four values: very untrustworthy vu, untrustworthy u, trustworthy t and very trustworthy vt. Abdul-Rahman and Hailes describe three uncertainty states, which complement the four trust values: more positive experiences u^+, more negative experiences u^-, and equal amount of positive and negative experiences u^0. Ratings are specified in a discrete metric: very bad vb, bad b, good g, very good vg.

To fit this into the generic trust model, the discrete trust values have to be mapped onto the scalar trust metric. The range $[0, 1]$ is split into three equally sized ranges. The values at the borders of these ranges represent the four values from the discrete metric $(0, \frac{1}{3}, \frac{2}{3}, 1)$. Each discrete value is assigned a single position number $(pos(0) = vu, pos(1) = u, pos(2) = t, pos(3) = vt)$. To map a value from the generic trust model (t_g) onto this discrete metric (t_d), the following calculation is applied: $t_d = pos(round(t_g \cdot 3))$. The same formulas are applied for mapping the four discrete rating values. This translation follows the reasoning that trust in this model cannot be greater than *very trustworthy*, which is represented by the value of 1 in the generic trust model.

The semantics of the uncertainty values is not defined in [5], therefore the mapping into our generic trust model is difficult. For the four trust values, no uncertainty is known, which is represented as a certainty of 1 in our generic trust model. The initial trust value (when no previous experiences are known) is represented by the u^0 uncertainty value, so it makes sense to keep the generic certainty value of 0 (the generic trust value is of no importance in this case, so we also keep it at the lowest level of 0). Rahman's paper does not give an explanation on how to interpret this uncertainty value in other situations. The uncertainty values u^+ and u^- represent states where slightly more positive (or negative) previous experiences have been recorded. This is expressed in our generic trust model by a slight mistrust $(1/3)$ or a small positive trust $(2/3)$. In these cases the uncertainty component is represented by a mean generic certainty value (0.5).

5.2   The Beta Reputation System

The Beta Reputation System [8] is based on Bayesian probability. The *posteriori* probability of future positive experience is represented as a beta distribution based on past experiences. The trust value, in this work called "reputation rating", is determined by the expectation value of the corresponding beta distribution. This is a probability value in the scalar range $[0, 1]$. A one-to-one mapping to our generic trust value is possible. The certainty of the trust calculation is defined in this paper by mapping the beta distribution to an opinion, which describes beliefs about the truth of statements $([14, 15])$. In this mapping the certainty starts at 0 and grows continuously to 1 with more experiences being considered. This metric also can be directly mapped to our scalar generic certainty metric $[0, 1]$. Experiences in the Beta Reputation System are rated through two values: $r \geq 0$ for positive evidence and $s \geq 0$ for negative evidence. The sum $r + s$ represents the weight of the experience itself. These two weighted rating values can be mapped to the generic rating value $(0 \leq R \leq 1)$ and the generic weighting metric $(0 \leq w \leq 1)$ as $r = w \cdot R$ and $s = w \cdot (1 - R)$.

In this trust model, the accumulation of ratings can make use of a forgetting factor, which is the equivalent to the generic aging factor. In the Beta Reputation System the forgetting factor (λ_{beta}) has a reversed meaning: $\lambda_{beta} = 1$ is equivalent of having no forgetting factor and $\lambda_{beta} = 0$ means a total aging (only the last experience counts). Thus $\alpha = 1 - \lambda_{beta}$ represents a simple mapping to our generic aging factor.

5.3   The ReGreT System

The ReGreT system [7] represents a reputation system which uses direct experiences, witness reputation and analysis of the social network where the subject is embedded to calculate trust.

Direct experiences are recorded as a scalar metric in the range $[-1, +1]$. Trust is calculated as a weighted average of these experiences and uses the same value range. A mapping to the generic values can be done by transforming these ranges to $[0, 1]$ (shifting and scaling). A reliability is calculated for each trust value, based on the number of outcomes and the variation of their values. This reliability is expressed as a value in the range $[0, 1]$ which directly matches the representation of our generic certainty value.

An aging factor is not used. Instead, the oldest experience is neglected ($w = 0$), the newest experience is fully weighted ($w = 1$). The weight of experiences in between grows linearly from 0 to 1.

5.4   The Original UniTEC Algorithm

In the first work on UniTEC [2], a trust update algorithm describes the trust dynamics. It calculates a new trust value based on the old trust value and the new rating. *Ratings* in the original UniTEC proposal are expressed as a binary metric of $\{0, 1\}$ (either bad or good experience). The trust update algorithm works as well with ratings in a scalar range of $[0, 1]$ instead, which then require no further mapping to the rating metrics of the generic trust model.

In UniTEC we specified the certainty of the trust assertion through a confidence vector, where the amount of direct and indirect experiences and a trail of the latest n direct experiences is recorded. A semantic interpretation of this vector was not given. We need to calculate the certainty as a single scalar metric as in the generic trust model. This can be accomplished in a similar manner as in the ReGreT System, where the number of experiences and the variability of its values are consolidated into a single value in the range $[0, 1]$.

We created a simple fading algorithm that works with the UniTEC update algorithm and uses the fading factor λ. In the time when no experiences are recorded, trust will linearly drop to the minimal trust value in $1/\lambda$ time units.

6   Test Scenarios

To assess the quality of the trust update algorithms presented in the previous section, a series of test scenarios was developed. Each scenario simulates a different behavior pattern of trustor and trustee as a list of ratings. This pattern is then reflected by each single trust algorithm as trust dynamics. A test scenario can bring forward a specific feature or a malfunction of a trust update algorithm.

As the test scenarios simulate the behavior of real-world people, there are certain expectations associated with the trust dynamics. A trust algorithm is expected to generate trust dynamics that satisfy these expectations. Failing to comply with the specified expectations can either be a consequence of the calculations themselves or it reflects a shortcoming of the adaptations and mappings necessary for the local trust model to work in the generic trust model.

We want to stress the fact, that due to the subjectiveness of trust in general, also the quality estimation of the behavior reflected in the trust dynamics is subjective. Therefore, we do not offer a ranking of trust update algorithms, but instead point out the distinctive features of the algorithms, so that each user can choose the algorithm that most closely reflects his own expected behavior.

OnlyMaximalRatings. Starting from the initial trust state, only maximal ratings ($= 1$) are given. We would expect the trust to grow continuously and approach the maximal trust value ($= 1$).

OnlyMinimalRatings. Starting from the initial trust, only minimal ratings ($= 0$) are given. If the initial trust is the minimal trust value ($= 0$), then trust should stay at this level. Otherwise, we would expect the trust value to decrease and eventually approach the minimal trust value.

MinimalThenMaximalRatings. First, a series of minimal ratings is given, which is followed by a series of maximal ratings. We would expect the trust dynamics to start as described in the test scenario *OnlyMinimalRatings*. After switching to maximal ratings, trust should rise again. The expected growth rate of trust after the start of the maximal ratings should be lower than in the *OnlyMaximalRatings* test scenario.

MaximalThenMinimalRatings. First, a series of maximal ratings is given, followed by a series of minimal ratings. We expect trust to rise as in the test scenario *OnlyMaximalRatings*. When the series of minimal ratings starts, trust should decrease again. The trust decrease rate in the second half of the test should be slower than in the test scenario *OnlyMinimalRatings*.

SpecificRatings. After the previous test scenarios, which work with extreme ratings, these four test scenarios make use of a specific set of ratings (the *SpecificRatings*) which simulate a real-world rating situation. The ratings are: 1.0, 0.8, 0.5, 0.4, 0.5, 1.0, 0.6, 0.7, 0.7, 0.8, 1.0, 0.4, 0.3, 0.2, 0.2, 0.5, 1.0, 0.3, 0.4, 0.3. These ratings are submitted in this original order (*-Normal*), in a reversed order (*-Reversed*), ordered by ascending (*-OrderedAsc*) and by descending rating value (*-OrderedDesc*). In the *Normal* order, there are more positive ratings in the first half of the rating sequence, whereas negative ratings predominate in the second half. The expectation is that the final trust value is slightly below the mean trust value ($= 0.5$). With the *Reversed* order the expectation for the final trust value is a value slightly above the mean trust value. If the ending trust values in all four scenarios are equal, it suggests that the trust algorithm uses an *indistin-*

guishable past (see [6]), which means that the order of previous experiences does not matter. This should not the case when using an aging factor.

KeepPositive. This scenario has a *dynamic* nature, in that it actively reacts on the resulting trust values after each individual rating. Maximal ratings are given until a certain level of trust is reached (> 0.8). This trust level is then "misused" in form of minimal ratings, until the trust value reaches a mistrust level (< 0.5). Then, maximal ratings are submitted to raise trust again. This process is repeated four times. Here the trust algorithm's reaction to attempts of misuse is analyzed. We would expect trust to quickly drop to a mistrust level when the minimal ratings occur. The *optimal algorithm* should quickly detect this misuse attempt and react appropriately, e.g. by reporting minimal trust or even blacklisting the user.

7   Evaluation

We subjected each trust update algorithm discussed in Sec. 5 with a variation of aging factors to each test scenario from the previous section. For each evaluation graph we use the representation of the algorithms presented in Fig. 2.

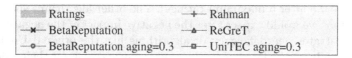

Fig. 2. Key for the trust dynamics presented in the evaluation

Test scenario *OnlyMaximalRatings* presented in Fig. 3 illustrates the different initial trust values of the algorithms: The trust dynamics start either with a trust value of 0 (UniTEC and Abdul-Rahman) or 0.5 (Beta Reputation and ReGreT). Trust rises monotonously for all algorithms. Trust in Beta Reputation with no aging factor and UniTEC approaches asymptotically the maximum trust value. Beta Reputation with an aging factor approaches a certain level of positive trust value. ReGreT and Abdul-Rahman reach maximum trust after just one maximal rating and remain at this level.

Similar effects can be noticed in the test scenario *OnlyMinimalRatings* (see Fig. 4). The trust algorithms that started with the lowest trust value (UniTEC and Abdul-Rahman) stay at this minimum trust level. ReGreT that started at 0.5 drops to the lowest trust value after just one bad experience. Beta Reputation also started with a trust value of 0.5. Without aging factor, trust approaches asymptotically the minimum trust value. With an aging factor, trust never drops below a certain level of mistrust.

Beta Reputation with an aging factor uses only a limited interval of the totally available trust value scope. This happens because the accumulation of the evidence (r and s) using a positive aging factor represents a geometric series. An upper limit for r and s thus limits the possibly reachable maximum and

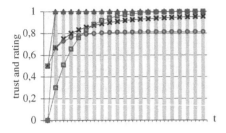

Fig. 3. OnlyMaximalRatings

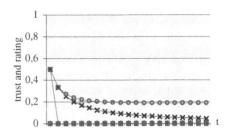

Fig. 4. OnlyMinimalRatings

minimum trust values. One possible solution to make use of the whole range regardless of an aging factor is to scale the possible output range to the whole generic trust value range. This can only be done if the aging factor remains constant throughout the relevant rating history.

In *MinimalThenMaximalRatings* (Fig. 5) when the maximal ratings start, trust starts rising again in all analyzed algorithms but Abdul-Rahman's. In this latter case, trust remains at the lowest level until as much maximal ratings as minimal ratings have been received. The discrete metrics of this trust model does not support other intermediate states. Another interesting observation is that UniTEC shows the same rise on trust as in the *OnlyMaximalRatings* test scenario (rising above 0.8 after 5 maximum ratings). The other algorithms show a slower rise of trust, as we would expect after the negative impact of the negative ratings. This demonstrates one deficiency of algorithms like the original UniTEC one, which rely solely on the last trust value and the new rating for their calculations and do not consider adequately the remaining history of ratings.

The *MaximalThenMinimalRatings* test scenario (Fig. 6) shows similar results as the previous scenario. It starts as expected like the *OnlyMaximalRatings*. When the minimal ratings start, trust drops with all but Abdul-Rahman's algorithm. Here, trust suddenly drops from maximum to the minimal value at the end of the scenario which is the point when more minimal than maximal ratings are recorded in the history.

In both scenarios we notice that Beta Reputation without an aging factor shows a slow reaction to the pattern change in the ratings.

The *SpecificRatings* test scenarios are depicted in Figs. 7, 8, 9 and 10. In *SpecificRatingsNormal* most algorithms follow the expected trust dynamics. The

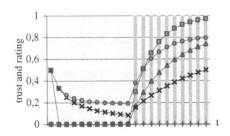

Fig. 5. MinimalThenMaximal

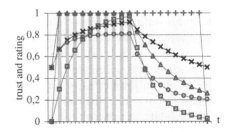

Fig. 6. MaximalThenMinimal

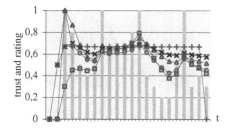

Fig. 7. SpecificRatingsNormal

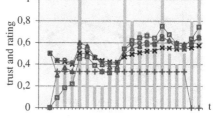

Fig. 8. SpecificRatingsReverse

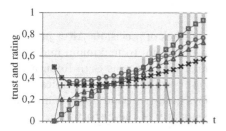

Fig. 9. SpecificOrderedAsc

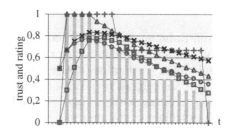

Fig. 10. SpecificOrderedDesc

ending trust value for UniTEC and Beta Reputation with aging factor of 0.3 is just below the average trust value of 0.5. ReGreT and Beta Reputation without an aging factor are a bit more optimistic ending just above 0.5. In *SpecificRatingsReversed* the opposite can be seen: The ending trust value is just above the trust value mark of 0.5.

In those four test scenarios Abdul-Rahman generates a trust dynamic that follows our expectations up until the end, when suddenly trust and certainty drop back to the lowest values. What happened here is that the algorithm reached the uncertainty state u^0. The most evident problem with this can be seen in Fig. 9. At the last couple of ratings this state of uncertainty is reached, which is not expected at all. The weakness lies in the lack of semantical meaning of the u^0 state. The only solution would be to alter the original algorithm and its underlying trust model to improve the way uncertainty is handled.

We see the characteristic of *indistinguishable past* with Abdul-Rahman and Beta Reputation without an aging factor: The ending trust values are the same regardless of the ordering of the ratings. All remaining algorithms use aging of ratings, leading to different ending values depending on the order of the ratings.

In our last test scenario, *KeepPositive*, the rating history depends on the calculated trust values. In Fig. 11 the reaction of the Beta Reputation algorithm to the scenario shows that the use of an aging factor helps with a fast reaction to the sudden minimum ratings, while it also makes the reaction speed more independent of the total history size. It can be noticed that without an aging factor, the dynamics of trust gets more steady as the history of ratings grows. The reaction of the remaining algorithms to this test scenario can be seen in Fig. 12.

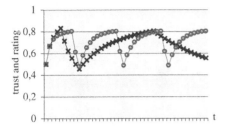

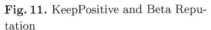

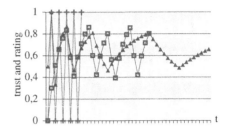

Fig. 11. KeepPositive and Beta Reputation

Fig. 12. KeepPositive and the other algorithms

Abdul-Rahman cannot really compete due to the lack of precision: After just one maximum or minimum rating trust flips from minimum to maximum and back to minimum trust value. ReGreT shows a similar deficiency as Beta Reputation without an aging factor: As more experiences are recorded, trust dynamics react slower to rating pattern changes. UniTEC shows quick reaction to the minimum ratings while maintaining this reaction independently of the history size.

8   Conclusion

In this work we investigated the various dimensions of trust relationships. Furthermore, we presented our approach towards a generic trust model which represents these dimensions and includes measures for trust, certainty, experiences and factors required for trust calculations. The model is based on observations gained through the analysis of a set of well-known trust models from the literature. It is generic in that it allows to plug in different specialized models and trust update algorithms and provides a bijective mapping between each local model and the generic trust representation. We discussed our adaptations of the original models which were necessary because we considered new trust relationship dimensions and ones that are not supported as such by all algorithms.

This generic trust model provides for the first time the possibility to compare various trust update algorithms through its common representation of algorithm inputs and outputs. We developed a set of test scenarios to assess the subjective quality of each supported algorithm. Our evaluation points out several important qualities but also deficiencies of the algorithms. To summarize our findings, we conclude that the Abdul-Rahman–Hailes algorithm in our generic trust model suffers from its discrete four step metrics in comparison to the field. The Beta Reputation system with an aging factor provides in our view the best overall results. The only drawback is the limitation of the trust value bandwidth which is proportional to the aging factor. The ReGreT algorithm provides responses to our test scenarios that meet our expectations, but its dynamics proved to be highly dependent on the history size: Too fast reactions without or with a small previous history of experiences, and slower dynamics as more experiences were collected. Finally the original UniTEC proposal provided a simple yet efficient algorithm and eased integration of the various dynamics. However, a deficiency of this algorithm lies in focusing merely on the current trust value and the latest experience and not taking into account patterns of past experiences.

Future work on trust update algorithms could consider giving more weight to negative experiences as opposed to positive ones. Furthermore, analyzing patterns of past experiences would be another interesting aspect to better detect misuse attempts and enhance the calculation of trust certainty. Besides improving existing trust update algorithms, we plan to investigate how to fit further algorithms into the generic model. Regarding the farther future, we consider to refine the representation of semantic distance in the model. In the current state of UniTEC, the semantic distances between the different trust context areas are specified by the applications and can be modified by each user. It would be challenging but surely interesting to investigate, whether and if yes how this process could be automated further.

References

1. Kinateder, M., Terdic, R., Rothermel, K.: Strong Pseudonymous Communication for Peer-to-Peer Reputation Systems. In: Proceedings of the ACM Symposium on Applied Computing 2005, Santa Fe, New Mexico, USA, ACM (2005)
2. Kinateder, M., Rothermel, K.: Architecture and Algorithms for a Distributed Reputation System. In Nixon, P., Terzis, S., eds.: Proceedings of the First International Conference on Trust Management. Volume 2692 of LNCS., Crete, Greece, Springer-Verlag (2003) 1–16
3. Gambetta, D.: Can We Trust Trust? In: Trust: Making and Breaking Cooperative Relations, Department of Sociology, University of Oxford (2000) 213–237
4. Jøsang, A., Gray, E., Kinateder, M.: Analysing Topologies of Transitive Trust. In Dimitrakos, T., Martinelli, F., eds.: Proceedings of the First International Workshop on Formal Aspects in Security & Trust (FAST 2003), Pisa, Italy (2003) 9–22
5. Abdul-Rahman, A., Hailes, S.: Supporting trust in virtual communities. In: Proceedings of the 33rd Hawaii International Conference on System Sciences, Maui Hawaii (2000)
6. Jonker, C.M., Treur, J.: Formal analysis of models for the dynamics of trust based on experiences. In Garijo, F.J., Boman, M., eds.: Proceedings of the 9th European Workshop on Modelling Autonomous Agents in a Multi-Agent World: Multi-Agent System Engineering (MAAMAW-99). Volume 1647., Berlin, Germany, Springer-Verlag (1999) 221–231
7. Sabater, J.: Trust and Reputation for Agent Societies. PhD thesis, Institut d'Investigaci en Intelligncia Articial, Bellaterra (2003)
8. Jøsang, A., Ismail, R.: The Beta Reputation System. In: Proceedings of the 15th Bled Conference on Electronic Commerce, Bled, Slovenia (2002)
9. Yu, B., Singh, M.P.: An evidential model of distributed reputation management. In: Proceedings of the first international joint conference on Autonomous agents and multiagent systems, Bologna, Italy, ACM Press (2002) 294–301
10. Blaze, M., Feigenbaum, J., Lacy, J.: Decentralized Trust Management. In: Proceedings of the 17th IEEE Symposium on Security and Privacy, Oakland (1996) 164–173

11. Yu, B., Singh, M.P.: A Social Mechanism of Reputation Management in Electronic Communities. In Klusch, M., Kerschberg, L., eds.: Proceedings of the 4th International Workshop on Cooperative Information Agents. Volume 1860., Springer-Verlag (2000) 154–165
12. Mui, L.: Computational Models of Trust and Reputation: Agents, Evolutionary Games, and Social Networks. PhD thesis, Massachusetts Institute of Technology (2003)
13. Marsh, S.P.: Formalising Trust as a Computational Concept. PhD thesis, Department of Mathematics and Computer Science, University of Stirling (1994)
14. Jøsang, A.: A Logic for Uncertain Probabilities. International Journal of Uncertainty, Fuzziness and Knowledge-Based Systems **9** (2001) 279–311
15. Jøsang, A., Grandison, T.: Conditional Inference in Subjective Logic. In: Proceedings of the 6th International Conference on Information Fusion, Cairns (2003)

A Probabilistic Trust Model for Handling Inaccurate Reputation Sources

Jigar Patel, W.T. Luke Teacy, Nicholas R. Jennings, and Michael Luck

Electronics & Computer Science, University of Southampton, Southampton SO17, 1BJ, UK
{jp03r, wtlt03r, nrj, mml}@ecs.soton.ac.uk

Abstract. This research aims to develop a model of trust and reputation that will ensure good interactions amongst software agents in large scale open systems in particular. The following are key drivers for our model: (1) agents may be self-interested and may provide false accounts of experiences with other agents if it is beneficial for them to do so; (2) agents will need to interact with other agents with which they have no past experience. Against this background, we have developed *TRAVOS* (Trust and Reputation model for Agent-based Virtual OrganisationS) which models an agent's trust in an interaction partner. Specifically, trust is calculated using probability theory taking account of past interactions between agents. When there is a lack of personal experience between agents, the model draws upon reputation information gathered from third parties. In this latter case, we pay particular attention to handling the possibility that reputation information may be inaccurate.

1 Introduction

Computational systems of all kinds are moving toward large-scale, open, dynamic and distributed architectures, which harbour numerous *self-interested* agents. The Grid is perhaps the most prominent example of such an environment and is the context of this paper. However, in all these environments the concept of self-interest, which is endemic in such systems, introduces the possibility of agents interacting in a way to maximise their own gain (perhaps at the cost of another). Therefore, in such contexts it is essential to ensure good interaction between agents so that no single agent can take advantage of the others in the system. In this sense, good interactions can be defined as those in which the expectations of the interacting agents are fulfilled; for example, if the expectation of one of the agents is recorded as a contract which is then fulfilled by its interaction partner, it is a good interaction.

We view the Grid as a multi-agent system (MAS) in which autonomous software agents, owned by various organisations, interact with each other. In particular, many of the interactions between agents are conducted in terms of Virtual Organisations (VOs), which are collections of agents (representing individuals or organisations), each of which has a range of problem-solving capabilities and resources at its disposal. A VO is formed when there is a need to solve a problem

P. Herrmann et al. (Eds.): iTrust 2005, LNCS 3477, pp. 193–209, 2005.

or provide a resource that a single agent cannot address. Here, the problem of assuring good interactions between individual agents is further complicated by the size of the Grid, and the large number of agents and interactions between them. Nevertheless, solutions to these problems are integral to the wide-scale acceptance of the Grid and agent-based VOs [4].

It is now well established that computational *trust* is important in such open systems [10]. Specifically, trust provides a form of social control in environments in which agents are likely to interact with others whose intentions are not known. It allows agents within such systems to reason about the reliability of others. More specifically, trust can be utilised to account for uncertainty about the willingness and capability of other agents to perform actions as agreed, rather than defecting when it proves to be more profitable. For the purpose of this work, we use an adaptation of the definition offered by Gambetta [5], and define trust to be *a particular level of subjective probability with which an agent assesses that another agent will perform a particular action, both before the assessing agent can monitor such an action and in a context in which it affects the assessing agent's own action.*

Trust is often built over time by accumulating personal experience with others, and using this experience to judge how they will perform in an as yet unobserved situation. However, when assessing our trust in someone with whom we have no direct personal experience, we often ask others about their experiences with this individual. This collective opinion of others regarding an individual is known as the individual's *reputation* and it is the reputation of a trustee that we use to assess its trustworthiness, if we have no personal experience.

Given the importance of trust and reputation in open systems and their use as a form of social control, several computational models of trust and reputation have been developed, each with requirements for the domain to which they apply (see [10] for a review of such models). In our case, the requirements can be summarised as follows. First, the model must provide a trust metric that represents a level of trust in an agent. Such a metric allows comparisons between agents so that one agent can be inferred as more trustworthy than another. The model must be able to provide a trust metric given the presence or absence of personal experience. Second, the model must reflect an individual's *confidence* in its level of trust for another agent. This is necessary so that an agent can determine the degree of influence the trust metric has on its decision about whether or not to interact with another individual. Generally speaking, higher confidence means a greater impact on the decision-making process, and lower confidence means less impact. Third, an agent must not assume that opinions of others are accurate or based on actual experience. Thus, the model must be able to discount the opinions of others in the calculation of reputation, based on past reliability and consistency of the opinion providers. However, existing models do not allow an agent to efficiently assess the reliability of reputation sources and use this assessment to discount the opinion provided by that source (see Section 5 for a detailed discussion). To meet the above requirements, therefore, we have developed TRAVOS, a trust and reputation model for agent-based VOs.

The remainder of this paper is organised as follows. Section 2 presents the basic TRAVOS model. Following from this, Section 3 provides a description of how the basic model has been expanded to include the functionality of handling inaccurate opinions from reputation sources. A scenario using these mechanisms is then presented in Section 4. Section 5 presents related work. Finally, Section 6 concludes the paper and provides an outline for future work.

2   The TRAVOS Model

TRAVOS equips an agent (the truster) with two methods for assessing the trustworthiness of another agent (the trustee). First, the truster can make the assessment based on the direct interactions it has had with the trustee. Second, the truster may assess the trustworthiness of another based on the reputation of the trustee.

2.1   Basic Notation

In a MAS consisting of n agents, we denote the set of all agents as $\mathcal{A} = \{a_1, a_2, ..., a_n\}$. Over time, distinct pairs of agents $\{a_x, a_y\} \subseteq \mathcal{A}$ may interact with one another, governed by contracts that specify the obligations of each agent towards its interaction partner. An interaction between a_1 and a_2 is considered successful by a_1 if a_2 fulfils its obligations. From the perspective of a_1, the outcome of an interaction between a_1 and a_2 is summarised by a binary variable[1], O_{a_1,a_2}, where $O_{a_1,a_2} = 1$ indicates a successful (and $O_{a_1,a_2} = 0$ indicates an unsuccessful) interaction[2] for a_1 (Equation 1). Furthermore, we denote an outcome observed at time t as O_{a_1,a_2}^t, and the set of all outcomes observed from time t_0 to time t as $O_{a_1,a_2}^{n:t}$.

$$O_{a_1,a_2} = \begin{cases} 1 \text{ if contract fulfilled by } a_2 \\ 0 \text{ otherwise} \end{cases} \tag{1}$$

At any point of time t, the history of interactions between agents a_1 and a_2 is recorded as a tuple, $\mathcal{R}_{a_1,a_2}^t = (m_{a_1,a_2}^t, n_{a_1,a_2}^t)$ where the value of m_{a_1,a_2}^t is the number of successful interactions of a_1 with a_2, while n_{a_1,a_2}^t is the number of unsuccessful interactions of a_1 with a_2. The tendency of an agent a_2 to fulfil or default on its obligations to an agent a_1, is governed by its behaviour. We model the behaviour of a_2 towards a_1, denoted B_{a_1,a_2}, as the *intrinsic* probability with which $O_{a_1,a_2} = 1$. In other words, B_{a_1,a_2} is the *expected value* of O_{a_1,a_2} given

---

[1] Representing a contract outcome with a binary variable is a simplification made for the purpose of our model. We concede that in certain circumstances, a more expressive representation may be appropriate.

[2] The outcome of an interaction from the perspective of one agent is not necessarily the same as from the perspective of its interaction partner. Thus, it is possible that $O_{a_1,a_2} \neq O_{a_2,a_1}$.

complete information about a_2's decision processes and all environmental factors that effect its capabilities (Equation 2). For simplicity, we admit the subscripts for B when the identity of the interacting agents is irrelevant to the discussion.

$$B_{a_1,a_2} = E[O_{a_1,a_2}], \quad \text{where } B_{a_1,a_2} \in [0,1] \tag{2}$$

In TRAVOS, each agent maintains a *level of trust* in each of the other agents in the system. Specifically, the level of trust of an agent a_1 in an agent a_2, denoted as τ_{a_1,a_2}, represents a_1's assessment of the likelihood of a_2 fulfilling its obligations. The *confidence* of a_1 in its assessment of a_2 is denoted as γ_{a_1,a_2}. Confidence is a metric that represents the accuracy of the trust value calculated by an agent given the number of observations (the evidence) it uses in the trust value calculation. Intuitively more evidence would result in more confidence. The precise definitions and reasons behind these values are discussed in Sections 2.2 and 2.3 respectively.

2.2   Modelling Trust

The first basic requirement of a computational trust model is that it should provide a metric for comparing the relative trustworthiness of different agents. From our definition of trust, we consider an agent to be trustworthy if it has a high probability of performing a particular action which, in our context, is to fulfil its obligations during an interaction. This probability is unavoidably subjective, because it can only be assessed from the individual viewpoint of the truster, based on the truster's personal experiences.

In light of this, we have adopted a probabilistic approach to modelling trust, based on the individual experiences of any agent in the role of a truster. If a truster, agent a_1, has complete information about a trustee, agent a_2, then, according to a_1, the probability that a_2 fulfils its obligations is expressed by B_{a_1,a_2}. In general, however, complete information cannot be assumed; the best we can do is to use the expected value of B_{a_1,a_2} given the experience of a_1, which we consider to be the set of all interaction outcomes it has observed. Thus, we define the level of trust τ_{a_1,a_2} at time t, as the expected value of B_{a_1,a_2} given the set of outcomes $O_{a_1,a_2}^{1:t}$ (3).

$$\tau_{a_1,a_2} = E[B_{a_1,a_2}|O_{a_1,a_2}^{1:t}] \tag{3}$$

The expected value of a continous random variable is dependent on the *probability density function* (pdf) used to model the probability that the variable will have a certain value. Thus, we must choose such a function that is suitable to our domain. In Bayesian analysis, the beta family of pdfs is commonly used as a prior distribution for random variables that take on continuous values in the interval $[0,1]$. For example beta pdfs can be used to model the distribution of a random variable representing the unknown probability of a binary event [2]— B is an example of such a variable. For this reason, we use beta pdfs in our model. (Beta pdfs have also been previously applied to trust for similar reasons by [7]).

The general formula for beta distributions is given in Equation 4. It has two parameters, α and β, which define the shape of the density function when plotted. Examples, plotted for B with various parameter settings are shown in Figure 1; here, the horizontal axis represents the possible values of B, while the vertical axis gives the *relative* probability that each of these values is the true value for B. The most likely (expected value) of B is the curve maximum. The width of the curve represents the amount of uncertainty over the true value of B. If α and β both have values close to 1, a wide density plot results, thus representing a high level of uncertainty about B. In the extreme case of $\alpha = \beta = 1$, the distribution is uniform, with all values of B considered equally likely.

$$f(b|\alpha,\beta) = \frac{b^{\alpha-1}(1-b)^{\beta-1}}{\int U^{\alpha-1}(1-U)^{\beta-1}dU}, \quad \text{where } \alpha, \beta > 0 \tag{4}$$

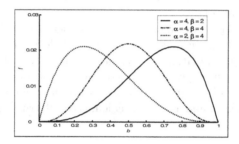

Fig. 1. Example beta plots, showing how the beta curve shape changes with the parameters α and β

Against this background, we now show how to calculate the value of τ_{a_1,a_2} based on the interaction outcomes observed by a_1. First, we must find values for α and β that represent the beliefs of a_1 about a_2. Assuming that prior to observing any interaction outcomes with a_2, a_1 believes that all possible values for B_{a_1,a_2} are equally likely, then a_1's initial settings for α and β are $\alpha = \beta = 1$. Based on standard techniques, the parameter settings in light of observations are achieved by adding the number of successful outcomes to the initial setting of α, and the number of unsuccessful outcomes to β. In our notation, this is given in Equation 5. Then the final value for τ_{a_1} is calculated by applying the standard equation for the expected value of a beta distribution (Equation 6) to these parameter settings.

$$\alpha = m^{1:t}_{a_1,a_2} + 1 \quad \text{and} \quad \beta = n^{1:t}_{a_1,a_2} + 1 \quad \text{where } t \text{ is the time of assessment} \tag{5}$$

$$E[B|\alpha,\beta] = \frac{\alpha}{\alpha+\beta} \tag{6}$$

2.3   Modelling Confidence

In the previous section, we showed how an agent can establish trustworthiness so that it can be used to compare the trustworthiness of different agents. However, this method is susceptible to two problems created by the need for adequate evidence (observations) to calculate a meaningful value for trust. Firstly, an agent may not have interacted with another agent for which it is calculating a level of trust. This means that it has no personal experience and $m_{a_1,a_2}^t = n_{a_1,a_2}^t = 0$. Secondly, an agent may have had few interactions and observed outcomes with another. In both these cases, the calculated value of τ_{a_1,a_2} will be a poor estimate for the actual value of B_{a_1,a_2}. Intuitively, having observed many outcomes for an event will lead to a better estimate for the future probability for that event (assuming all other things are equal). These problems create the need for an agent to be able to measure its *confidence* in its value of trust. To this end, we incorporate a confidence metric in TRAVOS, based on standard methods of calculating confidence intervals taken from statistical analysis.

Specifically, the confidence metric γ_{a_1,a_2} is a measure of the probability that the actual value of B_{a_1,a_2} lies within an acceptable level of error ϵ about τ_{a_1,a_2}. It is calculated using Equation 7. The acceptable level of error ϵ influences how confident an agent is given the same number of observations. For example, if the number of observations remains constant, a larger value of ϵ causes an agent to be more confident in its calculation of trust than a lower value of ϵ.

$$\gamma_{a_1,a_2} = \frac{\int_{\tau_{a_1,a_2}+\epsilon}^{\tau_{a_1,a_2}-\epsilon}(B_{a_1,a_2})^{\alpha-1}(1 - B_{a_1,a_2})^{\beta-1}dB_{a_1,a_2}}{\int_0^1 U^{\alpha-1}(1 - U)^{\beta-1}dU} \tag{7}$$

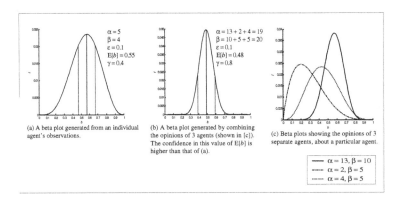

(a) A beta plot generated from an individual agent's observations.

(b) A beta plot generated by combining the opinions of 3 agents (shown in [c]). The confidence in this value of E[b] is higher than that of (a).

(c) Beta plots showing the opinions of 3 separate agents, about a particular agent.

Fig. 2. Example beta plots showing how 3 agents' opinions are aggregated to yield a more confident value of trust in a particular agent

2.4 Modelling Reputation

Until now, we have only considered how an agent uses its own direct observations to calculate a level of trust. However, by using confidence, we can specify a decision-making process in an agent to lead it to seek more evidence when required. In TRAVOS, an agent a_1 calculates τ_{a_1,a_2} based on its personal experiences with a_2. If this value of τ_{a_1,a_2} has a corresponding confidence γ_{a_1,a_2} below that of a predetermined *minimum confidence level*, denoted θ^γ, then a_1 will seek the opinions of other agents about a_2 to boost its confidence above θ^γ. These collective opinions form a_2's reputation and, by seeking it, a_1 can effectively obtain a larger set of observations.

The *true* opinion of a_3 at time t, about the trustee a_2, is the tuple, $\mathcal{R}^t_{a_3,a_2} = (m^t_{a_3,a_2}, n^t_{a_3,a_2})$, defined in Section 2.1. In addition, we denote the *reported* opinion of a_3 about a_2 at time t as $\hat{\mathcal{R}}^t_{a_3,a_2} = (\hat{m}^t_{a_3,a_2}, \hat{n}^t_{a_3,a_2})$. This distinction is important because a_3 may not reveal $\mathcal{R}^t_{a_3,a_2}$ truthfully. The truster, a_1, must form a single trust value from all such opinions that it receives. An elegant and efficient solution to this problem is to enumerate all the successful and unsuccessful interactions from the reports that it recieves (see Equation 8). The resulting values, denoted N_{a_1,a_2} and M_{a_1,a_2} respectively, represent the reputation of a_2 from the perspective of a_1. These values can then be used to calculate shape parameters (see Equation 9) for a beta distribution, to give a trust value determined by opinions provided from others. In addition, the truster takes on board any direct experience it has with the trustee, by adding its own values for n_{a_1,a_2} and m_{a_1,a_2} with the same equation. The confidence value γ_{a_1,a_2} for this combined distribution will be higher than for any of the component opinions, because more observations will have been taken into account (see Figure 2).

$$N_{a_1,a_2} = \sum_{k=0}^{p} \hat{n}_{a_k,a_2}, \quad M_{a_1,a_2} = \sum_{k=0}^{p} \hat{m}_{a_k,a_2}, \quad \text{where } p = \text{number of reports} \quad (8)$$

$$\alpha = M_{a_1,a_2} + 1 \quad \text{and} \quad \beta = N_{a_1,a_2} + 1 \quad (9)$$

The desirable feature of this approach is that, provided Conditions 1 & 2 hold, the resulting trust value and confidence level is the same as it would be if all the observations had been observed directly by the truster itself.

Condition 1. *The behaviour of the trustee must be independent of the identity of the truster it is interacting with. Specifically, the following should be true:* $\forall a_2 \quad \forall a_3, \quad B_{a_2,a_1} = B_{a_3,a_1}.$

Condition 2. *The reputation provider must report its observations accurately and truthfully. In other words, it must be true that:* $\forall a_2 \quad \forall a_3, \quad \mathcal{R}^t_{a_3,a_2} = \hat{\mathcal{R}}^t_{a_3,a_2}.$

Unfortunately, we cannot expect these conditions to hold in a broad range of situations. For instance, a trustee may value interactions with one agent over another, it might therefore commit more resources to the valued agent to increase its success rate, thus introducing a bias in its perceived behaviour. Similarly, in the case of a rater's opinion of a trustee, it is possible that the rater has an incentive to misrepresent its true view of the trustee. Such an incentive could have a positive or negative effect on a trustee's reputation; if a strong co-operative relationship exists between trustee and rater, the rater may choose to overestimate its likelihood of success, whereas a competitive relationship may lead the rater to underestimate the trustee. Due to these possibilities, we consider the methods of dealing with inaccurate reputation sources an important requirement for a computational trust model. In the next section, we introduce our solution to this requirement, building upon the basic model introduced thus far.

3   Filtering Inaccurate Reputation Reports in TRAVOS

Inaccurate reputation reports can be due to the reputation report provider being malevolent or having incomplete information. In both cases, an agent must be able to assess the reliability of the report passed to it. The general solution to coping with inaccurate reputation reports is to adjust or ignore opinions judged to be unreliable (in order to reduce their effect on the trustee's reputation). There are two basic approaches to achieving this that have been proposed in the literature; these can be referred to as *endogenous* and *exogenous* methods. The former techniques attempt to identify unreliable reputation information by considering the statistical properties of the reported opinions alone (e.g. [12, 3]). The latter techniques rely on other information to make such judgements, such as the reputation of the source, or the relationship with the trustee (e.g. [1]).

Many proposals for endogenous techniques assume that inaccurate or unfair raters will generally be in a minority among reputation sources. Based on this assumption, they consider reputation providers whose opinions deviate in some way from mainstream opinion to be those most likely to be inaccurate. Our solution is also based on an endogenous approach, but we make our judgements on an individual basis — we judge a reputation provider on the perceived accuracy of its past opinions, rather than its deviation from mainstream opinion. More specifically, we calculate the probability that an agent will provide an accurate opinion given its past opinions, and later observed interactions with the trustees, for which those opinions were given. Using this value, we reduce the distance between a rater's opinion and the prior belief that all possible values for an agent's behaviour are equally probable. Once all the opinions collected about a trustee have been adjusted in this way, the opinions are aggregated using the technique described in Section 2.4.

In the following subsections we describe this technique in more detail: Section 3.1 describes how the probability of accuracy is calculated and then Section 3.2 shows how opinions are adjusted and the combined reputation obtained.

3.1   Calculating the Probability of Accuracy

The first stage in our solution is to estimate the probability that a rater's stated opinion of a trustee is an accurate predictor of the trustee's behaviour towards the truster. More specifically, let $\hat{\tau}_{a_3,a_2}$ be the trust value calculated using $\mathcal{R}^t_{a_3,a_2}$.

With this in mind, our goal is to calculate the probability that $\hat{\tau}_{a_3,a_2} = B_{a_1,a_2}$. We denote this probability as ρ_{a_1,a_3} — the accuracy of a_3 according to a_1. If a_1 had observed sufficient direct interactions with a_2, then it would already have the means to calculate this probability: it is given using the beta pdf (Equation 4) with parameters set using a_1's direct experience with a_2. Unfortunately, the very reason that a_1 seeks reputation information about a_2 is because its direct experience with a_2 is not enough to make such a judgement accurately. However, we can avoid this problem by taking advantage of the fact that O_{a_1,a_2} is conditionally independent of the identity of a_2 given B_{a_1,a_2}. In other words, if we had a set of agents $\mathcal{C} \subseteq \mathcal{A}$, and $\forall a_k \in \mathcal{C}, \forall a_l \in \mathcal{C}, B_{a_1,a_k} = B_{a_1,a_l}$, then regardless of which member of $\mathcal{C}$ we interacted with, the probability of that member fulfilling its obligations would be the same. This means that we could calculate $E[B_{a_1,a_k}]$ using not only the outcomes of interactions with a_k, but the outcomes of all interactions with any member of $\mathcal{C}$. In light of this, we can derive a beta probability function based on the outcomes of all interactions for which a rater gives the same value for $\hat{\tau}$ — regardless of which agents these opinions were given for. Using the parameter settings of this distribution, we can use Equation 4 to calculate ρ_{a_1,a_3} for a given value of $\hat{\tau}_{a_3,a_2}$.

Two problems must be solved before this solution can work in practice. First, the number of possible values of $\hat{\tau}_{a_3,a_2}$ is infinite — we cannot in general expect to see the same value of $\hat{\tau}_{a_3,a_2}$ more than once, so will never observe enough contracts to estimate ρ_{a_1,a_3} confidently. Second, for the same reason, ρ_{a_1,a_3} will always be vanishingly small. We solve both of these problems by approximation. All possible values for $\hat{\mathcal{R}}_{a_3,a_2}$ are split into bins according to the expected value and standard deviation of the resulting beta distribution (Equation 10); a single beta distribution is generated from all observations for which $\hat{\mathcal{R}}_{a_3,a_2}$ belongs to a given bin. For each bin, the probability that the true value of B_{a_1,a_2} lies within the range of expected values belonging to that bin is calculated — it is this value that we use for ρ_{a_1,a_3}. Calculation of this value is done by integrating Equation 4 over the expected value range of the bin.

$$\sigma = \sqrt{\frac{\alpha\beta}{(\alpha + \beta)^2(\alpha + \beta + 1)}} \text{where } \sigma \text{ is the standard deviation} \qquad (10)$$

3.2   Adjusting the Reputation Ratings

Our goal in adjusting a reputation source's opinion is to reduce the *effect* of unreliable opinions on a trustee's overall reputation. To achieve this, we consider the properties of a beta distribution, based on a single rater's opinion, that determine its effect on the final reputation value. Specifically, we consider the expected value of the distribution and its standard deviation. Effectively, by adding a rating to a trustee's reputation (Equation 8) we move the expected value of the combined distribution in the direction of the rater's opinion. The standard deviation of the opinion distribution contributes to the confidence value for the combined reputation value but, more importantly, its value relative to prior standard deviation determines how far towards the rater's opinion the expected value will move. However, the relationship between the change in the expected value, and the standard deviation is non-linear. Consider as an example three distributions d_1, d_2 and d_3, with shape parameters, expected value and standard deviation (denoted σ) as shown in Table 1; the results of combining d_1 with each of the other two distributions are shown in the last two rows.

Table 1. Example beta distributions and the results of combining them

Distribution	α	β	$E[B]$	σ
d_1	540	280	0.6585	0.0165
d_2	200	200	0.5000	0.0250
d_3	5000	5000	0.5000	0.0050
$d_1 + d_2$	740	480	0.6066	0.0140
$d_1 + d_3$	5540	5280	0.5120	0.0048

As can be seen, distributions d_2 and d_3 have identical expected values with standard deviations of 0.025 and 0.005 respectively. Although the difference between these values is small (0.02), the result of combining d_1 with d_2 is quite different from combining d_1 and d_3. Whereas the expected value in the first case falls approximately between the expected values for d_2 and d_1, in the latter case, the relatively small parameter values of d_1 compared to d_3 mean that d_1 has virtually no impact on the combined result. Obviously, the reason for this is due to our method of reputation combination (Equation 8), in which the parameter values are summed. This is an important observation because it shows how, if left unchecked, an unfair rater could purposely increase the weight an agent puts in its opinion by providing very large values for m and n, which in turn determine α and β.

In light of this, we adopt an approach that significantly reduces very high parameter values unless the probability of the rater's opinion being accurate is very close to 1. Specifically, we reduce the distance between the expected value and standard deviation of the rater distribution, and the uniform distribution, $\alpha = \beta = 1$, which represents a state of no information; we denote the standard deviation of this uniform distribution as $\sigma_{uniform}$ and its expected value as $E_{uniform}$. Returning to our example scenario of a rater agent a_3 providing an opinion to agent a_1 about agent a_2, this is performed according to Equations 11 and 12 respectively. In these equations, we use the over-bar, for example $\bar{\alpha}$, to indicate that we are referring to the adjusted distribution. Adjusting the expected value as well as the standard deviation in this way results in a more conservative estimate. This is important in cases in which few more reliable ratings are available to mediate the expected value of the combined reputation.

$$\bar{E} = E_{uniform} + \rho_{a_1,a_3} \cdot (E - E_{uniform}) \tag{11}$$
$$\bar{\sigma} = \sigma_{uniform} + \rho_{a_1,a_3} \cdot (\sigma - \sigma_{uniform}) \tag{12}$$

Once all reputation opinions have been adjusted in this way, we sum the ratings as normal according to Equation 8. To do this, we must calculate the adjusted values for $\hat{m}_{a_3,a_2}$ and $\hat{n}_{a_3,a_2}$. It can be shown that the adjusted parameter values $\bar{\alpha}$ and $\bar{\beta}$, can be calculated according to Equation 13 and Equation 14. The new values for $\hat{m}_{a_3,a_2}$ and $\hat{n}_{a_3,a_2}$ are then given by subtracting the prior parameter settings from the adjusted distribution parameters (Eqn. 15).

$$\bar{\alpha} = \frac{\bar{E}^2 - \bar{E}^3}{\bar{\sigma}^2} - \bar{E} \tag{13}$$

$$\bar{\beta} = \frac{(1 - \bar{E})^2 - (1 - \bar{E})^3}{\bar{\sigma}^2} - (1 - \bar{E}) \tag{14}$$

$$\bar{m}_{a_3,a_2} = \bar{\alpha} - 1 \quad , \quad \bar{n}_{a_3,a_2} = \bar{\beta} - 1 \tag{15}$$

4   TRAVOS in Action

This section provides an agent-based VO scenario in which we demonstrate the use of TRAVOS. We begin by stating that there is a need to create a VO to meet a specific requirement to provide a composite multimedia communication service to an end user. The composite consists of the following basic services: text messaging, HTML content provision and phone calls (this example is taken from [9]). Now, assume agent a_1 has identified this need and wishes to capitalise on the market niche. However, a_1 only has the capability to provide a text messaging service. It can only achieve its goal by forming a VO with an agent that can supply a service for phone calls and one for HTML content. For simplicity, we assume that each agent in the system has the ability to provide only one service. Agent a_1 is aware of three agents that can provide a phone call service, and its interaction history with these is shown in Table 2. Similarly, it is aware of three agents that are capable of providing HTML content, and its past interactions with these entities are given in Table 3.

Table 2. Agent a_1's interaction history with phone call service provider agents

Agent	Past interactions	
	Successful	Unsuccessful
a_2	17	5
a_3	2	15
a_4	18	5

Table 3. Agent a_1's interaction history with HTML content service provider agents

Agent	Past interactions	
	Successful	Unsuccessful
a_5	9	14
a_6	3	0
a_7	18	11

Agent a_1 would like to choose the most trustworthy phone call and HTML content service provider from the selection. The following describes how this is achieved using TRAVOS. Before we calculate which of the possible candidates are the most trustworthy, we must specify certain parameters that a_1 requires. First, we specify the level of error that a_1 is willing to accept when determining the confidence in a calculated trust value as $\epsilon = 0.2$. Second, we specify that $\theta^\gamma = 0.95$, below which a_1 will seek other's opinions about the trustee.

4.1   Calculating Trust and Confidence

Using the information from Tables 2 and 3, a_1 can determine the number of successful interactions n, and the number of unsuccessful interactions m, for each agent it has interacted with. Feeding these into Equation 5, a_1 can obtain shape parameters for a beta distribution function that represents the behaviour of each service provider agent. For example, the shape parameters α and β, for a_2, are calculated as follows:

Using Table 2: $n_{a_1,a_2} = 17$, $m_{a_1,a_2} = 5$.
Using Equation 5: $\alpha = 17 + 1 = 18$ and $\beta = 5 + 1 = 6$.

The shape parameters for each agent are then used in Equation 6 to calculate a trust value for each agent that a_1 is assessing. For example, the trust value τ_{a_1,a_2} for a_2 is calculated as follows:

Using Equation 6: $\tau_{a_1,a_2} = \frac{\alpha}{\alpha+\beta} = \frac{18}{18+6} = 0.75$.

For a_1 to be able to use the trust values it obtains for each agent, it must also determine the confidence it has in the calculated trust value. This is achieved by using Equation 7 and the variable ϵ (which in this scenario has been set to 0.2). For example, the confidence γ_{a_1,a_2} that a_1 has in the trust value τ_{a_1,a_2} is calculated as shown below:

Using Equation 7:

$$\gamma_{a_1,a_2} = \frac{\int_{\tau_{a_1,a_2}+\epsilon}^{\tau_{a_1,a_2}-\epsilon} B^{\alpha-1}(1-B)^{\beta-1}dB}{\int_0^1 U^{\alpha-1}(1-U)^{\beta-1}dU} = \frac{\int_{0.95}^{0.55} B^{\alpha-1}(1-B)^{\beta-1}dB}{\int_0^1 U^{\alpha-1}(1-U)^{\beta-1}dU} = 0.98$$

Table 4. Agent a_1's calculated trust and associated confidence level for HTML content and phone call service provider agents

Agent	α	β	τ_{a_1,a_x}	γ_{a_1,a_x}
a_2	18	6	0.75	0.98
a_3	3	16	0.16	0.98
a_4	19	6	0.76	0.98
a_5	10	15	0.40	0.97
a_6	4	1	0.8	0.87
a_7	19	12	0.61	0.98

The shape parameters, trust values and associated confidence for each agent, a_2 to a_7, which a_1 computes using TRAVOS, are shown in Table 4. From this, it is clear that the trust values for agents a_2, a_3 and a_4, all have a confidence above θ^γ (=0.95). This means that a_1 does not need to consider the opinions of others for these three agents. Agent a_1 is able to decide that a_4 is the most trustworthy out of the three phone call service provider agents and chooses it to provide the phone call service for the VO.

4.2   Calculating Reputation

The process of selecting the most trustworthy HTML content service provider is not as straightforward. Agent a_1 has calculated that out of the possible HTML service providers, a_6 has the highest trust value. However, it has determined that the confidence it is willing to place in this value is 0.87, which is below that of θ^γ and means that a_1 has not yet interacted with a_6 enough times to calculate a sufficiently confident trust value. In this case, a_1 has to use the opinions from other agents that have interacted with a_6, and form a reputation value for a_6 that it can compare to the trust values it has calculated for other HTML providers (a_5 and a_7).

Lets assume that a_1 is aware of three agents that have interacted with a_6, denoted by a_8, a_9 and a_{10}, whose opinions about a_6 are $(15, 46)$, $(4, 1)$ and $(3, 0)$ respectively. Agent a_1 can obtain beta shape parameters based solely on the opinions provided, by using Equations 9 and 8, as shown below:

Opinions from providers: $a_8 = (15, 46), a_9 = (4, 1)$ and $a_3 = (3, 0)$
Using Equation 8: $N = 15 + 4 + 3 = 22, M = 46 + 1 + 0 = 47$
Using Equation 9: $\alpha = 22 + 1 = 23, \beta = 47 + 1 = 48$

Having obtained the shape parameters, a_1 can obtain a trust value for a_6 using Equation 6, as follows:

Using Equation 6: $\tau_{a_1,a_6} = \frac{\alpha}{\alpha+\beta} = \frac{23}{23+48} = 0.32$

Now a_1 is able to compare the trust in agents a_5, a_6 and a_7. Before calculating the trustworthiness of a_6, agent a_1 considered a_6 to be the most trustworthy (see Table 4). Having calculated a new trust value for agent a_6 (which is lower than the first assessment), agent a_1 now regards a_7 as the most trustworthy. Therefore a_1 chooses a_7 as the service provider for the HTML content service.

4.3   Handling Inaccurate Opinions

The method a_1 uses to assess the trustworthiness of a_6, as described in Section 4.2, is susceptible to errors caused by reputation providers giving inaccurate information. In our scenario, suppose a_8 provides the HTML content service too, and is in direct competition with a_6. Agent a_1 is not aware of this fact, which makes a_1 unaware that a_8 may provide inaccurate information about a_6 to influence its decision on which HTML content provider agent to incorporate into the VO. If we look at the opinions provided by agents a_8, a_9 and a_{10}, which are $(20, 46)$, $(4, 1)$ and $(3, 0)$ respectively, we can see that the opinion provided by a_8 does not correlate with the other two. Agents a_9 and a_{10} provide a positive opinion of a_6, whereas agent a_8 provides a very negative opinion. Suppose that a_8 is providing an inaccurate account of its experiences with a_6. We can use the mechanism discussed in Section 3 to allow a_1 to cope with this inaccurate information, and arrive at a better decision that is not influenced by self-interested reputation providing agents (such as a_8).

Before we show how TRAVOS can be used to handle inaccurate information, we must assume the following. Agent a_1 obtained reputation information from a_8, a_9 and a_{10} on several occasions, and each time a_1 recorded the opinion provided by a reputation provider and the actual observed outcome (from the interaction with an agent to which the opinion is applied). Each time an opinion is provided, the outcome observed is recorded in the relevant bin. Agent a_1 keeps information of like opinions in bins as shown in Table 6. For example, if a_8 provides an opinion that is used to obtain a trust value of 0.3, then the actual observed outcome (successful or unsuccessful) is stored in the $0.2 < E[B] \leq 0.4$ bin.

Using the information shown in Table 6, agent a_1 can calculate the weighting to be applied to the opinions from the three reputation sources by applying the technique described in Section 3.1. In so doing, agent a_1 uses the information from the bin, which contains the opinion provided, and integrates the beta distribution between the limits defined by the bin's boundary. For example, a_8's opinion falls under the $0.2 < E[B] \leq 0.4$ bin. In this bin, agent a_1 has recorded that $n = 15$ and $m = 3$. These n and m values are used to obtain a beta distribution, using Equations 4 and 5, which is then integrated between 0.2 and 0.4 to give a weighting of 0.0039 for a_6's opinion. Then, by using Equations 11 and 12, agent a_1 can calculate the adjusted mean and standard deviation of the opinion, which in turn gives the adjusted α and β parameters for that opinion. The results from these calculations are shown in Table 5.

Table 5. Agent a_1's adjusted values for opinions provided by a_8, a_9 and a_{10}

Agent	Weighting	Adjusted Values			
		μ	σ	α	β
a_8	0.0039	0.5	0.29	1.0091	1.0054
a_9	0.78	0.65	0.15	5.8166	3.1839
a_{10}	0.74	0.62	0.17	4.3348	2.6194

Summing the adjusted values for α and β from Table 5, a_1 can obtain a more reliable value for the trustworthiness of a_6. Using Equation 4, a_1 calculates a trust value $= 0.62$ for a_6. This means that from the possible HTML content providers, a_1 now sees a_6 as the most trustworthy and selects it to be a partner in the VO. Unlike a_1's decision in Section 4.2 (when a_7 was chosen as the VO partner), here we have shown how a reputation provider cannot influence the decision made by a_1 by providing inaccurate information.

Table 6. Observations made by a_1 given opinion from a reputation source. n represents that the interaction (to which the opinion applied) was successful, and likewise m means unsuccessful

	[0, 0.2]		[0.2, 0.4]		[0.4, 0.6]		[0.6, 0.8]		[0.8, 1]		Total
	n	m	n	m	n	m	n	m	n	m	
a_8	2	0	11	4	0	0	0	0	2	3	25
a_9	0	2	1	3	0	0	22	10	6	4	30
a_{10}	1	3	0	2	0	0	18	8	5	3	25

5   Related Work

There are many computational models of trust, a review of which can be found in [10]. Generally speaking, however, models not based on probability theory (e.g. [6, 11, 8]) consist of calculating trust from hand-crafted formulae that yield the desired results. For the purpose of our work, we only consider models that are similar to TRAVOS in the manner of calculating trust.

Probabilistic approaches are not commonly used in the field of computational trust, but there are a couple of such models in the literature. In particular, the Beta Reputation System (BRS) [7] is a probabilistic trust model like TRAVOS, which is based on the beta distribution. The system is specifically designed for online communities and is centralised. It works by users giving ratings to the performance of other users in the community. Here, ratings consist of a single value that is used to obtain positive and negative feedback values. The feedback values are then used to calculate shape parameters that determine the reputation of the user the rating applies to. However, BRS does not show how it is able to cope with misleading information.

Whitby et al. [12] also build on the BRS and show how it can be used to filter unfair ratings, either unfairly positive or negative, towards a certain agent. In their model, the ratings for an individual are stored in a vector, which is then used to obtain an aggregated reputation value for that individual (represented as a beta distribution). However, this method is only effective when there are sufficient ratings to allow successful identification of unfair ratings. Filtering in this manner disregards the possibility of ratings that may seem unfair, but which truthfully represent the perspective of the rater (as the rater may have an inaccurate view of the world). In TRAVOS, no opinion is disregarded, and, instead, the consistency between the reputation provider's opinion and the actual behaviour of an individual to which the opinion refers forms the weight that is to be placed in opinions provided by that particular reputation source.

6   Conclusions and Future Work

This paper has presented a novel model of trust, TRAVOS, for use in open agent systems. The main benefits in using TRAVOS are that it provides a mechanism for assessing the trustworthiness of others in situations both in which the agents have interacted before and share past experiences, and in which there is little or no past experience between the interacting agents. Establishing the trustworthiness of others, and then selecting the most trustworthy, gives an agent the ability to maximise the probability that there will be no harmful repercussions from the interaction. In particular, through the example scenario, we have demonstrated how TRAVOS can be used to handle inaccurate opinions expressed by reputation providers. Here, reputation providers are requested to provide opinions about a certain individual when an agent is not confident in the amount of evidence it has in order to assess the trustworthiness of that individual. In this situation, it is particularly important that the opinions that are given are accurate and based on past experiences. By using TRAVOS, an agent ensures that opinions from inaccurate reputation sources are not given equal weighting to those from accurate sources in the aggregation of reputation. This gives the agent the ability to handle inaccurate information effectively.

In the short term, we will be carrying out empirical analysis on TRAVOS, and evaluating it against similar approaches. As it stands, TRAVOS assumes that the behaviour of agents does not change over time, but in many cases this is an unsafe assumption. In particular we believe that agents may well change their behaviour over time, and that some will have time-based behavioural strategies. Future work will therefore include the removal of this assumption and the use of functions that allow an agent to take into account the fact that very old experiences may not be relevant in predicting the behaviour of an individual. In addition we will extend the model to represent a continuous outcome space, instead of the current binary outcome space. Further extensions to TRAVOS will include using the rich social metadata that exists within a VO environment in the calculation of a trust value. Thus, as described in Section 1, VOs are social structures, and we can draw out social data such as roles and relationships that exist both between VOs and VO members. The incorporation of such data into the trust metric should allow for more accurate trust assessments to be formed.

References

1. S. Buchegger and J. Y. L. Boudec. A robust reputation system for mobile ad-hoc networks ic/2003/50. Technical report, EPFL-IC-LCA, 2003.
2. M. DeGroot and M. Schervish. *Probability & Statistics*. Addison-Wesley, 2002.
3. C. Dellarocas. Mechanisms for coping with unfair ratings and discriminatory behavior in online reputation reporting systems. In *ICIS*, pages 520–525, 2000.
4. I. Foster, N. R. Jennings, and C. Kesselman. Brain meets brawn: Why grid and agents need each other. In *Proceedings of the 3rd Int. Conf. on Autonomous Agents and Multi-Agent Systems*, pages 8–15, 2004.
5. D. Gambetta. Can we trust trust? In D. Gambetta, editor, *Trust: Making and Breaking Cooperative Relations*, chapter 13, pages 213–237. Basil Blackwell, 1988.
6. T. D. Huynh, N. R. Jennings, and N. Shadbolt. Developing an integrated trust and reputation model for open multi-agent systems. In *Proceedings of the 7th Int Workshop on Trust in Agent Societies*, pages 62–77, 2004.

7. R. Ismail and A. Jøsang. The beta reputation system. In *Proceedings of the 15th Bled Conference on Electronic Commerce*, Bled, Slovenia, 2002.

8. A. Moukas, G. Zacharia, and P. Maes. Amalthaea and histos: Multi-agent systems for www sites and reputation recommendations. In M. Klusch, editor, *Intelligent Information Agents*, chapter 13. Springer-Verlag, 1999.

9. T. J. Norman, A. Preece, S. Chalmers, N. R. Jennings, M. Luck, V. Dang, T. D. Nguyen, V. Deora, , J. Shao, A. Gray, and N. J. Fiddian. Agent-based formation of virtual organisations. *Knowledge-Based Systems*, 17(2–4):103–111, May 2004.

10. S. D. Ramchurn, D. Hunyh, and N. R. Jennings. Trust in multi-agent systems. *Knowledge Engineering Review*, 19(1), 2004.

11. J. Sabater and C. Sierra. Regret: A reputation model for gregarious societies. In *4th Workshop on Deception Fraud & Trust in Agent Societies*, pages 61–70, 2001.

12. A. Whitby, A. Jøsang, and J. Indulska. Filtering out unfair ratings in bayesian reputation systems. In *Proceedings of the Workshop on Trust in Agent Societies, at the 3rd Int. Conf. on Autonomous Agents & Multi Agent Systems*, 2004.

Trust as a Key to Improving Recommendation Systems

Georgios Pitsilis[1] and Lindsay Marshall

School of Computing Science, University of Newcastle Upon-Tyne,
Newcastle Upon Tyne NE1 7RU, UK
{Georgios.Pitsilis, Lindsay.Marshall}@ncl.ac.uk

Abstract. In this paper we propose a method that can be used to avoid the problem of sparsity in recommendation systems and thus to provide improved quality recommendations. The concept is based on the idea of using trust relationships to support the prediction of user preferences. We present the method as used in a centralized environment; we discuss its efficiency and compare its performance with other existing approaches. Finally we give a brief outline of the potential application of this approach to a decentralized environment.

Keywords: Recommendation Systems, Subjective Logic, Trust Modeling.

1 Introduction

This paper introduces a method that can be used to improve the performance of recommendation systems using trust based neighbourhood formation schemas. In recommendation systems a typical neighbourhood formation scheme uses correlation and similarity as measures of proximity. With this approach, relationships between members of the community can be found only in the case when common properties or common purpose exists, where such properties can be for example, common experiences expressed in the form of opinions about an assessed property. This requirement appears to be a problem for the formation of communities especially at the beginning of the process when in general there is a low number of individual experiences and therefore the possibility of common experiences existing is also low.

·Our main idea is to exploit information, which at first glance may seem to be extraneous, in such a way that might be beneficial for the community. In a recommendation system, that benefit appears as improved accuracy, as well as improved capability in providing recommendations. We make use of any common experiences that two entities might have, to establish hypothetical trust relationships between them, through which they will then be able to relate to other entities. This would make it possible for entities which were unlinked before, to link together and use each other's experiences for their mutual benefit.

However, there are two challenges for recommendation systems which appear to be in conflict with each other : scalability and accuracy. Accuracy is proportional to

---

[1] Scholar of the Greek State Scholarships Foundation (IKY).

P. Herrmann et al. (Eds.): iTrust 2005, LNCS 3477 pp. 210–223, 2005.

the amount of data that is available but appears to work at the expense of scalability, since more time is needed to search for those data. In this paper we only deal with the first challenge, leaving the scalability issues for future work.

Our claim is that discovering trust relationships and thereby linking the users of a recommendation system together can have a positive impact on the performance of such a system.

To support our hypothesis we ran experiments on a small community of 100 nodes and compared the recommendations of our system against those that a plain collaborative filtering method would give. We also performed a comparison against the output that we would get if the choices were solely based on intuition. In our study we chose a centralized environment as our test-bed for evaluating the algorithms and for carrying out the processing of data. However, we do discuss the requirements, benefits and pitfalls if deploying it in a decentralized system.

The rest of the paper is organized as follows. In the next section there is a general description of recommendation systems, as well as related work in the field. In section 3 we explain the main idea of our work, the logic and calculus we have used in our model and we also focus on the trust modeling we have done for the purpose of our experiments. In Section 4 there are some performance measurements showing the benefits and the drawbacks of our system. In sections 5 and 6 we explain roughly how such a model might work in a decentralized environment showing some major drawbacks that have to do with the information discovery process and we also propose solutions that might help overcome these problems.

2   Motivation

2.1   Background Research

Recommender systems [1] are widely used nowadays and in simple terms their purpose is to suggest items, usually products, to those who might be interested in them. The main idea is to get the users that participate in such system correlated based on the opinions they have expressed in the past and then to provide as suggestion lists of products that might be of interest, or in the simplest form, predictions of ratings of services or products they want to know about.

Recommender systems often exist as services embedded into web sites which provide support for e-commerce activities. *epinions.com* [2], *amazon.com* [3] and *ebay* [4] are some of the most popular commercial sites. Some others, such as *Grouplens* [5] have been built with the sole purpose of supporting research activities in this area.

Technologies that have been applied to recommender systems include *Nearest-neighbor* (which includes *Collaborative filtering* (CF)), *Bayesian networks*, and *Clustering*. Bayesian networks create a decision tree based on a set of user ratings. Despite their speed in providing recommendations they are not practical for environments in which user preferences are updated regularly. In clustering, users are grouped by their similarity in preferences and predictions are made regarding the participation of a user in some cluster. In the case of participation in multiple clusters the prediction is a weighted average. As is shown in [6], algorithms based on Clustering have worse accuracy than nearest-neighbor therefore pre-clustering is recommended.

The basic idea behind CF is to make predictions of scores based on the heuristic that people who agreed (or disagreed) in the past will probably agree (disagree) again. Even though such a heuristic can be sufficient to correlate numerous users with each other, systems that have employed this method still appear to be highly sparse and thus are ineffective at making accurate predictions all the time. This ineffectiveness is proportional to how sparse the dataset is. By Sparsity we mean a lack of data required for a CF system to work, where in this specific case the data are in the form of experiences which users share with each other through the system. Sparsity appears mostly because users are not willing to invest much time and effort in rating items.

Conventional recommendation systems face other problems such as the *cold start problem* [7] and their *vulnerability to attacks*. The latter comes from the centralized nature of a collaborative filtering system and the fact that there are always users that have malicious intent and want to influence the system. The attacker can simply create a fake user with very similar preferences to that of the targeted user and thus he/she becomes highly influential to the victim. The cold start problem, is due to the low number of ratings that new users contribute to the system who thus becoming isolated and cannot receive good quality recommendations. Developing other types of relations between the users, especially new ones, could help increase their connectivity base and thus their contribution to the system.

2.2 Trust and Reputation in Computing Systems

Trust and *Reputation* have always been a concern for computer scientists and much work has been done to formalize it in computing environments [8]. In computing, *Trust* has been the subject of investigation in distributed applications in order to enable service providers and consumers to know how much reliance to place on each other. *Reputation* is a commonly held belief about an agent's trustworthiness. It is mainly derived from the recommendations of various agents.

Yahalom et. al in [9] distinguish between directly trusting an entity about a particular subject and trusting an entity to express the trustworthiness of a third entity with respect to a subject. These two types of trust are known as direct and indirect (or derived) trust. This raises the issue of how one can traverse a whole chain of intermediate entities to find a trust value for a distant one. In fact, there is a debate as to whether it is valid or not to consider transitive trust relationships. Even though it has been shown that trust is not necessarily transitive [10], there are various requirements such as the context, otherwise known as the trust purpose, that need to be specified and which indicate the ability to recommend [11]. This ability, if it exists, makes indirect trust possible. Assuming that this ability is present in a long chain then a recommendation can be made, as indirect trust can be calculated along the chain.

2.3 Trust Modeling

Trust can be thought as the level of belief established between two entities in relation to a certain context. In *uncertain probabilities* theory [12] *belief* is expressed with a metric that is called *opinion*. Because opinions are based on observations, there is always imperfect knowledge and therefore it is impossible to know for certain the real (objective) behavior of the examined entity. This theory introduces the notion of uncertainty to describe this gap of knowledge or else the absence of belief and disbelief. Uncertainty is important in trust modeling, as it is always present in human beliefs and thus is suitable for expressing these kinds of beliefs.

A framework for artificial reasoning that makes use of the uncertainty in the expression of beliefs is called *Subjective Logic* [13]. It has its basis in uncertain probabilities theory and provides some logical operators for combining beliefs and deriving conclusions in cases where there is insufficient evidence.

From a probabilistic point of view there would be both a certain amount of belief and disbelief which is used to express the level of trustworthiness with absolute certainty. As that absolute certainty can never exist, the uncertainty property (u) has been introduced to fill this gap and deal with the absence of both belief and disbelief. The probabilistic approach would treat trustworthiness by observing the pattern of an entity's behavior and using only two properties belief (b) and disbelief (d) where b+d=1, $b, d \in [0,1]$. Binary calculus assumes statements of trust as dual-valued; either *true* or *false*. As such, Subjective Logic can be seen as an extension of both binary calculus and probability calculus. The relationship between b,d and u is expressed as b+d+u=1 which is known as the *Belief Function Additivity Theorem* [13].

Subjective Logic also provides the traditional logical operators for combining opinions (e.g. $\wedge, \vee$) as well as some non-standard ones such as *Suggestion* and *Consensus* which are useful for combining series of opinions serially or in parallel.

A complete reference about the algebra of *Subjective logic* and on how the algebra is applied to *b,d* and *u* can be found in [14].

Even though opinions in the form (b,d,u) are more manageable due to the flexible calculus that opinion space provides, evidence is usually available in other forms, that are easier for humans to understand. In [13] there is a mapping between Evidence Spaces to Opinion Spaces based on the idea of coding the observations as elements of the Beta Distribution probability function. In this approach the uncertainty property (u) appears to be exclusively dependent on the quantity of observations. [15] has an alternative mapping that uses both quantitative and qualitative measures to transform observations into opinions.

In contrast, other similarity based approaches [16] use the idea of linking users indirectly with each other using predictability measures, but these have not been tested on real environments.

As we mentioned, the requirement for trust to become transitive in long chains requires that a common purpose will exist along the chain. Only the last relationship should concern trust about a certain purpose and all the other trust relationships in the chain should be with respect to the entities' recommending abilities for the given purpose.

It is worth mentioning the existence of another approach to making recommendation systems trust-enabled [17] which does not distinguish between functional and recommended trust.

3 Our Approach

3.1 Using Trust in Recommendation Systems

As we mentioned in 2.1, in standard collaborative filtering, the correlation of ratings is done on a nearest-neighbour basis, which means only users who have common experiences can be correlated. In that schema only knowledge within a radius of one hop from the referenced node can become useful. For example, in the simple scenario of figure 1, where 3 services are experienced by 4 entities, using the standard method, there is no way for any knowledge from entity A to be used for providing recommendations to entity D.

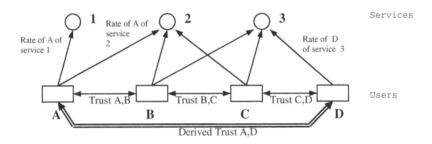

Fig. 1. Using Trust to link A B C and D together

Our idea is to exploit information from any experiences that can be reached beyond the barriers of the local neighborhood for the benefit of the querying entities. We deal with this issue by utilizing the trust that could exist between the entities and in this way build a web of trust within the system.

Then, those entities that may have experienced the services in question would be reachable through the web of trust, thus providing additional information to the querying entities for making predictions about services they might like, but where no relevant experiences have been found for them within their local neighbourhood.

However, this requires some way of mapping the experiences of each entity into trust measures and in the opposite direction, transforming the derived trust into some form of information that can provide useful recommendations.

Once all these issues are shorted our, the quality of the recommendation system should improve since more queries can now be answered and thus avoid the problems of Sparsity.

3.2 Our Trust Modeling

In general, trust models are used to enable the parties involved in a trust relationship to know how much reliance to place on each other and there are a few models that have been proposed to calculate trust, for instance [13][18].

The problem that emerges when Trust is to be used in a recommendation system is the fact that entities involved provide ratings of items rather than their trust estimates of other entities. That means, making the model trust enabled would require that all this information that has been expressed in the form of ratings be transformed into trust values, and this requires a transformation method.

In [15] we proposed a technique for modeling trust relationships between entities derived from evidence that characterize their past experiences. Our model aims to provide a method for estimating how much trust two entities should place on each other, given the similarities between them. In this model, the entities are considered as more similar the more accurately they predict each other's ratings. Predictions can be done using Resnick's [1] formula or some alternative to this [16][6].

$$p_{a,i} = \bar{r}_a + \sum_{u=1}^{n} w_{a,u} (r_{u,i} - \bar{r}_u) \tag{1}$$

where, $p_{a,i}$ is the querying user's predicted rating of product i, $\bar{r}_a$ is the average rating of the querying user a, $w_{a,u}$ is the *Coefficient* of the similarity correlation of user a with some user u (which appears as weight in the deviation) and expresses the similarity between the two entities a and u which are involved in the relationship. $\bar{r}_u$ is the average rating of each of the n other correlated users that provide recommendations and $r_{u,i}$ are the ratings of the same product i of all the other n users'.

As can be seen from the formula, the prediction is dependent on the number of correlated entities n and becomes noisy and unreliable when 5 or less entities are involved. Hence, higher accuracies become possible with the incorporation of more entities in the calculation.

In contrast to modeling trust using the Beta distribution function [13], our similarity based modeling technique can also be used in the opposite way for estimating similarities given the trust between the entities. Using this characteristic, a querying entity that can receive ratings about some distant entities for which it can make a trust estimate through the graph, will be able to use them in its prediction schema as similarity factors (w).

4 Our Experiments

As we mentioned in section 2.3, there is a requirement for a common trust purpose that has to be met in order to regard trust as transitive. In the trust graph idea we have used to bring users together, we assumed as the common purpose the involved party's ability to recommend. This ability comes from the way the trust relationships have been formed. Hereafter, in this experiment we assume that the entities, in fact, do have this ability to provide recommendations as soon as they appear to have a common taste on things.

We performed a series of tests to examine how efficient our method might be if applied to a real recommender system. Efficiency is measured as how successfully the system can predict the consumer's preferences. In our experiments we used data from the publicly available dataset of the MovieLens project [20]. MovieLens is a film recommendation system based on collaborative filtering, established at the University of Minnesota. The dataset that is publicly available contains around one million ratings of movies made by 6,040 users who joined the MovieLens in the year 2000. In our experiment we used a subset of 100 users which comprises only around 13,000 ratings. The size of the testing data set (100 users) was chosen to be that small because that made possible to receive the results within a reasonable period of time.

To avoid poor performance due to the noisy behavior of the Pearson Correlation, we applied some filtering to the existing relationships. Therefore, those relationships which were built upon 5 or less common experiences were not considered in our calculations.

The dataset also contains timestamps for every rating indicating when the rating took place, but that information was not considered at all in our correlations since at this stage we intended to study the static behaviour of the model. The timestamps might be useful in some future experiment if used as a secondary criterion for choosing ratings to be considered in the trust relationships. For example, only ratings that have been issued by both counterparts within a certain amount of time will be considered in a trust relationship.

In our analysis, we demonstrate how such system would perform in comparison to standard collaborative filtering. We also applied a comparison schema against a system that involves no use of recommendation system, but where the users make the choices themselves by using their intuition. For this comparison, every user's predictions were guided alone by personal, past experiences. Needless to say such a schema has meaning only to those users that share some significant number of personal experiences.

We introduce two notions that will be used in our measurements:

Computability: We define this as the total number of services for which a user can find opinions through the trust graph, divided by the total number of services that have been rated by all counterparts in the sample. This normalization value should be seen as a performance limit, as no more services can be reached by any of the counterparts. The Computability value is specific to a particular user since the number of services that can be reached is absolutely dependent on users' position in the graph as well as the number of their own experiences.

Recommendation Error (E): We define this as the average error of users when trying to predict their own impressions of those services they can reach when using the reputation system. It can be defined as the prediction rating divided by the rating that is given after the experience. Similar to *Computability*, this measure is also specific to a particular user.

To provide a unique metric of effectiveness, we also introduce the *Normalized Coverage* factor F. This measure combines *Recommendation Error* and *Computability* into a single value and is expressed as:

$$F = (1 - \overline{E}) \cdot C \qquad (2)$$

where:
$\overline{E}$ is the average recommendation error for a particular user and C is the Computability value for that user. F represents how much a user benefits from his participation in the community. High values of F should mean that participation is beneficial for the user.

4.1 Testing Method

For evaluation purposes we used two algorithms, one for the calculation of *Computability* and another one for the *Recommendation Error*. Due to the static nature of the data that we used in the experiment there was no way to simulate a real environment of users experiencing services. For that reason, to be able to measure the difference between a prediction and the actual experience, we used a technique called *leave one out* as our metric. In this method one rating is kept hidden and the system tries to predict it.

The pseudocode we used to evaluate the Recommendation Error of the recommendations is given in figure 2.

```
Let S the set of all services
Let f the filter used in the trust propagation
Let hop the number of hops the trust can be propagated
Let U the set of all users in the group
For each user U_A in U {
    Let S_A ⊂ S the experiences of U_A
    For each service s in S_A {
        Let r = R[U_A,s]                /* The rate given from U_A on s */
        Let B_s ⊂ U the users that have also experienced s
        For each user U_B in B_s {
            Trust_{A→B} = f(path_{A→B}, f, distance_{A→B} < hop)
            CC_{A,B} = f(Trust_{A→B})   /* similarity between U_A & U_B */
        }
        Let Sp = f(CC_{A,i}), ∀ i ∈ Bs  /* The predicted rating about s */
        Let Err = f(r,Sp)
    }
    RecomError = Average(Err)
}
```

Fig. 2. Pseudocode for evaluating the Recommendation error

The difference between the real rating – mentioned here as post-experience – and the predicted rating gives the error. Setting *hop*=1 in the algorithm returns the prediction error for the plain CF method which is based on examining the nearest neighbours only. In the same way, *hop*=0 can give the error if users were doing the choices guided by their intuition alone. In our experiments we run tests for *hop* ranging from 0 to 3.

For *Computability* (or *Coverage*), we also ran evaluations for values of *hop*=0,1,2,3. The pseudocode of the algorithm we used is shown in figure 3.

```
Let S the set of all services
Let f the filter used in the trust propagation
Let hop the number of hops the trust can be propagated
Let U the set of all users in the group
For each user UA in U {
  Let SA ⊂ S the set of services that UA has experienced
  For each user UB in U {
    TrustA→B = f(pathA→B , f, distanceA→B < hop)
    If TrustA→B > 0 {          /* B is reachable by A  */
      Let SB ⊂ S the set of services that UB has experienced
      SA = SA + SB        /* Add SB to A's potential experiences */
    }
  }
  Coverage = SA / S
}
```

Fig. 3. Pseudocode for calculating the coverage

For the calculation of trust between any two entities in the trust graph we used a parser to discover the accessible trust paths between the trustor entity and the trustee. Then we applied subjective logic rules (the *consensus* and *recommendation* operators) to simplify the resulting graphs into a single opinion that the trustor would hold for the trustee at distance k. It was necessary to do this separately for every individual entity to prevent any opinion dependency problems [14] that can be caused when hidden topologies exist. Therefore, the calculation of the resulting trust was left to be carried out by every trustor individually.

Moreover, in cases where trust paths couldn't be analyzed and simplified further by just using these two operators, we applied a simple pruning technique to remove those opinions that were found to cause problems in the simplification process. In this study, the selection of the pruned links was done at random, but we leave for future work an extensive study of the consequences of using pruning in trust calculations as well as the formulation of a policy that would minimize these consequences.

4.2 Results

Figures 4,5 and 6 show the results from the experiments we performed. Figure 4 shows how Prediction Error changes with regard to hop distance and various belief filtering policies in the propagation of trust. In total, we compared three filtering policies ($b>0.5$, $b>0.6$ and $b>0.7$), where b is the belief property. In this filtering policy, trust is not allowed to propagate to entities that are not considered trustworthy as defined by the filter. So, path exploration proceeds up to the point where it is found that the belief property of some neighboring entity does not exceed the value set on the filter.

The same diagram also shows the results from the plain CF method (1 hop) as well as the case where users make choices using only their intuition. For the latter, there is no categorization for various trust filters since there is no use of trust at all. The results represent average values taken over the series of 100 entities.

It seems that, on average, the intuitive rating appears to have the lowest error, but as we will see, this criterion is inadequate to be used for judging. An equally interesting fact is that in our method (Hop distance>1) the error is not affected significantly as the hop distance increases, which means there is no loss of precision if using the trust graph.

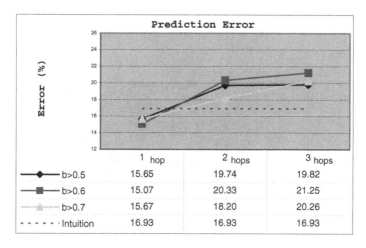

Fig. 4. Accuracy of Recommendations

Figure 5 shows the average Coverage ratio, that is, the number of reachable services for the group of 100 users divided by the total number of services that opinions can be expressed about. In all cases, our method appears to perform better against both the intuitive choice and the plain CF method. A strong filtering policy though has a negative impact especially for short hop distances, whereas applying an average filter (0.6) seems to improve the situation. (hop=2)

Finally, figure 6 presents the *Normalized Coverage Factor* we introduced and which can be thought as the total gain from using some policy. From the graph it seems that the participants do not benefit when strong filtering policies are applied. Strong filtering though is less consuming in resources due to the simpler graphs that have to be explored and be simplified. Therefore, such comparison without including the cost compared to the benefit would not be fair. We leave as future research a full performance analysis that would find the best policy.

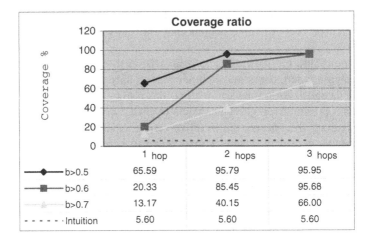

Fig. 5. Computability of Recommendations

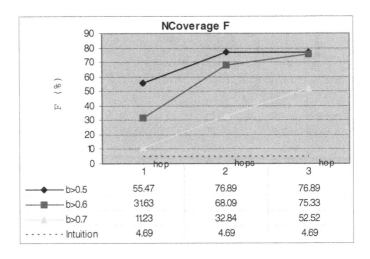

Fig. 6. Normalized Coverage F

5 Discussion

The increase in computability that our method can achieve also has a positive effect on the reduction of Sparsity. Our measurements show a significant fall of sparseness of 9.5%. The original 100 user dataset was found to be 97.85%. sparse. This calculation of sparseness is based on the 100 users we used in the evaluations over the whole set of items (6040), where the total number of ratings expressed by those 100 users was 12976.

By using our method, only 30% of the users benefited by using the trust graph. The remaining 70% were those who received the same benefit as when using the plain CF system (1 hop). This is because in the dataset it was likely for two users to have common experiences and this is dependent on how clustered the user communities in the dataset are. For example, if there were more than one clusters of user communities, then on average the benefit of using the graph would be higher because a very small number of users would be enough to bridge the gap between those separate clusters and thus to increase the number of recommendations that can be received from the other side.

That extra 30% benefit characterizes the potential of the proposed system with respect to the dataset used in the experiment. Speaking in terms of sparseness, that potential over the 100-user base, constituted a dataset that was 88.33% sparse. (fall by 9.5%).

The results justify the explanation we gave in section 2 saying that the plain method suffers from reduced coverage due to the small number of ratings that close neighbors can provide. This is because the nearest-neighbors algorithms rely upon exact matches.

For the prediction error, a comparison against a random choice of ratings instead of predicting them shows our method to be better even for hop distances of 3. Using our dataset, random generated values would give error rates as low as 24.5%, but such a comparison would be unfair for two reasons, first because it requires access to global knowledge which is unlikely to be possible, and second, because the error is highly dependent on the distribution of ratings over the classes of rates.

As can be seen, even though our method increases the system output by increasing the quality of recommendations as compared to the plain method, the algorithms do not scale to large amounts of data and thus performance degrades for a large number of users. In other words, the design will not lead to a system capable of providing quality recommendations in real-time. Even if the complex and expensive computation of direct trust vectors is done off-line there will be a bottleneck in calculating the indirect trust relationships and discovery of trust paths. This is because a direct trust vector needs to be recalculated whenever a new rating is introduced by either of the two sides in a trust relationship. However, these re-calculations could be done off-line as background processes, preserving the computing power for the graph analysis. This is feasible since in such recommendation systems the user and the item data do not change frequently.

For the above reasons, the method does not seem suitable for use in centralized systems. Cacheing techniques might provide some extra speed in calculations, provided that changes in the virtual trust infrastructure will not happen frequently.

6 Future Issues

In the future, we intend to perform a comparison of our method with other alternatives such as Horting [16] or others based on Dimensionality Reduction such as Singular value Decomposition [20]. As regards the depth we chose to do the graph analysis, we anticipate performing more analyses using greater depths than the 3 hops we used in this experiment. This would help us to study how the performance increases with the depth of search and also find the optimum depth given the high computational load that depth searching requires.

As we mentioned in the Discussion section, our method is not suitable for application in centralized systems because it is highly compute intensive. However, a promising solution to overcome this weakness would be to restructure the centralized system as a peer-to-peer recommendation system. In such an approach the benefit is two fold. It provides distributed computational load as well as higher robustness and it lowers vulnerabilities to the kinds of attacks we described in section 2. This architecture is also closer to the natural way that recommendations within groups of people take place.

As regards the requirement for a common purpose to exist in order for trust relationships to be used in a transitive way, we intend to alter the assumptions we have made about the existence of common purpose and re-run the experiment using pure recommender trust in the transitive chains. That requires though, that we can somehow model the trust placed on a recommender's abilities for the given purpose, using the existing set of evidence.

We also plan to investigate the model from a graph theoretical perspective and examine how the Clustering Coefficient of the trust graph might affect the quality of recommendations. Also a close analysis of every user separately could show better which users benefit most from their contribution in the system.

7 Conclusion

We proposed a method that is based on the idea of using trust relationships to extend the knowledge basis of the members of groups so they can receive recommendations of better quality. In this study we applied a model that uses quantitative and qualitative parameters to build trust relationships between entities based on their common choices. We used algebra for relating users together through the transitive trust relationships that can be built between them and we extended in this way their neighboring basis. For the evaluations we used real data from a publicly available centralized recommendation system and we presented some preliminary results about the performance of our method, we discussed the benefits and the pitfalls. Our first results show that despite the fact that the method seems incapable of providing recommendations in real time, it seemed to improve the efficiency of the system, which translates into increased computability without significant impact on the accuracy of predictions. We also pointed out how the disadvantages could be overcome if the method is applied in decentralized environments such as peer-to-peer.

References

[1] W., " Why isn't Trust Transitive?", In Proc. of the Security Protocols Workshop, p171-
     P.Resnick – H.R.Varian, "Recommender Systems", Communications of the ACM, 40(3):
     56-58, 1997
[2] http://www.epinions.com

[3] http://www.amazon.com

[4] [4] http://www.ebay.com

[5] P.Resnick - N.Iacovou - M.Suchak - P.Bergstrom - J.Riedl, "Grouplens. An Open Architecture for Collaborative filtering of Netnews, from Proceedings of ACM 1994, Conf. On Computer Supported Cooperative Work.

[6] Breese, J.S. Heckerman, D. Kadie,C. (1998). "Emperical Analysis of Predictive Algorithms for Collaborative Filtering". In Proc. of the 14th Conference on Uncertainty in Artificial Intelligence pp 43-52.

[7] D. Maltz and K.Ehrlish. "Pointing the Way: Active Collabortive filtering". In Proc. Of CHI-95,

[8] S.Marsh, "Formalizing Trust as Computational concept", PhD Thesis, University of Stirling, Scotland 1994.

[9] R.Yahalom, B.Klein, T.Beth, "Trust relationships in secure systems – A Distributed authentication perspective", In Proc. of the 1993 IEEE Symposium on Research in Security and Privacy, p 152. pages 202-209,Denver,Colorado 1995.

[10] Cristianson B.,Harbison p176, 1996

[11] A.Jøsang – E.Gray – M.Kinateder, "Analyzing topologies of Transitive Trust", In proceedings of the Workshop of Formal Aspects of Security and Trust, (FAST 2003), Piza September 2003.

[12] G.Shafer, "A Mathematical Theory of Evidence", Princeton University Press. 1976

[13] A.Jøsang, "A Logic for Uncertain probabilities", International Journal of Uncertainty, fuzziness and Knowledge based systems, Vol.9,No.3, June 2001.

[14] A.Jøsang, "An Algebra for Assessing Trust in Certification Chains", In proceedings of NDSS'99, Network and Distributed Systems Security Symposioum, The Internet Society, San Diego 1999.

[15] G.Pitsilis. – L.Marshall., "A model of Trust Derivation from Evidence for User in recommendation Systems", CS-TR-874, Technical Report Series, School of Computing Science, University of Newcastle , November 2004.

[16] Aggarwal, C.C. Wolf, J.L., Wu K. and Yu, P.S. (1999). "Horting Hatches an Egg: A New Graph-theoretic Approach to Collaborative Filtering". In Proceedings of the ACM KDD'99 Conference. San Diego, CA, pp.201-212

[17] P.Massa – P.Avesani, "Trust-aware Collaborative Filtering for recommender Systems", CoopIS/DOA/ODBASE (1) 2004: 492-508

[18] Rahman.A – Heiles.S, "Supporting trust in Virtual Communities", Proceedings of International conference on System Sciences, Jan 4-7 2000, Hawaii

[19] Bradley N. Miller, Istvan Albert, Shyong K. Lam, Joseph A. Konstan, John Riedl. (2003). "MovieLens Unplugged: Experiences with an Occasionally Connected Recommender System". InProceedings of ACM 2003 International Conference on Intelligent User Interfaces (IUI'03) (Accepted Poster), January 2003.

[20] Sarwar.B.M.,Karypis.G.,Konstan.J.A.,Riedl.J.T, "Application of Dimensionality Reduction in Recommender System-A Case Study", WebKDD Workshop, August 20, 2000.

Alleviating the Sparsity Problem of Collaborative Filtering Using Trust Inferences

Manos Papagelis[1,2], Dimitris Plexousakis[1,2], and Themistoklis Kutsuras[2]

[1] Institute of Computer Science, Foundation for Research and Technology – Hellas,
P.O. Box 1385, GR-71110, Heraklion, Greece
[2] Department of Computer Science, University of Crete,
P.O. Box 2208, GR-71409, Heraklion, Greece
{papaggel, dp}@ics.forth.gr, kutsuras@csd.uoc.gr

Abstract. Collaborative Filtering (CF), the prevalent recommendation approach, has been successfully used to identify users that can be characterized as "similar" according to their logged history of prior transactions. However, the applicability of CF is limited due to the *sparsity* problem, which refers to a situation that transactional data are lacking or are insufficient. In an attempt to provide high-quality recommendations even when data are sparse, we propose a method for alleviating sparsity using *trust inferences*. Trust inferences are transitive associations between users in the context of an underlying social network and are valuable sources of additional information that help dealing with the *sparsity* and the *cold-start* problems. A trust computational model has been developed that permits to define the *subjective* notion of trust by applying *confidence* and *uncertainty* properties to network associations. We compare our method with the classic CF that does not consider any transitive associations. Our experimental results indicate that our method of trust inferences significantly improves the quality performance of the classic CF method.

1 Introduction

Recommendation systems [1] have been a popular topic of research ever since the ubiquity of the web made it clear that people of widely varying backgrounds would be able to access and query the same underlying data. Both research and e-commerce applications have extensively adopted variations of recommendation algorithms in order to provide an intelligent mechanism to filter out the excess of information available to their users. *Collaborative filtering* (CF) [2] has almost certainly been the finest technique of choice for recommendation algorithms. CF tries to identify users that have relevant interests and preferences by calculating similarities among user profiles [3]. The idea behind this method is that, it may be of benefit to one's search for information to consult the behavior of other users who share the same or relevant interests and whose opinion can be trusted.

Regardless of its success in many application settings, the CF approach encounters two serious limitations, namely sparsity and scalability [4, 26]. In this paper we focus on the sparsity problem. The sparsity problem occurs when available data are insufficient for identifying similar users (neighbors) and it is a major issue that limits

P. Herrmann et al. (Eds.): iTrust 2005, LNCS 3477, pp. 224–239, 2005.

the quality of recommendations and the applicability of CF in general. The main objective of our work is to develop an effective approach that provides high-quality recommendations even when sufficient data are unavailable.

The remainder of the paper is organized as follows: Section 2 elaborates on the sparsity challenge and explains the weaknesses of already proposed methods for dealing with it. Section 3 presents our methodology that is based on trust inferences., while Section 4 presents experimental evaluation of our work.

2 Problem Statement

The numbers of users and items in major e-commerce recommendation systems is very large [5]. Even users that are very active result in rating just a few of the total number of items available in a database and respectively, even very popular items result in having been rated by only a few of the total number of users available in the database. This problem, commonly referred to as the *sparsity problem*, has been identified as one of the main technical limitations of CF and its further development and adoption. Because of sparsity, it is possible that the similarity between two users cannot be defined, rendering CF useless. Even when the evaluation of similarity is possible, it may not be very reliable, because of insufficient information processed. The cold-start problem emphasizes the importance of sparsity problem. *Cold-start* [6] refers to the situation in which an item cannot be recommended unless it has been rated by a substantial number of users. This problem applies to new and obscure items and is particularly detrimental to users with eclectic taste. Likewise, a new user has to rate a sufficient number of items before the recommendation algorithm be able to provide reliable and accurate recommendations.

There are several methods that have been proposed to deal with the sparsity problem. Most of them succeed in providing better recommendations, but fail to introduce a general model for dealing with sparsity. Most popular approaches proposed include dimensionality reduction of the user-item matrix, application of associative retrieval technique in the bipartite graph of items and users, item-based similarity instead of user-based similarity, and content-boosted CF. The dimensionality reduction approach addresses the sparsity problem by removing unrepresentative or insignificant users or items so as to condense the user-item matrix. More advanced techniques to achieve dimensionality reduction have been proposed as well. Examples include statistical techniques such as Principle Component Analysis (PCA) [7] and information retrieval techniques such as Latent Semantic Indexing (LSI) [8, 9, 10]. However, potentially useful information might be lost during this reduction process. Transitive associations of the associative retrieval technique [11], even if they have been successfully employed to deal with the sparsity problem, fail to express the subjective notion of the associations. Item-based [12, 13] in addition to Content-boosted CF [13, 14] approaches require additional information regarding items as well as a metric to compute meaningful similarities among them [25].

Our research work provides an alternative approach to deal with sparsity problem. Instead of reducing the dimension of the user-item matrix, in an attempt to make it more informative, we propose a method that permits to define transitive properties between users in the context of a social network. The consideration of these properties leads to extra information accessible for recommendation purposes. Our approach focuses on developing a computational model that permits the exploration of transitive user similarities based on trust inferences for addressing the sparsity problem.

3 Methodology

3.1 Social Networks in Recommender Systems

CF has been successfully employed to express the "word-of-mouth" paradigm in a computational context [15]. Common interactions that take place in a typical recommendation system include ratings, transactions, feedback data etc. For the rest of the paper we assume without loss of generality that interactions are based on rating activity. Based on these interactions, it is possible to express similarity conditions between pairs of users, according to the subset of their co-rated items. We view these similarity conditions as associations between users. It is then possible to consider these associations as links of a *social network*. If we define as user-item matrix the matrix having as elements the ratings of users to items, then a user's model [16] is represented in this matrix as an n-dimensional vector, where n is the number of items in the database. Figure 1 illustrates the process of the network construction, where a user's rating activity is used to define network associations.

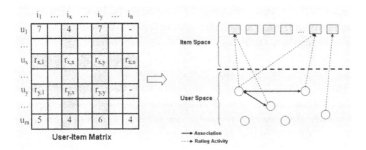

Fig. 1. Underlying Social Networks in Recommender Systems

As theories on social networks find application in completely diverse research areas, we need to properly describe their particularities in our context and most importantly identify the process of *membership* and *evolution*.

Membership: A user joins the underlying social network by submitting at least one rating to an item that has previously been rated by another user.

Evolution: Users' ratings to items are enabling the construction of new associations between users and thus new links in the underlying network are considered.

3.2 Trust Through User-to-User Similarity

We think of the associations between users as an expression of established *trust* between each other, as far as the specific application area is concerned. Since trust is defined in the context of similarity conditions, the more similar the two users are the greater their established trust would be considered [17]. In order to compute the similarity between users, a variety of similarity measures have been proposed, such as Pearson correlation, cosine vector similarity, Spearman correlation, entropy-based uncertainty and mean-square difference. However, Breese et al in [18] and Herlocker et al. in [19] suggest that Pearson correlation performs better than all the rest.

If we define the subset of items that users u_x and u_y have co-rated as $I=\{i_x: x=1, 2, ..., n\}$, r_{u_x,i_h} as the rating of user u_x to item i_h and $\overline{r_{u_x}}$, $\overline{r_{u_y}}$ as the average ratings of users u_x and u_y respectively, then the established trust between two users is defined as the Pearson correlation [20] of their associated rows in the user-item matrix (Eq. 1).

$$T_{x \to y} = sim(u_x, u_y) = \frac{\sum_{h=1}^{n'} (r_{u_x,i_h} - \overline{r_{u_x}})(r_{u_y,i_h} - \overline{r_{u_y}})}{\sqrt{\sum_{h=1}^{n'} (r_{u_x,i_h} - \overline{r_{u_x}})^2} \sqrt{\sum_{h=1}^{n'} (r_{u_y,i_h} - \overline{r_{u_y}})^2}} \qquad (1)$$

3.3 Trust Inferences

Due to the number of ratings that exist in recommendation systems, underlying social networks are very sparse. There are cases in which insufficient or loss of information is detrimental for the recommendation algorithms. Consider, for example, the case in which associations between users are based on very few data or the case in which there aren't any k users to employ in a k-nearest neighborhood algorithm. A motivating example is illustrated in Figure 2(a). Suppose that users S, N have rated item I_1 and users N, T have rated I_2. Classic CF will associate user S with user N and user N with user T, but not user S with user T. However, a more sophisticated approach that incorporates transitive interactions would recognize the associative relationship between user S and user T and infer this indirect association. To deal with this problem, we adopt a method of inferring trust between users that are not directly associated to each other. Thus, in the example, it is possible to infer trust between the source user S and the target user T through the intermediate user N. According to this process, trust is propagated in the network and associations between users are built, even if they have no co-rated item.

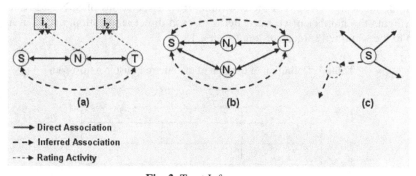

Fig. 2. Trust Inferences

Trust Paths

Propagation of trust [21, 22] implies the existence of *trust paths* in the network. Combination of consecutive direct associations between all intermediate users creates a trust path from a source user to a target user. Trust paths can be of variable *length*, depending on the number of associations that one needs to traverse in order to reach the target user. If k associations need to be traversed then the path is considered to be of length k. Direct associations are of length *1*, while when the target user is not accessible from the source user, the length of the supposed path is considered infinite.

While computation of trust in direct associations is based on user-to-user similarity, for length-k associations we need to adopt a transitivity rule that facilitates the computation of the inferred trust between the source user and the target user. If we define as N={Ni: i=1, 2, ...,k} the set of all intermediate nodes in a trust path that connects user S and user T, then their associated inferred trust is given by Equation 2.

$$T_{S\underset{N_1\to\ldots\to N_k}{\longrightarrow}T}=\left(\left(\left(\left(T_{S\to N_1}\oplus T_{N_1\to N_2}\right)\oplus\ldots\right)\oplus T_{N_{k-1}\to N_k}\right)\oplus T_{N_k\to T}\right) \qquad (2)$$

For example, in order to compute to what degree user S trusts user T in the example of Figure 2(a), we need to compute the inferred trust $T_{A\to C}=T_{A\to B}\underset{B}{\oplus}T_{B\to C}$.

In Equation 2, we employ the symbol $\oplus$ to denote that we need to apply a special operation in order to compute the inferred trust in the path. If I_x is the set of items that user u_x has rated, and $n(I_x)$ is the cardinality of the set I_x, then Equation 3 interprets the special operation employed.

$$T_{S\underset{N}{\to}T}=T_{S\to N}\oplus T_{N\to T}=\oplus\left(\frac{n(I_S\cap I_N)}{n(I_S\cap I_N)+n(I_N\cap I_T)}|T_{S\to N}|+\frac{n(I_N\cap I_T)}{n(I_S\cap I_N)+n(I_N\cap I_T)}|T_{N\to T}|\right)$$

$$where\ \oplus=\begin{cases}+,\ if\ T_{S\to N}>0\ and\ T_{N\to T}>0\\ -,\ if\ T_{S\to N}>0\ and\ T_{N\to T}<0\\ -,\ if\ T_{S\to N}<0\ and\ T_{N\to T}>0\\ \infty,\ if\ T_{S\to N}<0\ and\ T_{N\to T}<0\end{cases}\ and\ n(I_{S\to T})=\left\lceil\frac{n(I_S\cap I_N)+n(I_N\cap I_T)}{2}\right\rceil \qquad (3)$$

In plain words, in order to compute the inferred trust in a trust path that associates a source user S with a target user T through one intermediate node N, we first compute the weighted sum of the two direct trust associations of S, N and N, T using as weights the number of co-rated items of each direct association, and then apply a sign to the weighted sum according to table 1.

Table 1. Definition of the sign of the inferred trust in a trust path

	$T_{S\to N}\geq 0$	$T_{S\to N}<0$
$T_{N\to T}\geq 0$	+	-
$T_{N\to T}<0$	-	∞

The intuition behind this computation is that:

- If user S trusts user N and user N trusts user T then it is inferred that user S trusts user T
- If user S does not trust user N and user N trusts user T then it is inferred that user S does not trust user T
- If user S trusts user N and user N does not trust user T then it is inferred that user S does not trust user T
- If user S does not trust user N and user N does not trust user T then inference is not applicable and the length of the supposed path between user S and user T is considered infinite

The computed value of the inferred trust is a value that lies between the values of the two direct trust associations as indicated in Equation 4 and it is biased towards the value of the direct trust association with the most co-rated items. For example, if $T_{S \to N} = 0,7$ based on 5 co-rated items and $T_{N \to T} = 0,35$ based on 2 co-rated items, then $T_{S \underset{N}{\to} T} = 0,6$. In the same context, if $T_{S \to N} = 0,7$ and $T_{N \to T} = -0,35$, then $T_{S \underset{N}{\to} T} = -0,6$.

$$\min\{T_{S \to N}, T_{N \to T}\} \le T_{S \underset{N}{\to} T} \le \max\{T_{S \to N}, T_{N \to T}\} \tag{4}$$

3.4   Confidence and Uncertainty Properties of Trust Associations

Network evolution is based on individual rating behavior, thus it is reasonable to consider that available structural information defines multiple personalized webs of trust [22]. The *personal web of trust* or *local trust* for a user S is given through the set of trust paths originating from S and passing through users he or she trusts *directly* or *indirectly*. Figure 2(c) depicts the notion of personal web of trust. Consequently, a user S that interacts with other users in the system develops a *subjective belief* of the network. By subjective belief, we mean that probably what a user in the network believes about S is different from what another user in the network believes about user S. In order to express this subjective notion of trust we set up a confidence model able to respond to the following interrelated questions:

Q1: How confident user S feels of his or her opinion about user T?
Q2: What is the uncertainty enclosed in user's S opinion about user T?

Confidence Property
We define as *confidence*, a property assigned to each direct association of the network that expresses the reliability of the association. We make the assumption that confidence is directly related to the number of co-rated items between two users. This assumption indicates that (a) a user's opinion becomes more reliable as additional co-rated items become available and that (b) the reliability of an association between two users may be influenced by the change of the number of co-rated items between other users in the system. For that reason, the more items two users have co-rated, the higher the degree of confidence their association would have. Confidence is applied to

each one of a user's direct associations and it is based exclusively on the user's rating activity. In order to compute the confidence of all direct associations of a user, we initially identify the most confident association in an individual's personal web and then express all confidence values of the remaining direct associations in relation to the identified most confident association. We denote the user with which the most confident association has been created as u_{MAX_CONF}. If I_x is the set of items that user u_x has rated, and $n(I_x)$ is the cardinality of the set I_x, then the confidence $C_{S \to T}$ of the association between the source user S and the target user T is given by equation 5.

$$C_{S \to T} = \frac{n(I_S \cap I_T)}{n(I_S \cap I_{u_{MAX\_CONF}})} \qquad (5)$$

Figures 3(a) and 3(b) show how confidence values of direct associations derive from the number of co-rated items between the source user S and the remaining users in the system. The value of the most confident direct association is always equal to 1, while all other direct associations are equal to or less than 1 as depicted in Figure 3(b).

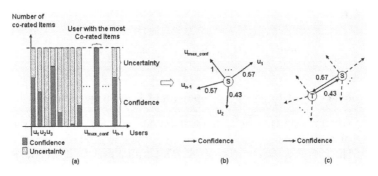

Fig. 3. Confidence Model to Define Uncertainty and Subjectiveness of Trust

Uncertainty Property

The confidence model described earlier can be employed to define *uncertainty* [23]. We define as uncertainty, a property assigned to each direct association of the network that expresses the unreliability of the association. Uncertainty, just like confidence is directly related to the number of co-rated items between two users. This assumption indicates that (a) the uncertainty enclosed to a user's opinion is greater when the number of co-rated items is small and that (b) the uncertainty of an association between two users may be influenced by the change of the number of co-rated items between other users in the system. It becomes obvious that in our model, confidence and uncertainty are contradictory and complementary. Consequently, the more confident one feels about his or her opinion of a user, the less uncertainty is enclosed in his or her opinion of that user and vice versa. Uncertainty $U_{S \to T}$ of the association between the source user S and the target user T is given by equation 6.

$$U_{S \to T} = 1 - C_{S \to T} \qquad (6)$$

Confidence and Uncertainty in Trust Paths
Confidence and uncertainty properties may also be assigned to trust paths. We adopt a transitivity rule that facilitates the computation of the confidence between a source user and a target user through a trust path [21, 22]. If we define the set of intermediate nodes in a trust path that associate a source user S with a target user T as $N=\{N_i: i=1, 2, ...,k\}$, then the confidence of the trust path is given by Equation 7. Accordingly, the uncertainty assigned to the trust path is given by equation 8.

$$C_{S\underset{N_1\to...\to N_k}{\to}T} = \left(\left(\left(\left(C_{S\to N_1}\cdot C_{N_1\to N_2}\right)\cdot...\right)\cdot C_{N_{k-1}\to N_k}\right)\cdot C_{N_k\to T}\right) \tag{7}$$

$$U_{S\underset{N_1\to...\to N_k}{\to}T} = 1 - C_{S\underset{N_1\to...\to N_k}{\to}T} \tag{8}$$

Subjectiveness
Since the evolution of personal webs is based on individual rating behavior one would expect that confidence and uncertainty are defined from a user's perspective. Indeed, confidence and uncertainty are *bidirectional* properties. This means that even if two users trust each other as much as what a similarity measure indicates, they do not necessarily have the same confidence in this association. Consider for example, the illustration of Figure 3(c) where there is a direct trust association between user S and user T. Since computation of trust is based on user similarities their associated trust would be the same for both users. However, user S is as much as 0.57 confident about this association, while user T is as much as 0.43 confident about this association. Therefore, our approach is in accordance with the widely accepted position that trust has a subjective notion [23] and reflects the way in which trust is raised in real world social networks.

3.5 Managing Multiple Trust Paths

Since trust inferences are based on traversal paths in a network, it is possible to find *multiple paths* that connect two users. Figure 4 depicts an example in which a source user S is connected to a target user T through two alternative trust paths P_A and P_B.

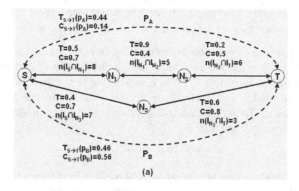

Fig. 4. Illustrating Example of Multiple Trust Paths

Path P_A passes through users N_1, N_2, while path P_B through user N_3. The inferred trust in each of these trust paths is independent of the other. Thus, our trust model needs to define a rule that decides which of these inferred trusts to take into consideration. We describe two approaches for inferring trust when there are multiple trust paths available; the first approach is based on *path composition*, while the other is based on *path selection*. For the following approaches we assume that there are p discrete paths between user S and user T.

Path Composition

The path composition approach tries to combine the values that are inferred by the multiple paths to one single trust value. We distinguish between two methods of composition; *Average Composition* and *Weighted Average Composition*.

- *Average Composition*: We compute the average of all the trust values that are inferred by each of the alternative paths according to Equation 9. Despite the fact that this approach is very cost effective it is considered too naive, because it doesn't take into consideration the confidence of each path.

$$T_{S \to T} = \frac{\sum\limits_{i=1}^{p} T_{S \to T \atop P_i}}{p} \tag{9}$$

- *Weighted Average Composition*: We compute the weighted average of the trust inferred by the alternative paths, using for weights the propagated confidence of each inferred association between user S and user T, according to Equation 7. This approach is more sophisticated since path confidence is taken into consideration. The final computed trust would be biased to the trust inferred by the most confident path.

$$T_{S \to T} = \sum_{i=1}^{p} \frac{C_{S \to T \atop P_i}}{\sum\limits_{i=1}^{p} C_{S \to T \atop P_i}} T_{S \to T \atop P_i} \tag{10}$$

Path Selection

The path selection approach tries to identify the most confident path among the paths available. We employ two methods of selection, one based on *Maximum Path Confidence* and one based on *Minimum Mean Absolute Deviation (MAD)*.

- *Selection Based on Path Maximum Confidence*: Based on the confidence of direct association we can compute the confidence of a path in the network according to Equation 7. Thus, it is possible to compute the confidence of all discrete paths and then to select the one with the highest degree of confidence. Then, we can use only this path to compute the inferred trust between user S and user T.

$$T_{S \to T} = \max\{C_{S \to T \atop P_i} : i = 1, 2, ..., p\} \tag{11}$$

- *Selection Based on Minimum Mean Absolute Deviation (MAD)*: It is possible to order the discrete paths that connect user S and user T, according to the Mean Absolute Deviation of their direct associations. We consider absolute deviation to be the difference between the confidence values of two consecutive associations. Once all MAD values are computed for each of the paths available we select the one with the minimum MAD as indicated by Equation 12, where N is the cardinality of nodes in the path p. This path selection method requires that the path comprises of at least 3 users (i.e. $N \geq 3$). The assumption of this approach is that a path would be more confident when consecutive values of confidence introduce smaller instability.

$$T_{S \to T} = \min\{MAD(P_i) : i = 1, 2, ..., p\}, \quad where \quad MAD(P_i) = \frac{\sum_{k=1}^{N-2} \left\| \left| C_{N_k \to N_{k+1}} \right| - \left| C_{N_{k+1} \to N_{k+2}} \right| \right\|}{N-2} \quad (12)$$

4 Experimental Evaluation and Results

In this section we evaluate our method for alleviating the sparsity problem using trust inferences. Our evaluation scenario spans across two dimensions. We first evaluate the *impact of trust inferences* to the sparsity problem and then evaluate the *quality of the recommendations* that are based on the underlying network of direct and inferred associations. The experimental data come from our movie recommendation system named *MRS*. The lowest level of sparsity introduced by the system is 0.972 which is a typical sparsity level for recommendation systems, while ratings range from 1 to 10.

4.1 Trust Inference Impact

Our first objective was to introduce a method that would lead to additional information accessible for recommendation purposes. We have run tests to discover how much more informative or "dense" is the user-item matrix after applying our method of trust inferences. However, since inferences are dependent on user rating activity we first provide an allocation of ratings that correspond to each user. This helps understanding the peculiarities of our network. Figure 5 illustrates the user

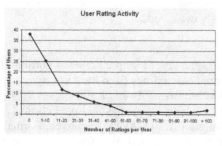

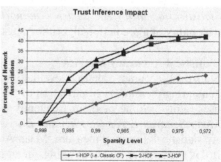

Fig. 5. User Rating Activity

Fig. 6. Impact of Trust Inference for Different Sparsity Levels

rating activity in our recommendation system, which seems to follow a *power law distribution* (Zipf distribution) [24]. There are a few users that have submitted many ratings, some users with normal number of ratings and many users with a few or even no ratings. It is essential to mention that 38% of users have no rating. This means that in our system there are some users for which no information is available, and therefore recommendations are not possible. However, for the rest users, which are members of the underlying social network, our methodology seems to be beneficial.

For our experiments, we define as *k*-HOP CF the method that employs neighbor users that are *k* hops away from the active user. We compute the percentage of user pairs that are feasible in the network when *1*-HOP, *2*-HOP and *3*-HOP CF algorithms are employed and for different sparsity levels. *1*-HOP CF represents the classic CF algorithm, while *2*-HOP CF and *3*-HOP CF represent our trust inference based transitive method for 2 and 3 hops away respectively. According to Figure 6, the percentage of network associations considered by the Classic CF are fewer than these considered by our transitive method. This is consistent with our theory, since Classic CF (*1*-HOP) employs only direct associations, while *2*-HOP CF and *3*-HOP CF apply transitive properties in the network. In addition, it is shown that for sparsity level of 0.972, the *1*-HOP CF considers approximately 24% of the total user pairs, while *2*-HOP and *3*-HOP consider approximately 43% of the total user pairs. It is also demonstrated that after a while *1*-HOP, *2*-HOP and *3*-HOP CF algorithms reach an *upper limit*. This limit is defined by the percentage of users that are inactive in the system, and therefore are not connected to the underlying network. Furthermore, it is depicted that *3*-HOP CF has similar results to *2*-HOP CF, thus for the recommendation quality experiments we only consider the *2*-HOP CF algorithm, which has better time performance.

4.2 Recommendation Quality

If a *prediction* is defined as a value that expresses the predicted likelihood that a user will "like" an item, then a *recommendation* is defined as the list of *n* items with respect to the top-*n* predictions from the set of items available. Thus we can reduce the problem of recommendation quality to the problem of prediction quality for our experiments. More accurate prediction algorithms indicate better recommendations. *Statistical accuracy* and *decision-support accuracy* are the key dimensions on which the quality of a prediction algorithm is usually evaluated.

Statistical Accuracy Metrics
Statistical accuracy metrics evaluate the accuracy of a prediction algorithm by comparing the numerical deviation of the predicted ratings from the respective actual user ratings. Some of them frequently used are *Mean Absolute Error (MAE)*, *Root Mean Squared Error (RMSE)* and *Correlation* between ratings and predictions [19]. As statistical accuracy measure, Mean Absolute Error (MAE) is employed. Formally, if *n* is the number of actual ratings in an item set, then MAE is defined as the average absolute difference between the *n* pairs $< p_h, r_h >$ of predicted ratings p_h and the actual ratings r_h and is given by equation 13.

$$MAE = \frac{\sum_{h=1}^{n} |p_h - r_h|}{n} \tag{13}$$

The lower the *MAE*, the more accurate the predictions are, allowing for better recommendations to be formulated. *MAE* has been computed for Classic CF and for the four variations of our 2-HOP CF method based on trust inferences. The prediction algorithms are tested for different levels of sparsity over a pre-selected *300-ratings set* extracted randomly by the set of actual ratings. Figure 7 illustrates the sensitivity of the algorithms in relation to the different levels of sparsity applied.

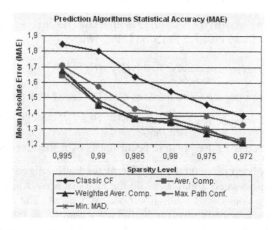

Fig. 7. MAE of the Classic CF and the variations of our CF method of trust inferences for different Sparsity lpevels

As far as statistical accuracy is concerned 2-HOP CF algorithm outperforms the *1*-HOP Classic CF for all sparsity levels. For typical sparsity levels of recommendation systems, such as 0.975 and 0.98, 2-HOP CF performs as much as 10.1% and 13.1% better than *1*-HOP CF respectively. In cases that data is extremely sparse, for example when it is equal to 0.99, 2-HOP CF performs as much as 17% better than *1*-HOP CF. Considering that most of the alternative methods proposed for dealing with the sparsity problem result in recommendation quality degradation, the quality performance of our prediction algorithms is very satisfactory.

Decision-Support Accuracy Metrics

Decision-support accuracy metrics evaluate how effectively predictions help a user to select high-quality items. Some of them frequently used are *reversal rate, weighted errors, Precision-Recall Curve (PRC) sensitivity* and *Receiver Operating Characteristic (ROC) sensitivity*. They are based on the observation that, for many users, filtering is a binary process. Consequently, prediction algorithms can be treated as a filtering procedure, which distinguishes "good" items from "bad" items.

As decision support accuracy measure, ROC sensitivity is employed. ROC sensitivity is a measure of the diagnostic power of a filtering system. Operationally, it is the area under the receiver operating characteristic (ROC) curve, a curve that plots the sensitivity and the 1-specificity of the test. Sensitivity refers to the probability of a randomly selected "good" item being accepted by the filter. Specificity is the probability of a randomly selected "bad" item being rejected by the filter.

If *PR, AR, QT* denote the predicted rating, the actual rating and a quality threshold respectively, then the following possible cases are defined by the filter for one item

- True Positive (TP) when $PR \geq QT \wedge AR \geq QT$
- False Positive (FP) when $PR \geq QT \wedge AR < QT$
- True Negative (TN) when $PR < QT \wedge AR < QT$
- False Negative (FN) when $PR < QT \wedge AR \geq QT$

For a set of items sensitivity is defined as the True Positive Fraction (TPF) and the 1-specificity as the False Positive Fraction (FPF) where

- $sensitivity = TPF = \dfrac{tp}{tp + fn}$, where tp, fn is the number of the true positive

  and the false negative occurrences over the set of items respectively.

- $1 - specificity = FPF = \dfrac{fp}{fp + tn}$, where tn, fp is the number of the true

  negative and the false positive occurrences over the set of items respectively.

ROC curve has been computed for different prediction algorithms and for quality thresholds ranging between 1 and 9, while the sparsity level was equal to 0,972. For each prediction we considered a neighborhood of 5 users. The area under the curve represents how much sensitive the prediction algorithm is, so the more area it covers the better for the prediction algorithm. Results are illustrated on Figure 8.

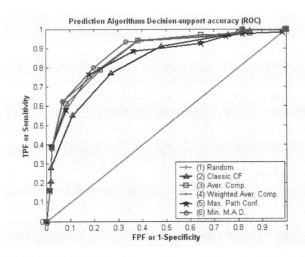

Fig. 8. ROC for the Classic CF and the variations of CF method of trust inferences

As far as decision-support accuracy is concerned the performance of the CF method based on our method of trust inferences is of superior quality than Classic CF prediction algorithms, while there is only slight difference between the accuracy performance of the four variations of our CF method. To obtain a clear view of the overall performance of each algorithm one needs to compute the area under the ROC curve. It is clear from Figure 8 that Classic CF performs much worse than every other algorithm employed based on our method of trust inferences.

5 Conclusions

Sparsity is one of the major aspects that limits the application of the CF method and provokes its success in providing quality recommendation algorithms. In this research, our main objective was to describe a method that is able to provide high-quality recommendations even when information available is insufficient. Our work employs theoretical results of research conducted in areas of social networks and trust management in order to develop a computational trust model for recommendation systems. To deal with the sparsity problem we proposed a method that is based on trust inferences. Trust inferences are transitive associations between users that participate in the underlying social network. Employment of this model provides additional information to CF algorithm and remarkably relaxes the sparsity and the cold-start problems. Furthermore, our model considers the subjective notion of trust and reflects the way in which it is raised in real world social networks. Subjectiveness is defined in terms of confidence and uncertainty properties that are applied to the network associations. We have experimentally evaluated our method according to the impact that trust inferences have to sparsity and according to recommendation quality. Our experimental results indicate that our method succeeds in providing additional information to the CF algorithm while it outperforms the quality performance of the classic CF method. The methodology described is general and may probably be easily adopted to alleviate the sparsity problem in other application areas, especially where underlying social networks can be identified.

References

1. Resnick P. and Varian Hal R. "Recommender Systems (introduction to special section)". Communications of the ACM, 40(3), 1997
2. Herlocker, J., Konstan, J. A., Terveen, L. and Riedl, J. "Evaluating Collaborative Filtering Recommender Systems". ACM Transactions on Information Systems, 22 (1), 2004
3. Herlocker, J. L., Konstan, J. A., and Riedl, J. "Explaining Collaborative Filtering Recommendations". Proc. of the ACM Conference on Computer Supported Cooperative Work, 2002
4. Sarwar, B., Karypis, G., Konstan, J., Riedl J. "Analysis of recommendation algorithms for e-commerce". Proc. of ACM Electronic Commerce, 2000
5. Linden, G., Smith, B., York, J. "Amazon.com Recommendations: Item-to-Item Collaborative Filtering". IEEE Internet Computing, January, 2003

6. Schein, A. I., Popescul, A., Ungar, L. H. "Methods and Metrics for Cold-Start Recommendations". Proc. of the 25th Annual International ACM SIGIR Conference on Research and Development in Information Retrieval, 2002

7. Goldbergh, K., Roeder, T., Gupta, D., and Perkins, C. "Eigentaste: A constant time collaborative filtering algorithm". Inf. Ret. 4, 2, 133–151, 2001

8. Billsus, D., and Pazzani, M. J. "Learning collaborative information filters". Proc. of the 15th International Conference on Machine Learning, 46–54, 1998

9. Deerwester, S., Dumais, S. T., Furnas, G. W., Landauer, T. K., Harshman, R. "Indexing by Latent Semantic Analysis". JASIS 41(6), 1990

10. Hofmann, T., 2003. "Collaborative Filtering via Gaussian Probabilistic Latent Semantic Analysis". Proc. of the 26th Annual International ACM SIGIR Conference on Research and Development in Information Retrieval, 2003

11. Huang, Z., Chen, H., Zeng, D. "Applying Associative Retrieval Techniques to Alleviate the Sparsity Problem in Collaborative Filtering". ACM Transactions on Information Systems, 22 (1), 2004

12. Sarwar, B., Karypis, G., Konstan, J., Riedl, J. "Item-based Collaborative Filtering Recommendation Algorithms". Proc. of WWW, 2001

13. Popescul, A., Ungar, L. H., Pennock, D.M., Lawrence, S. "Probabilistic Models for Unified Collaborative and Content-Based Recommendation in Sparse-Data Environments". Proc. of UAI, 2001

14. Melville, P., Mooney, R. J. and Nagaragan, R. "Content-Boosted Collaborative Filtering for Improved Recommendations". Proc. of the National Conference of the American Association Artificial Intelligence, 2002

15. Shardanand U. and Maes P. "Social information filtering: Algorithms for automating "word of mouth"", Proc. of CHI, 1995 -- Human Factors in Computing Systems, 210-217, 1995

16. Allen, R.B. "User Models: Theory, method and Practice". International Journal of Man-Machine Studies, 1990

17. Ziegler, C.N. and Lausen, G. "Analyzing Correlation Between Trust and User Similarity in Online Communities". Proc. of the 2nd International Conference on Trust Management, 2004

18. Breese, J. S., Heckerman, D. and Kadie, C. "Empirical analysis of predictive algorithms for collaborative filtering". Proc. of the 14th Conference on Uncertainty in Artificial Intelligence, 1998

19. Herlocker, J. L., Konstan, J. A., Borchers, A., and Riedl, J. "An Algorithmic Framework for Performing Collaborative Filtering". Proc. of the 22nd ACM SIGIR Conference on Research and Development in Information Retrieval, 1999

20. Pearson K. "Mathematical contribution to the theory of evolution: VII, on the correlation of characters not quantitatively measurable". Phil. Trans. R. Soc. Lond. A, 195, 1-47, 1900.

21. Guha,R., Kumar,R., Raghavan, P., Tomkins, A. "Propagation of Trust and Distrust". Proc. of WWW2004

22. Ziegler, C.N. and Lausen, G. "Spreading Activation Models for Trust Propagation". Proc. of IEEE International Conference on e-Technology, e-Commerce, and e-Service, 2004

23. Josang, A. "A Logic for Uncertain Probabilities". International Journal of Uncertainty, Fuzziness and Knowledge-Based Systems, Vol. 9, No. 3, June, 2001

24. Faloutsos, M., Faloutsos P., Faloutsos C. "On Power-Law Relationships of the Internet Topology". Proc. of SIGCOMM, 1999

25. Papagelis M., Plexousakis D. "Qualitative Analysis of User-based and Item-based Prediction Algorithms for Recommendation Agents". International Journal of Engineering Applications of Artificial Intelligence, vol 18(4), June, 2005
26. Papagelis M., Rousidis I., Plexousakis D., Theoharopoulos E. "Incremental Collaborative Filtering for Highly-Scalable Recommendation algorithms". Proc. of International Symposium on Methodologies of Intelligent Systems, 2005

Experience-Based Trust: Enabling Effective Resource Selection in a Grid Environment

Nathan Griffiths[1] and Kuo-Ming Chao[2]

[1] Department of Computer Science, University of Warwick, Coventry, CV4 7AL, UK
nathan@dcs.warwick.ac.uk
[2] School of MIS, Coventry University, Coventry, CV1 5FB, UK
k.chao@coventry.ac.uk

Abstract. The Grid vision is to allow heterogeneous computational resources to be shared and utilised globally. Grid users are able to submit tasks to remote resources for execution. However, these resources may be unreliable and there is a risk that submitted tasks may fail or cost more than expected. The notion of trust is often used in agent-based systems to manage such risk, and in this paper we apply trust to the problem of resource selection in Grid computing. We propose a number of resource selection algorithms based upon trust, and evaluate their effectiveness in a simulated Grid.

1 Introduction

Distributed computer systems can be viewed as multi-agent systems in which individual autonomous agents cooperate to achieve their objectives. It is through cooperation that such agents function effectively, since they typically lack the knowledge, capabilities or resources to achieve their objectives alone. Grid computing can be viewed as a multi-agent system that allows users to discover, select and use remote resources [15]. The process of a user submitting a task to a resource, and that resource performing the task, can be viewed as cooperation. Both users and resources have control over their own behaviour, and are autonomous agents having their own decision making mechanisms. By definition, however, autonomous agents also control how they cooperate. In particular, such agents determine for themselves when to initiate cooperation, when to offer it, and when to rescind cooperative commitments. Consequently, when agents cooperate, any one of them can cease cooperation at any time, (typically) causing the whole interaction to fail. In a Grid environment autonomy manifests itself through users and resources being able to change the nature of their cooperation, or even ceasing to cooperate, at any time. For example, a resource may reduce the priority of a user's task causing it to overrun, or may cease processing one user's task in favour of another.

When entering into cooperation, agents enter into uncertain interactions in which there is a risk of failure due to the decisions and actions of others. To function effectively agents must manage this risk, and the notion of trust can used to

P. Herrmann et al. (Eds.): iTrust 2005, LNCS 3477, pp. 240–255, 2005.

provide a suitable mechanism. In this paper, we describe how trust can be used to manage cooperative interactions in the context of Grid computing. In particular, we provide a mechanism for user agents to use trust for resource selection, i.e. choosing the most appropriate resource for a task. Although several researchers have considered the problem of resource selection in a Grid environment from the perspective of minimising cost [3, 16], relatively few have been concerned with minimising task failure [1, 2]. Those that do consider failure tend to use restrictive trust models, and often do not consider the cost of task execution[1].

In the following section, we introduce the Grid context in more detail and illustrate the problems that trust can address. In Section 3 we describe the notion of trust, and the trust model that we use, and in Section 4 we describe how trust can be compared using a strict, stratified, or windowed approach. The application of trust to the resource selection problem is described in Section 5. Our approach has been implemented in a simulated Grid, as described in Section 6, and in Section 7 we give details of our results. Finally, in Section 8 we give our conclusions and outline ongoing work.

2   Context: Grid Computing

Grid computing provides a mechanism for users to discover, select and utilise remote resources. Although most existing Grids are fairly localised, the Grid vision is to allow global resource sharing, where resources charge users for executing their tasks. Resources are heterogeneous, geographically distributed and locally controlled, and have specific individual capabilities in terms of their processor architecture, network bandwidth etc. that are made available for an associated cost. Grid resources may be unreliable and may erroneously fail to execute a task, or circumstances may cause them to delay or drop execution of a remote user's task. An example of the former is where hardware or network problems cause a task to fail. The latter case is illustrated by a resource dropping a task submitted by one user, in favour of that submitted by a higher priority user. For example, remote users' tasks may be dropped in favour of local users, or tasks submitted by low paying users may be dropped in favour of users who pay more.

When selecting a resource to submit a task to, a Grid user typically tries to minimise the execution cost (possibly considering time in addition to financial cost) and the risk of the task failing. These aims may conflict with each other, since cheap resources may be unreliable and reliable resources may be expensive. Therefore, a user must balance these criteria according to their own preferences. Additionally, users should generally aim to use a broad selection of resources, to avoid reliance on a narrow set. If a user interacts only with a small set of resources that subsequently become unreliable, there will not be familiar alternatives to submit tasks to, and alternatives must be source and familiarity rebuilt.

---

[1] There has been other work in minimising failure in Grid computing but not from a Grid user's perspective (e.g. [10]).

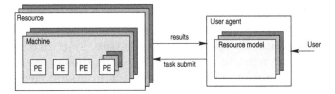

Fig. 1. A single user's perspective of the Grid as a multi-agent system

The factors that a user considers when selecting a resource depend both on its individual decision making mechanism, and on the nature of its individual Grid context. The context is important since it determines, among other things, the significance of failure in terms of cost. In this paper, we assume that all of a user's tasks must be completed and that failure has an associated cost penalty. Thus, if a resource fails to complete a task the user incurs a cost penalty (i.e. a fine) and must find an alternative resource to submit the task to. The overall cost of processing a task is therefore related to the risk of failure, since in addition to the execution cost there is an implicit cost overhead for resubmission and an explicit penalty for submitting tasks to an unreliable resource.

The Grid environment is illustrated in Fig. 1, where resources (which comprise a set of machines that in turn comprise a set of processing elements) are shown as resource agents and human users are represented by user agents. Users submit tasks to resources via their corresponding user agents. All of a user's interactions with resources are performed via its user agent which assists in managing these interactions. In particular, the responsibility of selecting an appropriate resource for a task is devolved to the user agent, which is configured to reflect the user's preferences (e.g. in balancing cost and risk). Our focus in this paper is primarily concerned with using trust for resource selection and, although cost is clearly relevant, we are not concerned with the details of specific economic models of Grid computing. Therefore, we adopt a simple flat commodity market model in which resources specify their service price and charge users according to how much resource is consumed [3]. There are many alternative market models, including tendering, auctions and negotiation. However, these add complexity both in themselves, and in terms of how they effect trust. For example, agents may build trust through a negotiation process, in addition to via their task interactions. Consideration of these alternative market models is beyond the scope of this paper, but is a potential area for future investigation.

3   Trust

The notion of trust is recognised as a means of assessing the potential risk in interactions [5, 7, 12]. Trust represents an agent's estimate of how likely another agent is to fulfil its cooperative commitments. When considering uncertain interactions, an agent can use its trust of potential cooperative partners to evaluate the risk of failure. There are two main categories of trust: experience-based and recommendation-based. In the former, an agent's assessment of trust is purely based on its own experiences, while in the latter trust is based on information provided by other agents (possibly supplemented by individual experience). Experience-based trust naturally fits the Grid context. Users interact with resources and infer trust based on their experiences and, over time, improve their trust models. Recommendation-based trust requires users to share information about their experiences with a resource with other potential users of the resource. Although this is certainly a potentially powerful mechanism, there are a number of obstacles to its use. In particular, there is no intrinsic motivation for information sharing. Indeed, if a user gives positive feedback about a resource this may jeopardise possible future use, since others are more likely to use the resource (reducing its availability). There are also general issues concerning the subjectivity and context-specific nature of feedback. Other researchers are, however, considering these problems to allow use of recommendation-based trust in the Grid domain [9, 14]. Our work is orthogonal to this, and we envisage experience-based and recommendation-based trust eventually complimenting each other to provide a single trust mechanism. For the purposes of this paper, however, we are solely concerned with experience-based trust.

3.1 Trust Framework

We base our model of trust on Gambetta's theoretical work [7], Marsh's formalism [12], and the work of Griffiths [6, 8], and define the trust T in an agent α, to be a real number in the interval between 0 and 1: $T_\alpha \in [0, 1]$. The numbers merely represent comparative values, and have no strong semantic meaning in themselves. Values approaching 0 represent complete distrust, and those approaching 1 represent complete blind trust. There is an inverse relationship between trust and the perceived risk of an interaction: cooperating with a trusted agent has a low perceived risk of failure, while there is a high risk associated with distrusted agents. Trust values represent the view of an individual agent, subjectively based on its experience, and are not directly comparable across agents.

Trust values are associated with a measure of confidence, and as an agent gains experience its confidence increases. With no prior experience, trust takes an initial value according to an agent's disposition: optimistic or pessimistic. Optimistic agents ascribe a high initial trust value to others (implying a low perceived risk), and pessimists ascribe low values. This disposition also determines how trust is updated after interactions [13]. After successful interactions, optimists increase their trust more than pessimists and, conversely, after unsuccessful interactions pessimists decrease their trust more than optimists. An agent's disposition comprises: the initial trust, $T_{initial}$, ascribed prior to interacting and functions for updating trust after successful and unsuccessful interactions, $update_{success}$ and $update_{fail}$ respectively. These functions for updating trust are simple heuristics, and there is no standard definition for them. Instead, it is the responsibility of the system designer to choose an appropriate heuristic. In this paper we use the following definitions for the update functions:

$$update_{success}(T) = T + ((1 - T) \times (d_s \times T))$$

$$update_{fail}(T) = T - ((1 - T) \times (d_f \times T))$$

where d_s and d_f are weighting factors defined by the disposition[2]. Other definitions are possible, and there is no "correct" definition; empirical evaluation is needed to determine appropriate functions for a given domain.

Over time trust values may become inaccurate and outdated if the experiences that gave rise to them are no longer relevant. The environment may change, and a resource that was reliable previously may no longer be so. To address this problem, we apply a decay function to converge each trust value to $T_{initial}$ in the lack of any subsequent experience. Thus, unless reinforced by recent cooperative activity, the positive effect of successful interactions reduces over time, as does the negative effect of failed interactions. The decay function is defined as:

$$decay(T) = T - ((T - T_{initial})/d_d)$$

where d_d a decay rate defined by the agent's disposition.

To improve its trust models an agent may also explore alternative resources for low priority tasks. Agents typically only interact with others that are considered trustworthy. Thus, there tends to be a subset of resources that are interacted with, and it is this subset for whom the agent will be confident about its trust values. To reduce the risk of a reliable agent being outside this subset, agents can periodically select resources from outside the set to verify its judgement is correct and attempt to discover additional trusted resources[3].

4   Numerical, Stratified and Windowed Trust

In our approach trust is modelled as a numerical value, however some researchers note that using continuous numerical values can introduce ambiguity since the semantics are hard to represent [1, 12]. The alternative approach is to divide the trust continuum into a set of labelled strata. Abdul-Rahman and Hailes, for example, take this approach, providing four distinct trust strata ("very trustworthy", "trustworthy", "untrustworthy", and "very untrustworthy") that they argue provides a clear semantics for different trust values [1]. The advantage of this approach is that "trustworthy" for one agent should correspond to "trustworthy" for another, avoiding the problem of defining the meaning of a numerical value. However, these semantics are still subjective, and different agents may ascribe the same experiences to different strata; experiences that rate as highly trustworthy for one agent may only rate as trustworthy for another. A further problem with stratifying trust is a loss of sensitivity and accuracy, since comparisons become coarse grained with no way to distinguish between agents within

---

[2] It is beyond the scope of this paper to discuss the impact of different dispositions, however our experiments have obtained similar results to those presented in Section 7 with different dispositions.

[3] This approach is analogous to the simulated annealing method for local search, where potentially suboptimal options are considered to avoid local minima [11].

a stratum. For this reason Marsh rejects the use of strata in favour of numerical values [12]. In our approach, to avoid loss of sensitivity and accuracy, we also represent trust by numerical values. Furthermore, updating trust after interactions is simple for numeric values, whilst those models that use stratification gloss over how agents determine a trust strata from their experiences [1, 2].

The primary advantage of trust strata is that selection between resources is simplified. In our model, suppose that a user must select between two resources with trust values 0.5 and 0.50001. The user must either conclude that this difference is insignificant and the resources are equally trusted, or that there is a real difference in trust and the latter resource is more trustworthy. The use of strata avoids this problem, since there are no numerical values for consideration. Ideally, a trust model would have the sensitivity and accuracy of a numerical approach, combined with the ease of comparison from a stratified approach. To this end, we propose two simple modifications to our trust model *at the time of trust comparisons*: variable stratification and windowed trust.

In the former, trust values are translated into strata immediately before comparison. The number of strata is variable, with fewer strata providing the simplest but least precise comparison, while more strata reduces the comparison advantage but retains precision. For example, Abdul-Rahman and Hailes' strata can be modelled by dividing the trust interval into the following equal parts: very trustworthy: $0.75 <= T <= 1$, trustworthy: $0.5 <= T < 0.75$, untrustworthy: $0.25 <= T < 0.5$, and very untrustworthy: $0 <= T < 0.25$.

The disadvantage of stratifying trust is that an equal difference in values is not significant within a stratum, but is when it lies across strata. For example, using the above strata a difference of 0.1 is not significant for agents with trust values 0.6 and 0.7 (i.e. both are "trustworthy"), but it is for agents with values of 0.7 and 0.8 (i.e. the former is "trustworthy" and the latter "very trustworthy").

Our second modification is to use a variable size window when considering trust values, such that values within the window are considered equal. This is a similar to stratified trust, but avoids the problems across strata boundaries. Windowed trust can be thought of as stratified trust with movable boundaries. For example, if we use a window size, or *trust distance*, of 0.1, then agents with trust values 0.6 and 0.7 are considered equal, as are agents with trust values of 0.7 and 0.8. However, the agent will still distinguish between trust values of 0.6 and 0.8. The trust distance is variable, and similarly to stratified trust, a larger distance provides the simplest but least precise comparison, while smaller values reduce the comparison advantages but retain precision.

5   Resource Selection

When selecting a resource a user must first consider whether the resource has the required capabilities (e.g. processor architecture, network bandwidth etc.), and second whether it is likely to complete the task successfully. The first of these considerations is simple — either a resource has the required capabilities or it does not. Those that do not can be rejected, otherwise factors such as cost and reliability must be considered. These factors are more complex, since they have varying degrees and may be based on uncertain information. Trust enables an agent to consider these factors. A user is likely to prefer a resource that generally completes tasks on time and rarely fails, to one that frequently fails. This is embodied by the trust ascribed to a resource. To select a resource an agent should balance trustworthiness against cost. Selecting a resource in this manner is a heuristic decision and there are several possible approaches. This paper proposes six fundamental options, as introduced below.

5.1   Cost

The simplest approach to minimising execution cost is to select the resource that has the lowest expected cost, based on its published cost-per-second. However, this will only be successful if resources are honest and reliable. If a resource takes longer than expected to process the task, or fails to execute it, then this approach will not result in the lowest overall cost. If execution takes longer than expected then the user will be charged for the additional processing time. Should task execution fail then an alternative resource must be found, and the user will be charged a penalty for failure. The problem is that the risk of resource failure and unreliability is not considered when selecting a resource.

5.2   Strict Trust

To minimise the risk of failure, an agent can select the most trusted capable resource (provided the agent is confident of its models[4]). If several resources are equally highly trusted, then one is selected arbitrarily. For low priority tasks the agent periodically selects an untrusted resource, by way of exploration as described in Section 3. This approach ensures that the resource that is perceived to be the lowest risk is selected. However, users are forced to distinguish between resources even where the numerical difference is small. Since trust is solely based on experience, small differences in the numerical value may not be sufficient to make *meaningful* judgements. Although small differences may arise from genuine differences in reliability, they may also arise from differences in the extent or recency of experiences. Thus, there is a risk of overfitting by drawing conclusions from trust values where differences arise from irrelevant artifacts of the data.

A further disadvantage to using strict trust is that it tends to lead to a very narrow set of resources being used. Since users may select resources based on small numerical differences, these small differences are reinforced by the resulting interactions. Over time, an insignificant difference in trust can be magnified significantly. For example, if resource R_1 is trusted only slightly more than R_2 then after a period of successful interactions the trust of R_1 may be significantly more than R_2. Thus, in future interactions R_1 is likely to remain more trusted that R_2 even if in reality there is no significant difference. This is problematic

---

[4] If the agent is not confident, it can do little more that choose arbitrarily to gain experience. In the remainder of this section we assume such confidence.

since, as described in Section 2, a broad selection of resources should be used to ensure resilience.

5.3   Stratified Trust

To avoid the narrow resource usage that results from strict trust we can use stratified trust at the comparison stage. The most trusted resource is selected, according to the trust stratum that the numerical value lies in. Where several resources are equally most trusted, one is selected arbitrarily. Again, where the task is of low priority the agent periodically selects a resource that is not trusted by way of exploration. This approach avoids the problem of overfitting small numerical differences, but at the cost of a loss of precision. The number of strata is variable, and the effect of strata size is discussed in Section 7.

5.4   Stratified Trust with Cost

Using stratified trust for resource selection minimises the risk of failure, and avoids overfitting, however no consideration is given to the task execution cost. Therefore, we propose a fourth selection method that initially uses stratified trust, but then selects the cheapest of the most trusted resources, based on their advertised cost-per-second. Thus, an agent first determines the capable resources, then extracts the most trusted of these, and finally selects the cheapest.

The choice of strata size is crucial to the effectiveness of this approach. If too few strata are used, an agent is unable to distinguish between resources according to reliability; if too many strata are used there is likely to be a single most-trusted resource leaving no opportunity to distinguish based on cost. The number of strata effectively determines the emphasis given to reliability versus cost — more strata emphasises reliability and reduces the influence of cost, and visa versa. Again, the effect of different strata sizes is discussed in Section 7.

5.5   Windowed Trust

Stratified trust avoids the overfitting associated with strict trust, however, as noted in Section 4, it suffers from problems at strata boundaries. The alternative is to use windowed trust, in which the most trusted resource is selected according to the trust window that the numerical value lies in. Where several resources are equally most trusted, one is selected arbitrarily. Again, agents periodically select a resource that is not trusted, by way of exploration. This approach avoids both the overfitting problem and the effects of strata boundaries. Similarly to stratified trust, the trust distance (i.e. the window size) is variable, with a larger distance giving higher precision, but at the risk of overfitting. Section 7 discusses the effects of trust distance.

5.6   Windowed Trust with Cost

Our final selection approach combines windowed trust with cost. Similarly to stratified trust with cost, a user first determines the capable resources, then determines the most trusted of these according to windowed trust, and finally selects the cheapest. Again, the size of trust distance is important, with smaller distances emphasising reliability and reducing the influence of cost, and visa versa. The effects of different trust distances are discussed in Section 7.

6   Experimental Scenario

The resource selection mechanisms described above have been explored using the GridSim simulation toolkit [4]. This toolkit provides a feasible way to experiment with such algorithms on a reasonably large-scale Grid of heterogeneous resources. The overheads and resource requirements of investigating these algorithms in a physical Grid are prohibitive, since significant access to Grid resources would be required. Our future aim is to instantiate the most effective of our resource selection mechanisms in a real Grid environment after validation via simulation.

In the GridSim toolkit, resources comprise a set of machines that in turn comprise a set of processing elements (PEs). Each resource has certain capabilities, defined by its communication bandwidth and the configuration and processor architecture of its PEs. At run-time resources have a variable load, due to tasks being processed on behalf of users and due to background processing. Resource load, at least in part, determines how long it takes to process a given task. In GridSim each resource has an associated "calendar", specified when configuring a simulation, that defines how background load varies according to time of day (i.e. peak and off-peak loads), day of the week and holidays etc. We have extended the GridSim toolkit to allow the simulation of unreliable resources, and in our GridSim extension resources have an additional characteristic defining their reliability in terms of a failure rate. Tasks are defined as Gridlets with attributes defining their length, disk I/O operations, and the size of input and output files. GridSim does not constrain the granularity of Gridlets, and in our simulations we view a single job as comprising several Gridlets. Thus, a users can allocate large jobs to several resources, by allocating the component Gridlets.

To test the validity of our approach, and the resource selection algorithms described above, a series of experiments were performed. A range of user agents with different dispositions (including varying values of d_s, d_f and d_d), from optimistic to pessimistic, were used in a selection of Grid contexts, ranging from the majority of resources being reliable, through a mixed set, to unreliable resources. Each of the resource selection proposed algorithms was used, with varying numbers of trust strata (from 1 to 5000) and trust distances (from 0.0001 to 1). For control purposes a random selection algorithm was also used, where user agents simply submitted tasks to random resources. Various numbers of users and resources were experimented with, however most of the results presented below are for 30 resources and 10 users. Each user generates a random set of 500 tasks to be completed with varying lengths, bandwidth requirements, and priorities. For each configuration of the experimental domain we performed 10 runs, and the results shown below represent the average values across those runs.

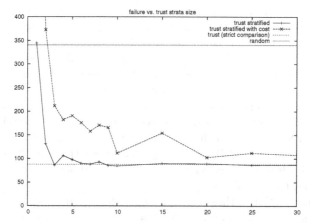

Fig. 2. Failure rate for the stratified trust and stratified trust with cost resource selection methods

7 Results and Evaluation

In this section we present results obtained from using the resource selection algorithms described above. We view these results as 'proof-of-concept', since empirical experimentation is needed to determine appropriate trust update functions and disposition values for a specific domain. Initial results with alternative update functions show broadly similar results to those given below. We are primarily concerned with the failure rate, execution cost, and total cost (i.e. execution cost plus any failure penalties) of the proposed strategies. We consider first the stratified trust methods, and then the windowed trust methods, in both cases investigating the impact of strata size and trust distance. Finally, we illustrate the effect of Grid context in terms of the proportions of reliable and unreliable resources, and identify the preferred proposed strategies in our simulated Grid.

7.1 Stratified Trust Approach

Fig. 2 shows the failure rate for the stratified trust and stratified trust with cost resource selection methods for a varying number of strata. The failure rate represents the average number of failed Gridlets. In our experiments users generate 500 Gridlets that must be completed, and so are resubmitted in the event of failure. Thus the failure rate is equivalent to the average number of resubmissions needed to complete all 500 Gridlets. These results represent the average of 10 runs in a "mixed" Grid resource environment, i.e. there is a mix of reliable and unreliable resources[5]. Fig. 2 also shows the failure rate for the strict trust and random selection methods. The failure rate for the cost based selection method

---

[5] It should be noted that the effect of the number of strata is broadly the same regardless of the mix of resources, as discussed later in this section.

is not shown, since it is too high (an average of 987) to appear on the graph. It can be seen immediately that the lowest failure rate is achieved for the strict trust method and, with the exception of very low numbers of strata, the random selection method gives the highest failure rate. It can also be seen that provided at least 3 trust strata are used then both strata-based methods perform better than a random selection (and significantly better than a cost-based approach). In both strata-based approaches lower failure rates are achieved as more strata are used. The simple strata-based approach tends to perform as well as the strict trust approach for 10 or more strata, while the strata-based with cost approach is consistently only around 10-15% worse than strict-trust for 20 or more strata (the trace for both methods continues to be flat for 30-5000 strata, but for clarity is omitted from the graph).

Recall from Section 5 that one significant disadvantage of using strict trust for resource selection is that a narrow set of resources tends to be used. In the experiments illustrated in Fig. 2, the strict trust approach led to a user generally interacting with a single trusted resource. The strata-based approaches led to a wider range of resources being used, where fewer strata gave a wider set of resources (a single strata leads to all resources being used equally). At the point where the failure rate for the strata-based approaches levels off (around 10 strata without cost and 20 with cost) then, as for strict trust, there is a single trusted resource being used. However, before this point there is a wider set of used resources, and so a higher resilience to change and a reduced likelihood of negligible differences being interpreted as significant. Moreover, a wider range of resources allows a user to allocate concurrent Gridlets to different resources.

The execution cost for the stratified trust methods is shown in Fig. 3, along with the execution cost for the cost-based, strict trust and random selection methods. It can be seen that a stratified trust with cost approach gives the least cost, followed by a cost-based approach, and then the random, strict trust, and stratified trust methods respectively. The reason that stratified trust with cost

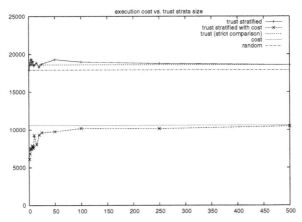

Fig. 3. Execution cost for the stratified trust and stratified trust with cost resource selection methods

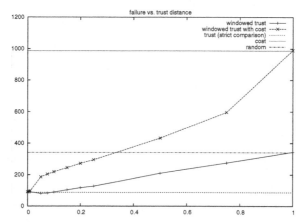

Fig. 4. Failure rate of the windowed trust and windowed trust with cost resource selection methods

gives a lower execution cost than a pure cost-based approach is that the execution cost is the *actual* execution cost, and the reliable resources that are favoured by the stratified trust with cost approach are those whose actual execution cost is likely to be closer to their advertised cost.

It can be seen from Figs. 2 and 3 that in general the stratified trust with cost approach gives better results in terms of execution cost than the strict trust, cost-based and random approaches. However, the stratified trust approach gives a lower failure rate, but only by around 10-14%.

7.2   Windowed Trust Approach

Fig. 4 shows the failure rate for the windowed trust and windowed trust with cost selection methods for varying trust distances. Again, results are averaged over 10 runs in "mixed" resource environment. It can be seen that the cost-based approach produces the highest failure rate while a strict trust approach gives the least. For a trust distance of less than 0.35 the windowed trust with cost method gave a lower failure rate than a random approach, while windowed trust was always better. The windowed trust approach gave significantly fewer failures than windowed trust with cost, and for both approaches larger trust distances increased failures. With a trust distance of 1, the windowed trust approach is equivalent to random selection, and the windowed trust with cost approach is equivalent to the cost-based approach.

Larger trust distances led to more resources being used. For a trust distance of 1, windowed trust uses all resources and windowed trust with cost uses all cheapest-cost resources. As trust distance is reduced, so is the set of used resources, such that very small values (< 0.001) are equivalent to using strict-trust.

The execution cost for the windowed trust methods is shown in Fig. 5, along with the execution cost for the cost-based, strict trust and random selection methods. It can be seen that a cost-based approach gives the least cost,

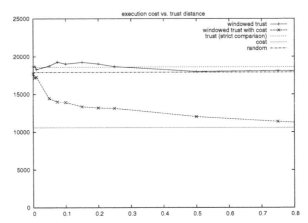

Fig. 5. Execution cost of the windowed trust and windowed trust with cost resource selection methods

followed by windowed trust with cost, random and strict trust. The windowed trust method is the highest cost for a trust distance of less than 0.25, while for larger window sizes it tends toward the cost of the random approach.

From Figs. 4 and 5 it can be seen that for trust distance of less than 0.35 both windowed trust approaches give a lower failure rate than a random or cost-based approach. The windowed trust with cost method gives a lower execution cost than all alternatives except cost-based, while windowed trust gives a lower failure rate than all except strict trust.

7.3   Resource Setting

The above results illustrate the characteristics of our proposed allocation methods. However, in order to select the most appropriate method for a given situation must consider the nature of the available resources and the penalty imposed for failure. To this end we consider three Grid environments, with differing resource reliabilities. Suppose that there are six levels of reliability, defined as follows.

reliability	failure rate
highly reliable (HR)	$0 \leq$ failure rate $\leq 3\%$
reliable (R)	$3\% <$ failure rate $\leq 10\%$
marginal unreliable (MU)	$10\% <$ failure rate $\leq 30\%$
unreliable (U)	$30\% <$ failure rate $\leq 60\%$
highly unreliable (HU)	$60\% <$ failure rate $\leq 90\%$
very highly unreliable (VHU)	$90\% <$ failure rate $\leq 100\%$

Using these definitions we define the following three sets of resources, according to the proportions of reliable and unreliable resources present.

	HR	R	MU	U	HU	VHU
reliable	60%	20%	10%	4%	3%	3%
mixed	20%	20%	20%	20%	10%	10%
unreliable	5%	10%	30%	20%	20%	15%

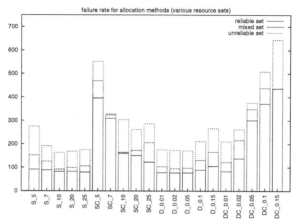

Fig. 6. Failure rate for different allocation methods in various resource sets (reliable, mixed, and unreliable)

Using these resource sets, we have experimented with each allocation method (for various strata sizes and trust distances) and obtained the average failure rates, execution costs, and total costs. The failure penalty was set to a cost of 100. This value is arbitrary, and in a real-world scenario is likely to be variable. However, it must be considered to determine total cost. Our aim in this section is to illustrate our proposed mechanism, rather than to identify exact values for agent disposition, strata size and trust distance. Empirical identification of these values is needed for real-world deployment of our proposed mechanism.

Fig. 6 shows how the failure rate varies for selected allocation methods according to resource set (reliable, mixed, and unreliable). In the figure, S_x and SC_x represent stratified trust and stratified trust with cost allocation methods with x strata respectively. Similarly, D_x and DC_x represent windowed trust and windowed trust with cost with a trust distance of x. As expected, the failure rate is least with reliable resources, rises in a mixed situation, and is highest where resources are unreliable. Furthermore, as expected from the above discussions, stratified trust and windowed trust have lower failure rates than stratified trust with cost and windowed trust with cost, and increasing the number of strata or decreasing the trust distance also reduces the failure rate.

Fig. 7 shows how the total execution cost varies according to resource set[6]. Again, it can be seen that the total cost is smallest where resources are reliable, rises in a mixed situation, and is highest when resources are unreliable. The total cost is determined by both failure rate (in terms of penalties) and execution cost. It can be seen that the lowest cost is obtained by the stratified trust with cost

---

[6] Random and cost-based allocation methods are not included because the total cost is too high. The strict trust method is not included since it is not practical due to the narrow set of resources that are used (although in pure cost terms it performs fairly well). Finally, note that the origin of the y-axis is non-zero.

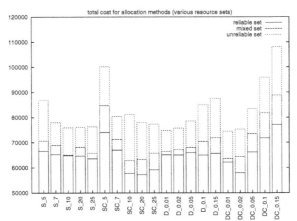

Fig. 7. Total execution cost for different allocation methods in various resource sets (reliable, mixed, and unreliable)

and windowed trust with cost algorithms, but only for certain values of number of strata and trust distances. In particular, the best results are obtained for 10-20 strata or trust distances of 0.01-0.02. Overall, for these values of strata and trust distance there is little to choose between the two approaches; stratified trust with cost is marginally better in a reliable resource context and windowed trust with cost is marginally better in an unreliable context.

8   Conclusions

In a Grid environment resource selection is fundamental to minimising the cost and failure rate that user incurs. We have shown how the notion of trust can be leveraged to implement a suitable resource selection method that minimises both cost and risk. In this paper we have presented several resource selection algorithms based on alternative methods for trust comparison namely, strict, stratified and windowed trust. We have demonstrated the use of these algorithms in a Grid context. Our results show that the use of trust significantly reduces the failure rate encountered by users when utilising Grid resources. Furthermore, where cost is factored into resource selection the overall cost of performing a task is reduced. We have shown that the most effective approaches are stratified trust with cost and windowed trust with cost with moderate strata numbers and trust distances (around 10-20 and 0.01-0.02 respectively). Both of these approaches ensure that users interact with a much wider set of resources than would occur with a strict trust approach, and so they are more resilient to environmental change or incorrect information. Our ongoing work is concerned with investigating further approaches to combining trust and cost information, in particular through the use of fuzzy logic, along with explicitly including the desire to maximise the number of resources used. Future work also includes the instantiation in a real Grid environment of the most effective of our proposed mechanisms, namely stratified trust with cost and windowed trust with cost. Finally, we also intend to apply the trust framework and resource selection algorithms to a peer-to-peer scenario.

References

1. A. Abdul-Rahman and S. Hailes. Supporting trust in virtual communities. In *Proc. of the Hawaii Int. Conf. on System Sciences 33*, 2000.
2. F. Azzedin and M. Maheswaran. Integrating trust into Grid resource management systems. In *Proc. of the Int. Conf. on Parallel Processing*, pages 47–54, 2002.
3. R. Buyya, D. Abramson, J. Giddy, and H. Stockinger. Economic models for resource management and scheduling in Grid computing. *Concurrency and Computation: Practice and Experience*, 14:1507–1542, 2002.
4. R. Buyya and M. Murshed. GridSim: A toolkit for the modelling and simulation of distributed resource management and scheduling for Grid computing. *Journal of Concurrency and Computation: Practice and Experience*, 14(13–15):1–32, 2002.
5. C. Castelfranchi and R. Falcone. Principles of trust for MAS: Cognitive anatomy, social importance, and quantification. In *Proc. of the 3rd Int. Conf. on Multi-Agent Systems*, pages 72–79, Paris, France, 1998.
6. J. R. D. Dyson, N. Griffiths, H. N. Lim Choi Jeung, S. A. Jarvis, and G. R. Nudd. Trusting agents for Grid computing. In *Proc. of the IEEE SMC 2004 Int. Conf. on Systems, Man and Cybernetics*, pages 3187–3192, 2004.
7. D. Gambetta. Can we trust trust? In D. Gambetta, editor, *Trust: Making and Breaking Cooperative Relations*, pages 213–237. Basil Blackwell, 1988.
8. N. Griffiths and M. Luck. Coalition formation through motivation and trust. In *Proc. of the 2nd Int. Conf. on Autonomous Agents and Multi-agent Systems*, pages 17–24, 2003.
9. T. D. Huynh, N. R. Jennings, and S. Shadbolt. Developing an integrated trust and reputation model for open multi-agent systems. In *Proc. of the 7th Int. Workshop on Trust in Agent Societies*, pages 65–74, 2004.
10. S. Hwang and C. Kesselman. A flexible framework for fault tolerance in the Grid. *Journal of Grid Computing*, 1:251–272, 2003.
11. S. Kirkpatrick, C. D. Gelatt, and M. P. Vecchi. Optimization by simulated annealing. *Science*, 220(4598):671–680, 1983.
12. S. Marsh. *Formalising Trust as a Computational Concept*. PhD thesis, University of Stirling, 1994.
13. S. Marsh. Optimism and pessimism in trust. In *Proc. of the Ibero-American Conf. on Artificial Intelligence*, 1994.
14. S. D. Ramchurn, C. Sierra, L. Godo, and N. R. Jennings. A computational trust model for multi-agent interactions based on confidence and reputation. In *Proc. of the 6th Int. Workshop of Deception, Fraud and Trust in Agent Societies*, pages 69–75, 2003.
15. O. F. Rana and L. Moreau. Issues in building agent based computational grids. In *Proc. of Third Workshop of the UK Special Interest Group on Multi-Agent Systems*, 2000.
16. K. Subramoniam, M. Maheswaran, and M. Toulouse. A micro-economic model for resource allocation in Grid computing systems. In *IEEE Canadian Conf. on Electrical and Computer Engineering*, pages 782–785, 2002.

Interactive Credential Negotiation for Stateful Business Processes[*]

Hristo Koshutanski and Fabio Massacci

Dip. di Informatica e Telecomunicazioni - Univ. di Trento,
via Sommarive 14 - 38050 Povo di Trento (Italy)
{hristo, massacci}@dit.unitn.it

Abstract. Business Processes for Web Services are the new paradigm for lightweight enterprise integration. They cross organizational boundaries, are provided by entities that see each other just as business partners, and require access control mechanisms based on trust management. Stateful Business Processes, enforcing separation of duties or service limitations based on past or current usage, pose additional research challenges. Clients, which may not know the right set of credentials to supply to each partner, may end up in dead-ends and servers should help them find out what must be revoked and what missing is that grant access to a particular resource.

We propose a logical framework and an interactive algorithm based on negotiation of credentials for access control that works for Stateful Business Processes. We show that our algorithm is sound (no grant is given to unauthorized clients), complete (authorized clients get grant) and resistant against DoS attempt.

1 Introduction

Business Processes (BPs) for Web Services (WS) are the new buzzword for e-commerce integration. BPs allow for a lightweight integration of partners' services and the establishment of virtual enterprises on the Web. To support this effort a number of standards have emerged: SOAP and WSDL for basic functionalities, BPEL4WS and ebXML for complex business processes.

Business Processes can be seen as workflows distributed among independent partners where all communication is channeled by the invocation of web services. Since each "task" of the workflow is offered as a web service that can be activated by anyone credentials must be used to enforce access control.

In this paper we discuss our system for reasoning about access control for Stateful BPs for WS. The basic intuition is that partners, offering web services in a BP, do not know a priori what credentials clients may need to present nor

---

[*] This work is partially funded by the IST programme of the EU Commission FET under the IST-2001-37004 WASP project and by the FIRB programme of MIUR under the RBNE0195K5 ASTRO Project and RBAU01P5SS Project.

P. Herrmann et al. (Eds.): iTrust 2005, LNCS 3477, pp. 256–272, 2005.

clients know exactly which services they want, as the BP may take different paths. So, we need an interactive process in which a client starts a business process and partners evaluate client's current credentials to determine whether they are sufficient to unlock a resource or something is missing. If missing is found then they communicate it back to the client which, in turn, may decline some of the requested credentials and a new path must be sought.

If Business Processes are stateless this can be accomplished using either trust negotiation by Yu et al. [1], Bonatti and Samarati's framework for access to Web Services [2] or our own framework for interactive access control [3] with various degree of automation, flexibility and restriction on policies. For example Yu et al. reassures monotone policies.

If the access control to a BP is stateful (i.e. access decision can change depending on past interactions or past presented credentials) this is no longer possible. For example separation of duties means that we cannot escalate privileges by supplying more credentials. Past requests or services may deny access to future services as in Bertino et al. [4] centralized access control model for workflows.

So, we need to find a way for BP partners to find a solution assuming they only know their policies. Further, it does not make sense for a BP to ask all potentially useful credentials (too demanding and privacy intruding for clients) nor such option is practical, considering that partners may prefer to ask for some credentials directly the clients rather than making them publicity available.

1.1   Our Contribution

In this paper we give an algorithm for full-fledged access control for stateful BP and show that it is correct, complete and resistant against malicious clients.

The intuition behind an interactive access control algorithm is the following.

- Initially a client submits a set of credentials and a service request.
- Then the algorithm checks whether the request is granted by the access policy according to the client's set of credentials.
- If the check fails the algorithm computes all credentials disclosable from the disclosure policy according to the presented credentials.
- After that, using abductive reasoning, the algorithm finds a (minimal) solution set of missing credentials that unlocks the desired resource and preserves consistency.
- If such a set cannot be found, the algorithm performs a recovery step in which it runs the abductive reasoning again to find a (minimal) set of excessing credentials that ban the client to get a solution for the resource.
- Once a solution (missing or excessing credentials) is found it is communicated back to the client so that he can provide the missing credentials and revoke the excessing ones.

We note that in contrast to intra-enterprise workflow systems [4], a partner offering a service has no way to assign to a client the right set of credentials which would be consisted with his future requests (because the partner cannot assign to or prohibit the client future tasks). So, we must have some roll-back procedure by which, if the user has sent "wrong" credentials, he can revoke them.

Following is a short introduction to the basic framework and reasoning services. Section 3 introduces the interactive access control algorithm for stateful BP. Next, Section 4 extends the interactive algorithm to cope with malicious clients and shows that the extended version is resistant to Denial of Service attacks. Theoretical part of the stateful framework together with the theorems for soundness and completeness is presented in Section 5. Then, Section 6 introduces the global management and initialization of session profiles in the framework. Finally, Section 7 looks through the related work and concludes the paper.

2   Basic Framework

This section shortly introduces the basic model in our framework and we refer the reader to [3] for more details. The formal model is based on normal logic programs under the stable model semantics [5]. We have predicates for requests, credentials, assignments of users to roles and of roles to services, see Figure 1. They are self explanatory, except for role dominance: a role dominates another if it has more privileges. We have constants for user's identifiers, denoted by $\mathsf{User}\!:\!U$, for roles, denoted by $\mathsf{Role}\!:\!R$, and one for services, denoted by $\mathsf{Service}\!:\!S$.

Policies are written as normal logic programs. These are sets of *rules*:

$$A \leftarrow B_1, \ldots, B_n, \ not\, C_1, \ldots, \ not\, C_m \tag{1}$$

$\mathsf{Role}\!:\!R_i \succ \mathsf{Role}\!:\!R_j$ when role $\mathsf{Role}\!:\!R_i$ dominates role $\mathsf{Role}\!:\!R_j$.
$\mathsf{Role}\!:\!R_i \succ_{\mathsf{Service}S} \mathsf{Role}\!:\!R_j$ when for service $\mathsf{Service}\!:\!S$, role $\mathsf{Role}\!:\!R_i$ dominates role $\mathsf{Role}\!:\!R_j$.
$\mathsf{assign}\,(P, \mathsf{Service}\!:\!S)$ when an access to the service $\mathsf{Service}\!:\!S$ is granted to P. Where P can be either a $\mathsf{Role}\!:\!R$ or $\mathsf{User}\!:\!U$.

(a) Predicates for assignments to Roles and Services

$\mathsf{declaration}\,(\mathsf{User}\!:\!U)$ it is a statement by the $\mathsf{User}\!:\!U$ for its identity.
$\mathsf{credential}\,(\mathsf{User}\!:\!U, \mathsf{Role}\!:\!R)$ when $\mathsf{User}\!:\!U$ has a credential activating $\mathsf{Role}\!:\!R$.
$\mathsf{credentialTask}\,(\mathsf{User}\!:\!U, \mathsf{Service}\!:\!S)$ when $\mathsf{User}\!:\!U$ has the right to access $\mathsf{Service}\!:\!S$.

(b) Predicates for Credentials

$\mathsf{running}\,(P, \mathsf{Service}\!:\!S, \mathsf{Number}\!:\!N)$ when the $\mathsf{Number}\!:\!N$-th activation of $\mathsf{Service}\!:\!S$ is executed by P.
$\mathsf{abort}\,(P, \mathsf{Service}\!:\!S, \mathsf{Number}\!:\!N)$ if the $\mathsf{Number}\!:\!N$ activation of $\mathsf{Service}\!:\!S$ within a workflow aborts.
$\mathsf{success}\,(P, \mathsf{Service}\!:\!S, \mathsf{Number}\!:\!N)$ if the $\mathsf{Number}\!:\!N$-th activation of $\mathsf{Service}\!:\!S$ within a workflow successfully executes.
$\mathsf{grant}\,(P, \mathsf{Service}\!:\!S, \mathsf{Number}\!:\!N)$ if the $\mathsf{Number}\!:\!N$ request of $\mathsf{Service}\!:\!S$ has been granted
$\mathsf{deny}\,(P, \mathsf{Service}\!:\!S, \mathsf{Number}\!:\!N)$ if the $\mathsf{Number}\!:\!N$-th request of $\mathsf{Service}\!:\!S$ has been denied.

(b) Predicates for System's History and State

Fig. 1. Predicates used in the model

where A, B_i and C_i are (possibly ground) predicates among those shown in Figure 1. A is called the *head* of the rule, each B_i is called a *positive literal* and each *not* C_j is a *negative literal*, whereas the conjunction of the B_i and *not* C_j is called the *body* of the rule. If the body is empty the rule is called a *fact*. In our framework, we also need *constraints* that are rules with an empty head.

$$\leftarrow B_1, \ldots, B_n, \; not\, C_1, \ldots, \; not\, C_m \qquad (2)$$

The intuition is to interpret the rules of a program P as constraints on a solution set S (a set of ground atoms) for the program itself. So, if S is a set of atoms, rule (1) is a constraint on S stating that if all B_i are in S and none of C_j are in it, then A must be in S. A constraint (2) is used to rule out from the set of acceptable models situations in which B_i are true and all C_j are false (those situations are not acceptable).

Definition 1 (Logical Consequence and Consistency). *We use the symbol $P \models L$, where P is a policy and L is either a credential or a service request, to specify that L is a logical consequence of a policy P. P is* consistent *($P \not\models \bot$) if there is a model for P.*

This reasoning service is used in most logical formalizations [6]: if the request r is a consequence of the policy ($\mathcal{P}$) and the credentials ($\mathcal{C}$) (i.e. $\mathcal{P} \cup \mathcal{C} \models r$), then access is granted otherwise it is denied.

A number of works have deemed such blunt denials unsatisfactory and therefore it has been proposed by Bonatti and Samarati [2] and Yu et al. [1] to send back to the client some of the rules that are necessary to gain additional access. Figure 2 shows the essence of the approaches. In their work it is revised to allow for the flow of rules and information to users.

---

1. verify that the request is a logical consequence of the credentials, namely $\mathcal{P} \cup \mathcal{C} \models r$,
2. if the check succeeds then grant access else
   (a) select some rule $r \leftarrow p \in \texttt{PartialEvaluation}(\mathcal{P} \cup \mathcal{C})$,
   (b) if r exists then send the rule back to the client else deny access.

Fig. 2. Disclosable Access Control

The systems proposed in [2,1] are flat, i.e. in p the client will find all missing credentials to continue the process until r is granted. In many cases this is neither sufficient nor desirable. If the policy is not flat, it has constraints on the credentials that can be presented at the same time (e.g., separation of duties) or a more complex role structure is used, these systems would not be complete.

Here, a partner must be able to infer the causes of a failed request and to ask a client the missing credentials. The corresponding logical process is no longer deduction but it is *abduction*. So we must have co-existence of deduction (for deciding access and disclosure of information) and abduction (for explaining failed requests).

Definition 2 (Abduction). *The abductive solution over a policy P, a set of predicates (credentials) H (with a partial order $\prec$ over subsets of H) and a ground literal L is a set of ground atoms E such that: (i) $E \subseteq H$, (ii) $P \cup E \models L$, (iii) $P \cup E \not\models \bot$, (iv) any set $E' \prec E$ does not satisfy all conditions above.*

Traditional p.o.s are subset containment or set cardinality.

How we bootstrap from the two basic reasoning services a comprehensive interactive access control algorithm for BPs is the subject of the next section.

3   Interactive Access Control for Stateful Systems

Stateful systems are systems where the status of the current state depends on the status of the system in past conditions, i.e. access decision can change depending on past interactions or past presented credentials.

In our framework each partner has a *security policy for access control* $\mathcal{P}_A$ and a *security policy for disclosure control* $\mathcal{P}_D$. The policy for access control is used for making decision about usage of all web services offered by a partner. The policy for disclosure control is used to decide credentials whose need can be potentially disclosed to a client.

To execute a service of the fragment of a partner, the user will submit a set of *presented credentials* $\mathcal{C}_p$, a set of *revoked credentials* $\mathcal{C}_r$ and a *service request* r. We assume that $\mathcal{C}_p$ and $\mathcal{C}_r$ are disjoint. We also need to keep a memory of past credentials submitted by a user. This is the role of $\mathcal{C}_P$, the set of *active credentials* that have been presented by the client in past requests to other services within the domain of a partner.

In many workflow authorization schemes, the policy alone is not sufficient to make an access control decision and thus we need to identify a *history of execution* $\mathcal{H}$ of services under the control of a partner. It keeps track on what has been done by the system and what is the current status of it. For instance a branch manager of a bank clearing a cheque cannot be the same member of staff who has emitted the cheque [4–pag.67]. If we had no memory of past credentials then it would be impossible to enforce any security policy for separation of duties on the application workflow.

Once a client makes a service request, the authorization mechanism starts a session in which the client iterates with the system until a final decision of *grant* or *deny* is taken. In the same session context, we keep a set of *declined credentials* $\mathcal{C}_N$, a set of *missing credentials* $\mathcal{C}_M$ and a set of *excessing credentials* $\mathcal{C}_E$. The set $\mathcal{C}_N$ consists of credentials that the client has declined to present to the system during an authorization session. The sets $\mathcal{C}_M$ and $\mathcal{C}_E$ keep information from the output of the last interaction. Once the session is started, the algorithm loads the policies for access and disclosure control $\mathcal{P}_A$

and $\mathcal{P_D}$ together with the two sets: the history of execution $\mathcal{H}$ and the client's active credentials $\mathcal{C_P}$.

Our interactive access control solution for stateful services and applications is shown in Figure 3. The logical explanation of the algorithm is the following. The algorithm's input consists of client's sets of currently presented credentials $\mathcal{C_p}$, revoked ones $\mathcal{C_r}$ and the service request r. When a client requests a specific service the authorization mechanism creates a new session and initializes to empty set the variables $\mathcal{C_N}$, $\mathcal{C_M}$ and $\mathcal{C_{\mathcal{E}}}$.

Then, the set of active credentials $\mathcal{C_P}$ is updated by removing the revoked ones $\mathcal{C_r}$ from it and then adding the newly presented credentials $\mathcal{C_p}$ (ref. step 1). The declined credentials $\mathcal{C_N}$ are updated by credentials the client was asked in the previous interaction minus the ones that he has currently presented. Step 3 prepares the two sets $\mathcal{C_M}$ and $\mathcal{C_{\mathcal{E}}}$ for the interaction output.

Next, the algorithm checks whether the request r is granted by $\mathcal{P_A}$ and $\mathcal{C_P}$ (step 4). If the check fails then in step 5a the algorithm computes all credentials disclosable from $\mathcal{P_D}$ and $\mathcal{C_P}$ and from the resulting set removes all already declined and presented credentials. In this way we avoid dead loops of asking something already declined or presented. Step 5b computes (using abduction reasoning) a (minimal) solution for r. Up to this point the algorithm is essentially our interactive access control algorithm for stateless WS described in [3].

Global vars: $\mathcal{C_N}, \mathcal{C_M}, \mathcal{C_{\mathcal{E}}}$;   Initially $\mathcal{C_N} = \mathcal{C_M} = \mathcal{C_{\mathcal{E}}} = \emptyset$;
Internal input: $\mathcal{P_A}, \mathcal{P_D}, \mathcal{H}, \mathcal{C_P}$;
Input: $\mathcal{C_p}, \mathcal{C_r}$ and r;
Output: grant/deny/$<$ask($\mathcal{C_M}$),revoke($\mathcal{C_{\mathcal{E}}}$)$>$;

1. update $\mathcal{C_P} = (\mathcal{C_P} \setminus \mathcal{C_r}) \cup \mathcal{C_p}$,
2. update $\mathcal{C_N} = \mathcal{C_N} \cup (\mathcal{C_M} \setminus \mathcal{C_p})$, where $\mathcal{C_M}$ is from the last interaction,
3. Set up $\mathcal{C_M} = \mathcal{C_{\mathcal{E}}} = \emptyset$,
4. verify whether the request r is a security consequence of the policy access $\mathcal{P_A}$ and presented credentials $\mathcal{C_P}$, namely $\mathcal{P_A} \cup \mathcal{H} \cup \mathcal{C_P} \models r$ and $\mathcal{P_A} \cup \mathcal{H} \cup \mathcal{C_P} \not\models \bot$,
5. if the check succeeds then return **grant** else
   (a) compute the set of *disclosable credentials* $\mathcal{C_D} = \{c \mid \mathcal{P_D} \cup \mathcal{C_P} \models c\} \setminus (\mathcal{C_N} \cup \mathcal{C_P})$,
   (b) use abduction to find a minimal set of *missing credentials* $\mathcal{C_M} \subseteq \mathcal{C_D}$ such that both $\mathcal{P_A} \cup \mathcal{H} \cup \mathcal{C_P} \cup \mathcal{C_M} \models r$ and $\mathcal{P_A} \cup \mathcal{H} \cup \mathcal{C_P} \cup \mathcal{C_M} \not\models \bot$,
   (c) if a set $\mathcal{C_M}$ exists then return $<$**ask($\mathcal{C_M}$),revoke($\mathcal{C_{\mathcal{E}}}$)**$>$ and iterate else
      i. for every $c \in \mathcal{C_P}$ introduce a new credential $\hat{c}$ in the language,
      ii. use abduction to find a minimal set of *missing credentials* $\mathcal{C_M} \subseteq \{\hat{c} \mid c \in \mathcal{C_P}\} \cup \mathcal{C_D}$ such that
         – $\mathcal{P_A} \cup \mathcal{H} \cup \{c \leftarrow \text{not } \hat{c}. \mid c \in \mathcal{C_P}\} \cup \mathcal{C_M} \models r$,
         – $\mathcal{P_A} \cup \mathcal{H} \cup \{c \leftarrow \text{not } \hat{c}. \mid c \in \mathcal{C_P}\} \cup \mathcal{C_M} \not\models \bot$,
      iii. if no set $\mathcal{C_M}$ exists then return **deny** else
         A. compute $\mathcal{C_{\mathcal{E}}} = \{c \mid \hat{c} \in \mathcal{C_M}\}$ and $\mathcal{C_M} = \mathcal{C_M} \cap \mathcal{C_D}$,
         B. return $<$**ask($\mathcal{C_M}$),revoke($\mathcal{C_{\mathcal{E}}}$)**$>$ and iterate.

Fig. 3. Interactive Access Control Algorithm for Stateful Services

If in step 5c no $C_\mathcal{M}$ was found then we come to the part of the algorithm devoted to stateful systems. The motivation here is that if a solution for r cannot be found in $C_\mathcal{D}$ it means that

- either the client *does not have enough privileges* to get the disclosure of more missing credentials so that the abduction can find a solution
- or in the client's set of credentials $C_\mathcal{P}$ there is *something "wrong"* that bans the client to get any solution, i.e. it makes $\mathcal{P}_\mathcal{A}$ inconsistent.

In the first case there is nothing you can do and we should just quietly deny access. In the second case we could have a possibility for recovery.

So, following the second case, in steps 5(c)i and 5(c)ii, we use abduction over the set of disclosable and active credentials $C_\mathcal{D} \cup C_\mathcal{P}$ searching for a possible solution $C_\mathcal{M}$ that unlocks r and preserves consistency in $\mathcal{P}_\mathcal{A} \cup \mathcal{H}$. If a solution for r is found it clearly indicates that this solution could not be found in step 5b because of the existence of "wrong" credentials in $C_\mathcal{P}$ that makes $\mathcal{P}_\mathcal{A}$ inconsistent. In this case we compute the set of excessing credentials $C_\mathcal{E}$ as the set difference $C_\mathcal{P} \setminus C_\mathcal{M}$. Here we separate the definitely good (consistent) solution $C_\mathcal{M}$ from the rest in $C_\mathcal{P}$.

Notice that steps 5(c)i–5(c)iii could be simplified by simply setting $C_\mathcal{E} = C_\mathcal{P}$ and $C_\mathcal{M} = \emptyset$, i.e. asking the client to revoke everything and restart from scratch. We believe that this is hardly practical. We want to have a more precise control on the revokable credentials i.e. of being able to compute a minimal set of revokable and missing credentials. To do so we introduce for each credential $c \in C_\mathcal{P}$ a new symbol for it $\hat{c}$ in the model, step 5(c)i in Figure 3. Then after obtaining the set of new symbols $\{\hat{c} \mid c \in C_\mathcal{P}\}$ we generate a set of rules $\{c \leftarrow \text{not } \hat{c}. \mid c \in C_\mathcal{P}\}$. The trick here is that negating all credentials in $C_\mathcal{P}$ using the newly introduced symbols and running abduction reasoning over the set union of $\{\hat{c} \mid c \in C_\mathcal{P}\} \cup C_\mathcal{D}$ (step 5(c)ii) allows us to find a *minimal* solution $C_\mathcal{M}$ for r that itself indicates what should be revoked and what should be asked from the client.

Let us consider the set $\{c \leftarrow \text{not } \hat{c}. \mid c \in C_\mathcal{P}\}$. Since we attach this set to $\mathcal{P}_\mathcal{A} \cup \mathcal{H} \cup C_\mathcal{P}$ so it follows that all credentials in $C_\mathcal{P}$ will be deduced again except those that the corresponding new symbol appears in $C_\mathcal{M}$. So, all new-symbol credentials appearing in $C_\mathcal{M}$, computed in step 7(c)ii, will be treated such that the absence of their respective credentials in $C_\mathcal{P}$ allows the abduction reasoning to find a solution set for r.

Remark 1 (Multiple Activations and Revocations of Credentials). In an interactive access control process the algorithm may ask the client to present credentials that he has revoked (was explicitly asked for that) in previous interactions or ask the client to revoke credentials that the same has activated.

Since we do not know what solution a client has for a particular resource so in the presence of alternatives in the access policy the system may choose the "wrong" one[1] such that later on when the right alternative is chosen it may require the

---

[1] Here we call "wrong" alternative a solution set that the client does not have it.

revocation/activation of credentials that were already activated/revoked by the client in the interactions with the "wrong" one.

Example 1. Abstracting from a specific meaning let us have the following scenario. A client with a set of available credentials $\{C_A, C_B, C_C\}$ wants to access a service r. The client's set of active credentials (already presented to the system) is $C_P = \{C_C\}$ and history $\mathcal{H} = \emptyset$. The policies for access and disclosure control are shown below.

$$
\mathcal{P}_A \left|
\begin{array}{l}
r \leftarrow C_A, C_B. \\
r \leftarrow C_C, C_D. \\
\leftarrow C_A, C_C.
\end{array}
\right.
\qquad
\mathcal{P}_D \left|
\begin{array}{l}
C_A \leftarrow . \\
C_B \leftarrow . \\
C_C \leftarrow . \\
C_D \leftarrow .
\end{array}
\right.
$$

Now, let suppose that the client initially requests service r with set of presented credentials $C_p = \{C_A\}$. According to the algorithm in Figure 3 the check in step 4 will fail, then in step 5b abduction will not find any solution because the policy is inconsistent with the client's set of credentials and so the algorithm will reach step 5(c)ii. The output of this step, considering the minimality criterion subset containment, is:

- Abduction output: $\left\{\hat{C}_A, C_D\right\}$, algorithm result: $\textbf{ask(\{C_D\})}, \textbf{revoke(\{C_A\})}$
- Abduction output: $\left\{\hat{C}_C, C_B\right\}$, algorithm result: $\textbf{ask(\{C_B\})}, \textbf{revoke(\{C_C\})}$

Since we do not know what solution the client has so we must choose one of the two outcomes listed above.

If we are lucky and choose the solution $<\textbf{ask(\{C_B\})}, \textbf{revoke(\{C_C\})}>$ then on the next interaction since the client has in possession $\{C_A, C_B, C_C\}$ the same presents C_B, revokes C_C and gets $\textbf{grant}$ r in step 5 in the next interaction.

In the other case, if we choose the solution $<\textbf{ask(\{C_D\})}, \textbf{revoke(\{C_A\})}>$ then on the next interaction the client will revoke C_A but will decline to present C_D, simply because he does not have it. Then the check in step 4 will not succeed because $C_p = \{C_C\}$ does not contain enough credentials to unlock r. Following that, the abduction reasoning is step 5b will not find a solution because in C_p there is a credentials C_C that is inconsistent with the only solution available in $C_D = \{C_A, C_B\}$.

Running again abduction reasoning with minimality according subset containment the only solution found is $\{\hat{C}_C, C_A, C_B\}$ and the respective outcome of the algorithm is $<\textbf{ask(\{C_A, C_B\})}, \textbf{revoke(\{C_C\})}>$. Essentially, we ask the client to restart from scratch.

On the next interaction since the client has in possession $\{C_A, C_B, C_C\}$ so he revokes C_C, presents $\{C_A, C_B\}$ and in step 5 gets $\textbf{grant}$ r.

4 Coping with Malicious Clients

We need to improve the algorithm in Figure 3 to protect the server against Denial of Service (DoS) attacks. To do so we consider the client as an entity that can manipulate the system only via its input sets of credentials C_p and C_r. Particularly, he may present in his input set C_p credentials, which he has revoked in past interactions with the system, without been explicitly asked for it and, respectively, may revoke credentials in C_r, which he has activated and presented to the system in past interactions, again without been asked for it. In both cases it would bring the system in a previous state (by letting it compute the same solution again and again). A malicious client could thus waste server's time forever.

The new algorithm is shown in Figure 4. In step 1, a new data set is introduced, the set of *revoked credentials* C_R, which accumulates all credentials revoked by a client in an interaction session for a particular service r. So, step 1 updates the set of revoked credentials by removing from C_R the set of missing credentials C_M, asked in the last interaction, and adding to the resulting set the newly revoked credentials C_r. The motivation for the set difference $C_R \setminus C_M$ is that whatever the client presents from C_M it is dropped from C_R because it is not any more revoked and whatever it is not presented in C_M but is dropped from C_R is added to the set of declined credentials C_N. In this case revoked and declined credentials are kept disjoint, i.e. $C_R \cap C_N = \emptyset$.

Global vars: C_N, C_R, C_U, C_M, C_E;   Initially $C_N = C_R = C_U = C_M = C_E = \emptyset$;
Internal input: $\mathcal{P}_A, \mathcal{P}_D, \mathcal{H}, C_P$;
Input: C_p, C_r and r;
Output: grant/deny/$<$ask(C_M),revoke(C_E)$>$;

1. update $C_R = (C_R \setminus C_M) \cup (C_r \cap C_E)$,
2. update $C_P = (C_P \setminus C_R) \cup (C_p \setminus C_R) \cup (C_p \cap C_M) \cup (C_p \cap C_N)$,
3. update $C_N = C_N \cup (C_M \setminus C_p)$,
4. update $C_U = C_U \cup (C_E \setminus C_r)$,
5. Set up $C_M = C_E = \emptyset$,
6. verify whether the request r is a security consequence of the policy access $\mathcal{P}_A$ and presented credentials C_P, namely $\mathcal{P}_A \cup \mathcal{H} \cup C_P \models r$ and $\mathcal{P}_A \cup \mathcal{H} \cup C_P \not\models \perp$,
7. **if** the check succeeds **then** return **grant else**
   (a) compute the set of *disclosable credentials* $C_D = \{c \mid \mathcal{P}_D \cup C_P \models c\} \setminus (C_N \cup C_P)$,
   (b) use abduction to find a minimal set of *missing credentials* $C_M \subseteq C_D$ such that both $\mathcal{P}_A \cup \mathcal{H} \cup C_P \cup C_M \models r$ and $\mathcal{P}_A \cup \mathcal{H} \cup C_P \cup C_M \not\models \perp$,
   (c) **if** a set C_M exists **then** return $<$**ask(C_M),revoke(C_E)**$>$ and iterate **else**
       i. for every $c \in (C_P \setminus C_U)$ introduce a new credential $\hat{c}$ in the language,
       ii. use abduction to find a minimal set of *missing credentials* $C_M \subseteq \{\hat{c} \mid c \in (C_P \setminus C_U)\} \cup C_D$ such that
           – $\mathcal{P}_A \cup \mathcal{H} \cup (C_P \cap C_U) \cup \{c \leftarrow \text{not } \hat{c}. \mid c \in (C_P \setminus C_U)\} \cup C_M \models r$,
           – $\mathcal{P}_A \cup \mathcal{H} \cup (C_P \cap C_U) \cup \{c \leftarrow \text{not } \hat{c}. \mid c \in (C_P \setminus C_U)\} \cup C_M \not\models \perp$,
       iii. **if** no set C_M exists **then** return **deny else**
           A. compute $C_E = \{c \mid \hat{c} \in C_M\}$ and $C_M = C_M \cap C_D$,
           B. return $<$**ask(C_M),revoke(C_E)**$>$ and iterate.

Fig. 4. Extended Access Control Algorithm

Extending further step 1, to prevent situations of revoking credentials not supposed to be revoked by the client, we update $C_{\mathcal{R}}$ by adding only those credentials from C_r that the client was explicitly asked in the previous interaction, i.e. adding only $C_r \cap C_{\mathcal{E}}$.

Step 2 updates the client set of active credentials by removing from $C_{\mathcal{P}}$ the set of all revoked credentials and adding to it the set of newly activated credentials C_p. First we use the set difference $C_{\mathcal{P}} \backslash C_{\mathcal{R}}$ to remove all revoked credentials and second, expanding the set of active credentials, we add from currently presented credentials C_p only the credentials that have not been revoked before – $C_p \backslash C_{\mathcal{R}}$ – and we add also those credentials in C_p that the system has asked the client – $C_p \cap C_{\mathcal{M}}$ – or the client has declined to present in past interactions but it is presenting now – $C_p \cap C_{\mathcal{N}}$.

In other words, step 2 allows the client to activate credentials among those:

- that the system has asked him to present in the last interaction or
- that he has denied to present in past interactions or
- brand new credentials[2] that the client has not supplied to the system at the time of interacting.

Then, in step 4, we introduce a new data set $C_{\mathcal{U}}$. The role of $C_{\mathcal{U}}$ is analogous of that for $C_{\mathcal{N}}$ and serves as a data store for those credentials that a client has declined to revoke in an interaction session. $C_{\mathcal{U}}$ is updated by adding to it the set difference of excessing credentials the client was asked in the last interaction minus the ones currently revoked. Similarly, once a client refuses to revoke a credential the same credential will not be considered in a possible output again.

We note that a client at any time can present credentials that he has declined to present in previous interactions, although he will never be asked for them again. Here, a client is not allowed (the system will not consider) to revoke credentials that he has refused to revoke before without been asked for it. The last requirement is mainly because the revocation of credentials is usually a cumbersome process and once the client refuses to revoke a credential then it is unlikely to expect him to do it later in a negotiation process.

The last key-point of the extended algorithm is in step 7(c)ii. Here we run the abduction reasoning over the set $\{\hat{c} \mid c \in (C_{\mathcal{P}} \backslash C_{\mathcal{U}})\} \cup C_{\mathcal{D}}$. The set difference $C_{\mathcal{P}} \backslash C_{\mathcal{U}}$ comes from the fact that we do not want to ask the client to revoke credentials that he has already refused to revoke. In this way we rule out those models where the client already denied to comply to. We also note that the two conditions in step 7(c)ii are analogous with their respective ones in Figure 3 because whatever we drop from $C_{\mathcal{P}} \backslash C_{\mathcal{U}}$ we add it by the intersection of $C_{\mathcal{P}} \cap C_{\mathcal{U}}$.

Now on, wherever we refer to the access control algorithm we refer to its extended model shown in Figure 4.

---

[2] Excluding the revoked credentials since the system is aware of them.

5   Correctness and Completeness

This section presents the theoretical part of the stateful framework together with theorems for soundness and completeness. We refer the reader to [7] for details on the proofs of the theorems.

At first we introduce some preliminary definitions.

Definition 3 (Solution Set for a Resource r). *Let $\mathcal{P}_\mathcal{A}$ is an access policy and r be a request. A set of credentials $\mathcal{C}_\mathcal{S}$ is a solution set for r according to $\mathcal{P}_\mathcal{A}$ if r is a security consequence of $\mathcal{P}_\mathcal{A}$ and $\mathcal{C}_\mathcal{S}$ ($\mathcal{P}_\mathcal{A} \cup \mathcal{C}_\mathcal{S} \models r$ and $\mathcal{P}_\mathcal{A} \cup \mathcal{C}_\mathcal{S} \not\models \bot$).*

Definition 4 (Completeness). *If a client has a solution for a request r then he always gets* grant r.

Definition 5 (Soundness). *If a client gets* grant r *then he has a solution for r.*

In the following we assume that the sets of missing and excessing credentials are disjoint, i.e. $\mathcal{C}_\mathcal{M} \cap \mathcal{C}_\mathcal{E} = \emptyset$, otherwise the server will reject the answer outright. Note that this is true for the interactive algorithm in Figure 4. We also assume that at any time in an interaction process the sets of currently presented and revoked credentials are disjoint, i.e. $\mathcal{C}_p \cap \mathcal{C}_r = \emptyset$.

Definition 6 (Powerful and Compliant Client). *A* powerful and compliant client *is a client that whenever receives $<$**ask**$(\mathcal{C}_\mathcal{M})$,**revoke**$(\mathcal{C}_\mathcal{E})>$ returns $<\mathcal{C}_\mathcal{M},\mathcal{C}_\mathcal{E}>$, i.e. activates all $c \in \mathcal{C}_\mathcal{M}$ and revokes any $c \in \mathcal{C}_\mathcal{E}$.*

Definition 7 (Cooperative and Compliant Client). *A client with ability to manage (obtain or revoke) a set of credentials $\mathcal{C}$ is a* cooperative and compliant client *if whenever receives $<$**ask**$(\mathcal{C}_\mathcal{M})$,**revoke**$(\mathcal{C}_\mathcal{E})>$ returns $<\mathcal{C}_\mathcal{M} \cap \mathcal{C}, \mathcal{C}_\mathcal{E} \cap \mathcal{C}>$, i.e. activates all $c \in (\mathcal{C}_\mathcal{M} \cap \mathcal{C})$ and revokes any $c \in (\mathcal{C}_\mathcal{E} \cap \mathcal{C})$.*

Definition 8 (Fair Access). *Let $\mathcal{P}_\mathcal{A}$ be an access control policy and let $\mathcal{C}_{\mathcal{P}_\mathcal{A}}$ be the set of ground instances of all credentials occurring in $\mathcal{P}_\mathcal{A}$. The policy $\mathcal{P}_\mathcal{A}$ guarantees* fair access *if for any request r there exists a set $\mathcal{C}_\mathcal{S} \subseteq \mathcal{C}_{\mathcal{P}_\mathcal{A}}$ that is a solution for r.*

Definition 9 (Fair Interaction). *Let $\mathcal{P}_\mathcal{A}$ and $\mathcal{P}_\mathcal{D}$ be, respectively, an access and disclosure control policies. The policies* guarantee fair interaction *if*

1. *$\mathcal{P}_\mathcal{A}$ guarantees fair access and*
2. *if $\mathcal{C}_\mathcal{S}$ is a solution for a request r then $\mathcal{C}_\mathcal{S}$ is disclosable by $\mathcal{P}_\mathcal{D}$, i.e. $\forall c \in \mathcal{C}_\mathcal{S}$, $\mathcal{P}_\mathcal{D} \models c$.*

Theorem 1 (Soundness). *Let $\mathcal{P}_A$ be an access policy, $\mathcal{P}_D$ be a disclosure policy and r a request. If a client gets grant r with the algorithm in Fig. 4 then he has a solution set $\mathcal{C}_S$ that unlocks r according to $\mathcal{P}_A$.*

Theorem 2 (Termination). *Let $\mathcal{P}_A$ be an access policy, $\mathcal{P}_D$ be a disclosure policy and r a request. The access control algorithm in Fig. 4 always terminates.*

We use the idea of well-founded tuples ordering so that at each interaction we associate the tuple $<\mathcal{C}_N, \mathcal{C}_U, \mathcal{C}_P \cup \mathcal{C}_R>$. Then we show that if the algorithm does not return grant or deny (it terminates) then the sets in the tuple always increase from one interaction to the next so that the maximal number of interactions is bounded by the credentials occurring in the access policy.

5.1   Completeness

Definition 10 (Monotonic and Non-monotonic Policy). *A policy P is monotonic if whenever a set of statements C is a solution set for r according to P then any superset $C' \supset C$ is also a solution set for r according to P.*

In contrast, a non-monotonic *policy is a logic program in which if C is a solution for r it may exists $C' \supset C$ that is not a solution for r, i.e. $P \cup C' \not\models r$*

Theorem 3 (Completeness for a Monotonic Access Policy). *Let $\mathcal{P}_A$ be a monotonic access policy, $\mathcal{P}_D$ be a monotonic disclosure policy and r a request. If $\mathcal{P}_A$ and $\mathcal{P}_D$ guarantee fair access and interaction then a powerful or cooperative client always gets grant r with the algorithm in Fig. 4.*

Of course the whole business of the stateful systems requires non-monotonic policies, so this result is not enough. Here we relax the policy access $\mathcal{P}_A$ from the assumption of monotonicity and consider it as an arbitrary non-monotonic policy. So, from now on we assume that $\mathcal{P}_A$ is *non-monotonic* and $\mathcal{P}_D$ *monotonic* unless explicitly specified otherwise.

In the same context, without loss of generality, we assume that whenever a client initially requests a service he submits $\mathcal{C}_p = \mathcal{C}_r = \emptyset$ and if hidden credentials $\mathcal{C}_\mathcal{H}$ needed then $\mathcal{C}_p = \mathcal{C}_\mathcal{H}$ and $\mathcal{C}_r = \emptyset$.

Theorem 4 (Completeness for a Powerful and Compliant Client). *Let $\mathcal{P}_A$ be an access policy, $\mathcal{P}_D$ be a disclosure policy, $\mathcal{H}$ be history of executions and r a request. If $\mathcal{P}_A \cup \mathcal{H}^3$ and $\mathcal{P}_D$ guarantee fair access and interaction then a powerful and compliant client always gets grant r with the algorithm in Fig. 4.*

Here the properties for fair access and interaction guarantee that it exists a solution $\mathcal{C}_S$ for r that is disclosable by the disclosure policy and so the abduction reasoning

---

[3] It is important to pose the property of fair access over $\mathcal{P}_A \cup \mathcal{H}$ because it guarantees fairness wrt other (possibly) environment constraints like limited number of executions on a service, limited number of users accessing a service and so on.

potentially can find it in step 7b in Figure 4. If it fails then in the next step 7(c)ii because of the existence of such solution and since it is contained in the set of disclosable credentials $\mathcal{C}_{\mathcal{D}}$ follows that abduction at least finds this solution together with the set of excessing credentials which is returned back to the client. Then because the client is a powerful one he presents and revokes what he was asked and on the next interaction gets grant.

Theorem 5 (Completeness for a Cooperative and Compliant Client). *Let $\mathcal{P}_{\mathcal{A}}$ be an access policy, $\mathcal{P}_{\mathcal{D}}$ be a disclosure policy, $\mathcal{H}$ be history of executions and r a request. If $\mathcal{P}_{\mathcal{A}} \cup \mathcal{H}$ and $\mathcal{P}_{\mathcal{D}}$ guarantee fair access and interaction then if a cooperative and compliant client has a set of credentials $\mathcal{C}_{\mathcal{S}}$ that unlocks r according to $\mathcal{P}_{\mathcal{A}}$ then the client always gets grant r with the algorithm in Fig. 4.*

We prove it in two parts. First part showing that if a client does not get grant he gets $<\mathsf{ask}(\mathcal{C}_{\mathcal{M}}), \mathsf{revoke}(\mathcal{C}_{\mathcal{E}})>$, i.e. he never gets deny. Second, we use Theorem 2 (for termination) and conclude that in a bounded number of interaction a cooperative client always gets grant.

6   Initialization and Service Management

Figure 5 gives the intuition of possible management of services wrt the access control decision process and its relevant data sets. The algorithm shown in Figure 5 works like web servers. A main web server listens to service requests and whenever a request is detected the server runs the algorithm in a new thread and initializes the global variables $\mathcal{H}$ and $\mathcal{C}_{\mathcal{P}}$ to empty sets. Of course here it should distinguish between the very first initialization and any further loading of those data sets simply because we do not want to loose any data from past interactions. For further loadings we keep a profile for each client with the respective data set $\mathcal{C}_{\mathcal{P}}$ so that when the client accesses again a service we just load $\mathcal{C}_{\mathcal{P}}$.

```
Global Vars: Cₚ, H;
Initially: Cₚ = ∅ and H = ∅;

ServiceRequest(r, Cₚ, Cᵣ){ // starts a new thread

  1. result_access = InteractiveAccessControl(r, Cₚ, Cᵣ);
  2. Update(H, result_access, r);
  3. if result_access == grant then
  4.    result_service = InvokeService(r);
  5.    Update(H, result_service, r);
  6. endif

}
```

Fig. 5. Global Initialization and Management of Services

Algorithm output	Status Predicates
grant	grant (User: U, Service: S, Number: N),
	running (User: U, Service: S, Number: N)
deny	deny (User: U, Service: S, Number: N)

Service Execution	Status Predicates
accomplished	success (User: U, Service: S, Number: N)
failed	abort (User: U, Service: S, Number: N)

Both $\mathcal{C_P}$ and $\mathcal{H}$ are local to a service provider and are managed and initialized independently. The history of execution $\mathcal{H}$ is set up to the empty set at the start when a particular business process is started[4]. Even a business partner may decide to have for each running business process separate histories $\mathcal{H}$. To this extend we assume that $\mathcal{H}$ is mapped to those business process(es) that are relevant to the authorization logic and is released when those processes complete their executions.

Another session profile is the set of active user's access rights $\mathcal{C_P}$ available to the partner's application domain. Each session is associated with a single user and each user is associated with a *single* session. This session profile is created[5] when the user for the first time requests a service under the partner's domain. In contrast to the history profile, the set of user's access rights is valid until a certain time slot expires. Even more, it is valid across multiple runnings of business processes within the entire scope of the partner's domain and it eventual deactivation depends on the partner's authorization logic.

The third session profile kept in the model is for the service level negotiation. Here, each session is associated with a single user but each user is associated with *one or more* negotiation sessions. Whenever a user requests a service (ref. ServiceRequest(...) in Figure 5) it is created a session within which the interactive access control algorithm is running. Once the session is created the user interacts with the system until a final decision of grant or deny is taken. Within these interactions a user (de)activates some subset of roles ($\subseteq \mathcal{C_P}$) that he or she is assigned.

In comparison with RBAC model, the service level agreement session corresponds to the *user_sessions(u:USERS)* function as introduced by Ferraiolo et al. [8], which is the mapping of a user u onto a set of active sessions. The user session of active rights corresponds to *avail_session_perms(user_sessions(u:USERS))* introduced in [8]. Where *avail_session_perms(s:SESSIONS)* returns the permissions available to a user in a session. We note that the user's session of active access rights in our framework extends Ferraiolo et al. [8] because in $\mathcal{C_P}$ one can also find access credentials from already concluded service level sessions but with still valid expiration dates.

To keep the history of execution $\mathcal{H}$ up-to-date, after each interaction step appropriate predicates should be added indicating what has been done by the system.

---

[4] It entirely depends on the provider's business logic and whenever an application business process is started we refer to it as an initial point to set up $\mathcal{H} = \emptyset$.

[5] The set $\mathcal{C_P}$ is strictly time-dependent and must be periodically cleared up from already expired credentials.

This is done by the function Update shown in Figure 5. The table below summarizes the possible updates of $\mathcal{H}$.

The temporal evolution of the access rights wrt the history of execution $\mathcal{H}$ can be complex because even the most simple constraint on executed actions may block a request. Indeed, the set of requests that must be grantable by the policy may change with the services that we have used. As intuitively expected, we may have access to less services if we have limitations on their usage. For instance the following constraint specifies that the service *reviewSellBids* cannot be executed more than three times in a workflow session:

$\leftarrow$ assign (User : U, Service : $reviewSellBids$),
$4 \leq \{N.$ success (User : U, Service : $reviewSellBids$, Number : N)$\}$.

7   Related Work and Conclusions

Access control for business processes borrows some aspect of trust management and some aspects of workflow security. Among these models we find a number of relevant works: for workflows [4], web services [9], role based access control on the web [10, 11], tasks [12] and DRM [9], possibly coupled by sophisticated policy combination algorithms. However, they have mostly remained within the classical framework – all decisions of grant/deny are based on checking that request would follow from the policy and the presented set of credentials.

The work on trust negotiations [13, 1] focuses on communication and infrastructure and assumes that requests and counter requests have been somehow calculated from the access policy. Also the formal models on credential-based access control and policy combination [4, 14, 15, 16] do not treat the problem of inferring missing credentials from failed requests.

Also the proposal by Bonatti and Samarati [2] that has the explicit focus on access and release control is not fully on target. In a nutshell, the request is received, the policy rules are filtered for relevance, the relevant rules are partially evaluated and sent to the client. The client will have to figure out which are the credentials and then will evaluate these credentials according its release policy.

The other key proposal on trust negotiation by Yu et al. [1], offers a dual view w.r.t Bonatti and Samarati [2]. Loosely speaking, each credential is associated to a policy (a boolean expression) denoting the credentials that a client must have already provided for its safe disclosure. By a step wise process the parties can exchange credentials or policy rules until the desired resource is released. The paper provides safe sequences of disclosure building upon trees rather than logical formalization. As a consequence they can only treat monotone policies and it is not possible to define notions of consistency of policies and disclosure of policies in presence of constraints (e.g. separation of duty). Another limitation of the paper is that it interlocks the access and the release policy into one. So, as the authors acknowledge [1–page 21], it is impossible to access resources if some of the needed credentials cannot be disclosed at some point.

In this paper we have presented a framework for interactive access control for stateful systems. The work is the continuation of [3] and goes beyond the model for stateless services. With the extended framework a service provider is able to reason of not only finding the missing credentials that compliment client's access rights to unlock the resource but also to resolve conflicts occurring in its security policy. The last thing is in the context of reasoning about the excessing credentials, among the client's ones, that make the provider's policy inconsistent. Even more, the proposed access control algorithm breaks off the monotonic policy paradigm so that now a service provider can control access to its resources written in an arbitrary non-monotonic policy language.

The work models two types of clients, a powerful and a cooperative, and together with the definitions for fair access and interaction they are stated theorems for soundness and completeness for the two clients.

Finally, we refer the reader to [17, 7] for an architectural approach and implementation of the interactive access control framework and to [18] for an extension of it that copes with bilateral negotiation of credentials.

References

1. Yu, T., Winslett, M., Seamons, K.E.: Supporting structured credentials and sensitive policies through interoperable strategies for automated trust negotiation. ACM Transactions on Information and System Security (TISSEC) **6** (2003) 1–42
2. Bonatti, P., Samarati, P.: A unified framework for regulating access and information release on the web. Journal of Computer Security **10** (2002) 241–272
3. Koshutanski, H., Massacci, F.: Interactive access control for Web Services. In: Proceedings of the 19th IFIP Information Security Conference (SEC 2004), Toulouse, France, Kluwer Press (2004) 151–166
4. Bertino, E., Ferrari, E., Atluri, V.: The specification and enforcement of authorization constraints in workflow management systems. ACM Transactions on Information and System Security (TISSEC) **2** (1999) 65–104
5. Apt, K.: Logic programming. In van Leeuwen, J., ed.: Handbook of Theoretical Computer Science. Elsevier (1990)
6. De Capitani di Vimercati, S., Samarati, P.: Access control: Policies, models, and mechanism. In Focardi, R., Gorrieri, F., eds.: Foundations of Security Analysis and Design - Tutorial Lectures. Volume 2171 of LNCS. Springer Verlag Press (2001)
7. Koshutanski, H., Massacci, F.: Interactive access control for stateful web services business processes. Technical Report DIT-05-002, Department of Information and Communication Technology, University of Trento (2005)
8. Ferraiolo, D.F., Sandhu, R., Gavrila, S., Kuhn, D.R., Chandramouli, R.: Proposed NIST standard for role-based access control. ACM TISSEC **4** (2001) 224–274
9. Park, J., Sandhu, R.: Towards usage control models: beyond traditional access control. In: Seventh ACM SACMAT, ACM Press (2002) 57–64
10. Giuri, L.: Role-based access control on the web. ACM Transactions on Information and System Security (TISSEC) **4** (2001) 37–71
11. Park, J.S., Sandhu, R.: RBAC on the Web by smart certificates. In: Proceedings of the fourth ACM workshop on Role-based access control, ACM Press (1999) 1–9
12. Joshi, J.B.D., Aref, W.G., Ghafoor, A., Spafford, E.H.: Security models for web-based applications. Communications of the ACM **44** (2001) 38–44

13. Roscheisen, M., Winograd, T.: A communication agreement framework for access/action control. In: Proceedings of the Symposium on Security and Privacy, IEEE Press (1996) 154–163
14. Li, N., Grosof, B.N., Feigenbaum, J.: Delegation logic: A logic-based approach to distributed authorization. ACM Transactions on Information and System Security (TISSEC) **6** (2003) 128–171
15. Jajodia, S., Samarati, P., Subrahmanian, V.S., Bertino, E.: A unified framework for enforcing multiple access control policies. In: Proceedings of the 1997 ACM SIGMOD conference on Management of data, ACM Press (1997) 474–485
16. Wijesekera, D., Jajodia, S.: Policy algebras for access control the predicate case. In: Proceedings of the 9th ACM conference on Computer and Communications Security, ACM Press (2002) 171–180
17. Koshutanski, H., Massacci, F.: An access control framework for business processes for Web services. In: Proceedings of the 2003 ACM workshop on XML security, Fairfax, VA, ACM Press (2003) 15–24
18. Koshutanski, H., Massacci, F.: An interactive trust management and negotiation scheme. In: Proceedings of the 2nd International Workshop on Formal Aspects in Security and Trust (FAST), Toulouse, France, Kluwer Press (2004) 139–152

An Evidence Based Architecture for Efficient, Attack-Resistant Computational Trust Dissemination in Peer-to-Peer Networks

David Ingram

dmi1000@cam.ac.uk

University of Cambridge Computer Laboratory,
15 JJ Thompson Avenue, Cambridge, CB3 0FD, United Kingdom

Abstract. Emerging peer to peer (P2P) applications have a requirement for de-centralised access control. Computational trust systems address this, achieving security through collaboration. This paper surveys current work on overlay networks, trust and identity certification. Our focus is on the particular problem of distributing evidence for use in trust-based security decisions. We present a system we have implemented that solves this in a highly scalable way, and resists attacks such as false recommendations and collusion.

1 Introduction

1.1 A Metaphor for Trust-Based Security

In the physical world, there are three main approaches to access control. If we wish to secure a building, we could lock the door and issue keys only to those who work in the building. This makes access less convenient though, so it could be better to leave the door unlocked and save time for our legitimate users. Alternatively, we might choose to leave the door unlocked but employ a security guard who sits in the lobby keeping an eye on those who pass by. The guard won't often have to stop anyone because he will recognise those who work in the building; also he can make an assessment on whether strangers are a threat, based on factors such as if they are being accompanied by someone he does know.

In the online world, typically we can only choose the first two alternatives – either to secure the resource and issue (digital) keys to those who are permitted access, or to allow anyone access. Computational trust modelling is a way of implementing the third option (a decision-making security guard) in an internet environment. For many applications this enables a new and more acceptable combination of security and convenience.

1.2 Our Approach

We form models for **trust** and **risk** in online entities, and use this information to make access control decisions. This is useful in many application domains, such as Internet auctions, spam filtering, P2P storage services and so on. A key feature of our model

P. Herrmann et al. (Eds.): iTrust 2005, LNCS 3477, pp. 273–288, 2005.

is its use of **recommendations** to exchange trust information between principals. This creates a requirement for an effective and scalable mechanism to distribute such information across the network.

A typical scenario involves millions of principals, most of whom do not know each other. Patterns of interaction may be random and not exhibit much locality of reference. Furthermore, any information sent via the network can be falsified, including recommendations and routing information, yet the system must be secure.

Overlay networks can be used to provide deterministic, scalable data access for P2P applications. Using such techniques we can look up any piece of evidence with a logarithmic number of messages and collate all that is known about each principal in **behaviour profiles**. We combine this with a set of Certification Agencies to limit attacks by making it expensive to obtain extra identities.

Our prototype is named ENTRAPPED (Efficient Network Trust & Recommendation Access by Peer-Peer Evidence Distribution).

1.3   Example: Internet Auctions

Internet auction sites such as E-bay are a familiar example of e-commerce based on trust between mutually unknown participants. E-bay works by allowing buyers to provide feedback on sellers (recommendations). In the case of serious complaints the management can act to bar participants from the site.

Consider what would happen if there were no central authority to police the system, no human being in the decision loop for making purchases, and attackers colluding to recommend each other. If we would like our machine to authorise micropayments automatically when we click on links on the web, for example (desirable since popup windows seeking confirmation are tedious and tend to be dismissed without much thought) then this is exactly the case. The rest of this paper addresses this type of scenario. Note in particular that reading E-bay reports on sellers and judging their legitimacy is an AI-complete task, hence difficult to automate!

1.4   Trust Application Framework

The general requirements for applications to which this framework can be applied are that they should consist of pairwise interactions, and that actions have objective success criteria, so we can exchange information about what has happened.

All entities that can exchange information, and it is meaningful to trust or distrust, are **principals**. Principals are pseudonymous; they are authenticated and named typically by public keys, but we don't know their real-world identity. Pairs of principals may perform **actions**, such as exchanging goods or opinions. A trust-based security decision must be made by one party to determine whether to allow each action.

Trust is seen as a quantified predictor of the principal's future behaviour based on **evidence** of the outcomes of previous interactions, both from direct **observations** and **recommendations**. The established trust in a principal is used to determine the likelihood that they will perform a new action in a cooperative manner. This is combined with the cost of any potential negative consequences and a **risk** analysis is done to determine if they may proceed. The dataflow between components is shown in Fig. 1.

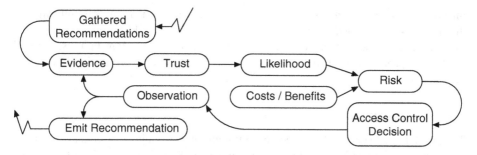

Fig. 1. Framework dataflow

2 Background: Overlay Networks

2.1 Distributed Hash Tables

To make trust decisions we need efficient random access to evidence that is widely distributed throughout the network. To solve this problem, it is natural to apply a Distributed Hash Table (DHT), such as Chord [19], Kademlia [15] or Pastry [16]. We therefore pause to consider how these operate. Distributed Hash Tables perform the basic function of mapping keys (associated with data items to be accessed) onto host addresses (such as IP and port number). In our case the data items are collections of trust information and the hosts are members of the P2P network.

In an evidence distribution scenario, it is important that each of the N hosts do not have to be aware of the identities of most other hosts, since that would require $O(N)$ storage per node. Furthermore a steady state is impossible since nodes join and leave the network continuously. Network traffic must be kept to a modest number of messages, both during data lookups and when nodes are added or removed. The system should not require a top-level authority (unlike the DNS, for example).

DHT's have the following useful properties:

– Data lookups take place in $\log N$ steps
– Only $\log N$ storage is required per node for routing tables
– Routing tables can be updated with $\log N$ messages when nodes arrive or depart
– The table can restore consistency after nodes fail silently
– Data item keys are distributed evenly amongst the nodes

The basic operation is to hash keys and node IDs onto the same linear (circular) keyspace, and then place data at the node whose ID is numerically closest to that data's key. The logarithmic properties arise because each node maintains its own small routing table containing complete information about nearby nodes, but also a few routes to more distant nodes. A target can be reached quickly by starting with approximate, large hops and homing in with smaller ones.

To guard against unexpected node failure, data items are actually replicated at a number of locations (typically three or more). If node IDs are essentially random it is convenient to place the replicas on adjacent nodes in the keyspace so they can all be located with a single search. Replication is also essential when we are storing trust information, as it protects against a single malicious peer changing trust information that it has been assigned to store. The replication factor should be set conservatively to guard against such attacks occurring at the same time as random failures. We will see how to protect against malicious collectives (multiple attackers acting in concert) below.

2.2   Secure DHT's

The problem of making a DHT secure (in the presence of deliberate attacks) has been considered by Sit and Morris [18] and largely solved by Castro et al [5] in the context of secure Pastry (their solutions are also applicable to other DHT's). They identify three requirements: secure node ID assignment, secure routing table maintenance and secure message forwarding. We shall describe the first of these in more detail.

2.3   Secure Node ID Assignment

The first step to making a DHT secure is to generate node IDs from a hash of the principal's IP address and their public key. Linking node IDs to the public key means that nodes can definitely prove their identity once they have been contacted. Including a hash of the IP address makes it hard for attackers to assume control of chosen parts of the keyspace, because their IP address is verifiable and they do not have free choice of addresses.

Chord node IDs used in CFS[7] are SHA-1(IP address, virtual node index). Virtual node indices are present to allow for NAT, but must be small integers, which limits a node's choice of Chord ID. The authors observe that "owners of large blocks of IP address space tend to be more easily identifiable (and less likely to be malicious)".

Unfortunately however, IPv6 is likely to give attackers enough IP addresses to exceed the total number of nodes, whereas DHCP (or mobile clients) and NAT cause problems by changing and hiding actual IP addresses. For this reason Castro recommends using Certification Agencies (CAs) that sign certificates binding a random node ID (generated by the CA) to the public key that speaks for it and its IP address. We shall have more to say about this in Section 4 on Identity.

3   Computational Trust

The trust and risk models we employ are based on our experience within the SECURE project (Secure Environments for Collaboration among Ubiquitous Roaming Entities) [4, 17, 11].

3.1   Trust Values

Trust values may be stored in arbitrary formats. For example, Yu and Singh [22] use belief and disbelief values from Dempster-Shafer theory to measure trust and recommendations. We believe it is better to store the evidence itself rather than derived trust attributes, since transformations lose information. For this reason we restrict to storing raw observations, or in the aggregate case event frequency counts. Probabilities, confidence intervals and so forth can be derived from the evidence by higher layers; our goal is to distribute relevant information in an efficient and secure way.

In our system, trust values are represented by pairs (m, n), where m is the number of successful interactions (good outcomes) and n the number of failures (bad outcomes). The use of a DHT gives us sufficient space to record each individual observation, without any need to amalgamate the evidence (requiring summaries). This is because nodes are assumed to have, on average, enough storage to remember everything they have personally observed (multiplied by a small constant factor to handle fault-tolerance replication), and this information is distributed evenly around the entire network by the DHT.

3.2   Recommendations

Formally, a **recommendation** is information passed from principal W, the **witness**, to principal E, the **evaluator**, describing their judgement of principal S, the **subject**. The use of recommendations increases the amount of evidence we have regarding the subject's expected behaviour, but we must decide if we can trust the advice itself (see the next section on meta-trust).

One solution to scaling the distribution of recommendations is to form recommendation *chains*. Trust chains have been analysed in detail by Jøsang and Gray [13]. The difficulty with recommendation chains is that of actually finding them.

An alternative is to directly look up all reports of interactions with the subject and to make a statistical assessment from this. Even newcomers to the system can then decide who to trust by correlating the opinions of multiple independent strangers. A problem with the statistical method is that we will be fooled if all those who have interacted with the subject so far are their accomplices (a malicious collective).

The essential problem of accessing evidence is that observations are initially indexed by *observer*, and need to be looked up by *subject*. Furthermore if the population is large we can only hope to store partial information at each node.

3.3   Meta-trust

Our **meta-trust** (MT) in another principal measures the accuracy of their recommendations. The value of evidence delivered by a trust chain is **discounted** (scaled down) at each stage in the chain by the meta-trust for each principal in turn. One purpose of meta-trust is to identify principals who perform acceptable interactions, but give misleading positive recommendations to a series of bad collaborators. Without it they could get away with this repeatedly and give a trust "boost" to each bad newcomer. It must be tracked *independently* from ordinary trust so that such behaviour cannot be masked by numerous records of performing good actions.

3.4   Searching for Chains

Small world theory has found that, for certain types of graph arising naturally in social networks, short chains of connections exist between any two individuals, and that they can be found efficiently by a greedy algorithm. We investigated whether this can be used to help locate trust chains.

The Freenet information storage system [6] is notable for searching along paths within a graph. It falls somewhere between systems that flood the whole network, and those which deterministically route to the required data. It employs *directed routing* based on nodes' best guesses at where the data will be stored, combined with back-tracking if it doesn't happen to be there. Data is cached nearby while retrieving it. The premise is that over time nodes will come to specialise in parts of the keyspace, making searches more efficient. It provides no guarantees, so paths may be long and the system will fail to locate data when the maximum hop count is exceeeded.

Guided search algorithms such as Freenet and DHT's work by looking up IDs which have an *order* defined upon them. A structure can be imposed on this which gives a notion of "nearer" and "further away" to guide and prune the search (this is deterministic for DHT's and probabilistic for Freenet). In our case the objects we are looking for are *paths* themselves (we must find a route via the subgraph of trust relationships, the structure of which is outside our control). There is no ordering on paths, so looking for chains reduces to a graph search problem, which cannot be made to scale. Also, so-called "super nodes" (particularly well-connected principals) do not help unless they are an immediate neighbour of the target – we're still no closer to knowing which route to leave them by.

N	k	Localities				Unrelated			
		Fail	Obs	d	Visit	Fail	Obs	d	Visit
64K	3	11%	4%	4	29K	10%	0%	5	40K
64K	5	2%	4%	3	17K	1%	0%	3	35K
64K	10	0%	13%	1	5700	0%	0%	2	35K
64K	20	0%	20%	1	2900	0%	0%	2	31K
1M	3	11%	2%	6	489K	13%	0%	6	688K
1M	5	3%	3%	4	274K	1%	0%	4	614K
1M	10	0%	7%	2	62K	0%	0%	3	585K
1M	20	0%	10%	1	24K	0%	0%	2	544K

N = population size, k = average acquaintances, d = search depth,
Fail = chain non-existance, Obs = direct observations, Visit = nodes visited during search

Fig. 2. Searching for chains

We ran simulations to test our conjecture. Fig. 2 shows the results of a breadth-first search for chains between two randomly selected nodes. We used networks with either 64,000 or a million nodes. In each case we varied the average number of direct acquaintances each principal had, from 3 (a sparsely connected network) up to 20 (a well connected network). The columns marked "Unrelated" refer to networks where acquaintances are formed at random, whereas "Localities" are those with a significant amount of clustering (two corresponding bits in the ID numbers of two acquaintances only differ 10% of the time, to be precise). Partners for new interactions were chosen in the same way.

Note that when the average number of direct acquaintances is only 3, the search fails some of the time (no chain connecting the two participants existed). In the case of localities however sometimes there was already a direct observation link between the two participants, making a chain of length one; this never happened with unrelated acquaintances. The average search depth to find a chain is given by d, and the exact number of nodes visited before hitting the target in the "Visit" columns. When nodes are unrelated, this is generally about half the population. In the case of localities it is lower, and more so in graphs with a higher degree of connectivity. Unfortunately even in the best case we still have to visit thousands of nodes before we find a chain.

Our simulation results suggest that short MT chains exist, but can't be found efficiently. If we look for trust chains we must either flood the whole network or accept a low chance of finding a chain. In the light of these results we have chosen a statistical method for collecting recommendations and evaluating meta-trust called "behaviour profiles", instead of building chains.

4   Newcomers, Identity and Sybil Attack Protection

Newcomers present a particular problem for recommendation systems. We would like to allow bona-fide newcomers to start to participate, but also without risking an action on an unproven entity. The Eigentrust [14] system solves this by directing 10% of all actions to a pool of newcomers. We could also allow acquaintances to initially vouch for them using pre-trusted peers (statically configured and set per user, not globally, in their policy configuration files).

Friedman and Resnick present a very thorough analysis of "The Social Cost of Cheap Pseudonyms" [10] in the context of game theory. Specifically, they look at a massive online pairwise prisoners dilemma with a changing set of pseudonymous players, some of whom may be irrational. It is assumed that the whole interaction history is common knowledge. They note that suspicion of strangers is costly to society, but prove that distrust of newcomers is an inherent cost of easy identity changes.

4.1   Sybil Attacks

Untrustworthy newcomers are not too serious a problem if there are is only one of them per attacker. A Sybil Attack [9] is a situation whereby a single malicious participant creates multiple apparently unrelated identities and uses them in concert to defeat the system. It occurs whenever there is pseudonymity and no cost associated with the formation of new unlinked identities.

We might consider placing restrictions on principals who have recently joined the system (in a chronological sense); however a "Rolling Sleeping Army" attack may then be employed. In this situation, an attacker creates a large number of new identities each day, continues until the first set of them are eligible to perform risky actions and then deploys them in their respective batches every day from then on.

A group of identities under the control of a single real-world entity is described as a **collective**. In our experiments, for simplicity, the behaviour of each member of a collective follows a uniform policy. We assume however that it is impossible to identify collectives by spotting patterns, since in reality a large enough group could configure its interactions in arbitrarily complicated and realistic-looking ways, so as to resemble a normal part of the population.

Behaviour profiles are directly susceptible to Sybil attacks. MT chains are also vulnerable since new principals may initially agree with your opinions in order to build meta-trust chains, and then start to mislead.

4.2   Certification Agencies

A Certification Agency (CA) is a special trusted entity which signs others' public keys to show they are valid for use in the system. Note that a CA is a central point of failure, and hence undesirable.

There is an emerging consensus that Certification Agencies in some form are required to counter Sybil attacks. Douceur [9] has established that in the absence of CAs a Sybil attack can undermine *any* recommendation system. It should be noted that CAs may be *implicit* (for example CFS uses IP addresses; DNS approaches implicitly rely on ICANN as the trusted agency) as well as explicit (such as Verisign).

Castro [5] notes that Sybil attack protection can be achieved by charging for identity certificates, or binding them to real-world identities, and suggests that in practice different forms of CA are appropriate for different situations.

Friedman and Resnick [10] recommend free but unreplaceable pseudonyms which they call "once in a lifetime IDs". A CA is shown proof of real-life identity before issuing a single corresponding ID. Anonymity is preserved with blind signatures, so that even the CA itself does not know the mapping between real identities and keys, but can ensure it is 1-1. Names are valid within different "arenas" (namespaces used for different types of application); this is a tradeoff between accountability and anonymity. The authors suggest auctioning off the ID server franchise.

Before returning to Certification Agencies we first consider some possible alternatives for regulating the creation of new identities.

4.3   Rate Limits

There have been several proposals for ways to restrict the *rate* at which attackers can generate new identities. A feasible rate limit would be very useful as we could then quantify how much damage a limited proportion of attackers can do, and express this as an overhead loss expected by legitimate principals.

Hash Cash [3] addresses this by making it computationally expensive to generate IDs. To do so one is required to find a partial hash collision, i.e. two numbers which match in a given number of bits after passing through a one-way function. One number can be derived from your e-mail address (or in our case, public key, to preserve anonymity) so that others can't reuse it. Douceur [9] also considers other types of resource game, including those which require bandwidth or a lot of storage space.

The problem with all such approaches (taking computation power as an example) is that the puzzle must be easy enough for the slowest legitimate node to solve in a reasonable time, but hard enough to seriously slow down a determined attacker. It does not seem likely that this will be possible, particularly given the disparity between resource-light mobile nodes and the cost-effectiveness of purpose-built crypto hardware.

Another possibility suggested by Eigentrust [14] and others is to require the user to solve a CAPTCHA [20] to receive an ID. This is a task such as obfuscated picture recognition that a human can perform which requires too much AI for a computer to solve, thereby preventing automated attacks. The difficulty with this is that a central component is required to administer the test; it is unclear how it could be used in a distributed fashion.

For these reasons we are not convinced that an effective rate limiting solution for identity generation exists at present.

4.4   Entry Fees

Freidman and Resnick [10] describe several techniques for charging newcomers an entry fee in order to join the system.

Payment can be made to a special agency or distributed amongst the whole population, for example. Of course the former is not a decentralised solution, and takes utility away from the participants. The shared-fees method however leads to entities lurking in the system in a dormant state simply to collect entry fees.

The biggest problem is trying to find an "optimal entry fee" when payoffs are heterogeneous. One is faced with a choice between high registration fees, which discourage poor participants, or the need to set low maximum transaction amounts to keep them below the value of an identity.

An alternative to entry fees is for newcomers to "pay their dues" by accepting poor treatment from principals with established positive reputations. For example they may have to pay up front, accept shipping delays or higher prices. One problem with this is that for many applications it is hard to pay "in kind". A scenario may have arbitrary non-monetary costs, for example. Another serious issue is that collaborators might "pay their dues" to each other.

4.5   ENTRAPPED Approach

Our approach is to make large quantities of fake IDs expensive, without needing to charge for a reasonable number or limiting legitimate participants to a single ID. These might be described as "few in a lifetime IDs".

We achieve this by allowing existing well-known companies, whom the participants have a prior business relationship with, to act as (multiple) Certification Agencies. They have already seen participants' real IDs and need not charge a fee since this can be viewed as a "value-added" service. CAs use blind signatures to preserve anonymity. Attackers will find it increasingly expensive to obtain more identities, since each CA will only issue one and they will run out of easy-to-obtain sources.

Typical companies might include ISP's, banks, phone companies, utility companies, the post office, vehicle licensing agency, passport agency, solicitors, Verisign, VISA and large shopping chains. The cost to attackers is initially due to the need to open accounts with companies or pay registration fees, and eventually becomes the cost of fabricating a complete new identity (forged passport etc) in order to access another batch of IDs.

Making some identities free is useful because it ensures a low cost of entry. Allowing users to have multiple IDs is very important since they can use different personas for sensitive topics, such as commenting on a political forum that their employer or state might disapprove of. Users may choose how they wish to partition their own identity since we do not enforce particular namespaces on them.

The restriction on CAs issuing a second ID is time-based, for example one per year. This allows legitimate users to discard and eventually replace their IDs if they get stolen, say. Attackers can get replacement IDs too but only at a very slow rate.

Identity Presentation Protocol. An ENTRAPPED identity is a vector, which allows signatures from multiple CAs to be presented at once. Each principal also has a list of CAs which they accept as valid. The following process describes what happens when an identity is presented to another principal:

1. The requester's public key has been signed by various CAs.
2. CAs publish nominal value pairs (registration fee, cost of real-world credentials).
3. The recipient masks off CAs he/she doesn't recognise.
4. Component CA values are adjusted according to local policy (maximum amounts, etc) and then a combined ID value function is evaluated. This could be a simple sum of the components, or it might be superlinear since extra IDs are progressively harder to find. It could also insist that at least two or more components match.
5. This value is the cost to the requester if their identity becomes unusable due to low trust and MT. If non-zero, it indicates the maximum recommended transaction value.

The third step is most important – a match is made between the CAs offered and those recognised by the recipient. We anticipate a market for identity servers; agencies will try to become sufficiently well known that the chance of being mutually listed is high. To facilitate commerce we also recommend an API for principals to publish which CAs they accept. This gives requesters a clue as to which identities they need to acquire, and lets friends learn what is considered valuable or reputable.

ENTRAPPED is suitable for a range of transaction sizes from tiny (micropayments) up to medium value (a few $100). Free transactions are not relevant, because there is no risk. Large transactions are unsafe since they may exceed the value of identities, but fortunately users are generally happy to use conventional credit card mechanisms for these, since convenience is not so important.

We also envisage *Transaction Guarantors*, which are Certification Agencies that also provide *insurance* for actions, up to a transaction limit. Care must be taken over timing attacks – distributed locks are needed on identities during transactions. Again, participants will prefer well-known but also lower commission agencies.

5   The ENTRAPPED Platform

We now describe our solution for distributing trust information. Our implementation is built from four main components; a Distributed Hash Table, a Statistical Correlator, the SCOP[12] events system and a distributed database of tables stored at each node.

5.1   State Tables

ENTRAPPED is designed to work with any DHT. We prefer Chord or similar, due to the availability of neighbour sets for efficient replica location and the strong security constraints on routing table entries. Three-way application-level replication and comparison is used to detect attempts by an attacker to substitute false evidence for a given key (if they are lucky enough to control the node it hashes to). Each node is responsible for storing seven different tables; their own personal observations together with behaviour and meta-trust profiles for three other principals. The DHT ensures that a node cannot predict which subjects they will be maintaining profiles for.

Personal observations are the most direct and hence most useful source. If they exist they are used first. Recommendations are fetched from behaviour profiles and weighted equally for each recommending principal, except those which are eliminated by meta-trust. Meta-trust profiles tell us what is known about the accuracy of the recommendations from a particular principal. They are replicated and distributed in a similar manner to behaviour profiles. Information from meta-trust profiles is fed back to the "global outlier" column in behaviour profiles.

The format of behaviour profiles is shown in Fig. 3. Each behaviour profile stores a complete dossier about a given principal. For example, Alice's behaviour profile contains recommendations about Alice made by everybody who has interacted with her. This table is the only information which is needed when one makes a decision about whether to perform an action with Alice.

In the example table, principal David has been detected as a local outlier given his unusual success rate of 95% (suggesting he is an accomplice of Alice). Emily isn't an outlier with regard to Alice but her meta-trust profile has reported she was unreliable elsewhere, so we have marked her as a global outlier. The remaining recommendations from Claire, Bob and Fred lead to an overall trust value of 6.7%.

Subject	Witness	Action	Success rate	Local Outlier	Global Outlier
ALICE	EMILY	ECOM	50%	0	1
ALICE	CLAIRE	" "	10%	0	0
ALICE	DAVID	" "	95%	1	0
ALICE	BOB	" "	0%	0	0
ALICE	FRED	" "	10%	0	0
ALICE	*Overall*	ECOM	6.7%		

Fig. 3. Behaviour Profile Format

5.2   Data Exchange Between Tables

Fig. 4 shows how data is exchanged between the three different sorts of table. A row is copied from an observation table to the relevant behaviour profile locations whenever a new observation occurs. The destination is looked up using the DHT so this is a point-to-point operation (in fact there are three replica destinations, of course).

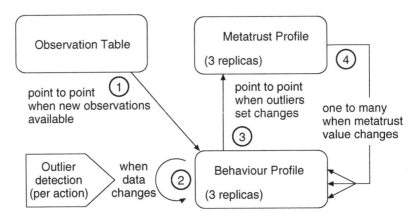

Fig. 4. Dataflow between Tables

Whenever the data in a behaviour profile changes, the rows with the same action type are compared to detect outlying recommendations. For example, most of the witnesses might report a high proportion of successes but one witness may state that they had many interactions with the subject all of which were failures. Such a witness is an outlier and is marked as such in the Local Outlier column.

When the set of local outliers in a behaviour profile changes, the row in question is sent to the three locations of the meta-trust profile for that witness. The meta-trust profile is used to calculate *global outliers*. This is a more accurate measure of whether recommendations should be believed and it is actually the global outlier state that is used to determine which rows in the behaviour profile are included in the overall summation.

6   Threat Analysis

We now describe our threat model by enumerating a large number of different attacks, with some notes as to how they can be neutralised. The attacker knows the parameters of the system and can tune his parameters to manipulate trust and meta-trust. We cannot prevent all attacks from succeeding, but we can ensure that all attacks cost an attacker more than they benefit them (so it isn't possible to make a profit by cheating).

Human error is a major problem with security systems, especially if users must create their own policies. ENTRAPPED helps to avoid this because the main trust components are shared; everyone is working from the same data, hence although decisions are made autonomously the same core policy can be used for most clients. Examples of user-controlled configuration parameters are pre-trusted peers and risk sensitivity.

Software error is a problem which scales based on the size of the TCB. We can counter it with simplicity and by providing strategies for recovery in the event of an exploit. The timeouts on user identities help ensure they can be replaced if compromised.

Identity theft has a well-defined meaning here – it is achieved by breaking into another machine and harvesting the private key (we assume passphrases are not used, or if they are they can be obtained as well by keyboard sniffers).

Routing attacks target the P2P overlay network, and are countered by the use of a secure DHT.

Bad guys are principals which always behave badly, making them the easiest kind of attacker to spot!

The **Newcomer attack** consists of a principal who joins the system, performs a single bad interaction, and then leaves. A stronger version of this is the **Basic Sybil attack**, in which the attacker employs a long series of badly behaved principals with throwaway IDs. We counter widespread adoption of both of these by economic means, due to "few-in-a-lifetime" certified identities.

The **Waiting attack** consists of performing a series of good interactions in order to build up a positive trust value, and then cheating. A stronger version is the **Oscillation attack**, whereby the principal switches between well-behaved and hostile modes in an attempt to manipulate its own trust value. In a variant which we call the **Mixed behaviour attack**, the principal chooses a mode (cooperate or defect) for each separate interaction probabilistically. Again the objective is to manipulate their trust value to stay just below the threshold for identification as a bad guy.

This has been studied in the context of the Eigentrust [14] project, in which the most effective probabilty of defecting was found to be 50% (in this case their simulation measured that 28% of all interactions in the system were actually successful attacks). In defence this strategy comes at a cost to the malicious nodes, since performing some good interactions may be undesirable for them; however this is application-dependent and will not always be the case.

Misconfiguration and **Chaotic behaviour attacks** lead to either random or constant, incorrect behaviour.

Carelessness is not strictly speaking an attack, but may be even more common in practice. Careless principals are generally good but suffer from "trembles", which means they will occasionally behave badly by mistake (at random). Our system is able to distinguish clearly between careless and bad principals (in fact in our implementation the "good" principals were all modelled as careless 10% of the time).

Peer-specific attack: Pseudonymity should prevent an attacker matching the real identity of principals and hence attacking a named target (but see concerns under privacy attack below). However an attacking node might try a policy which involves cheating only a subset of other principals (say arbitrarily those whose IDs equal 0 modulo 4), so that the rest give it good recommendations.

A Collusion Clique is an attack on the recommendation system using false praise. All principals in a clique behave badly, but provide articifially good recommendations for each other.

Collusion with Supporters is a more subtle approach whereby just one principal behaves badly, and the others in the collective simply recommend it (they may themselves not perform any actions or perform good ones, depending on the application). Note that systems which do not have a separate meta-trust concept such as [14] never discover supporters, making this attack more effective.

Collusion with Camouflage is a combination of supporters and mixed behaviour in which the active principal only misbehaves some of the time (and the supporters not at all) in order to try and escape detection whilst making a profit.

Defamation consists of attacking a good principal's reputation. This attack is one reason why we cannot simply treat any negative recommendations as proof that the subject is bad (another reason is trembles, as described under carelessness above).

An **Indirect Sybil attack** involves a stream of colluding recommenders boosting the trust of one badly behaved principal; A **General Sybil attack** might include many teams of colluding recommenders and arbitrary numbers of badly behaved principals. These are both limited by identity certification.

Privacy attack: Behaviour profiles reveal a great deal of information about the interaction pattern for a principal. If they can be correlated with some external piece of known data (perhaps a shipment of a certain size last week, or an expected pattern of suppliers), a correspondence with a real identity might be established. Even without this, anonymous "shopping pattern" information can be collected, correlated with known demographics and principals treated differently on this basis.

ENTRAPPED provides a partial defence against privacy attacks by masking off principal IDs in behaviour profiles when they are made visible to the network. The statistical trust value calculation only requires that users know the pattern of interactions, not who observed them. Only the three replica nodes who are randomly assigned a given behaviour profile can see the real node IDs. Data integrity is ensured since the identity-masked copies can be compared; if the pattern is not the same then tampering has occurred.

Denial of service attacks are possible at the network layer, DHT layer, evidence distribution layer, and/or application layer. Care must be taken so that DoS against a third party cannot mislead a target and cause incorrect decisions to be made, as well as merely preventing actions.

We have already seen that **Resource costs** (CPU, storage, connectivity) for each node are acceptable. A larger issue is that of **Deployment costs**. In particular a critical mass user-base may be required for adequate functioning. Our system helps address this by warning when there is insufficient evidence to make a decision.

7   Related Work

Abdul-Rahman and Hailes [1] have identified similar concepts to trust and meta-trust, as well as recommendations and trust categories (their name for trust in different actions). However they have a very basic notion of trust value, with only a few possible states, and the lack of an efficient distribution system makes their trust chains and revocations unconvincing.

Aberer and Despotovic [2] present an efficient, scalable peer to peer evidence locator, based on their "P-Grid" data structure. They monitor "complaints" between principals which have interacted and provide a number of replicas of the information tuned to provide acceptable fault-tolerance. Unfortunately they don't consider routing attacks or different types of action, and don't distinguish trust and meta-trust.

The work by Xiong and Liu [21] is similar to our own. They advocate the use of an overlay network to locate what we call behaviour profiles, in a peer to peer envionment. Their implementation uses a P-Grid. They also recognise that recommenders should not be believed to an equal degree, but rely on a cache for this information rather than distributing meta-trust.

The EigenTrust [14] project is closest to our approach, in particular using behaviour profiles in much the same way. This is done in the context of a file-sharing application. It solves the problem of finding trust chains (transitive trust) by iteratively multiplying a global trust matrix until it converges. We believe this creates a scalability problem, however. Everyone has to participate in calculating the global trust in lock step, which creates inter-dependency and a lot of communication. No distinction is made between trust and meta-trust; the algorithm requires a set of globally pre-trusted peers to break attacks by malicious collectives.

8   Conclusion

We have created a mechanism for the distribution of trust information, using a Distributed Hash Table to store statistical *Behaviour Profiles*.

The system returns all that has been observed about a given principal in $log\ N$ steps. All trust values are pre-computed and do not require a process of convergence over multiple iterations. There is a distributed, shared evaluation of the accuracy of recommendations (meta-trust). Trust and meta-trust are represented distinctly.

The system does not depend on caches (which require locality of reference amongst accesses) or trust chains, which we have shown cannot be found efficiently. It is scalable to very large populations: there's no centralised component, no multicast messages, and the storage requirements per node are modest.

The system applies to any kind of evidence-based application. Certification Agencies are used to protect against Sybil attacks by creating "few in a lifetime IDs". Multiple CAs are supported via vector IDs. Finally it has been designed to be reliable in the presence of a range of deliberate attacks, and to protect participants' privacy.

Acknowledgements. This work was funded by the European Commission Information Society Technologies SECURE project, IST-2001-32486. I would like to thank my colleagues at the University of Cambridge Computer Laboratory, at BRICS in the University of Aarhus, the Trinity College Dublin DSG, Université de Genève Object Systems Group and SmartLab at the University of Strathclyde.

References

1. A. Abdul-Rahman, S. Hailes. "Using Recommendations for Managing Trust in Distributed Systems". *Proceedings of the IEEE Intl. Conference on Communication*, Malaysia, November 1997.
2. K. Aberer, Z. Despotovic. "Managing Trust in a Peer-2-Peer Information System". *Proceedings of the 10th Intl. Conference on Information and Knowledge Management*, 2001.
3. A. Back. "Hashcash - A Denial of Service Counter-Measure".
   http://www.hashcash.org
4. V. Cahill, et al. "Using trust for secure collaboration in uncertain environments". *IEEE Pervasive Computing, 2(3):52-61*, August 2003.

5. M. Castro, P. Druschel, A. Ganesh, A. Rowstron, D. Wallach. "Secure routing for structured peer-to-peer overlay networks". *Proceedings of the 5th Usenix Symposium on Operating Systems Design and Implementation*, Boston, December 2002.

6. I. Clarke, O. Sandberg, B. Wiley, T. Hong. "Freenet: A Distributed Anonymous Information Storage and Retrieval System". *Proc. ICSI Workshop on Design Issues in Anonymity and Unobservability*, 2000.

7. F. Dabek, F. Kaashoek, D. Karger, R. Morris, I. Stoica. "Wide-area cooperative storage with CFS". *Proc. 18th ACM Symposium on OS Principals (SOSP '01)*, October 2001.

8. N. Dimmock, I. Maddison. "Peer-to-Peer Collaborative Spam Detection". *ACM Crossroads Magazine*, Dec 2004.

9. J. Douceur. "The Sybil Attack". *Proc. 1st Intl Workshop on Peer-to-Peer Systems (IPTPS'02)*, March 2002.

10. E. Friedman, P. Resnick. "The Social Cost of Cheap Pseudonyms". *Journal of Economics and Management Strategy 10(2): 173-199*, 2001.

11. D. Ingram. "Trust-based Filtering for Augmented Reality". *1st Intl. Conference on Trust Management*, Crete, May 2003.

12. D. Ingram. "The SCOP Events Library". `http://www.srcf.ucam.org/~dmi1000/scop/index.html`

13. A. Jøsang, E. Gray, M. Kinateder. "Analysing Topologies of Transitive Trust". *Proc. Workshop Formal Aspects of Security and Trust (FAST)*, September 2003.

14. S. Kamvar, M. Schlosser, H. Garcia-Molina. "The EigenTrust Algorithm for Reputation Management in P2P Networks". *Proc. 12th Intl WWW Conference*, May 2003.

15. P. Maymounkov, D. Mazières. "Kademlia: A Peer-to-peer Information System Based on the XOR Metric". *Proceedings of the 1st Intl. Workshop on Peer-to-Peer Systems*, March 2002.

16. A. Rowstron, P. Druschel. "Pastry: Scalable, decentralized object location and routing for large-scale peer-to-peer systems". *Proceedings of the 18th Intl. Conference on Distributed Systems Platforms (Middleware)*, Germany, November 2001.

17. SECURE: Secure Environments for Collaboration among Ubiquitous Roaming Entities. *EU Project IST-2001-32486*, December 2002. `http://secure.dsg.cs.tcd.ie/`

18. E. Sit, R. Morris. "Security Considerations for Peer-to-Peer Distributed Hash Tables". *Proc. 1st Intl Workshop on Peer-to-Peer Systems (IPTPS'02)*, March 2002.

19. I. Stoica, R. Morris, D. Liben-Nowell, D. Karger, M. Kaashoek, F. Dabek, H. Balakrishnan. "Chord: A Scalable Peer-to-peer Lookup Service for Internet Applications". *Proceedings of the ACM SIGCOMM Conference*, San Diego, August 2001.

20. B. Watson. "Beyond Identity: Addressing Problems that Persist in an Electronic Mail System with Reliable Sender Identification". *1st Conference on Email and Anti-Spam (CEAS)*, 2004.

21. L. Xiong, L. Liu. "Building Trust in Decentralized Peer-to-Peer Electronic Communities". *5th International Conference on Electronic Commerce Research*, October 2002.

22. B. Yu, M. Singh. "An Evidential Model of Distributed Reputation Management". *Proc. 1st Intl. Joint Conference on Autonomous Agents and MultiAgent Systems*, Italy, July 2002.

Towards an Evaluation Methodology for Computational Trust Systems

Ciarán Bryce[1], Nathan Dimmock[2], Karl Krukow[3],
Jean-Marc Seigneur[4], Vinny Cahill[4], and Waleed Wagealla[5]

[1] University of Geneva, Switzerland
[2] University of Cambridge, UK
[3] University of Aarhus, Denmark
[4] Trinity College Dublin, Ireland
[5] University of Strathcylde, UK

Abstract. Trust-based security frameworks are increasingly popular, yet few evaluations have been conducted. As a result, no guidelines or evaluation methodology have emerged that define the measure of security of such models. This paper discusses the issues involved in evaluating these models, using the SECURE trust-based framework as a case study.

1 Introduction

Over the past few years, the computer security field has seen the emergence of trust-based models for access control and security decision optimisation, e.g., [7, 3, 18, 19]. Their goal is to permit interacting principals to build trust in one another, in an analogous way to humans. This approach removes the need for pre-configured access control rules, which is advantageous for two reasons. First, modern infrastructures do not necessarily have an administration that is capable of making security decisions for all principals, either due to the decentralised nature of the network or to the exceedingly large number of principals. Second, the trust-based approach scales better since the principals being controlled need not be known in advance; rather, the onus is placed on each principal to become known and trusted through its actions in the system.

To employ the trust-based approach in a computer system, a model is required that provides a *computational representation* of trust. Modern trust models tend to be evidence based, in that a principal's decision to trust another is directly related to the evidence available to the former concerning the latter's behaviour. In effect, trust values – that represent the trustworthiness of principals – encode the history of a principal's behaviour. Examples of this include EigenTrust [7] and the trust model component of the SECURE framework [4].

Trust-based security frameworks are complex and, as a result, many papers only address a small number of the problem-space's facets. As a result, the authors know of few systems which have implemented **and** completely evaluated. In undertaking to address this gap, it is necessary to define exactly *how* to go about analysing a complete computational trust-system. Part of the challenge in

P. Herrmann et al. (Eds.): iTrust 2005, LNCS 3477, pp. 289–304, 2005.
© Springer-Verlag Berlin Heidelberg 2005

evaluating a trust-based security model is that the computation of a trust value for a principal is only the first step. The goal of any security model is to take a decision, so the remaining steps include establishing confidence in the identity or credentials of the requesting principal(s), and depending on the framework, calculating the risk involved in permitting or refusing the requested action. Only then is the final security decision taken.

In this paper, we address the issue of evaluation. The first task is to clearly delimit the role of each component of the security framework. This is particularly important for the trust model component since trust in the human world is subject to various interpretations, and arguments on its semantics can have a confusing impact on the evaluation of computational trust systems. Once the precise role of each component is clarified, an analysis of the component is undertaken to determine how failures of, or attacks on, the component influence the outcome of the decision making process. These attacks are added to a system attack profile against which the whole security system is empirically evaluated. By evaluating all components together, one can also measure the effectiveness of computational trust against weaknesses in other components, e.g., the usefulness of recommendations when principal authentication is weak.

In this paper, we use the SECURE model [4] as an example trust framework, and a SPAM filter that we built over it as an example application. SECURE is an application-neutral framework that allows principals to represent trust in other principals. Trust in a principal $\mathcal{P}$ is established through observation of action outcomes, or from recommendations received for $\mathcal{P}$. The framework makes risk modelling explicit. A trust value is used to estimate the cost-benefit of collaborating with $\mathcal{P}$, and a final decision is made from this cost. The SPAM filter application uses SECURE to classify a message as valid or SPAM. Each message downloaded from the mail server is processed by the user's local SECURE framework instance, where a decision is made on the message's classification. The outcome depends on the trust in the message sender and the cost associated with a false SPAM classification.

The remainder of this paper is organised as follows. Section 2 outlines our evaluation approach. Since the SECURE framework is our running example, we give a brief overview of it in Section 3 and discuss the impact of each of its components on evaluation. We use our approach to analyse a SPAM filtering application in Section 4. Related work is presented in Section 5 and we conclude in Section 6.

2   Evaluation Criteria

The fundamental purpose of SECURE and other trust-based frameworks is to automate a decision process for security. The decision to take is whether a requesting principal should be allowed access to a resource. Another interpretation of the decision process is that it should select an interaction partner principal such that the risk of interacting with that principal is deemed to be acceptable to the decision-maker.

Numerous security frameworks have been designed over the years to implement this decision making process, e.g., [3, 11, 8]. The originality of trust-based frameworks is that they include a computational treatment of trust in the process. There are thus two basic questions that an evaluation methodology must answer:

1. *The Question of Security* How good is the framework at automating the decision making process, and how likely is it to take the right decision?
2. *The Question of Trust* How does the computational treatment of trust improve, or impact upon, the security question?

It is important to distinguish these two questions. The Security Question is the fundamental one, and depends not only on the trust component, but also on the framework's risk assessment and principal recognition or authentication components. The basic assumption of researchers working on trust-based models is that these models yield better decision making for security.

2.1   The Question of Security

There are four major elements to all security infrastructures, as suggested in Figure 1. One element is the principal authentication or recognition phase. The goal of authentication is to ascertain the identity of the requesting principal; recognition is used when the system does not guarantee a fixed identity for principals, and seeks to determine if a requesting principal has been previously encountered [15]. Authentication and recognition are done at runtime, once the requesting principal furnishes its identifying information.

The goal of the risk assessment phase is to attribute a cost to permitting or refusing each request, and perhaps the likelihood of that cost occurring. The cost might be represented as the loss of information, privacy being compromised or it might even be a monetary value. Trust attribution to a principal $\mathcal{P}$ is a definition of the level of risk that one is willing to take with $\mathcal{P}$. Finally, the decision phase of a security framework decides whether a request from $\mathcal{P}$ should be permitted based on the risk and trust calculations.

Context. The key difference between access control based security infrastructures, e.g., [11], and trust-based frameworks concerns when and how risk assess-

Fig. 1. Security Decision Framework

ment and trust attribution are done. In a Unix environment for instance trust attribution and risk assessment are implicitly made by a user when he decides what access rights to accord to users of his group and to others for his files. The trust value of each user is indirectly represented in these rights since they determine what actions the user is allowed to undertake. The decision phase in Unix simply checks whether the requesting principal (process) has been accorded the necessary rights for the requested action. In trust-based security frameworks, e.g., [13, 12], the trust decision is made at run-time, and is not guaranteed to be the same between two successive requests. It generally based on observations of the requesting principal's behaviour. Risk assessment is generally included in the decision phase policy. This policy is defined as a mapping from trust values to permitted actions, and an implicit risk assessment guides this mapping. One of the originalities of the SECURE project is that the risk assessment phase is carried out at runtime, as we describe in Section 3.

Clearly, the difference between access control-based security frameworks and emerging trust models is that the former are *administration-oriented* while the latter are built for *autonomous* decision making. The former are preferred in environments where the users are known in advance and the owner of resources wishes complete control over the access that others have to his resources. The latter are required when there is no centralised control in the system, where the total number of principals cannot be identified or where there is no commonly trusted party to store security data. Here, the trust approach is required so that an unknown principal can show itself to be trustworthy and thus interact with others. Thus the *context* for the two classes of models are different. The context defines the set of use cases and *attack scenarios* against which a security model must be measured. An attack by a principal or group of principals is *any behaviour that aims to influence a security decision in such a way as to be detrimental to the decision maker.*

The John Smith Test. The security subsystem implements a *decision-making process.* The obvious evaluation criteria is its ability to make the right decision. Consider the example of a Bayesian SPAM filter. Here, the strength of the mechanism is given by the number of correct message classifications, the number of false positives and false negatives. If we abstract away from the application-specific nature of this example, we can quantify the strength of a security mechanism by the triple $< \mathcal{E}, \mathcal{P}, \mathcal{N} >$. $\mathcal{E}$ represents the total number of events that need to be controlled by the security subsystem; $\mathcal{P}$ represents the number of false positives (decisions where access was incorrectly refused) and $\mathcal{N}$ represents the number of false negatives (decisions where access was incorrectly granted). The number of correct decisions is given by $\mathcal{E} - (\mathcal{P} + \mathcal{N})$. It is useful to distinguish $\mathcal{P}$ and $\mathcal{N}$ since the cost of a wrong decision can be different when a request is incorrectly refused from when it is incorrectly permitted.

The notion of right decision is not only application specific, but also varies from principal to principal. In the case of SPAM for instance, a message considered SPAM by a principal named John Smith might be considered as valid by another. The notion of right decision is best determined by a, possibly imaginary, human user who surveys the system. In this respect, the strength of the security subsystem is determined by a Turing-like test that is run for all events and which measures $\mathcal{P}$ and $\mathcal{N}$.

Profile. There are two profiles that are used when deciding the strength of a decision making process.

1. John Smith's profile, where John Smith is the decision making principal. His profile defines the correct outcome to each decision. That is, it defines the outcomes to the decision process that John Smith would give if he were asked rather than have the decision taken by the security framework.
2. The community profile is made up of the messages for John Smith from principals. These messages represent requests, recommendations and evidence. The community profile models all principals that can influence John Smith's security decision.

Different attack scenarios are modelled using different community profiles, e.g., a collusion attack can be modelled by a profile where different principals send incorrect recommendations for each other. $< \mathcal{E}, \mathcal{P}, \mathcal{N} >$ values are only comparable for the same profiles. We define $\mathcal{E}_\mathcal{P}$ as the profile, and refine our metric to $\mathcal{E}_\mathcal{P} \to < \mathcal{P}, \mathcal{N} >$, where the number of events of the profile $\mathcal{E}_\mathcal{P}$ is $\mathcal{E}$.

The Turing-test nature of the evaluation suggests that empirical measurements for a range of profiles is required to evaluate the strength of the security mechanism. Indeed, several systems have been evaluated in this manner, e.g., [7], and we use this approach ourselves in Section 4 to evaluate a SPAM-filter application that employs SECURE. There are however two important considerations:

1. The number of events $\mathcal{E}$ that all profiles generate can be very large or even unbounded, which makes a complete analysis unfeasible. When we use a subset of profiles, we must be able to argue that the subset used is sufficient to yield a meaningful measure of security. For this reason, the evaluation criteria are defined in terms of the select attack scenarios that the model must withstand, and is measured against them.
2. An analysis and measure of the value of security is still required, to be able to extract useful information from the myriad of simulation data. Simulation data alone do not tell us *why* results are good or bad. We need to understand how potential weaknesses in each of the components lead to incorrect decisions being taken.

Computational Cost. The cost of the decision making process is its efficiency with respect to CPU, memory and network, as well as more abstract resources such as the number of OS processes or databases employed. For general evaluation, there are three resources of particular importance. The first is *network*, which can be abstractly measured as the number of messages exchanged in the model, i.e., for evidence distribution. This is important to measure since security relies on being able to exchange information between principals – one thus needs to measure the level of security as a function of collaboration. The second cost is *memory*, which can be abstractly measured as the number of items of evidence (observations and recommendations) in a principal's evidence store. This aspect is important since autonomous computing devices might not have a lot of memory available. The importance of the figures for network and memory consumption is that they give a measure of the model's *scalability*. The final measure is CPU: though verifying the presence of an access right is single-instruction, policies can be expressed as code units, which means that the number of instructions becomes a measure. We aggregate these three costs to $\mathcal{C}$. We thus extend our security metric to $\mathcal{E_P} \rightarrow < \mathcal{P}, \mathcal{N}, \mathcal{C} >$.

Implementation and Operation. There is a difference between a framework *model* and its *implementation*. One could measure the ability of engineers to implement secure channels or a tamperproof kernel that can store data. This is a challenge in the design of any system[1].

Another measure is the ease with which one can express policies using the framework. The is important since most security breaches in system arise from incorrect use or non-use of the system's security mechanisms [2]. The limit of most users' policy expressions are the access control lists they set on their files. This nonetheless is deceptively easy: though bits on a file can be changed with the chmod command, there is no guarantee that the policy is meaningful from a security viewpoint.

Summary. Comparison of trust based models to existing security architectures is not completely meaningful, since the latter are aimed at autonomous systems. To evaluate the model, one must identify the application specific profile $\mathcal{E_P}$ that encapsulate the attacks that the framework is designed to withstand; the number of these events is $\mathcal{E}$, and the measure of security for these events is $\mathcal{E_P} \rightarrow < \mathcal{P}, \mathcal{N}, \mathcal{C} >$. In a second stage, the role of each component needs to be clearly delimited so that the impact of each on the security decision process can be measured via associated attack scenarios.

2.2   The Question of Trust

Trust frameworks rely on evidence exchanged between principals. This allows a principal to learn about principals that are behaving badly. Traditional architectures do not have this possibility, so make no distinction between well-behaving and badly-behaving principals at runtime. *The added value of a trust model is to render it possible to make this distinction.*

No trust model can predict the future behaviour of a principal. The assumption behind the models where trust values encode history is that *the best available indicator of a principal's expected behaviour is its previous behaviour*; see Assertion T below. Evidence distribution systems seek to maximise the knowledge available to one principal concerning the behaviour of others. This is considered

---

[1] The challenge we undertook in SECURE was to implement the framework in a safe programming language so that the resulting kernel could be ported to any device.

essential for security since, even if principal Alice believes Bob to be honest, she may learn that Bob was dishonest with Charlie, and thus revise her trust in Bob.

Assertion T. The more one knows about a principal's previous behaviour, the better one can judge its future behaviour.

Assertion T encapsulates the fundamental strength and limitation of trust models. The same assertion is often employed in the human world. In any case, it shows that the trust model can do nothing against a random failure, i.e., where a well-behaving principal abruptly becomes malicious. The assertion sums up the best we can do concerning security, and represents a sort of *undecidability* for trust based models. This limit is illustrated by the line separating the security state in Figure 2. The security state can be defined as $< \mathbf{min}(\mathcal{P}), \mathbf{min}(\mathcal{N}), \mathbf{min}(\mathcal{C})>$ for the set of profiles $\mathcal{E}_\mathcal{P}$ of the system under evaluation.

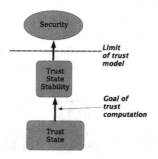

Fig. 2. Security Decision Framework

The intermediate state in Figure 2, denoted *trust state stability*, represents a state where every principal has an accurate account of the past behaviour of all other principals. The role of the trust model, and its evidence distribution framework, is to ensure a transition from any state to trust stability. *A measure of the trust component is its ability to achieve trust state stability or to reach a better understanding of principals' behaviour.* Many of the evaluations taken of trust models actually measure this, e.g., [13, 7, 12].

Trust stability in practice is very hard to achieve in a reasonably sized system for two reasons. First, there is simply too much information for principals to exchange and store. Second, principals are faulty and malicious and may be unable or unwilling to exchange correct trust values. Further, they can collude with false trust values, e.g., Alice creates false recommendations for Bob to help Bob cheat by making Charlie accord too much trust in him. A trust model must work with *partial and uncertain information.* Nevertheless, the exchange of trust values should bring the system closer to stability. For this reason, the attack scenarios of $\mathcal{E}_\mathcal{P}$ must model insufficient numbers of and false recommendations.

3   Evaluation of Secure Framework Components

The background to our work is the SECURE framework [4], see Figure 3. A principal consults the framework when it receives a request for an action a from another principal $\mathcal{P}$. There are three phases in the decision process. The first is to attribute a trust value to $\mathcal{P}$ for a. The second is *risk assessment*. Each action outcome has a pre-defined cost function associated with it. For instance, the cost of marking a valid message as SPAM has a higher cost associated than the cost of letting a SPAM message pass. The trust value of $\mathcal{P}$ is then applied to the cost functions for all outcomes of the action to give an *estimated cost*. In the SPAM filter for instance, if the trust value for $\mathcal{P}$ indicates that $\mathcal{P}$ has sent a lot of SPAM, then the estimated cost for the action will be closer to the pre-defined costs of accepting SPAM messages. The third phase of the decision process is the access control policy. This is a threshold type policy: it considers the estimated cost of undertaking the action and then makes a decision.

To model trust formation and evolution, principals can exchange *recommendations*. Trust also evolves by observing the outcome of an action. Recommendations and observations are collectively known as *evidence*. The trust life-cycle manager is responsible for producing new trust values based on accumulated evidence. The other major element of the framework is entity recognition; its role is to assign principal identifiers to requesting entities.

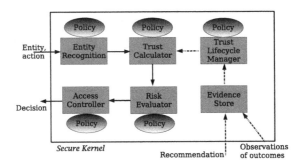

Fig. 3. The SECURE Framework

In the remainder of this section, we clarify the role of each major component on the decision making process.

3.1   Risk Evaluator

The risk evaluation phase of SECURE applies a pre-defined cost function for an action to a request for that action. Consider an e-purse, where a request for a payment action is made for the amount m. One cost function (policy) might by $a.m$, where a is a weight, meaning that the cost (of risk) is directly proportional to the amount of money transferred. In the overall decision framework, the importance of trust is that it determines the amount of risk that one is willing to take; in this example, this translates to the amount of payment [4].

In contrast to trust which may be considered to be globally computed, risk evaluation is a local process in which a principal assesses its personal exposure that results from trusting another principal. In this way, a principal may make a local evaluation of global information (trust) to ensure that the views of others cannot contravene its own security policy, or force it to take a decision that it would not otherwise wish to make.

Risk is defined in terms of likelihood and impact, and the method of evaluation is outcome-based analysis [16]. If the analysis is static, that is, pre-computed and does not evolve throughout the lifetime of the principal, then it effectively forms part of the principal's *policy* and the key aspects that should be evaluated are the expressiveness, completeness, computational efficiency and ease-of-use for the policy-writer.

However, given the dynamic nature of trust, the SECURE consortium have also proposed that risk should similarly evolve to take account of changing environments, contexts and circumstances [5]. Such a dynamic risk evaluator would need to be evaluated using quite different criteria, namely the rate of adaption to changes in context and circumstance and, as with the trust model, appropriate attack scenarios must be constructed and the risk evaluator shown to respond in the expected manner.

3.2   Trust Lifecycle Management

The Trust Lifecycle Manager (TLM) provides trust functions that facilitate evidence processing, in terms of how trust is formed, how it evolves over time and how it is exploited in the decision making process. The TLM is a policy that deals with issues such as whether a received recommendation should be believed, and if it is not totally believed, what alternative trust value should be assigned to the referenced principal. TLM also abstracts behaviour *patterns* from the reported behaviour of principals, and models how the decision maker's trust in others builds and erodes in the light of evidence.

The evaluation criteria of the TLM were demonstrated in the simulation of an e-purse [17]. The scenario involved an e-purse that a passenger uses to pay for a ticket on a bus (the decision making principal). In this scenario, a passenger's trustworthiness reflects the expected loss or gain in a transaction involving him. Our main aim was to measure how effective the TLM is at expressing how gathered evidence of a particular principal becomes a trust value for the decision maker, e.g., how a recommendation received – containing a trust value – gets turned into a local trust value. We conducted numerous experiments that use a wide variety of principals' behaviour profiles (i.e. norm behaviour, complex behaviour, and indiscernible or inconsistent behaviour) to verify that the TLM manages to run its functions on the accumulated evidence from previous interactions, and accordingly, give a better representation of the accurate trustworthiness of the principal in question. The simulation also focused on how the TLM abstracts the patterns of principal behaviour in their interactions to ease the decision making process for the bus company.

In the security evaluation, the impact of TLM is measured by varying the manner in which received recommendations are translated into local trust values.

3.3   Entity Recognition

The goal of Entity Recognition (ER), as suggested in Figure 4, is to bind a virtual identity to an interacting entity. When the ER component recognises a virtual identity, it means the entity has been met before; a new identity means that the entity has not previously been met. An attack on ER is one that leads to either premise being violated:

1. *Identity Usurption.* This occurs when a real-world identity obtains the information required to have itself identified as another. Common examples include password and private key stealing.
2. *Identity Manufacture.* This happens when a real-world identity can fabricate the data needed to have itself recognised as a new principal, and is also known as the Sybil attack [6]. An example of this is faked e-mail address used by a spammer. It is a particular problem in networks where identity management is decentralised or non-existent but where newcomers must be allowed.

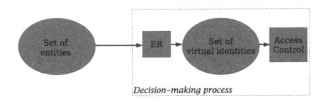

Fig. 4. ER maps interacting entities to virtual identities

Two key parameters need to be considered for ER evaluation. The first is whether the component relies on a centralised repository of information – as is the case with a public key system. A second parameter to consider is the information that a principal must furnish to have itself recognised. This is important in helping to judge the strength of the mechanism. For instance, IP addresses as ER information have proved to be fairly unreliable; DNA sampling on the other hand where real-world identities correspond to people is very reliable. Other factors to consider are privacy (whether the information furnished can be protected by the decision making principal), and responsibility (whether the link between the virtual identity and the real-world identity is strong enough for prosecution or insurance).

An example evaluation of the ER mechanism for SECURE is described in [14]. The outcome of this evaluation is a *confidence factor ER_C*. This is a percentage that indicates the level of confidence that the ER is able to accord to the virtual identity that it binds to the requesting entity. This value is then used in the security decision-making process.

With respect to a security framework evaluation, the ER evaluation must help us to answer the question: *what is the impact of an ER attack on the decision-making process?* The most likely way for an attacker to exploit ER attacks is *spoofing*, i.e., have itself recognised as an honest principal, either during an access request, or to create false recommendations for his buddies. For this reason, such collusion attacks should be part of the profile $\mathcal{E}_P$.

4   The SPAM Example

In this section, we apply the methodology to a simulation of a SPAM filter for e-mail messages where a message gets classified as SPAM or as valid, based on trust in the message sender. One reason for choosing the SPAM-filter application is that it is an example application for a highly distributed environment, where there is no global agreement as to what is a good decision, i.e., whether a specific message is valid or not.

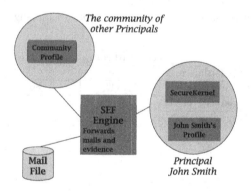

Fig. 5. The SECURE Evaluation Framework Configuration

The experimental set-up is illustrated in Figure 5. The environment models and evaluates mail messages sent to principal John Smith. The evaluation uses a fixed set of mail messages that are stored in the mail file. Each message is processed by the policies that are plugged into the SECURE kernel, where a classification is assigned. Each message is pre-tagged as SPAM or valid, and for each evaluation run profile, the accuracy of the results – $\mathcal{P}$ and $\mathcal{N}$ – is obtained by comparing the calculated SECURE classification to the pre-assigned SPAM tags of the messages.

The community profile of $\mathcal{E}_P$ being evaluated includes spoofing attacks, for sending SPAM and false recommendations. As mentioned in the previous section, the key attack scenarios of the profile concern the impact of false and insufficient recommendations as well as the impact of weak recognition.

The mail message file is compiled from the **SpamAssassin** benchmark [1]. We used the easy_ham and spam files, composed respectively of valid messages and SPAM messages, and randomly merged the contents into the benchmark. There are 3051 messages in the benchmark, of which 2551 are valid and 500 are SPAM. The messages are sent from a community of 846 different senders. Of these, 425 senders are spammers, and 51 are repeat offenders (send more than 1 SPAM message). The number of valid mail senders is 421. Of these, 213 are once-off message senders and 208 send more than one message.

Figure 6 shows the results for two profiles. There are four rows: the first row gives the number of correct classifications, and the second gives the percentage. The third and fourth rows give the breakdown on false positives and negatives respectively. The left column shows what happens when no SPAM filtering mechanism is used. Obviously, all SPAMs arrive in the Inbox, so the number of false negatives equals the number of SPAM messages in the benchmark. The second column considers the case where no recommendations are received, and where John Smith relies on his own observations. The most natural policy is to classify as SPAM any message received from a sender that previously sent SPAM – this is the learning effect brought by observations. For messages received from first time senders, the message will be classified as valid since no previous experience exists. $\mathcal{C}$ is the cost of observations – the number of messages received.

	No Filtering	Observations Only
Valid Classifications	2551	2626
Percentage	71.84%	86.07%
False Positive (FP)	0	0
False Negative (FN)	500	425

Fig. 6. Results when no filter is used, and when observations of previous spammers are taken into account

The main benefit of a trust framework is the exchange of evidence, though the evidence can be falsified. In Figures 7 and 8 we model the effect of recommendations on the result. We simulate the arrival of recommendations for all principals. Each column deals with a different truth factor t for recommendations, from 0 (all recommendations are false) in the left column to 1 in the right-most column (all recommendations are true). The factor increases by 0.1 in each column. The right-most column of Figure 7 resembles trust stability since all past behaviour is known, so we detect all spammers. The policy used by John Smith is to consult recommendations when he has no experience concerning an email sender: he prefers observations to recommendations. This explains why the validity is not so bad when all recommendations sent are false, i.e., his own observations act as a safety net against poor recommendations. This illustrates the importance of meta-trust, i.e., buddy principals in whom John Smith can trust for good recommendations. It shows that profiles with principal collusions are contained by this observation effect.

t	0	0.1	0.2	0.3	0.4	0.5	0.6	0.7	0.8	0.9	1.0
V	2205	2290	2375	2460	2545	2630	2715	2799	2883	2967	3051
%	72.27	75.06	77.84	80.63	83.42	86.2	88.99	91.74	94.49	97.25	100
FP	421	378	336	294	252	210	168	126	84	42	0
FN	425	383	340	297	254	211	168	126	84	42	0

Fig. 7. The correctness of the recommendations increase incrementally by 0.1

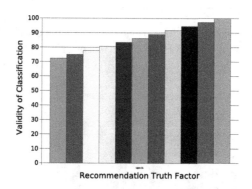

Fig. 8. Effect of recommendations - ranging from truth factors of 0 to 1 in units of 0.1

The result of the security decision is heavily dependent on the entity recognition confidence factor ER_C. John Smith is in a quandary if his ER component recognises a principal p but with a low confidence value. In such a case, he might not even be able to use his trust value for p.

We can expect two kinds of behaviour for John Smith with respect to ER_C. If the calculated factor is low, then he might assume that the ER is unable to recognise the principal, and simply classifies the message as SPAM or as valid. These two cases are termed Easy Reject (ER) and Easy Accept (EA) respectively, and we evaluated with threshold ER_C factors of 25%, 50%, 75% and 100%. An alternative approach is to take product of the trust value for the recognised p and the ER_C factor for p, and to classify a message if a threshold has been reached. If the threshold is not reached, the message can be classified as SPAM or as valid. We name these cases Statistical Reject (SR) and Statistical Accept (SA) respectively. We evaluated for threshold values of 25%, 50%, 75% and 100%. In all experiments, the messages received have a confidence factor randomly distributed between 10% and 100%. Results are shown in Figures 9 and 10. These confirm that the best decisions are made when both trust in a principal's recommendations and ER confidence values are used. The reason is that even if the ER_C factor is low, the possibility of a useful recommendation can help to avoid a valid message being classified as SPAM.

Tol	25	50	75	100	25	50	75	100
V	2539	2030	1252	742	2952	2851	2714	2614
%	83.22	66.54	41.04	24.32	96.76	93.44	88.95	85.68
FP	512	1021	1799	2309	0	0	0	0
FN	0	0	0	0	99	200	337	437
V	2903	2757	2513	2344	2958	2855	2719	2627
%	95.15	90.36	82.37	76.83	96.95	93.58	89.12	86.10
FP	148	294	538	707	0	0	0	0
FN	0	0	0	0	93	196	332	424

Fig. 9. The table is divided into four parts. The top left part models the Easy Reject (ER) policy and the top rightmost the Easy Accept (EA). The bottom left and right sub-tables implement the Statistical Reject (SR) and Statistical Accept (SA) policies

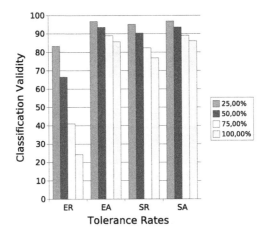

Fig. 10. Different treatments of Entity Recognition Confidence

5   Related Work

A quantitative approach for assessing the security properties of trust metrics is described in [16]; the authors describe an analytical evaluation approach, but only apply it to the graphs of trust relations. Our work in this paper completes this by assessing the security properties of the trust-based model as a whole by including aspects such as identity, trust life-cycle management and risk.

Massa and Bhattacharjee analyse a recommendation system in [13]. In particular, they consider the weaknesses of sparseness, cold start and vulnerability to fake reviews of items. Trust information can treat these issues, mainly since the sparseness level drops. Cold start users supply a friend's name. The mechanism is robust so long as fake users are not considered as friends.

Liu and Issarny present a recommendation distribution system and its evaluation in [12]. Recommendation is context-specific and evolves over time. The system is designed to overcome free-riders (principals that do not share recommendations), defamation attacks (propagation of incorrectly low recommendation values) and collusion attacks (propagation of incorrectly high recommendation values). The experiments indicate that the reputation adapts correctly to these attacks. Like for [13], the validation criteria proposed include validity (ability to distinguish between honest and dishonest principals), timeliness or response, robustness under attacks and resource economical. The evaluation is thus with respect to a single component – aspects such as trust in principal recognition and policy expression. More importantly, the evaluation does not link the recommendation system to the strength of a security process that employs it.

Other researchers have attempted to evaluate the mapping between trust model and actual human intuitions of trust by psychological experiment [9, 10]. Their results so far are very insightful concerning to how humans really do *trust*, but as yet not detailed enough to really give much guidance to designers of computational trust systems.

6   Conclusion

This paper discussed the evaluation of the SECURE framework, along with a methodology for evaluating trust-based frameworks. We believe that it is important to distinguish the evaluation of security, from the evaluation of the trust subsystem and of other components, and to clearly delimit the role and functionality of each component. A meaningful analysis is otherwise not possible.

Our own work on evaluation is continuing. One further area of investigation is another application that uses SECURE ; we currently have an eBay-like application in mind. The community profile of this application differs from the SPAM filter since cheating requires collaboration, so the key attack scenarios change.

References

1. Spamassassin, http://spamassassin.apache.org.
2. Ross J. Anderson. *Security Engineering — A Guide to Building Dependable Distributed Systems*. John Wiley & Sons, 2001.
3. Matt Blaze, Joan Feigenbaum, and Jack Lacy. Decentralized Trust Management. Technical Report 96-17, DIMACS, June 28 1996.
4. V. Cahill and etal. Using Trust for Secure Collaboration in Uncertain Environments. In *IEEE Pervasive*, volume 2(3), pages 52–61. IEEE, April 2003.

5. Nathan Dimmock, Jean Bacon, David Ingram, and Ken Moody. Trust-based access control model. EU IST-FET SECURE Project Deliverable, September 2004.

6. John R. Douceur and Judith S. Donath. The Sybil Attack. February 22 2002.

7. Hector Garcia-Molina, Mario T. Schlosser, and Sepandar D. Kamvar. The Eigen-Trust Algorithm for Reputation Management in P2P Networks, November 18 2002.

8. Li Gong. *Inside Java 2 Platform Security*. The Java Series. Addison Wesley, 1999.

9. Catholijn M. Jonker, Joost J. P. Schalken, Jan Theeuwes, and Jan Treur. Human Experiments in Trust Dynamics. In *Proceedings of the 2nd International Conference on Trust Management, LNCS 2995*, pages 206–220, March 2004.

10. Tim Kindberg, Abigail Sellen, and Erik Geelhoed. Security and Trust in Mobile Interactions: A Study of Users' Perceptions and Reasoning. In *Proceedings of the Sixth International Conference on Ubiquitous Computing (UbiComp 2004)*, 2004.

11. Butler Lampson and Ronald L. Rivest. SDSI – A Simple Distributed Security Infrastructure. Technical report, July 26 1996.

12. J. Liu and V. Issarny. Enhanced Reputation Mechanism for Mobile Ad Hoc Networks. In *Proceedings of the 2nd International Conference on Trust Management, LNCS 2995*, pages 48–62, March 2004.

13. Paolo Massa and Bobby Bhattacharjee. Using Trust in Recommender Systems: an Experimental Analysis. In *Proceedings of the 2nd International Conference on Trust Management, LNCS 2995*, pages 48–62, March 2004.

14. Jean-Marc Seigneur, Nathan Dimmock, Ciaran Bryce, and Christian Jensen. Combating SPAM with Trustworthy Email Addresses. In *Proceedings of the 2nd International Conference on Privacy, Security and Trust*, pages 228–229, New Brunswick, June 9–19 2004. ACM Press.

15. Jean-Marc Seigneur and Christian Damsgaard Jensen. Privacy Recovery with Disposable Email Addresses. *IEEE Security & Privacy*, 1(6):35–39, November/December 2003.

16. Andrew Twigg and Nathan Dimmock. Attack Resistance of Computational Trust Models. In *IEEE International Workshops on Enabling Technologies: Infrastructure for Collaborative Enterprises — Enterprise Security*, pages 281–282, June 2003.

17. Waleed Wagealla, Sotirios Terzis, Colin English, and Paddy Nixon. Simulation-based Assessment and Validation for the SECURE Collaboration Model. Technical report, University of Strathcylde, 2005.

18. Li Xiong and Ling Liu. A Reputation-based Trust Model for Peer-to-Peer Ecommerce Communities. In *Proceedings of the 4th ACM Conference on Electronic Commerce (EC-03)*, pages 228–229, New York, June 9–12 2003. ACM Press.

19. Nicola Zannone. A Survey on Trust Management Languages. Technical report, University of Verona, August 01 2004.

Trusted Computing: Strengths, Weaknesses and Further Opportunities for Enhancing Privacy

Siani Pearson

Hewlett-Packard Laboratories, Bristol, BS34 8QZ. UK
Siani.Pearson@hp.com

Abstract. This paper assesses how trusted computing technology can enhance privacy, both in the short and long term, and provides a variety of examples. In addition, potential negative privacy implications are assessed and outstanding issues are highlighted that need to be addressed before trusted computing could be provided in a privacy-friendly manner within the consumer space.

1 Introduction

Open networks are a fact of modern life, giving us all the advantages of connectivity but also bringing heightened security risks. Once our computers start communicating with each other, it is very difficult to know if they are behaving as we expect. We continuously expose our infinitely reprogrammable computers to the Internet and download and process arbitrary data all the time. Who can really say that they know what's going on in their computer? And how can they be sure that their privacy is being protected?

This should be of major concern to those of us who want to maintain control over our identity, maintaining personal freedom, and guard against increased fraud. And it applies across a whole range of domains from e-commerce to e-government, because just as the amount of on-line information is increasing exponentially there is a correspondingly growing need to ensure that these new technologies benefit people and organizations to their full potential, while protecting their privacy. Moreover, data privacy is an enabler for any future business, addressing both on- and off-line data about individuals.

So what is the nature of current threats against our privacy? As considered further in Section 2, current privacy technologies tend to focus on giving the user greater anonymity and control over the use of their data. On-line privacy breaches can vary a great deal in scope, but in this paper I focus on the following:

User profiling: compilation of information about someone, perhaps involving the abuse of cookies on their machine, tracking their behaviour, and/or distribution of the resultant profiles to third parties without the consent or even knowledge of that person.

IT insecurity: for example, Trojan horses, viruses, or software bugs that can expose secrets.

P. Herrmann et al. (Eds.): iTrust 2005, LNCS 3477 pp. 305 – 320, 2005.

In this article I suggest ways of helping address these problems using trusted computer technology [13]. As described more fully in Section 3, the term 'trusted computing' can apply to a range of similar technologies for developing 'more secure' computing platforms in a cost-effective way. At best, this is only a partial solution to the privacy problem, because there are some business issues it is unlikely to address (such as unwanted marketing or being forced to give personal information to obtain a service). In addition, there are numerous classes of technical problems that are not addressed by trusted computer technology, such as spyware, adware, keystroke loggers, network sniffers, and wireless interception. Moreover, in being a technical approach it does not help address relative privacy threats, for example which may involve employer rights, local legal frameworks, and so on, or involve abuse of personal information that is provided voluntarily.

Trusted computer technology has been seen by some as a threat to privacy and freedom; however I argue that it also has tremendous potential for enhancing and protecting privacy. This is an important aspect of this new technology that has not been fully appreciated to date. For example, trusted (computing) platforms can be used to provide many pseudonymous identities, each of which nevertheless inherit the trustworthiness of the basic platform, hardware protection for secrets and independent mechanisms for verifying the trustworthiness of users' own systems and those they interact with. I assess counterarguments that are based on misconceptions, and highlight where there are still further privacy-related issues to be resolved before such technology should be applied.

The paper includes the following: a brief overview of current privacy-enabling technology; an assessment of how trusted computing platform technology can enhance privacy; consideration of privacy enhancing safeguards of trusted computing technology; analysis and examples of how such building blocks can be used; an assessment of the potential negative privacy implications of trusted computing; concluding remarks.

2   Current Privacy-Enabling Technologies

Various solutions are already available for enhancing users' on-line privacy, but with the advance of technology, these will soon fall far short of providing comprehensive, cheap, scalable solutions for real-world use. Current privacy-enabling tools include cryptographically secured protocols (for example, to encrypt credit card information during transit when an on-line purchase is being made), digital certificates, cookie management software, privacy policy languages (most notably P3P – Platform for Privacy Preferences) and infomediaries that allow users to surf the web in such a way that destination sites do not acquire personally identifiable information. In addition, various anonymising techniques are currently being developed such as mix cascades and anonymous authentication protocols. There are also techniques for carrying out data mining and database queries in a privacy-friendly way, as well as enterprise privacy auditing and enforcement of user privacy preferences at the back end. In addition there are specialised privacy techniques applicable to particular areas such as biometrics and radio frequency identity tags (RFID). Detailed discussion of these techniques is out of the scope of this paper, but the reader is referred to [2] for comprehensive details of current techniques.

As we shall see in the following section, trusted computing technology has particular relevance to the provision of anonymity or pseudonymity ('reversible anonymity') and to security-related features and its approach includes some similar aspects to the following separate mechanisms for providing pseudonymity:

- *The use of a third party* trusted by the user to act as a mediator, vouching for the user or their computing device but removing any information identifying the user.
- *Digital pseudonyms* being public keys for testing digital signatures where the holder of the pseudonym can prove holdership by forming a digital signature using the corresponding private key. Such keys could be bound to attributes within digital certificates to form *attribute certificates*.
- *Proof of knowledge protocols* (such as those developed by Chaum [5] and Brands [1]) that provide credentials whose inspection the holder actively participates in, proving entitlement to the credential without revealing any persistent information.

3 How Trusted Computing Platform Technology Can Enhance Privacy

Computer platforms are central to electronic business and commerce, and the need for information protection is increasing, not least on client platforms. However, the degree of confidence in software-only security solutions depends on their correct installation and execution, which can be affected by all other software that has been executed on the same platform. Trusted hardware provides a reliable foundation to protect against software attacks, without the danger that the foundation will itself be modified by a non-physical attack without being able to detect this.

These factors, combined with increasing privacy issues and emerging e-business opportunities that demand higher levels of confidence, have led the industry-wide *Trusted Computing Platform Alliance* (TCPA) (and now its successor the *Trusted Computing Group* (TCG)) to design and develop specifications for computing platforms [13;14] that create a foundation of trust for software processes, based on a small amount of hardware. TCG has adopted all the TCPA specifications, and so for consistency we shall henceforth refer to TCG technology.

The only trusted platforms on the market today are the first generation of products that incorporate this standard hardware solution; these only provide very limited functionality (protected storage) with little support from the operating system and without secure boot. They prevent someone trawling the hard disk to find keys if your computer is lost (since this information is stored in an encrypted form) but only provide a standard protection for direct physical attack, dependent upon the degree of tamper-resistance provided. The current solutions are only for laptop and desktop PCs, but other types of trusted platform are likely to be available shortly.

Allied protected computing environments under development by certain manufacturers and open source operating systems such as Linux can support TCG facilities further and allow their widespread and convenient use. Intel's LaGrande hardware and chipset modifications [7] are designed to provide access-protected memory, and give greater support to secure operating systems. Microsoft's Next-Generation Secure Computing Base (NGSCB), formerly known as Palladium, is a secure computing environment that can run in parallel with Windows [9]. It provides additional protection beyond that defined by the TCG specification, including some protection of the video output and keyboard input. All these different types of platform are trusted platforms; they differ in that some are designed to be backwards compatible with existing platforms and others include enhanced security features and hardened infrastructure and hence a greater level of trustworthiness, but all of them accord to the basic underlying philosophy of trusted platforms, as espoused in [13] and considered further below.

3.1 What Is "Trusted Computing" About?

As illustrated in Figure 1, trusted computing addresses some central concerns of people using PCs: it protects data that is stored on those machines (even while they are interacting with other machines over the Internet) and it aims to put everyone in the position where they can feel confident that they can:

- Protect their data
- Find out whether their platform is in a trustworthy state
- Have the means to decide whether it is reasonable for them to trust other platforms

Fig. 1. What is 'trusted computing' about?

But what exactly is the nature of this 'trust'? Broadly speaking, the view taken by the proponents of trusted computing (see for example [13]) is that we can think of something as being trusted if it operates in the expected manner for a particular purpose, or can be relied upon to signal clearly if it does not. (For a discussion of how this approach relates to a broader understanding of trust, see [12].) Within the platform is a "root of trust" – the ultimate layer of the actual device that can be trusted intrinsically, and can report on other aspects of the system. Such a root of trust is missing from existing computers; there is no obvious way to check if the system is running correctly, as expected, and has not been deliberately or inadvertently tampered with in some way. In TCG technology, the "root of trust" takes the form of a cost-effective security hardware device (roughly equivalent to a smart card chip) known as a *Trusted Platform Module* (TPM). The TPM, as described in the TCG specifications [13;14], is tamper-resistant and has cryptographic functionality. It is a passive chip that is only called by other hardware; for the full range of functionality to be available, a secure BIOS (boot block) is needed, together with special processes that dynamically collect evidence of the platform's behaviour and provide evidence of its behaviour.

Basically, a trusted platform is an open computer platform that has been modified to maintain privacy using a trusted component. It does this by:

- reporting on the platform integrity
- protecting private and secret data and identity information against subversion
- attesting to the properties of the platform to a challenging party while maintaining anonymity (if required)

Proof that a platform is a genuine trusted platform is provided by cryptographic attestation identities. Each identity is created on the individual trusted platform, with attestation from a Public Key Infrastructure (PKI) Certification Authority (Privacy-CA), which is an organisation chosen by the user to return pseudonyms for the platform. To obtain attestation from a CA, the platform's owner sends the CA information that proves that the identity was generated on a genuine trusted platform. This process uses signed certificates from the manufacturer of the platform and uses a secret endorsement key installed in the Trusted Platform Module (TPM). That secret is known only to the TPM and is used only under the control of the owner of the platform. In particular, it is not divulged to arbitrary third parties. The platform owner may choose different CAs to certify each TPM identity in order to prevent correlation. As we discuss further below, a more recent option allows the platform owner to obtain attestation identities without the issuing CA knowing their platform's identity. For further information about trusted computing see [10].

3.2 Building Blocks for Privacy

Trusted computing provides the following key features, based on the basic functionalities described above, that provide building blocks for privacy:

- *protection for users' secrets*: 'protected storage' functionality binds secrets to a platform and can even prevent the revelation of secrets unless the software state is approved.

- *potential for remote trust*: users or enterprises can recognise that a platform has known properties and identify that a system will behave as expected. The technology can for example allow users to trust the platform in front of them to handle their banking or medical data.

In essence, these features allow privacy-protecting software, like any other software, to be more certain about the software environment under which it is running and to utilise more secure storage for private data and secrets.

Lurid media reports may refer to a TCG device as a spy-in-the-box, covertly gathering and reporting information on the user to the unprincipled giant corporation, and incidentally ensuring that only their products are compatible with the system. But with appropriate industry-agreed safeguards the reverse can be the case: the device can guarantee certain privacy and security aspects in the on-line marketplace and be broadly compatible with all products and systems. It is therefore vitally important that appropriate safeguards are agreed and introduced.

4 Privacy Enhancing Safeguards

Various fundamental privacy-enhancing safeguards are integral to the TCG specifications, as follows.

4.1 Owner Control

Ultimate control over activation and the functionality of the TPM must be given to the platform owner, and users can deactivate it if desired. Also, the TCG organisation does not endorse any particular supplier or certifier of TCG-compliant hardware or software, nor does it provide such a role itself; notably, the choice of software to be run on a platform is entirely under the owner's control.

4.2 TCG Pseudonymous Identities

The TCG specification deliberately does not include attempts to identify which platform is making statements or communicating; instead it prefers to allow the use of attributes or credentials and gives the communicating entity better reason to trust these attributes. There is no need to have a single stable identity across transactions, thereby avoiding the privacy-related pitfalls of having a unique identity (which has affected some previous technologies). The only cryptographic key that is permanently associated with the TPM (the endorsement key) is designed to never sign or encrypt data, in order that an outside observer will not see anything traceable back to that TPM, and is only used to decrypt the response from a Privacy-CA within the TPM identity creation process.

TCG platform attestation therefore protects users against correlation and tracking of their activities as follows:

- TCG provides for the TPM to have control over "multiple pseudonymous attestation identities"

- There is no need for any identity to contain owner or user related information, since it is a platform identity to attest to platform properties.
- The identity creation protocol allows the choice of different Privacy-CAs to certify each TPM identity, and thus helps prevent correlation of such identities.

The origin of a specific identity cannot be tracked further, except by the Certification Authority (CA) that issues a certificate for that attestation identity. So appropriate selection of CAs enables the owner to control traceability from an attestation identity to the certificates that attest to a specific TPM and a specific platform. Identities can only be correlated with other identities by the CA that certifies these identities – and the owner chooses that CA (admittedly, negotiation with the communication partner may be needed to find a CA that is trusted by both parties). So the owner can choose a CA whose policy is not to correlate identities, or whose policy is to correlate identities, according to the wishes of the owner. Different identities are used for different purposes and in particular, separate identities would usually be given to different users of the trusted platform.

The latest version of the TCG specification [14] includes the option of using a zero-knowledge protocol to obtain platform identities; this enables a CA to issue identity certificates without having to see platform credentials.

4.3 Data Protection

Each user's data can be kept private such that even the platform owner or administrator cannot access that data without the necessary access data. Furthermore, the revelation of secrets can be prevented unless the software is in an approved state. (However, as mentioned above in Section 3, only a standard protection against direct physical attack is provided).

The TCG specifications have been designed in full support of data protection legislation. For instance, if you are handling personal data, you need to have reasonable assurances about the software you are using that handles these data, and trusted computing helps provide this. As a platform for *handling* personal data, a trusted platform allows you to comply more effectively with the requirement to handle Personally Identifying Information (PII), or other types of sensitive personal data, in a suitably secure manner. By effectively isolating certain classes of data from the rest of the system, you can significantly reduce the risk that such protected data will 'leak' to, or be actively 'stolen' by, other software. In addition, you want to minimise the personal data that is revealed, and as we have seen the TCG specification deliberately minimises both the potential for identifying a platform across multiple uses, and the use of identifying data.

5 How Can These Building Blocks Be Used?

We have seen that trusted computing provides useful building blocks for privacy, but additional mechanisms such as identity management will need to be used in addition in order to provide a complete privacy solution.

5.1 Properties and Enhancements

Broadly speaking, trusted platforms provide the following properties, which are useful for a range of services including electronic business, corporate infrastructure security and e-government:

1. **recognizing that a platform has known properties, both locally and remotely.** This is useful in scenarios such as deciding whether to allow mobile platform access to a corporate network and providing remote access via a known public access point.
2. **identifying that a system will behave as expected, both locally and remotely.** Again, this property can be exploited in order to allow mobile access to a corporate network only with appropriate security measures (e.g. firewall and antivirus requirements) or to verify the integrity of a service provider platform.
3. **enabling a user to have more confidence in the behaviour of the platform in front of them.** In particular, users can have more trust in a platform to handle private data. A trusted platform helps provide assurances about software that handles personal data or personally identifying data in a suitably secure manner.

Specifically, the following enhancements provide greater confidence in protection of private data:

- Increasing users' confidence about their data residing on the server: It becomes possible not only to store personal data on the server more safely but also for the data owner to restrict the conditions under which that data can be used (more specifically, to specify appropriate software environments in which the data can be used or exposed). An example of where this would be useful would be in healthcare, where, say, a patient may need to send details of medication to a doctor in order to receive advice, but they would want to be assured that this information would be adequately protected within the on-line medical system.

- Confidence in an appropriate form of data being disclosed: The amount and type of data disclosed could be dependent upon the perceived trustworthiness of the receiving party. For example, data could be generalised, sent with policy conditions attached or not sent at all.

- Checking for appropriate treatment of data: Enforcing privacy policies via an extension of TCG software verification: it is possible to check that there is appropriate technology for enforcing policies on a remote platform before making the associated information available. This is particularly relevant in multi-party scenarios where there needs to be privacy-related controls over how sensitive or personal information is passed around between the involved entities. This could be the case in federated identity management (cf. arranging a holiday via a travel agent), or in on-line e-commerce involving multiple parties (cf. buying a book that needs to be delivered to your address).

- <u>Preventing disclosure of personal data or secrets in an adverse software environment</u>: Integrity metrics relating to the server platform could be sent to the user when authorisation was needed, so that the user could assess trustworthiness of the server platform before making a decision of whether to authorise the key. TCG technology provides a special wrapping process that allows the authorised owner of a secret to state the software environment that must exist in the platform before the secret will be unwrapped by the TPM. This allows prevention of disclosure of customers' data and other confidential data or secrets stored on the server in an adverse software environment. Such an environment might masquerade as a safe software environment, and in particular enable undesirable access to, alteration of or copying of the data.

TCG technology not only allows existing applications to benefit from enhanced security but also can encourage the development of new applications or services that require higher security levels than are presently available. Applications and services that would benefit include electronic cash, email, hot-desking (allowing mobile users to share a pool of computers), platform management, single sign-on (enabling the user to authenticate himself or herself just once when using different applications during the same work session), virtual private networks, Web access, and digital content delivery. In general, applications which would benefit from trusted computing technology, as opposed to other secure hardware solutions with enhanced OS, are those that need the properties described above, provided in a cost-effective manner without the need for cryptographic acceleration or physical security.

5.2 Example Applications

This section considers some examples of how trusted computing technology might be applied in the future. The examples build from the more straightforward to the less obvious, but no less promising applications; however, the need for a secure OS probably makes examples three and four unrealistic in the short term.

In order to make use of trusted computing, it is not necessary that all the communicating computers are trusted computers. Firstly, it is not necessary to be a trusted computer in order to challenge a trusted computer and to analyse the resulting integrity metrics, although it helps to verify this on a trusted computer, since one might have more confidence in the result. Secondly, it is not necessary to use a trusted computer to produce pseudonymous identities (although the provision of such identities is a useful feature of trusted computers); in any case the trusted hardware can be used to generate new key pairs such that the private part is never exposed outside the trusted hardware and identity certificates can be created that bind the public part of such key pairs to privileges, authority or attributes of users. Trusted computers provide additional useful functionality in the form of protected storage and remote verification (aka integrity checking). Hence, depending upon the service model or application, it could be of benefit to have the clients and/or severs as being trusted platforms.

Example One – Controlling Remote Access to Corporate Networks

Imagine that an employee wants to connect to his or her corporate network to read their email, either from their laptop in a hotel room or from a PC in an internet café. The company might adopt the policy that the machine must prove that it is in a trusted state. Part of this proof is that it is a trusted platform, in order that it can measure and report the state of the platform reliably. The platform could also have to demonstrate that appropriate security precautions such as current anti-virus software were running, as would comply to the company policy.

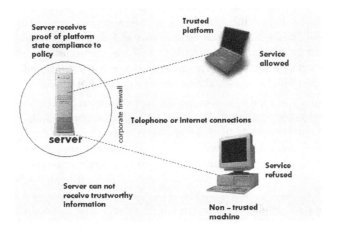

Fig. 2. Remote access

Example Two – Privacy-Enhanced Insurance

In order to satisfy the goal of putting users in control of their Personally Identifiable Information (PII), and to avoid privacy infringements when gathering customer information, we can design architectures such that there is selective disclosure and generalization of attributes based on the trustworthiness of the receiver. Notably, platform integrity information could be included within such an assessment. If someone wants to provide high confidence in digital signatures they use while protecting their anonymity, pseudonymous TCG identity keys can be used to vouch for TP signing keys (by 'certifying' those keys), and these may incorporate information about the software state of the platform into their value. This approach can be used for example in various types of e-commerce model in which a buyer or supplier makes anonymous bids and reveals its true identity only after a bid has been accepted in principle, or reveals only the minimum amount of information necessary at each stage of the transaction.

One such architecture in the field of insurance is illustrated in Figure 3. Presently, when a person applies for insurance (e.g. life, motor, holiday, etc.) they fill in a form revealing their true identity and documenting the necessary information for a premium to be derived. The procedure is not transparent from the user's point of view. Does the insurance company make its decision simply on the advertised criteria (e.g. age, gender, make of vehicle, in the case of car insurance), or do they make additional checks on the buyer's identity that are not advertised and are possibly illegal? Some examples of when this might happen are as follows:

1) If in the future all or part of our genomes are individually sequenced and illegally held, an insurer might furtively access such information even though they advertise insurance where such information is not required.
2) Perhaps an insurer might refuse car insurance to someone with a criminal record even if it was not an advertised criterion for deciding a premium.

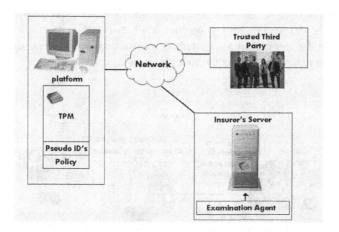

Fig. 3. Privacy-enhanced insurance

Many other possibilities exist, such as an insurer checking credit rating, shopping patterns and other personal information that is increasingly becoming available in large databases.

To limit such profile building and misuse of PII, people could apply for insurance through a pseudonymous identity, giving the requested information and no more. A pseudonymous user identity (perhaps created for that particular purpose) can be associated with selected policy attributes from a user policy, and it is only these selected attributes (possibly generalized to ranges etc.) that are made available to the insurer. Other attributes, including the real identity of the user, are 'hidden'. If a claim is made under the policy, the person could reveal their true identity and prove that the details given pseudonymously were correct at that time. Alternatively, a trusted third party could validate the information at the time of application for an insurance policy. Figure 3 shows an example of how this process could work, using trusted software agents on both the client and server side.

Software whose integrity is attested by trusted platform mechanisms could vouch to both sides that the process of selective disclosure and generalization of attributes has been carried out properly [11]. The TPM protects this mechanism via software authentication and also can protect policies and secrets. The model still provides some benefit if there is a trusted server only, because users can still check that the server will protect their information and operate as expected.

Note that if desired, the identity of the applicant need *never* be divulged to the insurance company since for example a trusted third party could vouch that the applicant satisfies the criteria for insurance, or did satisfy them at the time of application.

Example Three – Untraceable Digital Cash

With an extremely secure implementation of TCG, untraceable and pseudonymous digital cash could be achieved without the need for complicated or inefficient cryptographic protocols, as follows. The user has an account of digital cash (sometimes called a digital "wallet") that is stored in secure storage, and a trusted program is in control of the user's account, such that it is not possible for any other software to change the value of the cash stored in the account. (The secure implementation would need to provide secure communication channels between the program and the account and guard against 'replay' attacks attempting to utilize backup and data restoration mechanisms to replenish the account to a previous higher value.)

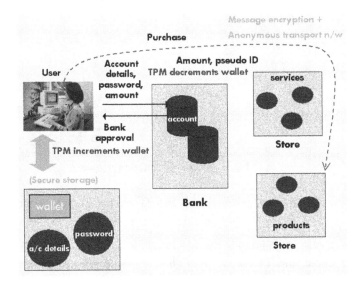

Fig. 4. Digital cash

When the user wants to load the account, then the trusted program just needs to send the user's bank account details and some other form of identification such as an account-related password (which are also stored in secure storage) to the bank. Once the bank approves the withdrawal, the program can increment the account accordingly. Similarly, the program will decrement the account when the user wishes to make a payment. All such communication would be carried out using an anonymous transport network (e.g. using mix cascades [3]) and using encryption of messages, for example via TLS (Transport Layer Security).

Integrity checks are used to insure that the client, bank and recipient bank platforms are trusted platforms in a trustworthy state (with the integrity of the trusted programs in tact), to guard against cheating. Trusted computing technology also increases trustworthiness of likely auxiliary measures such as OS compartmentalization and Chaum observers [4].

Example Four – Protection Against Game Cheating

Internet technology has made it possible for games players to engage in interactive games with other players who are geographically remote from them. Indeed, several companies make money at present by hosting servers running real time interactive games that have multiple players playing against each others, and the monetary value of the winners' prizes may be quite significant. The problem is that a cheating player can have an unfair advantage over fellow players and exploit this to win the game. Cheating is possible because, in general, games engines are written so that a given game can be added to by other programmers in order to add extra levels and hence provide a more interesting gaming experience for the game players, but this also allows software 'patches' to be applied in order to modify operation of the game and specifically to be applied locally to make a participant's game easier to play.

How may this be countered in such a way that people's privacy is protected as much as possible? Trusted computing allows the performance of a participant to be validated by means of issuing a challenge to the participant's computer to determine whether it is trustworthy, and if it is then testing the integrity of the games software running on the participant's computer. By these means a game's provider can detect the presence of software augmenting a player's performance and thereby remove such a player from the game.

6   Potential Negative Privacy Implications of Trusted Computing

The type of techniques I describe can be applied to benefit users in a variety of situations. They can also be applied to benefit corporations, sometimes at the expense of users' freedoms. It is this latter case that is often highlighted (and sometimes exaggerated) within recent publicity about trusted computing, but there is bound to be a spectrum of opinion about trusted computing technology largely depending upon the standpoint or vested interests of the holders. For a précis of a recent debate about trusted computing, see [15]. It is true that technical and legal solutions to such privacy issues are less well developed than for the enterprise space, largely because consumer issues are not the initial focus for TCG. However, for this very reason there is still time to engage in such a debate and it is important that we do so, particularly because privacy concerns are very relevant at the user level.

Much of the public discussion about trusted computing is demonstrably factually incorrect, or coloured by people's worst fears – hardly surprising when there is a new technology or initial lack of information. Popular misconceptions include that the technology cannot be disabled and that unapproved, uncertified and open-source software cannot run on a trusted platform.

This is not to deny that there are problematic aspects for the consumer space. Trusted computing does provide a building block for privacy, as considered above, but it is only a building block and not a complete solution. Most notably, when you apply for credentials, you might reasonably need to provide personal information (as in the case of insurance), and this could be passed on to others. Whether any personal data is required by a given Privacy-CA when it issues a pseudonym is a matter for that Privacy-CA to decide. The TCG specification makes no such requirement:

national legislation may (in different jurisdictions) either prohibit or mandate such linkage.

Probably the most important objection to trusted computing that is commonly made is against customer lock-in via 'trusted' applications. As with any technology, and especially one which is powerful enough to provide high levels of protection against accidental and malicious disclosure, there is potential for commercial abuse in that a content provider or software supplier might require a user to provide excessive personally identifying data, or to use only 'approved' software that is not produced by competitors. The TCG specification does not give a controlling position to any particular commercial body, but this is only part of the solution. Any such abuse of market dominance needs to be prevented using relevant laws and agreements, including anti-monopoly and data protection legislation, and it is important that this does happen.

Concerns have also been voiced in the public arena about the potential use of trusted computing for:

- *remote censorship*: This should not be a major issue since TCG does not help at all with deleting selected files on other platforms and in order to find them, the owner of a trusted platform would have to agree to the appropriate measurements being made and in any case such a comparison could be easily subverted by storing the same content in a slightly modified way.
- *increased tracking of users, even to the extent of 'spying' on users*: Trusted computing does not make the situation worse, so long as 'trusted' source code were published to show that tracking mechanisms were not secretly hidden. This is one of several good reasons why TCG-compliant open source software should be encouraged and supported.
- *loss of user control through having keys on the platform that are controlled by third parties:* I do not see a problem in the endorsement key pair being generated within the TPM. This is independently trustworthy and it is necessary to have some private key within the machine associated with an authorisation secret that can still be used in some restricted ways if the machine is compromised. The problem is rather that you need to trust that the key has been generated, or put in properly, and so we need to guard against the possibility of chip vendors storing the private key and modulus, even if they deny doing this.

There are two further outstanding issues related to privacy and personal choice, both of which are a long way from being resolved. These are:

1. *If you have a platform that provides you with mechanisms to protect your information, should a third party be able to use these mechanisms in your computer to protect their information from you?* This question is particularly contentious because of the issues that certain groups have with the use of Digital Rights Management (DRM), particularly in circumstances when the users affected do not want to be governed by such enforcement and may lose 'fair rights' usage as a result. For discussion of how fair use might be achieved when building DRM technologies on top of TCG, see [6]. Note however that TCG does not address DRM directly and it is certainly possible to carry out DRM without TCG. Concerns by anti-DRM proponents would be greatly reduced if it could be guaranteed that in

given situations output from applications belongs to the owner of the platform or user of the application rather than the application provider, and can always be accessed by the owner or user, using the viewer of their choice.

2. *How will the open-source community self-certify software, and will owners of commercial data trust that software?* The problem is essentially that if a data owner cares enough to protect his or her data, he or she would probably not want an arbitrarily modified software environment to operate on those data, yet should be able to choose to use open source products. Open source suppliers could certify certain software distributions, to say that these distributions will operate as they should, but this takes money and time, and restricts the revisions that can easily take place. Furthermore, there is the issue of whether owners of commercial data would trust such distributions to respect the use of those data. Related discussion is given in [8].

7 Conclusions

The first trusted computing platforms are already available for purchase and several more types will be appearing over the next few years. These are designed to be a cheap, exportable and ubiquitous way of improving the security of personal, corporate and government data.

However, trusted platforms are not yet intended for ordinary consumers. This paper aims to highlight how trusted platforms can, in the near future, provide building blocks for privacy and thereby bring widespread benefits for consumers.

Before this can be done, however, various unresolved issues need to be addressed. First of all, it must be acknowledged that trusted computing technology does not provide a complete privacy solution, even for those technological aspects of privacy that it can help enhance. In particular, mechanisms such as identity management and privacy policy specification and enforcement are needed as part of a solution (so that you can keep control over personal data once it has been released via the TPM, for instance), along with appropriate interpretation of current data protection principles, for example regarding the treatment of personal information given when applying for credentials. Secondly, development of open source TCG-compliant software and products needs to be encouraged. Thirdly, the potential for commercial abuse must be countered.

Trusted computing technologies can be used to provide better data protection and consumer control over Personally Identifiable Information (PII) [11]; however, similar technologies can be used for more controversial technologies such as Digital Rights Management (DRM). So, as with many other technologies, trusted computing could be used as a basis for applications or services that individuals might regard as desirable or otherwise. An analogy would be the telephone, which brings many benefits but can also be used for surveillance. Just as we would not think of surveillance as being the inspiration or a necessary part of telephony, we are liable to miss out on many potential benefits for individual users if we do not adopt the technology with appropriate safeguards.

In this article, various examples have been given of how rich the potential application of such trusted computers could be and how this may benefit users in a variety of circumstances. As with many technologies, trusted computing *could* be used for constraining applications or protection of proprietary interests. As such uses are inconsistent with users' needs, we may expect both market and regulatory pressures to direct that its use will instead focus on enhanced privacy and the benefits that increased trust of computers can bring to a wide variety of users. In order to do this, technical mechanisms, standards and laws are insufficient enough by themselves. These need to be developed in parallel, and in addition a political framework is needed in which to guide operation of such solutions.

Acknowledgements. The author is grateful for feedback and input from reviewers.

References

[1] S. Brands, "A Semi-Technical Overview of Digital Credentials", **International Journal on Information Security**, August 2002. Available via http://www.credentica.com.

[2] J.C. Cannon, **Privacy**, Addison-Wesley, 2004.

[3] D. Chaum, "Untraceable electronic mail, return addresses and digital pseudonyms", **Communication of ACM**, vol 24, no 2, February 1981.

[4] D. Chaum, "Security without Identification: Card Computers to make Big Brother Obsolete", **Communication of ACM**, vol 28, no. 10, pp. 1030-1044, 1985.

[5] D. Chaum, "Achieving Electronic Privacy", **Scientific American**, pp. 96-101, August 1992.

[6] J. Erickson, "Fair Use, DRM and Trusted Computing: Friends or Foes?", **Comm. of ACM**, November 2002.

[7] Intel, "LaGrande Technology Architectural Overview", September 2003. Available via http://www.intel.com/technology/security/downloads/LT_Arch_Overview.pdf.

[8] D. Kuhlmann, "On TCPA", **Financial Cryptography**, R.N. Wright (ed.), LNCS 2742, pp. 255-269, Springer-Verlag, Berlin, 2003.

[9] Microsoft, Next-Generation Secure Computing Base home page, http://www.microsoft.com/resources/ngscb.

[10] S. Pearson (ed.), **Trusted Computing Platforms**, Prentice Hall, 2002.

[11] S. Pearson, "A Trusted Method for Self-profiling in e-Commerce", **Trust, Reputation and Security: Theories and Practice**, R. Falcone et al. (eds.), LNAI 2631, pp. 177-193, Springer-Verlag, Berlin, 2003.

[12] S. Pearson, M. Casassa Mont and S. Crane, "Persistent and Dynamic Trust: Analysis and the Related Impact of Trusted Platforms", LNCS, Proceedings of iTrust 2005, ed. P. Herrmann, V. Issarny and S. Shiu, France, May 2005.

[13] Trusted Computing Group, **TCG Main Specification**, Version 1.1b, 2003. Available via http://www.trustedcomputinggroup.org.

[14] Trusted Computing Group, **TCG TPM Specification**, Version 1.2, 2003. Available via http://www.trustedcomputinggroup.org.

[15] M. Yung, "Trusted Computing Platforms: The Good, the Bad and the Ugly", **Financial Cryptography**, R.N. Wright (ed.), LNCS 2742, pp. 250-254, Springer-Verlag, Berlin, 2003.

Trust Transfer: Encouraging Self-recommendations Without Sybil Attack

Jean-Marc Seigneur[1], Alan Gray[1], and Christian Damsgaard Jensen[2]

[1] Trinity College Dublin, Ireland
Jean-Marc.Seigneur@trustcomp.org, Alan.Gray@cs.tcd.ie
[2] Technical University of Denmark, Lyngby, Denmark
Christian.Jensen@imm.dtu.dk

Abstract. Trading privacy for trust thanks to the linkage of pseudonyms has been proposed to mitigate the inherent conflict between trust and privacy. This necessitates fusionym, that is, the calculation of a unique trust value supposed to reflect the overall trustworthiness brought by the set of linked pseudonyms. In fact, some pieces of evidence may overlap and be overcounted, leading to an incorrect trust value. In this approach, self-recommendations are possible during the privacy/trust trade. However, this means that Sybil attacks, where thousands of virtual identities belonging to the same real-world entity recommend each other, are potentially easier to carry out, as self-recommendations are an integral part of the attack. In this paper, trust transfer is used to achieve safe fusionym and protect against Sybil attacks when pieces of evidence are limited to direct observations and recommendations based on the count of event outcomes. Trust transfer implies that recommendations move some of the trustworthiness of the recommending entity to the trustworthiness of the trustee. It is demonstrated and tailored to email anti-spam settings.

1 Introduction

According to Romano [15], trust is not multiple constructs that vary in meaning across contexts, but a single construct that varies in level across contexts. We adopt this position in this paper as well as her definition of trust:

"Trust is a subjective assessment of another's influence in terms of the extent of one's perceptions about the quality and significance of another's impact over one's outcomes in a given situation, such that one's expectation of, openness to, and inclination toward such influence provide a sense of control over the potential outcomes of the situation" [15].

Throughout this paper, we refer to trust in a given situation as *trust context*. Social research identifies three main types of trust [13]: interpersonal trust, based on past interactions with the trustee; dispositional trust, provided by the trustor's general disposition towards trust, independent of the trustee; and system trust, provided by external means such as insurance or laws. Depending on the situation, a high level of trust in one of these types can be sufficient to make the decision to trust. For example, when there is insurance against a negative outcome, or when the legal system acts as a credible deterrent against undesirable behaviour, it means that the level of system trust is high and the level of risk is negligible - therefore the levels of interpersonal

P. Herrmann et al. (Eds.): iTrust 2005, LNCS 3477, pp. 321–337, 2005.

and dispositional trust are less important. It is usually assumed that by knowing the link to the real-world identity, there is insurance against harm that may be done by this entity: in essence, this is security based on authenticated identity. In this case, the level of system trust seems to be high but one may argue that in practice the legal system does not provide a credible deterrent against undesirable behaviour, e.g., it makes no sense to sue someone for a single spam email, as the effort expended to gain redress outweighs the benefit. In this paper, we focus on scenarios where the level of system trust is low. Dispositional trust is reflected in the user setting manually general trust values (for example, for newcomers) and the chosen risk policy (that is, how the user is disposed towards accepting risk). Interpersonal trust is represented as a computed *trust value*. A trust value, that is the digital representation of the trustworthiness or level of trust in the entity under consideration, can be seen as a non-enforceable estimate of the entity's future behaviour in a given context based on past evidence. The basic components of a computational trust engine (depicted in Figure 1) should expose a decision-making component that is invoked when a requested entity has to decide what action should be taken with respect to a request made by another entity, the requesting entity.

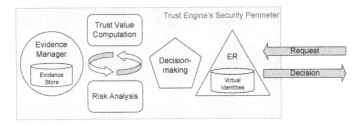

Fig. 1. High-level View of a Trust Engine

In order to make the decision to grant the request, two sub-components are needed:

- a trust module that can dynamically assess the trustworthiness of the requesting entity based on pieces of evidence (such as, observations or recommendations);
- a risk module that can dynamically evaluate the risk involved in the interaction.

The chosen action should maintain the appropriate cost/benefit ratio. Depending on dispositional trust and system trust, the weight of the trust value in the final decision may be small.

In the background, another component is in charge of gathering evidence (for example, recommendations or comparisons between expected outcomes of the chosen actions and real outcomes). This evidence is used to update risk and trust information. Thus, trust and risk follow a managed life-cycle. The Entity Recognition (ER [16]) module is in charge of recognising the interacting entities, called virtual identities or pseudonyms.

There is an inherent conflict between trust and privacy because both depend on knowledge about an entity, albeit in opposite ways. Trust is based on knowledge about the other entity: the more evidence about past behaviour is known, the better the prediction of future behaviour should be. However, the more one entity knows about another, the less privacy they have. Although trust allows us to accept risk and engage in actions with a potentially harmful outcome, a computational trust engine must take into account that humans need (or have the right to) privacy. We believe that it is therefore important that any trust engine supports privacy. This is why we have proposed to use pseudonymity as a level of indirection at the identity layer [16], which allows the formation of trust without exposing the real-world identity. It is sufficient to recognise a virtual identity to build trust on past interactions.

However, depending on what benefits can be reaped through trustworthiness, people may be willing to trade part of their privacy for increased trustworthiness: hence, contextual *privacy/trust trade* is possible in our model for privacy/trust trade based on linkage of pieces of evidence [16]. If insufficient evidence is available under the chosen pseudonym, more evidence may be linked to this pseudonym in order to improve trustworthiness and grant the request. In our model, a protocol is given for explicitly disclosing to the requested entity that some evidence can be linked. Some thresholds should be set concerning the acceptable evidence that should be disclosed. An algorithm is used to ensure the *Minimal Linkability principle* [16] – no more evidence than needed to create the link is taken into account.

It may be beneficial to make the link between some pseudonyms explicit (for example, to avoid discounted evidence or reduce the time to reach trustworthiness due to division of evidence between pseudonyms). However, care should be taken when linked evidence on multiple pseudonyms is assessed. The most important requirement is to avoid counting the same evidence twice when it is presented as part of two different pseudonyms or overcounting overlapping evidence. This is especially true when pseudonyms are linked during the privacy trade/process. A *fusionym* is the result of linking two or more pseudonyms together, based on some proof of their linkage, so that they can be regarded as a single pseudonym whose overall trust value is calculated based on the pieces of evidence associated with each composing pseudonym.

The solution to calculating the correct trust value for fusionym proposed in this paper works under the following assumptions:

- the trust value is based on direct observations or recommendations of the count of event outcomes from one specific entity; reputation from a number of unidentified entities and credentials generally used in credential-based trust management [18] are not covered by the solution described in this paper;
- the *link* function is only used for linkage at the level of pseudonyms (p): $link(p_1,...,p_n)$ for n linked pseudonyms; the linkage is supposed perfect, unconditionally true and proven by some means beyond the scope of this paper (such as cryptographic signatures, as in [16]);
- a pseudonym can neither be compromised nor spoofed; an attacker can neither take control of a pseudonym nor send spoofed recommendations;
- everyone is free to introduce as many pseudonyms as they wish;
- all messages are assumed to be signed and time stamped.

The next section describes how to achieve safe fusionym based on direct observations and discusses issues introduced by allowing recommendations. Section 3 explains how we use trust transfer to achieve safe fusionym whilst encouraging self-recommendations. The trust transfer approach is tailored to the email and anti-spam sphere in Section 4. Section 5 surveys related work and Section 6 draws conclusions.

2 Fusionym

First we give the formula for the calculation of a fusionym trust value based only on direct observations. We then discuss the issues associated with the use of recommendations in decentralised systems using pseudonyms. Finally, we discuss some of the approaches that others have taken to address the Sybil attack [5].

2.1 Direct Observations

Given the assumptions in the introduction, a trust value is based on the count of event outcomes. Different formats can be used to represent the trust value. A simple scenario is when there is one type of outcome and the trust value is represented as a tuple (g,b) counting the number of good (g) outcomes and bad (b) outcomes. Another format compliant to our assumption is the SECURE trust value [14]. An event outcome count is represented as a (s,i,c)-triple, where s is the number of events that supports the outcome, i is the number of events that have no information or are inconclusive about the outcome and c is the number of events that contradict the expected outcome. The trust value consists of a tree of (s,i,c)-triples, corresponding to a mathematical event structure. This format takes into account the element of uncertainty via i.

With such a trust value format and a perfect linkage, it is sufficient to add all elements of the same type. For example, the fusionym trust value of $link(p_1, ...,p_n)$ would be:

$$\sum_{i=1}^{n}(g_i,b_i) \text{ or } \sum_{i=1}^{n}(s_i,i_i,c_i) \text{ in the whole event structure.}$$

2.2 Self-recommendations

In open environments, security through collaboration allows the computing entities to deal with the high-level of uncertainty by sharing knowledge [14]. Recommendations exchanged between trust engines are the means to share knowledge between the computing entities. Therefore, when the fusionym trust value is calculated, it should be possible to utilise recommendations in addition to direct observations.

However, when recommendations are used and pseudonyms are allowed, *self-recommendations*, that is, recommendations from pseudonyms belonging to the same real-world entity challenge the use of event outcome counts for the calculation of a trust value. In such a system, a real-world entity can use self-recommendations as a low cost mechanism for introducing new pseudonyms in order to protect his/her privacy. If this is the case, then it is difficult to determine how to fairly incorporate this into a trust system based on the count of event outcomes, as the self-recommendation is not based on a history of interactions. If a linkage is performed explicitly after self-recommendations, it may be correct to simply discard the recommendations in the calculation (which means, that the count of recommendations must be stored separately from direct observation and identified with the pseudonym of the recommender). However, if no linkage is done, then we cannot know if there has been a self-recommendation. Permission to make self-recommendations at will, without cost, paves the way for a Sybil attack, unless explicitly addressed.

2.3   Sybil Attack

A well-known attack in the field of computational trust is Douceur's Sybil attack [5]. Douceur argues that in large scale networks where a centralised identity authority cannot be used to control the creation of virtual identities, a powerful real-world entity may create as many virtual identities as it wishes and in doing so challenge the use of a majority vote and flaw trust metrics. This is possible in trust engine scenarios where the possibility to use many pseudonyms is facilitated by the trust engine. In fact, a sole real-world entity can create many pseudonyms who blindly recommend one of these pseudonyms in order to fool the trust engine. The level of trust in the latter virtual identity increases and eventually passes above a threshold which makes the decision to trust (the semantics of this depend on the application).

One approach proposed to protect against the Sybil attack is the use of mandatory "entry fees" associated with the creation of each pseudonym [1, 6]. This approach raises some issues about its feasibility in a fully decentralised way and the choice of the minimal fee that guarantees protection. Also, "more generally, the optimal fee will often exclude some players yet still be insufficient to deter the wealthiest players from defecting" [6]. An alternative to entry fees may be the use of once in a lifetime pseudonyms (1L [6]), a.k.a. pseudonym commitment, where an elected party per "arena" of application is responsible to certify only 1L to any real-world entity, which possesses a key pair bound to this entity's real-world identity. Blind signatures are used to keep the link between the real-world identity and its chosen pseudonym in the arena unknown to the elected party. However, there are still three unresolved questions about this approach: how the elected party is chosen; what happens if the elected party becomes unreachable; and how much the users would agree to pay for this approach. More importantly, a Sybil attack is possible during the voting phase, so the concept of electing a trusted entity to stop Sybil attacks is fundamentally flawed.

Bouchegger and Le Boudec envisage the use of expensive pseudonyms [6], cryptographically generated unique identifiers and secure hardware modules to counter the Sybil attack. This may overcome the Sybil attack, but at the same time it may exclude poor users as said in [6]. Similarly, Kinateder et al.'s workarounds [10] are two-fold. Firstly, some of the risks of pseudonymity are alleviated via trusted hardware including a trusted certificate agency that would certify the pseudonym without disclosing the real-world identity until legal bodies want to retrieve the link. Secondly, the trust engine should be combined with electronic payment systems, which allow the creation of an originality statement during the payment process which can be included in a recommendation in order to prove that a transaction regarding the recommendation in question really took place. However, relying on real money turns the trust protection into a type of system trust, which is high enough to make the use of interpersonal trust (that is, the trust value) almost superfluous. In the real world, tax authorities are likely to require traceability of money transfers, which would completely break privacy in a money-based system.

A real-world application where Sybil attacks occur is the email system. The success of spammers has proven that it is still cheap enough to create text email addresses, which act as pseudonyms in order to carry out profitable, large-scale spam attacks. It is for this reason that we give an example application of our solution in the email and anti-spam domain in Section 4.

3 Trust Transfer for Recommendations

In addition to considering trust to be a single construct, Romano also notes that trust is "functional, such that trusting behaviours are attempts to attain desirable outcomes by protecting one's interests through actions that either increase or decrease influence in accordance with one' assessment of such influence" [15]. When someone recommends another person, he/she has influence over the potential outcome of interaction between this person and the trustor. The inclination of the trustor with regards to this influence "provides a goal-oriented sense of control to attain desirable outcomes" [15]. So, the trustor expects to be able to increase/decrease the influence of the recommenders according to his/her goals. The goal in this paper is to build a trust engine, which allows recommendations without being vulnerable to the Sybil attack, so the mechanism used to control the recommender's influence must achieve this goal. We conclude that the overall trustworthiness depends on the complete set of trust contexts. This overall trustworthiness must be put in context: it is not sufficient to strictly limit the domain of trustworthiness to the current trust context and the trustee; if recommenders are involved, the decision and the evaluation of the expected outcome should impact their overall trustworthiness according to the influence they had.

La Rochefoucauld [12] highlighted that when one recommends another, they should be aware that the outcome of their recommendation will reflect upon their trustworthiness and reputation since they are partly responsible for this outcome.

With this idea in mind, we argue for the revision of the handling of recommendations in order to achieve safe fusionym and prevent Sybil attacks. In this section, we first examine how others address trust using recommendations. Then we present our model for trust transfer that allows and even encourages self-recommendations from pseudonyms of the same real-world entity. Finally, we present an example of trust transfer in action.

3.1 Adjusted Recommendations Based on Recommending Trustworthiness

This is not the first time that the handling of recommendations has been addressed. Since some recommenders are more or less likely to produce good recommendations, the notion of recommending trustworthiness has been added to advanced trust engines. Intuitively, recommendations must only be accepted from senders that the local entity trusts to make judgements similar to those that it would have made itself. Assuming the user has a metric for measuring the accuracy of another sender's recommendations then Abdul-Rahman and Hailes [2], Jøsang [8] and others have suggested models for incorporating that information into the local trust decision. In many cases, the final trust value, which is used locally, may be different to the recommended one. For example, a recommender with trust value of *0.6* on a *[0,1]* scale giving a recommendation of *0.8* provides the discounted trust value:

$$0.6 \times 0.8 = 0.42$$

The overall amount of trust in the system is higher after the recommendation ($0.6+0.8+0.42 > 0.6+0.8$). In a system where there are pseudonyms that can potentially belong to the same real-world entity, a transitive trust process is open to abuse. Even if there is a high discounting factor, the real-world entity can diminish the impact of this discounting factor by sending a huge number of recommendations from his/her army of pseudonyms in a Sybil attack. Additionally, obtaining a measure of recommending trustworthiness is rather difficult, for example, the "semantic distance" [2] between recommendations and local outcomes has to be calculated and that involves the (rather arbitrary) choice of a number of parameters.

It has been noted in the literature that there are issues "with trusting recommenders to recommend arbitrarily deep chains" [2]. They argue that trust at level n is independent of trust at level $n+1$. However, this contradicts Romano's view of trust as a single construct that varies across contexts: there is a dependency between trust contexts as they are not independent multiple constructs. Kinateder et al. [10] also take the position that there is a dependence between different trust contexts. For example, a chef known to have both won cooking awards and murdered people may not be a trustworthy chef after all. In the next subsection, we present our view on the dependence between trustworthiness and recommending trustworthiness in the same trust context.

3.2 Trust Transfer

Trust transfer implies that recommendations cause trust on the trustor (T) side to be transferred from the recommender (R) to the subject (S) of the recommendation. A second effect is that the trust on the recommender side for the subject is reduced by the amount of transferred trustworthiness. If it is a self-recommendation, then the second effect is moot, as it does not make sense for a real-world entity to reduce trust in his/her own pseudonyms. So, the overall level of trust in the entire network does not increase via recommendations, in contrast to transitive trust schemes. Even if there are different trust contexts (such as trustworthiness in delivering on time or recommending trustworthiness), each trust context has its impact on the single construct trust value: they cannot be taken separately for the calculation of the single construct trust value. A transfer of trust is carried out if the exchange of communications depicted in Figure 2 is successful. A local entity's *Recommender Search Policy (RSP)* dictates which contacts can be used as potential recommenders. Its *Recommendation Policy (RP)* decides which of its contacts it is willing to recommend to other entities, and how much trust it is willing to transfer to an entity.

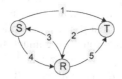

Fig. 2. Trust Transfer Process

Trust Transfer (in its simplest form) can be decomposed into 5 steps:

1. The subject requests an action, requiring a total amount of trustworthiness *TA* in the subject, in order for the request to be accepted by the trustor; the actual value of *TA* is contingent upon the risk acceptable to the user, as well as dispositional trust and the context of the request; so the risk module of the trust engine plays a role in the calculation of *TA*;

2. The trustor queries its contacts, which pass the *RSP*, in order to find recommenders willing to transfer some of their positive event outcomes count to the subject. Recall that trustworthiness is based on event outcomes count in trust transfer;

3. If the contact has directly interacted with the subject and the contact's *RP* allows it to permit the trustor to transfer an amount *(A≤TA)* of the recommender's trustworthiness to the subject, the contact agrees to recommend the subject. It queries the subject whether it agrees to lose *A* of trustworthiness on the recommender side;

4. The subject returns a signed statement, indicating whether it agrees or not;

5. The recommender sends back a signed recommendation to the trustor, indicating the trust value it is prepared to transfer to the subject. This message includes the signed agreement of the subject.

Both the *RSP* and *RP* can be as simple or complex as the application environment demands. In this instance, we limit the policies to simple ones based on trust values. For example, a more complicated *RSP* could be based upon privacy considerations (as is highlighted in the email anti-spam application in Section 4.2). An advanced *RP* could be based upon level of participation in the collaborative process and risk analysis.

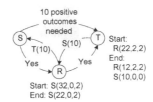

Fig. 3. Trust Transfer Process Example

The trust transfer process is illustrated in Figure 3 where the subject requests an action, which requires *10* positive outcomes (recall that the system uses interpersonal trust based on the outcome of past events). The *RSP* of the trustor is to query a contact to propose to transfer trust if the *balance (s-i-c)* is strictly greater than *2TA*. This is because it is sensible to require that the recommender remains more trustworthy than the subject after the recommendation. The contact, having a balance passing the *RSP* *(s-i-c=32-0-2=30)*, is asked by the trustor whether he/she wants to recommend *10* good outcomes. The contact's *RP* is to agree to the transfer if the subject has a trust value greater than *TA*. The balance of the subject on the recommender's side is greater than *10 (s-i-c=22-2-2=18)*. The subject is asked by the recommender whether he/she agrees *10* good outcomes to be transferred. Trustor *T* reduces its trust in recommender

R by *10* and increases its trust in subject S by *10*. Finally, the recommender reduces his trust in the subject by *10*.

The recommender could make requests to a number of recommenders until the total amount of trust value is reached (the search requests to find the recommenders are not represented in the figures but the issue is further discussed in Section 4.2). For instance, in the previous example, two different recommenders could be contacted, with one recommending *3* good outcomes and the other one *7*. A recommender chain in trust transfer is not explicitly known to the trustor. The trustor only needs to know his/her contacts who agree to transfer some of their trustworthiness. This is useful from a privacy point of view since the full chain of recommenders is not disclosed. This is in contrast to other recommender chains such as public keys web of trust [8]. Because we assume for this paper that the entities cannot be compromised, we leave the issue surrounding the independence of recommender chains in order to increase the attack resistance of the trust metric for future work. The reason for searching more than one path is that it decreases the chance of a faulty path (either due to malicious intermediaries or unreliable ones). If the full list of recommenders must be detailed in order to be able to check the independence of recommender chains, the privacy protection is lost. This can be an application-specific design decision.

Thanks to trust transfer, although a real-world identity has many pseudonyms, the Sybil attack cannot happen because the number of direct observations (and hence, total amount of trust) remains the same on the trustor side. Still, local newcomers can be introduced thanks to collaboration. In the previous example, if the subject and the recommender are pseudonyms of the same real-world entity, they remain unlinked. If the proof is given that they can be linked, the fusionym trust value can be calculated as in Section 2.1 with a guarantee of no overcounting of overlapping evidence or self-recommendations.

One may argue that it is unfair for the recommender to lose the same amount of trustworthiness as specified in his/her recommendation, moreover if the outcome is ultimately good. It is envisaged that a more complex sequence of messages can be put in place in order to revise the decrease of trustworthiness after a successful outcome. This is left for future work, because it can lead to vulnerabilities (for example, based on Sybil attacks with careful cost/benefit analysis). The current approach is still limited to scenarios where there are many interactions between the recommenders with the overall trustworthiness in the network (that is, the global number of good outcomes) is large enough that there is no major effect on the trustworthiness of entities when they agree to transfer some of their trust (such as in the email example below). Ultimately, without sacrificing the flexibility and privacy enhancing potential of limitless pseudonym creation, Sybil attacks are guaranteed to be avoided, which is a clear contribution to the field of decentralised, computational trust.

4 Application to Email Anti-spam

In the following subsection, we explain how a trust engine can be used to prioritise emails according to the trustworthiness of their senders. Then, we slightly modify the search for recommenders in order to put more work on the spammer side and take privacy considerations into account.

4.1   Trust Value-Based Email Prioritisation

There are different techniques to obtain anti-spoofing of email addresses. We assume that each email user uses our Claim Tool Kit [16] proxy, which allows email users to sign their emails based on a key pair. This key pair does not require to be bound to the user's real-world identity. The proxy also runs a trust engine, which is our Java implementation of the SECURE trust engine [16]. The use of the proxy is transparent to the user, who has just to change the mail server IP address to the IP address of the proxy in his/her preferred email client. The trust value is composed of one triple, which represents the number of emails considered of good quality from the point of view of the email user. The emails in the *Inbox* are prioritised according to the trust value of the sender thanks to a column in the email client graphical user interface ordered by:

$$\frac{s}{s+i+c}$$

In this situation, s and c correspond respectively to the number of good and bad quality emails from the sender. The i element of the triple corresponds to unread email in the *Inbox*. Several unread emails from the same sender are prioritised from the oldest received email to the most recent. Many email addresses can be *pre-trusted* by external means, for example, the email addresses in the *to:*, *cc:* and *bcc:* fields and those appearing in the address book. Pre-trusted email addresses get the value *(1,0,0)*.

If the email is considered too highly prioritised by the user at time of reading, the user can specify in one click that the email prioritisation is wrong and c is increased by *1*; otherwise the sender's s value is increased by one after the email is closed. The trust values are recomputed and emails are reorganised in the folders after each user reading and feedback cycle.

In this example, we assume that compromising email accounts and spoofing are not possible. So, the spammers can only rely on the creation of pseudonyms that will collude to try to get spam emails through. If a spammer sends an email with a disposable email address that will never be reused, the email will end up with the lowest prioritisation, which is *0*. Emails with priority *0* are left in a different folder called *Spam*. Collaboration between email users is used to prioritise emails from legitimate users. Thanks to the user's feedback with regards to the quality of the emails received, the trust value may also be used as the recommending trustworthiness of the sender since senders with higher trust values are likely to prioritise senders of emails of the same good quality.

However, it is possible to engineer advanced attacks on social networks, where the most well-connected users (according to importance metrics such as PageRank, Betweeness Centrality, Degree Distribution Ranker and HITS [9]) are targeted. The success of these attacks hinges on the ability of the attacker to gain information about the topology of the network. This underlines another disadvantage of public online networks of contacts, which goes beyond privacy issues. For example, we mined Google's archive from February 2001 to September 2004 of the *rec.arts.books.hist-fiction* newsgroup. It corresponds to a network of *909* email users. Each contributor to the same email discussion thread is considered a contact of the other contributors to the thread. The threads with only one contributor are discarded. Two contributors appearing in two different threads are not considered to be contacts if they have never contributed to the same unique thread.

Figure 4 gives the overhead of collaboration email when 5 or 25 email users of this network are attacked, either randomly selected or according to an importance metric. The spammer *pleases* them by sending relevant emails from one email address and the remaining users are requested (attacked) by this apparent honest email address, who is considered trustworthy if at least one recommender is found starting from their direct contacts. If the attacker is considered trustworthy, we say that the user has been *fooled*. Breadth-First-Search (*BFS*) and Random Walk (*RW*) without back-tracking, both limited in number of hops, are compared. Among these Sybil-related attacks, the engineered ones introduce many more collaboration emails, especially when *BFS* is used because the most well-connected nodes have a great number of contacts.

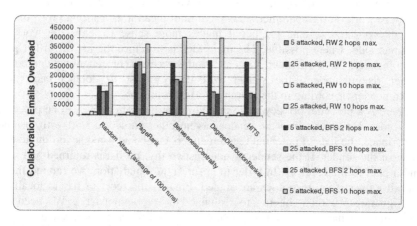

Fig. 4. Overhead due to Attacks Caused by No Network Privacy

At first glance, the email infrastructure may be challenged by trust transfer because of the overhead of emails to find potential recommenders. However, in the modified search we present in the next section, the spammer must start the search with his/her own friends. This means that the network load is localised to the spammer's network of honest friends (of whom there are unlikely to be many). As a rule of thumb [1], increasing the cost to the spammer for an attack is desirable and our new trust transfer further increases this cost when engineered attacks are used. In addition to this, recommendations are usually only required for newcomers. Finally, the overhead of collaboration is limited by the *RSP* and more intelligent directed search schemes, for example [7] based on local knowledge about similarity between the sender and the local contacts, do not flood the network.

Concerning the impact of *networked topology engineered* (that we call *NETOPE* in short) attacks, an attack with 5 attacked email users approximately corresponds to 0.55% of the total email users. An attack with 25 attacked email users approximately corresponds to 2.75% of the total email users. For 5 attacked email addresses (0.55%), the worst case scenario varies from 1.5% to 91.5% of fooled email users in random configurations and from *5.8%* to *91.2%* in importance-based configurations. For 25 attacked email addresses (*2.75%*), the worst case scenario varies from *7.4%* to *92.5%* fooled email users in random configurations and from *33.7%* to *91.2%* in importance-based configurations. The greatest difference of impact between the random attack and the engineered attack happens with the following configuration: *5* attacked email users, the *RW* search scheme limited to two hops and PageRank. In the latter configuration, *5.9* times more email users fall in the *NETOPE* attack than in the random attack.

4.2   Proof of Friends (PoF) for Privacy and Sender-Borne Search Work

It is not acceptable to leave the legitimate user proxies to carry out the recommender search on behalf of the spammer. So, we revise the trust transfer process in order to put more work on the spammer side. We do not mean it as a strong proof-of-work or bankable postage scheme [1] but it makes more sense to leave the work on the spammer side, where possible. The main idea is to return the list of further potential recommenders to the sender. Instead of the receiver or recommender contacting further recommenders, the sender will use the list to contact each potential recommender (according to the search algorithm chosen).

There is a potential privacy issue in giving the lists of contacts to be processed by the sender. However, since the sender has no other choice to start with his/her own best friends, the lists of potential recommenders can be adjusted according to the trust value of the sender. If the sender is not trustworthy, no list is returned and it cannot find a path to the receiver. In order to ensure non-repudiation, we remind the reader that all requests and responses are signed. Finally, the receiver has to locally verify the signatures (without having to recontact the recommenders). We need another protection mechanism related to privacy disclosure. Each time an email is sent to a new receiver, the email sender sets two local values on a *[0,1]* scale. The first value corresponds to the level of privacy information that the receiver is allowed to see from *0* (none) to *1* (full information). The second value, which is also specified in the sender's email when the receiver must change it, corresponds to the level of privacy required by the contacts of the receiver to be allowed to use the sender as a recommender. A shop may set the second value pretty high since it is in its interest to know as many customers as possible. $Contact_{Privacy}(0.8,0.7)$ means that the contact has a privacy level of *0.8* and allows the recommender to disclose their relationship to subjects with privacy level greater than (or equal to) *0.7*.

Thus, the default trust transfer is changed to the one in Figure 5 (the search requests for the different recommenders are not represented).

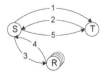

Fig. 5. Proof of Friends Trust Transfer

The trust transfer consists of the following steps:

1. The subject requests an action of the trustor;
2. The trustor replies that an amount of trustworthiness, *TA*, is required before it will grant the request; Until a complete recommender chain is found (or the search's time-to-live expires):
3. The subject starts to query his/her contact email addresses, who pass the *RSP*, to find a recommender chain to the trustor;
4. If the privacy test is passed and the recommender does not know the receiver, it sends back the list of privacy checked contacts to the sender, including a statement signed by the recommender that he/she is willing to recommend the sender as part of a recommender chain, if one can be found; Once the recommender chain is found, every recommender involved confirms that they have transferred trustworthiness accordingly by signed statement;
5. The subject sends the recommendation to the trustor.

In the example of Figure 6, the sender has only one contact, who does not know the receiver target. However, this contact has one contact who knows the receiver. In this scenario, the *RSP* requires that a potential recommender must have a balance of at least *2TA* on the trustor side. The *RP* is that the subject must have a balance strictly greater than *TA* on the recommender side.

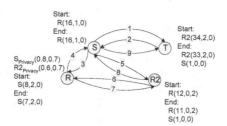

Fig. 6. PoF Trust Transfer Example

In our default collaboration scheme, the following emails are exchanged:

1. The sender sends an email to a new receiver;
2. The receiver replies that the proof of having sent one legitimate email is needed to get the email out of the spam folder. In other words, *TA* is *(1,0,0)*;
3. The sender starts contacting his/her list of contacts; in this case, there is only one contact;
4. The sender's only contact is queried; it does not know the receiver, so it starts checking its list of contacts to see if the privacy test is passed; in this case, the sender has a privacy disclosure trust value of *0.8*, which is higher than the threshold specified by the potential recommender *R2*; therefore, the contact is passed back to the sender: more precisely, the contact signs an email stating that it is inclined to recommend *(1,0,0)* for the sender. based on a recommender chain including *R2*;
5. The recommender's contact is queried by the sender and is found to be a contact of the receiver; it agrees to recommend *(1,0,0)* for the sender to the receiver as

long as it receives a confirmation from R. This is because R has a balance of 10 on $R2$'s side, which is greater than TA. S has a balance of 6 on R's side, so the RP is passed on all nodes in the recommender chain;

6. An email is sent to R in order to confirm that the trustworthiness in the sender has been decreased by $(1,0,0)$ on R's side;
7. The trustworthiness in the sender is decreased by one and a confirmation email is sent back to $R2$;
8. $R2$ transfers some trustworthiness (one supporting outcome) from R to the sender; then, an email confirming that $R2$ recommends $(1,0,0)$ is sent back to the sender;
9. The recommendation is passed to the receiver, who transfers $(1,0,0)$ trustworthiness from $R2$'s trust value to the sender's trust value.

5 Related Work

PoF are pushed recommendations similar to credential chains: "multiple chains can be submitted to establish a higher degree of trust" [18]. However, credential-based trust management misses the possibility of direct observations, which can be used to incrementally form the trust value.

Although we have considered the email system in its current form, others [4] have envisaged deploying structured peer-to-peer layers on top of the email infrastructure and these could be used to facilitate the retrieval of recommenders. However, the change may not be feasible on a worldwide scale as it requires all mail servers to participate. Our proxy solution works for adopters of the proxy, but also for legacy users, although they do not benefit from the anti-spam features. Others have used centralised social networks, such as in TrustMail [7], which does not claim to be a spam filter but prioritises good quality email, as is done in this paper. Our approach is different to TrustMail as it relies on the count of event outcomes, rather than on user defined trust values for prioritisation.

Rahman et al's [2] recommendation protocol is carried out by the trustor and entities involved in the recommendation chain search. We envision that their protocol could be carried out as our PoF protocol, if the trustee is supposed to do most of the work.

Our definition of self-recommendation is different to the one used in [17], where pushed trustworthiness is possible by exhibiting buddy relationships. Roughly, PoF can be considered to be pushed trustworthiness. Furthermore, their buddy relationships may be considered to be wrapped recommendations. So, both their and our approaches provide some kind of pushed recommendations. Finally, successful introduction of local newcomers is possible in both their and our approaches, since pseudonyms with a high PoF can be selected, which is equivalent to a high number of buddy relationships. In contrast to our approach, their approach does not protect against Sybil attacks: to have a high number of buddy relationships does not mean the newcomer is not a spammer because a Sybil attack can be used to fake a great number of buddy relationships between his/her own faked email addresses.

Ziegler and Lausen's trust metric, called Appleseed [19], is possible when it is assumed that all users make their trust values publicly available. Although this can be true in the Semantic Web, due to the publicly crawlable Friend-Of-A-Friend (FOAF) files extended with Golbeck's framework [7] and its trust assertions, this assumption is a threat to privacy since a clear view of the network of acquaintances can be obtained. This is in contrast to our decentralised solution, which permits personalisable levels of privacy. Their trust value ranges from 0 (lack of trust) to 1 (blind trust). Recommending trustworthiness does not explicitly appear, but is reflected in the choice of the "spreading factor" [19], which is recommended to be set to 0.85 and "may also be seen as the ratio between direct trust [...] and trust in the ability [...] to recommend others as trustworthy peers". Appleseed spreading factor enables trustworthiness gained by an entity to be passed to another entity. If the spreading factor is below 0.5, most of the granted trustworthiness is kept by the receiving peer and small portion of the trustworthiness is passed to their direct contacts. This is an example of a system where trustworthiness is shared between entities and is in line with the concept of trust transfer. However, this factor is not set by the recommender, but by the computing trustor and is the same for all entities in the network. In a peer-to-peer way, the recommender should be able to specify the factor itself. An improvement to the scheme may be to use the recommending trustworthiness stated by the receiving peer. In contrast to our solution, their solution creates the problem of the choice of the spreading factor, which, we argue, make no sense to be randomly chosen by the trustor without feedback from the recommender. This is because the recommender is the only entity who has experienced the recommending trustworthiness of his/her contacts.

Ziegler and Lausen [19] also make the distinction between global group trust metrics, which compute a single, global trust value for each entity. This does not allow for the personal bias of any entity and also requires the complete trust network information for all entities. For example, Google's PageRank [3] can be considered here, as pseudonyms and their contacts can be replaced by pages and their hyperlinks. Another type of trust metric, called local [19], takes into account personal bias. Local trust metrics have two sub-types [19]: local group metrics and local scalar metrics. The local group metrics, such as Appleseed, return a subset of the most trustworthy peers from the point of view of the local trustor over a partial view of the trust network, given the amount of trustworthiness desired. Local scalar metrics compute the trust value of a specific entity from the point of view of the local trustor "tracking trust paths from source to target" [19]. Finally, the computation may be centralised or distributed, meaning that the recommendation received is evaluated before being passed to the successor in the recommender chain. Appleseed is a local centralised group metric. Our trust transfer metric is a local decentralised scalar metric.

The OpenPrivacy's "nym manager" [11] allows the user to use different pseudonyms corresponding to public keys. According to the trust context, different pseudonyms can be used. It is possible that a parent pseudonym generates different child pseudonyms. Then, they argue it is possible to prove to an external entity that two children were generated from the same parent anonymously by generating a certificate (or non-anonymously). Of course, they underline that long-lived pseudonyms are preferable in order to be granted interactions requiring a great trust value. In our approach, fusionym is provided to combine the trust values of different pseudonyms once a link has been proven between them.

6   Conclusion

Self-recommendations are the potential means for Sybil attacks in decentralised computational trust systems where virtual identities can be cheaply created and used. Self-recommendations are even a greater issue when the trust engines explicitly support the feature to use multiple virtual identities per user. This enhances the privacy of the system, but it must still be possible to compute accurate trust values.

When trust values are based on direct observations of counts of event outcomes, fusionym provides accurate trust values even if multiple virtual identities are used per user. Still, thanks to trust transfer, safe fusionym is possible even if self-recommendations are used at some stage before the disclosure of the link between the pseudonyms. At the same time, it removes the risk of Sybil attacks.

When evaluated according to the trust metric classification, trust transfer is an instance of a new type of trust metric, local decentralised scalar trust metric.

The evaluation of trust transfer in the email application domain highlights that different search algorithms are possible for trust transfer and some search algorithms are more suitable than others. For example, in email anti-spam settings, it makes sense that the search load is borne by the sender of the email rather than the network, as demonstrated by our proof of friends search for recommenders.

An extended version of this paper, to be published elsewhere, would present that negative recommendations consist of similar trust transfer based on the verification of signed real events recommended to have ended up with a harmful outcome, obviously without the agreement between the trustee and the trustor but followed by a warning of the trustee of this negative recommendation to insist on reciprocity. No incentive has been put in place to force collaboration further since it challenges privacy and some entities are simply not active and not at the centre of the network. Further work including incentives may be interesting in scenarios where privacy is not required.

This work is sponsored by the European Union (IST-2001-32486 SECURE and IST-2001-34910 iTrust) and Enterprise Ireland (grant number CFTD/03/219).

References

1. M. Abadi, A. Birrell, M. Burrows, F. Dabek, and T. Wobber, "Bankable Postage for Network Services", in Proceedings of ASIAN, Springer, 2003.
2. A. Abdul-Rahman and S. Hailes, "Using Recommendations for Managing Trust in Distributed Systems", in Proceedings of the Malaysia International Conference on Communication'97, IEEE, 1997.
3. S. Brin and L. Page, "The Anatomy of a Large-Scale Hypertextual Web Search Engine", in 30(1-7), Computer Networks, 1998.
4. E. Damiani, et al., "P2P-Based Collaborative Spam Detection and Filtering", in Proceedings of the Conference on Peer-to-Peer Computing, 2004.
5. J. R. Douceur, "The Sybil Attack", in Proceedings of the 1st International Workshop on Peer-to-Peer Systems, 2002.
6. E. Friedman and P. Resnick, "The Social Cost of Cheap Pseudonyms", vol. 10(2), pp. 173-199, Journal of Economics and Management Strategy, 2001.

7. J. Golbeck and J. Hendler, "Accuracy of Metrics for Inferring Trust and Reputation in Semantic Web-based Social Networks", 2004.
8. A. Jøsang, "A Subjective Metric of Authentication", in Proceedings of ESORICS, Springer, 1998.
9. JUNG, "JUNG, the Java Universal Network/Graph Framework", http://jung.sourceforge.net/index.html.
10. M. Kinateder and K. Rothermel, "Architecture and Algorithms for a Distributed Reputation System", in Proceedings of the First Conference on Trust Management, LNCS, Springer, 2003.
11. F. Labalme and K. Burton, "Enhancing the Internet with Reputations", 2001, www.openprivacy.org/papers/200103-white.html.
12. La Rochefoucauld, "Réflexions", 1731.
13. D. H. McKnight and N. L. Chervany, "What is trust? A Conceptual Analysis and an Interdisciplinary Model", in Proceedings of AMCIS, 2000.
14. N. Mogens, M. Carbone, and K. Krukow, "An Operational Model of Trust", SECURE Deliverable 1.2, 2004, http://secure.dsg.cs.tcd.ie.
15. D. M. Romano, "The Nature of Trust: Conceptual and Operational Clarification", in PhD Thesis, Louisiana State University, 2003.
16. J.-M. Seigneur and C. D. Jensen, "Trading Privacy for Trust", in Proceedings of the Conference on Trust Management, Springer-Verlag, 2004.
17. F. Stefan and O. Philipp, "The Buddy System - A distributed reputation system based on social structure", Technical Report 2004-1, Universitat Karlsruhe.
18. W. H. Winsborough, K. E. Seamons, and V. E. Jones, "Automated Trust Negotiation", DARPA Information Survivability Conference, 2000.
19. C.-N. Ziegler and G. Lausen, "Spreading Activation Models for Trust Propagation", in Proceedings of the International Conference on e-Technology, e-Commerce, and e-Service, IEEE, 2004.

Privacy-Preserving Search and Updates for Outsourced Tree-Structured Data on Untrusted Servers

Tran Khanh Dang

School of Computing Science,
Middlesex University,
London, United Kingdom
k.dang@mdx.ac.uk

Abstract. Although tree-based index structures have proven their advantages to both traditional and modern database applications, they introduce numerous research challenges as database services are outsourced to untrusted servers. In the outsourced database service model, crucial security research questions mainly relate to data confidentiality, data and user privacy, authentication and data integrity. To the best of our knowledge, however, none of the previous research has radically addressed the problem of preserving privacy for basic operations on such outsourced search trees. Basic operations of search trees/tree-based index structures include *search* (to answer different query types and *updates* (modification, insert, delete). In this paper, we will discuss security issues in outsourced databases that come together with search trees, and present techniques to ensure privacy in the execution of these trees' basic operations on the untrusted server. Our techniques allow clients to operate on their outsourced tree-structured data on untrusted servers without revealing information about the query, result, and outsourced data itself.

Keywords: Outsourced search trees, data and user privacy, oblivious search and updates, encrypted data, untrusted servers.

1 Introduction

Advances in the networking technologies and continued growth of the Internet have triggered a new trend towards outsourcing data management and information technology needs to external service providers. Database outsourcing is a recent manifestation of this trend [28]. In the outsourced database service (ODBS) model, clients rely on the premises of the provider, which include hardware, software and manpower, for the storage, maintenance, and retrieval of their data. This ODBS model introduces numerous research challenges and thus has rapidly become one of the hot topics in the research community [15, 30, 23, 6, 13].

As mentioned, in the ODBS model, a client (e.g., an organization) stores its private data at an external service provider, who is typically not fully trusted. Therefore, securing outsourced data, i.e. make it confidential, is one of the foremost challenges in this model. Basically, regardless of the untrusted server at the provider's side, the final goal that clients want is that they can use the outsourced database service as an in-

P. Herrmann et al. (Eds.): iTrust 2005, LNCS 3477, pp. 338–354, 2005.

house one. This includes a requirement that clients can operate on their outsourced data without worrying about leak of their sensitive information. This requirement in turn poses several additional challenges related to privacy-preserving for client's queries as well as for the outsourced data during the execution of operations at the untrusted server. Overall, with an assumption that client's side is trusted[1], the following security requirements must be met:

- *Data confidentiality*: outsiders and even the server's operators (database administrators) cannot see the client's outsourced data contents in any cases (including when the client's queries are performed on the server).
- *User privacy*: clients do not want the server to know about their queries and the returned results.
- *Authentication and data integrity*: clients are ensured that data returned from the untrusted server is originated from the data owner and has not been tampered with.

The above security requirements are different from the traditional database security issues [7, 33] and will in general influence the performance, usability and scalability of the ODBS model. Among the three, the last security objective (i.e. authentication and data integrity) is out of the scope of this paper and we refer interested readers to a recent publication [28] for more details. In this paper, we concentrate on addressing the first two security objectives for the outsourced databases that come together with search trees as discussed below.

To deal with the data confidentiality issue, outsourced data is usually encrypted before being stored at the external server. Although this solution can protect the data from outsiders as well as the server, it introduces difficulties in querying process: It is hard to protect the user privacy as performing queries over encrypted data. The question is *"how will the server be able to perform client's queries effectively, efficiently and obliviously over encrypted data without revealing any information about both data and queries?"*. The problem has been quite well-solved (even without help of special hardware) if the outsourced data contains only encrypted records and no tree-based index structures are used for the storage and retrieval purposes [10, 16, 22, 6, 15, 32]. However, no solution has been developed to radically solve the problem in case such search trees are employed although some preliminary proposals have been made as [13, 27, 17, 16]. In our previous work [13], we proposed an extreme protocol for this ODBS model based on private information retrieval (PIR)-like protocols [2]. However, it would become prohibitively expensive in case only one server is used to host the outsourced data [8]. In Damiani et al.'s work [17, 16], they gave a solution to query outsourced data indexed by B+-trees. Their approach, however, does not provide an oblivious way to traverse the tree and this may lead to compromise the security objectives [13, 27]. Of late, Lin and Candan [27] introduced an approach to solve the problem with a computational complexity security algorithm and the experimental results reported are sound. Unfortunately, their solution only supports oblivious *search* operations on the outsourced search trees, but *insert*, *delete*, and *modification* ones. That means their solution can not be applied to dynamic outsourced search trees

---

[1] There are some cases in which clients are not allowed to receive data that does not belong to the query result. In these cases, clients are considered untrusted and more *data and user privacy-preserving* requirements must be taken into account (cf. section 5).

where new items may be inserted into and removed from, or existing data can be modified. In this paper, we will analyse and introduce techniques to solve the concerned problem completely.

The rest of this paper is organized as follows: Section2 briefly introduces search trees and their important role in database applications. Section 3 summarizes Lin and Candan's approach and discusses its limitations. Section 4 is dedicated to presenting our contributions to solve the problem radically. Section 5 presents other related work and discussions. Eventually, we give conclusions and present future work in section 6.

2   Tree-Based Index Structures and Applications

The basic structure of trees is organized into *nodes*. Each node in the tree, except for a special one called the root, has one parent node and several (may be zero) child nodes. The root node has no parent and a node that does not have any child nodes is called a leaf node. A node is called an internal node if it is neither the root nor a leaf node. The number of child nodes in an internal node is called the *fanout* of that node.

Generally, a search tree/tree-based index structures is a typical type of tree that is used to guide the search for data items, given some search criteria. Basically, the search trees are multilevel indexes which can be employed to cluster many types of data, ranging from one-dimensional to multi-dimensional/spatial data sets. They have played a fundamental and vital role in both traditional and modern database application domains. As an example, B+-trees among the most traditional search trees have become a commonly accepted default structure for generating indexes on demand in most DBMSs. Coming along with the development of real world applications as well as theoretical research problems, many multi-dimensional access methods (MAMs) have also been invented [18, 4, 11, 12]. They are an indispensable factor for modern database applications domains due to their efficiency in managing the storage and retrieval of data. Some specific examples of typical real-world application areas comprise information retrieval (IR), data mining, digital libraries, time-series databases, geographical information systems, and many others come together with the fast continued development of computer science (see [12] for more detailed discussions).

Basic operations of search trees include search (to answer different types of queries) and updates (modification, insert, delete). In practice, updates are the most critical operations, especially in *dynamic databases*, because they heavily form the structure of the resulting search trees and the achievable performance. As we will show later, the previous work of Lin and Candan fails to protect privacy for the users and such dynamic outsourced databases.

3   Oblivious Traversal of Outsourced Search Trees: Access Redundancy and Node Swapping Techniques

As private data is outsourced with search trees, the tree structure and the outsourced data should all be confidential. Otherwise, relations between the data items as well as the data distribution will be revealed, hence the data confidentiality and user privacy will be compromised. As shown in [16], encrypting each tree node as a whole is preferable because protecting a tree-based index by encrypting each of its fields would disclose to the untrusted server the ordering relationship between the index values. Lin and Candan's approach also follows this solution. Moreover, like other approaches [13, 17, 16], the unit of storage and access in their approach is also a tree node. Each node is identified by a unique node identifier (NID). The original tree is then stored in the server as a table with two attributes: NID and an encrypted value representing the node content. A client retrieves a node from the server by sending a request including the NID of the node. Let's see an example: Figure 1(a) shows a B+-tree built on an attribute *CustomerName* with sample values; Figure 1(b) shows the corresponding plaintext and encrypted table used to store the B+-tree at the external server. As we can see, that B+-tree is stored at the external server as a table over schema B+EncryptedTable= {NID, EncryptedNode}.

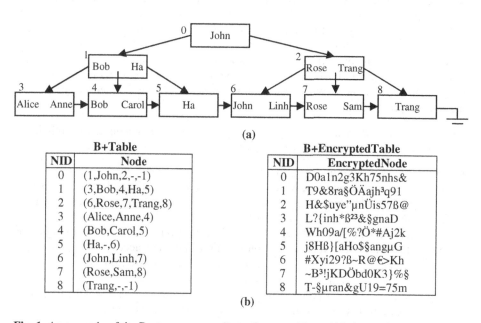

(a)

	B+Table			B+EncryptedTable
NID	**Node**		**NID**	**EncryptedNode**
0	(1,John,2,-,-1)		0	D0a1n2g3Kh75nhs&
1	(3,Bob,4,Ha,5)		1	T9&8ra§ÖÄajh³q91
2	(6,Rose,7,Trang,8)		2	H&$uye"µnÜis57ß@
3	(Alice,Anne,4)		3	L?{inh*ß²³&§gnaD
4	(Bob,Carol,5)		4	Wh09a/[%?Ö*#Aj2k
5	(Ha,-,6)		5	j8Hß}[aHo$§angµG
6	(John,Linh,7)		6	#Xyi29?ß~R@€>Kh
7	(Rose,Sam,8)		7	~B³!jKDÖbd0K3}%§
8	(Trang,-,-1)		8	T-§µran&gU19=75m

(b)

Fig. 1. An example of the B+-tree on an attribute *CustomerName* with fanout 3 (a) and the corresponding plaintext and encrypted table used to store the B+-tree at the external server (b)

Based on the above settings, Lin and Candan proposed an approach to oblivious traversal of outsourced search trees using two adjustable techniques named access redundancy and node swapping. We summarize these two techniques and related important procedures, and then discuss issues arisen from this approach below.

Access Redundancy. This technique requires that whenever a client accesses a node, called the target node, it asks for a set of m-1 randomly selected nodes in addition to the target node from the server. By this access redundancy, the probability that the server can guess the target node is 1/m. Here, m is an adjustable security parameter and the authors also gave discussions about how to choose the value of this parameter in the paper. This technique is different from those presented in [17, 16], where only the target node is retrieved (this may lead to reveal the tree structure as shown in [13]). Also, it bears another weakness: it can leak information about the target node. This is easy to observe: multiple access requests for the root node will reveal its position by simply calculating the intersection of the redundancy sets of the requests. If the root position is disclosed, there is a high risk that its child nodes (and also the whole tree structure) may be exposed [27]. This deficiency is overcome by secretly changing the target node's address after each time it is accessed.

Node Swapping. Each time a client requests to access a node from the server, it asks the server for a redundancy set of m nodes consisting of at least one *empty* node along with the target one. The client then (1) decrypts the target node; (2) manipulates its data; (3) swaps it with the empty node; and (4) re-encrypts nodes in the redundancy set and writes them back to the server. As presented in [27], with this technique, the possible position of the target node is randomly distributed over the data storage space at the untrusted server, and thus the weakness of the access redundancy technique is overcome. Note that, however, in order to prevent the server from differentiating between read and write operations, a read operation is always followed by a write operation. This technique, in turn, requires re-encryption of nodes using a different encryption scheme/key before they are rewritten to the server. More detailed discussions of the re-encryption technique are presented in the original paper.

Additional Procedures. To realize oblivious traversal of outsourced search trees, some more critical issues must be addressed:

- *Managing root node address:* In order to traverse a search tree, clients must first know the root node address, which can be dynamically changed by the node swapping technique. The authors proposed a solution by employing a special entry node called SNODE whose NID is known to all clients. This node is encrypted by a fixed secret key known to all legal clients. It keeps pointers ROOTS pointing to the root nodes of all outsourced search trees that the client can access.

- *Managing empty node lists:* Empty nodes are stored in hidden linked lists. Each of the empty nodes (data + pointer) is also encrypted. To help clients find out the empty nodes, two other types of pointers are also stored in the SNODE: EHEADS and ETAILS point to the heads and the tails of empty node lists, respectively.

- *Managing random choice of the redundancy set:* A redundancy set consists of the target node, an empty node, and m-2 randomly selected nodes. To enable clients to do this, the SNODE records the range of NIDs of nodes in the data storage space at the server. The client will then be able to generate m-2 random NIDs within the range that are different from NIDs of both target node and selected empty node.

- *Managing the tree structure integrity:* This aims to maintain node/parent-node relationships after the node swapping. The authors proposed two solutions to this issue. Shortly, the first solution is to find the empty node to be swapped with the child node and update the parent node accordingly before actually swapping the child node. The second solution is to let clients keep track of all nodes from the root down, deferring all the swaps until the node containing the data is accessed.

- *Concurrency control in the multi-user environment:* The authors' solution is to organize nodes in the data storage space at the server into d levels. Each level requires an empty node list to store empty nodes at this level. Besides, the client always asks for *exclusive locks* (because there are no pure read operations) of parent-level nodes before that of child-level ones, and always asks for locks of nodes in the same level using some predefined order. Therefore, all clients access nodes in some fixed predetermined order, ensuring deadlock-free accesses.

Searching on the Tree. As pointed out in the paper, the first solution to the tree structure integrity maintenance is better than the second one in terms of the space complexity, O(m) vs. O(d x m), and the concurrency perspective. Both of them have the time complexity of O(d x m), where d denotes the depth of the tree storage space and m denotes the redundancy set size. We summarize below Lin and Candan's algorithm for oblivious traversal of outsourced search trees based on the first solution to the tree structure integrity maintenance as mentioned above:

__Algorithm 1:__ Oblivious Tree Traversal/Search

1. Lock and fetch the SNODE, let it be PARENT. Find the root and let it be CURRENT.
2. Select a redundancy set for the CURRENT, lock nodes in the set, and let the empty node in the set be EMPTY.
3. Update the PARENT's pointer to refer to the EMPTY, and release locks on the PARENT level.
4. Swap the CURRENT with the EMPTY.
5. If the CURRENT contains the needed data, return CURRENT. Otherwise:
6. Let the CURRENT be PARENT, find the child node to be traversed next, let it be CURRENT, and repeat steps 2 through 5.

Note that a client has to keep two redundancy sets of both PARENT and CURRENT after step 2. The exclusive locks on nodes of the redundancy set of the PARENT can only be released after the locks on nodes of the redundancy set of the CURRENT are gained and necessary information of the PARENT is updated.

Issues and Limitations of Lin and Candan's Approach. We identify and discuss critical issues and limitations of Lin and Candan's work below, and present our solutions to solve all of them in section 4:

- *Maintenance of empty node lists and inefficiency in storage space usage:* As presented, for each node swapping operation, the target node is swapped with an empty node. Nevertheless, the authors did not show how the empty node list is updated or how such target nodes can be reused.
- *Insert and delete operations on outsourced search trees:* In case dynamic databases with search trees are outsourced, the system has to facilitate these basic operations. Lin and Candan's work fails to support such basic operations. However, insert and delete are not simple operations in search trees [12], and the previous work cannot be applied to these operations directly.
- *Maintenance of the tree structure integrity:* It is easy to observe that the first solution to the tree structure integrity maintenance can not be applicable to insert and delete operations in dynamic outsourced databases due to the split and deletion of over-full and under-full nodes (see [12, 18]).

- *Using more empty nodes for a redundancy set:* The node swapping technique using only one empty node for each redundancy set is not suitable for cases in which an overfull node is split into two new nodes.
- *Modification of indexed data:* Whenever attributes or feature values of a data object are modified, the object location in the search tree may be changed as well. This basic operation closely relates to inserts and deletes, which are not supported by the previous work.

4 Privacy-Preserving Search and Updates on Outsourced Search Trees

In this section, we will present techniques to ensure privacy for basic operations on outsourced search trees. First, we introduce a full-fledged solution to maintain empty node lists and manage the target nodes swapped with empty nodes during the execution of the operations, which has not been addressed by the previous work.

4.1 Node Swapping and Managing Empty Nodes

Our main aim is twofold: (1) to provide a solution to keep information about empty nodes up-to-date after a node swapping operation is carried out, and (2) to provide an efficient use for the database storage space at the server. For the ODBS model, the latter is not less important because it relates directly to costs that the data owner has to pay for the service provider.

In the same line as [27], we also use hidden linked lists to keep empty nodes and information about these lists (i.e., EHEADS and ETAILS) is stored in the SNODE. The difference is that when the target node is swapped with the empty node (all nodes are in the same redundancy set – cf. section 3), information in the SNODE must be updated accordingly to reflect the changes. Concretely, as a client receives a redundancy set of m nodes, including an empty node ENODE, for a certain target node TNODE, it will then have to perform the following tasks:

1. Decrypts TNODE.
2. Manipulates its data as needed.
3. Swaps TNODE with ENODE.
4. Inserts ENODE (this is the *new* empty node with the NID is the old target node's NID) into the end of the corresponding empty node list and amends the head pointer of the list so that it points to the next member of the list, i.e. corresponding information in the SNODE must be updated.
5. Re-encrypts the redundancy set and write it back to the server.

As we can see above, there is a new task the client must tackle: As TNODE is swapped with ENODE, the new ENODE, i.e. the old TNODE, becomes useless for the current tree structure, and thus the new ENODE is inserted into the end of the empty node list (so the ETAILS must be updated) to reuse later. Moreover, information about the first member in the corresponding empty node list, which is the old ENODE itself, must be changed as well (so the EHEADS must be updated). With these changes, our main aim as stated above is satisfied, hence the corresponding issue in the previous work is solved.

There is another issue in this approach: Because the (new) ENODE is inserted into the end of the *corresponding* empty node list at a predefined level (nodes are organized into d levels - cf. section 3), it may provide a clue for some statistical attacks afterwards. To deal with this issue, we propose not to insert the new ENODE into the same empty node list from which the old ENODE was picked up, but choose another list to put it in. This can be easily done because information about all empty node lists is stored in the SNODE (by the pointers EHEADS and ETAILS).

4.2 Search Operation

Basically, besides changes to the node swapping technique and the maintenance of empty nodes as noted above, the oblivious search algorithm remains quite similar to Algorithm 1. We present our algorithm for this operation as follows:

Algorithm 2: Oblivious Tree Search

1. Lock and fetch the SNODE, let it be PARENT. Find the root and let it be CURRENT.
2. If PARENT <> SNODE, lock and fetch the SNODE.
3. Select a redundancy set for the CURRENT, lock nodes in the set, and let the empty node in the set be EMPTY.
4. Update information in the SNODE to reflect changes to the empty node lists as described above in section 4.1 (here, the CURRENT and EMPTY take the role of the TNODE and ENODE, respectively).
5. If PARENT <> SNODE, write the SNODE back to the server and release the lock on it.
6. Update the PARENT's pointer to refer to the EMPTY, re-encrypt nodes of the PARENT redundancy set, write them back to the server, and release locks on the PARENT level.
7. Swap the CURRENT with the EMPTY.
8. If the CURRENT contains the needed data, manipulate that data as required, then re-encrypt nodes of the CURRENT redundancy set, write them back to the server, and release locks on the CURRENT level. Otherwise:
9. Let the CURRENT be PARENT, find the child node to be traversed next, let it be CURRENT, and repeat steps 2 through 8.

In general, whenever a client asks for a data object, the outsourced search tree must be traversed from the root down to the leaf node in which that object should reside. In step 1, our algorithm locks and fetches the SNODE to find the root address. To manage empty nodes the algorithm has to lock and fetch the SNODE if it has not been done (step 2). Obviously, this step is not performed in the first loop. When we have already locked and fetched nodes in the redundancy set of the CURRENT (step 3), the algorithm has to update information related to the empty node in the SNODE as discussed in the previous section (step 4). The SNODE is then encrypted (using a fixed key known to all clients), written back to the server and the exclusive lock on it is released (step 5). In step 6, the PARENT's pointer referring to the CURRENT will be changed to refer to the EMPTY, which will take the CURRENT's role after the swap is carried out in step 7. After being swapped, the CURRENT is checked if it contains the needed data to further process (step 8). Otherwise, a new loop is triggered, repeating steps 2 through 8, with new PARENT and CURRENT nodes (step 9).

We should note that the number of child nodes to be traversed next in step 9 may be more than one in some situations:

- The client asks for more than one data object.
- The asked (spatial) data object overlaps more than one node along the search path.
- Nodes in a search tree can overlap (see [12, 18, 4, 11]) and the asked object overlaps the intersection of some nodes.
- Some outsourced search trees may store a data object over several leaf nodes, for example R+-trees [31], UB-trees [3].

Our algorithm as presented above also follows the first solution to the tree structure integrity maintenance (cf. section 3). Let d denote the depth of the tree storage space and m denote the redundancy set size, intuitively the space complexity of the algorithm is $O(m)$ and the time complexity is $O(d \times m)$.

4.3 Insert Operation

As a new data object needs to be inserted into a search tree, we first have to look for a leaf node that is *most suitable* to keep the new object. It is out of the scope of this paper to discuss which leaf node can be considered most suitable, and we refer interested readers to [18, 12] for detailed discussions. After a leaf node is determined and if it still has at least one free entry, the new object will be inserted into that leaf. Otherwise, the leaf is a full node and needs to be split into two leaf nodes, and the new object will be inserted into one of them. In this case, corresponding updates on the parent node must be performed to reflect the split, and such updates may propagate up the tree if the parent node is also already full. In the worst case, the splits propagate up to the root, and if the root is also full, it must be split and a new root is created, so the tree height increases.

In the case of outsourced search trees and with the node swapping technique, we have to lock nodes along the traversal path on the tree. If the nodes are not locked, later necessary updates are impossible because the NIDs can be changed by other oblivious operations. Furthermore, because there are not pure read operations existing with the node swapping technique, we have only exclusive locks on tree nodes. Obviously, exclusively locking all nodes along the traversal/search path from the root will penalize the concurrency degree of the outsourced database. In this section, we will present a new locking scheme for outsourced search trees that can be used for *oblivious insert* operations (with a modified node swapping technique) but does not have to lock *all* nodes along the traversal path.

The philosophy of our locking scheme is as follows: Lock and fetch nodes in the root redundancy set in exclusive mode and find an appropriate child node of the root to access next. Lock and fetch nodes in the redundancy set of this child node and check if the child node is not full. If it is, the locks on nodes of the root redundancy set can be released. Otherwise, continue traversing down the tree and whenever a non-full node on the traversal path (would be a leaf) is found, the locks on all nodes in *all* previous redundancy sets can be released (cf. Figure 2). The reason behind this locking scheme is that if a node on the traversal path is not full, the insertion of a new object into a leaf in its sub-tree will not cause changes to higher level nodes, even if there are node splits in this sub-tree. In database textbooks, this approach is called the *conservative approach* for concurrency control in indexes.

We present below the high level pseudo-code of an algorithm for the oblivious insert operations, which can be applied to a wide range of outsourced search trees. With some special search trees, such as SH-trees [14], UB-trees [3], R+-trees [31], the algorithm can be easily adapted, but we will not go further into such details because of the space limitation.

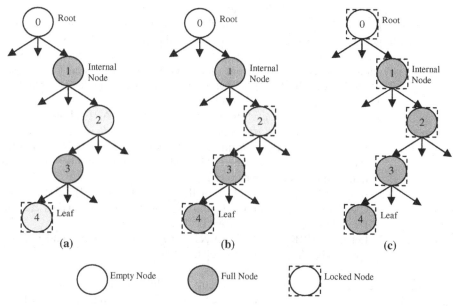

Fig. 2. Examples for the *conservative* locking scheme on outsourced search trees

Algorithm 3: Oblivious Insert Operations

1. Find the root, let it be CURRENT.
2. Initialize a stack variable called STACK.
3. Get a redundancy set for the CURRENT so that this set contains the target node and at least *three* empty nodes if the CURRENT itself is the root or at least *two* empty nodes, otherwise.
4. If the CURRENT is not full, empty the STACK.
5. If the CURRENT is an internal node:
    5.1. Update some meta-information in the CURRENT if necessary.
    5.2. Push its redundancy set in the STACK.
    5.3. Find its child node to be traversed next, let it be CURRENT and go back to step 3.
6. Else (i.e. the CURRENT is a leaf node):

6.1. If it is not full (so the STACK is empty now because of step 4): insert the new object into it, swap it with one of the empty nodes in the redundancy set, and finalize the algorithm.

6.2. Else (i.e. this leaf node is full, and thus either the leaf itself is the root node or the STACK is not empty), do the following tasks:

    6.2.1. Insert (M+1) data objects, M in the CURRENT and a new one, into the two empty nodes (E1, E2) in the redundancy set of the CURRENT. Note that M denotes the maximum number of objects that a leaf node can keep.

    6.2.2. If the STACK is empty (i.e. the CURRENT itself is the root node): empty out the CURRENT, insert E1, E2 into the CURRENT, swap the CURRENT with the third empty node (E3) in its redundancy set, and finalize the algorithm. Otherwise:

    6.2.3. Pop an item (a redundancy set in this case) out from the STACK. Let the target node (an internal node) in this redundancy set be PARENT.

    6.2.4. If the PARENT is not full (so the STACK is empty now because of step 4): delete the CURRENT from the PARENT, insert E1 and E2 into the PARENT, swap the PARENT with one of the empty nodes in its redundancy set, and finalize the algorithm.

    6.2.5. Else (i.e. the PARENT is full, and thus either the PARENT itself is the root node or the STACK is still not empty):

        6.2.5.1. Delete the CURRENT from the PARENT (so the PARENT now consists of M'-1 entries, where M' is the maximum number of entries that an internal node can keep).

        6.2.5.2. Insert (M'+1) entries, M'-1 in the PARENT and E1, E2 from the CURRENT redundancy set, into the two empty nodes (E1', E2') in the redundancy set of the PARENT.

        6.2.5.3. Let the CURRENT be PARENT, let E1 and E2 be E1' and E2', respectively, then go back to step 6.2.2

Although the above algorithm is not difficult to follow, we have some important notes as follows. First, for each redundancy set, we need to lock and fetch at least two (or three if the target node itself is the root) empty nodes in order to support the possible node splits afterwards (step 3). If no split is required for a certain node (steps 6.1 and 6.2.4), one of these empty nodes is employed to swap with the target node as described in section 4.1. On the contrary, the target node is split and its entries as well as the new objects are inserted into these two empty nodes (steps 6.2.1 and 6.2.5.2). Note that, in a special case where the root is full and needs to be split: After its entries and the new objects are distributed over the first two empty nodes, it is emptied out and these two empty nodes are inserted back into the root, then the root itself is swapped with the third empty node before the algorithm is finalized (step 6.2.2).

Second, as mentioned in step 5.1, because the algorithm does not keep the full search path so some meta-information stored in the internal/root nodes, which are no longer kept track of once the nodes are removed from the STACK, needs to be updated soon before the new item is actually inserted. For example, information about the boundary of the subspace, that is stored in an internal node, needs to be updated as soon as this internal node is visited.

Last, as mentioned before, the main advantage of our approach is that it is unnecessary to lock all nodes visited along the search/traversal path as the second solution to the tree structure integrity maintenance in [27], hence the higher concurrency degree can be achieved while the tree structure integrity is still ensured. This advantage relies on the fact that we are able to find some non-full nodes along the traversal path from the root down the tree to the target leaf node. In most practical cases, as discussed in [12], this fact is affirmative, and thus our conservative approach is quite practical.

4.4 Delete Operation

When an object is deleted from a leaf, more issues are arisen if that leaf becomes under-full (i.e., its remaining item number is less than kM, where k is the *minimum fill factor* of the tree). There are several solutions to this problem [21]: An under-full leaf node can be merged with whichever sibling that needs to have the least enlargement or its objects can be scattered among sibling nodes. Both of them can cause the node splits, especially the latter can lead into a propagated splitting. Therefore, R/R*-trees [21, 5] and many new MAMs as [26, 34, 9, etc.] employ re-insertion policy instead of the two above. With the re-insertion policy, all objects in an under-full leaf are reinserted after this leaf is removed from the tree structure. Note that the same issue can happen to internal nodes and the same technique can also be used to solve this issue.

Some other modern MAMs employ a "delete-borrow-reinsert" policy: after an object is deleted from a node and if this node becomes under-full, it tries to "borrow" some objects from its siblings and if this is impossible, the re-insertion policy is applied. As shown in [12], this "delete-borrow-reinsert" policy is desired for the storage utilization but not usually good for the search performance. Again, as we discussed before in section 4.3, this will lead to decrease the concurrency degree for the insertions of outsourced search trees. So we will follow the re-insertion policy to deal with under-full nodes in R-trees and the GiST [24] in order to control under-full nodes in outsourced search trees:

Algorithm 4: Oblivious Delete Operations

1. Search for the leaf node L containing the deleted object O. Lock all nodes in the redundancy sets along the search path from the root node. Stop if O is not found. Note that, each redundancy set needs to have only one empty node E, not two or three as in Algorithm 3.
2. Remove O from L.
3. Let CURRENT be L. Set Q, the set of deleted nodes, to be empty.
4. If the CURRENT is the root, go to step 8. Otherwise, let PARENT be the parent of the CURRENT, and let E_N be the CURRENT's entry in the PARENT.
5. If the CURRENT has fewer than kM entries (i.e. it is an under-full node):
   5.1. Delete E_N from the PARENT and add the CURRENT to set Q.
   5.2. Add the CURRENT to an empty node list.
6. If E_N has not been removed from PARENT, adjust the meta-information in E_N and at higher levels accordingly to reflect the deletion of O.
7. If E_N has been removed from PARENT: Let the CURRENT be PARENT, and go to step 4.

8. Reinsert all entries of nodes in set Q. Entries from deleted leaf nodes are reinserted into tree leaves as described in Algorithm 3, but entries from higher level nodes must be placed higher in the tree at the corresponding levels.
9. If the root has only one child, make the child the new root.
10. Release the locks on nodes and finalize the algorithm. Note that, swapping the node with the empty node in the corresponding redundancy set may need to be conducted in this step.

Algorithm 4 can easily be adapted to support the B+-tree and its variants, as well as other special MAMs like R+-trees, UB-trees, etc. Furthermore, as argued in [25], in some implementations of tree-based indexes it is preferable to leave the under-full nodes after a delete in the expectation that it will be filled up soon thereafter. To support such behaviour, we can replace all steps 3 through 10 with only one step to carry out three tasks at each *locked* target node along the search path as presented in Algorithm 5 below. Note that, similarly to Algorithm 3, in this case we also do not have to lock all nodes along the search path, but just nodes that their meta-information should be updated if O is deleted from the tree.

Algorithm 5: Oblivious Delete Operations (under-full nodes are accepted in the tree)

1. Search for the leaf node L containing the deleted object O. Lock nodes in the redundancy sets along the search path if the target node in that redundancy set should be updated in the case O is actually removed from the tree. Stop if O is not found. Note that, each redundancy set needs to have only one empty node E, not two or three as in Algorithm 3.
2. Remove O from L.
3. With each locked target node from L's parent node up the tree:
    3.1. Adjust the meta-information stored in the node accordingly to reflect the deletion of object O in step 2.
    3.2. Apply the node swapping technique as described in section 4.1 to the redundancy set of this node.
    3.3. Re-encrypt nodes in the redundancy set of this node, write them back to the server, and release the locks on them.

As shown in [27], a critical weakness of the node swapping technique is that if a query Q occurs at a very high frequency, the intersections introduced by random nodes cannot hide the intersections between Qs. We observe that the above assumption can be slightly changed, but the consequence: It is easy to see that reinserting a large number of *near* objects consecutively may lead to reveal information about the tree structure. The main reason is that there is a high probability that a part of the traversal paths as inserting two near objects is the same because near objects are usually stored in the *same or near* nodes (e.g., nodes having the same parent) [18]. Therefore, if a large number of near objects are inserted consecutively, part of the tree structure may be disclosed with a high probability. Attackers may make use of this aspect to find out the whole tree structure. In [27], the authors mentioned that dummy calls and intersections can be introduced to overcome this issue. Although the authors have not realized this idea, it can be foreseen that this solution would be prohibitively expensive. However, Algorithm 5 above can be employed to overcome this critical weakness of the node swapping technique because the insertions are completely omitted.

4.5 Modification Operation

If an indexed data object is modified so that its feature values (or attributes) related to its location in the search tree are changed, the object must be deleted, updated, and then reinserted, so that it will find its way to the right place in the tree. For example, when the shape of an object in the R-tree is changed, its covering rectangle will be changed as well, and this leads to the possible movement of its location in the tree. This basic operation relates closely to inserts and deletes, and in the context of outsourced search trees it can be done easily with the support of oblivious insert and delete operations as introduced in previous sections.

5 Other Related Work

Most similarly to our work, there are two approaches aiming to protect the data confidentiality for outsourced indexed data [16, 22]. Both approaches protect the outsourced data from intruders and the server's operators by some encryption methods. To process queries over encrypted data, they introduced two different solutions. In [22], the authors proposed storing, together with the encrypted data, additional indexing information. This information can be used by the untrusted server to select the data in response to a user's query. The main idea to process a query in this scheme is to split the original query into: (1) A corresponding query over encrypted relations to run on the untrusted server; and (2) a client query for post processing the results returned from the server query. Although this approach is suitable for both exact match and range queries, it still has several critical security limitations [35, 16]. In [16], the authors analyzed some potential inference and linking attacks, and proposed a hash-based indexing method, which is suitable for exact match queries. To process range queries they proposed a solution employing B+-trees. But, as shown in [13], their solution does not provide an oblivious way to traverse the B+-tree and this can be exploited by the untrusted server to carry out inference and linking attacks. Besides, none of the two above approaches supports outsourced MAMs.

In a quite different scenario, when the data owners outsource their private data and allow other clients to access the outsourced data, the *data privacy* may also become important [19, 15, 13]. By the data privacy, the client is not allowed to receive data that does not belong to the query result. In this scenario, the data owner needs to protect their data from both clients and the server. Clients, in turn, may not want to reveal queries and results to both the data owner and the server. Therefore, additional data and user privacy-preserving issues must be taken into account. In [19], the authors introduced an approach to the data privacy in PIR schemes but this approach is not for the outsourced data. Du and Atallah [15] introduced a solution to this outsourcing model, but their approach cannot be applied to outsourced search trees. In our recent work [13], we proposed a solution resorting to a *trusted* third party in order to bring this outsourcing model back to the ODBS model considered in this paper.

In [8], Chor et al. first time introduced the PIR protocol and it has been investigated by many researchers thereafter [2]. This protocol supports the user privacy, allowing a client to access a database without revealing to the server both the query and result. In [13], we also introduced a solution to the ODBS model based on PIR-like protocols. Although this approach would become prohibitively expensive if there is no replication for the outsourced data and an information-theoretic PIR protocol is used, it would be practical if some efficient computational PIR protocol, such as [1], is employed instead.

Last, apart from the software-based approaches as shown above, hardware-based approaches to the problem of secure computations have also been investigated and developed at IBM [29, 30]. In their project, IBM has been developing special security hardware equipment called *secure coprocessors* that can support secure computations at both client and server sides. Although this hardware-based solution may satisfy security objectives, there is still a matter of opinion [20, 29].

6   Conclusions and Future Work

In this paper, we presented full-fledged solutions to the problem of preserving privacy for basic operations on outsourced search trees. Based on the access redundancy and node swapping techniques introduced in [27], we proposed practical algorithms for privacy-preserving search, insert, delete, and modification operations that can be applied to a variety of outsourced search trees. Moreover, we also proposed a complete solution to maintain empty node lists and to use the database storage space at the server efficiently, which was not clarified in [27]. To the best of our knowledge, none of the previous work has dealt with the oblivious updates on outsourced search trees. Our presented work therefore provides the vanguard solutions for this problem.

Our future work will focus on evaluating the efficiency of the proposed solutions in real-world applications. Specially, evaluating the efficiency of Algorithms 5 and investigating its impact on various outsourced search trees will be of great interest because, as introduced in [25], the technique used in this algorithm has been designed to work only with B-trees. Furthermore, comparing our approach with the one introduced in [13] using efficient computational PIR protocols as mentioned in section 5 will be interesting. Last but not least, because there are various search trees, developing generalized oblivious tree algorithms will also be worth considering.

References

1.   D. Asonov, J.C. Freytag. Repudiative Information Retrieval. ACM Workshop on Privacy in the Electronic Society, USA, 2002
2.   D. Asonov. Private Information Retrieval - An Overview and Current Trends. ECDPvA Workshop, Informatik 2001, Austria, 2001
3.   R. Bayer. The Universal B-Tree for Multidimensional Indexing: General Concepts. Int. Conf. on Worldwide Computing and Its Applications (WWCA'97), Japan, 1997

4. C. Boehm , S. Berchtold , D.A. Keim. Searching in High-Dimensional Spaces: Index Structures for Improving the Performance of Multimedia Databases. CSUR, 33(3), Sept. 2001, 322-373
5. N. Beckmann, H-P. Kriegel, R. Schneider, B. Seeger. The R*-tree: An Efficient and Robust Access Method for Points and Rectangles. ACM SIGMOD 1990, pp. 322-331
6. L. Bouganim, P. Pucheral. Chip-Secured Data Access: Confidential Data on Untrusted Servers. VLDB 2002
7. S. Castano, M.G. Fugini, G. Martella, P. Samarati. Database Security. Addison-Wesley and ACM Press 1994, ISBN 0-201-59375-0
8. B. Chor, O. Goldreich, E. Kushilevitz, M. Sudan. Private Information Retrieval. IEEE Symposium on Foundations of Computer Science, 1995
9. K. Chakrabarti, S. Mehrotra. The Hybrid Tree: An Index Structure for High Dimensional Feature Spaces. ICDE 1999, pp. 440-447
10. Y-C. Chang, M. Mitzenmacher. Privacy Preserving Keyword Searches on Remote Encrypted Data. Cryptology ePrint Archive: Report 2004/051
11. E. Chávez, G. Navarro, R. Baeza-Yates, J.L. Marroquín. Searching in Metric Spaces. CSUR, 33(3), Sept. 2001, 273 – 321
12. T.K. Dang. Semantic Based Similarity Searches in Database Systems (Multidimensional Access Methods, Similarity Search Algorithms). PhD Thesis, FAW-Institute, Johannes Kepler University of Linz, Austria, May 2003
13. T.K. Dang. Extreme Security Protocols for Outsourcing Database Services. The 6th Int. Conf. on Information Integration and Web-based Applications and Services-iiWAS 2004, Jakarta, Indonesia, Sept. 27-29, 2004, pp. 497-506
14. T.K. Dang, J. Kueng, R. Wagner. The SH-tree: A Super Hybrid Index Structure for Multidimensional Data. The 12th International Conference on Database and Expert Systems Applications-DEXA 2001, Munich, Germany, Sept. 3-7, 2001, pp. 340-349
15. W. Du, M.J. Atallah. Protocols for Secure Remote Database Access with Approximate Matching. The 7th ACM Conference on Computer and Communications Security, the 1st Workshop on Security and Privacy in E-Commerce, Greece, 2000
16. E. Damiani, S.D.C. Vimercati, S. Jajodia, S. Paraboschi, P. Samarati. Balancing Confidentiality and Efficiency in Untrusted Relational DBMSs. The 10th ACM Conference on Computer and Communication Security, USA, 2003
17. E. Damiani, S.D.C. Vimercati, S. Paraboschi, P. Samarati. Implementation of a Storage Mechanism for Untrusted DBMSs. The 2nd International IEEE Security in Storage Workshop, USA, 2003
18. V. Gaede, O. Guenther. Multidimensional Access Methods. CSUR, 30(2), June 1998, 170–231
19. Y. Gertner, Y. Ishai, E. Kushilevitz, T. Malkin. Protecting Data Privacy in Private Information Retrieval Schemes. STOC'98, USA, 1998
20. O. Goldreich, R. Ostrovsky. Software Protection and Simulation on Oblivious RAMs. Journal of the ACM, 43(3), May 1996, 431-473
21. A. Guttman. R-Trees: A Dynamic Index Structure for Spatial Searching. ACM SIGMOD 1984, pp. 47-57
22. H. Hacigümüs, B.R. Iyer, C. Li, S. Mehrotra. Executing SQL over Encrypted Data in the Database-Service-Provider Model. ACM SIGMOD 2002, pp. 216-227
23. H. Hacigümüs, S. Mehrotra, B.R. Iyer. Providing Database as a Service. ICDE 2002
24. J.M. Hellerstein, J.F. Naughton, A. Pfeffer. Generalized Search Trees for Database Systems. TechnicalReport #1274,University of Wisconsin at Madison, July 1995
25. T. Johnson, D. Shasha. Inserts and Deletes on B-trees: Why Free-At-Empty is Better Than Merge-At-Half. Journal of Computer Sciences and Systems, 47(1), Aug. 1993, 45-76
26. N. Katayama, S. Satoh. The SR-Tree: An Index Structure for High Dimensional Nearest Neighbor Queries. ACM SIGMOD 1997, pp. 369-380

27. P. Lin, K.S. Candan. Hiding Traversal of Tree Structured Data from Untrusted Data Stores. WOSIS 2004, Porto, Portugal, April 2004, pp. 314-323

28. E. Mykletun, M. Narasimha, G. Tsudik. Authentication and Integrity in Outsourced Databases. NDSS2004, San Diego, California, USA, February 5-6, 2004

29. S.W. Smith. Secure Coprocessing Applications and Research Issues. Los Alamos Unclassified Release LA-UR-96-2805. Los Alamos National Laboratory, 1996

30. S.W. Smith, D. Safford. Practical Server Privacy with Secure Coprocessors. IBM Systems Journal, 40(3), 2001

31. T.K. Sellis, N. Roussopoulos, C. Faloutsos. The R+-Tree: A Dynamic Index for Multi-Dimensional Objects. VLDB1987

32. D.X. Song, D. Wagner, A. Perrig. Practical Techniques for Searches on Encrypted Data. IEEE Symposium on Security and Privacy, 2000

33. A. Umar. Information Security and Auditing in the Digital Age - A Managerial and Practical Perspective. NGE Solutions, December 2003 (e-book version)

34. D. A. White, R. Jain. Similarity Indexing with the SS-Tree. ICDE 1996, pp. 516-523

35. K.C.K. Fong. Potential Security Holes in Hacigümüs' Scheme of Executing SQL over Encrypted Data. http://www.cs.siu.edu/~kfong/research/database.pdf

Persistent and Dynamic Trust: Analysis and the Related Impact of Trusted Platforms

Siani Pearson, Marco Casassa Mont, and Stephen Crane

Trusted Systems Laboratory, Hewlett Packard Research Labs, Filton Road, Stoke Gifford, Bristol, BS34 8QZ, UK
{Siani.Pearson, Marco.Casassa_Mont, Stephen.Crane}@hp.com

Abstract. This paper reviews trust from both a social and technological perspective and proposes a distinction between persistent and dynamic trust. Furthermore, this analysis is applied within the context of trusted computing technology.

1 Introduction

This paper demonstrates how trusted computing can provide both persistent and dynamic trust, and assesses the role of both of these within the context of on- and off-line trust provision. Specifically, it provides:

- background analysis of trust (in the form of a summary of trust aspects emerging from the social sciences, cross-disciplinary backgrounds, and e-commerce)
- contrast between persistent v. dynamic trust, together with analysis of how both social and technological means can be used to support such trust
- linkage of this analysis to the real world deployment of Trusted Platforms.

2 Analysis of Persistent and Dynamic Trust

To date, we have no universally accepted scholarly definition of trust. Evidence from a contemporary, cross-disciplinary collection of scholarly writing suggests that a widely held definition of trust is as follows [22]: "Trust is a psychological state comprising the intention to accept vulnerability based upon positive expectations of the intentions or behaviour of another". Yet this definition does not fully capture the dynamic and varied subtleties considered below.

In this section we analyse the complexities of the notion of trust; this supports further consideration in Section 3 of the extent to which trust is increased by using trusted computing technology.

2.1 A Social Science View of Trust

Approaches to modelling trust in social science include:

- **Temporal aspect.** Trust has been considered to have a temporal aspect for a long time, ever since Aristotle stressed that friendship cannot exist without trust and that

P. Herrmann et al. (Eds.): iTrust 2005, LNCS 3477 pp. 355–363, 2005.

trust needs time. In the twentieth century, Niklas Luhmann viewed trust as a representation of the future. This is rather similar to the belief we hold when reasoning inductively that after experiencing a historical pattern of behaviour, similar behaviour can be expected in the future. In the personal sphere, trust is a historical process of individuals learning to trust others without having to give unlimited trust. However, according to [14], we do not really understand the process.

- **Risk aspect.** Social scientists have strongly stressed that risk is a central aspect of trust. For example, Luhmann believed that trust is an investment that involves risky preliminary outlay, where we accept risk in order to reduce the complexity of what we think about the world, in order that we may function [14]. In a similar vein, Georg Simmel believed that trust is an intermediary state between ignorance and knowledge, and the objective of gaining trust may fail [23]. Again, more recently, Nissenbaum in [17] stressed how trust involves vulnerability.

- **Delegation.** One reason why trust is necessary is because we do not have the resources on a personal level to analyze all the information that we need during our working life. Therefore, as societies become more advanced, social order is replaced by legal order and delegation increasingly requires trust in functional authorities and institutions, particularly in the area of knowledge (and technology). However, if these institutions or powerful individuals let down the people who trust them, there is the risk of a big change of attitude towards them. This leads us to the following point...

- **Dynamic aspect.** There can be differing phases in a relationship such as building trust, a stable trust relationship and declining trust. Trust can be lost quickly: as Nielsen states [16]: "It [trust] is hard to build and easy to lose: a single violation of trust can destroy years of slowly accumulated credibility".

2.2 Analysis of On-line Trust

In this section, some additional issues that relate to on-line trust are highlighted. These include:

- **Brand image.**   Reputation is perhaps a company's most valuable asset [17] (although a company's reputation may not be justified), partly because trust is a better strategy than power games [13]. Brand image is associated with trust and suffers if there is a breach of trust or privacy.

- **Delegation and provision of assurance information.** Due to a lack of information and time, together with the huge complexity of IT security, it is impossible for users of IT products to identify the level of security offered by individual products. They need to rely upon the reliability of a product being assessed by experts via evaluation and certification procedures, such as using criteria catalogues (e.g. the 'orange book', ITSEC, Common Criteria in ISO/IEC). The idea is that if a certain assurance level is reached after testing and evaluation of a product, it is worthy of trust being invested in it. Such delegation of trust underpins security certification and privacy seals.

- **Security and privacy.** Enhancing security will not necessarily increase trust, but it is an important enabler and can do so. Some would argue that security is not even a component of trust. For example, Nissenbaum argues that the level of security does not affect trust [17]. She argues that security is increased in order to reduce risk, and not to increase trustworthiness. However, we would argue that, according to the situation, security may increase the level of trust, decrease the level of trust or indeed be neutral as Nissenbaum suggests. An example of increasing security to increase trust comes from people being more willing to engage in e-commerce if they are assured that their credit card numbers and personal data are cryptographically protected [8].

Note that there can be a conflict between security and privacy. For example, some methods of enhanced authentication can result in privacy concerns (such as manufacturers' issue of identification numbers associated with networked devices). Indeed, in order for users who value privacy highly to regard a computing system as trusted, it is important that increased security does not have an adverse effect on privacy.

For further general discussion related to trust in Information Technology, see [1;4] and various recent research studies that analyse trust in relation to the e-commerce domain [5;6;7].

2.3 Assessing the Impact of Computer Systems: Persistent and Dynamic Trust Underpinned by Social and Technological Mechanisms

When assessing how trust may be increased by computer systems, we see it as helpful in distinguishing between persistent and dynamic trust, and between social and technological means of achieving such trust:

Persistent trust is trust in long-term underlying properties or infrastructure; this arises through relatively static social and technological mechanisms. Social mechanisms, behaviour and values contributing to this include sanctions, assurance and vouching (including seals of approval): such examples are of infrastructural mechanisms that may vary over time, but in general are relatively stable. Technological mechanisms include underlying security infrastructure, well-known practices and the technological features corresponding to static social mechanisms; these can involve the following, for example:

- Certified hardware (for example, tamper-resistant hardware)
- Protocols
- Certified cryptographic techniques
- Assurance
- Other security features
- Audit and enforcement

Dynamic trust is trust specific to certain states, contexts, or short-term or variable information; this can arise through context-based social and technological mechanisms. The content of social mechanisms would be liable to substantial change at short notice, such as brand image, look and feel, reputation and history of interactions. The technological mechanisms give confidence that a particular environment or system state is trusted (at a given time, for a particular purpose).

A system's behaviour can change according to a given context, and in particular if it has been hacked, and in some cases system behaviour can be driven by policies (dictated by people, business needs or even malicious people) that change over time. For example, dynamic trust could be affected by the following information being divulged:

- A particular system has been compromised (for example, spyware is running on it)
- The location of the system or user has changed
- Software is in a certain state
- Policy enforcement has not been carried out

The relationship between these categories can be complex, and in particular the distinction between persistent and dynamic trust should be viewed as a continuum because there is not always a clear-cut distinction between these categories. For example, recommendation could be considered to be in-between these categories as it is in general fairly static but could still change in the short term.

The focus of this paper is on a subset of persistent (social and technological-based) and of dynamic (technological-based) trust. Both social and technological aspects of trust are necessary when designing online systems, quite apart from additional social guarantees of privacy and security.

2.4 Summary

Trust is a complex notion and a multi-level analysis is important in order to try to understand it. There are many different ways in which on-line trust can be established: security may be one of these (although security, on its own, does not necessarily imply trust [18]). When assessing trust in relation to computer systems, we have distinguished between social and technological means of providing persistent and dynamic trust. All of these aspects of trust can be necessary.

Persistent social-based trust in a hardware or software component or system is an expression of confidence in technological-based trust, because it is assurance about implementation and operation of that component or system. In particular, there are links between social-based trust and technological-based trust through the vouching mechanism, because it is important to know who is vouching for something as well as what they are vouching; hence social-based trust should always be considered.

Mechanisms to provide dynamic technological-based trust need to be used in combination with social and technological mechanisms for providing persistent trust: as we shall see in the following section, if software processes provide information about the behaviour of a platform, that information can only be trusted if entities that are trusted vouch both for the method of providing the information and for the expected value of the information.

3 Deploying Trusted Technologies

In this section we explore the deployment of trusted technologies in relation to the framework described in the previous section.

3.1 Trusted Platforms

A Trusted Platform (TP) is designed to create a foundation of trust for software processes, based on a cost-effective security hardware device that is tamper-resistant and has cryptographic functionality, called a Trusted Platform Module (TPM). Documents that specify how a TP must be constructed have been produced by the Trusted Computing Platform Alliance (TCPA) (and now its successor the Trusted Computing Group (TCG)) [24;26]. TCG has adopted all the TCPA specifications, and so for consistency we shall henceforth refer to TCG technology.

The TCG-enabled computers which are already commercially available include little support from the operating system. Allied protected computing environments under development by certain manufacturers and open source operating systems such as Linux can support TCG facilities further and allow their widespread and convenient use. Intel's LaGrande hardware and chipset modifications [10] are designed to provide access-protected memory, and give greater support to secure operating systems. Microsoft's Next-Generation Secure Computing Base (NGSCB), formerly known as Palladium, is a secure computing environment that can run in parallel with Windows [15]. It provides additional protection beyond that defined by the TCG specification, including some protection of the video output and keyboard input. These different trusted computing implementations are all TPs since they accord to the same underlying philosophy and basic principles of operation, as espoused in [25].

Trusted computing addresses some central concerns of people using PCs: it protects data that is stored on those machines (even while they are interacting with other machines over the Internet) and it aims to put everyone in the position where they can feel confident that they can:

- Protect their data
- Find out whether their platform is in a trustworthy state (i.e. its integrity has not been compromised)
- Have the means to decide whether it is reasonable for them to trust other platforms

Although the technology is at least initially targeted at corporate environments, the introduction of trusted computing has been the focus for an open debate about whether or not this technology will be beneficial for ordinary people – for discussion of some of the issues, see [2;20;28] as further consideration of that issue is out of the scope of this paper.

3.2 How TPs Can Provide Persistent and Dynamic Trust

Broadly speaking, the view taken by the proponents of trusted computing (see for example [25]) is that we can think of something as being trusted if it operates in the expected manner for a particular purpose, or can be relied upon to signal clearly if it does not. The TCG definition of trust is that something is trusted "if it always behaves in the expected manner for the intended purpose" [25]. A similar approach is also adopted in the third part of ISO/IEC 15408 standard [11]: "a trusted component, operation or process is one whose behavior is predictable under almost any operating condition and which is highly resistant to subversion by application software, viruses and a given level of physical interference".

We believe that categorizing trust in terms of the analysis presented in Section 2 helps in understanding further how TPs enhance trust.

- **Dynamic v. persistent trust.** Within a TP, a trust hierarchy operates such that such behavioural trust in the platform is underpinned by trust that the platform is at that time properly reporting and protecting information (dynamic trust), again underpinned by another layer of trust that that platform is capable of properly reporting and protecting information (persistent trust). Both dynamic and persistent trust are involved in the decision by an enquirer (either local user or remote entity) whether a platform is trusted for the purpose intended by that enquirer: if the enquirer trusts the judgment of the third parties that vouch for the system components, and if the platform proves its identity and the measurements match the expected measurements, then the enquirer will trust that the platform will behave in a trustworthy and predictable manner. The platform reports information to the enquirer to enable that decision to be made [26], and analysing this requires intelligent application of cryptographic techniques; optionally, use could be made of a third party service to perform or help with this analysis. In reality, the enquirer might want to be reassured about a set of platforms running services, managing their personal data. Analysing such composite assurance is an open issue that we are currently addressing [21].

In relation to the aspects of trust that were discussed above:

- **Temporal aspect.** Some trust is based on our use of similar technological products beforehand, and our history of interactions with companies (see the discussion about brand image below). In the shorter term, trust sustainability should be addressed: in order to maintain a trust relationship between service requester and provider over time, or at least until a service is completed, the service requester may periodically re-challenge the provider to check the latest integrity metrics. The analysis required may need to take account of other factors too, such as time and history. Another approach is to have enhanced trusted software on the provider platform that monitors any changes to the platform state against pre-registered conditions provided by the service requester and notifies the requester if the changes impact the conditions [27]. This can be more efficient but requires additional initial setup and infrastructure; moreover, it can potentially lessen trust and security if the root of trust for reporting is no longer the TPM hardware chip.

- **Risk aspect.** Risk can operate at various levels, including business with strangers being risky (no less so for business partners online than it is off-line [12]) and threats from hackers. Trust in a TP ultimately reduces to trust in social entities, which involves risk. On the technological side, there are risks arising from the necessity to reduce complexity of platform state during analysis for practical reasons (and hence a focus on checking only selected integrity metrics) and privacy or security risks that trusted computing does not protect against – for example, unauthorised keystroke logging. The first generation of TPs only provides a protected storage capability – it does not expose the full functionality described in the TCG specifications and can only be trusted to protect secrets in a certain way since there is no trusted boot process. TPs that do provide the full functionality described in the TCG specifications provide roots of trust for systems, but even so they do not provide a complete trust solution: instead, additional trust functionality should be built on top of them. In the short term, this must include security enhancements at the operating system level (as mentioned above), right up to trust management techniques (see for example [3;9]). Even if all this functionality were provided in a system, no system is ever completely secure, so there is some risk, however unlikely.

– **Delegation.** Trust in a computer system is underpinned by trust in individuals, in companies, and in brand names who vouch for the system. Lack of trust by some people in some entities involved in the production of trusted computing is a reason for them to distrust the technology as a whole (see for example [2;28]). The (persistent) social basis for trust is that trusted third parties vouch (a) for the mechanisms that collect and provide evidence of dynamic trust as well as (b) that particular values of integrity metrics represent a platform that is behaving as it should. In essence, delegation is centrally involved: certain third parties are prepared to endorse a platform because they have assessed the platform and others are willing to state that if measurements of the integrity of that platform are of a certain value, it can be trusted for particular purposes.

In order to do the former, an endorsement key is embedded into the TPM. The public endorsement key is signed by the manufacturer and published in the form of a digital certificate. Social trust is used to recognise a specific genuine TPM: you trust a specific TPM because it is an assertion made by the trusted manufacturer that produced it. In a similar way, other elements of a TP also have certificates, and delegation of trust to authorities is needed in order to provide such certification material: TCG provides this in conformance with the Common Criteria.

– **More on dynamic aspect.** In order to know whether a platform can be trusted at a given time, there are processes in a TP that dynamically collect and provide evidence of platform behaviour. These processes carry out measurement and provide a means for the measurement method to show itself to be trustworthy. When any platform starts, a core root of trust for measurement (inside the BIOS or the BIOS Boot Block in PCs) starts a series of measurements involving the processor, OS loader, and other platform components. The TPM acts as a root of trust for reporting and dynamically stores and protects against alteration the results of this measurement process, as well as reliably cryptographically reporting the current measured values. To find out if a service executes properly (in a dynamic way) you check these measurements against values that have been created and signed by someone that you trust, as discussed above.

– **Brand image.** Brand image can be leveraged to sell trusted systems. Someone's willingness to carry out business with a TP will depend on the intended use and on the level of trust in the platform and the owner of the platform. In particular, the manufacturer of a platform is visible to a third party communicating with that platform. For example, Original Equipment Manufacturers (OEMs) can exploit their reputation for quality to make their platforms the preferred solution for business-critical services.

– **Security and privacy.** Trusted computing is designed to provide enhanced security at an affordable price. Trusted computing is also designed to provide this security in a privacy-friendly manner – for example, it provides pseudonymous or anonymous attestation identities: see [20] for discussion of this issue.

4 Conclusions

In conclusion, answers to questions about technology-mediated trust involve a combination of technology and also (changing) human attitudes and behaviour. In order to determine whether a system is trustworthy, we have to ask whether we have assurance that the system will behave as it should and also whether we trust the people behind the technology. TPs help in doing this, but note that still we trust these people if we believe that they will not exploit their potential to hurt us. By the mechanisms described above the next versions of TPs will aim to provide a root of trust for other trust service technologies.

Acknowledgements. Our ideas on this topic benefited from useful input and discussions with Graeme Proudler (HP) and Giles Hogben (JRC).

References

1. ACM, Special Issue on "Trusting Technology", *Communications of the ACM,* vol 43, no 12, December 2000.
2. Anderson, R., "'Trusted Computing' Frequently Asked Questions", v1.1, August 2003. Available via http://www.cl.cam.ac.uk/~rja14.
3. Blaze, M., Ioannidid, J. and Keromytis, A.D., "Experience with the KeyNote Trust Management System: Applications and Future Directions", Proceedings of the First International Conference on Trust Management (iTrust 2003), Crete, Greece, pp. 284-300, May 2003.
4. Castelfranchi, C. and Y.-H. Tan, eds., *Trust and Deception in Virtual Societies,* Kluwer Academic Publishers, 2001.
5. Cheskin, "Research and Studio Archetype", *eCommerce Trust Study,* University College London. January 1999. Available via http://www.sapient.com/cheskin/.
6. Egger, F. N., *Increasing Consumers' Confidence in Electronic Commerce through Human Factors Engineering,* MSc project, University College London, 1998.
7. Friedman, B., P. H. Kahn Jr. and D. C. Howe, "Trust Online", *Communications of the ACM,* 43, no. 12, December 2000, pp. 34-40.
8. Giff, S., *The Influence of Metaphor, Smart Cards and Interface Dialogue on Trust in eCommerce,* MSc project, University College London, 2000.
9. Grandison, T. and Sloman, M., "Trust Management Tools for Internet Applications", Proceedings of the First International Conference on Trust Management (iTrust 2003), Crete, Greece, pp. 91-107, May 2003.
10. Intel, "LaGrande Technology Architectural Overview", September 2003. Available via http://www.intel.com/technology/security/downloads/LT_Arch_Overview.pdf.
11. ISO/IEC 15408 (all parts), "Information technology – Open Systems Interconnection – Evaluation criteria for information technology security", *International Organization for Standardization,* Geneva, Switzerland, 1999.
12. Jupiter, *Trust Online: Barrier Today, Strength Tomorrow,* Research Report, 4 April 2001.

13. Kumar, N., "The Power of Trust in Manufacturer-Retailer Relationships", *Harvard Business Review*, Nov-Dec 1996, pp92-106.
14. Luhmann, N., "Trust as a Reduction of Complexity", *Trust and Power: Two works by Niklas Luhmann*, New York: John Wiley & Sons, 1979, pp. 24-31.
15. Microsoft, Next-Generation Secure Computing Base home page, http://www.microsoft.com/resources/ngscb.
16. Nielsen, J., "Trust or Bust: Communicating Trustworthiness in Web Design", *Jacob Nielsen's Alertbox*, 1999. Available via http://www.useit.com/alertbox/990307.html.
17. Nissenbaum, H., "Can Trust be Secured Online? A theoretical perspective", *Etica e Politica*, no. 2, Dec 1999.
18. Osterwalder, D., "Trust Through Evaluation and Certification?" *Social Science Computer Review*, 19, no. 1, Sage Publications, Inc., Spring 2001, pp. 32-46.
19. Pearson, S., "A Trusted Method for Self-profiling in e-Commerce", *Trust, Reputation and Security: Theories and Practice*, R. Falcone et al. (eds.), LNAI 2631, pp, 177-193, Springer-Verlag, Berlin, 2003.
20. Pearson, S., "Trusted Computing: Strengths, Weaknesses and Further Opportunities for Enhancing Privacy", LNCS, Proceedings of iTrust 2005, ed. P. Herrmann, V. Issarny and S. Shiu, France, May 2005.
21. PRIME: Privacy and Identity Management for Europe, European RTD Integrated Project under the FP6/IST Programme, http://www.prime-project.eu.org/, 2004
22. Rousseau, D., S. Sitkin, R. Burt and C. Camerer, "Not so Different after All: a Cross-discipline View of Trust", *Academy of Management Review*, 23, no. 3, 1998, pp. 393-404.
23. Simmel, G., *Soziologie*, 5th ed., p. 263, Berlin, 1968.
24. Trusted Computing Group, *TCG Main Specification*, Version 1.1b, 2003. Available via http://www.trustedcomputinggroup.org.
25. Trusted Computing Group, *TCG Specification Architecture Overview*, Version 1.2, 2004. Available via www.trustedcomputinggroup.org.
26. Trusted Computing Group, *TCG TPM Specification*, Version 1.2, 2003. Available via http://www.trustedcomputinggroup.org.
27. Yan, Z. and Cofta, P., "A Mechanism for Trust Sustainability Among Trusted Computing Platforms", S. Katsikas, J. Lopez and G. Pernul (eds): TrustBus 2004, LNCS 3184, pp.11-19, Springer-Verlag Berlin Heidelberg, 2004.
28. Yung, M, "Trusted Computing Platforms: The Good, the Bad and the Ugly", *Financial Cryptography*, R.N. Wright (ed.), LNCS 2742, pp. 250-254, Springer-Verlag, Berlin, 2003.

Risk Models for Trust-Based Access Control (TBAC)

Nathan Dimmock*, Jean Bacon, David Ingram, and Ken Moody

University of Cambridge Computer Laboratory,
JJ Thomson Ave, Cambridge CB3 0FD, UK
`Firstname.Lastname@cl.cam.ac.uk`

Abstract. The importance of risk in trust-based systems is well established. This paper presents a novel model of risk and decision-making based on economic theory. Use of the model is illustrated by way of a collaborative spam detection application.

1 Introduction and Background

Autonomous decision-making is an increasingly popular application of Trust Management systems. This is particularly true for security and access control in emerging fields such as pervasive and autonomic computing, where existing techniques are seen as inadequate. However, *trust* in itself is an abstract concept and, in order to take a decision, how much trust is required must be balanced against other factors. These are normally quantified as the *risk* of the various courses of action available to a decision-maker.

Proposition 1. *Trust is unnecessary unless there is something at risk.*

1.1 What Is Risk?

Previously the SECURE project [1] has explored risk [2] as being a combination of two components, *likelihood* and *impact*. Economists take an alternative approach, defining it as a special type of *uncertainty* [3].

Risk applies to situations when one is unsure of the outcome, but the odds are known.
Uncertainty applies to situations when one is unsure of the outcome and the odds are unknown.

When interacting with autonomous agents in a global computing environment the uncertainty in the outcome is usually due to uncertainty as to the future behaviour of the other agents. Computational trust models of evidence and reputation ultimately allow this uncertainty about potential actions be transformed into risk, and consequently the uncertain situation can be reasoned about as a risky one, using trust-based decision engines such as SECURE [1].

---

* Supported by the EU SECURE project, IST-2001-32486.

P. Herrmann et al. (Eds.): iTrust 2005, LNCS 3477, pp. 364–371, 2005.

1.2   Decision-Making Under Uncertainty in Economics

Hirshleifer's state-preference theory [4] aims to reduce choice under uncertainty to a conventional choice problem by changing the commodity structure appropriately. Thus preferences are formed over state-contingent commodity-bundles or, if we assume the commodity is currency, then *state-payoff* bundles. To use Hirshleifer's classic illustration, "ice cream when it is raining" is a different commodity from "ice cream when it is sunny".

Given a suitable formulation of the situation, the von Neumann-Morgenstern (vNM) expected utility rule ([5], see below) can then be applied to choose the best course of action given our beliefs about which state is likely to obtain. This approach fits nicely with the concept of Trust-Based Access Control (TBAC) used in the SECURE project [6], since it allows for reasoning about outcomes where a number of different states could obtain.

1.3   Suitability of the Expected Utility Theory for TBAC

Extensive experimental research has resulted in many concluding that the expected utility theory is not an accurate model of how humans make decisions, and much debate on this subject continues [7]. We feel that the psychological side of this debate — such as the supposition that humans do not meet the criteria for being rational[1] agents, and issues of the way in which the problem is framed [8] — is irrelevant to our model. *We are looking to build autonomous agents, not artificially intelligent ones.* [7] details a number of phenomena that are not well-modelled by the vNM utility rule, but since no unified model for all the phenomena described by [7] has yet been found, for simplicity we shall restrict our initial experiments to using the vNM rule.

2   A Trust-Based Access Control Model for SECURE

The state-preference model has the following five components:

- a set of acts available (X) to the decision-maker;
- a set of (mutually exclusive) states available to Nature (S);
- a consequence function, $c(x, \varsigma)$, showing outcomes under all possible combinations of acts and states[2];
- a probability function, $\pi(\varsigma)$, expressing the decision-maker's trust beliefs;
- an elementary-utility function (or preference scaling function), $v(c)$ measuring the desirability of the different possible consequences.

The von Neumann-Morgenstern theory then gives the utility of each act, $x \in X$ as:

$$U(x) \equiv \sum_{\varsigma \in S} \pi_\varsigma v(c_{x,\varsigma})$$

---

[1] That is, will act to maximise their personal utility.

[2] NB: ς is used to denote elements of S to avoid clashing with the existing SECURE terminology of using s as part of an (s, i, c) trust-triple.

2.1   Defining Preference Using Utility

Previous models of risk have expressed preference over outcomes in the form of monetary costs and benefits. This approach has been criticised as being inappropriate because in many situations financial valuation is difficult or impossible. In this new model the abstract metric of (economic) utility is used. This represents money adjusted for time-effects (such as inflation and interest) and relative wealth, thereby overcoming the drawbacks associated with using actual money.

Whilst [9] observes that economists have proved that there is no meaningful measure of utility, the following definition from page 73 of [9], seems well-suited to our purposes:

Definition 1. *A real-valued function of consequences, v, is a utility if and only if $f \leq g$ (i.e. g is preferred to f) is equivalent to $v(f) \leq v(g)$, provided f and g are both with probability one confined to a finite set of consequences.*

We note that the concept of monetary costs and benefits satisfies this definition, which could be useful in applications where financial considerations are already present, for example the e-purse scenario outlined in [1].

2.2   Access Control Policy

A simple access control policy would be to choose any act, $a \in A$ where:

$$A = \left\{ a \mid a \in X \wedge U(a) = \max_X [U(x)] \right\}$$

If $|A| > 1$ then we choose the action $a' \in A$ with the smallest variance of utility.

Unfortunately this model does not yet address the problem of reasoning about the uncertainty and information content of trust-values. Intuitively a person will not feel confident in taking a course of action based upon a decision about which they have too little information. The quantity of the information required to satisfy them that this is the correct course of action will depend on their risk-aversity, and therefore must be encoded as part of the person's policy. Therefore we allow the policy-writer to set a lower-bound l for the number of bits of information known about the chosen action a, in order for it to be executed. If this check fails, then the system may test other actions in the set A or fall back to a pre-defined, "default" action.

2.3   Integration with the SECURE Trust Model

While this model is designed to be used with any suitable trust metric, we will now summarise how it is expected to integrate with the SECURE Trust Model [10]. This trust model provides for a principal to compute a set of beliefs about the likely outcome of interacting with another principal. Outcomes are defined in event structures and beliefs have the form (s, i, c) where s is the number of pieces of evidence supporting that outcome, c is the number of pieces of evidence contradicting that outcome, and i is the number of inconclusive pieces of evidence. By defining a mapping from the event structure of outcomes, E, to the states of Nature, S, it is trivial to compute a similar mapping from the set of beliefs in (s, i, c) form to a set of $\pi(\varsigma)$.

Entity Recognition (ER) also plays an important part in the SECURE model and the required level of confidence in the recognition of a principal should be determined by the risk associated with the decision. Intuitively, if an entity is incorrectly recognised, then the estimates for $\pi(\varsigma)$ are likely to be completely invalid. One way of representing this in the model would be to use the confidence in entity recognition to scale the measure of information the decision is based upon — the decision to perform act a is known to be based upon trust-values of the form (s, i, c) and since states are mutually exclusive, $\sum_S \pi(\varsigma) = 1, \forall \varsigma \in S, s + i + c = I$, which is the quantity of information, upon which the decision is based. This is then reduced in magnitude by the probability of incorrect entity recognition, $(1 - p_{er})$ before being compared to the information threshold l, described above.

An alternative method would be to perform a second risk analysis using the state-preference approach, once the set A has been determined. In this second analysis there would be just two states, {entity recognised correctly, entity recognised incorrectly} and the acts would be A plus a fall back act for the eventuality that the risk of mis-recognition is too high to take any of the acts in A.

3   Selection Under Uncertainty as a Decision Problem

One of the weaknesses of the current SECURE trust model is that it is optimised for yes/no style decisions. For example, making a selection, such as choosing the best principal (or principals) from which to request a service, is very inefficient. This new model may be used to make a selection in the following way:

- The set of acts available (X) to the *selector* is equal to the set of potential service providers, P, or the power-set of P if combinations of providers are to be considered.

- The set of (mutually exclusive) states available to Nature (S). Each state represents whether each particular principal was "good" or "bad". For example, $\varsigma_1 = \{p_1\}, \varsigma_2 = \{p_1, p_2\}$ means that only p_1 satisfied us in state ς_1, while in state ς_2, p_1 and p_2 satisfy us, and so on.

- The consequence function, $c(x, \varsigma)$, showing outcomes under all possible combinations of acts and states — so $P \times S$ in the simple case where $X = P$. Good consequences, (x_i, ς_j) are those where $p_i \in \varsigma_j$.

- The probability function, $\pi(\varsigma)$, expressing the user's beliefs.

- The elementary-utility function (or preference scaling function) $v(c)$, measuring the desirability of the different possible consequences — so those that are "good" consequences, as mentioned above, have higher utility than those that are "bad". This function could also encode constraints such as a budget.

4   Example Application: Spam Detection

4.1   Risk Analysis of Spam Filtering

When considering whether an e-mail is spam or not, the decision-maker must decide whether to *mark* a message as spam or allow it to *pass* into the inbox. The situation can therefore be modelled as follows:

- The set of acts available to the decision-maker is $X = \{mark, pass\}$.
- The set of (mutually exclusive) states available to Nature is $S = \{spam, notspam\}$.
- The consequence function, $c(x, \varsigma)$ with example utilities for each consequence shown (where E is a parameter that allows the sensitivity of the filter to be adjusted):

X/S	spam	notspam
mark	1	-E
pass	0	0

- The probability function, $\pi(\varsigma)$, expressing the decision-maker's beliefs in whether the message is spam or not. How this is determined is discussed below.

4.2   Collaborative Spam Detection

Determining the belief function, $\pi(\varsigma)$, is difficult when dealing with spam. The lack of reliable authentication mechanisms in Internet e-mail makes forgery of existing identities and the creation of new ones too easy. This makes it difficult to make trust assessments about the sender of a message. An alternative mechanism, described in [11], uses a peer-to-peer (p2p) collaborative network to detect spam. It takes the view that, since identifying spam is an AI problem that can never be entirely solved using rule-based systems, even advanced ones based on Bayesian inference, the best method of identifying spam is still a human. Therefore the first human to identify a spam publishes a hash of the message to a p2p network and then each member of that network compares their incoming e-mail with the published hashes, as shown in figure 1. A trust and risk analysis is used to determine whether to mark the message as spam or allow it to continue into the user's inbox, given the opinion of other trusted nodes on the p2p network. Since spam e-mails increasingly have added random noise to try to defeat filters, fuzzy signature algorithms such as Nilsimsa[12] must be used to generate the *fingerprint*.

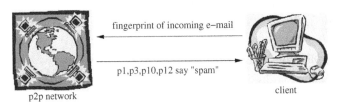

fingerprint of incoming e–mail

p1,p3,p10,p12 say "spam"

p2p network   client

Fig. 1. Overview of the operation of a Collaborative Spam Detector

4.3 Trust and Identity

For simplicity each principal is represented by a public key so entity-recognition does not have a large role to play in the current implementation of this application.

In the trust model, each client locally stores a (s_j, i_j, c_j) triple for each principal, p_j, indicating how much they trust their judgement. s_j is the number of times they have given a correct opinion on whether an e-mail is spam or not, c_j is the number of times they have incorrectly described an e-mail and i_j is the number of opinions received that have yet to be confirmed as correct or incorrect.

The probability that a mail is spam given that p_j says it is spam is then given by:

$$\rho_j = p(\text{spam}|p_j) = \frac{s_j}{s_j + c_j}$$

The probability that a mail is spam given that p_j says it is **not spam** is given by:

$$\rho_j = p(\text{spam}|\overline{p_j}) = \frac{c_j}{s_j + c_j}$$

The information from each principal is then weighted, based upon the number of previous interactions we have had with them and using a weighted-mean, to determine an overall probability of whether a message is spam or not:

$$p(\text{spam}) = \frac{w_1\rho_1 + w_2\rho_2 + ... + w_j\rho_j}{\sum w_j}$$

where $w_j = s_j + c_j$. Information from principals with w_j below the information threshold, l, is ignored.

When the owner of the system reads their mail they give feedback to the system as to whether or not it made the correct decision. This may be implemented implicitly by monitoring how the user deals with the e-mail (such as moving it to a certain folder), or an explicit feedback channel exclusively for correcting errors (as used in [11]).

Once a message has been verified by the human operator of the system, the (s, i, c) triples for each principal that published an opinion are updated.

4.4 Recommendations

If there is insufficient information (as determined by the information threshold, l) in the local trust database about principal Alice who offers an opinion on a particular e-mail, then the trust engine may also query the p2p network for recommendations from other principals about their experiences with Alice. To avoid problems with second-hand information and loops, only information from direct experiences is published, in the form of (s, i, c) triples.

Clearly, naïvely trusting recommendations from other p2p users is dangerous. In order to incorporate these recommendations into the probability calculation, they are first discounted [13], using the belief in the principal's *recommendation integrity*; they are then averaged over all principals who supplied a recommendation, before being added to any local trust information.

Recommendation integrity (also known as "meta-trust") is calculated using the concept of *semantic distance* from [14]. Received recommendations are stored in a cache and then, after a certain number of interactions with the subject of the recommendation have taken place (arbitrarily chosen as five in the initial prototype), the value of the (newly obtained) local *observed* trust value is compared with the *received* trust value. The main difficulty here is that the information content of the received value is likely to be far higher than the experience value. The two trust values are therefore normalised, giving (where $info = s + i + c$):

$$\left(\frac{s_o}{info_o}, \frac{i_o}{info_o}, \frac{c_o}{info_o} \right), \left(\frac{s_r}{info_r}, \frac{i_r}{info_r}, \frac{c_r}{info_r} \right)$$

The recommendation integrity, RI, is then given by the ratio:

$$\frac{s_o}{info_o} : \frac{s_r}{info_r}$$

We observe that if $RI < 1$ then the recommendations tend to be better than the behaviour we experience, and so any recommendation should be scaled down accordingly. In contrast, if $RI > 1$ then the recommendations are more negative than our observations indicate. Note, we do not scale up in this instance as this would allow an attacker to manipulate trust values by giving negative recommendations about those it wished to make appear more trustworthy. Instead we observe that anyone who is guilty of "bad-mouthing" another principal is unlikely to be very trustworthy at all and ignore any recommendation they may give if $RI > 2$.

The RI for a recommender is calculated at most once per recommendation received to ensure that principals are not overly penalised if the principal they recommend subsequently changes their behaviour. Since principals are likely to make many recommendations, the RI value for a principal is an average over all recommendations that principal makes.

4.5   Evaluation

A comprehensive evaluation of this application has been undertaken, using both analytical and empirical approaches. Unfortunately space constraints preclude any detailed discussion here. The approach was threat-based, analysing what type of behaviour individual attackers might use to influence decisions, and simulation was then used to determine how these individual behaviours would interact at a system-wide level.

The results indicated that the attackers operating in isolation were quickly identified and ignored and so their best strategy was to co-operate in a co-ordinated manner. To mitigate the Sybil Attack [15], policies were used that forced principals to supply more correct than incorrect information in order to be able to affect decisions.

5   Research Context and Conclusions

This paper has presented a novel model of risk and trust-based access control based on the economic theory of decision-making under uncertainty. This model has been evaluated through the implementation of a p2p collaborative spam detection application which demonstrated its effectiveness.

This work builds on the authors' experiences of developing and using the SECURE risk model [2], which whilst being flexible and expressive was found to have a number of weaknesses in practical deployment. Jøsang and Presti [16] also use the expected utility theory to model agent risk aversity, but their model concentrates on using risk to deduce trust rather than for access control. Further work could involve integrating our approach with Jøsang and Presti's, and an investigation of more complex expected utility functions.

References

1. Cahill, V., et al.: Using trust for secure collaboration in uncertain environments. IEEE Pervasive Computing **2** (2003) 52–61
2. Dimmock, N.: How much is 'enough'? Risk in trust-based access control. In: IEEE International Workshops on Enabling Technologies: Infrastructure for Collaborative Enterprises — Enterprise Security. (2003) 281–282
3. Knight, F.H.: 1. In: Risk, Uncertainty, and Profit. Library of economics and liberty. 8 September 2004 edn. Hart, Schaffner & Marx; Houghton Mifflin Company, Boston, MA (1921)
4. Hirshleifer, J., Riley, J.G.: The analytics of uncertainty and information. Cambridge surveys of economic literature. Cambridge University Press (1992)
5. von Neumann, J., Morgenstern, O.: Theory of Games and Economic Behavior. Second edn. Princeton University Press (1947)
6. Dimmock, N., Belokosztolszki, A., Eyers, D., Bacon, J., Moody, K.: Using trust and risk in role-based access control policies. In: Proceedings of Symposium on Access Control Models and Technologies, ACM, ACM (2004)
7. Machina, M.J.: Choice under uncertainty: Problems solved and unsolved. The Journal of Economic Perspectives **1** (1987) 121–154
8. Simon, H.A.: Models of bounded rationality. Volume 1. MIT Press (1982)
9. Savage, L.J.: The foundations of statistics. Second edn. Dover, New York (1972)
10. Carbone, M., Dimmock, N., Krukow, K., Nielsen, M.: Revised computational trust model. EU IST-FET Project Deliverable (2004)
11. Dimmock, N., Maddison, I.: Peer-to-peer collaborative spam detection. ACM Crossroads **11** (2004)
12. cmeclax: Nilsimsa codes. http://ixazon.dynip.com/~cmeclax/nilsimsa.html (2004) Accessed 22 November 2004 17:30 UTC.
13. Jn++sang, A.: A logic for uncertain probabilities. International Journal of Uncertainty, Fuzziness and Knowledge-Based Systems **9** (2001)
14. Abdul-Rahman, A., Hailes, S.: Supporting trust in virtual communities. In: Hawaii International Conference on System Sciences 33. (2000) 1769–1777
15. Douceur, J.R.: The Sybil attack. In: Proceedings of the First International Workshop on Peer-to-Peer Systems (IPTPS'02). Number 2429 in LNCS, Springer-Verlag (2002) 251–260
16. Jn++sang, A., Presti, S.L.: Analysing the relationship between trust and risk. In: Proceedings of the Second International Conference on Trust Management (iTrust'04). Number 2995 in LNCS, Oxford, UK, Springer (2004) 135–145

Combining Trust and Risk to Reduce the Cost of Attacks*

Daniel Cvrček and Ken Moody

University of Cambridge, Computer Laboratory,
15 JJ Thomson Avenue, Cambridge, CB3 0FD, United Kingdom

Abstract. There have been a number of proposals for trust and reputation-based systems. Some have been implemented, some have been analysed only by simulation. In this paper we first present a general architecture for a trust-based system, placing special emphasis on the management of context information. We investigate the effectiveness of our architecture by simulating distributed attacks on a network that uses trust/ reputation as a basis for access control decisions.

1 Introduction

Many large-scale systems span multiple autonomous administrative domains. In such environments there are both economic and technological obstacles to system-wide user enrolment, and it is not feasible to establish a flexible centralised administration. Emerging environments such as ubiquitous computing and sensor networks also pose significant management challenges. Traditional security mechanisms, based on the assignment of privileges according to each user's known identity, cannot be employed, yet cooperation between diverse, autonomous entities is essential. Security decisions can only be based on (partial) information about a principal's previous behaviour. Such systems are called *trust-based systems* [1, 2, 3, 4] or *reputation systems* to characterise their nature.

This paper describes a formal model for such systems, based on concepts derived from intrusion-detection and anomaly-detection architectures. The design follows the principles of common security systems. We assume the existence of a multitude of log files each containing a large number of events, each event useless on its own because of its low-level origin. We also assume that trust and risk are two conceptually different qualities, and that we can exploit this difference to increase the efficiency (security) of the model framework.

The second part of the paper covers some of the experiments that we have run in order to estimate the seriousness of Sybil attacks, and we argue that trust-based access control can help to defend against such attacks on distributed systems. We argue that there is a fundamental difference between conventional

---

* The research is supported by the EU project SECURE (Secure Environments for Collaboration among Ubiquitous Roaming Entities), IST-2001-32486.

P. Herrmann et al. (Eds.): iTrust 2005, LNCS 3477, pp. 372–383, 2005.

mechanisms and trust-based systems, and this difference may be exploited to improve the overall security of a system.

The paper is structured as follows: a short background section is followed by an overview of the general framework we are proposing for trust-based systems. The next section describes our view on the role of risk in evidence-based systems. Section 5 briefly discusses the importance of trust dynamics. This concept is used in the subsequent section, which outlines some of the results obtained when simulating a network under Sybil attack. We conclude by outlining the contribution that the paper makes towards effective trust-based security.

2   Background

The aim of the SECURE project [5] is to solve security problems related to access control of ubiquitous entities in a global and mobile environment. The demands of the environment prevent the use of centralised solutions, and entities must solve most problems in a distributed and scalable manner [6, 7, 8].

The reasoning introduced in this paper is based on the following general idea of reputation (or trust) systems. Systems do not enroll users – there is no prior objective knowledge about computational entities [9, 10]. All that the system can use is evidence about the previous behaviour of recognisable digital identities. Functionally, there are three types of node in the system. There are *requesters* (clients), exploiting services and resources offered by the second type of nodes – *servers*. Servers may benefit from information supplied by *recommenders* that have an interaction history with requesters. Kinateder and Pearson [11] use a slightly refined description of recommenders, in which they define recommenders as having their own direct experience, and *accumulators* with mediated evidence.

Each user may adopt a large number of distinct digital identities (pseudonyms). One of the implications is the possibility that a number of different *valid* trust values exist for a single physical identity. We cannot, and often do not even want to, prevent this, in order to preserve a certain level of privacy. On the other hand, we need to identify the properties and behaviour of the underlying physical identity as accurately as possible. Each system incorporating trust is based on two paradigms:

1. **Local trustworthiness evaluation** allows any system to make use of its local behavioural evidence to form an opinion of the trustworthiness of users.
2. **Distribution of trust** makes it possible for nodes to propagate the results of local trust evaluation to other nodes in the network.

Some trust-based systems do not support mechanisms for trust propagation. Such systems introduce poor correlation between the trustworthiness of digital identities in different parts of a network, and lose the advantage of aggregating experience.

3   General Framework

Establishing a framework for trust- and evidence-based security systems has been a long-term goal of the SECURE project [5]. Research in this area has produced a reasonable consensus regarding a suitable high-level system architecture, but the nature of the interaction between risk and trust computations remains open. Existing models for trust-based systems do not solve this problem; most systems take only trust into account, while risk is regarded merely as a complement of trust, or is even ignored altogether [12, 13, 14, 15].

Our present opinion is that an important semantic distinction is that trust is established with respect to entities/principals (a user, a process, implementation of a service), while risk is a property of particular processes (e.g. service invocations, protocol instances, ...). Both are subject to context. In this way we identify orthogonal qualities that can be exploited to establish a framework. However, this distinction is not sufficient in itself to specify their mutual relationship, or to establish ways of combining risk and trust. The crucial step in developing the final model was to return to the basics – definition of a transaction, risk analysis as used in IT risk management (e.g. CRAMM, or BSI's IT Baseline Protection Manual), and architectures for intrusion detection and anomaly detection systems (e.g. [16, 17]).

The first results of our analysis are in the diagram with basic data flows (fig. 1), giving an idea of how the framework of a trust-based system should work. All data used as evidence in a trust-based system are derived from transactions. Any interaction encompasses a user (or process) able to start an activity, a service (or more likely services) invoked by the user, and resources being accessed. The role of the trust-based system is to issue grant/reject decisions about access to resources, including services. That is represented by the A/C (access control) component in the diagram.

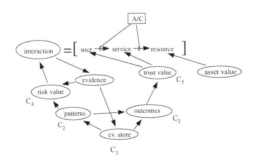

Fig. 1. Data flows and context information for the system framework

The figure shows separate data flows for trust and risk that may converge in the A/C component. The complexity of the model is apparent when we realise that each data type has a different set of contexts that characterise its elements (contexts are marked C_1, C_2, ..., C_5). Let us briefly describe the mechanics of the framework and the relations between the various contexts.

Contexts of evidence (C_1) are determined by the system and its evidence sources. Users and administrators form a separate source of evidence, since they can identify and provide high-level information (outcome) that partially defines a context for trust (C_5). These two sets of contexts express low-level (system) and high-level (user) points of view. C_1 contains contexts that characterise e.g. IP-based messages, access to particular configuration files, IP addresses of servers handling requests, IDs of ports accessed, IP/MAC addresses of clients, and so forth. User level contexts C_5 will describe attributes important from a "managerial" viewpoint, such as the specific service offered (e.g. creating an account, processing a loan application, overdraft management, etc., in a banking environment).

Obviously, a single high-level transaction with an outcome relevant to business policy decisions will encompass tens or hundreds of low-level pieces of evidence. The quantity of low-level evidence is an essential premise (and a source of data management problems) for intrusion-detection systems (IDSs), as well as for the risk part of our framework. IDS systems do not meet problems in gathering sufficient data to start searching for changes in behaviour; the difficulties arise when starting to reason about the changes detected in such large volumes of evidence, in that it is hard to distinguish real threats from random fluctuations or minor nuisance.

There is a direct relation between transaction outcomes and C_5. The types of outcome define contexts for trust values. This mapping can be expressed by a set of functions. When linear, each function defines a distinct weight for each type of outcome:

$$\forall\, c_i \in C_5, \; c_i = \phi_i(o_1, .., o_k) = \sum_{j=1..k} w_i^j.o_j$$

where o_j are the aggregates of all outcomes (the set C_3) of a given type j.

These functions, ϕ_i, will be usually defined on the basis of a business model, and as such are set explicitly by users. However, one can imagine that if the framework is to be used in an automated way, the parameters can be established simply on the basis of the expected high-level results of the system, for example according to the success or failure of transactions.

Contexts of patterns (C_2), on the other hand, are the product of an automated process. We have already mentioned that our knowledge of any large system is limited, and it is therefore necessary to introduce mechanisms that detect new dependencies and relationships in the behaviour of the system. Contexts of patterns describe sequences of events (and pieces of evidence describing them) that lead to similar outcomes (positive or negative) with sufficient probability. The occurrence of such contexts may indicate undesirable changes of risk, and it may be appropriate to terminate transactions as a security measure. Outcomes of the patterns will be characterised by a value (positive/negative) and a probability representing likelihood. These can be used directly for probabilistic computations of trust values.

Contexts of risk values C_4 are derived from patterns akin to trust value contexts. In detail, the IDs of C_4 patterns characterise dimensions of risk values, and the probability that such a pattern leads to a particular outcome could be used to identify specific aspects of risk.

So far, we have not discussed the processes that cause the data flows. We have to define at least three, and the most important: threat assessment, risk analysis, and trust computation. All are depicted in fig. 2 together with the data flows for risk and trust computations to show their independence.

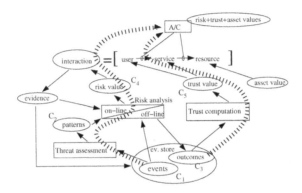

Fig. 2. Three most important processes in the framework

Threat assessment should be run each time the system receives a new outcome. The aim is to identify all patterns that lead to a predictable negative outcome. These patterns represent threats in our model. This is the most demanding part of the framework, as the implementation may have to mine for patterns in all the evidence available in the evidence store. Such patterns should be as specific as possible, and clearly distinguishable from events generated by transactions that have different outcomes.

Once such patterns have been derived, there is an opportunity to share a well-defined means of identifying supposedly fraudulent behaviour across a network, or to allow quick revision of patterns if other nodes in the network possess contradictory evidence. This is especially important when threat analysis becomes so complex that thorough analysis of all the evidence is infeasible for individual nodes. In this case, risk analysis may become non-deterministic, and nodes in the network must cooperate to identify potential threats.

Another notion from IT risk management is risk analysis. In our model, risk analysis may occur either when a transaction is requested, or on a prompt from the evidence store. The latter is initiated whenever threat assessment induces a change in the set of threats. The output of risk analysis can be in the form of a list containing instances of threats – possible attacks identified on the available evidence. Each record in this list represents an outcome that can be used during trust computations. Risk analysis on "live" transactions (whose access requests have not yet been granted) has one important difference; the results can be available before a request for access is made. This allows much faster reaction to such changes in behaviour as happen when e.g. a virus takes over a client, or a Sybil attack [18] is launched and a number of entities are switched into "attacking mode". We shall use risk analysis to refer to both risk analysis and threat assessment in order to simplify the following description.

4   Risk as a Distinct Quality

Current research in the area of trust-based systems is based on the idea that each event has an assigned outcome. However, the usual situation with information systems is slightly different – a huge number of events without particular meaning (outcome) take place (and are logged) in the system. In the conventional approach trust-based systems would ignore all evidence lacking a distinguishable outcome. We argue that it is dangerous to ignore such a rich source of data about system behaviour just because there is no instant meaning, and that to do so makes the system vulnerable to any threat that lies outside the existing analysis of outcomes.

The crucial aspect of trust-based systems is the role of contexts. It is evident that trust is not universal, one always has to specify in what context someone is trusted (Jean trusts Ken to buy a good wine, but she does not trust him to get home on time). The same holds for digital systems, and we have to satisfy certain restrictions. The contexts need to be fairly abstract, in order to allow users to manage security policy in a reasonable way. However, systems are complex, and most low-level events are too fine-grain to be appropriate for specifying the conditions under which access requests are presented. To put it another way – the user cannot specify ways of determining whether an individual request will result in a successful transaction. Worse, we cannot list all the contexts relevant to the trust decisions for a given request; users will be aware of some of the contexts, but because of the complexity of the system the list will be incomplete. A better approach is to use risk analysis to uncover the factors relevant to each request.

Risk analysis takes the form of pattern mining on that large set of elementary data that we have just discussed – the more data there is, the better the chance of obtaining useful results. Individual data items (evidence) have no particular meaning in themselves, but when considered collectively as parts of sequences – patterns – they may say a lot. What we propose therefore is to regard risk analysis as the search for patterns that are precursors of particular outcomes. This approach offers an elegant solution to another problem, namely that of identifying the high-level contexts useful when expressing access control policy at user level. These types of pattern will form the contexts for high-level evidence. In this way we can change abstraction levels between *system-level* and *user-level* events, by assigning names to patterns and using them to create a set of *user-level* contexts. We can thus free users from the burden of low-level data management without losing all of the information that it offers. We should emphasise that the approach is that of non-classical pattern recognition, in which we do not seek to define the relevant patterns a priori, but instead identify them empirically through data mining.

Risk analysis is similar to principles of artificial immune systems [19], but the basic assumption is reversed. We assume, unlike the situation for immune systems, that all events are harmless unless a pattern known to be a predictor of sinister outcomes has been identified. What is similar is that we do not repeat the same risk analysis all over again, but instead change the conditions by specifying subsets of evidence to be analysed for particular runs. If the amount of possible contexts becomes so large that it is impossible to evaluate them thoroughly at each local system, randomness can be introduced to the selection process, resulting in a non-deterministic parallel search in a distributed system (this is similar to random creation of receptor proteins by an immune system). The possible wide spread of such contexts and their deployment to all nodes in a distributed system is once again analogous to the idea of an immune system.

From the security point of view, the success of an attack depends among other things on the time during which the attack may be successfully deployed. This time can be inferred from two intervals: the delay before the detection of an attack, and the reaction time to repel the attack. The former is the time needed for successful risk analysis and identification of the appropriate pattern in evidence; the reaction time is determined by the speed with which trust values can be adjusted to respond to changes in behaviour.

5   Trust Dynamics

As we argued earlier in [20], the dynamics of trustworthiness is crucial if trust-based systems are to be usable as a security mechanism. Our research analysed use of the arithmetic mean as the simplest possible aggregate function, and Jøsang et al. went in the same direction when defining the consensus operator for dogmatic beliefs [21].

The problem with the arithmetic mean is that it is very stable when a large number of pieces of evidence are used, but we need the system to be able to react swiftly to attacks. After experimenting with several approaches, we recalled the *Dirac impulse* and its use for measuring system reactions [22]. We found this to be an appropriate way to establish objective parametrisation of a system's reaction to attacks. One can model the reaction of a system in a computationally simple way, i.e. with a linear function, see fig. 3. Three basic parameters represent the maximum response (r_m), the level of sensitivity (Δr) necessary for invocation of the correction mechanism, and the duration of response (t_{res}).

When using the Dirac impulse to define a normalised reaction of a system, and it happens that several behavioural deviations appear in a row, we merely

Fig. 3. Dirac impulse and a system response

sum the system responses and ensure that the result fits between values 0 and 1 – the boundary values for trust. More details can be found in [20].

6   Sybil Attack Revisited

The notion of Sybil attack comes from the paper of Douceur [18]. He formalised the threat posed by an attacker able to create an arbitrary number of digital identities acting on her behalf. His assumptions are somewhat simplistic, but the results have been taken quite seriously as an important threat for P2P systems, and for distributed systems in general. Let us briefly summarise his points:

1. The cost of creating new identities is nearly zero.
2. Digital identities represent users that are unknown to each other – a kind of anonymity exists that shields the user behind each digital identity.
3. Any user is able to create as many digital identities as she wants.
4. Servers communicating with identities cannot distinguish them from one another.

Commonly used P2P clients cannot find out what physical entity lies behind each digital identity, and whether some of them are likely to behave in a similar manner – for example, through being run by the same user. The question is whether trust-based systems can help us to defend against Sybil attacks.

In order to build a defence against the attack we have to break one of the assumptions in Dourceur's threat model. Our idea is to link digital identities together according to their behaviour – risk analysis from the framework architecture presented above seems to be designed specifically for this purpose.

6.1   Simulation Scenarios

The simulations introduced here are based on research in network resiliency. We realised that similar models may be used to evaluate attacks on trust-based systems – one has merely to add trust-based intelligence to nodes and change the attack model. In our case, the nodes are not being removed, but the system incurs a cost as its resources are misused.

The simulations were run on random and scale-free topologies. There were separate sets of users and nodes. Nodes represent servers running trust-based systems to evaluate the trustworthiness of users, while users represent clients of nodes. This separation means that nodes in the network are all of the same credibility; we do not study the impact of attacking cliques inside the network in this paper.

The results presented below are averaged results from 10-20 randomly generated networks consisting of 200 nodes with 400 edges in total – very sparse networks. We have 1000 users, and 60% of these are attackers (controlled by one user). The attack is realised in rounds in which fifty randomly selected attackers target one node each at random. We have lowered the number of attacks per round to increase the influence of recommendations. The cost of each attack on a node is zero or one; this value is assigned according to the actual level of the user's trustworthiness and the evidence that the node possesses.

Actual trust values are computed as described in section 5. The static parts of random initial trust values based on arithmetic means are assumed to be the result of a large quantity of evidence, so they are fixed during attacks. It is the dynamic part of trust, defined with the help of Dirac impulses, that actually changes the trust values.

6.2   Results

To demonstrate the Sybil attack, we first run a scenario when nodes under attack can detect only the identities that targeted them, but cannot link identities together.

The question that we are investigating here is, what is the impact of evidence allowing more precise description of transactions and therefore allowing recognition of similar behaviours? Figure 4 shows the impact of this capability on costs (when compared with the Sybil attack as defined by Douceur).

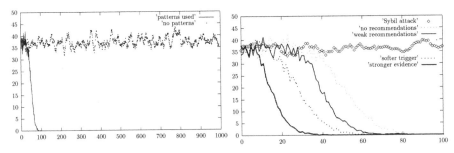

Fig. 4. Sybil attack and the decrease of costs when patterns are introduced

Fig. 5. Cutting costs by changing trust model parameters

As mentioned above, the simulated system was parametrised in a number of ways. The following figure 5 depicts the impact of some configuration changes in the overall cost induced by Sybil attacks. The rightmost curve represents the situation in which no information about attacks is exchanged among the nodes of the network. This setting results in the highest costs, but the difference from the following settings is not so radical. We believe that two reasons are crucial for this situation – the low connectivity of the network (only immediate recommendations are modelled, when only witnesses can send them), and random selection of the nodes to be attacked. The latter represent the strongest possible attacks, as the whole network may be targeted at once. A much more common situation is when attacks spread from one or two hot spots – in this case, the network would be more resistant to the attack, as patterns could be distributed before the attack reached nodes distant from the hot spots. The second curve demonstrates the situation when recommendations are enabled. Trustworthiness is updated according to linear equations, in which trust values become zero when twenty observations are made or forty recommendations are delivered (or some linear combination of these).

The third curve was obtained by softening the triggers – conditions determining when recommendations are sent. The original trigger was switched when about ten pieces of evidence about a particular attack had been collected; the softer trigger required only three appearances. The last curve comes from simulations in which the rules for computing trustworthiness were further tightened.

6.3   Risk v Trust Again

The graphs in figure 5 show a characteristic curve for the costs. There is an initial phase when patterns are being formed and recommendations are not yet being exchanged. It is followed by an exponential curve as information about the attack is spread throughout the network. We can also see the different effects of trust and risk computations in this graph. As mentioned above, 50 nodes are attacked at each round. However, the average cost of a round is about 38; the rest survive because of the protection of the trust values used for access control. Risk, on the other hand, causes the exponential decay in cost, and with trust determines the slope and length of the curve. The time to detect an attack is the interval needed to identify a pattern in attackers' behaviour, while the time to react is determined by the way in which the patterns are propagated, and how they are used for security decisions.

7   Conclusions

The paper introduces a novel approach to trust- and evidence-based systems. The framework that we introduce is based on independent definitions of risk and trust. This allows access control decisions based on risk to terminate interaction even before a trust evaluation is requested. The relevant rules are orthogonal to trust-based reasoning. Trust-based systems assume that there is evidence defining the outcomes of interactions, and we exploit this data to identify system states (contexts) in which unwanted as well as positive events have happened. This allows explicit specification of "anomalies", with the potential for considerable improvement in the process of analysing events for patterns that lead to particular outcomes. Patterns identified in this way are used as new types of identified threat, and as such are used to improve trust computation and refine the trust-values of appropriate subjects.

This framework solves two important problems of trust-based systems: (1) it establishes trust and risk as orthogonal qualities and (2) it creates a system exploiting a two-layer evidence base that expresses the distinction between system and user viewpoints. Our architecture not only defines risk as a first-class property for describing the behaviour of groups of subjects, but also enables the system to learn from the evidence it has gathered, and to pass this knowledge on to cooperating subsystems.

The second part of the paper uses a naive scenario to demonstrate that a system based on our framework can defend itself against Sybil attacks by recognizing specific threats on the basis of similar behaviour. Action can be taken to block attacks initiated following the generation of multiple identities, which must now behave uniquely to prevent quick detection of their intentions. The success of the framework is based on the assumption that it is possible to profile attacking identities from their behaviour. This is supported by a number of results, e.g. in the area of traffic analysis. It also raises certain concerns related to privacy issues.

References

1. Abdul-Rahman, A., Hailes, S.: Using recommendations for managing trust in distributed systems. In: IEEE Malaysia International Conference on Communication '97 (MICC'97), IEEE (1997)
2. Abdul-Rahman, A., Hailes, S.: Supporting trust in virtual communities. In: Hawaii International Conference on System Sciences 33. (2000) 1769–1777
3. Bacon, J., Moody, K., Yao, W.: Access control and trust in the use of widely distributed services. Middleware 2001, Lecture Notes in Computer Science (2001) 295–310
4. A. Jøsang, Daniel, M., Vannoorenberghe, P.: Strategies for combining conflicting dogmatic beliefs. In: Proc. of the 6th International Conference on Information Fusion. (2003) 1133–1140
5. : RTD Proposal - SECURE: Secure Environments for Collaboration among Ubiquitous Roaming Entities (IST-2001-32486)
6. Blaze, M., Feigenbaum, J., Lacy, J.: Decentralized trust management. In: Proc. of The IEEE Symposium on Security and Privacy, AT&T (1996) 164–173
7. Blaze, M., Feigenbaum, J., Keromytis, A.D.: The role of trust management in distributed systems security. In: Secure Internet Programming, Springer-Verlag (1999) 185–210
8. English, C., Terzis, S., Wagealla, W., Lowe, H., Nixon, P., McGettrick, A.: Trust dynamics in collaborative global computing. In: IEEE International Workshops on Enabling Technologies: Infrastructure for Collaborative Enterprises (WETICE). (2003) 283–290
9. Shand, B., Dimmock, N., Bacon, J.: Trust for Ubiquitous, Transparent Collaboration. Special issue: Pervasive computing and communications 10 (2004) 711 – 721

10. Cahill, V., et al.: Using trust for secure collaboration in uncertain environments. IEEE Pervasive Computing Magazine **2** (2003) 52–61
11. Kinateder, M., Pearson, S.: A privacy-enhanced peer-to-peer reputation system. In: Proceedings of the 4th International Conference on Electronic Commerce and Web Technologies, EC-Web 2003. LNCS 2738, Prague, Czech Republic, Springer-Verlag (September 2003) 206–215
12. Jøsang, A.: A logic for uncertain probabilities. International Journal of Uncertainty, Fuzziness and Knowledge-Based Systems **9** (2001) 279–311
13. Twigg, A., Dimmock, N.: Attack-resistance of computational trust models. In: IEEE International Workshops on Enabling Technologies: Infrastructure for Collaborative Enterprises. (2003) 275 – 280
14. Weeks, S.: Understanding trust management systems. In: IEEE Symposium on Security and Privacy. (2001) 94–105
15. Winsborough, W.H., Li, N.: Towards practical automated trust negotiation. In: Proceedings of the Third International Workshop on Policies for Distributed Systems and Networks (Policy 2002), IEEE Computer Society Press (2002) 92–103
16. Lane, T., Brodley, C.: Temporal sequence learning and data reduction for anomaly detection. In: Proceedings of the 5th ACM conference on Computer and communications security, ACM Press (1998) 150–158
17. Lee, W., Stolfo, S.: A framework for constructing features and models for intrusion detection systems. ACM Transactions on Information and System Security **3** (2000) 227–261
18. Douceur, J.: The sybil attack. In: 1st International Workshop on Peer-to-Peer Systems (IPTPS'02). LNCS 2429, Springer-Verlag (2002) 251–260
19. Harmer, P.K., Williams, P.D., Gunsch, G.H., Lamont, G.B.: An artificial immune system architecture for computer security applications. IEEE Transactions On Evolutionary Computation **6** (2002) 252–280
20. Cvrček, D.: Dynamics of reputation. In: Proc. of the Ninth Nordic Workshop on Secure IT Systems. Publications in Telecommunications Software and Multimedia, Helsinki, Finland, Helsinki University of Technology (2004) 1–7
21. Jøsang, A.: The consensus operator for combining beliefs. Artificial Intelligence Journal **141** (2002) 157–170
22. Bracewell, R.: 5. The Impulse Symbol. In: The Fourier Transform and Its Applications. McGraw-Hill, New-York (1999) 69–97

IWTrust: Improving User Trust in Answers from the Web

Ilya Zaihrayeu[1,*], Paulo Pinheiro da Silva[2], and Deborah L. McGuinness[2]

[1]ITC-IRST, Trento, Italy
[2]Stanford University, Stanford, USA

Abstract. Question answering systems users may find answers without any supporting information insufficient for determining trust levels. Once those question answering systems begin to rely on source information that varies greatly in quality and depth, such as is typical in web settings, users may trust answers even less. We address this problem by augmenting answers with optional information about the sources that were used in the answer generation process. In addition, we introduce a trust infrastructure, IWTrust, which enables computations of trust values for answers from the Web. Users of IWTrust have access to sources used in answer computation along with trust values for those source, thus they are better able to judge answer trustworthiness.

1   Introduction

The number of information sources available to web applications is growing. As information source breadth increases, so does the diversity in quality. Users may find growing challenges in evaluating the quality of web answers, particularly in settings where answers are provided without any kind of justification. One way our work improves a user's ability to judge answers is by including *knowledge provenance information* along with answers. Knowledge provenance includes information about the origin of knowledge and a description of the reasoning processes used to produce the answers [8]. This paper describes our new work, which supports justifications that may include *trust values* with answers. The computation process takes into account the user's (stated or inferred) degree of belief in the sources, question answering engines, and in other users who provide sources and/or answering engines. Our framework allows users to define and (locally) maintain individual trust values, and use those values in their evaluation of answers from their own trust "viewpoint".

In recent work, we have addressed the problem of improving user's trust in answers by providing information about how an answer was calculated [5].

---

* A part of the work had been done when the author was affiliated with the University of Trento, Italy.

P. Herrmann et al. (Eds.): iTrust 2005, LNCS 3477, pp. 384–392, 2005.

That work provides an infrastructure, called Inference Web (IW), which allows proofs and proof fragments to be stored in a portable, distributed way on the web by using the proof Interlingua called the Proof Markup Language (PML) [7]. Proofs describe information manipulation processes (i.e., information extraction, reasoning, etc.) used to answer questions providing full support for tracking knowledge provenance related to answers. In addition to PML, which serves as a proof interlingua, IW provides IWBase [4], which is a distributed repository of *knowledge provenance elements*. Knowledge provenance elements contain proof-related meta-information such as information about *question answering engines*, *inference rules*, *representation languages*, and *sources* such as ontologies or documents. PML documents can represent answers varying from a single database lookup operation to a derivation of complex answers in a distributed fashion, involving multiple sources, and using distinct answering engines.

Knowledge provenance alone may not provide enough information for users to determine trust levels of answers. For example, a user may be unfamiliar with a question answering component that was used to find (a part of) the answer. A user may not know much about the question answering system (e.g. reasoning method, correctness and completeness of the reasoner, reasoning assumptions, etc.). Alternatively, a user may know something about the reasoner and would normally expect to trust answers from the reasoner, however when answers appear to be incomplete or conflict with a user's expectations, a user may need more information before trusting the answer. Also, users may trust a question answering system completely however if the system relies on information from sources that the user does not trust, then the user may not trust the answer. Additional considerations include situations where a source is used that is unknown to the user but the source is known to be trusted by another user (human or agent) who is trusted by the user.

In this paper we introduce an extension of IW, called *IWTrust*, which can quantify users' degree of trust in answers obtained from web applications and services. IWTrust uses trust values between users as well as trust values between users and provenance elements. Trust values for answers are computed relative to a particular user's perspective. The final trust value for the answer uses both a user's trust value of the sources used in the answer as well as a user's trust in other user's trust of sources used to obtain the answer.

The paper is organized as follows. Section 2 provides an abstract view of how trust components interact with question answering components. Section 3 provides the details of our trust model for IW. Section 4 provides an example use of IWTrust and the final section summarizes our work.

2   Trust for Question Answering

In the Inference Web context, a question *answering engine* is any kind of software system providing services able to produce answers in response to queries. From this general definition, answering engines may vary from retrieval-based services, such as database management systems and search engines, to reasoning-based services such as automated theorem provers.

We assume an environment where a user interacts with a *query front-end* component to formulate and ask a query q. The query front-end responds with a set of answers A. The query front-end is also responsible for forwarding the query q to the answering engine, grouping answers from the answering engine into a set of answers A, and forwarding A to the user. Optionally, the user may provide a set S of information sources to be used by the answering engine when retrieving information. On demand, answering engines may also provide $N(A)$, a set of justifications for answers in A.

Query languages for q vary accordingly to the kinds of answering engines used in the environment. For example, q may be a SQL query if the answering engine is a relational database management system or q may be an OWL-QL [2] query if the answering engine is a hybrid automated reasoner such as JTP [3]. The set of justifications $N(A)$ is represented in PML [7].

In general, *trust components* are responsible for computing trust values for resources such as users. In a question answering environment, we believe *trust components* should be also able to compute trust values for trust graph resources such as sources, told information, and derived information.

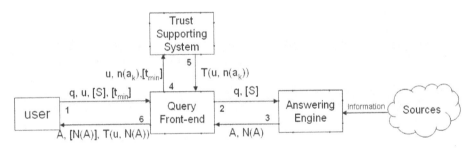

Fig. 1. Trust component in question answering systems

The computation of trust values for answers presented in Figure 1 provides a scenario where the trust component tries to assign trust values to every (intermediate) conclusion c_m during the question answering process. Trust is user-specific information; and, different users may trust other users and sources differently. Trust values for answers are computed on demand in the same way that justifications are computed on demand. Thus, if positive answer trust values are required, the answering engine should return answer justifications (step 3 in Figure 1), even if justifications are not asked by the user. From an answer and its justifications, the trust component computes (using the underlying trust network) user's trust values $T(u_i, n(a_k))$ for answer a_k, which are returned to the query front-end (step 5). The query front-end consolidates available trust values for justifications of answers in A into a single set $T(u_i, N(A))$[1]. Finally, the query front-end returns $T(u_i, N(A))$ to the user (step 6).

3   IWTrust Framework

In this section we introduce the IWTrust framework, referred to in the rest of the paper as IWTrust. Figure 2 shows IWTrust in action where a user u_1, submits a query q and obtains a set of answers $\{a_1, \ldots, a_n\}$ with their associated trust values $\{t_{11}, t_{12}, \ldots, t_{1m}, t_{21}, \ldots t_{n1}, \ldots\}$. The user is connected by trust relations to provenance elements (sources and answering engines in the diagram) that are used in answering the query. The user, u_1, is directly connected to some of them such as e_2. The user is connected to other provenance elements through other users (e.g., u_1 is connected to s_2, s_3 through u_3 and u_4). Provenance elements are connected to told assertions in proofs by provenance relations. Finally, Figure 2 identifies proof fragments, queries, IWBase and TrustNet as IW components supporting the trust graph as discussed in this section.

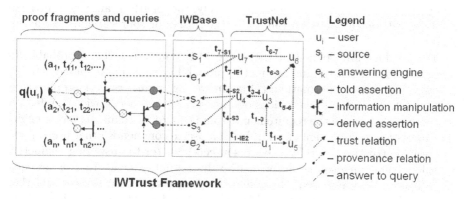

Fig. 2. IWTrust Framework

3.1   Proof Fragments and Queries

PML is used to build OWL documents representing proof fragments and queries. A PML *NodeSet* is the primary building block of proofs and is used to represent information manipulation from queries to answers and from answers to sources. A PML *Query* is used to represent user queries; it identifies the node sets containing conclusions used in answering the query. PML is an ontology written in W3C's OWL Semantic Web representation language [6] allowing justifications to be exchanged between Semantic Web services and clients using XML/RDF/OWL.

A node set $n(c)$ represents a step in a proof whose conclusion c is justified by a set of inference steps associated with the node set. The conclusion c represents

---

[1] $T(u_i, N(A))$ is defined as $\{X \mid \forall a_k \in A, T(u_i, n(a_k)) \in X\}$.

the expression concluded by the proof step. Every node set has one conclusion which is the element in the trust network that requires a trust value. Each inference step of a node set represents an application of an inference rule that justifies the node set's conclusion. The antecedents of an inference step form a sequence of node sets each of whose conclusion is a *premise* of the application of the inference step's rule. Each source of an inference step refers to an entity representing original statements from which the conclusion was obtained. An inference step's source supports the justification of the node set conclusion when the step's rule is a *DirectAssertion*.

3.2   TrustNet

TrustNet is a trust network, where users may define trust values w.r.t. other users, answering engines, and sources. In addition to these trust relations, the TrustNet trust graph represents provenance relations between sources. An edge in the graph may connect a source node to a created source node, provided that the source is the author (publisher or submitter) of the created source. Using the information in these edges, we can compute trust for a created source based on the trust of the source that created it. All edges in the graph are associated with two values: *length* and *trust value*. Intuitively, the length of an edge represents the trust "distance" between the origin (i.e., users or sources) and destination nodes.

Trust values are defined in the range [0,1], and are given a probabilistic interpretation. A trust value means the probability that: (1) a source contains relevant and correct information; (2) an answering engine correctly applies rules to derive statements (as conclusions of node sets); (3) a user provides a reference to a source that meets the requirements from (1), and/or to an answering engine that meets the requirements from (2); (4) a user recommends other user(s) who can provide trustworthy references to source(s) and/or to answering engine(s).

Edges connecting sources have length values equal to 0 and trust values equal to 1. These values represent the connection between created sources and their associated sources. All other edges have length 1 and may have an arbitrary trust value, which is computed as follows: each statement, used in query answering, and originated from some source, may be evaluated by the user either as correct or as incorrect. Users aggregate this information, and define their trust value of a source as the ratio of correct statements w.r.t. all evaluated statements from the source. The general formula for computing trust values follows: $t = \frac{t_p * n_p + n_t}{n_p + n_t + n_u}$, where n_t is the number of interactions evaluated as trustworthy; n_u is the number of interactions evaluated as untrustworthy; t_p is the level of prejudice; and n_p is a hypothetical number of interactions. t_p predetermines the starting trust level; and n_p defines the level of confidence of the user that t_p is correct – the higher n_p, the slower t changes its value, while "recording" actual interactions of the user, from the value of t_p. This approach is not absolutely new, and used in a similar form, for instance in [9].

4   Trusting Answers: An Example

IWTrust's typical use of trust values is for comparison and ordering of answers. We do not expect that typical users will be interested in looking at raw trust values such as 0.234 but we do expect that they will be interested in knowing that some answers were trusted more than others. In this section, we present an example showing how trust values can be used to rank both answers and justifications, as well as briefly discussing the algorithms used for trust computation[2].

   Figure 3 shows a proof tree supporting the answer to a question concerning the type of Tony's specialty (TonysSpeciality in Figure 3). This particular proof tree encodes information justifying that Tony's specialty is a shellfish dish. In this example, Source 2 states that Tony's specialty is a CRAB dish, and Source 1 states that the type is transitive (thus if a dish is of type crab and crab is a kind of shellfish, then the dish is of type shellfish). Thus, using generalized modus ponens (GMP), the proof concludes that Tony's specialty has the type of all of the superclasses of CRAB. Further, Sources 2 and 3 state that SHELLFISH is a superclass of CRAB. Thus, using GMP again, the proof concludes that Tony's specialty is a SHELLFISH dish.

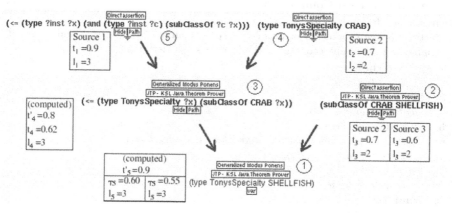

Fig. 3. Trust Composition Algorithm: an example

   The proof shows that the question has at least two answers: one that Tony's specialty is a SHELLFISH dish, and also that it is a CRAB dish. The proof also shows that the SHELLFISH answer has two justifications: one based on statements from Sources 1, 2 and 3; and the other based on statements from Sources 1 and 2 only.

   Trust rankings may be valuable for ranking of justifications and their components. For instance, if the user asks for a list of sources for the SHELLFISH

---

[2] See the full version of the paper for comprehensive details of the algorithms.
   Link: http://www.ksl.stanford.edu/people/pp/papers/Zaihrayeu_iTrust_2005.pdf.

answer, we may not include Source 3 since the justification based on Source 3 has a trust value (t=0.55) lower than the justification without it (t=0.60). Source 4, also stating that SHELLFISH is a superclass of CRAB, could be listed if its trust value was high enough to make a justification (based on its statement) with trust value higher than 0.60. The trust composition algorithm (see Algorithm 1) is used to compute these values. Thus, starting from the last step of the proof, i.e., node 1 in Figure 3, and proceeding through the set of antecedents of node 1, i.e., nodes 2 and 3, the algorithm computes t_c and l_c recursively (lines 6, 12 and 13 in Algorithm 1). The algorithm terminates when conclusions inside a proof have no antecedents ($C = \emptyset$), i.e., when it reaches nodes 2, 4 and 5 in our example. In this case, we assume an implicit trust relation with value 1.0 and length 1 between the conclusion and its source s; whereas t_c and l_c for the resulting tuple are inferred as the trust and length values for s (line 3). We adopt Agrawal's generalized version of the *semi-naive* algorithm to compute trust values between users and from users to sources [1]. In our case, the algorithm computes the transitive closure of a (trust) relation in an iterative manner, producing at each iteration a set of new transitively held relations.

Algorithm 1 Trust Composition

---

input: u_i, R_a, j; **output:** $< u_i, c, t_c, l_c >$
note: c is the conclusion of proof j; s is the source of c, if any; e and C are the engine and set of antecedents for the last step in j deriving c

1: **if** $C = \emptyset$ **then**
2:     $t_c, l_c \leftarrow R_a(u_i, s)$;
3: **else**
4:     $watv, wl, length \leftarrow 0$;
5:     **for all** $c_j \in C$ **do**
6:         $t_j, l_j \leftarrow trustCompositionAlgorithm(u_i, c_j, R_a, t_{min})$;
7:         $watv \leftarrow watv + (t_j/l_j)$;
8:         $wl \leftarrow wl + (1/l_j)$;
9:         $length \leftarrow total + l_j$;
10:    **end for**
11:    $t_e, l_e \leftarrow R_a(u_i, e)$
12:    $t_c \leftarrow (watv/wl) * t_e$;
13:    $l_c \leftarrow INT(length/|C|) + 1$
14: **end if**

For a conclusion c from a proof step with one or more antecedents, the algorithm works as follows: it first computes a weighted average over t_j for all $c_j \in C$, whereas the weights are inversely proportional to the path lengths of nodes in C. $watv$ and wl are used to compute the answer weighted average trust value. By computing a trust value for the answering engine input as the ratio between $watv$ and wl we are fully trusting the answering engine. However, we may have reasons for not trusting an engine that much. For instance, the engine may not be sound for some kind of questions. Thus, we "weigh" the input trust values against path lengths as shorter paths are likely to be more "credible" than longer ones. Then, we compute the trust value for t_c, l_c, by multiplying the weighted average trust value ($watv/wt$) by t_e (line 12). We compute the path length to c as the integer part of the average of all c_j, incremented by 1 (line 13).

5   Conclusions

In this paper, we have introduced IWTrust as a solution supporting trust in question answering environments. IWTrust leverages the Inference Web infrastructure to provide explanations from many question answering environments ranging from retrieval-intensive systems, such as database management systems and search engines, to reasoning-intensive systems such as theorem provers. It then enhances these explanations with user-customized trust values, which can then be used to determine trust of answers, sources, and answer justifications.

We present two primary contributions. First we provide an implemented solution infrastructure that can generate explanations for a wide range of question answering systems that has been integrated with a trust network. Second, we provide a design and prototype of a trust network with trust functionalities supporting trust computation in a distributed question answering environment such as the web. While others have provided trust algebras previously, and implemented explanation solutions exist for different types of question answering paradigms, our work is the first we know of that provides explanations with integrated trust values for a wide range of question answering systems and simultaneously provides an extensible architecture (allowing integration of other trust algorithms). Our primary contributions in the trust area include our design in the TrustNet layer presented in Section 3.2 and the answer trust computation algorithms used in Section 4.

References

1. R. Agrawal, S. Dar, and H. Jagadish. Direct transitive closure algorithms: Design and performance evaluation. *ACM Transactions on Database Systems.*, 15(3):427–458, September 1990.
2. Richard Fikes, Pat Hayes, and Ian Horrocks. DAML Query Language (DQL) Abstract Specification. Technical report, W3C, 2002.
3. Richard Fikes, Jessica Jenkins, and Gleb Frank. JTP: A System Architecture and Component Library for Hybrid Reasoning. Technical Report KSL-03-01, Knowledge Systems Laboratory, Stanford University, Stanford, CA, USA, 2003.
4. Deborah L. McGuinness and Paulo Pinheiro da Silva. Registry-based support for information integration. In S. Kambhampati and C. Knoblock, editors, *In Proceedings of IJCAI-2003's Workshop on Information Integration on the Web (IIWeb-03)*, pages 117–122, Acapulco, Mexico, August 2003.
5. Deborah L. McGuinness and Paulo Pinheiro da Silva. Explaining Answers from the Semantic Web. *Journal of Web Semantics*, 1(4):397–413, October 2004.

6. Deborah L. McGuinness and Frank van Harmelen. OWL Web Ontology Language Overview. Technical report, World Wide Web Consortium (W3C), February 10 2004. Recommendation.
7. Paulo Pinheiro da Silva, Deborah L. McGuinness, and Richard E. Fikes. A Proof Markup Language for Semantic Web Services. *Information Systems*, 2005. (to appear).
8. Paulo Pinheiro da Silva, Deborah L. McGuinness, and Rob McCool. Knowledge Provenance Infrastructure. *In Data Engineering Bulletin Vol.26 No.4*, pages 26–32, December 2003.
9. Wang Y. and Vassileva J. Trust-based community formation in peer-to-peer file sharing networks. *Proc. of IEEE/WIC/ACM International Conference on Web Intelligence (WI 2004), Beijing, China*, September 2004.

Trust Record: High-Level Assurance and Compliance

Adrian Baldwin, Yolanta Beres, David Plaquin, and Simon Shiu

Trusted Systems Laboratory, Hewlett Packard Labs, Bristol, UK
{Adrian.Baldwin,Yolanta.Beres,David.Plaquin,Simon.Shiu}@hp.com

Abstract. Events such as Enron's collapse have changed the regulatory and governance trends increasing executive accountable for the way companies are run and therefore for the underlying critical IT systems. Such IT functions are increasingly outsourced yet executives remain accountable. This paper presents a Trust Record demonstrator that provides a real time audit report helping to assure executives that their (outsourced) IT infrastructures are being managed in line with corporate policies and legal regulations.

1 Introduction

Image you are a CIO for a large company – you will be under pressure to make the IT systems more responsive to better support business processes and changing company needs and at the same time you have a very tight budget. Do you outsource your IT to save money, do you use service providers for certain IT functions, or perhaps utility data centre services to save on infrastructure costs? The post Enron world means that it is not enough to simply do more for less but you must be able to demonstrate that the IT systems are compliant with the IT governance policies [1][2] set out by the board and perhaps more worryingly maintain your freedom by demonstrating you have maintained compliance with Sarbanes Oxley (SOX) [3]. Outsourcing may help you meet budgetary constraints but you know you cannot outsource your accountability.

Whether your IT systems are internal, outsourced or some mixture you must know and be able to demonstrate that the systems are well run compliant with your corporate policies and various pieces of legislation. In the past you have relied on trusting staff to do the right thing along with regular 6 monthly or yearly audits. The climate created by Sarbanes Oxley makes this seem insufficient and instead you need a more strategic approach to assurance and IT risk management moving from these regular reviews to ongoing assurance. As such you need systems to support real time transparency into the IT systems and associated operating environment.

Trust record is such a system providing model based assurance of your IT systems and their environment. This paper describes a demonstrator that produces a high-level assurance report showing that the financial systems are compliant with SOX (amongst other factors) and hence reassuring our imagined CIO.

2 Trust Record

The trust record system (figure 1) provides an assurance report showing that an IT system is being run in line with corporate policies and operational procedures you

P. Herrmann et al. (Eds.): iTrust 2005, LNCS 3477 pp. 393–396, 2005.
© Springer-Verlag Berlin Heidelberg 2005

have agreed compliant with these policies. We develop a model of these policies, processes and the way they affect the underlying infrastructure. This model is used to deploy a series of agents (using SmartFrog [4]) that monitor the IT environment and send events to an analysis engine. The analysis engine interprets the events in light of the model using the results to produce a web based trust record. Events are stored within an event store that is built on top of a trusted audit system [5]; thereby ensuring their integrity is maintained.

The trust record is driven from a model of the infrastructure and the operational procedures (e.g. those defined within ITIL [6]) which it then maps back to high level concerns such as those defined within COBIT [1]. The model may contain a number of different aspects from policies that refer to system statistics (eg availability or percentage of staff completing security training) through administration processes to monitoring door locks and ensuring physical access policies are maintained. The analysis engine supports a number of different techniques including monitoring processes, and combining the system statistics. The analysis engine can add status information in the form of a colour from green to red as well as a trend, as compared to the previous report. This status information is included in a web based report covering the highest level of the model on the top page and allowing the user to dig down and further explore details and problems.

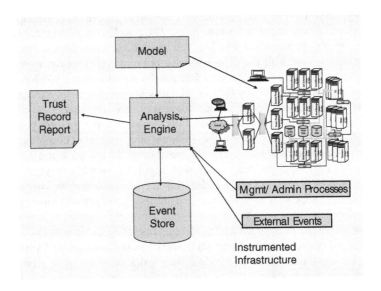

Fig. 1. Trust Record Architecture

3 SOX Example

As our imagined CIO one aspect you are particularly concerned with will be SOX compliance. The demonstrator shows how a trust record can be used to monitor the way a SAP finance application is being run. SOX compliance depends both on the integrity of the financial processes and the supporting IT infrastructure. Being the

CIO you are mainly concerned with the IT systems view. It is of course hard to test the trust record system on a live SAP system so we have created a simulator that generates events associated with various management processes along with a set of significant system statistics. This is used to demonstrate the effects of process and system failures on the trust record report.

3.1   The Trust Record Model for SOX

In setting up a trust record system a consultant would work with you, as our imaged CIO, to capture some of your main concerns and policies or processes that help ensure they are mitigated. SOX compliance will be one of these high level concerns and having discussed it with your auditors you decide there are three key aspects relating to how the SAP finance system is run: the infrastructure integrity; availability; and account management. These in turn can be further refined so the infrastructure integrity is dependant on the security of various components and ensuring change management and patching processes are well run. The account management again is highly dependant on the processes used for adding, changing and removing accounts here the model may include refer to various statistics that are indicative of well run accounts as well as tracking each process instance. Modelling the account adding process involves modelling both the workflow that should be followed and the way it affects certain system components (e.g. a SAP user database). Modelling these dependencies ensures the analysis covers various levels of system architecture from management through to system and network views.

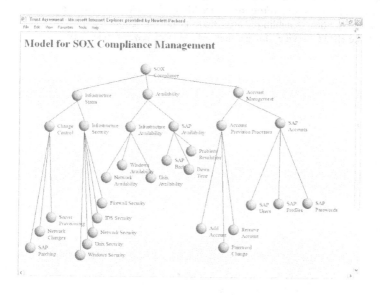

Fig. 2. An example model for monitoring compliance with SOX

3.2 Trust Record

As the CIO you get a web based report reflecting your concerns; either assuring you that the systems are compliant or indicating the impact of failures. The report has some high level traffic light based indicators as well as trends showing whether the situation has improved or is worsening. You have the ability to dig down to explore concerns; for example, you, or a member of your staff, may explore reports associated with change control and patching if critical patches have been raised in briefings or the press. In this way you can alleviate your concerns.

4 Conclusions

The trust record system generates regular high level assurance reports reflecting various concerns that have been captured within a model. As such this helps bridge the gap between high level governance policies and the IT management and IT operations layers. In doing this, trust record can help engender trust in flexible and outsourced IT environments.

References

[1] ITGI, "Control Objectives for Information and related Technologies (CobiT) 3rd Edition" 1998
[2] Salle, M IT Service Management and IT Governance. HP Labs Report HPL-2004-98
[3] USA, "Sarbanes Oxley Act of 2002" HR 3763
[4] Goldsack, P. *et at* "SmartFrog Reference Manual" www.smartfrog.org
[5] Baldwin, A. Shiu, "Enabling Shared Audit Data" IJIS 2004
[6] HP, "The HP IT Service Management (ITSM) Reference Model" 2003

Implementation of the SECURE Trust Engine

Ciarán Bryce[1], Paul Couderc[1], Jean-Marc Seigneur[2], and Vinny Cahill[2]

[1] University of Geneva, Switzerland
firstname.lastname@cui.unige.ch
[2] Trinity College Dublin, Ireland
firstname.lastname@cs.tcd.ie

Abstract. We present the implementation of SECURE and a SPAM filter that uses it to classify messages as SPAM based on trust in senders.

1 Introduction

The main elements of SECURE are illustrated in Figure 1. Each principal has its own instance of the framework that it consults when it needs to make a decision about entering into a collaboration with another principal. The boxes of the framework are programmable policy components that implement the decision process for the principal in the context of a specific application.

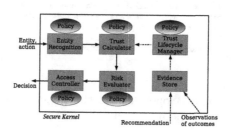

Fig. 1. SECURE framework components

Entity Recognition attaches a virtual identity to a requesting principal; it determines whether the requester has previously been encountered. The *Trust Calculator* retrieves a trust value for the requester. A trust value is formed based on *Observations* of the outcomes of actions with the requester, and on *Recommendations* received. Observations and recommendations are known as *Evidence*. The *Trust Lifecycle Manager* processes evidence about a principal and decides on a trust value for it. The *Risk Evaluator* calculates an estimated cost for the decision maker in permitting the action; the trust value is used in this calculation since trust is proportional to the degree of risk that a decision maker is willing to take. The *Access Controller* takes takes the final decision and generally uses a threshold policy that bases its decision on estimated the cost.

P. Herrmann et al. (Eds.): iTrust 2005, LNCS 3477, pp. 397–401, 2005.
© Springer-Verlag Berlin Heidelberg 2005

This paper presents an API for SECURE (Section 2), and its use in a
SPAM filter (Section 3). The SPAM application is representative of an autonomous system since each principal takes its own decision about whether
a message is SPAM, perhaps using recommendations from others. Section 4
concludes.

2   An API for SECURE

The framework is programmed in Java [1] because of its type-safety and availability of the JRE on a range of platforms. The kernel contains over 4000 lines
of code. Figure 2 lists some classes from the API. The classes correspond to
the key abstractions of the framework. The main class is SecureKernel whose
decide method is invoked by a principal's application code whenever a decision
needs to be taken by the application. The trust engine implements a *consulta-
tive mediation* approach, in much the same way that the current Java security
model works, in that an application explicitly invokes the kernel for a decision,
e.g.,

```
public MailMessage fetch(User name, Password passwd) {
    SecureKernel kernel = SecureKernel.getSecureKernel();
    MailMessage message = server.getNextMessage(name, passwd);
    PrincipalInformation pi = new PrincipalInformation(message.getSender());
    if ( kernel.decide(ReceiveAction, pi, message) == MessageIsSpam )
        message.addHeader("X-Spam-Value", "Spam");
    else
        message.addHeader("X-Spam-Value", "SECURE-OK");
    return message;
}
```

To use the API, the developer defines the policies for trust, risk, access
control, etc. This done by coding by coding an Action (e.g., ReceiveAction in
the SPAM filter), in which one specifies the Action.Outcomes and Outcome-
Costs, and then coding the appropriate subclasses of TrustLifecycleManager,
AccessController, etc. to represent the trust, access control policies, etc. A class
must be coded for each component plugged into the kernel, as suggested in
Figure 1.

3   SPAM Filter Example

The structure of the application is illustrated in Figure 3. A user – John Smith –
has an email client that is configured to use an IMAP and SMTP proxy. The role
of the proxy is to interpose on messages received from the server, and to declare
the message as SPAM or as valid, based on a SECURE decision. Each SPAM
message detected by the SECURE framework is marked. This is done through the
addition of a message header field **X-Spam-Value**. The email client employs a
filter to send SPAM messages to a special folder.

```
public final class SecureKernel {
    public Decision decide(Action, PrincipalInformation, Object[]);
    public void registerEvidence(Evidence);
    public static SecureKernel initialise(AccessController, Transport, EvidenceManagement, ....);
}

public final class Action {
    public static Action defineAction(String, Eventstructure);
    public TrustDomain getTrustDomain();
    public Outcome getOutcome(String);
    public Outcome[] getAllOutcomes();
    public void makeEncryptionKey();
}

public final class Outcome {
    public OutcomeCosts getOutcomeCosts();
}

public final class TrustDomain {
    public TrustValue getBottom();
    public TrustValue valueOf(TrustValue, Outcome, Triple);
}

public final class TrustValue {
    public boolean isLessTrustedThan(TrustValue, Outcome);
    public boolean isLessPreciseThan(TrustValue, Outcome);
}

public abstract class EntityRecognition {
    protected final RecognisedPrincipal createPrincipal(PrincipalInformation, Confidence);
    public abstract RecognisedPrincipal recognise(PrincipalInformation, Object);
}

public final class RecognisedPrincipal {
    protected final TrustValue trustInPrincipal(RecognisedPrincipal);
    public PrincipalInformation getPrincipalInformation();
    public EntityRecognition.Confidence getConfidence(); // ER confidence level
}

public final class Recommendation {
    public Recommendation(PrincipalInformation, PrincipalInformation, TrustValue);
    public PrincipalInformation getReferee();
}

public abstract class AccessController {
    public abstract Decision isAllowed(Action.Execution, TrustValue, RiskMetric);
}

public final class RiskEvaluator {
    public RiskMetric evaluateRisk(Action, RecognisedPrincipal, TrustValue);
}

public abstract class TrustLifecycleManager {
    private EvidenceStore; // For recommendations and observations
    protected abstract void update(Evidence);
    public final TrustValue trustIn(RecognisedPrincipal);
    public final void setTrust(RecognisedPrincipal, TrustValue);
}

public abstract class TransportLayer {
    private ListenerThread;
    public void distributeEvidence(Evidence, RecognisedPrincipal);
    public final TrustValue getTrustValue(RecognisedPrincipal, PrincipalInformation);
}
```

Fig. 2. Extract of SECURE API

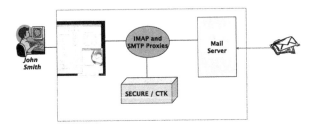

Fig. 3. The SECURE SPAM filter

In this application, a principal represents an email user, or more specifically, an email address. An email proxy runs as a separate process, on a machine that is specified by the email client configuration. In the case of a false positive or false negative, the user can move the message from or to the SPAM folder. This move request is intercepted by the proxy and interpreted as an observation of an outcome (of a message being SPAM or valid). This is why the SPAM filter acts as a proxy on the IMAP protocol – used by clients to download messages from the email server – since this protocol allows clients to create email folders on the server and to copy messages between them. All standard email clients today can be configured to use IMAP and SMTP proxies, i.e., the open source Mozilla clients, Netscape, as well as Microsoft's Outlook (Express). Thus, the SECURE filter is client-independent. The code that processes the IMAP commands and implements the policy components contains around 3000 lines of pure Java code.

Entity Recognition is got by the Claim Tool Kit (CTK) [3]. This is a reusable software tool kit of 22000 lines of code with 30 core classes. The receiver's and sender's CTK SMTP proxy store and exchange customised hashes of previous emails exchanged between the two, and are able to bootstrap each other using an augmented challenge/response technique [2]. Recognition is sufficient to build trust based on pieces of exchanged evidence. There is no need to authenticate the real-world identity with a certified binding to the public key, so registration is cheap, fast and convenient for users. This is in contrast to public key webs of trust schemes or ones requiring manual enrolment.

4   Conclusions

An evaluation of SECURE is currently ongoing. It is clear to us that the true value of trust-based models is best gauged from implementation experience. In the case of SPAM filtering, trust models give an interesting alternative[1].

---

[1] This work is sponsored by EU, grant *IST-2001-32486*, and by Swiss Confederation, grant *OFES 01.0210*.

References

1. K. Arnold and J. Gosling. *The Java Programming Language*. The Java Series. Addison-Wesley Publishing Company, 1996.
2. J.-M. Seigneur, N. Dimmock, C. Bryce, and C. Jensen. Combatting SPAM with trustworthy Email Addresses. In *3rd Conference on Privacy, Security and Trust*, pages 391–403, New Brunswick, Canada, Oct. 2004. ACM.
3. J.-M. Seigneur and C. D. Jensen. The Claim Tool Kit for Ad-hoc Recognition of Peer Entities. In *Journal of Science of Computer Programming*. Elsevier, 2004.

The CORAS Tool for Security Risk Analysis

Fredrik Vraalsen, Folker den Braber, Mass Soldal Lund, and Ketil Stølen

SINTEF, Norway
{fvr, fbr, msl, kst}@sintef.no

Abstract. The CORAS Tool for model-based security risk analysis supports documentation and reuse of risk analysis results through integration of different risk analysis and software development techniques and tools. Built-in consistency checking facilitates the maintenance of the results as the target of analysis and risk analysis results evolve.

1 Introduction

The CORAS framework for UML-based security risk analysis, in the following referred to as security analysis, consists of among other things a methodology, a language, and a tool. The CORAS methodology integrates aspects from partly complementary risk analysis techniques, like HazOp [1], FMEA [2], and FTA [3], with state-of-the-art system modeling methodology based on UML 2.0 [4]. A graphical UML-based language has been developed to support documentation and communication of security analysis results [5].

The integration of different risk analysis approaches facilitates the analysis of different aspects of a system or organisation, e.g. security, legal issues and business processes, resulting in a combined picture of the relevant risks. For example, the notion of trust is tightly interwoven with notions like security and usability [6, 7]. Furthermore, it is difficult to separate trust from the expectation of a legal framework that offers protection in the cases where the trust relationship fails [8]. An analysis of trust should therefore encompass a number of issues including technological, legal, sociological and psychological aspects.

This paper presents the CORAS Tool which has been developed to provide computerized support for performing security analysis in accordance with the CORAS methodology using the graphical CORAS language. Section 2 describes the CORAS Tool itself, while Sect. 3 outlines plans for future work.

2 The CORAS Tool

Security analysis is a highly elaborate and prolific process which involves many different types of documentation, such as UML models, tables with analysis data, and natural language descriptions of the target of evaluation. Access to this information and its change history needs to be provided. The information also needs to be shared between the various modelling and analysis tools used

P. Herrmann et al. (Eds.): iTrust 2005, LNCS 3477, pp. 402–405, 2005.

by the analyst. In addition, it is important to maintain consistency between all the different pieces of information. Computerised support for documentation, maintenance and reuse of analysis results is thus of high importance.

The CORAS Tool has been developed based on the principles and requirements outlined above and is publicly available as open source [9]. The tool follows a client-server model and is developed entirely in Java. The security analyst uses the CORAS client application to create new analysis projects, document and edit security analysis results, generate analysis reports, and manage and reuse experiences from previous analyses. Help is provided to the user in the form of integrated electronic versions of the CORAS methodology as well as user guides. A screenshot of the CORAS client application is shown in Fig. 1.

Analysis data is stored in a centralised database on the server, enabling multiple users to collaborate on the same analysis project. The server is based on standard Enterprise Java Beans (EJB) technology and runs on top of the open source JBoss application server. Figure 2 shows an overview of the structure of the CORAS tool.

There are two databases in the CORAS Tool, called repositories. The assessment repository stores results from the actual security analyses, while the experience repository contains reusable results from previous analyses in the form of UML-models, checklists, procedures and more. By facilitating reuse, the tool helps the user avoid starting from scratch for each new analysis. The repositories are versioned, so that all changes are maintained and the user can go back and look at the state of a security analysis at a previous point in time. The repositories are implemented on top of the open-source XML database eXist [10].

A wide variety of UML modelling tools and security analysis tools exist and are in use by security analysts and system engineers today. It is therefore important for our tool to provide flexible support for integration with external tools. Though the security analysis process is model-driven, the tool does not

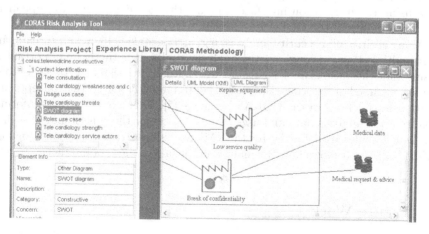

Fig. 1. Screenshot of the CORAS Tool

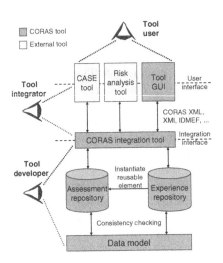

Fig. 2. Overview of the CORAS Tool

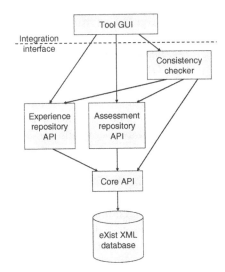

Fig. 3. Integration interface

deal exclusively with UML models, but must also be able to include tables and other constructs such as fault tree diagrams, intrusion detection logs and natural language descriptions. To satisfy these requirements, the tool provides an integration layer with a defined API which can be used by other tools to integrate with the CORAS tool. Standardised XML formats are utilised for data integration, such as XMI for the interchange of UML models.

Three different viewpoints or roles are defined in Fig. 2. The *tool user* represents the end-user, e.g. a security analyst who uses the CORAS tool together with various modelling and security analysis tools The *tool integrator*, on the other hand, is responsible for integrating the various external tools with the CORAS tool, using the integration interface. Finally, the *tool developer* will implement the functionality of the CORAS tool itself.

Many entities of a security analysis, e.g. assets, stakeholders and threats, appear multiple times throughout the analysis results. It is therefore important to ensure that the various analysis results are mutually consistent with each other. We have defined an internal risk analysis data model based on the concepts and relationships defined in the CORAS language [5]. This model extracts information from the analysis data and uses this as a basis for the consistency checking. Consistency rules are defined using the XML Stylesheet Transformation Language (XSLT). Figure 3 shows how the main components of the tool interact.

3   Future Work

Although the CORAS project was completed in 2003, development of the CORAS tool and methodology is continuing in a number of other projects. Support for creating and editing UML diagrams directly in the CORAS application is under development, as well as improvements to the security analysis methodology and language to facilitate e.g. legal risk analysis [11]. Integration of process and workflow techniques to facilitate a more methodology-driven approach is being investigated. We are also working on upgrading the consistency mechanisms, e.g. to support consistency languages such as CLiX [12] and to provide consistency repair functionality.

Acknowledgements

The work on which this paper reports has partly been carried out within the context of the EU-projects TrustCoM (IST-2003-01945) and CORAS (IST-2000-25031) as well as the SECURIS (152839/220) project funded by the Research Council of Norway.

References

1. Redmill, F., Chudleigh, M., Catmur, J.: HazOp and software HazOp. Wiley (1999)
2. Bouti, A., Kadi, D.A.: A state-of-the-art review of FMEA/FMECA. International journal of reliability, quality and safety engineering **1** (1994) 515–543
3. IEC 1025: Fault Tree Analysis (FTA). (1990)
4. OMG: UML 2.0 Superstructure Specification. (2004) OMG Document: ptc/2004-10-02.
5. Lund, M.S., Hogganvik, I., Seehusen, F., Stølen, K.: UML profile for security assessment. Technical Report STF40 A03066, SINTEF Telecom and informatics (2003)
6. Jøsang, A., Ismail, R., Boyd, C.: A Survey of Trust and Reputation Systems for Online Service Provision. Decision Support Systems (to appear) http://security.dstc.edu.au/papers/JIB2005-DSS.pdf.
7. Egger, F.N.: Towards a model of trust for e-commerce system design. In: CHI 2000: Workshop Designing Interactive Systems for 1-to-1 E-commerce. (2000) http://www.zurich.ibm.com/~mrs/chi2000/contributions/egger.html.
8. Jones, S., Wilikens, M., Morris, P., Masera, M.: Trust requirements in e-business. Communications of the ACM **43** (2000) 81–87
9. CORAS: The CORAS project (2005) http://coras.sourceforge.net/ (visited February 2005).
10. Meier, W.: eXist: An Open Source Native XML Database. In Chaudri, A.B., Jeckle, M., Rahm, E., Unland, R., eds.: Web, Web-Services, and Database Systems. Volume 2593 of LNCS., Erfurt, Germany, NODe 2002 Web- and Database-Related Workshops, Springer (2002)
11. Vraalsen, F., Lund, M.S., Mahler, T., Parent, X., Stølen, K.: Specifying Legal Risk Scenarios Using the CORAS Threat Modelling Language - Experiences and the Way Forward. In: Proceedings of 3rd International Conference on Trust Management (iTrust 2005). LNCS, Roquencourt, France, Springer (To appear 2005)
12. Systemwire: Clix: Constraint language in xml (2003) http://www.clixml.org/ (visited February 2005).

Towards a Grid Platform Enabling Dynamic Virtual Organisations for Business Applications

T. Dimitrakos[*,1], G. Laria[2], I. Djordjevic[1], N.Romano[2], F.D'Andria[2],
V. Trpkovski[1], P. Kearney[1], M. Gaeta[2], P.Ritrovato[2], L.Schubert[3],
B.Serhan[3], L. Titkov[1], and S.Wesner[3]

[1] BT Security Research Centre, BT Group Research Labs, Adastral Park, IP5 3RE, UK
[2] CRMPA, Università di Salerno, DIIMA, via Ponte Don Melillo, Fisciano, 84084, Italy
[3] HLRS, High Performance Computing Centre, Stuttgart, Germany

Abstract. In this paper we describe the demonstration of selected security & contract management capabilities of an early prototype infrastructure enabling dynamic Virtual Organisations for the purpose of providing virtualised services and resources that can be offered on-demand, following a utility computing model, and integrated into aggregated services whose components may be distributed across enterprise boundaries. The ideas underpinning this prototype have been investigated in the context of European projects TrustCoM [1], ELeGI [2] and GRASP [4] where initial prototype development has taken place.

1 Introduction

This paper summarises an infrastructure that gives enterprises the ability to take advantage of Grid and Web services technologies in order to virtualize their services, make them available to others on a charge-per-use basis, and form Virtual Organizations (VO) in order to selectively outsource components of end-to-end application services (AS) to other providers that participate in a VO. Particular emphasis is placed on the aspects of the infrastructure that relate to security and Service Level Agreement (SLA) management [8].

One of the key architectural elements of the middleware platform to be demonstrated is the distinction between the AS delivered to a client and the component Grid services used to implement this. The component Grid services are provided on demand by 3rd party Service Providers running Virtual Hosting Environments (VHE), which may consist of many individual hosts actually running the services. From a management perspective each VHE provides capabilities for the creation, virtualisation and management of the Grid services within it. The AS provider (ASP) can selectively integrate application components that are virtualised as services and that are offered by different VHE, on a charge-per-use basis subject to SLAs. The infrastructure enables the VHE manager to optimise resource usage within their VHE and also to control the operation of and access to the services that are hosted in their VHE as necessary in a commercial environment, while still exploiting

---

[*] Correspondence author: theo.dimitrakos@bt.com

P. Herrmann et al. (Eds.): iTrust 2005, LNCS 3477 pp. 406–410, 2005.

the power of the underlying Grid technology to deliver the overall AS whose components may be distributed across multiple VHE. The basic business functionality that Application and Service Provider require is provided as default capability by the infrastructure, therefore, simplifying the building Grid-based ASs.

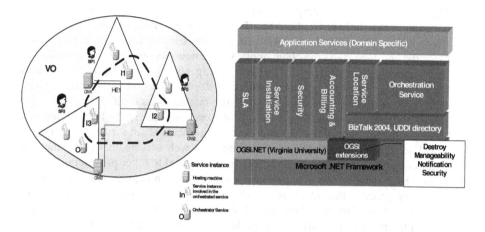

Fig. 1. VO concept (left) and High Level Architecture of underlying infrastructure (right)

Fig. 1. shows the high level architecture of the VO ecosystem infrastructure composed by three VHE. Building on top of existing OGSA compliant middleware (in the current prototype implementation this is OGSI.NET [5]). A first layer of extension relates to the functionality of Location, Instantiation and Orchestration:

- *Locator*: it allows publishing business services in the VHE and offers a discovery service that can meet a specified QoS/SLA constraint; it returns the endpoint for the *Instantiator* to create this service
- *Instantiator*: selects an appropriate host and invokes the appropriate Grid Service Factory (-ies), initiates SLA monitoring and Accounting & Billing services and interacts with the security manager service that is responsible for securing the group of GRASP services executing an AS
- *Orchestration*: orchestrates potentially transient Grid services On top of this extension, further business functionality is provided as part of this VO Ecosystem Infrastructure including:
- *SLA Management:* SLA (templates) used in selection of a VHE; monitoring of services to ensure compliance; mapping of monitored data to SLA concepts;
- *Accounting & Billing:* collection of performance/resource data (shared with SLA monitoring); combining different costing methods; applying pricing algorithms;
- *Security:* securing complete AS (multiple component Grid Services on multiple VHEs); handling securely life-time, as well as the addition and expulsion of component Grid service instances that collectively execute a complete application.

See [6],[7] for further details.

2 The Basic Demonstration Scenario

The demonstration will follow the following service aggregation scenario. (For simplicity, we refrain from elaborating the application specific functionality.)

1. The functionality of a composite service is captured within a business process description that is held by the ASP. The process is virtualised as a (composite) AS instance with a front-end GUI that facilitates interaction with the end-user. Once the end-user starts the client application a new AS instance is activated.
2. The activation of new AS instance instigates the activation of a new GroupManager service instance, which in turn creates of a security context defining a new Service Instance Group (SIG) that includes itself.
3. Using a graphical application interface, the end-user enters its UserID and sets some parameters that define the end-user requirements about service provision.
4. The UserID and requirements are passed to a web service that maps them to requirements for component services to be outsourced to other providers.
5. Using these outsourcing requirements, an orchestration engine initiates a service discovery process that inspects a VO registry for advertised capabilities[1] that meet these requirements. If successful, this process retrieves a list of capabilities offered by different providers for each description of requested service.
6. If discovery is successful then the creation of service instances by the providers that are top in the list is requested, and (upon successful instantiation) the orchestration engine retrieves their virtual addresses.
7. With each service instance, an SLA instance describing the terms of service provision is created and a dedicated monitoring capability is activated.
8. All new instances crated are included in the same SIG as the AS instance. The underlying security infrastructure ensures that service instances can interact only with other service instances in the same SIG or with pre-determined groups of infrastructure services (mainly within their own VHE).
9. The business process capturing the application logic is now executed within the security perimeter that is effectively defined by the SIG within which the AS instance and all component services instances are contained.
10. During the execution of this business process, each service instance is monitored and accounted against the constraints. Depending on the threshold violation of SLA constraints can lead to penalty (e.g. discount) or the graceful shut-down of a component and/or the aggregated service.
11. During the process execution the composite AS will interact with the end-user via its application interface at specific interaction points, as described in the business process specification capturing the application logic.
12. Upon the completion of the application or a user requesting to shut-down the application instance, the infrastructure manages the shut-down of all component

---

[1] The term "capability" is used here to denote the ability of a VHE to commit to creating or activating a service instance that offers the requested functionality at a service level within the requested boundaries. Each capability is associated with the address of an *Instantiator* service which is responsible for managing the creation of such service instances within its VHE and returning virtual address for each such service instance to the requestor.

service instances, the nullification of agreement instances and the dissolution of the SIG, including the invalidation of the associated security context.

3 Conclusion

This is an early prototype of an infrastructure for enabling dynamic Virtual Organisations for the purpose of providing services that can be used on-demand. Summarizing the main objectives of the demonstration are: *1)* To introduce a service instantiation process that allows choosing a suitable host matching the parameters specified in an SLA offer, if such a host is available. This instantiation process provides a substantial improvement to the concept of Grid service factories. *2)* To provide an example of SLA monitoring with violation notification that leads to the application of penalties to the final accounted charge. *3)* To provide a first proven concept of a Grid platform that allows to charge service use on the basis of granular parameters, explaining the real use of the instance (e.g. number/type of invocations, amount/type of exchanged data, etc). *4)* To show how the possibility to automate the on-demand creation and management of virtual secure perimeters that span across security/administrative domains, maintain security context across a transaction and permit message exchanges only between instances that are contained within the perimeter itself.

The prototype developed so far represents a significant milestone towards the convergence of Web Services and Grid Computing approaches into a new network-centric, inter-enterprise computing paradigm. However, the current state of the implementation provides a limited functionality for trust management and security policy specification and analysis, and its dependence on OGSI implies that resource management and virtualization mechanisms are not always compliant with more traditional Web Services. In the period 2005-2008, we plan to continue pursuing a conceptually similar approach, while adapting and/or rebuilding the prototype infrastructure as appropriate in order to address the need for such further development while ensuring alignment with the parallel evolution of the web service oriented architecture and web services paradigms, which we intend to influence. Such further applied research and development plans have been accommodated in the European Integrated Projects: TrustCoM [1], ELeGI [2] and Akogrimo.

References

[1] TrustCoM, European Integrated Project, information portal www.eu-trustcom.com
[2] ELeGI, European Integrated Project, information portal at www.elegi.org
[3] Akogrimo European Integrated Project. Information portal at www.mobilegrids.org
[4] GRASP, European targeted research project, information portal www.eu-grasp.net
[5] Glenn Wasson, Norm Beekwilder, Mark Morgan and Marty Humphrey OGSI.NET: OGSI-Compliance on the .NET Framework. In Proceedings of CCGrid 2004, the 4th IEEE/ACM International Symposium on Cluster Computing and the Grid.
[6] S.Wesner *et al.* Towards a platform enabling Grid based Appl. Service Provision. In [9]
[7] T. Dimitrakos *et al.* Enabling Dynamic Sec. Perimeters for Virtual Collaborations. In [9].

[8] P. Ritrovato, T. Dimitrakos, et al. Trust, Security and Contract Management Challenges for Grid-based Application Service Provision. In iTrust2004, Springer-Verlag LNCS.

[9] P. Cunningham et al. Building the Knowledge Economy: Issues, Applications, Case Studies. IOS Press Inc.

Multimedia Copyright Protection Platform Demonstrator

Miguel Soriano, Marcel Fernandez, Elisa Sayrol, Joan Tomas, Joan Casanellas,
Josep Pegueroles, and Juan Hernández-Serrano

Escola Tecnica Superior d'Enginyeria de Telecomunicacio de Barcelona (ETSETB),
C/ Jordi Girona 1 i 3, Campus Nord, UPC, 08034 Barcelona, Spain
{soriano, marcelf, josep, jserrano}@entel.upc.es
elisa@tsc.upc.es

Abstract. The work presented in this paper consists in the development of a
portable platform to protect the copyright and distribution rights of digital
contents, and empirically demonstrate the capacity of several marking and
tracing algorithms. This platform is used to verify, at a practical level, the
strength properties of digital watermarking and fingerprinting marks. Initially,
two watermarking algorithms, one based on spread-spectrum techniques and the
other based on QIM (Quantization Index Modulation), have been implemented.
Moreover, we use these watermarking algorithms to embed a fingerprinting
code, based on code concatenation, equipped with an efficient tracing
algorithm. In this paper we focus on the implementation issues of the Java-
based platform, that consists of three main packages that are fully described.

1 Introduction

The distribution and playback of digital images and other multimedia products is easy
and fast. Thus, its processing in order to achieve satisfactory copyright protection is a
challenging problem for the research community. Encrypting the data only offers
protection as long as the data remains encrypted, since once an authorized but
fraudulent user decrypts it, nothing stops him from redistributing the data without
having to worry about being caught. A watermarking scheme [1,2], which embeds
some owner information (mark) into host images, is regarded as a possible solution to
this problem. Nevertheless, digital watermarking is not strong enough to offer
protection against illegal distributors. In this environment, digital fingerprinting
techniques [3] provide a good solution to dissuade illegal copying. To make such
distribution systems work securely, the embedded marks in those systems must be
resistant to powerful attacks such as common image processing operations, lossy
image compression, geometric transforms, combination addition of random noise
(errors) and/or collusion attacks.

The work presented in this paper consists in the development of an empirical and
portable platform with the following objectives:

- To offer a practical platform where digital video can be protected against
  dishonest users.
- To verify at a practical level the strength properties of digital watermarking
  and fingerprinting marks.

P. Herrmann et al. (Eds.): iTrust 2005, LNCS 3477, pp. 411–414, 2005.

- To compare different watermarking algorithms. In this first version, spread-spectrum and QIM (Quantization Index Modulation) based watermarking algorithms have been implemented.
- To offer a platform over which we can embed different digital fingerprinting codes, and verify its behaviour. In the first version, we have developed the proposal presented in [3]

An entire platform for digital video has been developed. The MPEG2 video format has been selected since the necessary Java libraries are available and already developed. The following section shortly describes the implementation issues. The platform front-end is showed in section 3. Finally, section 4 is devoted to some conclusions.

2 Platform Implementation

The platform consists of five different blocks, regarding its functionality: Web Server, MuxDemux Server, MarkAudio Server, MarkVideo Server and Mark Generator. Figure 1 illustrates the platform structure and the process flow to mark the multimedia contents that should be protected.

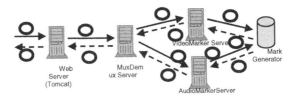

Fig. 1. Platform structure

As example of the marking operation system, the MPEG2 copyright protection process is detailed. The overall procedure consists on the following steps: a) demultiplexing the MPEG-2 sequence into video and audio bitstreams, b) extraction of DCT coefficients from the sequence, and c) the embedding of a mark (only for traceability purposes) according to the chosen method (spread spectrum technique or QIM). The coefficients are then put back into the sequence and multiplexed with the audio sequence.

To achieve the functional objectives in an efficient manner, the following features have been established:

- **Web interface:** a common implementation with server technology based on servlets 2.4 on top of Tomcat has been adopted. Each time that a client generates a request the corresponding servlet establishes a socket connection to the MuxDemux server.
- **Modularity:** The system is designed to be highly modular so to allow in a simple manner: the interaction, the addition of new functionalities and the reuse of the implemented classes. When a bitstream is analyzed, all the

MPEG2 hierarchy is identified and properly encapsulated into the corresponding objects.

- **Execution time minimization:** the MPEG2 hierarchy objects are fully stored in memory. Once loaded in memory, the marking process and the sequence reconstruction is efficiently done.
- **Platform portability:** all the system has been developed using Java.
- **Scalability:** the modular design allows incorporating new watermarking and fingerprinting algorithms. Moreover, the system can be easily modified and adapted to any number of concurrent requests.
- **Design robustness:** the system has been designed in a way that prevents from modifying essential values that are necessary to recompose the MPEG2 sequence.

Figure 2 shows the sequential steps during the marking process.

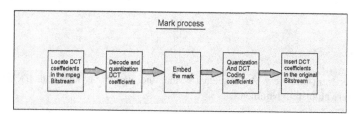

Fig. 2. General marking process

Some difficulties have been tackled during the implementation process:

a) No native Java libraries exist that allow an easy access to the DCT coefficients.

b) The mark embedding should not alter the sequence quality considering the *Human Visual System (HVS,)* this is why the quantization of the DCT coefficients has to produce the minimum possible loss. So, the Java *rounding functions* have been slightly modified to avoid additional losses and to ensure a video sequence with the required robustness and imperceptibility properties.

c) To improve the codeword search during the run-length decoding, the codewords are ordered as a binary tree.

d) The minimum working size in Java is a byte. So, some tools have been developed to read and write at the bit level (the minimum working size in MPEG2).

e) The MPEG2 standard supports a large quantity of user extensions. To have a complete implementation, the *Abstract Factory* model has been utilized.

3   User Platform Front-End

The platform can be accessed and tested through the following web site:
http://isg.upc.es/ongoing.html

When a user accesses the platform, he/she has to select the kind of document (image, MPEG2 file, video bitstream ...) and the desired service (watermarking, fingerprinting). Later the user has to choose the corresponding algorithms and their parameters if necessary. Next, the user uploads the document or selects one from the platform gallery. Finally the user can download the marked document.

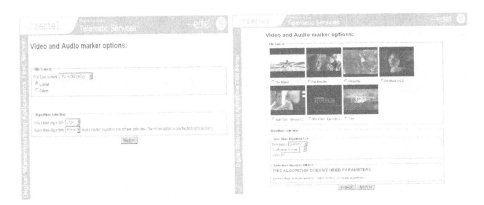

Fig. 3. User front-end view. A) Sequence format and algorithms selection. B)Chose sequence and configure algorithm parameters

4   Conclusions

This paper presents the implementation of a portable, modular and robust platform, that can be used to test watermarking and fingerprinting algorithms for video sequences. The associated drawbacks encountered during the process of implementing the platform are discussed. Classical spread spectrum techniques have been used for watermarking the DCT coefficients. Also, an algorithm based on dither modulation-quantization index modulation techniques is introduced. At the present moment spread-spectrum-based techniques have shown a better performance, however DM-QIM techniques offer many possibilities still to be fully exploited. With respect to fingerprinting, we use of a 2-secure fingerprinting code based on code concatenation.

References

1. B. Chen and G.W. Wornell. "Quantization index modulation: A class of provably good methods for digital watermarking and information embedding". IEEE Trans. Inform. Theory, 47:1423–1443, 2001.
2. I. Cox, J. Killian, T. Leighton, and T. Shamoon. "Secure spread spectrum watermarking for multimedia". IEEE Trans. Img. Process., 6(12):1673–1687, 1997.
3. M. Fernandez and M. Soriano. "Fingerprinting concatenated codes with efficient identification". In Information Security Conference–ISC, LNCS, volume 2433, pages 459–470, 2002.

ST-Tool: A CASE Tool for Modeling and Analyzing Trust Requirements*

P. Giorgini[1], F. Massacci[1], J. Mylopoulos[1,2], A. Siena[1], and N. Zannone[1]

[1] Department of Information and Communication Technology,
University of Trento - Italy
{giorgini, massacci, asiena, zannone}@dit.unitn.it
[2] Department of Computer Science,
University of Toronto - Canada
jm@cs.toronto.edu

Abstract. ST-Tool is a graphical tool integrating an agent-oriented requirements engineering methodology with tools for the formal analysis of models. Essentially, the tool allows designers to draw visual models representing functional, security and trust requirements of systems and, then, to verify formally and automatically their correctness and consistency through different model-checkers.

1 Introduction

Requirement Engineering is the phase of the software development process that aims at understanding the organization of a system, the goals of system actors and social relationships among them. This phase is critical since a misunderstanding may raise expensive errors during later development stages.

Visual modeling has been recognized as one of the relevant aspects in Software Engineering for aiming the parties involved in the development process at understanding requirements. However, though a graphical notation is useful for human communication, graphical models cannot be used for an accurate system verification. To do this, we need transformation mechanisms to support the translation from graphical model to formal specification languages.

This paper presents ST-Tool, a CASE tool for design and verification of functional, security and trust requirements. It has been designed to support the Secure Tropos methodology [3]. Specifically, this tool provides advanced modeling and analysis functionalities based on the Secure Tropos methodology. Main goals of the tool are:

- Graphical environment: provide a visual framework to draw models;
- Formalization: provide support to translate models into formal specifications;
- Analysis capability: provide a front-end to external tools for formal analysis.

---

* This work has been partially funded by the IST programme of the EU Commission, FET under the IST-2001-37004 WASP project, by the FIRB programme of MIUR under the RBNE0195K5 ASTRO Project and by PAT MOSTRO project.

P. Herrmann et al. (Eds.): iTrust 2005, LNCS 3477, pp. 415–419, 2005.

The remainder of the paper is structured as follows. Next (§2) we provide a brief description of Secure Tropos concepts and diagrams. Then, we describe ST-Tool and its components (§3). Finally, we conclude with some directions for future work (§4).

2   Background

Secure Tropos [3] is an agent-oriented software development methodology, tailored to describe both the organization and the system with respect to functional, security and trust requirements. Secure Tropos extends the Tropos methodology [1] and has the concepts of actor, goal, task, resource and social relationships for defining the obligations of actors to others. A full description of these concepts is provided in [3].

Various activities contribute to the acquisition of a first requirement model, to its refinement into subsequent models: Actor modeling, Permission Trust modeling, Execution Trust modeling, Execution Delegation modeling, Permission Delegation modeling, and Goal refinement (see [3] for full details). A graphical representation of the model obtained following the first five modeling activities is given through four different kinds of *actor diagrams*: *permission trust model*, *execution trust model*, *functional requirements model*, and *trust management implementation*. In these diagrams, actors are represented as circles; goals, tasks and resources are respectively represented as ovals, hexagons and rectangles. In the remainder of the paper, we refer to services when we don't need to distinguish goals, tasks and resources. Goal refinement aims to analyze any goals of each actor, and is conducted by using AND/OR decomposition. A graphical representation of goal refinement is given through *goal diagrams*.

Due to lack of space, we have focused on the key modeling aspects of the framework and refer to [3] for the introduction of the formal framework based on Datalog.

3   Overview of ST-Tool

ST-Tool is a CASE tool that provides a user interface for designing Secure Tropos models, support for translating automatically graphical models into formal specifications and a front-end with external tools for model checking. To manage visual editing

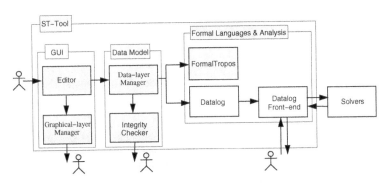

Fig. 1. The Architecture Overview

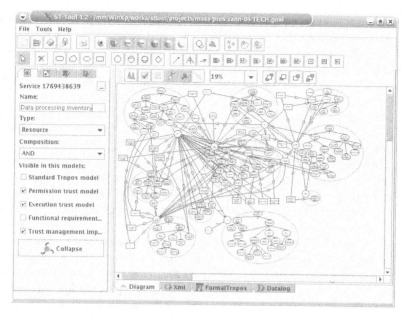

Fig. 2. ST-Tool screenshot

features and data management consistency at the same time, we have adopted a two-layer solution: a graphical layer and a data layer. In graphical layer, models are shown as graphs where actors and services are nodes, and relations are arcs. Each visual object refers to a data object. The collection of data objects is the data layer.

ST-Tool is mainly composed of two parts: the ST-Tool kernel and external solvers. ST-Tool kernel has an architecture comprised of three major parts, each of which is comprised of modules. Next, we will discuss these modules and their interconnections. In Fig. 1, the modules of ST-Tool are shown, their interrelations are also indicated.

The tool provides a graphical user interface (GUI), through which users can manage all the components and functionalities of the tool. A screenshot of the interface is shown in Fig. 2. The GUI's key component is the *Editor Module*. This module allows the user to visually insert, edit or remove graphical objects in the graphical layer and object properties in the data layer. A second GUI component is the *Graphical-layer Manager (GM) Module* that manages graphical objects and their visualization. GM supports goal refinement. A goal diagram is associated to each actor. When systems are very large, it could be difficult to read their models. To this end, GM aids users by supporting two types of collapsing nodes: service and actor collapsing. GM also allows users to display one or more Secure Tropos diagrams listed in Section 2 at the same time.

The *Data-layer Manager (DM) Module* is responsible for building and maintaining data corresponding to graphical objects. For example, DM manages misalignments between social relations and their graphical representation. Actually, GM uses arcs to connect two nodes to each other, while many Secure Tropos relations are ternary. DM rebuilds these relations by linking two appropriate graphical objects (the two arcs) to the same data object (the relation). ST-Tool allows users to save models through the

DM module that stores a neutral description of the entire model in .xml format files. A support for detecting errors and warnings during the design phase is provided by the *Integrity Checker Module*. Integrity Checker analyzes models stored in the DM module and reports errors such as "orphan relations" (i.e. relations where an arc is missing) and "isolated nodes" (i.e. services not involved in any relations). Warnings are different from errors: they are failure of integrity constraints, like errors, but the designer may be perfectly happy with a design that does not satisfy them. Integrity Checker reports warnings, for example, when more than one service have the same name. More than one service with the same name are needed to represent delegation and trust chains.

After drawing so many nice diagrams, system designers may want to check whether the models derived so far satisfy some general desirable properties. To support formal analysis, ST-Tool allows an automatic transformation from .xml files stored by DM into formal languages. Currently, two languages are supported: Formal Tropos [2] and Datalog. These transformations are performed, respectively, by two different modules: *Formal Tropos Module* and *Datalog Module*. *Datalog Front-end (DF) Module* provides direct support for model checking by using external Datalog solvers, namely ASSAT[1], Cmodels[2], DLV[3] and Smodels[4]. DF guarantees flexibility since it allows users to select which security properties they want to verify [3] and to complete models with additional "ad-hoc" Datalog statements related to the specific domain users are analyzing. Once a user is confident with the model, DF passes the specifications given by Datalog Module, the axioms and properties defined in the Secure Tropos formal framework, and the additional Datalog statements to the external solver. Once the solver ends its job, the output is parsed and presented in a more user-readable format by the DF module.

4   Conclusion

We have presented a tool for modeling and verifying functional, security and trust requirements. We have already used the tool to model a comprehensive case study of the application of the Secure Tropos methodology for the compliance to the Italian legislation on Privacy and Data Protection by the University of Trento, leading to the definition and analysis of an ISO-17799-like security management scheme [4].

Future work will involve a front-end with T-Tool [2] for automatically verifying Formal Tropos specification. Further, Secure Tropos is still under work, so is ST-Tool, too. We are also considering to integrate our tools into the ECLIPSE platform.

References

1. P. Bresciani, P. Giorgini, F. Giunchiglia, J. Mylopoulos, and A. Perini. TROPOS: An Agent-Oriented Software Development Methodology. *JAAMAS*, 8(3):203–236, 2004.
2. A. Fuxman, L. Liu, M. Pistore, M. Roveri, and J. Mylopoulos. Specifying and analyzing early requirements: Some experimental results. In *Proc. of RE'03*, page 105. IEEE Press, 2003.

---

[1] http://assat.cs.ust.hk/

[2] http://www.cs.utexas.edu/users/tag/cmodels.html

[3] http://www.dbai.tuwien.ac.at/proj/dlv/

[4] http://www.tcs.hut.fi/Software/smodels/

3. P. Giorgini, F. Massacci, J. Mylopoulous, and N. Zannone. Requirements Engineering meets Trust Management: Model, Methodology, and Reasoning. In *Proc. of iTrust'04*, *LNCS* 2995, pages 176–190. Springer-Verlag, 2004.
4. F. Massacci, M. Prest, and N. Zannone. Using a Security Requirements Engineering Methodology in Practice: The compliance with the Italian Data Protection Legislation. *Comp. Standards & Interfaces*, 2005. To Appear. An extended version is available as Technical report DIT-04-103 at `eprints.biblio.unitn.it`.

The VoteSecure™ Secure Internet Voting System

Periklis Akritidis[1], Yiannis Chatzikian[2], Manos Dramitinos[3],
Evangelos Michalopoulos[2], Dimitrios Tsigos[2], and Nikolaos Ventouras[3]

[1] Institute of Computer Science, Foundation for Research and Technology –Hellas,
GR-71110, Heraklion, Crete, Greece
akritid@ics.forth.gr
http://www.ics.forth.gr/
[2] VIRTUAL TRIP Ltd, Science and Technology Park of Crete, GR-71110, Heraklion,
Crete, Greece
{hatzikia, mihalop, tsigos, venturas}@vtrip.net
http://www.vtrip.net
[3] Athens University of Economics and Business, Computer Science Department, Patission,
76, Athens, GR 104 34, Greece
mdramit@aueb.gr

Abstract. We have developed a system that supports remote secure internet voting and ensures the secrecy of the voting process by means of employing advanced cryptography techniques. In this paper, we present this system, called VoteSecure™. The cryptography-related part performs the encryption and "breaking" of the ballots submitted to parts that are distributed to tally members. These ballots can be later reconstructed by means of the cooperation of at least T out of N tally members. We argue that our system is both innovative and useful; it can be used as a stand-alone system or integrated with an existing e-government and/or e-community platform that could take advantage of its functionality.

1 Introduction

Recent elections whether at a local, national or European level have been characterised by growing voter non-participation. One cannot separate this phenomenon from wider issues of growing voter apathy and aloofness from the political system, but there are signs that by enabling the easier exercise of voting rights remotely, authorities might be able to improve voter participation. Traditionally, remote voting has involved postal ballots, but issues of security have dogged the process. The alternative is an internet-based system that is not only cheaper, but more convenient, more secure, allows people to vote from work, and also provides for geographically distributed and long running elections. Apart from internet polling and surveying, internet voting can by divided into two broad categories: (a) Remote internet voting, and, (b) Poll-site internet voting. The VoteSecure™ system focuses on providing a internet voting solution that address the problem of voter participation by providing an easy to implement, convenient, secure, and easy to use internet-based remote voting application. The key characteristics of the Virtual Trip VoteSecure™ remote internet voting

P. Herrmann et al. (Eds.): iTrust 2005, LNCS 3477, pp. 420–423, 2005.

platform include: (a) PKCS#12 key storage format supported by both popular MS Internet Explorer and Netscape Navigator, both of which export keys in this format, (b) Talliers are participants responsible for tabulating the votes without compromising privacy, (c) No single party other than the voter can compromise vote privacy, and, vote privacy can be maintained against collusion of talliers up to a predefined threshold, (d) Disputes over vote delivery are resolved using receipts, (e) Even passive observers can verify the election results long after the fact, (f) The operator of the system is only responsible for service quality and availability and cannot compromise vote privacy or forge the results without being detected, (g) The system can be delivered by a service provider and is flexible enough to allow the easy design of bespoke ballots.

2 The VoteSecure™ Platform

The programming platform used for VoteSecure™ is the Java plugin by Sun. It provides certain valuable features such as allowing multiple experts who have individually evaluated the code to sign it, thus increasing trust in that code. Another feature is the support for PKCS12 keystores, which is the representation used by Internet Explorer and Netscape Navigator for their exported private keys. This simplifies the use of the existing public key infrastructure (PKI). A relational database is used at the back end for data storage. The system is loosely coupled to the underlying database, but transactional capabilities are required.

2.1 Protocols

An important component of an internet voting system is the underlying cryptographic secure voting protocol. A voting protocol is defined as a set of sub-protocols that allow a set of voters to cast their votes securely and with privacy, while enabling a set of talliers to compute and communicate the final tally that is verified by a set of observers. These sets need not be disjoint sets. These fundamental requirements of privacy and integrity must be addressed by the protocol. There are the following protocol types in Voting Systems: (a) Mixing Protocols, (b) Blind Signatures, and, (c) Protocols Based on Homomorphism. Mixing protocols are based on voters mixing each other's votes so that no one can associate a vote with a voter. There are no separate talliers or observers. These protocols are impractical for elections with more than a handful of voters. Blind Signatures use an anonymous channel to cast ballots preventing association of votes and voters. Authentication is preserved through the use of blind signatures. Blind signatures allow a document to be signed without revealing its contents and were originally used for untraceable digital cash. These protocols are very flexible and even allow write-in options. Finally, Protocols Based on Homomorphism are protocols where individual votes are split up among different tallying authorities so that no single one of them can compromise the privacy of an individual voter. These protocols are based on homomorphic encryption and homomorphic secret sharing and allow for universal verifiability. VoteSecure™ uses a protocol based on homomorphism which introduces publicly verifiable secret sharing that makes it more robust and convenient than earlier protocols. The protocol used assumes the availability of a so-called bulletin board in which each entity can post a message exclusively to its own section, but cannot erase or overwrite previously posted messages.

3   The VoteSecure™ Voting Process

Voters cast their votes by posting ballots to the bulletin board. The ballot does not reveal any information on the vote itself but its validity is ensured by an accompanying proof that the ballot contains a valid vote. Then, Talliers compute the final tally from an accumulation of the valid ballots. Privacy of individual votes is ensured against coalitions of talliers up to a configurable threshold T. Robustness against N-T faulty talliers is also maintained, where N is the number of Talliers. The final tally can be verified by any observer against the accumulation of the valid ballots, thus the protocol provides for universal verifiability. All communication through the bulletin board is public and can be read by any entity. No entity can erase any information from the bulletin board, but all active participants can append messages to their own designated section. Digital signatures are used to control access to the various sections of the bulletin board. This realises the requirement of limiting each entity's messages to its own section. VoteSecure addresses the denial of service attacks issue using Replicated Servers and by postulating that all participants can append messages only to their section. This, together with the write-once requirement can be realised by designing the bulletin board as a set of replicated servers implementing Byzantine agreement. Such a system is described in [1]. In VoteSecure we approximate the ideal bulletin board by using receipts. The bulletin board issues digital signatures for each transaction. The transaction is considered committed by the entity performing it only after the receipt and verification of a digital signature of the exchanged messages. Thus failure to post a message can be immediately detected and dealt with. In the case of a dispute about the delivery of a message (e.g. vote dropping), the involved entity can present the receipt and challenge the bulletin board to present the corresponding messages. A malicious voter may pretend to lose his or her vote, and claim it was the server's fault in order to 'frame' the server. However, it would take a co-ordinated effort among many voters to truly cast suspicion on the voting process in this manner, which is unlikely. The amount of complaints can be used as an indication of the validity of the election.

3.1   The VoteSecure™ Voter/Tallier Implementation

Both the voters and the talliers are implemented as client programs accessing the bulletin board, which acts as a server. A party must completely trust the system on which these programs are executing on his behalf as well as their code. Sensitive information is never leaked outside these programs unencrypted. Trust in the system is achieved by using the user's own computer to execute the client programs. It is the responsibility of the user to maintain the security of his computer. The client program has access to the user's private key in order to post messages to the bulletin board server. The key is stored in password protected PKCS12 format on the client machine, as exported by the user's browser. To allow this kind of access one must either deploy the program as a signed applet, or install it locally on the client machine. Care must be taken for sensitive input such as a vote. Applet input is not considered a privileged operation by the Java plugin and this could be exploited if regular use of the system was through an applet. Malicious applets could disguise as a voting client program. To prevent this we use a special way to deploy the client program.

3.2 Deployment

To enable the use of the system on a machine, the user invokes a signed applet that will install the client program on the user's machine. This operation is considered privileged and the signers of the applet are clearly indicated to the user while asked for permission. For regular use, the user invokes the program directly from his or her machine. This ensures that the executed program is the intended one. To increase trust in the code of the client program, multiple experts have evaluated and digitally signed the code. Recall that this is possible using Java plugin's applet signing mechanisms.

4   Conclusions

VoteSecure™ is a secure internet voting system that effectively addresses the issue of vote-privacy and voting-results verifiability based of principles of Trust-Management and ICT Security. The system can by used in a broad spectrum of application domains, ranging from secure gallops / opinion research to Secure Auction systems.

References

1. M. Reiter: The Rampart toolkit for building high-integrity services
2. R. Cramer, M. Franklin, B. Schoenmakers, and M. Yung. Multi-authority secret ballot elections with linear work. In Advances in Cryptology---EUROCRYPT '96, volume 1070 of Lecture Notes in Computer Science, pages 72--83, Berlin, 1996. Springer-Verlag.
3. R. Cramer, R. Gennaro, and B. Schoenmakers. A secure and optimally efficient multi-authority election scheme. In Advances in Cryptology---EUROCRYPT '97, volume 1233 of Lecture Notes in Computer Science, pages 103-118, Berlin, 1997. Springer-Verlag
4. B. Schoenmakers. A simple publicly verifiable secret sharing scheme and its application to electronic voting. In Crypto'99, 148--164. Springer-Verlag. LNCS Vol. 1666.

Author Index

Lecture Notes in Computer Science

For information about Vols. 1–3391

please contact your bookseller or Springer